The Second World War By Those Who Were There

"*I am near the spot where so many boys from home lost their lives during the last war. You remember that company from home? Well I suppose, anyway it's not far from their final resting place. I bet you would find them all turned over in their graves if they knew that we were back to finish the job they thought they were finishing. 25 years ago we were fighting to save Democracy. Today it's the same story only under a new banner. Fighting to end all wars. What a futile idea. Human nature is the same today as it was a quarter century ago and until you change the heart and soul of man, then and only then can you expect to have a change in man's nature and hence hoping for a peaceful life. Let us resolve that after the victory which is surely ours that we try a stab at reforming man's nature by the educational method. Don't make a mistake by trying to force democracy on the world. From my knowledge of these countries they can't handle it.*"

American soldier to his mother
Alsace-Lorraine, January 1945.

Veteran Nellis VerHey, G Company, 508th Parachute Infantry Regiment, 82nd Airborne Division, at the Utah Beach Museum on the 70th anniversary of the Normandy Landings.

A survivor of D-Day, Nellis was wounded in France and the Netherlands.

British veteran Cecil Newton, tank crewman of the 4th/7th Dragoon Guards (whose story you will discover on page 221) and the author on the day they met in 2017.

FOREWORD
How it all began

GENESIS OF THE PROJECT

The first time I ever heard about the Second World War, I was just a child. On holiday in Brittany, my family used to visit an old lady who cooked the local cake to perfection. One day, she received friends, including a man who left his mark on my mind: all he had left on his hands were his thumbs. Seeing the look on my face, he told me his story. As a member of the Resistance, he had lost his fingers while sabotaging a railroad track. I had probably heard about the war before, but I was too young to understand it. I was simply impressed by this vision and even today, at 30 years old, I still remember his hands as if I'd seen them yesterday. Later, my father, who was very interested in the subject, took me to visit the beaches of Normandy. We passed through the Colleville cemetery with its white crosses as far as the eye can see. I finally took stock of the events that had taken place there some sixty years earlier and began to take an interest in this period. My father then bought me the book *Mémoires d'objets, histoires d'hommes* by François Bertin (Ouest-France Editions, 2004), which presented military equipment produced in millions of quantities, but which all had incredible and unique destinies. It triggered the desire in me to collect these pieces of history, and my discovery of a famous online auction site marked the beginning of belt-tightening measures at home...

As soon as I obtained my driver's license, I returned to the beaches of Normandy for the first of my many annual pilgrimages. As I write these lines, the commemorations of June 6, 1944 are still an opportunity to shake hands with those men who liberated our country from Nazi rule. It is hard to believe when I say, "Thank you" to this former 82nd Airborne pathfinder and he humbly replies with a simple "You're welcome", that at my age he was one of the first Allies to land on French soil, in enemy territory, aware that he would probably never return. How can we not reflect on our own lives and accomplishments when meeting men and women with such exceptional backgrounds? I quickly understood that I had to fulfill my duty of remembrance, paying tribute to them in my own way. Alberg Figg, a former British gunner with the 43rd (Wessex) Division, told me in June 2017, just a month before his death: *"It's good that young people like you are interested in what we've done. You need to talk to your children and grandchildren about it, so that we are not forgotten."* Fortunately, many comrades of my generation have taken on the mission to save their testimonies, as long as we still can. I am thinking of Florent Plana, who traveled across the United States to video interview as many veterans as possible, or Bertrand Froger, who welcomed many veterans' families to Normandy and actively participated in preserving their memory. Many other young people maintain websites dedicated to a forgotten unit or perpetuate their memory through reconstitution.

In 2015, at the beginning of this book project, hundreds of veterans from the United States, the United Kingdom, Canada, France and other Allied nations were dying every day. While their attics were emptied by the movers, the memories and correspondence of our liberators often ended up in antique shops or auctioned on the Internet. Over the years, I have sought to collect and safeguard these direct testimonies of the conflict, before they were lost forever. To the frontline soldier, these letters were worth all the money in the world. They are now of inestimable value. The book you are about to read compiles nearly fifteen years of collecting and carefully selected writings.

These are stories that have never been told before, for those who think they have read everything about this war, as well as historical context provided for those who might be new to the subject.

THE RESEARCH PROCESS

The letters of hundreds of soldiers were read, and in the end only a very small percentage were used. Deciphering the handwriting of each of these correspondences (often retrieved in batches of several dozen letters) could take days. I then had to translate and transcribe in full those that I thought were interesting. However, in the 1940s, the censors were (more or less) vigilant and few ventured to disclose information about their living conditions and combat experience. The majority of the messages were of no historical interest. But from time to time, a real gem caught my eye and it was put aside.

The second step was to research the history of each soldier in order to better understand the context in which these letters were written. There is no shortage of online sources for American archives, but it was often necessary to use the archives at Kew for the British, or the Service historique de la Défense in Vincennes for the French. Sometimes, associations or enthusiasts' forums were able to help me complete my work. I then spent whole days going through old handwritten documents, loaded with military abbreviations, hastily photocopied decades ago and then scanned in low resolution, to walk in these soldiers' shoes. Some documents were over 1,000 pages long.

Finally, when I had been able to mix the individual stories with history and I was sure I wanted to publish a correspondence, there was one last crucial step: finding the soldier's descendants, in order to ask his family for permission to honor him in my project. I could find some clues about the existence of possible children in the letters, but the information was mostly incomplete... The unfortunate habit of online dealers to maximize their profits by splitting batches of old letters (and then selling them individually) made a large number of leads disappear and the investigation much more complicated. Fortunately, I had other means at my disposal: many genealogy sites, obituaries, veterans' associations... For some soldiers, contacting their descendants proved to be a real challenge, especially in the United Kingdom, which keeps many archives closed to the public. Finding information about the Royal Marine Michael Davey and his wife Phyllis took nearly five months: buying marriage and death certificates from the British General Register Office, applying to open the Naval Party 1645's file using the Freedom of Information Act (refused), sending emails to the Royal Marines and Royal Navy's museums, contacting many strangers on Facebook and even the cemetery where Phyllis was buried in 2007... Michael's name, quite common, did not make my job any easier. It was finally by sheer luck, after months of unsuccessful research, that I got in touch with Phyllis' family.

The daughter of a former brother-in-arms of Michael put me in touch with a journalist from Teignmouth who turned out to know her! As for the many dead ends, I have left enough clues in some anonymous portraits for their potential descendants to perhaps recognize a relative. I would be happy to meet them and honor one more soldier in a future edition of this book.

For others, however, a simple Internet search was enough, and my work was immediately rewarded. The first family found was of Ray Alm, an elite American soldier from the 2nd Ranger Battalion, who landed on Omaha Beach. His son Rick, who unfortunately lost his battle with cancer on February 16, 2017, was an extremely kind man and interested in my project. As a great journalist (and a Pulitzer Prize winner), he always had a good anecdote to tell about his father. One of them was about the secret language that Ray and his wife Audrey had developed. Censorship didn't allow Ray to reveal his location, so he used his signature in a clever way: closing his letters with *"With love"* meant he was in England, *"All my love"* in Scotland and France was *"Lovingly"*. Not knowing where he would go, they prepared many codes in advance for countries such as Italy, Japan, Russia, Australia, and even Guatemala or Somalia. As you've probably guessed, *"Till Victory"* was the signature for Germany.

His son's kindness and trust gave me the courage to find more than forty other families. Before Rick sadly passed away in 2017, I promised him that the title of the book would honor his father. Beyond the anecdote, *Till Victory* represents optimism and determination, while carrying the uncertainty that this horrible war could bring to two young lovers' lives. The title perfectly sums up the content of the book: hope and fear, love and sacrifice, the home and the front, "until victory".

After the book was released in France in October 2018, there was still one huge task ahead: translating it into English so that these heroes' stories are known throughout the world. I did it myself as best as I could, although my English may not be as rich as my French, my native language. The most important thing, however, is that you are now able to read most of these letters as they were originally written, in English.

DUTY OF REMEMBRANCE

I am neither a historian by training nor a full-time writer. Only a young Frenchman trying to honor those who fought for our freedom. Despite all my efforts to find the rightful owners of all the content published here,

FOREWORD

I hope that I will be forgiven for any omissions. All letters, items and uniforms presented here are, or have been, part of my personal collection (unless otherwise stated). In this way, I wanted to guarantee the independence of this project and bring new elements forward that were previously unknown to the public. Each piece worn by the models in this book, from helmets to shoulder patches, from ties to cigarette packs, are wartime originals: they have all been authenticated by experts as far as possible (unfortunately, counterfeiters have been getting rich for decades now). Only the weapons carried are reproductions (except for the M1 Garand from 1943, which was graciously lent to me). As a matter of principle, I have always refused to own a weapon, even if it's decommissioned, so have instead used these faithful resin replicas. The M1A1 Thompson machine-gun and the M1 Carabine were used during the filming of the television series *The Pacific* (2010) and the movie *Monuments Men* (2014).

Expressions of the time have been preserved and the letters published as they were written. Some terms such as 'Huns', 'Jerries' or 'Japs' may seem offensive now, but these are from an era when the human race was divided in this way and such language was not only tolerated but encouraged by propaganda. I use the term 'enemy' in my narrative (in the present tense) to refer to Germans or Italians, but it is only to put the reader in the context of the time. We have since built peace with our former adversary, and it has been going on for a long time. Punctuation has sometimes been modified to make it easier to read and notes added in square brackets. Paragraphs of no historical interest (often personal stories related to acquaintances or family) were also cut.

There is no shortage of books on the Second World War, but this one was written on the battlefields of Europe, amidst bombs and tracer bullets, by the heroes themselves. Through the letters of these young men and women sent to the hell of Africa, Italy, France or the heart of the Third Reich, we discover the Allies' daily lives, their doubts, fears and hopes. They offer a new perspective on these events, beyond the staggering figures and dates that seem to be from another time. Whether they are simple GIs, British tank crews, Canadian airmen or frontline medics, their fates deserve to be known and their memory preserved. It should be remembered that, apart from elite volunteer soldiers, most were only very young armed citizens who were just waiting for the war to end. I have also written this book for my generation and those to follow, who are enjoying and will continue to enjoy for a long time, I hope, a freedom that is so dearly acquired, but so fragile. It is easy to forget that it is worth dying for. Thank you to the veterans who gave their youths for ours. These few men and women are honored here because their letters were sold at the right place, at the right moment… This book would certainly have been very different if I had written it at another time. Millions of other anonymous heroes could have been featured in their place, and this book is dedicated to them as well.

I hope that the words of those you are about to discover reflect the state of mind and experience of this entire generation that has suffered so much. I like to think of this book as a book about peace.

CLÉMENT HORVATH

Below, the author at work in 2015, and on the left, more than twenty years earlier, on a remnant of a German bunker and an American Sherman tank.

GLOSSARY

Definitions and essentials to make your reading easier

ORGANIZATION OF AN ALLIED ARMY

The armed forces have three main branches: the Army, Air Force and Navy. An **Army Group** oversees a whole campaign in a 'theater of operations' (such as the European Theater of Operations, ETO). It is divided into different formations of infantry, armored (tanks) and artillery (guns firing from behind the lines) units, supported by military engineers, signal technicians (communications), or logistical, administrative and medical support.

ARMY GROUP	Lead by a Field Marshal
	at least 2 armies / 400 000 soldiers
ARMY	Lead by a General
	2 to 5 corps / 80 000 soldiers
CORPS	Lead by a Lieutenant-General
	2 to 5 divisions / 40 000 soldiers
DIVISION	Lead by a Major-General
	2 to 5 brigades or regiments / 10 000 soldiers
BRIGADE / REGIMENT	Lead by a Colonel
	3 battalions and support / 3 000 soldiers
BATTALION	Lead by a Lieutenant-Colonel
	3 to 5 companies / 500 to 900 soldiers
COMPANY	Lead by a Captain
	3 to 4 platoons / 60 to 200 soldiers
PLATOON	Lead by a Lieutenant
	3 to 4 squads / 16 to 40 soldiers
SQUAD	Lead by a Staff Sergeant
	4 to 10 soldiers

While an American **Infantry** Division is divided into three regiments and its supporting units, the British case is more complex. Their regiments are composed of different 'active' battalions, but also reserve and territorial defense battalions that may be called upon to serve abroad. As their members are recruited by locality, the British prefer not to risk seeing a whole region mourning their dead if a regiment is decimated. Thus, for instance, the seven battalions of the King's Own Scottish Borderers were assigned to different brigades: the 2nd KOSB served with the 89th Brigade of the 7th (Indian) Division in Burma, the 6th KOSB with the 44th Brigade of the 15th (Scottish) Division in France, and the 7th KOSB became an airborne unit attached to the 1st Airborne Division (where it would suffer 90% casualties in the Netherlands). A battalion can even be duplicated when a territorial battalion goes to war and must be replaced in the United Kingdom: thus the 1/6th and 2/6th (Territorial Force) South Staffordshire (or '1st and 2nd versions of the 6th territorial battalion of the South Staffordshire Regiment') were raised, and both served in the 177th Brigade, 59th (Staffordshire) Infantry Division in Normandy.

Armored divisions are divided into tank battalions, mechanized infantry, field artillery and supporting units grouped into three 'Combat Commands'. Their companies are called 'Troops', which are grouped into 'Squadrons'. These companies are known as 'Batteries' in the **artillery**. The latter was widely used by the British, who, because of their centuries of military experience, preferred to attack a specific point after a long and powerful artillery preparation (while the Americans launched large and rapid assaults). 18% of the British troops served behind an artillery gun, ahead of the infantry (14%) and engineers (13%). Their weapons are listed by caliber, which refers to the largest diameter of their projectiles. The most common are 75 mm (anti-tank

FOREWORD

guns for example), 88 mm (such as the German anti-aircraft gun, very effective against tanks and causing terror among the Allies), 105 mm (heavy howitzers) or 155 mm (powerful artillery guns). The **Air Force** has several components, such as Bomber Command (strategic bombardments), Fighter Command, and Coastal Command (defense). Each Air Force base or 'Station' hosts several 'Wings', themselves divided into two 'Groups' (US only), which contain five 'Squadrons'. Each of these Squadrons has about a hundred men, divided into 'Flights' and 'Squads'.

On the German side, the **Wehrmacht** (Armed Forces of the Reich) included the **Heer** (Army), the **Kriegsmarine** (Navy) and the **Luftwaffe** (Air Force). Alongside the Heer was the **Waffen-SS**, the armed wing of one of the main organizations of the Nazi regime, which hosted divisions of foreign volunteers. Motivated by their belief in a superior race, they became as famous for their fighting spirit as for their crimes (against both prisoners of war and civilians).

In order to avoid confusion, the ranks and names of foreign units have been kept in their original language. You will have no difficulty understanding the meaning of very similar words such as 'Infanterie' and Infantry, but it should be remembered that tank units are called 'Armored' on the US side, 'Armoured' (with a 'u') on the British side, 'Blindées' in French, and 'Panzer' on the German side. The abbreviation of the ordinals (1st in English) is written with a period in German, as in *1. Panzer-Division*.

You will probably be surprised by the small number of **women** in this book, as it focuses primarily on letters written on the Allied front in Western Europe. At the time, fighting troops in Western armies were mainly made up of men (which was not the case in the Red Army or in Eastern countries: Russian, Polish, Chinese, Czech, Greek or Yugoslav women fought alongside their male counterparts). The British created women's branches such as the **ATS** (Auxiliary Territorial Service) for the Army, the **WRNS** (Women's Royal Naval Service) for the Navy or the **WAAF** (Women's Auxiliary Air Force), but their members mainly performed support tasks (defense, cooking, administration, transport, maintenance...). Women also played a major role in the country, replacing men in factories and fields.

THE LANGUAGE OF THE FIGHTER

I will regularly mention the **losses** suffered by a unit: a distinction must be made in military language between 'casualties' (all losses) and 'fatalities' (deaths). Casualties refer to soldiers who are no longer part of a unit because they are dead, wounded or missing. Many of these disappeared soldiers may have been captured by the enemy or will never be found (the violence of war not sparing the integrity of the bodies). The most common cause of casualties during the Second World War was '**shrapnel**': exploding grenades, mortar or artillery shells which threw up white-hot metal fragments of various sizes several hundred feet into the air, which were often more dangerous than the original explosion itself. To protect themselves, men would dig '**foxholes**'. These were often a simple hole in the ground, just big enough to lie in, but soldiers sometimes increased its comfort by fitting it out or by placing boards and camouflage on top for more protection and to make them waterproof.

Soldiers use rather flowery language to talk about their allies or opponents. The French are familiar with the word '**Boche**', which was used a lot during the First World War to refer to the German invader. The Anglo-Saxons gave them many nicknames, such as the **Heinies** (for 'Heinrich'), the **Krauts**, the **Fritz**, the **Huns** (barbarians of Eastern Europe) and especially **Jerry** or Jerries (probably the root of 'German'). The latter came to us under the name 'Jerrycan', the Germans having invented gasoline or water containers in the 1930s that the Allies simply called the 'Jerry-Can'. The American soldier is nicknamed '**GI**' (for 'Government Issue'), '**Yank**' or 'Yankee', and the British '**Tommy**' or '**Limey**'.

A 1943 British Jerrycan, souvenir of the Mayenne fighting of August 1944, discovered by the author in 2017 in an old farm. It is stamped with the initials WD (War Department) and with the British Broad-Arrow. Note the sand painting is still visible, applied for the previous campaign in North Africa (1940-1943).

Sorting the mail.

THE CORRESPONDENCE

Besides food, nothing is more important to the warrior than news from home. The long separations and the fear of losing a loved one encourage soldiers and their families to write almost daily. Civilians are asked to talk about even their most routine activities and give news from the community, to maintain the link between the soldier and his home. But the latter cannot talk about his recent actions, or even his exact position, for fear that the mail could be intercepted and read by the enemy. Each letter is therefore controlled by a **censor**, sometimes the officer in charge of the company or a controller at the Military Post Office, who can blacken or cut out certain parts of the letters that reveal sensitive information. Officers therefore spent their rest periods reading about fifty letters a day... While some do their job in a hurry and avoid getting too involved in their men's private lives, others take this opportunity to gauge the morale of the troops.

Aware that their correspondence is being scrutinized by a third party, soldiers have fun with it or develop coded message systems, but in the end, few dare reveal the slightest detail about the reality of life at the front... However, the need to clear one's conscience or express one's opinion occasionally takes over and some people try their luck. Officers censoring their own mail also allow themselves to tell their experience of the war in detail (at the risk of disturbing their relatives). Fortunately, many 'unfiltered' testimonies have fallen through the cracks of censorship, without which this book would not have been possible!

THE V-MAIL

In times of war, postal workers were quickly overwhelmed, especially since soldiers could send free mail. Transporting such quantities of letters across continents was costly in terms of scarce resources essential to the war effort. Also, convoys were sometimes destroyed and correspondence lost. Everyone quickly got into the habit of numbering each letter, in order to know which ones had reached home or the front. To optimize the space and to increase speed and security, the mail changed shape with the appearance of **V-mail** ('Victory Mail'), a specific letterhead which was then distributed by postal workers (sometimes free of charge and up to two per day). Composed of blocks delimited for the censor's stamp, the addressee's and sender's addresses and the letter's content (too restricted according to the users' opinion), the sheet measured 7 by 9 1/8 inches (18 x 23 cm). It was then folded in three to be sent without an envelope to a V-mail processing center (although some forms were sent as regular mail).

At harbors or in remote locations, the Eastman Kodak Company and specially trained military personnel photographed the letters on microfilm using the Recordak machine. Each 16 mm strip sent could contain 1,700 letters! The Post Office and War Department then worked together to ensure the delivery of the valuable messages, which followed a complex process between personnel, photographic and printing equipment, ships and aircrafts. The strips were finally printed in the destination country on small sheets of paper measuring approximately 4 1/4 by 5 1/4 inches (11 x 13 cm), wrapped and distributed.

The British were the first to use this process with their Airgraph service in April 1941. The US War Department then contacted the Eastman Kodak Company on May 8, 1942 to develop the V-mail. The service officially started on the following June 15. Hundreds of millions of V-mails were exchanged until the end of the service in November 1945. The benefit of the system was obvious to the user: while a simple letter could take a month to arrive by sea, V-mail arrived at its destination in less than twelve days by air. Moreover, if the microfilm was lost, the original form could be found and photographed again. However, the system was not to everyone's liking. In addition to the impossibility of attaching a photo, a press article, a souvenir or perfuming it, the idea had several disadvantages. Limited to less than 300 words, the author was tempted to write small, or to fill as much space as possible. But once photographed and printed, the form reduced to a quarter of its original size was then unreadable. Similarly, the writing needed to be clear, and the form kept clean: such a thing is difficult in a foxhole. It was also a constraint for soldiers' wives, whose lipstick kisses clogged microfilm machines... All in all, the V-mail did not completely replace Air Mail, far from it.

Below, wartime advertising for Kodak explaining the concept of V-mail. On the right, a full-size promotional copy.
The microfilm used to print it is stapled here in the upper left corner of the V-mail, where the censor's stamp should be.

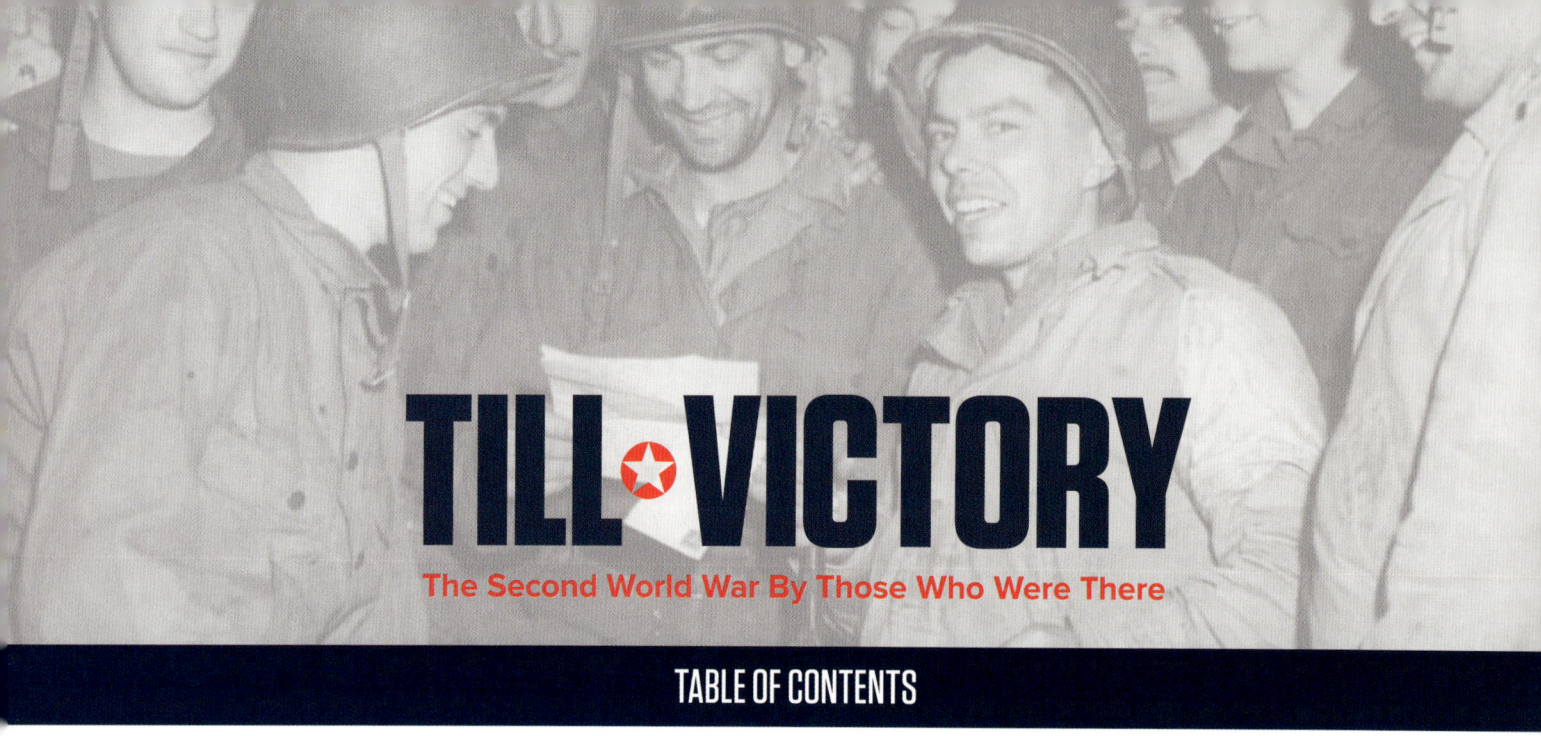

TABLE OF CONTENTS

I - THE DARK YEARS 1939-1942 page 13

Hitler invades Poland, and the French and British are waiting for an attack that seems will never come. When it finally occurs on May 10, 1940, the French army (then one of the most powerful in the world) is defeated in a few weeks. The United Kingdom now stands alone against Germany and Italy, in the air, at sea and in North Africa. A glimmer of hope emerges following the Japanese attack on Pearl Harbor: the Americans enter the conflict.

II - THE COUNTER-ATTACK 1942-1943 page 67

The Canadians make a massive commitment to defend their cousins across the Atlantic, but their first major operation in Dieppe is a disaster. American recruits, many of whom were drafted, discover the harsh military life in training. While the bombings on Germany intensify, in Africa the British regain the advantage at El Alamein. As soon as the Americans land during *Operation Torch*, the Allies advance towards Tunis.

III - THE SOFT UNDERBELLY 1943-1944 page 107

The Allies take Sicily quickly, leading to the Italian surrender in September 1943. Seizing the opportunity to land on the continent, the British 8th Army and the American 5th Army keep their eyes on Rome. But first, they have to break the Gustave line of defense, which will only fall in May 1944, after four costly assaults on Monte Cassino and a diversionary landing in Anzio. Italy is, in fact, nothing like the 'soft underbelly of a crocodile' (Winston Churchill), and the fight for its liberation will continue until May 1945.

IV - OVERLORD SUMMER 1944 page 149

On the morning of June 6, 1944, the largest armada in history heads for five Normandy beaches, coded *Utah* and *Omaha* for the Americans, and *Gold*, *Sword* and *Juno* for the British and Canadians. While the latter are delayed around Caen, the Americans advance through the Cotentin Peninsula and seize Cherbourg. After bitter fighting in the numerous traps of the bocage (hedgerows), the Allies finally surround the enemy south of Falaise, putting an end to the Battle of Normandy and opening the road to Paris.

V - VICTORY BY CHRISTMAS? END OF 1944 page 209

More French and American divisions land in Southern France in August. Boosted by the recent Allied successes, Montgomery launches *Operation Market Garden* in the Netherlands: it is a tragic failure. Meanwhile, in September 1944, Anglo-Canadians advance along the French coast to Holland. The port of Antwerp is liberated but unusable: the Germans have installed impenetrable fortresses that control the Scheldt estuary. On the Italian peninsula, the war is not over yet: as the 'D-Day Dodgers' face the Gothic Line, tragedies and heroic acts multiply. It becomes clear that no one would be home for Christmas.

VI - THE LONGEST WINTER WINTER 44-45 page 259

The Allies, who had made rapid progress to the east after Normandy, are stopped abruptly by the impressive defences protecting the Reich's borders: the Siegfried Line. In front of it, the smell of death hangs in the Vosges, on Aachen, in the Hürtgen forest or the streets of Metz, while the weather conditions deteriorate. Hitler launches the last chance offensive shortly before Christmas. He strikes with all his might through the Ardennes forest (again), with the hope of reaching Antwerp. Taken by surprise, the Americans manage to regain the upper hand in January 1945. They finally cross the Roer and the border for good.

VII - INTO THE REICH SPRING 1945 page 297

Communication with German civilians is not easy, and the Allies discover a country devastated by the bombardments. With the capture of the Remagen bridge and then *Operation Plunder* allowing them to cross the Rhine, nothing can stop their progress into the heart of the Reich. However, the war is far from won and the hastily trained replacements die by the thousands. A large part of the German army is destroyed in the Ruhr Pocket, but isolated and fanatical elements refuse to surrender. The liberation of the concentration camps found along the way finally give meaning to all these years of fighting.

VIII - VICTORY SUMMER 1945 page 331

The Wehrmacht in Italy falls first, then the rest of Western Europe hears its last shots. However, the celebration quickly gives way to boredom. The soldiers who do not have enough 'points' to return home will have to participate in the occupation or worse: continue the fight in the Pacific. Indeed, the Japanese have been waging a bitter war against the Allies for the past four years. But two atomic bombs on Hiroshima and Nagasaki officially lead to the end of the Second World War on September 2, 1945.

EPILOGUE page 371

CREDITS page 373

THE HEROES (whose identities are revealed)

- 🇫🇷 Maurice Balloux, 155e rég. inf. de forteresse (page 14)
- 🇫🇷 Roger Vallières, 105e rég. artillerie lourde hip. (page 20)
- 🇬🇧 Desmond Finny †, R.A. Service Corps (page 24)
- 🇫🇷 Charles Desrue, 136e rég. inf. de forteresse (page 32)
- 🇫🇷 Paul Clavier, 9e escadron du train (page 36)
- 🇫🇷 Alexis Wolff, 98e régiment d'infanterie (page 39)
- 🇫🇷 Jean Vacher-Corbière, France libre (page 47)
- 🇳🇿 Harold McOnie, 2nd New Zealand Div. (page 50)
- 🇬🇧 William Brown, R.A. Ordnance Corps (page 56)
- 🇺🇸 Thomas Friedrich, 56th Coast Artillery (page 63)
- 🇨🇦 Jim & Vernon Miller †, Royal Can. Air Force (page 70)
- 🇺🇸 Ronald Whitehead †, 15th Air Force (page 82)
- 🇨🇦 Laurence Alexander, 14th Can. Tank Reg. (page 91)
- 🇺🇸 Alan Morehouse †, 1st Infantry Division (page 98)
- 🇺🇸 Voyd Tromblee, 34th Inf. Division (page 101)
- 🇺🇸 Ernest "Bud" Siegel, 509th Para. Inf. Reg. (page 118)
- 🇨🇦 John Leslie Harris, 11th Can. Tank Reg. (page 122)
- 🇫🇷 Paul Pirat, 3e div. inf. algérienne (page 130)
- 🇺🇸 Joseph Nemec, 3rd Inf. Division (page 140)
- 🇺🇸 Willard Purdy †, 895th AAA Battalion (page 142)
- 🇺🇸 Andrew Gagalis, 45th Inf. Division (page 144)
- 🇺🇸 Baldwin Chambers †, 1st Armored Division (page 147)
- 🇬🇧 Michael Davey, Royal Marines (page 156)
- 🇺🇸 Murray Goldman, 82nd Airborne Division (page 161)
- 🇺🇸 Ray Alm, 2nd Rangers Battalion (page 164)
- 🇨🇦 James P. C. Macpherson, Cam. Highl. Ottawa (page 174)
- 🇬🇧 George E. E. Ross, 2nd Warwickshire Reg. (page 178)
- 🇬🇧 Leonard Wood †, 1/5th Queen's Royal Reg. (page 186)
- 🇺🇸 John Irvine †, 4th Inf. Division (page 194)
- 🇺🇸 Leo Brown, 90th Inf. Division (page 196)
- 🇺🇸 Cortland Kester †, 9th Inf. Division (page 200)
- 🇺🇸 Melvin Berg, 4th Quartermaster Company (page 203)
- 🇫🇷 André Bonnafous, 2e Division blindée (page 210)
- 🇫🇷 Jean Denise, FFI and 1re Armée française (page 214)
- 🇬🇧 Cecil Newton, 4th/7th Dragoon Guards (page 221)
- 🇺🇸 Paul L. Williams, IX Troop Carrier Com. (page 233)
- 🇬🇧 Raymond Edwards †, 4th/7th Dragoon Guards (page 239)
- 🇬🇧 Basil Taylor, 1st Airborne Division (page 242)
- 🇨🇦 Kenneth Royan †, H. & Prince Edward Reg. (page 257)
- 🇺🇸 Wendell Follansbee, 10th Armored Division (page 261)
- 🇺🇸 Gordon Pierson, 17th Airborne Division (page 269)
- 🇺🇸 Duette Mills, 101st Airborne Division (page 271)
- 🇺🇸 Raymond Hurd, 1st Inf. Division (page 275)
- 🇨🇦 Eugene Cleroux †, A. & S. Highlanders (page 284)
- 🇺🇸 Melvyn Roat †, 102nd Inf. Division (page 288)
- 🇺🇸 Kenneth Glemby, 9th Air Force (page 293)
- 🇺🇸 Henry Crookhorn, 303rd Signal Op. Bn. (page 301)
- 🇺🇸 Guenther Ahlf, 95th Inf. Division (page 303)
- 🇺🇸 Carl Holmberg, 4th Inf. Division (page 308)
- 🇺🇸 Archibald Sayce †, 4th Inf. Division (page 318)
- 🇬🇧 Hugh Stewart, Army Film & Photo. (page 322)
- 🇨🇦 Albert Vardy †, Royal Can. Air Force (page 326)
- 🇺🇸 Barbara Stuart, Camp Shows, USO (page 345)
- 🇨🇦 Fleming McConnell, Occupation Forces (page 347)
- 🇬🇧 Harrison Forrester, 7th Armored Division (page 358)

THE BIRTH OF EVIL

The Great War, which lasted for four years and ended in 1918 with 10 million dead and 21 million wounded, was to be "the last of the last". The Americans, arriving late in the conflict, wanted to apply moderate sanctions to the defeated Germany, but France demanded colossal reparations that plunged their aggressor into poverty and mass unemployment. This crisis would be the breeding ground for National Socialism ('Nazism' for short), a far-right party founded in 1920 and led by a deeply anti-Semitic former German soldier, Adolf Hitler, who was given a parliamentary majority in the 1932 elections. Appointed Chancellor by President Hindenburg on January 30, 1933, in less than a year Hitler succeeded in obtaining full powers, opening the first concentration camps, and reigning terror with the SA ('Sturmabteilung', or 'Storm Detachment') and the SS ('Schutzstaffel' or 'Protection Squadron'). When Hindenburg died in 1934, Hitler became head of state and the Führer of the Third Reich. The following year, with the Nuremberg Laws, Hitler made racial hatred an official doctrine: he undertook to purify Europe of the Jews and many others whom he considered inferior to his ideal, the Aryan race. Soon, the swastika flag would be flown all over Europe...

I
THE DARK YEARS
From the Invasion to the End of a World

When the Western democracies began to run out of steam, totalitarian regimes took advantage of the economic crisis of 1929. Benito Mussolini had created the fascist party and marched on Rome in 1922, while two years later Joseph Stalin succeeded Lenin in the young communist state that replaced the Russian Empire in 1917 (during the Bolshevik revolution). With his country excluded from negotiations at the end of the First World War, Stalin wanted to get closer to the Reich and lead a great military power. The Union of Soviet Socialist Republics (USSR) was thus built with major reforms, purges, repression and deportations. His Red Army had been fighting on its border against the Japanese since 1932, but the Soviet victory in Khalkhin Gol on 16 September 1939 prompts the Japanese to attack in the Pacific rather than in the North. The latter has been involved in the second Sino-Japanese war since 1937 and has invaded China, killing more than 20 million Chinese (military and civilian) in eight years. It was also in 1937 that Italy (which had been at war for a year in Ethiopia) joined the Anti-Comintern Pact (meaning 'Against the International Communist Organization') with Germany and Japan. They form the Axis forces at the signing of the Tripartite Pact on September 27, 1940, and are soon joined by Hungary, Romania, Slovakia and Bulgaria.

Hitler and Mussolini made their common baptism of fire in the Spanish Civil War, sending their troops to support the insurrection of General Franco, who had refused the election of the Spanish Popular Front (1936). The USSR supported the Republicans, but the Francoists won in April 1939 after the deaths of nearly 500,000 people. Meanwhile, Hitler launched the expansion of the *Lebensraum* (the living space of the German people). The *Anschluss*, the annexation of Austria, took place on March 13, 1938, then of the Sudetenland (Czechoslovakia) at the end of September. Hitler wanted to integrate the German-speaking people of this region into Germany, but above all to test the reaction of the other European powers. Their answer is very satisfactory. When he invades Czechoslovakia on March 15, 1939, no one reacts for fear of going to war with the Third Reich. Protecting its eastern flank by signing a non-aggression pact with Stalin on August 23, Hitler crosses the red line when he attacks Poland on September 1, 1939. The military alliance that France and the United Kingdom had signed with Poland brings old enemies back into conflict: this is Hitler's perfect excuse to take revenge on the 1918 defeat and war is declared on September 3. The resistance of the Polish Army is as heroic as it is futile, crushed by a German Army superior in number, tactics, and technology. As Warsaw is about to surrender, the USSR invades its eastern 'share' of the country on September 17, as agreed with Hitler on August 23. The Soviet secret police would later execute 22,000 captured officers in the Katyn forest in Russia. Germany, for its part, annexes the Danzig Corridor, Posnania and Silesia. Poland surrenders on September 27 and its government in exile moves to France, where it rebuilds an army of 90,000 men ready to fight in the Battle of France. Meanwhile, a large underground army in Poland, *Armia Krajowa*, is organizing itself.

Stalin invades Finland on November 30, triggering the Winter War. The first few months are disastrous for the unprepared Soviets and their primitive tactics, but they regain the upper hand in February. An armistice is signed on March 12, ceding vast Finnish territories to the USSR (taken over by Finland in the Continuation War alongside the Wehrmacht in June 1941). Hitler attacks Denmark, which is to serve as his base for invading Norway, on April 9, 1940. He invokes an operation aimed at "protecting the neutrality of these countries against a Franco-British invasion". Norway's many ports are of strategic importance to the Reich: they can accommodate a considerable fleet and allow crucial trade, providing access to Sweden's mineral wealth. Around 10,000 French and British troops land on both sides of Trondheim and Narvik to keep one foot in Norway, but the position is difficult to maintain and at the end of May they are ordered to withdraw to strengthen the front in France. Indeed, Hitler is trying to find his way to Paris. However, faced with the Maginot Line of fortifications stretching from Belgium to the Mediterranean and even to Tunisia (with the Mareth Line), attacking France head-on could cost him dearly. The French therefore expect to stop the Germans, just as they had in 1914.

MAURICE BALLOUX

21e bataillon d'instruction, 155e régiment d'infanterie de forteresse

Maurice is in position behind the Maginot Line, which he has been fortifying for several months. On the eve of the invasion of Poland, his wife Marthe is worried about a possible German attack... Indeed, after the 'phoney war', her husband would experience a bitter defeat.

Maurice Balloux was born on June 28, 1912 in Charmes, in the Aisne region of France. His military service in 1934 had assigned him to the 8th Company of the 2nd Engineer Regiment. Based in Metz, he was in charge of the mechanical and electrical maintenance of the Maginot Line, a network of fortifications that runs along the German border. In December 1937, he married Marthe, who gave him a son, Serge, a year and a half later. Maurice was still working at the factory, but was recalled to the army shortly before the general mobilization as tensions with Germany continued to rise.

THE MAGINOT LINE

The French Army was first put on alert in 1936 when Hitler sent elements from the Wehrmacht to the Rhineland. This territory in West Germany had been demilitarized as agreed in the Treaty of Versailles at the end of the First World War. A second alert took place two years later when the Reich annexed Austria, with everyone then expecting Hitler to attack Poland afterwards. France, which at the time had one of the most powerful armies in the world, mobilized 2.8 million men and was preparing to go to war, certain to be well protected by the Maginot Line.

Maurice in Bitche in 1934, and the insignia of the French fortress troops.

I - THE DARK YEARS 1939-1942

This is a formidable line of defense consisting of a long chain of casemates, turrets and fortifications, and equipped with an important underground communication system. It was designed after the First World War to combat the most violent offensives and the colossal budget allocated to its construction in the 1930s reassured the French of their ability to stop a possible German attack. On the other hand, the line is deliberately interrupted in the Ardennes, whose forest is considered impenetrable, and in northern France in order not to offend the Belgian allies. Of course, the Germans would take advantage of this and bypass the Maginot Line, which would prove to be completely useless. On August 21, 1939, the 'Fortress' regiments, specialized in the defense of its works and whose motto is 'One does not pass', are assigned to their posts on the Maginot Line. Three days later, the reservists in these regiments (like Maurice) are called upon to reinforce the machine gun and artillery positions in the casemates. Marthe writes to her husband the day before the invasion of Poland:

"Charmes, August 31, 1939
My dear little Maurice,
I reply to both your letters because you see, I received them at the same time. What made me very happy was having so much to read. Honey, I'm so depressed to know you're so far away. I see from your letter that you have not yet received any news from me, as you say, it is that they are late, because I always answer right away. I answered your first letter as soon as I received it. Now you tell me you've gone up the line and you're well hidden, you're not unhappy. Are you telling me this to calm me down? So that I can really believe you, you see, darling, I would like you to swear on your little Serge's head. I hope that in your answer you will do so. [...]

Now I see, darling, that you don't forget me, but don't worry, it's the same on my side. I always think of you and what all this will bring, because you see nothing good is said here, because the situation is much more critical than last year, it is not at all the same now. We put our lives on hold, waiting for a move from that HITLER PIG. This is all very sad, but despite everything, let's keep faith until he makes his decision, that's all I can say. Now, I was telling you that we were housing a soldier, and there are a lot of them in the city and in Andelain, well, everywhere, and we're talking about 3,000 British coming to the area. Robert is still there, and as long as he is, everything's okay.

Now, darling, how are you, and what do you eat? Tell me in your reply. We were very happy to know that you were in good health, for us it is the same and so is little Serge [...]. Now, while waiting to hear from you, I send you our tender kisses, I also send you kisses from our little Serge. Your little wife is thinking about you. Your mother kisses you also and will answer your letter immediately. Above all, to calm me down, darling, swear to me, if you can, what I asked you to do. Quick, write to me!"

THE WAIT

The next day, Hitler's troops invade Poland. However, Maurice is not yet in danger, as he will be waiting for the Germans... for nine long months. This period will be remembered on the French side as 'La drôle de guerre', the 'Phoney War' on the British side, or the 'Sitzkrieg' (the 'sitting war') among the Germans, which is obviously a pun following the 'Blitzkrieg' or 'lightning war' that Germany has waged in Poland.

Even if the French soldier is poorly equipped, sometimes still armed with the old Lebel rifle of 1914-1918, without an effective anti-tank gun or even a modern communication system, Germany is not in a position of strength. In front of the Maginot Line, it only has 23 divisions in September 1939, compared to 108 French divisions. On the other hand, the rumors heard by Marthe would prove true and the French are quickly reinforced by the BEF (British Expeditionary Force). Deployed in September 1939 and commanded by General Lord Gort, it takes up positions on the Franco-Belgian border alongside the 1st French Army Group. As Belgium wishes to preserve its neutrality, the British cannot advance before the German attack and remain confined to northern France.

There is no joint command yet and the British receive their orders from the French Commander-in-Chief, General Maurice Gamelin. Their four divisions represent only 10% of the defensive forces, but the BEF's strength increases from 158,000 men in October 1939 to 316,000 men in May 1940 (divided into ten divisions).

Reginald is a member of the 4th Searchlight Battery (Royal Artillery). Its role is to monitor the sky in order to prevent a Luftwaffe raid. He writes to his wife in January 1940: *"I am still at the same place Boulogne-sur-Mer and I don't know anything about what is happening. Of course, I couldn't tell you if I did. The place is not too bad, but we have not got a very good officer and of course that makes a big difference. We get fairly decent food considering there is a war on, but it amounts to stews for dinner nearly every day. We are still getting our bacon nearly every morning for breakfast and we are getting fed up with it. We are about 3 miles out of a big town, but there is not much we can do in there because nearly everything is restricted for British troops, and the pictures are all in French, so it is not much good going to them. Any how we have a walk round the shops and one thing and other and pass the evening away. Our biggest difficulty is with the language. We have to do most of our talking by signs in the shops..."*

The presence of the BEF greatly reassures the civilians, who already have a great deal of confidence in the French Army. A family expresses its optimism at the beginning of 1940: *"Many English troops arrived in Boulogne and the land where they built barracks was leased for five years. We cannot believe that the war can go on for so long. I have heard here, often by soldiers, that the war would be over by next spring. May God hear them and may this nightmare end soon. [...] Robert, whom you saw at the communion, is on leave. He is in the Ardennes and not exposed at the moment. It's a good thing, because when you think of his poor little girl who already has no mother, it's very sad. Let's hope that 1940 will be a little better for everyone and that it will be the end of this damn war."*

At the other end of France, near the German border, civilians also feel relatively safe when they see soldiers. They rely heavily on the Maginot Line, held by the 2e and 3e Armées, and on the Ardennes forest, which is reputed to be impassable: *"Here, every day, soldiers have to clean up the road and go to the supply station. Nothing can diminish their good mood, they are always smiling, they have an amazing morale. Despite everything, they firmly believe in victory, and watching them makes me as optimistic as they are."*

This is where Maurice is located. With the 155e régiment d'infanterie de forteresse, of the 103e Division, he is sheltered in a casemate in Mouzay, near Montmédy (not far from Sedan). His 21st Training Battalion (which includes about 700 men) has to train soldiers and workers in defense construction while providing frontline soldiers to the regiment. However, Maurice is running out of patience. He writes to Marthe on March 27, 1940: *"Don't be so depressed, and you don't have to worry about me, darling. I'm not unhappy here, except that I'm very bored."* Indeed, with the exception of a small incursion into Saarland and the capture of a few German villages on September 12, the French Army waits patiently and without a fight for an attack that seems will never come.

Maurice is also very confident, although his wife's absence lowers his morale. He writes on April 22, less than three weeks before the German attack: *"Speaking of furloughs, I can tell you, my sweet darling, that they have been restored and I see that by the end of May there will be good news for me. And you know, honey, I would love to be there already, because I have a crazy urge to embrace you. [...] Poor darling, you still ask me very kindly if I can bring you to me; you know how much I love you and how happy I would be to see you again, but to my great regret, I swear on the head of our dear little one that you can't come to me. You would not be allowed to pass and even if you could make it this far, you would be immediately dismissed and prosecuted. No, honey, believe me, give up this project, you know that if I could do it, I would have done it a long time ago."*

English and French soldiers entertaining themselves near a shelter in November 1939.

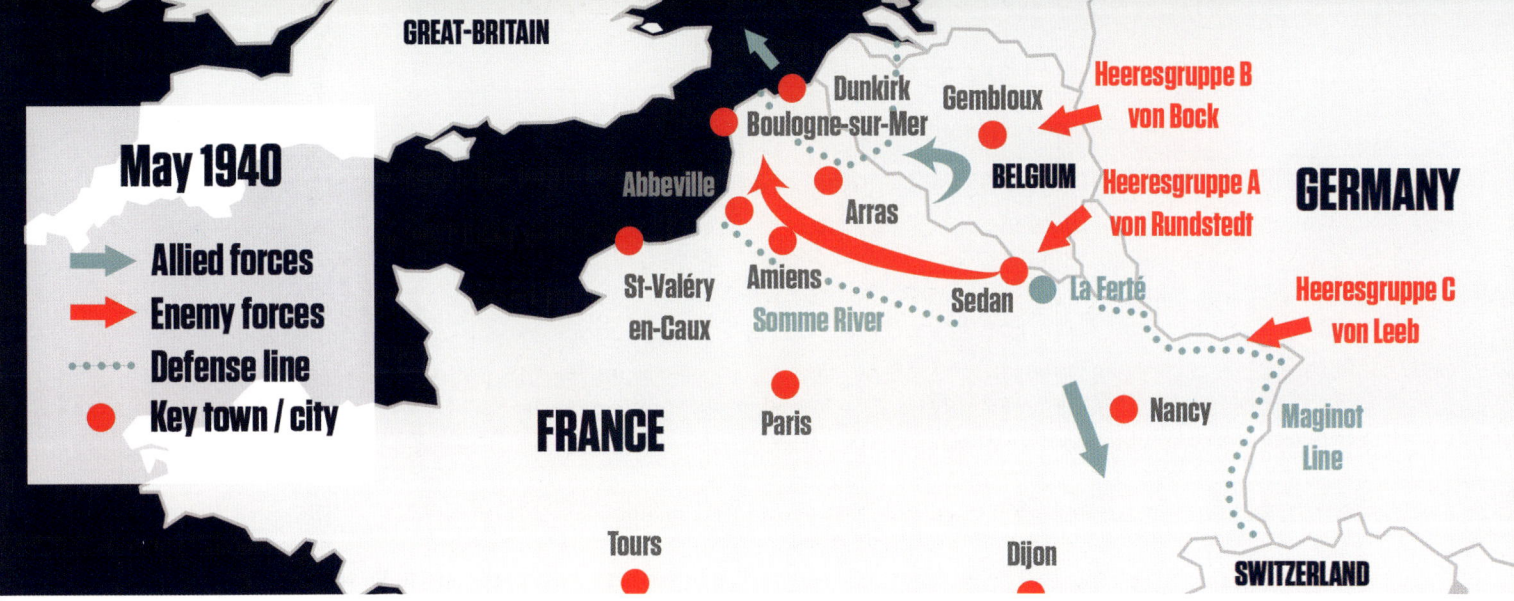

THE GERMAN ATTACK

Maurice and his comrades are alerted on May 10, 1940 that the Germans are launching their assault. *Fall Gelb* (*Plan Yellow*) involves more than 40 German divisions (out of the 141 they now have at the border), among the best in the Wehrmacht. Ten of them are armored or motorized. Although French tanks had long been superior both in numbers and technology, only the Germans understood their offensive value. The concentrated use of the new Panzer III and IV in deep breaches has a devastating effect on defensive lines. They are also supported by the Luftwaffe, led by former pilot Hermann Göring, who dominates the air after attacking more than fifty French airfields. Luxembourg, the Netherlands and Belgium are quickly invaded by Fedor von Bock's Army Group B (Heeresgruppe B).

The Dutch Army is defeated in a few hours and the country surrenders on May 15. Further south, Belgian defenses fall rapidly, such as the Eben-Emael Fort between Liege and Maastricht, which is taken by only eighty-five German parachutists. The enemy is simply bypassing the impregnable Maginot Line (which faces von Leeb's Army Group C). In response, the French launch the Dyle Plan, which consists of sending thirty-five divisions (including almost the whole BEF) to the river of the same name in Belgium. The French 7e Armée rushes towards Breda in the north, the British towards the south of Brussels, the 1re Armée towards Liège and the 9e Armée towards Dinant. In reality, the poorly equipped, poorly trained and understaffed units rushing into Belgium are heading straight for the trap set by Hitler. Against all odds, his Army Group A, commanded by von Rundstedt, goes through the Ardennes to launch the main attack. The breakthrough happens in Sedan, behind the back of the French who had gone to Belgium. Tactics from another time and serious command errors precipitate France's defeat.

Half a million men are now trapped on the Maginot Line. The positions north of the line are then quickly attacked and Maurice and his comrades jump to their guns under the Luftwaffe bombardments. The French air force, in a deplorable state, can't stand up to the onslaught, despite the courage of its pilots. The soldiers cross paths with Belgian and Luxembourg refugees and Maurice's company is tasked with guiding these displaced people to Montigny-sur-Meuse, although no accommodation or shelter has been planned. As a result, 8 million civilians fleeing the fighting will try to take refuge behind the Maginot Line. However, the latter would not last long, and a company of Maurice's regiment would face a tragic fate there.

LA FERTÉ

During the winter, the regiment occupied and reinforced the defenses around the bunker of La Ferté, located in the villages of Villy and La Ferté-sur-Chiers (French Ardennes). This fort, perched on a hill, is composed of two blocks connected by an underground gallery. It is equipped with only a few machine guns, grenade launchers and small caliber anti-tank guns. One hundred and seven men are present in the bunker, while the 23e régiment d'infanterie coloniale defends the village of Villy. In the north, the XIX. Panzer Korps commanded by Heinz Guderian reaches the Meuse between Dinant and Sedan on May 12. The powerful German artillery and Luftwaffe bombers allow the Germans to break through the disorganized French lines and then cross the river the next day.

On the 14th, the men in the bunkers on the Chiers and Meuse rivers are ordered to evacuate the positions, depriving La Ferté of its artillery and infantry support in the face of the inexorable advance of the Wehrmacht.

The bunker at La Ferté.

Above, a view of Block 1 protected by its anti-tank rails and anti-personnel barbed wire.

Below, the bell of Block 2 has several German 88 mm shell impacts. Three French soldiers were killed inside.

Villy would resist for three days, slowing the Germans' progress, until the enemy attacks towards its objectives of hills 223, 331 and the village of Vigny, which helps them take the bunker from a poorly defended blind spot. Despite many casualties inflicted on the attackers, the French soldiers fighting in the village surrender on the 18th and La Ferté finds itself totally isolated. On the same day, the bunker is pounded by heavy artillery and at 7:20 pm, German engineers reach Block 2 with explosive charges, destroying the turrets and creating openings through which they throw grenades. The defenders find shelter in the underground tunnel, soon joined by those of Block 1 which is attacked three hours later. Unfortunately, the many fires breaking out there, caused by German grenades, emit toxic fumes in the unventilated gallery. The French put on their gas masks, but as they are intended for battle gases and not against carbon monoxide and lack of oxygen, the poor men gradually suffocate.

At 5:40 am on May 20, La Ferté's phone stops answering: of the 107 French soldiers in the bunker, there are no survivors. The Germans take the bodies out, burying some in a mass grave in the village and others in a shell hole in front of Block 2. Some bodies would not be found until 1990. The lucky few sent to defend the village are taken prisoner.

THE END OF THE WAR FOR MAURICE

The following day, Maurice's training battalion hears about the destruction of La Ferté. Tasked with defending Dun (on the Meuse River), they organize themselves to block the passage of German tanks, which according to some reports had been pushed back at Montmédy. Maurice's company, with two complete sections, have been positioned on the road linking Murvaux to Milly, a little further south, since May 24. In foxholes and armed with machine guns, 25- and 37-mm guns and 81-mm mortars, they assist sappers of the French 618th Pioneer Regiment while the latter install roadblocks, barbed wire, anti-tank mines and an AAA (anti-aircraft) position. In reality, they have already been bypassed by the tanks and these defenses will never be used. The Germans have cut the Allied lines in half and reached the English Channel. An armored counter-attack led by Colonel Charles de Gaulle on May 17 at Montcornet only slowed them down, the Germans pulverizing his tanks with their Stukas dive bombers and artillery guns. The situation is so critical that General Gamelin, considered too passive, is replaced as Supreme Commander by Maxime Weygand, head of the Middle East forces.

Without receiving any information from the front, Maurice's battalion holds its line until June 10. They are then relieved by the 12th Zouave Regiment and withdrawn behind the Meuse River in Dun. Heavy shelling falls on the city on June 11, when the battalion is ordered to wait there for the enemy. The first enemy tanks appear on the edge of the wood the next day, greeted by a barrage of French artillery. At 9 pm, Maurice and his men are ordered to retreat, while the engineers blow up the bridges. Just on the other side of the Meuse, the Germans are trying to capture Sivry-sur-Meuse, which is on fire. Maurice and his battalion have to prevent the crossing of the canal, but at 3:30 pm on June 13, the enemy attacks the city with a rare violence. The fighting lasts all afternoon, until the men gradually withdraw, leaving Maurice's 1st Company alone against the Germans.

I - THE DARK YEARS 1939-1942

They would hold until 8 pm and eventually follow the rest of the battalion. At 2 am on June 14, the French soldiers set up their defences in Vacherauville, just north of Verdun. They must allow the entire 103e Division to retreat, but the Germans are already there. The men of the 2nd Company are lost, killed or captured. As it receives a new retreat order, the 3rd Company (which is located to the right of Maurice's) is destroyed. Lieutenant-Colonel Henri of the 155e régiment de forteresse orders the captain of the 1st Company to *"Hold on no matter what, the 21e bataillon is sacrificed, with the division légère, it must ensure the withdrawal of the entire 3e Armée."* Maurice and his company are therefore positioned at the entrance to the village, which they would defend house by house, and from 3 pm until nightfall, they repel three German attacks under a continuous bombardment. Receiving his orders to withdraw at 9 pm, Maurice is unable to extract himself from the firefight until midnight and finally rushes towards Verdun, which he discovers in flames. The bridges explode in the background. Now that the encirclement by the German forces is almost complete, the exhausted men withdraw on foot towards the Vosges, without any map to direct them. They also lack food and ammunition and have no idea of the overall situation. What remains of Maurice's company loses contact with the battalion on June 18 and with all the elements of the regiment they can find, they march through Toul, Vézelise (south of Nancy) and Saint-Dié.

It is here that at 6 am on June 22, the enemy enters the city and captures Maurice and his comrades.

Maurice Balloux is sent to Stalag XVII-B, in Krems, Austria, on a plateau overlooking the Danube. His camp is the one where prisoners will be treated the worst after Stalag II-B. Hygiene conditions are inhuman and dysentery epidemics will become common place. Food will be scarce and moldy most of the time: prisoners will often try to find a place in the dark so they won't see what they are eating. During his captivity, Maurice will be transferred to Stalag XVIII C Markt Pongau, also known as Stalag No 317 (north of the village of Sankt Johann im Pongau, also in the Austrian Alps). It will simultaneously accommodate up to 30,000 prisoners from nine different nations, even though it was designed for only 8,000 people.

When Maurice finally returns home to Charmes in the summer of 1945, he is unrecognizable due to the weight he lost in captivity. By then, little Serge will already be 5 years old. Going to the bakery with his paternal grandmother, Serge will pass by a man on the sidewalk wearing a large khaki woolen coat and a long beard. Seeing his grandmother burst into tears and jump into the arms of this stranger, the little boy will say to him, *"Hello sir"*. This will be Serge's first meeting with his father.

Maurice, still skinny from his captivity, Marthe and Serge shortly after the war.

Maurice died in 1978 and Marthe in 1998.

ROGER VALLIÈRES

105e régiment d'artillerie lourde hippomobile

While Maurice is holding the Maginot Line, Roger is sent to Belgium as part of the Dyle Plan. The operation turns into a disaster when the Germans break through the lines at Sedan: his unit is rushed to Dunkirk in the hope of being evacuated there. Sent back to France to continue the fight, Roger is taken prisoner and will spend the war in Germany, until his liberation by the Red Army in 1945.

Roger in full uniform. Note the French 'Adrian' helmet with the artillery emblem of two crossed guns.

Roger Vallières, born near Blois (France), is 25 years old when the war breaks out. Mobilized on September 3, he joins the 1st battery of the 105e régiment d'artillerie lourde hippomobile (RALH) (horse-drawn heavy artillery) in Bourges as a 2nd gunner. The means of towing the guns, using horses, is not the only primitive tool still in use in the French Army. Roger writes: *"With two others, I am assigned a Saint-Etienne [or Hotchkiss] anti-aircraft machine gun, model 1898, firing six hundred shots a minute* [the German MG34 has a rate of more than a thousand shots a minute]. *After a few shots, it's jammed! We got into a flat wagon, the battery ready to fire."* The regiment is on its way to the North of France to spend its 'drôle de guerre' there.

THE TRAP

The 105e RALH is part of the 2e Division nord-africaine (mainly Zouaves and Algerian riflemen), III Corps, 1re Armée of General Blanchard. It leaves with the BEF to support the Belgian Army and try to counter the German offensive in Belgium (*Dyle Plan*). Roger sets up his battery near Gembloux, north of Namur, on May 14, 1940. The same day, the 3. Panzer-Division attacks the area. The French air force is systematically shot down by the Flak (anti-aircraft guns) accompanying the assault troops. However, French tanks, infantry and especially Roger's artillery manage to stop the German aggression for a while. French guns fire as long as ammunition stocks permit, when they are not destroyed by 88 mm shells and Stuka bombs. The French count 2,000 killed, wounded and missing in their ranks, while they have inflicted less than half that number on the enemy. Roger recalls: *"After 24 hours of bombing, in the morning, the 105e fires at a distance of 8 km and in the evening at only 500 meters. As we see the Germans approaching, our regiment retreats to Waterloo [south of Brussels] and sets up the guns behind the electrified anti-tank line. Everything is moved the same day and ready to fire further east. I almost get taken prisoner, left alone with the machine gun I am forced to abandon. I use the moon to get out of the woods, but I lose the battery. After a long walk, I find some guys from the 105e, but from the 2nd battery."*

It is already becoming urgent to retreat to Lille, since the news has spread that the Germans have managed to break through the Ardennes and are threatening to surround the French and British troops in Belgium. Roger finally finds his unit in Neufmaison, then crosses the French border. Unfortunately, it is already too late as von Rundstedt's Army Group A is already heading from Sedan towards the English Channel. The British 5th and 50th Infantry Divisions attempt a counter-attack at Arras with the French 3e Division légère mécanique. But against two Panzer divisions and one Panzer-SS division, they have no choice but to withdraw.

The commemorative medal for the Battle of Gembloux, awarded to Roger on April 5 1987.

German troops capture Amiens on May 20 and seize an opportunity to encircle British, Belgian, and thirty French divisions in Boulogne-sur-Mer, Dunkirk and Calais. The Wehrmacht thus drives along the Somme towards Abbeville to form the 'pocket'. On the 28th, another counter-attack by the recently promoted General Charles de Gaulle's 4e Division cuirassée cannot stop the Panzers' progress, although it does achieve some success. Winston Churchill, who became British Prime Minister on the day of the German attack in France, decides to evacuate the BEF from French harbors to save it from certain destruction. On May 27, Roger's unit is violently bombed, particularly in Péronne-en-Mélantois: *"Sixteen dead soldiers, as many wounded, forty-six horses killed. In Péronne, I bury a guy with my bare hands in a shell hole with another man."*

Roger and a 155C Schneider gun, model 1917, the most widely used 155 mm gun by the French field artillery.

THE EVACUATION... ALMOST

The situation being desperate, the artillerymen are ordered to retreat to Dunkirk to be shipped to England. On May 28, the regiment is in Neuve-église: *"Battery ready to fire at 6 pm, and at 8 pm, we are ordered to destroy our own guns. We are surrounded and running for our lives... See you in Bray-Dunes! I jump into a truck to Poperinge (Belgium). From there, I walk to Bergues after only an hour of rest. I walk one night and one day and another part of the next night. On May 30, when I arrive in Bray-Dunes, I see comrades from the 3rd battery."* It's in Malo-les-Bains, just east of the great harbor of Dunkirk, that Roger is evacuated on May 31 in absolute chaos. While immersed in the fuel oil of the ships sunk by the Luftwaffe, he is recovered by the British dredger ship *Foremost 101*: *"I reach the Foremost 101 at 6 pm, completely exhausted. We climb on board using a net hanging along the side. Two Englishmen help me on each side otherwise I would fall back into the sea. Then I undress and dry near the boat's boiler. I lay down and think to myself: 'I don't care if we're sunk, I can't take it anymore!'"*

Roger arrives the next day at noon in Ramsgate, England. He is very well received by the English, but like most French soldiers, he doesn't stay there for long: he has to continue the fight in France. Of the 100,000 French soldiers evacuated to Britain, only 3,000 would stay to join the British Army (and later, the Free French of General de Gaulle, exiled in London on June 17). Roger leaves Plymouth on June 5 aboard the ship *La Ville D'Alger*. He arrives in Brest the next day at 11 am, takes many trains and walks many miles to reach Caen, where the regiment is reformed. Yet the battle is already lost. When the armistice is signed, only half of the repatriated French soldiers have time to return to combat against the Germans. Roger will be angry all his life with Marshal Pétain for *"delivering the French soldiers to Hitler"*.

The military dog tag worn by Roger on his wrist throughout this period. As part of the 1933 class, he had completed his military service that year with the 103e régiment d'artillerie lourde automobile (Automobile Heavy Artillery Regiment).

On June 26, 1940, Roger is interned in the Vannes arsenal with nearly 15,000 men, surrounded by watchtowers and machine guns. He is entitled to 500 grams of bread, 50 grams of meat, 20 grams of fat, 10 grams of coffee, 90 grams of dried vegetables or 50 grams of cheese per day. On August 12 he is transferred to Abbeville camp, after fifty hours of train travel, suffering from a nasty dysentery. His daily rations are getting smaller: he is now entitled to only one substitute of coffee or nettle, 200 grams of bread, 10 grams of pork fat and a liter of water.

The mayor of the town of Saint-Claude-de-Diray, near Blois, asks for Roger's release in a letter to the German authorities: *"[...] certifies that Private Vallières Roger, born on 26 October 1913 in Montlivault, Loir-et-Cher, soldier in the 105e RALH, interned at the Vannes arsenal on 26 June, transferred to the Champ de Mars camp, Abbéville, Somme on 12 August, is a farmer on a farm of about fifteen hectares located in the communes of Saint-Claude, Montlivault, Huisseau and Vineuil. Given the lack of labor in the municipality, the person concerned is essential to the resumption of economic life. To this end, I ask for his release or permission to help his wife work in the fields, as she lives alone. The mayor vouches for his accommodation, his good conduct, and affirms that he will not be a burden to the German authority."* No release will be granted to Roger.

Postcard sent by Roger from Guildford (as he crosses England in early June to be taken back to Plymouth), simply marked *"Good kisses"* on the back, and a photo booth picture taken with a comrade shortly after the evacuation. On the left, his medal commemorating the Battle of Dunkirk.

I - THE DARK YEARS 1939-1942

Roger's prisoner's plaque, bearing the Stalag name and his POW number. The latter is also written on a piece of fabric sewn to his work uniform.

On January 9, 1941, he begins a long journey to his prison camp (Stalag) abroad: *"On January 13, 1941, we arrive at the Kaisersteinbruck camp in Austria, 30 km southeast of Vienna, after ninety-six hours spent in the closed cattle wagon, packed with sixty-five to seventy men. To go to bed, you always need someone standing up: one hour lying down, one hour standing up. Instead of toilets, you have to use a mustard bucket."* However, this is not yet his final destination. After many more hours of train travel and miles of mountain walking, he arrives in Heilbrunn (Austria) on January 23. He is interned at Stalag XVIII-A, where he shares 25 m² with fifteen men. During the day, Roger does forced labor in the fields of the Paller and Kratzer families (whose sons serve on the Russian front). A farmer by trade, he is appreciated by the latter and will even visit them again after the war (in this photograph, taken during his captivity, Roger is on the right).

He would only be 'liberated' on May 8, 1945 by the Red Army: the Soviets would intern him for a while and send him to Hungary to unload wagons. Their trucks will finally take him near Linz, where the Americans will take over. At last, he will return home in the afternoon of June 4, 1945, after six years of absence.

Letter for Roger's release:
*"To the military commander of the city of Veszprém. I hereby request the release of a Frenchman and of an Italian, former prisoners of war.
Red Army military commander, city of Szombathely."*

DESMOND FINNY

Royal Army Service Corps, British Expeditionary Force HQ

As an experienced officer, Desmond deals with the evacuation operations on the pier at Dunkirk with typically British courage and optimism. His actions will earn him the Military Cross, but he will be killed in a motorcycle accident shortly before receiving it.

THE BEF UNDER PRESSURE

Desmond Marriott Finny was born on September 12, 1906 at Hill House, Finchingfield, Essex, England. He was quickly attracted to the army, despite coming from a family that was known in the medical field. Desmond was very impressed by his uncle, an Irish veteran of the Great War, who was seriously wounded in Passchendaele. Leading a company of Dublin Fusiliers, he had had the top of his head blown off during an assault but survived into his nineties! A graduate of the Royal Military College at Sandhurst, Desmond began his career in China with the Bedfordshire and Hertfordshire Regiment (Shanghai Defence Force) and then in Mhow (now the Ambedkar Nagar district) in India in 1928. On February 3, 1930, tired of the infantry, he was transferred to the Royal Army Service Corps five days after being promoted to lieutenant. He married Elsie the following year, an English woman he met in India, who gave him a son, John, in 1933. The latter would say of his father: *"He was a remarkable man, an exceptionally gallant and slightly eccentric officer with a multi-faceted intellect; indeed, he was rather typically Anglo-Irish."*

Desmond served in Egypt in 1936. He was made captain there, then mentioned in dispatches for his actions during the great Arab revolt in Palestine. On April 8, 1938, he started working under the Chief Inspector of Armaments in Manchester, a position he held until the declaration of war. Desmond then joined the BEF and landed in France on September 19, 1939, assigned to the railway communication lines of the Royal Army Service Corps (RASC). As the 'Phoney War' dragged on, he took the opportunity to attend a special training course at Staff College in Camberley, England. In May 1940 he then took on a new position at the BEF headquarters in Arras, just in time to see the Nazi armies set foot on French soil. Attached to the staff of General John Gort (Commander-in-Chief of the BEF), he carried orders from HQ to the various units scattered on the front, using his motorcycle.

Following the failure of the Dyle Plan, as the BEF withdraws in a hurry to the French coast, Desmond continues his round trips from HQ to the front under German bombardment until May 22. His role is starting to become crucial, when he is ordered to lead the way to Dunkirk for the units lagging behind.

Desmond's ID card and
Royal Army Service Corps collar badge.

Among those lost behind enemy lines, he runs into his uncle, Major-General Charles Finney, former head of the Royal Army Medical Corps (retired but recalled to the head of a field hospital) whom he recognizes at a distance in a deserted village by his monocle. *"Desmond, what the hell are you doing here?"* says Charles. *"Uncle, that is the question I have for you"* replies Desmond, returning him to safety.

Around 400,000 British, French, Belgian, Polish and Dutch soldiers await a hypothetical ship in Dunkirk. Most of them would embark from the east mole, an area where Desmond will be particularly active. Unfortunately, time is running out: despite the determination and sacrifice of British and French rearguard troops protecting the beaches, German troops are closing in and Churchill estimates that he can save some 45,000 men at best. Miraculously, on May 24, Hitler orders his tanks be stopped on the outskirts of the city, once the beach is within artillery range. The Panzers have been in constant combat for weeks and need to be preserved for the rest of the invasion. Moreover, seven German divisions remained blocked for five days in front of Lille: the courageous and desperate resistance of a corps of the French 1re Armée (half of them being North African troops) slowed down the German advance. This unexpected respite allows the Allies to evacuate large numbers of soldiers and organize their defense. The operation, code named *Dynamo*, is launched on May 27, 1940.

OPERATION DYNAMO

The Führer's order is finally lifted two days later, and so begins the battle for Dunkirk, on a front around 5 miles long and 12 miles wide. The Luftwaffe would drop more than 4,000 bombs on the city over the course of a thousand daily missions. Desmond is present on the pier during the German air attack of May 29, when several British ships are lost, including two destroyers. On many occasions, he helps the men get on a boat. Upon their return to England, many would visit Elsie and little John's home to express their gratitude: *"What I myself do remember, even as a small boy, was the constant stream of odd, dirty strangers coming by our Camberley house to give us messages from my father, of being patted on the head by a huge Guards Sgt. Major saying 'your father, lad, is a wonderful man; he saved all our lives, we'll never forget'* – and I bet they never did."

In a letter from Dunkirk on May 25, Desmond describes to his wife the atmosphere in the pocket: *"My own precious sweetheart, dreadfully sorry to have missed writing; I'm afraid one has been more than quite busy – bed at 12 or 1, and up at 5 or 6. Flat out, and no meal times. Heavens, what have I been doing? Or rather, what haven't I been doing? It has been utterly heavenly weather – the Devil has held Hitler's hands. I have beetled and beetled, principally on a motorcycle. My tail and hands are sore from bumping along cobbled roads!*

We are near the coast at one of the ports and it is very fresh and nice. Yesterday I had to run out on a special job, just behind the fighting. It was exciting, in the last four miles or so, approaching corners carefully in case a Boche tank should be around the corner! None was there however, and I got into some lovely rolling country, so green and wooded. It was exquisite. The usual hoo-hah, 'German motorcyclists are coming over the hill' was sprung, which I was able to quash with my glasses. Today was principally spent in the dock area – in the smoke of the fires. Bombing has been – is – very heavy in all the ports, but the work goes on just the same. Anti-aircraft fire is terrific. The sky is darkened with shell bursts, and the Boche keeps very high and zigzags. I saw one shot down this evening that came in cautiously low. A great sight! Every so often Spitfires or Hurricanes turn up, so terrific air battles eventuate. One can see them with glasses, specks in the sky, wheeling and turning, with the roar of machine guns and the periodic fall of a plane, the pilot sometimes jumping for it in a parachute. The films are very accurate! I saw a Spitfire shot down through my glasses – exactly as per films! The pilot jumped, and I think he was all right. A German was floating down similarly, about two miles away. They took ten minutes to float down from the great height they were up. I've heard bombs whistle too. Most gratifying, because from any reasonable height you can hear the whistle for two or three seconds before the crumps, which gives plenty of time to lie down. I still haven't had one near me (touch wood). Oh sweet my sweet, I love you so terribly much. I am not brave or adventurous at all these days. I only plot to get back rapidly to my dear, dear Elsie. God bless you, sweet, sweet love, and tell Poosle I love him. I am half asleep and must go to bed.

What adventures I will have to tell when I come back! I am feeling awfully fit and am doing myself very well. Ever your own, Des."

During the first few days, evacuation is very slow and the men waiting on the beaches make easy targets for enemy aircraft. The role of the Royal Navy in the operation is vital, but not sufficient, and the French and Merchant navies must provide full support to *Operation Dynamo*. Following the Admiralty's call on the BBC, many British, French, Belgian and Dutch fishermen and yachtsmen, who also volunteered for the evacuation of Calais and Boulogne-sur-Mer, start putting their boats to work. In addition to the 200 warships, 700 private boats (coasters, barges, yachts, tugboats, ferries, trawlers...) are requisitioned to hastily recover BEF and Allied soldiers. On the beach, General Harold Alexander himself, commander of I Corps, asks Desmond to leave the pocket as he has done more than his share. Desmond's last action in France is to push out a raft with a mixed Anglo-French band of non-swimmers to a waiting boat. He finally leaves Dunkirk on the night of June 2-3 with some of the last soldiers and the staff of John Clouston, the Canadian commander of the Royal Navy (in charge of the east mole, killed during the day). All in all, 338,226 soldiers have been evacuated, including more than 120,000 French soldiers (many of whom will be sent back to France, as we have seen earlier) but also Belgians, Dutch, Poles and Norwegians, during what Churchill will later call "the miracle of Dunkirk".

At the end of the operation, in his speech to the House of Commons on June 4, Churchill reminds everyone that wars are not won with evacuations, while at the same time galvanizing the British and calling on the Americans: *"Even though large tracts of Europe and many old and famous States have fallen or may fall into the grip of the Gestapo and all the odious apparatus of Nazi rule, we shall not flag or fail. We shall go on to the end. We shall fight in France, we shall fight on the seas and oceans, we shall fight with growing confidence and growing strength in the air, we shall defend our island, whatever the cost may be. We shall fight on the beaches, we shall fight on the landing grounds, we shall fight in the fields and in the streets, we shall fight in the hills; we shall never surrender, and if, which I do not for a moment believe, this island or a large part of it were subjugated and starving, then our Empire beyond the seas, armed and guarded by the British Fleet, would carry on the struggle, until, in God's good time, the New World, with all its power and might, steps forth to the rescue and the liberation of the old."*

When Dunkirk falls into German hands, 40,000 French and British defenders are taken prisoner, after receiving the order to stop their heroic fight to protect the boarding operations. According to Desmond, *"they saved the show".*

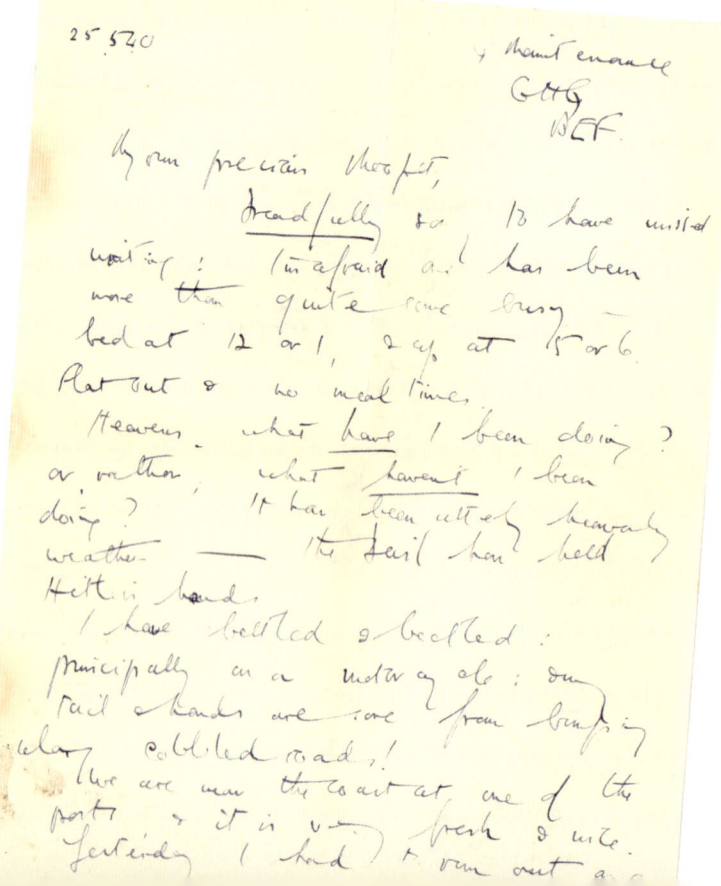

I - THE DARK YEARS 1939-1942

Among the defenders of the Dunkirk Pocket sacrificed for the BEF's embarkment are the Royal Scots, the oldest infantry regiment in the British Army (1633). The 1st Battalion was deployed with the 2nd Division (BEF), alongside the Border Regiment (1st Battalion) and the Royal Norfolk Regiment (2nd Battalion). After they were sent to Belgium, they are now responsible for protecting the evacuation. The Royal Scots move into position at Le Paradis, near Béthune, on May 25. They are ordered as follows: *"You will hold your positions. You will either be killed, wounded, or taken prisoner."*

The 3. SS-Division Totenkopf ('Death's Head' or 'Skull and Crossbones'), strongly indoctrinated by Nazi ideology and which has just executed 200 Moroccan prisoners in Cambrai, faces the Royal Scots and the Royal Norfolk who are entrenched near a farm. The British are enduring repeated attacks from German tanks, with only their rifles and a few machine guns to defend themselves. They are forced to surrender in the afternoon of the 27th, out of ammunition. The ninety-nine surviving soldiers are then placed in a line along a wall by the SS, and two machine guns get ready to fire at will on the prisoners.

Hauptsturmführer Fritz Knöchlein then orders that the men who somehow survived the bullets are finished off with a bayonet or with a rifle butt strike to the head. Miraculously, two British soldiers would survive and hide in a pigsty for three days before being captured by Wehrmacht soldiers. Upon their return from captivity, they would testify against Fritz Knöchlein who will be tried and executed in 1949. One of the two survivors, Private Albert Pooley, remembers: *"We turned off the dusty French road, through a gateway and into a meadow beside the buildings of a farm. I saw with one of the nastiest feelings I have ever had in my life two heavy machine guns inside the meadow... pointing at the head of our column. The guns began to spit fire... For a few seconds the cries and shrieks of our stricken men drowned the crackling of the guns. Men fell like grass before a scythe... I felt a searing pain and pitched forward... My scream of pain mingled with the cries of my mates, but even before I fell into the heap of dying men, the thought stabbed my brain 'If I ever get out of here, the swine that did this will pay for it'."*

However, these ninety-seven prisoners of war murdered by the SS are not the only ones. In 2007, a mass grave will be discovered nearby, containing the bodies of twenty-one soldiers from the 1st Royal Scots. They were lined up in front of a trench they had probably been ordered to dig, before being shot in the back of the head. Other units that have carried out their desperate rearguard mission would suffer the same fate at the hands of the Waffen-SS.

This representation of a resting Royal Scot wears an original Tam O'Shanter hat, adorned with a two-piece, two-color badge 'The Royal Scots', representing Saint Andrew, Scotland's patron saint. The red felt piece between the badge and the Scottish tartan designates the 1st Battalion. It will soon be reformed in England and serve in Burma.

The pier of the east mole at Dunkirk, where Desmond helped hundreds of soldiers evacuate the pocket.

Despite the many evacuees, in addition to the men captured on June 4, nearly 200 boats sank, including 6 British destroyers and 3 French; 177 aircraft were lost defending the pocket, while inflicting 240 losses on the Luftwaffe, and 11,000 men died in the bombings or during the street fighting.

Upon his return to England, Desmond is reunited with his wife and son, accompanied by a few officers in pitiful condition but determined to celebrate their survival. He would soon join the Headquarters Staff, X Corps, Northern Command, in Yorkshire. For his bravery during the evacuation, he is awarded the Military Cross, one of the highest military honors in the United Kingdom, and promoted to major. Unfortunately, his promising career is abruptly interrupted on the evening of July 30, 1940. Summoned to HQ at a late hour, his motorcycle collides with a truck: Desmond is killed instantly at the age of 33. He was to receive his medal a week later from King George VI at Buckingham Palace. His widow Elsie will take his place at a special ceremony in the King's personal air raid shelter on 17 September. Holding back her tears with courage, she would only announce his death to little John once the family had settled with her grandparents in January 1941. Elsie will never remarry... According to her, Desmond had been enough for a lifetime.

PANIC IN THE RANKS

Not all the British were evacuated from Dunkirk and a second operation, code named *Cycle*, takes place in Le Havre from 10-13 June. At the same time, the 52nd (Lowland) Infantry Division and the 1st Canadian Infantry Brigade land in France in the futile hope of creating a second BEF. They return to their ship a few days later with many other Tommies who were still cut off from the allied lines, trying by any means to reach a port to return to England. Among them, a member of a Royal Air Force (RAF) ground crew recounts the horror of the debacle in his diary. Near the Berry-au-Bac airfield, northwest of Reims, its personnel had taken the full force of the attack from the Ardennes:

"What I shall never forget:
May: *Attack after attack on us at Berry, those terrific moments in the gun pits, the lads going 'West' hour by hour, Dusty and me holding the 'Musette' cross roads, and getting through, Jessie in my mind pushing me every minute. 'B' Flight in the trenches holding the parachutists with fixed bayonets and we came out 75% strong. The start of the big retreat at 3 am on the Friday.* [...]
June: *Losing my pals day by day, writing optimistically to my mum and to dear Jessie when after so many near ones I never thought I could last out. The big fall back to the coast, bombing and machine gunning on the road. Max and Bill being killed beside me. Our lorry breaking down. Getting out, going mad, seeing red, fighting, running, fighting, etc. Reaching Brest, missing Lancastria, catching next boat. Listening to the boys on Lancastria singing 'Roll out barrel' as they went down.*"

The *RMS* (Royal Mail Ship) *Lancastria* was a liner requisitioned only one month earlier by the British Army. While France was on the verge of defeat, it helped evacuate the rest of the BEF to Brittany. After a passage through Brest, it hastily embarked nearly 9,000 soldiers and civilians in Saint Nazaire

I - THE DARK YEARS 1939-1942

(although it was designed for 3,000 passengers) as part of the third evacuation, *Operation Ariel* (from 15 to 25 June). Unfortunately, it was bombed at 4 pm on June 17 by German Junkers Ju 88s and sank in twenty minutes at the mouth of the Loire River, in a burning oil slick. Between 3,000 and 5,800 people died in the shipwreck, the largest maritime disaster in the history of the United Kingdom. The news is quickly suppressed by Churchill, so as not to further demoralize British citizens (this was more than the losses of *RMS Titanic* and *RMS Lusitania* combined). By missing the Lancastria, the author of this diary probably escaped death. He will be one of the 191,000 additional BEF soldiers repatriated from an Atlantic harbor and will reunite with his Jessie in England.

Some BEF units, attached to the French Army on the Maginot Line and which therefore escaped the encirclement of Dunkirk, are still in France: this is the case of the Gordon Highlanders, 51st (Highland) Infantry Division, who are still south of the Somme with three other British divisions. Following the evacuation of Dunkirk, the Highlanders are tasked with recapturing Abbeville and maintaining the communication lines with the French 10e Armée. For fear that it would be surrounded by the Germans approaching from all directions, the order is given on June 10 to extract the division by the small seaside town of Saint-Valéry-en-Caux. Battalions of the Gordon Highlanders, Seaforth Highlanders, Cameron Highlanders, Black Watch and French troops thus position themselves in a semi-circle around the city to prepare for the evacuation.

On June 11, the Germans arrive on the perimeter and the various battalions retaliate. The lines are quickly penetrated, and the first British troops are surrounded. However, when the order to embark is given, the Royal Navy ships withdraw, blinded by an impenetrable fog offshore and harassed by the Luftwaffe and German guns that have an unobstructed view of the coast. The miracle of Dunkirk will therefore not happen again. The Gordon Highlanders, under heavy machine gun fire, out of ammunition and suffering heavy casualties, realize with horror that no ship is waiting for them. Major-General Victor Fortune leaves his men of the 51st (Highland) Division in enemy hands on the morning of June 12, 1940. More than 10,000 soldiers are taken prisoner and sent to Poland in cattle wagons. Many Gordon Highlanders fell that day, as evidenced by the graves in the Saint-Valéry cemetery. The street leading to it is also renamed 'Avenue of Scotland'.

In total, 68,980 British soldiers and officers were killed, wounded or missing, mostly in the infantry, from May 10 to the end of the evacuation. The loss rate was 16.6%, almost as high as in the First World War (17%), demonstrating the violence of the fighting in the summer of 1940.

This Glengarry bonnet, with the Gordon Highlanders badge, belonged to Private George Fisher, who was taken prisoner in France during the battle. Two thousand Gordons of the 4th and 6th Battalions were evacuated from Dunkirk, but almost as many men from the 1st and 5th Battalions were captured in Saint-Valéry. They will be reformed in Great Britain, and the 51st (Highland) Division will be one of the most experienced divisions of the war.

This Scottish soldier wears his gas mask bag on his chest and his 37 Pattern webbing set. Two large ammo pouches are attached to its straps. As required by the regulations, the entire set is coated with Blanco, a powder mixed with water intended to camouflage the equipment: the color for the BEF in 1940 is No. 97 Khaki Green, or 'pea green'.

The retreat was so fast and chaotic that the BEF left behind all of its equipment: almost all its 445 tanks, 2,472 guns, 85,000 trucks and various vehicles, with more than 147,000 tons of gasoline, and 445,000 tons of small equipment and ammunition.

A witness of the debacle, this Large Pack was abandoned in the north of France. According to the military serial number handwritten on its back, it belonged to a soldier of the King's Own Scottish Borderers, a Scottish regiment attached to the 3rd Infantry Division, BEF. They were evacuated from Dunkirk during the night of May 31 to June 1. The division will train for four years and come back for revenge on June 6, 1944, from Sword Beach (Normandy) to Bremen (Germany). Bigger than the Small Pack carried on the back during combat (and which contains a bowl, cutlery, emergency ration and a sweater), the Large Pack is often carried in a vehicle to lighten the load of infantrymen. It holds the heavy wool coat, the cap comforter (a woolen scarf foldable into a hat), the toilet and sewing bags, spare socks and soap. Often, soldiers add the poncho (which also serves as a floor mat) folded behind the closing straps.

Next to it is an impacted British canteen. This example, with the ring on the side used to tie the cord connected to the cork, is a model from the inter-war period and was used by BEF troops in France in 1940. The next model will be in green enamel, although a few blue canteens will still be seen in 1944. This one, which received a bullet that has barely penetrated the metal, was found during excavations in Normandy. It may have belonged to a Tommy fleeing south in 1940, or to another who returned to France four years later.

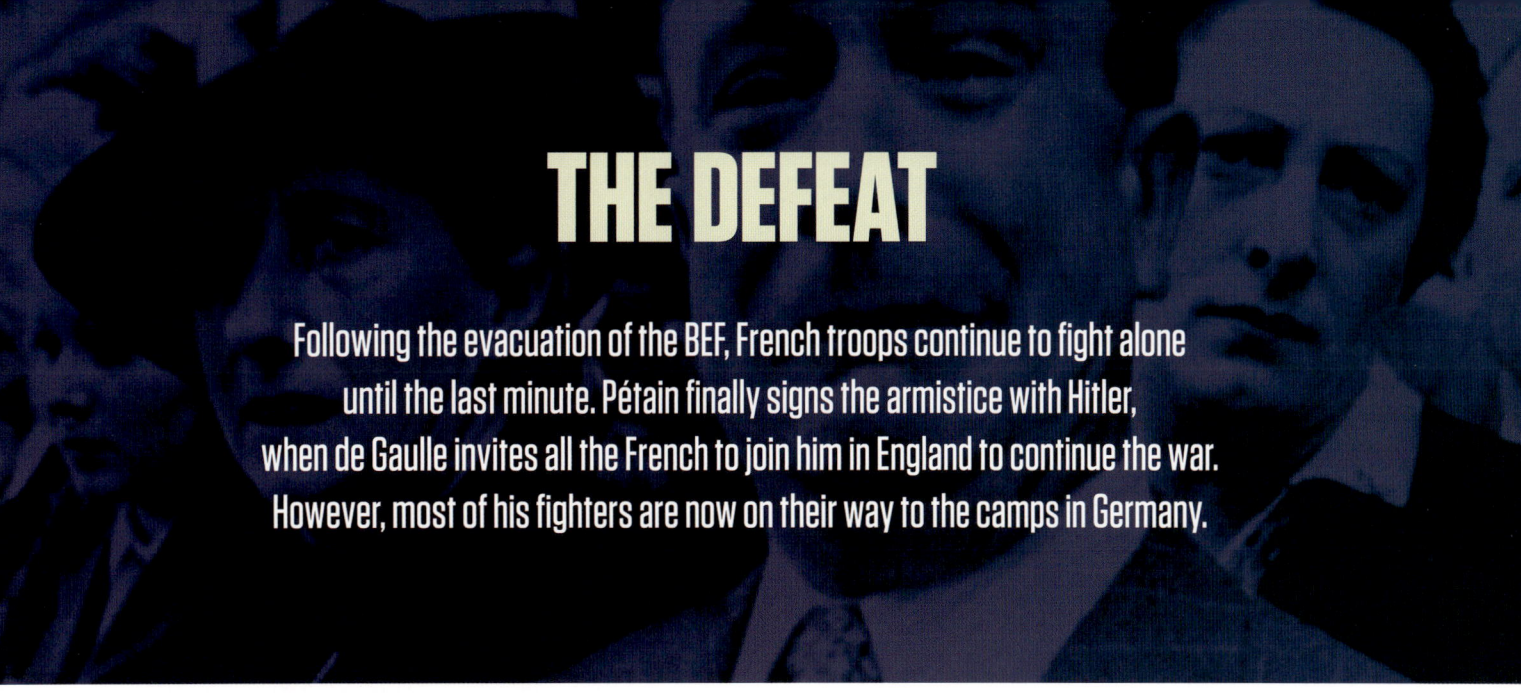

THE DEFEAT

Following the evacuation of the BEF, French troops continue to fight alone until the last minute. Pétain finally signs the armistice with Hitler, when de Gaulle invites all the French to join him in England to continue the war. However, most of his fighters are now on their way to the camps in Germany.

FOR THE CIVILIANS: EXODUS

Eight million French people leave their homes to flee the German advance. Optimism has given way to panic, and many are abandoning congested roads to rush to ports in the hope of being evacuated to the south. Thus, in Boulogne-sur-Mer, civilians mingle with soldiers to gain a place on a boat, while bombs fall on the city.

Marie was evacuated without her husband, Jules, from the docks of Boulogne on May 21 to the south of the Somme and the lines still held by the French Army. She writes the following letter from Ille-et-Vilaine, as she finds herself alone with her very young daughter and mother-in-law: *"For us, events have been rushing by with dizzying speed and my pain is great not to have Mother with me. With Renée and Jacqueline, she stayed in Hucqueliers. Were they able to escape? [...] The cars, the trains were no longer passing, and we had to flee on a small fishing boat that had accepted all three of us. Jules was on another one,* Le Surcouf, *and I haven't seen him for eight days, but I think he's safe, because* Le Surcouf *arrived in Cherbourg harbor despite an engine failure along the way. We stayed at sea for five days on this nut shell and we suffered a lot more morally than physically. We lost everything because we had taken few things, having only had an hour to save ourselves, a suitcase each containing a little laundry and clothes, but we still have our lives and our freedom. We only hope that our suffering will not be in vain and that victory will be swift to crown the efforts of our Allied soldiers. The unspeakable conduct of the King of the Belgians has caused consternation everywhere and to overcome it will be necessary to fight even harder!* [Belgium fell on May 28, after the Belgians' defeat on the Lys: the Belgians were supposed to prevent a German crossing of the river while the British were preparing to evacuate Dunkirk. After five days of bloody fighting, King Leopold III ordered the surrender, at the risk of weakening the left flank of the pocket. The Belgians suffered 23,350 killed and wounded.] *Poor young men! Last Tuesday at 2 am I was still hosting two exhausted Belgians and at 3 am I was leaving my poor house. What is left of it, alas! All three of us have a heavy heart, but Jeannette is a role model and never complains. She slept three nights on straw and ate dry bread without any objection."* Indeed, Marie's husband arrived in Cherbourg on May 22, and waited for his wife and daughters there for several scary days. They will be lucky enough to be reunited shortly afterwards and take refuge in the lower Loire region.

In Paris, concern is beginning to spread among the inhabitants. After destroying the Dunkirk Pocket, the Germans attack the Somme on June 5 at dawn, throwing no less than 138 divisions at the remains of the French Army, with three objectives: Dijon, Rouen, and the capital. On June 3, a Parisian woman writes to friends who had been evacuated: *"What a horrible thing this war is. Here we were at peace believing that the Germans were forgetting Paris... We had a first bombing today. Simone is always close to me and I don't want the holidays to start. There are good shelters in schools! I often think of you, and I fear very much that the Germans will not give us a better fate than you. There is only one thing left to do, and that is to pray to God to keep those who are dear to us. We feel so small in the face of events and what tomorrow will bring!"* The same day, the capital is bombed, killing 254 people and injuring 652.

On the front, the Panzers encounter fortified villages where the French use all the guns at their disposal. Nevertheless, on June 8, the Germans cross the Somme.

The French lines are broken, the Seine is reached the next day, then the Marne on the 12th. On that day, while the government is moving to Tours, Weygand (the first to demand an armistice with Germany) orders a general withdrawal to spare Paris, which is declared an 'open city'. Two days later, its deserted streets are occupied by the Wehrmacht. After heated debates, President Paul Reynaud resigns on June 16 and is succeeded by Marshal Philippe Pétain, former hero of the Battle of Verdun in 1916. The latter asks for the armistice the next day and from then on, as they advance southward, German troops encounter both fugitives dropping their weapons at the first sight of a gray uniform and resistance nests fiercely defending themselves.

FOR THE SOLDIERS: HUMILIATION

Charles Desrue was born on June 18, 1910 in Romorantin-Lanthenay. In October 1931, he served with the 131e régiment d'infanterie before returning to civilian life to become a postman. He was recalled to the army on September 7, 1939 and joined the 331e régiment d'infanterie, part of the 55e Division (X Corps) which formed the left wing of the 2e Armée (in charge of the defence of Sedan in the event of an invasion). Meanwhile, his wife was delivering letters in his place, even though pregnant with their third child. The birth of the latter could have allowed Charles to avoid the war, if he was not already on the front. On April 1, when his son was born, he got a three-day leave to go and see him and the army offered him a supposedly better position: 'safe' behind the Maginot Line.

Transferred to the 136e régiment d'infanterie de forteresse in Mouzon, he is only a few miles from Sedan, where the Germans would make their breakthrough barely a month later (his former 55e Division will be nearly destroyed there). After heavy fighting in the woods of Inor, Charles and his comrades head for Nancy and then Switzerland, before being surrounded and forced to surrender on the eve of the armistice. The French debacle would haunt Charles for the rest of his life, but he wouldn't say a word about it to his loved ones. It will only be just before his death at the age of 95 that he would confide in his family, with a trembling hand, in a letter to be opened after his passing: *"I had a little horse and a cart to put the machine gun in. On the first day, I led the machine gun to the bunkers' positions, then on the way, the bombers passed me a hundred meters above my head, and their bombs kept falling wave after wave, tearing our guts out. I couldn't hear anything anymore. Next door, in a farm, a regiment of Algerian Tirailleurs was leaving, I followed them, and I found my regiment three kilometers away. How lucky! This was on the first day of the war.*

Charles Desrue during his service with the 131e régiment.

We were in the Inor forest, machine-gunned and bombed. During the night of May 14 to 15, 1940, the 136e RIF was ordered to leave its pillboxes and withdraw to the woods [The fighting was terrible from the first day, but French positions resisted until they were relieved on May 21 by the 11e régiment de la Légion étrangère (Foreign Legion). The latter would inflict nearly 2,500 casualties on two German divisions. Also suffering heavy losses and completely surrounded, the legionnaires would hold until the end, outnumbered, at 6 to 1!]. *The days passed and everything remained the same, but several days later we moved to another place. There was the whole company. As the days went by, things got worse, the Germans followed us to the high ground, we were bombed. Once, we returned from positions at a junction of the road from Thonne-les-Près to the citadel of Montmédy and the shells began falling: as I had my*

I - THE DARK YEARS 1939-1942

little horse with me, I had to tie it up. The tree branches were falling on me. I took shelter in the citadel, it was a block of stone. The next day, we went on the road, the captain directed us to Nancy, but we didn't go very far. There were French anti-tank guns, so we turned back [Did he mean French anti-tank guns firing on approaching Panzers? The Germans were in Nancy on June 16]. *We were surrounded, we stopped in a forest near Switzerland, and the same thing: anti-tanks. The cruelest day was in a poplar wood. The Germans were following us, I tied my little horse to a tree, and myself and a friend from Seine-et-Oise named Binet stood behind a large poplar tree. But the air bursts* [a shell that explodes in the air, then shatters in all directions, unlike a percussion shell that explodes when it hits the ground] *kept falling, and my poor little horse was killed. My poor friend Binet was killed too, two meters from me. I had to carry the heavy machine gun and tripod on my own (my poor horse stayed there) and take my bag on my back."*

In the last few days, the Germans have already invaded the entire northern half of France and have reached Royan, Angoulême, Clermont-Ferrand, Lyon, Grenoble and Geneva. There is no hope of stopping the Wehrmacht anymore and many give up the fight. Charles says: *"In the last days of June, it was no longer possible to move around without being bombed.*

We were in an orchard in Marainville, in Meurthe-et-Moselle. They were still bombing us, we were surrounded. The captain left with a car and a white flag. An hour later, a German came, he spoke good French, it was June 21. He told us: 'You are no longer considered prisoners; the armistice is signed'. None of this was true [It would only be signed the next day, but cut off from allied lines of communication, the French are in total ignorance of the political situation. This technique, called 'the armistice trick', will be used regularly by German officers in the hope of taking prisoners without a fight and progressing faster]. *They put us in groups of four, with machine guns on each side, and there, in a well-guarded pasture, we had a pig for food. But it was impossible to cook it, as the first smoke was sprayed by a bombardment. Constant rain, no food, no water, we stayed in this pasture for two days."*

THE END

As a final blow, Hitler receives the French surrender in the wagon where the armistice of November 11, 1918 took place, at Rethondes, in the Compiègne Forest. The German victory is formalized on June 22, 1940 at 4:40 pm, but the armistice doesn't come into effect until the 25th, once signed by the Italians. Yet, the latter, who had only been at war with France since June 10, had never succeeded in breaking through the French lines. Around 312,000 Italians crashed into the fortresses held by far fewer alpine troops between Mont Blanc and Menton. On the 25th, the defenders had to abandon their intact pillboxes, after inflicting more than 6,000 Italian casualties, for only a few dozen French soldiers lost. In northern France, on the other hand, the French Army reported 92,000 deaths and twice as many wounded during a forty-five-day battle. However, it cost the Wehrmacht nearly 60,000 lives and higher daily losses than the Germans will suffer in Russia the following year.

On June 25 1940, France is divided in two and Alsace and Moselle are annexed to the Reich. A demarcation line separates the area occupied by the German army (from the north of the country to the Loire and the entire Atlantic coast) and a 'free' area administered by Pétain's regime, as permitted by the armistice.

Based in Vichy, the latter works closely with the Third Reich, both in the economic and military fields, and in the persecution of the Jews. The new coins bear the traditional values of 'Work, Family, Homeland' and the emblem of Marshal Pétain's government.

33

On the day of the armistice, the Germans take Charles and the others to the Lorraine-Dietrich car factory in Luneville, where 30,000 soldiers are imprisoned. The next day, after a 30-mile walk, some raw potatoes await them at Dieuze. Charles says in his letter: *"We stayed in Dieuze for about ten days and ate very little. The Germans were having fun with us, throwing scraps of bread and rushing up and bayoneting our behinds."* A few days later, a dozen trucks finally come to pick them up. Charles, too exhausted and sick, cannot climb in, but is kicked inside with a heavy boot. On their way, desperate and angry women block the convoy in an attempt to stop it and throw food at the prisoners.

The men finish their journey in a barracks in Sainte-Menehould. Fortunately for Charles, like railway workers and other men considered important to the proper functioning of occupied France, he is liberated thanks to his profession as a postman. Thus, of the 2,600,000 French soldiers captured, nearly a third are immediately released.

Charles' certificate states in German: *"POW district of Sainte-Menehould, July 24, 1940: prisoner Desrue Charles, born on June 18, 1910 and living in Fontaine-les-Coteaux, belongs according to his declarations to the railways staff of the French Post Office. He will be asked to exercise his profession in his office and he has committed to refrain from any act of hostility towards Germany and the German army."*

Charles is officially released on September 23, 1940, while his comrades leave for Germany.

This officer is wearing the Adrian 1926 (infantry type) helmet, a 1932 model coat identified to the 21e régiment, an officer's belt with a binocular case and a map holder (and a pistol on the other side), as well as a musette bag for the gas mask worn on the shoulder. After occupying the southern Maginot Line and participating in the Battle of the Somme from May 27, the 21e régiment fought until the end.

It tried to delay the German advance on the Poix River, on the Oise River, on the Orge River then on the Loire on June 17. However, the Germans were on their heels, and on the same day, Pétain ordered them to put down their weapons, while many units were still resisting with courage and declaring that the conditions had not yet been negotiated. Dissolved in August, the regiment had suffered more than 600 fatalities.

PRISONERS

For 1,850,000 French soldiers, the war ends in the Stalag. They will wait helplessly for their liberation, by the Western Allies or the Red Army. Despite the precarious conditions, a new life begins, punctuated by forced labor and letters from relatives.

THE STALAG

Nearly 2 million French soldiers are now waiting for their transfer to *Frontstalags*, improvised camps in fields. The final destination for the officers is an *Oflag*, and for the troops a *Stalag* (a contraction of *Kriegsgefangenenen-Mannschafts-Stammlager*). Scattered throughout Germany and its neighboring countries (Poland, Austria...), these camps consist of several wooden huts, surrounded by 13-foot high barbed wire walls, constantly watched by guards posted in towers equipped with machine guns and projectors. In total there are 260 such camps, including transit (*Dulag*) and interrogation camps, aviators (*Luftlager*) or sailors (*Marlag*) camps and civilian internment camps (*Ilag*). Divided into several military regions (*Wehrkreise*), they bear the number of the latter and a letter to indicate the camp. Thus, the Berlin region is in zone III and hosts four Stalags (A, B, C, and D): the closest to the capital is Stalag III-D.

It is precisely this Stalag III-D, created on August 14, 1940, that Émile goes to. A gunner in the French 406th Anti-Aircraft Regiment, he was taken prisoner when his unit, reduced to firing at close range at German tanks with parts intended for aviation, was forced to retreat. In a 1941 letter to his wife, who also seems to be suffering under the German occupation, he complains about the outcome the Battle of France and his new living conditions: *"About Tony, it hurt me that you gave him away. You must be having a really hard time if you're not able to feed a dog. Ah, what a comedy this fake war we fought is, and now we're paying for it. Remember what I said before I left, that it was all a bluff. We're tired of living like dogs, locked up in a cage!"*

All these men are terribly missed by their families, but also by the French economy, which is losing a large workforce to agricultural and industrial production. On the other hand, they are good news to the Germans, who also need to replace their men who had gone to the front. Around 95% of prisoners of war are sent to an *Arbeitskommando* ('working detachment'), small labor camps dependent on a Stalag. There are more than 82,000 *Arbeitskommandos*, which can sometimes hold 1,000 prisoners, mainly assigned to work in fields and farms, but also in mines, factories or on railways. In exchange for their hard work, they receive a meager salary in the form of special tickets called *Kriegsgefangenenen-Lagergeld*.

Only the officers in the *Oflags*, in accordance with Article 27 of the Geneva Convention, do not have to work. They occupy their time however they can, doing sports or artistic activities.

50 and 10 Reichspfennig banknotes for prisoners of war.

**Mess kit belonging to Alfred Cucchietti,
149e régiment d'infanterie de forteresse.
His unit remained true to its motto 'Resist and Bite',
pushing back the German offensive on the Maginot Line.
But when the regiment received the general order to withdraw
on June 13, it was surrounded during the Battle of Darmannes.
Alfred was sent to Frontstalag 190 in Charleville (France),
before being deported to other POW camps.
On the lid of his mess kit, he engraved the letters 'KG',
for 'Kriegsgefangener' (prisoner of war).**

At the very beginning of the war, the prisoners in Germany were mainly French (about 70%), British, Belgian or Polish. As early as 1941, they are joined by Russian prisoners. Indeed, Hitler has decided to take over the enormous resources of the USSR and breaks the Molotov-Ribbentrop Pact now that the West is almost under his control. After massing 3 million soldiers and 3,600 tanks at the Soviet border, he launches *Operation Barbarossa* on June 22, 1941 and quickly drives to Moscow, crushing the Red Army in its path. The latter, which has therefore switched to the Allied side, would not take the upper hand before the end of the year, once the Wehrmacht is slowed down by the harsh Russian winter. Although the Germans lose 750,000 men, they take more than 5 million prisoners in the USSR. The following year, American soldiers will join the POWs of the many Allied nations in the camps. On Christmas Day 1943, a South African sergeant captured in North Africa writes from Stalag VIII-A: *"I think every nationality in the world is represented in this camp, and colour too. It's a big place."* The prisoners are grouped by nationality and separated by barbed wire that divides each Stalag into sections.

LIFE IN THE CAMPS

Prisoners can receive letters and parcels from France, which transit in their millions. They are allowed to write to their families, after buying a regulated mail sheet of twenty-five lines within the camp. These letters are often written in pencil, as ink is prohibited to avoid the manufacture of false stamps. However, there is little they can say about their living conditions, as German censorship is strict: many letters do not get the 'geprüft' mark (verified by censorship), because their authors have overflowed lines, written in an illegible way or expressed opinions that are not appreciated by their jailers. However, the letters that have escaped their attention provide a striking picture of the atmosphere in the Stalags.

Paul Clavier was born on May 22, 1911 in Saint-Pierre-des-Corps, near Tours. Mobilized on September 4, 1939, he joined the 9e escadron du Train, whose mission was to ensure the support and movement of troops on the battlefield. Before his departure for the front, Paul became engaged to his girlfriend, Agnes, in February 1940.

**On this regulatory letter for prisoners,
a French soldier attached a flower
for his wife using a piece of bandage.**

POW Raymond Poidevin made this bracelet with his military dog tag and souvenirs from the various countries he crossed during his captivity: coins from the USSR, Czechoslovakia or Germany, and the medal of Notre-Dame de la Merci, patron saint of prisoners.

She writes to him a year later: *"On the 17th at 1 am, it will be a year since I left you. I gave you one last kiss through our gate and you left, bravely. The night was black, but the earth was white. The snow had covered everything with a beautiful carpet, but it was sad, because it was the departure, the separation, and for how long? God only knows."* Agnes has also left to take refuge with one of her sisters in a convent near Bordeaux.

Taking part in the defence of the Atlantic ports, Paul's unit quickly collapsed under the power of the German Panzers in Boulogne-sur-Mer and then Calais. When the latter city fell on May 26, he tried to reach Dunkirk in the hope of being evacuated from there. Unfortunately, Paul did not have this chance. Captured, he suffered three weeks of forced marching to Brussels. On the way, he witnessed the execution of black French soldiers on the side of the road: Nazi ideology encouraged the Germans to separate the colonials from the metropolitans, so as not to *"soil the Reich's soil"* with what they called 'sub humans'. Furthermore, African troops fought with fierce resistance, encouraging German propaganda to present them as 'savages' who *"do not hesitate to cut off the ears of their enemies to wear them as pendants, or to gouge their eyes out"*. Nearly 3,000 Senegalese tirailleurs were murdered.

On the day of Paul's capture, thirty-two Moroccan soldiers (all volunteers, unlike the Algerians who were most often conscripted) were also executed by the Waffen-SS in the Pas-de-Calais region. Many other massacres were reported throughout France, but 80,000 soldiers from the French colonies survived their capture. They would remain imprisoned in *Frontstalags* in France, in even more precarious conditions than in German Stalags. As for Paul, his road ends at Stalag II-B. Located in German Pomerania, near Czarne (now Poland), it was one of the first Nazi concentration camps in 1933, which later served as a Stalag when the first Polish prisoners arrived in September 1939. Paul had to undergo his first winter in a tent, because the first barracks there would not be built until 1941. Hygiene is very precarious and in June, the camp is expanded for the arrival of Russian prisoners: 45,000 of them would die in a typhoid fever epidemic that would last until the spring of 1942.

Paul works with an *Arbeitskommando* in potato picking and other agricultural activities. On the occasion of his fiancée's birthday, he writes on March 22, 1942: *"I kiss you very affectionately and very tenderly, hoping that next year on such an occasion I will have the joy of embracing you.*

I work alone on a farm, and in the evening, I come back to bed in a barrack with the seventeen French prisoners who work in the town. It's been two years since I left you. Time seems terribly long, and I wonder if it will end soon. Now I'm gloomy all the time, I'm completely discouraged. Ah, you will advise me once again patience and courage, but since this has been going on, all my will is running out. Would you be as kind as to include a washcloth, a dictionary and some wool with one of your next packages? And to think that I'm going to spend Easter here again, how sad."

Paul regularly receives parcels, to which the Germans help themselves when they are not sufficiently wrapped, and in July 1942 he writes to Agnes: *"Just got your package on my birthday, it's really providential and gave me great pleasure. Unfortunately, the parcel was damaged. I couldn't find the cigars. I had recommended that you sew a canvas around all your packages. Do so from now on and tell everyone to do it."* He is sent food, books and clothing, which provide much-needed comfort, but also a bargaining chip within the camp. His family is certainly generous, since they also suffer from deprivation: Agnes can only buy 75 grams of bread per day, which she buys with her ration coupons. She writes to him in June 1941: *"This month, there is a rumor about clothing coupons. What are we going to wear? Vine leaves? I have some beautiful ones in my garden, so I might be okay."*

Prisoners often seek hope in religion and find comfort in packages from home.

Paul near the Stalag in 1941.
He wears rabbit skin mittens, sent by his fiancée.

Paul will leave Stalag II-B in August 1943, thanks to false documents made by his brother saying he is a medic. He will be reunited with Agnes, whom he will marry a year later. As for his comrades who remain at Stalag II-B, they will be liberated by the Red Army in April 1945.

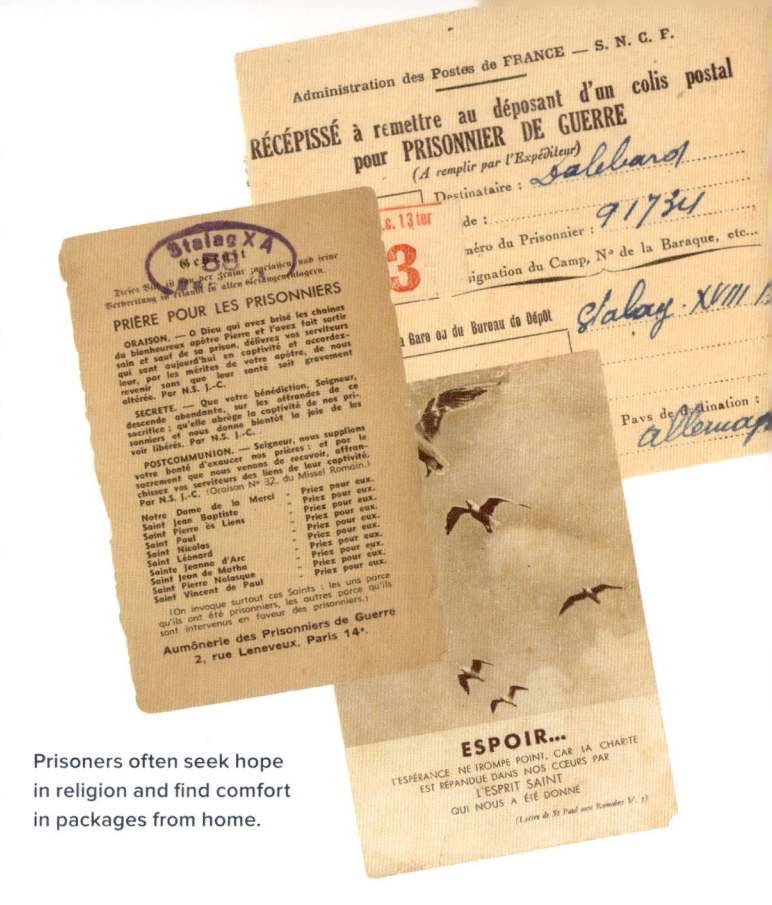

A TASTE FOR 'TRAVEL'

Living conditions improve in 1941, thanks to the reports from Red Cross delegates who visited the Stalags. Boredom and individual talents give birth to genuine small cities within each camp: there is soon a theater, a library, a church, a radio station, exhibitions, concerts, fairs, workshops, courses for students, sports clubs, and more. Life is no less gloomy, but the men are making the most of their situation.

A sergeant in the French Engineers, André, was taken prisoner on May 15, 1940, a few days after the start of the German invasion. He is first sent to Stalag IV-B, one of the largest camps in Germany, near Mühlberg, and writes his first letter on June 25, 1940 to his relatives and his wife (who managed to cross the demarcation line and move to the free zone): *"I think you have not been evacuated, and are still at home. When you write to me, make your letters short, very legible and few, and only give me news from the family or acquaintances. Do you have any [news] of Jacques? If you think it is useful, you can send me packages; we are entitled to three packages per month, including one of five kilograms free of charge. Make sure you don't ship more than one a week. Do not put any cash, money or preserves in it. What I would like: chocolate, snacks, gingerbread and tobacco, no laundry or money. Make the packaging strong and put the address inside the package as well. Please pass on my news to the whole family. I hope that we will all meet again soon, and in anticipation of this great joy, I give you all my best regards."*

I - THE DARK YEARS 1939-1942

In February 1941, Stalag IV-F opens near Chemnitz (south of Stalag IV-B), where André is transferred. As well as many Frenchmen, the camp also holds British soldiers captured in North Africa. André is busy in the carpentry workshop and even writes a theater play with other prisoners. However, he admits that they are *"a little too well-guarded at the moment, because two of our comrades have escaped, even though we are housed in a prison."*

Indeed, the number of escapes increases, which makes conditions of captivity even more difficult, as he writes on April 19, 1942: *"I have little hope of returning home for several years unless we take our destiny in our own hands. That's what two comrades did again yesterday, which makes four in one month. As you'd expect, the captivity is starting to weigh on us. No, during the Easter holidays, we didn't go out; we stayed locked up for the four days. As I thought, I wasn't given the newspapers you put in my last package. They will be sent to the censors and I will probably not see them again, like several books you sent me that didn't come back, even though they are allowed. As for shoes, many of us have complained to our families about the shortage. The French POWs' service replied that they had sent some to Germany especially for us, but we have never seen any, or rather yes, we have, but not on the prisoners' feet."*

Two weeks later, he adds: *"We still have no news of the comrades who have left. There are many people right now who have suddenly discovered a taste for travel and quite a few, I think, are succeeding. As for me, I'll wait and see."* Not all escapes are successful, as evidenced by his letter of 17 May: *"Our other two escaped prisoners have reportedly been taken back and sent to special labor camps in Poland. All the escapees that get caught are sent there now, which doesn't stop any new endeavors, given the length of time we spend here. The day before yesterday marked the day when, two years ago, my freedom was ended."*

Starting from March 1944 and the 'Aktion K' decree, all captured escapees will be executed with a bullet to the head.

THE ESCAPEES

In 1942, the Vichy regime signs agreements with the Reich resulting in the release of nearly 100,000 prisoners of war as part of the 'relief' (but at the cost of three French skilled workers sent to work in Germany for the return of one prisoner). Around 324,000 additional troops are released for health or other reasons. As for the others, they will have to wait for their liberation by the Allied armies (for more than two thirds of the French prisoners). In five years of captivity, 58,000 prisoners will have died or gone missing, and many find it hard to accept such a figure. In the same way as the black-market pharmacies flourish around the camps, some prisoners develop 'travel agencies'. Out of 1.8 million French prisoners of war, the Germans will face almost as many escape attempts! However, only about 70,000 of them will succeed, which amounts to around 4% of all attempts.

Among those who have chosen not to let fate decide for them, Alexis Wolff has an exciting story. After a one-year military service with the 152e régiment d'infanterie ('the Red Devils') in 1933, Alexis was recalled to the army on September 2, 1939. Within the 6e compagnie of the 98e régiment, 26e Division d'infanterie, he was sent to the Maginot Line with the VI Corps, 3e Armée of General Condé. His unit took up positions on March 13, 1940 in the Houve Forest (northwest of Saint-Avold, between Metz in France and Saarbrücken in Germany). It repelled many German attacks there until June 12, before retreating to the Seille and then the Nied rivers. On June 18, the enemy launched a violent attack in Maixe, east of Nancy, capturing a large part of Alexis' regiment.

A few souvenirs belonging to Alexis, including, the escapees' medal (right).

With the few survivors, he retreated southwards towards Charmes, in the Vosges. Concussed and slightly burned by the bursting of a shell, Alexis never reached the city: he was taken prisoner on June 20, near a level crossing just south of Bayon (Meurthe-et-Moselle). The rest of the 26e division fell into German hands a few hours later in the Charmes Forest. Alexis had to walk around 75 miles to Germany before reaching Saarbrücken on July 1 and was then transported by train to Stalag XII-D, not far from the Luxembourg border. He joined an *Arbeitskommando*, and started his forced labor on July 15. With eighty comrades, Alexis worked in fields in Leiwen, 20 miles from Trier. Although he was guarded at night by German soldiers, he spent his days alone with the peasants. Several men from his former unit were with him: privates Aufort, Lafranchise, Tripier, and sergeants Gidel, Michard, Dousset and Racles. The latter two would also escape.

In June 1941, Alexis began to develop an escape plan. Making rings by punching old coins that were no longer in circulation, he earned German and French money by selling his creations to the inhabitants. His home being in the 'free zone' between Vichy and Clermont-Ferrand (under Pétain's collaborationist regime, but not yet invaded by the Germans), he knew that his journey would be long and dangerous. On November 22, 1941, just demobilized, Alexis writes a report detailing his escape: *"I had saved my French money from the searches by hiding it in the lining of my clothes so I was able to buy a map and a compass, as well as food to take away. On the afternoon of August 22, 1941, going alone to work in the vineyards, I took my food in a bag and as soon as night fell, I set off across the fields towards the southwest. I didn't know if I'd been followed. I left dressed in a French Army uniform. I stopped walking before daybreak and hid carefully in coppices, doing the same for the next eleven days. For eleven days and eleven nights, I avoided any contact with anyone. I only walked at night, guiding myself with my compass, avoiding roads, towns, etc. On the night of 28 to 29, I crossed the old border, around Buschdorf* [40 miles from his starting point].

I crossed the Maginot Line on the night of August 30 to 31. Finally, on September 2, around 10 pm, near Louvigny (Moselle), when I approached a farm, I heard French; I went in to ask for some information for the crossing of the new border. A young man offered to act as my guide for the sum of 200 francs. I accepted and around midnight we crossed the Seille on a railway bridge and the border about 300 meters from that bridge. My guide left me there and I continued alone on to Pont-à-Mousson, where

I - THE DARK YEARS 1939-1942

I arrived in the morning. There again I went to a farm where I was very well received, I was given all the information I needed to travel to the forbidden zone and I was helped to get civilian clothes, civilian shoes and food. The same evening, September 3, I took the train to Nancy where I spent the night."

Alexis then walked more than 90 miles in enemy territory without being caught. Now in civilian clothes, he ran fewer risks, but still had to cross the demarcation line to reach the free zone. He now traveled by train, passing through Saint-Dié, Épinal, Vesoul, then Besançon. There, a railroad employee gave him the address of a guide in Mouchard, in the Jura, to cross the line. Unfortunately, the guide didn't show up, and Alexis had to spend another night on a farm. *"The next day, September 6, having the address of another guide in Champagnole (Jura), I took the train back to that place. There I found the guide who asked me for 300 francs for the crossing; I accepted and at 3 pm, I walked across the demarcation line. The first village I came to in the free zone was Crotenay (Jura) where I found a youth camp* [paramilitary camp for young people, a substitute for military service after the armistice]. *I took the bus and arrived in Lons-le-Saunier around 7 pm.*

I ate and slept at the Reception Center. The next day, September 7, I went to a 151e régiment d'infanterie barracks where I was fed at noon and given a road map to the Demobilization Center in Bourg (Ain), where I arrived the same evening. I didn't meet anyone I knew during my trip in the forbidden zone."

Alexis is lucky that the Vichy administration doesn't hand over the escaped prisoners to the Germans, as it wants to find labor for its industry. This actually benefits the occupiers, who therefore simply look away. Alexis is demobilized on September 9, 1941 in Bourg-en-Bresse and receives his bonus, which covers only half of his escape expenses in Germany, in the forbidden zone and in the free zone (purchase of compass, map, food, trousers, jacket and shoes, train tickets, guides...). As he says in his letter to the colonel commanding his region, to claim the bonus reserved for escapees, *"I repatriated myself by my own means"*. As soon as he returns home, he changes his name, probably with the complicity of the town hall in his commune or a network of resistance fighters. He receives food coupons and a fake identity card. He now calls himself René Pelletier (his middle name, and a surname inspired by his mother's maiden name).

Alexis' real ID card (left) and his fake papers (right). Note the very basic signature 'Pelletier'.

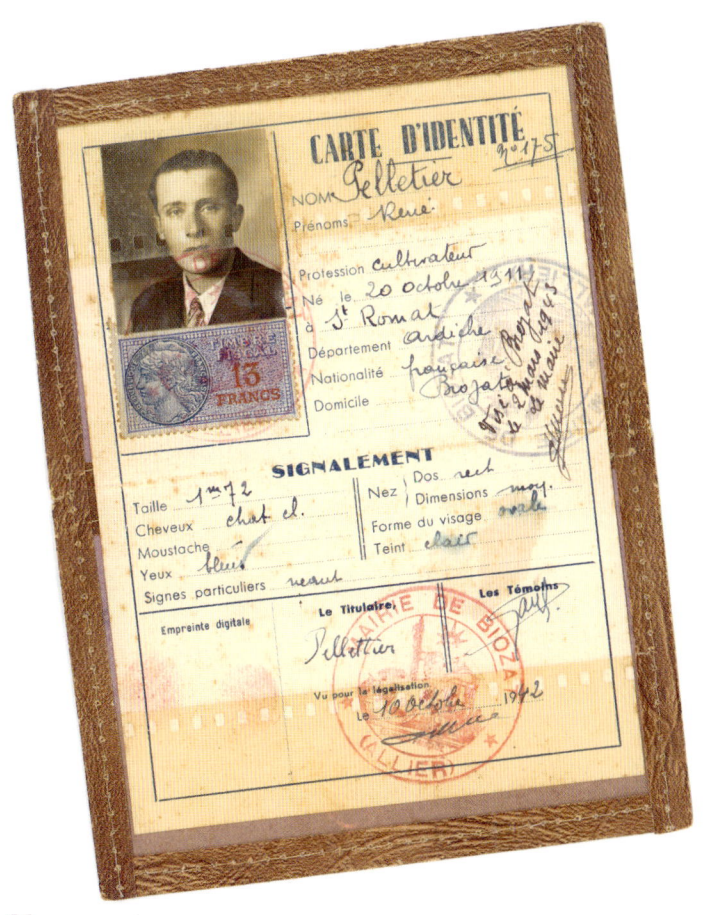

UNDER THE BOOT

Hitler reigns over most of Western Europe, and the isolated British await their turn.
In conquered countries, civilians are under occupation.
But those of the few great powers who are still free also suffer deprivation and constant danger.

GREAT BRITAIN STANDS ALONE

Apart from the occupied Channel Islands, Great Britain has not fallen yet. Betty lives in Glasgow, Scotland. She writes to Laura, an American friend who lives in California, about her daily life in August 1941. In a few lines, Betty summarizes the situation faced by millions of British people (certain points will be developed in the following pages):

"Dear Laura, our summertime ended yesterday, so now we are back to the 'Blackout' nights again, and inevitably, air raids. I just returned from my summer vacation last week which I spent at Edinburgh. I had a swell time although I only had 10 days. We could not get any snaps taken as it is very difficult to obtain spools for the camera, otherwise I would have sent you some snaps. I also went to have my photograph taken twice, and each time I moved, so I was so disgusted I haven't gone back again. If you have any more snaps Laura, I should be very pleased if you would send me one. I suppose you will have read about our clothes being rationed now. It's a bit of a problem trying to figure out how to spread them over. The worst item is stockings, as we have to give up two of our precious coupons for a pair of stockings, so most of the girls, including myself, have stopped wearing stockings and paint our legs. It feels nice and free in the summertime but I'm not so sure about the winter, as our legs will be rather cold.

You know, I was thinking seriously of joining one of the Services, as a shorthand typist. I had the 'Wrens' in mind, but I am in a reserved occupation and may not be released from my job. I saw the Philadelphia Story *the other night, with Cary Grant and Katherine Hepburn. It was very funny, though rather a silly story. Most of the pictures we see now are British and they are no good. [...] Well, Laura, as I am writing this in the office, I guess I'd better get a spot of work done. So cheerio just now, Betty."*

BLITZ AND BLACKOUT

Hitler dreams of invading his last opponent in the West. Before thinking of landing on the English coast (*Operation Seelöwe*), the Germans must take control of its sky. On the *Adlertag* ('Eagle Day'), August 13, 1940, the Luftwaffe attacks the Royal Air Force (RAF). The German Messerschmitt, Heinkel and Junkers planes face the famous English Hurricanes and Spitfires, which, although few in number, have the advantage of being guided by a new technological innovation: the radar. However, though it's deployed all along the coast, it's still not sufficient enough, and Fighter Command is in a very bad position. It loses dozens of pilots every day, but suddenly, Hitler changes his strategy on September 7, 1940.

A German bomber had mistakenly attacked London on August 24 without the Führer's agreement, triggering the bombing of Berlin the next day in retaliation. British cities have therefore become the new targets of the Germans. The 'Blitz' thus aims to terrorize civilians, but unintentionally, it mainly allows the RAF to rebuild its strength. British industry will indeed succeed in producing the impressive number of 132,500 aircraft out of its factories! The air battle ends in October, when the Luftwaffe has lost 1,733 planes (half as many as the RAF), but it still carries on its bombing raids. London (where the first bombardment would last fifty-seven consecutive nights, killing more than 30,000 civilians) and Coventry are the Luftwaffe's most famous victims, but the cities affected are far more numerous: Plymouth, Birmingham, Liverpool, Manchester, Canterbury, Exeter and many more. Scotland (where Betty lives) and its many coal mines and factories suffer a similar fate, as does Ireland (which remains neutral) and Wales. All in all, more than 50,000 British civilians would die under the bombs.

I - THE DARK YEARS 1939-1942

Betty writes about the end of the late summer sun and the blackout. As the bombardments take place at night (the pilots try to escape anti-aircraft fire), the British must completely remove urban lighting in order to avoid offering targets to the Luftwaffe. The inhabitants therefore hunt for the slightest light leak and seal their windows with cardboard, paint or thick curtains. This is particularly necessary in coastal cities, since German submarines use the city lights in the background to see the silhouettes of the ships they torpedo. In addition to its negative impact on morale, the blackout has much more tangible consequences. Cars need to be driven with headlights off, causing thousands of fatal accidents in the first few months of the war (despite the introduction of a 20 mph speed limit). Captain Desmond Finny (page 24) is one of the victims. White paint is used on vehicles and sidewalks, and pedestrians who really need to leave their homes make themselves visible by waving a white handkerchief. The blackout began on September 1, 1939 and would last until the end of the war. Around 300,000 civilian volunteers are trained to become ARP (Air Raid Precautions) wardens, who must guide residents to underground shelters during alerts.

However, not only does the Blitz fail to break British morale, it also has tragic consequences for the Germans. The RAF responds violently with Berlin in particular being attacked more than 350 times. The Germans, therefore, also experience a blackout, particularly from 1942 onwards, when Allied bombing campaigns intensify with the arrival of the US Army Air Forces. When Air Marshal Arthur Harris, quickly nicknamed 'Bomber Harris', takes over Bomber Command in February 1942, he begins a genuine campaign of blind revenge and in July 1943, 30,000 German civilians are killed in Hamburg. At the Casablanca Conference in January 1943, his orders are clear: *"Your main objective is the progressive destruction and dislocation of the German military, industrial and economic system, and the undermining of the morale of the German people to a point where their capacity for armed resistance is fatally weakened."* Yet, despite their intensity and the colossal loss of life, these bombing campaigns will not have the expected decisive effect.

RATIONING

The problem of rationing is directly linked to the Blitz. The Luftwaffe and the Kriegsmarine's U-Boats (submarines) are a constant threat to the frequently sunk maritime transport convoys. Gasoline is the first resource to be rationed. The quantity of imported food is reduced by 80% in the first month of the war, and food rationing is then introduced in early 1940. After the great census of September 29, 1939, each inhabitant receives a ration book, the quantity of which varies according to the age and condition of each person.

In France, personnel from the 'Défense passive' (DP) come to the rescue of civilians affected by the bombardments (mainly from the Allies after 1941).
From left to right: Adrian helmet painted white for the medical personnel, armband with blue cross for the unqualified medical personnel, civilian gas mask with case (produced in Belgium in 1940 for export to France), French TC-38 mask dated 1939 (civilian model based on the army's ANP31) with Czech origin filter cartridge, and Adrian helmet bearing the DP emblem.

The message on the back of this sheet of ration coupons for bread is very clear: *"So that those at the front have what they need every day, remove everything that is superfluous from your meals!"*

Of course, you still have to pay for your purchases, but they are now limited to a certain quantity, so that everyone can have a fair share of what is available. Great Britain is in such a situation of shortage that rationing will last until 1954.

On June 1, 1941, rationing is extended to the fabric used for parachutes and uniforms and, like food and gasoline, it will last until well after the war, until 1949. It will become common practice for Allied paratroopers to keep their silk parachutes to make a wedding dress when they return. Nylon stockings, which appeared in the late 1930s and are very popular, are also becoming a rare commodity. To the great displeasure of British women, nylon is now used to produce military equipment and ropes. However, despite the shortages, Betty and many others still find a way to stay pretty, by having a black line painted on the back of their legs to simulate the stitching from the stockings. For the less do-it-yourselfers, the black market is in full flow following the arrival of the first American soldiers in England (early 1942). The GIs brought with them products that were still unknown to the British, such as the canned ham 'Spam'. It will become so popular that the comedy band Monty Python, when joking in 1970 about the omnipresence of these preserves, will later give Spam a new meaning in the Internet age.

In France, shortages began as soon as the war broke out. Civilians lack everything, as Sophie writes in March 1940: *"We have difficulties here as far as supplies are concerned, coal and coffee were totally unavailable at one point. We're going to have three days without meat, and cafés will no longer be allowed to serve alcohol for three days as well."* The situation will worsen: the Germans, who were already suffering from hunger long before the conflict began, would exacerbate this phenomenon by taking resources from the occupied countries. Even the Americans on the other side of the Atlantic must 'tighten their belts'. After the attack on Pearl Harbor, civilian consumption becomes limited when factories are put to work for the US Army and its allies.

The first product affected is tires: the synthetic rubber industry in the United States is not yet very developed, and the Japanese have invaded the most important production sites in southeast Asia. The rationing of petrol quickly follows, and from 1942 onwards, it is no longer possible to buy a new car in the country. Motor racing is prohibited, speed is limited to 30 mph, and gasoline ration books are only distributed if the family provides proof of a genuine need. Automobile factories now devote themselves entirely to the manufacture of weapons, tanks, aircraft, vehicles and military equipment.

Although they were 'free', American civilians would learn how to ration.

According to this letter from a GI to his parents in October 1944, these deprivations would eventually pay off: *"It sure is too bad you can't get gasoline to do what little traveling you folks do, but if you only could see the vehicles of ours on the roads here in France it sure would make you feel your sacrifice has not been in vain. I know you don't mind the gas shortage, but I thought you should know we have the best motorized army in the world."*

Clothing and household appliances cease to be produced in the United States. As medicines must be supplied to the army in large quantities, hospitals are also rationed. Doctors must therefore estimate which patients to treat first, often unable to care for everyone. Food is also severely affected. Coffee becomes a rare commodity when the Kriegsmarine first attacks Brazilian convoys. Sugar is limited to 200 grams per person, per week, while other rationed foods include bread, cheese, butter, margarine, milk, bacon, dried fruit, jam, canned and frozen foods. However, the Americans are still safe from the famine that is wreaking havoc in Europe.

THE HOME FRONT

Despite these drastic measures, the British keep smiling, with their gas mask at hand, the sirens ringing daily and the endless waiting for a letter from a husband or son who has gone to the front. At the cinema, where they seek a little escape from the harsh reality of their daily lives, they watch news reels of the war and politically-oriented movies, which distill precious information on the behavior they must adopt daily (beware of spies, stay alert, participate in the war effort...).

Although Betty complained in August 1941 about the near absence of foreign films in the United Kingdom, the United States use Hollywood to promote the heroism of the US Army around the world, even before it arrives on the battlefield. For instance, when a British soldier attends a screening of the *Cargo of Innocents* (1942), he makes fun of it in his letters: *"Charles Laughton, Robert Taylor and Brian Donleve (I think that's how it's spelt) are the stars. It contained bags of American propaganda, but I quite enjoyed the show. An old pre-last war American destroyer meets a modern Japanese battleship. It tackles this battleship by herself and sinks her without much trouble. American casualties were one man killed and a few injured but what else can one expect when Robert Taylor is in command. I wish the Yanks would hurry up and put him into action for I'm sure the war couldn't last much longer. [...] I saw* Eagle Squadron. *It wasn't such a bad picture, but as usual full of propaganda. These Yanks sure are hell on wheels, aren't they? Makes such things as invasions look proper child's play. I only hope they come up to scratch when the real show starts."*

I - THE DARK YEARS 1939-1942

Nobody forgets that the country is threatened, and the British expect a German invasion at any time. One and a half million men join the Home Guard, created in May 1940, to defend the territory. During the following summer, civilians gather everything that can be considered a weapon (from old rifles to golf clubs) and prepare shelters. A Canadian soldier arriving in London discovers these defenses during a ride on a double-decker bus: small reinforced concrete bunkers in public gardens, roadblocks, or houses transformed into fortresses. He asks his parents in a letter: *"How would you react if someone installed an anti-tank gun in your bedroom?"*

As for women, they join the Women's Land Army to replace men in the fields, or the female branches of the armed forces. For example, the WRNS (Women's Royal Naval Service) that Betty wants to join offers volunteers jobs as telegraphers, radar operators, cooks, mechanics or drivers. She could also become an anti-aircraft gunner or a member of the military police by joining the ATS (Auxiliary Territorial Service), or even a parachute packer, meteorologist, or air reconnaissance photo analyst in the WAAF (Women's Auxiliary Air Force). Of the more than 500,000 British female soldiers, 800 would die in service. However, those who already hold a job deemed vital to the proper functioning of the country can neither go to the front nor volunteer to defend their homes. The list of 'reserved' occupations will constantly evolve during the war, depending on the demand for products and services and the available workforce. For instance, because jobs in coal mines were not reserved at the beginning of the war, Britain would soon face serious shortages, threatening their war machine. One out of ten conscripts will therefore be randomly selected and sent to the mines from December 1943 onwards and are know as the 'Bevin Boys' (after Ernest Bevin, the Labor Minister). Also, the war effort would generate constant tension and numerous strikes, and the presence of Allied camps will pose new social problems.

TAKING UP ARMS

In France, the German occupier (who costs the State about 400 million francs a day) behaves relatively correctly until 1942. The Wehrmacht wants to show itself at its best to avoid having to deploy too many law enforcement troops. Most French people are resigned to this new situation, despite the agricultural production diverted by the Reich, leading to scarcity, rationing and hunger. In June 1941, the end of the Molotov-Ribbentrop Pact turned the French Communist Party towards the Resistance, but the first murders of German officers by partisans gave more power to the Waffen-SS, vowing to massacre 100 civilians for every German killed by the 'terrorists'.

To maintain control over the French population, the occupier prohibits all communication between civilians in the free and occupied zones. However, from September 1940, it allows the sending of pre-filled postcards called 'interzones'.

The content must remain strictly family-based, as censorship and regulations are strict. This copy was stamped 'refused', since its author had gone over the lines. Nearly half a million of these cards are exchanged every day, until the unrestricted correspondence gradually resumes from the summer of 1941 to the invasion of the free zone in November 1942.

Therefore, Vichy promises to strengthen the 'security' of the French territory: its police thus organizes the first roundups of Jews (it will deport 75,721 of them) and Vichy creates a paramilitary force (the 'Militia') in January 1943. Meanwhile, the Resistance becomes organized thanks to the support of agents sent from England on General de Gaulle's orders. One of these agents, Jean Moulin, will unify the various movements under the Resistance Council before his arrest in June 1943. Thousands of its members will carry out spontaneous armed actions against the Germans in the occupied zone, and political acts against Vichy's propaganda in the free zone. In March 1944, they are assimilated to General de Gaulle's 'Armée de la France Combattante' as the French Forces of the Interior (FFI), except for communist resistance fighters who wish to keep the name 'Francs-Tireurs Partisans' (FTP).

Despite the increasing number of Resistance attacks, the German soldier no longer feels like he is at war and enjoys all that France has to offer. In the summer of 1941, his only fear is to be sent to the East to fight his new enemy: the Soviet.

This is the fate of Wilhelm, who is regretfully leaving Belgium and France, which were occupied for a year by his construction battalion. He's being transferred to the 269. Infantry Division to participate in *Operation Barbarossa*. **As indicated in his military notebook below, Wilhelm will die of his wounds in February 1942, after being hit by shrapnel south of Leningrad. Soon, the Soviets will take the upper hand. As for the tens of thousands of Germans still in France, they will face the growing hostility of the occupied population.**

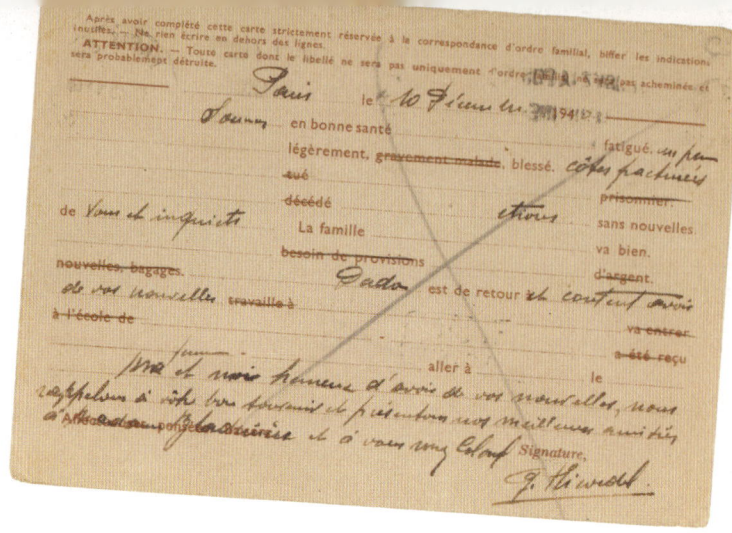

In reality, the renaissance of Europe is being organized from England. Several representatives of occupied countries in exile in London (France, Poland, Norway, Netherlands, Belgium, Czechoslovakia, Denmark...) send messages via British radio waves to resistance movements in the country. Some are symbolic, such as this Belgian encouragement to draw great 'V' in the streets (for 'Victoire' in French, and 'Vrijheid', 'freedom' in Flemish), but others are more tangible. On June 17, 1940, when Marshal Pétain asked the French to *"stop the fight"* on the French national radio, Charles de Gaulle intervened at the BBC the next day to call for the war to continue alongside the British. However, few French people heard this call on the English airwaves (as few could actually listen to the radio). Unfortunately, the message wasn't recorded and will therefore never reach us. The famous 'Appeal of 18 June' as it is known, is in fact a new message, delivered on Armistice Day (June 22). A summary of the speech was printed, giving birth to the famous poster 'à tous les Français' posted in British streets and published in the newspapers.

The General's second call ends with this sentence: *"I invite all French soldiers of the land, sea and air forces, I invite French engineers and workers specialized in armaments who are in British territory or who could get here, to meet with me."* From then on, the French Army is divided into two: on the one hand, the armistice army loyal to Pétain and the German authorities, and on the other, the Free French Forces of General de Gaulle, recognized by the British as the leader of Free France (June 28, 1940).

This leaflet-sized version of the summary of the Appeal of June 18 was printed in London from September 1944 onwards.

A TOUS LES FRANÇAIS

La France a perdu une bataille!
Mais la France n'a pas perdu la guerre!

Des gouvernements de rencontre ont pu capituler, cédant à la panique, oubliant l'honneur, livrant le pays à la servitude. Cependant, rien n'est perdu!

Rien n'est perdu, parce que cette guerre est une guerre mondiale. Dans l'univers libre, des forces immenses n'ont pas encore donné. Un jour, ces forces écraseront l'ennemi. Il faut que la France, ce jour-là, soit présente à la victoire. Alors, elle retrouvera sa liberté et sa grandeur. Tel est mon but, mon seul but!

Voilà pourquoi je convie tous les Français, où qu'ils se trouvent, à s'unir à moi dans l'action, dans le sacrifice et dans l'espérance.

Notre patrie est en péril de mort.
Luttons tous pour la sauver!

VIVE LA FRANCE !

18 Juin 1940

GENERAL DE GAULLE
QUARTIER-GÉNÉRAL,
4, CARLTON GARDENS,
LONDON, S.W.1.

Shortly after his call, 53,000 volunteers would sign for the land forces (*Forces Françaises Libres*), the navy (*Forces Navales Françaises Libres*) or the air force (*Forces Aériennes Françaises Libres*), gathered under the emblem of the Lorraine cross (province lost to the enemy and therefore a symbol of reconquest). Volunteers come from all over the world. The following letter is written on July 3, 1940, two weeks after General de Gaulle's call, by Jean Vacher-Corbière, of the French Consul in Durban (South Africa). He addresses a Royal Navy captain in English in the hope that his message would be conveyed to London: *"My dear Captain, I wanted to call on you but as I believe you are very busy I thought it [is] better to write. As I told you before I am determined to stand by the cause which up to now I have been serving and I am considering steps to offer my services to the French National Committee in London. Before doing so formally I have however to wait a few days as you know what it means to me: I lose everything I possess, my belongings which are all in France, my pension, and the possibility to see my people again! It is a heartbreaking problem to me. I would be alone I would not hesitate one minute, but I have to think of my wife and little daughter. What will become of them?*

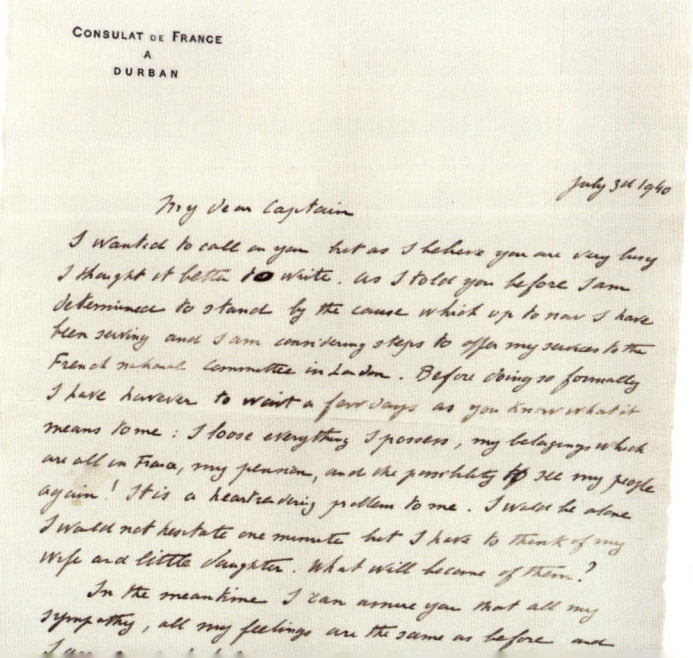

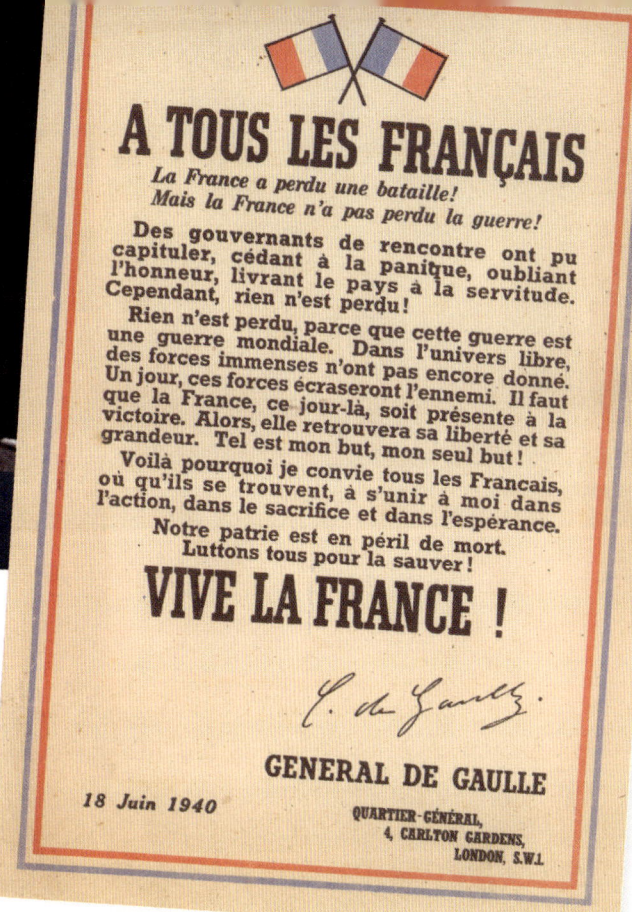

In the meantime, I can assure you that all my sympathy, all my feelings are the same as before and I am ready to help you as much as I can. If I find here a job [sic] then my decision will be easy, I shall relinquish my position as consul immediately and devote entirely myself to what I believe can still be hoped for: the downfall of Nazism! If you have time one day, I would like to have a talk with you in your office. Yours faithfully, Vacher-Corbière."

Charles de Gaulle replies in person to his request, in a telegram dated August 11, 1940: *"Congratulate you on the sentiments expressed in your letter. Ask you to stay for the moment at your post and serve French cause. Will send you by letter the information you request. Cordial sympathy."* (Charles de Gaulle, *Letters, notes and notebooks, volume 3: 1940-1941.*) Jean Vacher-Corbière, at the age of 54, is finally appointed representative of Free France in South Africa by General de Gaulle on July 15, 1941. Heavily involved in the establishment of his army, the general writes to him again in October: *"I remind you that it is your responsibility to inform me as soon as possible of everything that interests Free France and, above all, of all the still important rallying issues that frequently arise in these two cities. In a country where a notorious part of the population expresses its sympathy to us, please try, through your personal action and possibly, through the action of volunteer collaborators, to make the French soldiers passing through the South African Union understand where their duty lies. You must also inform them that I have decided to consider as a deserter any military person who, after being approached, has refused to join."*

NAVAL BATTLES

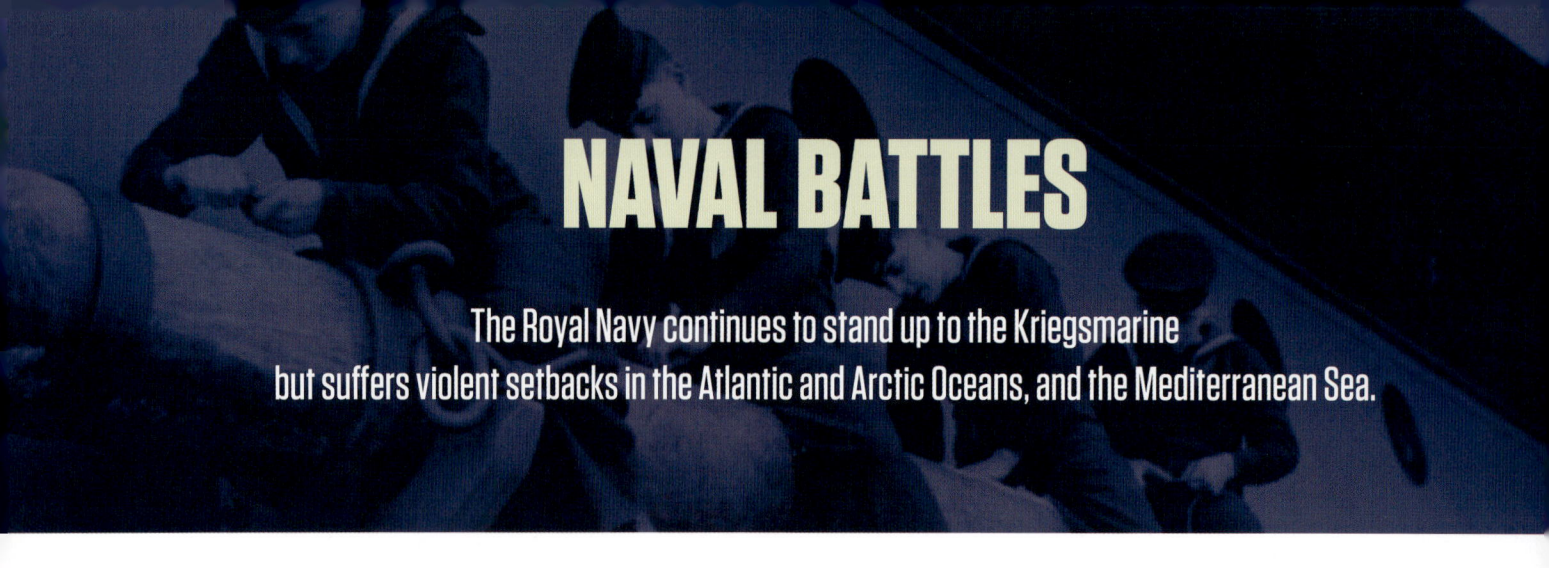

The Royal Navy continues to stand up to the Kriegsmarine but suffers violent setbacks in the Atlantic and Arctic Oceans, and the Mediterranean Sea.

At the beginning of the Second World War, the British Navy is the largest naval force in the world. Among its 332 ships, it counts a majority of destroyers, but also many cruisers, submarines and aircraft carriers. Its ranks would continue to grow until they reach 553 vessels in 1945. However, in the early years of the conflict, it is in a tough position finding itself alone against the German and Italian fleets, especially as the powerful French fleet, although immobilized and supposedly independent (as stipulated in the terms of the armistice), risks falling into enemy hands - Churchill doesn't trust Hitler. On July 3, 1940, the Royal Navy carries out *Operation Catapult*, the unpleasant mission of attacking its French ally at its naval base of Mers el-Kebir, Algeria. Some ships manage to escape (they would later participate in Allied operations in Europe), but the Royal Navy put a large part of the French fleet out of action, killing 1,297 sailors.

THE BATTLE OF THE ATLANTIC

The Battle of the Atlantic would last from September 3, 1939 to the end of the war, the control of this ocean being a key objective for both sides. To establish a blockade on Great-Britain, German U-boats (submarines) bring terror to the seas: Admiral Karl Dönitz developed the technique of the 'wolf pack', a coordination of his U-boats in the attack on commercial convoys. It's only in 1943, with the appearance of long-range bombers, that the Allies would regain control of the seas (for the Germans, it would mark the end of the 'glory days').

For the Allied sailors involved, this battle is not epic, but more like a long, boring hunt. Henry has been serving as a gunner on HMS *Exmoor* since November 1941. This 280-foot-long Hunt-class destroyer takes part in convoy escorts and is credited with having sunk the German submarine *U-131* off Portugal. For a sailor, Henry has the particularity of not knowing how to swim. However, he prefers to face his fear rather than be bored, as he explains to his girlfriend in the spring of 1942: *"We have been in harbour for about a week darling, and this is about the longest we've been in harbour since we've been out here. I did not go ashore all last week but yesterday I got so fed up with the ship and everybody on it that I had to go ashore to break the monotony. [...] There is not much to occupy your mind though on board, and you have to go ashore now and then. We have got plenty of books on board as we have a library and there is [sic] always plenty of magazines knocking about the mess-deck. We are allowed to go swimming as I told you before darling and I've been going in with my life belt on and I am getting along alright, today I let the belt right down and swam alright, so tomorrow I'll go in without it. When I come home we will be able to go swimming together darling."*

Others, however, would see their daily routine disrupted by an invisible and terrifying enemy. By the end of the battle, which will extend to the Arctic Ocean and the Mediterranean Sea, the Allies will have lost more than 70,000 men and 175 warships. Once the tables had turned, however, they would inflict losses on the Germans amounting to 757 U-boats (nicknamed 'iron caskets'), and 25,870 submariners (63% of the crews). During the war, there will be more than 300,000 successful Allied crossings of the Atlantic, with less than 5,000 ships of all types sunk (more than half of them British).

PROTECTING THE CONVOYS

Although the Americans have not yet entered the conflict militarily, they provide valuable assistance to the Allies thanks to the 'Lend-Lease Act' signed on March 11, 1941. Food, oil and equipment are delivered by sea from the United States to Great Britain, the Free French Forces, the Republic of China and the USSR, which since *Operation Barbarossa* has now been fighting against Germany. As a result, 1,400 American merchant ships now transit across the Atlantic and Arctic oceans to the Soviet Union. Escorted by Royal Navy

I - THE DARK YEARS 1939-1942

(British and Canadian) and US Navy ships, they mainly throw their anchors in the harbors of Arkhangelsk in the summer or Murmansk in the winter. $11 billion in steel, guns, planes (11,400 units), tanks (7,000), Jeeps (400,000), trucks and 1.75 million tons of food from the United States will eventually contribute greatly to the mobility, armament and the final victory of the Soviets. Among those participating in these convoy escorts, Archibald is busy in the engine room of the British minesweeper HMS *Gossamer*, a veteran of the evacuation of Dunkirk and the very first convoy to Russia, among others. On the morning of June 24, 1942, while anchored in Kola Bay (near Murmansk), HMS *Gossamer* is attacked by five Stuka dive bombers. Despite the response of the ship's guns and machine guns, the ship is hit by a bomb at 9:12 am. The order is given: *"Every man for himself, evacuate the ship!"* It sinks in eight minutes, killing three officers and twenty crew members. Of these, it's estimated that fifteen of them die in the explosion, while the others are trapped underwater. Archibald saves an injured sailor from drowning at the last minute, pulling him out of the debris just before that part of the ship is engulfed. HMS *Hussar* and several Russian ships immediately come to the rescue of the survivors, many of whom are wounded.

Archibald writes to his parents on July 1, 1942, a week after the events: *"Dear Mum and Dad, you will have had a couple of letters from me before so you should have a good idea how things stand. We are living ashore here at present waiting to take passage back to the United Kingdom so you will be seeing me at some future date. The ship was struck by a bomb and sank shortly after so most of us had to swim for it but we were very fortunate and had a very small percentage of casualties considering the damage done to the ship. I was fortunate myself and got away with my wallet and watch and most of my photographs and more important still without a scratch, otherwise I have lost everything I had on board so I will have to start again collecting my kit including a tool kit and that is going to be a hard job the way things stand these days. We were landed ashore and billeted in a big school building. After we had dried ourselves out we were kitted out in all sorts of gear so we are walking around here looking something like an out of work concert party. The weather here is scorching and we have a small lake or pond next door but we can't swim in it, but we do our washing. I've done my washing this forenoon so now I have to walk around nearly naked until it dries. We have to troop about two miles three times a day for our meals, it's good exercise and helps you to eat the food they dish out, the walk could be twice as long and the food twice as good but nevermind we will all be home someday soon so if a tramp comes to the door don't lock him out, it's me. [...] The skipper had just told us the day before we were hit that we were going home with the convoy but it's gone now and we will probably have to wait for the next one. [...]*

Well we have moved now from Polyarny to an army camp and if anything it's worse here. The grub shack is next door but they only feed us on black bread now so roll on the U.K.! There is a chance we will be moving down south to Archangel by train or series of trains but it has already been cancelled once so it may not come off. We have just had another batch of merchant seamen arrive [probably the American sailors of the *Alcoa Cadet*, which hit a mine nearby on June 21] *and some of them have been eight days in the boats but they seem to be OK and have brought most of their gear with them. I'm afraid none of the Yanks will ever do this trip again, once they get back in the States they will stay there. As one nigger* [sic] *said 'Lordie Lordie turn dem bombs to snowball, I shoo am skaird!'"*

Archibald and the survivors of HMS *Gossamer* will return to the United Kingdom aboard HMS *Marne*, which they will board on August 24. However, they will be attacked again the next day, killing three people and injuring five. They will reach Scapa Flow base in Scotland on August 28, 1942.

**The enemy is also wreaking havoc in the Mediterranean. These two Royal Navy hats and this sailor's collar belonged to the electrician William Widdowson, who died on HMS *Bonaventure*. On March 31, 1941, protecting convoy GA8 south of Crete, this 510-foot-long Dido-class light cruiser was torpedoed by the Italian submarine *Ambra*.
It sank in six minutes, taking the lives of 139 sailors and soldiers, including William's. The ship's name is embossed on the box and written in the hats. In wartime, the name on the headband is replaced by the initials 'HMS' (His Majesty's Ship) for safety.**

HAROLD McONIE

10 Railway Construction Company, 2nd New Zealand Expeditionary Force

The British also continue the fight on land, alongside their colonies and dominions (Australia, New Zealand, South Africa and Canada) in the Middle East. After the disasters in Greece and Crete, Harold will reinforce New Zealand's Expeditionary Force, supporting *Operation Crusader*.

THE DESERT WAR

The 'Desert War' (June 1940 - May 1943) consists of a long series of advances and retreats for both sides. The attacker, when pulling too much on his supply lines, becomes vulnerable and is eventually forced to fall back. For this reason, port cities such as Tripoli, Benghazi and Tobruk in Libya or Alexandria in Egypt are strategic targets and some of them will change hands several times. Constrained by the hostile terrain, the belligerents will thus fight over more than 1,200 miles from the Tunisian border to Egypt without really venturing more than 100 miles away from the Mediterranean coast.

As soon as he entered the war on June 10, 1940, Mussolini planned to attack the British in Egypt and Somalia from his colonies in Libya and Ethiopia. Four days later, British tanks entered Libya and took Fort Capuzzo. The 10a Armata (10th Italian Army) counter-attacked in September 1940, but encountered the 7th Armoured Division near Marsa Matruh and stopped its progress. The 36,000 British members of the Western Desert Force (soon to be renamed XIII Corps) advanced in early December (*Operation Compass*) and pushed the Italians back more than 500 miles to El Agheila. On the way, they seized the Libyan port of Tobruk on January 23, 1941. In two months, they broke the ten divisions of the 10a Armata, and took more than 130,000 prisoners. The Italians were forced to surrender on February 7. However, for the first time, the British were confronted with the problem of supply lines and couldn't progress any further. The Germans took this opportunity to help their allies: by landing armored troops in Tripoli (including the Italian division Ariete), they prevented the Italian surrender scheduled for the following day. The German troops formed the formidable Afrika Korps led by Generaloberst Erwin Rommel, one of Hitler's favorite generals, who would be nicknamed 'the Desert Fox' and who dreamed of seizing Egypt and the Suez Canal.

DIFFICULT START FOR THE 2 NZEF

New Zealand distinguished itself during the First World War with the 1st New Zealand Expeditionary Force, a member of the famous ANZAC (Australian and New Zealand Army Corps). When the country declared war on Germany on September 3, 1939, it set up the 2nd New Zealand Expeditionary Force. Under the command of General Bernard Freyberg, it had only

50

Spring 1941

- → Allied forces
- → Enemy forces
- ··· Defense line
- • Key town / city

one division: the 2nd New Zealand Division. Fully deployed at the end of September 1940, it participated in the first attacks in the desert two months later (some of its support units took part in *Operation Compass*), but its real baptism of fire took place in Greece. Mussolini, who after the Alpine disaster wanted to prove himself to Hitler, tried to invade the country from Albania on October 28, 1940. The Italians faced the courageous Greek Army, which not only pushed them back to the border, but even captured enemy ground. Churchill, who had an interest in the Balkans and Central Europe, decided to make this theater a priority: its bombers would be within range of the oil fields of Ploiesti (Romania), essential to the German war machine. Therefore, 58,000 men and their equipment were sent from Africa to Greece, including New Zealanders accompanied by a British armored brigade, two Australian divisions and a Polish rifle brigade. Landing on March 6, 1941, the 'Kiwis' took up position on the Aliakmon Line north of Mount Olympus. Unfortunately, this redeployment was taking place at the expense of the British lines of defense in Libya. The Afrika Korps jumped on this occasion to push the Allies back to Egypt on March 24, isolating the small port of Tobruk, which was nevertheless firmly held by the 9th Australian Division. Rommel's siege of the city would now begin.

In the meantime, the Germans were preparing to come to the rescue of their Italian allies in Greece, who had been humiliated once again. On April 6, the Wehrmacht launched a major offensive alongside the Italians and Bulgarians (*Operation Marita*). The New Zealanders, Greeks and other Allies were unable to contain the attack, and fell back to the east coast. A week later, the Germans broke the line in Klidhi's pass, forcing the defenders to withdraw in a hurry. In the north, Yugoslavia also fell after eleven terrible days, during a campaign in which the Germans only lost 151 killed. Commonwealth troops in Greece were evacuated from April 22: some to Crete, the others to Egypt. The Germans entered Athens on April 27, precipitating the surrender of Greece. Two of the three brigades of the 2nd NZ Division were sent to Crete (7,700 men), with 9,000 Greeks and 26,000 British and Australians. General Freyberg then had to organize the defense of the island against a forthcoming invasion of 14,000 *Fallschirmjäger* (German paratroopers), but he had very little armament. When the German *Operation Merkur* was launched on May 20, the British fought bravely against the paratroopers, with the help of the local population defending itself as best they could. The Germans suffered huge losses, but regained the advantage when they landed reinforcements in the north of the island and pushed the Allies southwards.

After twelve days of desperate fighting, particularly around Maleme airfield, 671 New Zealanders were killed and more than 2,000 taken prisoner (out of a total of 12,000 Allies captured). On May 31, the survivors were evacuated from the island and regrouped in Egypt.

HAROLD ARRIVES IN AFRICA

At the beginning of 1941, Harold George McOnie is a 24-year-old New-Zealander. He has just married and drives a tractor in his father-in-law's sawmill in a remote community in northeastern New Zealand called Motu. Even though married men don't yet have to serve their country (this wouldn't come into effect until July 31 of the same year, following the disaster in Greece), Harold volunteered for the army in March 1941, as did two of his brothers, joining the HQ of the New Zealand Railway Construction & Maintenance Group (Engineers), 2 NZEF, as a sapper. His unit maintains the railway tracks and transports the troops and their equipment to the front line and will therefore play a crucial role during the Desert War.

Up to ten convoys of reinforcements would leave New Zealand. Harold arrives in Egypt with the 6th Reinforcements (145 officers and 3,663 soldiers), which left Wellington on board the *Aquitania* on June 27, 1941. He lands on July 29, not far from Cairo. Harold is bombed in early September during a raid that kills one person and injures twenty-one, but he is unharmed. However, he suffers from chronic abdominal pains that lead him to the hospital and he writes from there on September 14, 1941:

Harold (left) and his brother Claude (right).

"Dear Auntie May, thank you ever so kindly for the very welcome letter which I received today. I haven't had any letters from home for three weeks now so you can guess how I welcomed yours. You warned me not to eat too much sand here. Just how did you know we were coming to the land of sand & flies? I have had a good time since being here, there are some wonderful things to see here and some things I don't ever want to see or hear after this business is all over. We aren't allowed to tell much of anything that happens here. I suppose Cairo's first air raid will be stale news to you by this time. I was pretty lonely at the time and not in the best of circumstances but I didn't panic. You see it is my first time near a raid. I wouldn't like to tell you what I think the results will be, however I am sure we can take it whatever it may be. [...] I don't blame you for not being too keen to see your boys leave home. Tell them for me they are foolish to come if they can do otherwise. Uncle Joe has done enough for your family. Was he in this part of the globe? [...] By the way, have you had a roster of the ship that brought us here? Let me know about it if you have. I suppose the seventh reinforcements will not be in NZ by this time. I have a brother coming with them and am very anxious to get some idea when they might be here."

I - THE DARK YEARS 1939-1942

The 7th Reinforcements from New Zealand. Harold's brother Claude is one of these passengers. He will serve in the 24th Auckland Battalion (infantry) during Operation Crusader.

The 2nd NZ Division regroups on November 11, in the desert near the Libyan border, south of Marsa Matruh. This is the first time that the entire 2 NZEF has been brought together, assembling more than 20,000 men. A week later, it takes part in *Operation Crusader* to lift the siege of Tobruk. Harold leaves the hospital at the same time and joins the 10 NZ Railway Construction Company along the way.

CRUSADER AND THE TOBRUK FORTRESS

Tobruk has been holding on since April 1941. The Australians repelled three assaults in two weeks, stopping Rommel's tanks at the city's gates. Their counter-attack stabilized the front on May 1, inflicting twice as many casualties on the Germans as on their ranks. Despite their relief by British, Polish and Czech units landing in the port, it becomes urgent to help Tobruk: Rommel can crush it at any minute.

Two Allied operations have already failed. *Brevity* in mid-May was a rapid attack on the border between Egypt and Libya, which was aborted after only one day. The second attempt, *Operation Battleaxe*, was also a bitter failure: the British 7th Armoured Division and the Indian 4th Infantry Division clashed with the 15. Panzer-Division in Sallum, near the coast, and on the same border. From June 15 to 17, the Allies lost many of their tanks there and narrowly missed a catastrophic encirclement. As a result, General Archibald Wavell, then Commander-in-Chief of Middle East Operations, was replaced by General Claude Auchinleck. The latter was supported by Winston Churchill and the Americans, who provided new tanks to the British Army. The newly created XXX Corps (British 7th Armoured Division, 1st South African Infantry Division, and 22nd Guards Brigade) was added to the XIII Corps in Egypt (which then included the 2nd New Zealand Division, the 4th Indian Infantry Division and the 1st Armoured Brigade). Together, they formed the soon to be famous 8th Army in September 1941.

This new operation *Crusader* consists of heading south towards Tobruk, while the garrison of 23,000 men trapped in the city is supposed to try to break the encirclement to join them. Bad surprise: Rommel, who was planning another assault on Tobruk, circumvents the British attack from the southwest and takes it from behind. As a result, the operation seems to turn once again into a disaster. The tank battles in Sidi Rezegh will be among the most violent and chaotic in the entire Desert War. They are so confusing that at one point both sides manage to launch an attack in two opposite directions without ever meeting each other. British tanks, already in a difficult situation because they're technically inferior to German tanks, charge enemy guns with disastrous results. On November 23, the 7th Armoured Division alone only has 60 tanks left out of the 477 it had a few days earlier. Nevertheless, Rommel is in an even more critical situation: he only has about 100 left for all his divisions. While the Allies have the luxury of waiting for reinforcements, the Royal Air Force cuts off any German hope of receiving fresh troops from Tripoli.

On November 26, the New Zealanders attack Sidi Rezegh while the Tobruk garrison attempts to flee. Rommel, now on the defensive, knows that the battle is lost. On December 7, after a final failed assault, he withdraws what he can save from the Afrika Korps and the line falls back to Gazala. The German resistance pockets of Bardia and Halfaya, which cannot be evacuated, would continue to fight until January 1942. Tobruk is liberated after a 242-day siege, and the British set out in pursuit of the enemy, which they chase from Gazala in mid-December to Tripoli. Harold and the other engineers play a major role in the rapid advance of the 8th Army, replacing the rails bent by German bombs. They sometimes lay more than 4 miles of track every day! Harold writes to his wife on January 10: *"I haven't had any word from you since last year. I don't suppose I can really grumble dear because I am never in the one place very long. We have once again moved, forward much to our pleasure, we don't seem to be able to go forward fast enough to satisfy everyone here."*

Operation Crusader cost the Allies more than 800 tanks, 2,900 killed, 7,300 wounded and more than 7,500 missing. As for the Afrika Korps, its losses amount to 340 tanks, 3,300 killed, 6,100 wounded, and nearly 30,000 missing (including many prisoners). Sadly, all these men were sacrificed for nothing. Indeed, as we will soon see in more detail, a new offensive by Rommel at the end of January 1942 would bring him back to the positions he held before *Operation Crusader*. Tobruk will even be surrounded again in June. As Rommel pushes the 8th Army eastward, Harold is working on the extension of a railway line from El Adem (south of Tobruk) to Fort Capuzzo (near Sallum, over the Egyptian border). During their retreat, the railways are responsible for keeping the Allies supplied with water, ammunition and gasoline, and are therefore regularly targeted by the Luftwaffe. Harold's company counts seven dead and fifteen wounded during the period.

He tells his wife: *"We had a hot week or so and then a speedy move out altogether. I never wished as much in all my life that I was with you Eva as I did when we were coming out of Libya. I thought of all the times I've treated you wrong darling and I am sure I paid for them then."*

While his unit leaves for Syria on June 9 (trading places with South African engineers), Harold is transferred to an armored cavalry unit in early July. However, his stomach still hurts, and he has to leave the front again on the 27th: combat rations and desert living conditions seem to be awakening an old ulcer. Harold thus spends several more weeks in the hospital, from where he writes: *"Sometimes, when I feel lonely, I wish I could go back to fight with the boys."*

Finally declared unfit for duty, he will board a ship on September 17 in Egypt and disembark on a stretcher in Wellington a month later. Harold will return to civilian life in January 1943 and despite his service, he will always be reluctant to receive the pension to which he is entitled. He will rarely talk about the war, never wear his uniform again, or even attend the commemorations for the ANZAC troops. Like many veterans, he considered that the war must remain in the past. Harold died in Tauranga on August 30, 1987, at the age of 70. He is buried with his wife in the Thames Valley, Bay of Plenty, New Zealand.

Thereafter, the 2 NZEF would participate in the victories in El Alamein and Tunisia, then in the Italian campaign. A total of 140,000 New Zealanders served in the Second World War, the vast majority of them in the 2 NZEF (104,000), but also in the British RAF and Royal Navy. With 11,928 killed in action, the country holds the Commonwealth's unfortunate record for the highest number of deaths per million inhabitants (6,684), ahead of Great Britain (5,123) and Australia (3,232).

In the desert, Harold (right) is seen apparently guarding a railway line from his dug-out.

I - **THE DARK YEARS** 1939-1942

A British 8th Army captain in North Africa.

The Khaki Drill shirt and shorts set belonged to Captain H. B. Stevens. On his shoulders you can see the three Bath Stars that indicate his rank.

He wears a Mark II helmet dated 1939 with a field-made cover cut from a burlap bag and sprayed with black paint. This practice was very common in North Africa for reasons of camouflage, temperature, and noise or sun-reflection reduction. The soldier added a strip of hessian cloth attached to the helmet cover with 1930s wire. According to the remains of a blue circle painted on the front of the steel helmet, underneath the cover, it could have belonged to an engineer in the 2nd New Zealand Division.

This model also wears the MKVI gas mask bag, as the threat of such an attack was still significant in the early 1940s. He's watching the enemy through his 1943 Bino Prism No.2 Mk.III binoculars (manufactured by Taylor Hobson), which belonged to a veteran whose mission was to make military maps in Europe: he painted the first letter of his name, an M, in red on the front of the binoculars.

WILLIAM BROWN

Royal Army Ordnance Corps

Although he wouldn't take part in tank fighting in the desert, William would experience the 'other war': the war against sandstorms, heat and thirst, insects, dysentery, and German bombardments. In charge of an ordnance store in Tobruk, he will be surrounded when Rommel returns in the summer of 1942. But this time the port city will fall, and William will be among the many prisoners.

WITH THE 8TH ARMY

William 'Bill' Brown is a passionate photographer from Derbyshire, England. His father is a veteran of the First World War, who received the Military Medal with the Royal Army Medical Corps. It was therefore natural for Bill to volunteer for the army in June 1940, shocked by the news of a German invasion. He joined the Royal Army Ordnance Corps, which manages the supply and maintenance of weapons, vehicles, spare parts, clothing and other equipment. Bill serves more specifically in an Ordnance Store Company, where he is in charge of the 'depots'.

Royal Army Ordnance Corps badge. It bears in French 'Honi soit qui mal y pense', (Shame on him who thinks evil of it) an old Anglo-Norman motto, seen on the badges of many British Army corps.

Bill arrives in Egypt in the spring of 1941. He's relatively far from the fighting, in Cairo, but still affected by extreme temperatures: although it's over 50°C (120°F) in the shade during the day, he needs to sleep with no less than six blankets at night. He describes the country in his letters to his wife Vera: *"We don't have much chance to get around in the day-time, but we do get a half-day off per week. I spent mine having a trip to one of the local spots of interest, one of the wonders of the world* [the pyramids]. *I should like to tell you of all I have seen here but censor says no so that's that, but there are a few things which stand out: mosquitoes, flies, donkeys, ants (about three-quarters of an inch long), beetles, camels (which smell!), women draped from head to foot in black with nearly all their faces covered, men and boys wearing gowns and trying to twist us every step. Those are a few. Every step you take seems to take you to a street vendor, and how they use their persuasion when exercising their salesmanship!!"*

In August, Bill leaves the lush gardens of Cairo for the merciless desert of El-Geneifa. The city is located near the Suez Canal, the main point of entry for goods to the Middle East. The following month, he meets men from the British 8th Army. Bill expresses his admiration for the number of

I - THE DARK YEARS 1939-1942

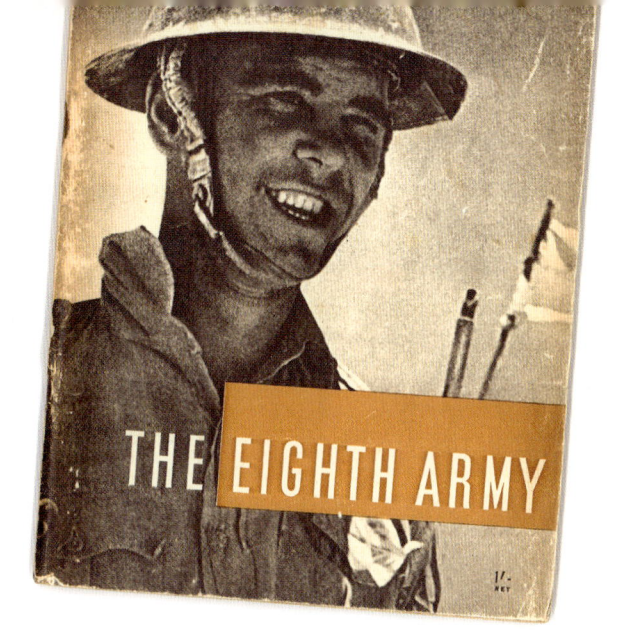

countries represented: there are Australians, New Zealanders, including Maori, *"New Zealand natives, very rich, receiving rents"*, Indians *"with their hair wrapped in a small ball above their heads"*, *"strong and blond South Africans"*, French (FFL), Sudanese, Poles, Czechs, Maltese, and many others. Some have already seen heavy fighting. A man from Bill's company told him one evening in the tent about the terrible British retreat from Crete, from which he returned to the great surprise of his comrades, who thought he had been captured or killed.

TOBRUK IS THREATENED AGAIN

A few weeks later, Bill leaves Egypt in the middle of a sandstorm and joins a forward supply depot a few miles from Tobruk. Unable to reveal his position, he sends his wife a pretty obvious clue – a poem from November 1941 called *The Tale of Tobruk*. Probably written by an Australian soldier, it tells the story of the city from its conquest by the Astralians until the siege in the summer of 1941:

*"We got in a ship and we sailed out to sea,
And each of us then was in spirits of glee,
For 'twas farewell to Egypt and old King Farouk,
We were bound for the beautiful town of Tobruk.
A night and a day we sailed o'er the waves,
Then arrived at Tobruk with its harbour of graves.
There were ships all around us, but, sad to relate,
They were all under water – a terrible state.
We gazed and we thought as our eyes met that sight,
Of all the good ships in that terrible plight.
There were British and Jerries, and Eyeties galore.
Oh! The price that we pay when we're forced into war.
Now we sighted the town that before us did lie,
And most of us then heaved a mighty big sigh.
For this was our home, right down by the sea;
But none of us knew for how long it would be.
We walked through the streets – 'twas a pitiful sight,
Each house in a turmoil – a ragman's delight.
Devastation lay 'round us, where bombs had come down.
Man's folly had wrecked this once beautiful town.
As weeks passed to months, the weather grew hot,
Each mother's son groused a terrible lot.
With fags unobtainable, and no hope of beer,
We all cursed the man who had sent us out here.
We worked with a will and enjoyed all the fun,
For the Eyeties turned tail, and started to run;
But we worked just as hard – we couldn't relax,
For our troops reached Benghazi and stopped in their tracks.
They had fought a long way, their strength was depleted.
When they met Jerry's Army our boys soon retreated.
For Jerry's were strong, and fresh in the fray.
We were vastly outnumbered that terrible day.
You've all heard the story of the long, thin, red line.
Our boys' rear-guard action was equally fine;
But the tenth day of April the bugle was sounded.
Alas and alack – Tobruk was surrounded.
We couldn't surrender, our morale was high,
When suddenly there came a roar in the sky.
They machine-gunned us, bombed us, and shelled us as well.
To be in Tobruk was like being in Hell.
We all now look forward to that glorious day,
When once more we hope, we shall sail out the bay;
And as we glide out we shall take a last look
At the wreck that was once the proud town of Tobruk."*

As we saw in the previous pages, after liberating the port city during *Operation Crusader*, the 8th Army then pushed the Germans back to El Agheila. Bill's unit is in charge of supplying the XIII Corps (which has by then progressed 500 miles), by air via a runway at Msus. He doesn't know yet that Rommel would push east again, and so in early January 1942, the British focus on their extended depots and supply lines, rather than on strengthening their front line. At the same time, they are also sending troops to fight the Japanese in Burma. This mistake is reminiscent of their deployment to Greece, which had made them neglect these same defenses less than a year earlier, but it's true that the situation in the Mediterranean has changed, and the *K-Force* (a fleet of Allied warships based in Malta) is now tasked with destroying enemy convoys bound for Africa. Unfortunately, the Germans had just started a campaign to destroy this same *K-Force*, already severely damaged in an underwater minefield not far from Tripoli, and the Luftwaffe has given back control of the area to the Axis. Rommel therefore receives 50,000 Germans and 30,000 additional Italians, while Auchinleck estimates the size of the whole Afrika Korps at only 35,000 men.

THE TALE OF TOBRUK

We got in a ship and we sailed out to sea,
And each of us then was in spirits of glee,
For 'twas farewell to Egypt and old King Farouk,
We were bound for the beautiful town of Tobruk.

A night and a day we sailed o'er the waves,
Then arrived at Tobruk with its harbour of graves.
There were ships all around us, but, sad to relate,
They were all under water - a terrible [fate].

We gazed and we thought as our eyes m[...]
Of all the good ships in that terrib[...]
There were British and Jerries, and [...]
Oh! The price that we pay when we're [...]

Now we [...] the town that before u[...]
[...] then heaved a mighty b[...]
[...] home, right down by t[...]
[...] w for how long it wo[...]

[...] the streets - 'twas [...]
[...] moil - a ragman's [...]
[...] nd us, where bo[...]
[...] ked this once [...]

[...] nths, the weathe[...]
[...] used a terrible [...]
[...], and no hope [...]
[...] who had sent [...]

[...] d enjoyed [...]
[...] ail, and [...]
[...] d - we [...]
[...] nghazi [...]

On January 21, 1942, after a simple reconnaissance of the British lines, which proved to be thin, Rommel seizes this chance and recaptures Benghazi and At Tamimi in just a few days.

On February 4, the British withdraw to a line of defense stretching from Gazala (30 miles west of Tobruk) to Bir Hakeim, occupied by the 1st Free French Brigade (50 miles further south). They now find themselves in positions from which they had driven their enemies only seven weeks earlier. The Gazala Line is a succession of defensive points, spaced a few miles apart and protected by minefields and barbed wire. While the rest of his unit retreat to Marsa Matruh in Egypt, Bill and 124 other soldiers are in charge of the remaining depots in Tobruk with a number of natives and Indians. Bill sets up his store in a building that has already been heavily damaged by the bombs. He sells everything to everyone, from privates to generals, and manages almost all the depots on his own to equip the 33,000 men in the garrison. It's difficult to maintain morale, especially since the rumors are not good: Rommel is approaching. Bill and his comrades, in addition to their daily duties, are preparing to defend the depots just like any infantryman. They are also the targets of numerous Luftwaffe attacks, including Messerschmitt 109 fighters converted to low-level bombers, making them similar to the Junkers Ju 87, or 'Stukas'.

I - THE DARK YEARS 1939-1942

Bill writes to his wife on March 8: *"In this letter I am going to give you a little idea of the comparisons – us out here and the boys at home [British reserve or territorial defense forces] – mainly for the benefit of these grumblers for I don't begrudge them in their luck but I think the grumblers ought to have a packet out here!! That would shake 'em. I read the letters in* Professional Photographer Magazine *and noted your remarks!! How inconsiderate of the army to put them twelve miles from the nearest town!! Why, on our day off we travelled between 90 and 100 miles for a glimpse of civilization and to be among our own 'people'; I fancy them having the initiative and courage to make the best of it and amuse themselves; the letter written in answer told them a thing or two!! How would they like bully biscuits for four meals out of six? Salt water tea!! Trying to shave three or four days growth of beard off with salt water (which will not lather). No dear, don't think I am grumbling, far from it because we just accept these things. I could tell you loads of them, but a better, cheerful and courageous crowd you will not find. Just another thing regarding food – often even if the food is good, a sand storm blows up and before you can eat it or drink the 'tea' it is all covered with sand, but you are so hungry, a little sand doesn't matter. [...]*

Darling, although I told you of those things don't class me as fed up entirely; it has been such an experience!! But then every day is that out here. During that journey we slept in a small utility truck (very small) and I leave you to guess what it was like travelling all that time with no roads and clouds of dust, but everyone laughed – the British soldier always laughs. He is crazy and doesn't know when he has had enough. Whilst on the job – these Stukas raids you read of in the papers, they don't last long but they are sometimes rather intense. One instance I had a grand view: a sky with puffy white clouds; a roar is heard and then appear three Stukas, then three more, more still – fifteen in all. Then they start diving through intensive AA fire – one is hit and the crew bale out, perhaps none were hit for we heard later that a few were fetched down further away. A little later along comes another plane, low and flying inland – 'one of ours' someone said, OK. Bang! Bang! goes machine gun. We were wrong, it was one of theirs with no markings. You have often told me to get into the shelter from shrapnel!! Have you heard it come down? Buzz-buzz-zzz just like a bee humming. Only the other day, three of us were together and found ourselves listening to it, then simultaneously we made a dive. Although I have told you all this don't go worrying your head off. Your own intelligence tells you an AOD [Advanced Ordnance Depot] must be in an advanced position but that doesn't mean constant danger, and we don't look for trouble, oh no!!

A few days ago, I went to a place [...] and bought some chocolates for the boys. We pulled in the place for the stores when Bang! Bang! Ack-ack fire. On with the helmet and out of the cab and down we dived into a shelter. No sooner had we arrived that mmm-mmm-mmm the scream of an engine – the bastard was diving and it sounded as if he was making straight for our shelter. Such a clatter as he drops his stuff... then all quiet. It was all over. Not stopping for details we load up and are away in hell of a dust, I can tell you. Since I have told you some of the things for I don't think I have given any vital secrets away, I will go further and tell you another story. A Stuka raid was on, and a bomb dropped right by a church, unfortunately there were some chaps near with a wagon. I was not there, but I am told it was horrible. I need not say the men were killed, about six I believe and to enlighten you further there was little left to bury. The wagon was lifted bodily and deposited about fifty yards away. Incidentally the plane came down and the pilot killed but again another life was lost when it crashed. As I said before I heard of this and was not there. I had better ease up on the letter my dear of you will think I am trying to scare you – far from it, but that letter did rouse me a little and if the subject comes up you can at least let them know a little of what happens out here. It doesn't happen to everyone, but on the other hand many are worse off, much worse off. There are good spots and bad in this part of the world, and good luck to the chaps in the good spots. I have had a share so why grumble. [...] Darling, please, I repeat that too my dear do not get alarmed at reports you get for we are bound to get a little activity which will creep into the news. [...]

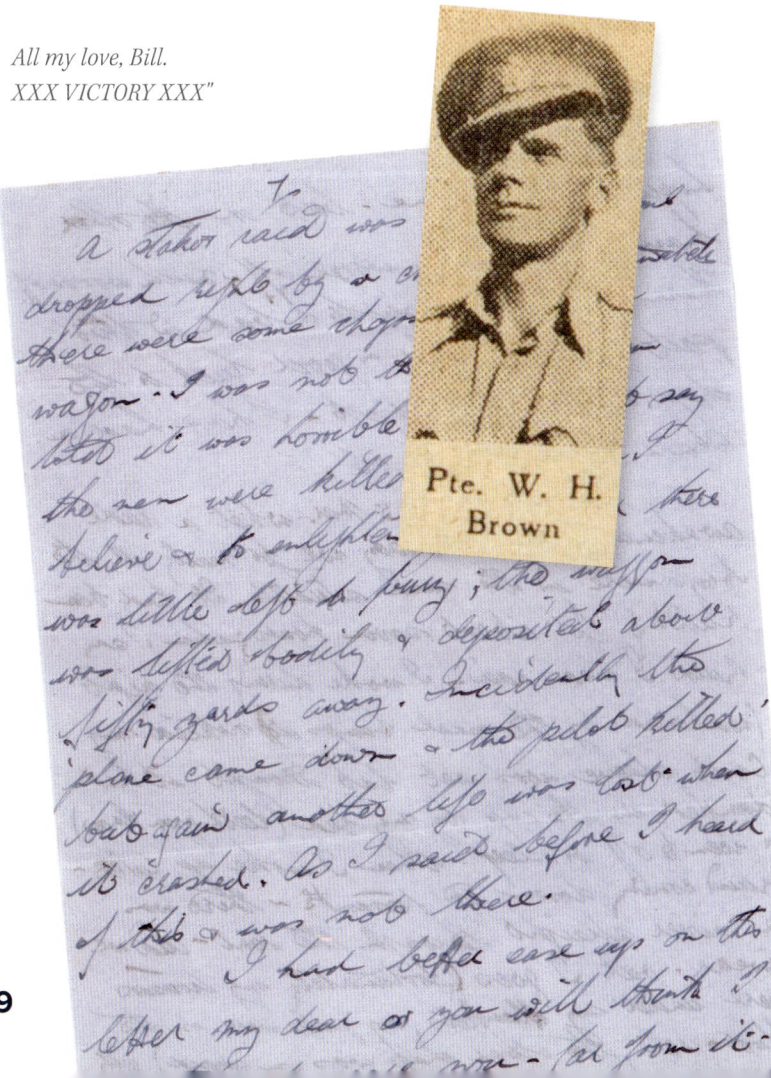

All my love, Bill.
XXX VICTORY XXX"

Pte. W. H. Brown

Living in a large hole in the ground with seven of his comrades, Bill describes his home in March 1942 as *"a crater on the Western Desert somewhere in Libya. Originally the hole was dug or blasted for a machine-gun or as protection from the air. We have rigged up this hole as a cook-house, orderly room, regimental headquarters and debating room. From nowhere we found a small table, seats cut out of the sides, rations on ledges all around and in one corner a couple of petrol fires."*

He sometimes has to leave his shelter and travel through places where both sides have moved forward and backward many times: *"A few days ago I had to join my proper depot which meant a ride of about twenty miles. Although I had done the trip a few times, that day was one which made your whole being feel glad to be alive; the sun shone gloriously and the wind coming from the coast was lovely and fresh; yet there we were driving through a devastated area dotted with wrecks of machines of all kinds; airplanes, motorcycles, tractors, fighting vehicles of all descriptions; here and there a grave or two, then a cluster and in one place a fair number set out in neat order. We passed the various 'lines' which, if only they had voices, would tell stirring stories of brave men who held that territory. My dear, war is a terrible thing, we all know only too well, but to get the right idea of the waste of useful resources of the word, the sacrifice of human lives, and above all the futility of its purpose one has to travel where it has laid its iron hand."*

ROMMEL ATTACKS GAZALA

Rommel still hasn't launched his attack on the Gazala Line, restoring the Allies' confidence. After all, they have received new American equipment, and a total of 110,000 troops, 843 tanks and 604 aircraft.

Bill writes to his wife on May 8: *"I'll bet your ears are glued to the wireless these days with all the action in the desert. We have just returned from hearing tonight's news which was very cheerful, we seem to be doing pretty well, but what a battle!! The ordnance are coming in for a lot of praise again too, and believe me they are earning it as are the other boys too. I expect you know of our Corps being a combatant corps now... don't we know it!! Still on with the show and let's have the curtain down soon. I wonder if the people at home realise half of what this battle in the desert is like?"*

On May 26, Rommel finally launches *Operation Venezia*. He first charges the positions of the 1st South African Infantry Division and the 7th British Armoured Division to the north, which proves to be a diversionary maneuver. Still, he inflicts heavy casualties, as evidenced by this letter between two senior officers, praising the courage of the commander of the 9th Queen's Royal Lancers: *"The battle started for the 2nd Armoured Brigade on the 27th May and the IX Lancers were in the van. From the very start the skill of their commander and the utter determination of all ranks to close with enemy tanks was most evident. The third day of the battle was the culminating triumph to a series of short sharp and well conducted actions. The 29th May will always be a memorable date in the annals of the Regiment. All day they, together with the remainder of the brigade, fought and held off the combined efforts of the 15. and 21. Panzer Divisions. Over 100 German tanks were bearing down on our already depleted numbers from one direction, whilst 70 more advanced from another: the odds were over two to one. All day the Regiment fought, using its Crusader tanks with the greatest tactical skill and hitting the Germans hard with its Grant tanks. By the fifth day the Regiment which had fought brilliantly and continuously was down to four tanks and I was compelled to relieve them. The moment they were re-equipped they were back again [...]. The Regiment has suffered but it has inflicted many more casualties on the enemy. I mourn for many good friends amongst the officers and men, but the way in which they died for their Country and their Regiment will be an inspiration to all for years to come."*

On May 27, Rommel attacks General Koenig's 1st Free French Brigade further south at Bir Hakeim. Some 3,700 Free French soldiers occupy a former Ottoman fortress in appalling living conditions. From the first day, the temperature is just under 50°C (120°F) in the shade and water is scarce. Still, despite their overwhelming numerical superiority, the Italians of the Ariete Division would suffer a painful defeat, wave after wave, against French mines and guns. The fighting would last for ten days, until the French positions are finally overrun on June 9, when the Italians receive reinforcements from the 21. Panzer-Division. A German officer then observes the only survivor of a of French battery, a legionnaire with his hand torn off, reload his 75 mm gun by pushing the shell in with his bloody stump. Nevertheless, two-thirds of Koenig's survivors would manage to escape after a 5-mile walk in the desert.

Lastly, Rommel heads for the remaining points of resistance, which the South Africans of the 1st Division and the British of the 50th (Northumbrian) Division can no longer hold. The Allies leave Gazala for Tobruk, which Churchill still wants to keep at all costs. Fortunately, Rommel's long drive jeopardized Germany's supply lines, forcing him to withdraw and organize them. The 8th Army takes this opportunity to counter-attack, but its assault is unprepared and fails. Many tanks are lost, and the Germans take the upper hand again. The Allied columns have no choice but to retreat to El Alamein, abandoning Tobruk to the Afrika Korps.

I - THE DARK YEARS 1939-1942

This old Kodak handheld camera, made in the United States in the mid-1920s, is a relic of the battle of Tobruk. It probably belonged to a South African or British soldier.

The latter, likely a photography enthusiast like Bill, narrowly escaped death when a German bullet passed through his camera. The bullet hit the front of the closed case, tore the bellows and exited from the back. As a souvenir, the soldier wrote on the camera: *"Shot by the Hun at the Battle of Tobruk 1942. Fritz missed me!!"*

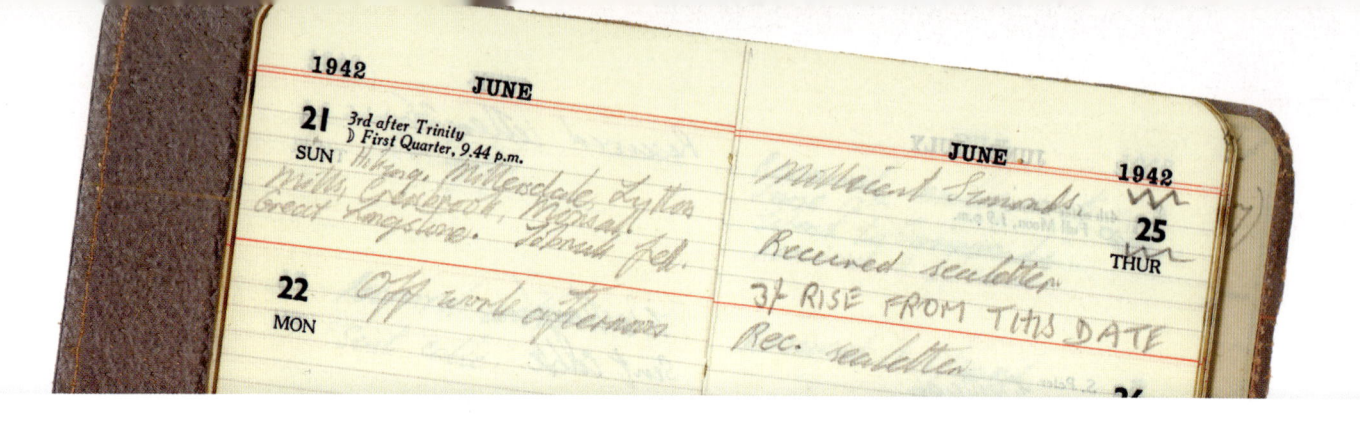

THE FALL OF TOBRUK

The Afrika Korps reaches the port city on June 17. All men able to fight, like Bill, do their best to defend the lines. However, Rommel doesn't want another never-ending siege. On June 20, the Germans send all their bombers to pound the area, and their troops enter the city at 8:30 am. In the evening, they get to the port, and the Tobruk garrison is captured: the 'bag' totals 35,000 men, mainly from the 2nd South African Division and the 201st Guards, 32nd Armoured and 29th Indian Brigades. Bill's unit managed to evacuate some of his officers and 186 men, but poor William is not so lucky. The supply depots in which he worked are destroyed and looted by the enemy, who lays his hands on 2,000 vehicles, including 30 tanks in working order, 4,000 tons of oil, and a colossal quantity of food (chocolate, biscuits, preserves, etc.), weapons and clothing.

For the German soldiers, this is a real treat after the hard fighting in the desert, but the joy for Hitler is so great that Rommel is immediately promoted to Generalfeldmarschall. As for the British Prime Minister, he hears about Tobruk's fall on the same day, while visiting Roosevelt in the United States. The latter, seeing Churchill depressed and humiliated, finally approves the idea of an Allied landing in North Africa: *Operation Gymnast* (later renamed *Torch*). For the Americans who were previously reluctant to the idea, this would be their first large-scale invasion, and a mandatory exercise before any successful operation in Europe.

Meanwhile, the fight in Africa continues. Rommel has a new port, and large quantities of captured equipment that will allow him to attack in Egypt, which he had been unable to do a year earlier. It will only be stopped 85 miles from Alexandria, in El Alamein on July 1, 1942. Because of this debacle, British General Auchinleck is replaced by General Harold Alexander, and Lieutenant-General Bernard Montgomery is put in charge of the 8th Army.

On Sunday, June 21, as she returns from her walk, Bill's wife learns of Tobruk's capture. She simply notes *"Tobruk fell"* in her diary (above: last line of June 21). Worried, she takes an afternoon off the next day, but isn't informed of her husband's disappearance until July 23. Although Bill is first listed as 'missing in action', she would learn on September 8 that he is, in fact, in Italian hands (as often happens with Allied soldiers taken prisoner in North Africa) when she receives her first card from him. After a few days in a temporary camp, a simple piece of desert surrounded by barbed wire, he is sent with other prisoners to Lucca, Italy. Bill will work there as a medical assistant in a military hospital, which had been recently established in a large monastery. In July 1943, shortly before the Italian surrender and as the Allies move up through Italy, the Germans will take over the Italian camps. Bill will be sent to Germany shortly after the summer, to Stalag VIII-B in Lamsdorf (now Łambinowice, in Poland). He will only be released at the end of the war, from a camp in Bavaria, and will afterwards run a clothing shop before passing away in 1988.

Bill's prison in Lucca, Italy, in 2016.

THOMAS FRIEDRICH

HQ Battery, 2nd Battalion, 56th Coast Artillery Regiment

On the morning of December 8, 1941, the Americans learn of the Pearl Harbor attack that took place the day before. For Thomas and other conscripts, this tragedy destroys any ambition of returning to civilian life. For the rest of the world, the entry of the United States into the conflict is a ray of hope. However, in 1941, the US Army, smaller than Romania's, has only 243,095 soldiers equipped with obsolete weapons...

Thomas Jefferson Friedrich was born on May 7, 1916 in Milwaukee, Wisconsin. After graduating with a degree in electrical engineering, Thomas worked for six months as a telephone electrician. He was called up with his older brother Woodrow on June 28, 1941, while his younger brother Andy joined the Air Force in September. Thomas was assigned to the 56th Coast Artillery Regiment, near San Francisco.

THE ATTACK ON PEARL HARBOR

The Japanese Imperial Army invaded Manchuria in September 1931, then advanced through China against the nationalists of Chiang Kai-shek and the communist revolutionaries of Mao Zedong (rivals during the civil war, and therefore poor allies). The mass rape and massacre of Nanking (China) by the Japanese in December 1937 shocked European and American public opinion. In total, more than 20 million Chinese people were killed between 1937 and 1945. Worried about Japanese expansionism threatening his interests in Asia and supporting the Chinese nationalists, President Roosevelt imposed a complete steel and oil embargo on July 26, 1941. Five months later, the Japanese Emperor Hirohito's forces (part of the Axis) decide to take revenge by raiding the US Navy's Pacific Fleet. Although the Americans are expecting an attack, they still don't know where and when it will happen.

On Sunday, December 7, 1941, at 7:49 am, the signal *"Tora! Tora! Tora!"* sounds. More than 400 Imperial Navy planes strike the American naval base at Pearl Harbor, Hawaii. The losses are very heavy, with 2,403 dead and 1,178 wounded as a result of the bombardments. Ten warships and 188 aircraft are also destroyed (most of them, however, will eventually be repaired, with the US Navy permanently losing only two obsolete battleships). At the same moment, other military bases in the Aleutians (near Alaska), Wake Island, Guam and the Philippines come under fire. Thailand is invaded (it will then join the Axis camp on December 21), and in Hong Kong, the Volunteer Defence Corps, assisted by Canadian soldiers, is unable to withstand the Japanese offensive, after more than two weeks of fighting.

In 1942, Ronald Whitehead (page 82) trains to become a bomber pilot. Some of the mechanics who repair the planes are survivors of Pearl Harbor. He writes to his parents: *"There are fellows in my group that were at Hickam Field, Hawaii, during the Japanese attack Dec. 6, 1941. The one fellow told me all about it. He said only four or five planes actually got off the ground. The camp had [a party] that Saturday evening and being regular soldiers they were really drunk. He said he had a .45 pistol and was trying hard to hit planes 10 to 15 thousand feet in the air, so you can imagine how he felt. Then the Japs were good at aiming with the bombs, they were hitting barracks at 8,000 feet high.*

He said when they pushed a plane out of the hangar, it was shot up by a Jap Zero (good ships). There was a Jap club there near the field [160,000 Hawaiians of Japanese origin were living on the island]. *That Saturday all the officers were invited to the club for a party. The Japs had all the officers drunk, so you can see everything was well planned. The first thing the Japs aimed for was the fire house in the port, and they really ruined that place. You remember the fellow that was decorated for hearing the planes and they wouldn't believe him? The reason the sergeant over him didn't believe him was because they had trouble with him before. He was a nut (crazy in the head they thought), they even had him up for a mental exam thinking he was crazy. This exam was about a month before the war. The sergeant just said he was drunk again and should forget about it. This guy is a captain in the army now."*

DAY OF INFAMY

US President Franklin Roosevelt said the day after the attack: *"Yesterday, December 7, 1941 – a date which will live in infamy – the United States of America was suddenly and deliberately attacked by naval and air forces of the Empire of Japan. The United States was at peace with that Nation and, at the solicitation of Japan, was still in conversation with its government and its Emperor looking toward the maintenance of peace in the Pacific. [...] I ask that the Congress declare that since the unprovoked and dastardly attack by Japan on Sunday, December 7, 1941, a state of war has existed between the United States and the Japanese Empire."*

Roosevelt signing the declaration of war against Japan, December 8, 1941.

The war in the Pacific will cover a very large area, including the Pacific Ocean islands, Southeast Asia, India and China. Great Britain, in turn, will declare war on Japan when the two warships HMS *Repulse* and HMS *Prince of Wales* are sunk off Malaysia on December 10. Roosevelt also wants to enter the war against Germany, to help Churchill, but Congress does not. Hitler's declaration of war on December 11, 1941, which follows that of his Japanese ally, finally lifts Roosevelt out of his embarrassment. The Allies even agree on the principle of 'Germany First': the fall of the Reich is a priority.

Thomas Friedrich has just discovered that his country has entered the war. He leaves Camp Callan, California, where artillery units train, for Fort Cronkhite, near the Golden Gate of San Francisco. This base is part of the bay's defense network, in the event of a Japanese attack. There are about 100 artillery guns, underwater mines, anti-aircraft batteries, radars, searchlights, observation posts, air patrols, and various fortifications. The 'old' 6th, and new recruits of the 18th, 54th and 56th Coast Artillery Regiments are now on alert. At 11 am on December 8, Thomas shares his feelings with his mother:

"Dearest Ritzy [the nickname he gives her, because of her coquetry], *at this time, I'd only like to tell you things which might make you feel good and less afraid of the future. It must be mentioned, though, how odd I felt, over reading about what you thought about my furlough, now that war has officially been declared. That was just a dream that can't be realized anymore. I can just imagine how the news has struck you, Ritzy, honey. It must have been tough on Evie* [Evelyn, Thomas' girlfriend] *too. I hope that the two of you can get together and console each other. I see that Evie has told you our idea of being married on my furlough. All I can say now, is that I must have been very selfish to even think of dragging her into anything like this. But, at least, I have the pride of knowing that I again changed my mind about marrying her, before this war was started. It was hard for me to do it, but last Saturday I wrote her a long letter saying that we had better reconsider and wait. I was hard, because I knew that her decision was made against her Dad's will. Well, the war has settled the question for us* [they will finally marry on March 27, 1943, in Alexandria, Virginia].

Naturally I hate to think of fighting, but the worst feeling I have at present is that one caused because I won't be able to get home for Christmas. Now I must send Evie back the train fare. Also, I must try to send home some very cheap little gifts which I hoped to be able to deliver personally. I may send them soon because there may be no chance later on. You can always wait until Christmas before you open the package though. We all know you shall not have a very pleasant Christmas, but maybe

I - THE DARK YEARS 1939-1942

you can make believe I'm with you when you see the presents. Ritzy, I just hope no one sends me anything. You see, we don't know a thing about the future, and we may not even have room to keep any kind of a gift. That even holds good with money. You see, we are not allowed to leave camp now. If we could, we would only spend it on foolishness, so you see to it that everyone at home spends their money on themselves. Maybe we will just have to forget that December 25 is Christmas this year.

Due to my job here, I was hopping around pretty fast yesterday afternoon and evening. For the time being I am through here, but that isn't true for the rest of the camp. Many of the boys haven't been to sleep since Saturday night. I had some interrupted sleep last night in full dress, and today I have time to write. Half of our 6" cannons have been set up right here. The rest were sent about 50 miles up the coast. The men not needed for setting up the cannons are either hauling ammunition or standing guard. The guard strength has been tripled, and they're not fooling either. For the first time, we are carrying bullets for our rifles too. I don't carry a rifle because it would be in the way. I'm supposed to have a pistol, but don't, because they aren't any. Other equipment which I have been unable to get is sleeping material, field bag, and a gas mask [at the time, the US Army wasn't yet the incredible war machine that it would become a few years later]. *Everything is pretty orderly around here. The main difficulty being that so many of our men were home on furlough (I wish, again, that I had taken my furlough on the early shift). All furloughs have been canceled, so these men should soon be back with us. San Francisco's defense seems to be none too strong. I hope that will be reason enough, for the time being, to keep us stationed here. I certainly do not want to be sent out on a boat at this time. On land we at least have a chance to run. I guess I'll quit before I get you to worrying too much. Please don't, Honey girl, this way, at least, this thing will be settled. Before, we could only worry about how much longer we'd have to stay in the Army, wasting time. It's funny, now, to think of all the better things we could have been doing during the time we spent planting that damn ice-plant all over the camp. Time for chow now.*

From now on, the grub shall start to get even worse than it has been. Besides, we eat everything out of mess kits now, no more plates for us. But perhaps that is just as well. Now, I may be able to redeem myself and again have my slim figure returned to me.

I expect the letters will probably all be censored now. For other reasons, too, they might be delayed. You and Evie may have to get together, even more, now, to learn all the news. You see, I may not be able to write as often as I have been doing. I'll try though. Well, Chicken Shit, that's all for now. Keep your pants up (I mean your chin) and please worry about yourself instead of me and Andy. I also expect I will soon have to include Woody again. That sure will be tough. Love & Kisses, Tom."

Thomas eating lunch from an army mess kit.

GETTING READY FOR WAR

In mid-December, the men are sent to a new camp. They leave Fort Cronkhite for Camp San Luis Obispo, halfway between Los Angeles and San Francisco. The torrential rain and deep mud make it difficult to work. As the soldiers are soaked to the bone, cases of pneumonia are common. However, Thomas now has the luxury of having a 4-man tent and cots to lay the sleeping bag he's just received on. Realistic about the fact that the war may continue, Thomas asks his mother to sell his car for him. He knows that sooner or later, he will most likely be sent abroad, a prospect that is ultimately much less enviable than his current situation.

He writes: *"No doubt, after we leave this camp, we may be sorry, and might change our ideas about it. At least we have cots and barracks to sleep in. Also, we have toilets and lots of hot water in the showers. Yes, we shall find it hard to give all that up. We don't know just what we can expect to run into when we move. [...] I imagine we shall sorta revert back to more of an animal state again. Who knows how long we might have to go without a bath or a shave? What can we expect to eat? And like a cat, I suppose we shall bury everything in a hole. Beyond a doubt, pants rabbits or bloomer beetles or whatever they are called shall thrive on us. Oh well, nothing like lots of company. No, if we look for the worst, it isn't a pretty picture. But the war can't last forever. Even if we go through dirt and suffering somewhere along this coast, I imagine we shall be thankful. Isn't that much better than being in the thick of the battle where your chances of living aren't very good? I sometimes wonder if we would be better off if we knew just what is in store for us. Will we stay here or be sent overseas? Truthfully, I believe we have good chances of seeing foreign service. After all, can this fight be settled definitely just by destroying the enemy's navy? It almost seems like we must hunt them down in their own land after the seas have been cleared of their boats."*

The soldiers now each carry forty bullets for their rifles, and keep a gas mask nearby at all times. In four years' time, the US Army will be the best equipped in the world, and the industrial production of the United States will be higher than that of all the other countries combined. Under the leadership of General George Marshall, appointed Chief of Staff on the day Germany invaded Poland, the US military will grow from 200,000 to 8 million men.

THE ENEMY DOESN'T COME

Soldiers fill sandbags, install barbed wire, dig trenches, camouflage concrete defenses, set up guns and scan the horizon in search of the Japanese fleet, which would never come. Thomas, who was refused his furlough, will not spend Christmas with his family. Weeks pass by, and the Navy, which is looking for Japanese submarines near the coast, only fires on a few whales by mistake. San Francisco Bay will never really be threatened, and the soldiers assigned to defend it are gradually sent to the Pacific front. Thomas wonders: *"Someone must be kept here for defending the West Coast – why can't it be me?"*

He will finally be sent to Barcelona (Venezuela) with part of the regiment in February 1942, where he'll try to become an officer. He will serve there with the 130th Engineer Combat Battalion, which will be deployed in Panama and in the Philippines. His brother Woodrow will serve in Europe with the 772nd Field Artillery Battalion, landing in France in the fall of 1944, and will finish his career as a lieutenant-colonel. Andy will be part of a bomber crew in the 367th Bomb Squadron of the 8th 'Mighty Eighth' Air Force. Arriving in England with his 'Flying Fortress' (nickname of the B-17 bomber) in September 1942, his missions will be successful, and he will receive two Air Medals. Unfortunately, while bombing U-boats in Lorient on March 6, 1943, his B-17 will be hit and crash into the sea. Three crew members will be killed instantly, but Andrew and six other men will manage to bail out. They will be captured by a German patrol boat and Andrew will remain in captivity at Stalag Luft III (a Stalag for Allied airmen, made famous by the 'Great Escape' of March 1944), then at Stalag VII-A (Moosburg) until April 1945. He will end his career as a major in the US Air Force.

Following the peace treaty with Japan and the development of modern defense weapons, San Francisco will reassess the relevance of its fortifications and destroy the last one in 1948. Thomas will return to his job at AT&T, which he will only leave upon his retirement in 1970. He will die after his brothers on September 23, 2007.

Found under a pile of helmets in an antique shop in Maine (USA), this model, nicknamed 'dishpan hat' for its shape, was probably used by a soldier in the American coastal defense (note the brushed blue camouflage, under the storage marks). As the famous round M1 helmet had not yet been invented in 1941, soldiers still used flat helmets from the First World War, or the M1917A1 model inspired by the British 'Brodie'. The one presented here is composed of a British steel shell from 1914-1918, and various other elements intended for passive defense, revealing the state of US Army equipment in 1941.

II

THE COUNTER-ATTACK
Conscripts and Volunteers

The armistice of June 1940 only allowed the French to keep a small army of 100,000 men in the southern free zone, which was there to maintain order and be controlled by the Vichy regime. On the other side of the Channel, Great Britain now calls for national service for all men aged 18 to 51 and, with a few exceptions, women aged 20 to 30. Elsewhere in the world, powerful armies are being formed to provide help.

THE US ARMY

In response to the rise of Nazism and fascism in Europe, in the United States the Selective Training and Service Act was signed on September 16, 1940, marking the first peacetime conscription (compulsory military service) in American history. On February 3, 1941, National Service for all was established, meaning of the 16 million Americans who will serve in the Second World War (representing more than one in ten inhabitants!), only 38.8% are, in fact, volunteers. Most of them join the army at the beginning of the war, following the patriotic momentum generated by the attack on Pearl Harbor. Conscripts (or 'draftees'), called up at the age of 18, are assigned to the various branches of the army according to its needs. Young high school students, who know that they will be drafted at some point anyway, often volunteer before the age of enlistment to ensure that they can express their preference for a service.

Those who volunteer are often in a more combative state of mind and receive preferential treatment from their instructors. A volunteer writes to his parents from the Reception Center in Camp Beale, California: *"Well here I am, and so far it's been so soft that I'm getting suspicious. All we have done today is learn how to make beds, to eat. Oh yes, we saw a training film on 'Courtesy & Discipline'. Tomorrow we get our shots, and will probably get another physical, and a mental (also cigarette rations).*

These 'Son in Service' flags, bearing a star for each child in the army, quickly multiply at the doors and windows of American homes.

FACTS REGARDING ENLISTMENT IN THE UNITED STATES ARMY

67

Distributed in rations as a source of comfort, and regularly sent to the front by families, cigarettes have never been smoked in such large quantities. They are a symbol of freedom and courage in the advertisements of the time. In 1942, Lucky Strike packs change to white to save pigment for uniforms, and the brand uses the slogan *"Lucky Strike GREEN has gone to war!"*. Taxes aren't enough to finance a conflict that will cost the United States $304 billion (ten times more in today's money), and 'War bonds' loans are established. Many ads encourage citizens to invest in the war effort, such as on this small pack of matches.

We have only five of us enlisted men here in our barracks of about sixty men, and I can't say much for the looks or language of the draftees, most of whom are older men. We five ERC [Enlisted Reserve Corps] men are all previously ACER [Air Corps Enlisted Reserve] and are all about eighteen and six months, so it makes it nice for us. They keep us more or less separated from the draftees. All our records are kept in separate files and they're (the Sergeants) always asking where we are (I think the sarge likes us better than the draftees, I hope). Oh yes, we have to mop the barracks floor every morning first thing, as well as making the bed, and straightening everything else in sight. Right now all five of us ERCs are considering joining the paratroopers. [...] Do not write me until I get to basic. We will only be here for about a week (I hope), so we'll be gone by the time your letters reach here."

CANADIAN VOLUNTEERS

The country of Canada was only 75 years old when it entered the war on September 10, 1939, to fulfill its commitment to the Commonwealth. A conscription had been put in place for a national defense service (The National Resources Mobilization Act), but the Canadian Army has the unusual position of only sending volunteers abroad. Despite everything, half of the men aged 18 to 45 will choose to serve their country and Canadians will fight all over the world: from Europe to the Pacific, in the Aleutian Islands or Hong Kong. Eventually, there were enough volunteers to form five divisions (including two armored ones).

John Leslie Harris (an immigrant from England whose adventures in Italy can be followed on page 122) is one of them. He joins an armored regiment in 1941 and trains at Camp Borden, Ontario. In a letter he writes from his barracks to his little sister Maisie, John talks about a film they both saw that led him to talk about his enlistment: *"As to your remark regarding the tidiness of the boy on the picture, well all I can say is we are no parade ground soldiers, we did not join up in a peace time army for a lot of swank and showy exhibition, some of the boys naturally joined from a spirit of adventure, but I know the majority figured there was a pretty big job to do and were willing to sacrifice good jobs, homes and people they loved in order to do it and can say with a good deal of pride that there is not one soldier in the Canadian Army over here today who had to be conscripted but all joined of their own free will in the hopes that out of this war might come a better deal for the everyday working man. The Canadian Army of the last war made a great History for themselves and I hope no doubt that this bunch of boys will do just as well given the chance. If you were here a few days you would get some idea of why we look like a bunch of tramps at times, we have to work in dust and mud and grease all the time and have not the conveniences for keeping just as tidy as civilians. Still if you see some of the pictures of Frenchy in civilian life you will see he looks just as good as anyone else. However this cuts no ice with me, we judge the boys how we find them and have our own standards, and he measures up OK by me. He would share anything he has and if he just had one cigarette would break it in half so the other guy could have a smoke too."*

A 'Red Ensign' Canadian flag from the Second World War era. The one we know today, with its large red maple leaf, was not adopted until 1965.

The youngest Allied soldier killed in Western Europe was a 16-year-old Quebecker who lied about his age to enlist. Alongside the Fusiliers Mont-Royal, Gérard Doré was killed during the Battle of Verrières Ridge (Operations *Atlantic* and *Spring*), south of Caen, on July 23, 1944. A monument is erected to his memory near the place where he fell.

However, the system will have its limits. As news of the harsh reality on the front lines reaches the public, the situation will become critical: the number of volunteers (on the decline) will no longer be sufficient to replace the high Canadian losses in Italy and France. In November 1944, following considerable political pressure, the government will have no choice but to send 17,000 conscripts from the National Defence Service abroad. Only 2,463 of them will actually serve on the front, and 69 will lose their lives in combat.

In any case, almost all Canadian soldiers preparing to liberate Europe do so by choice, with the sole purpose of rescuing their cousins on the other side of the Atlantic. In anticipation of the worst, as he crosses the ocean to land in France, Fleming McConnell writes: *"My dearest Mother, not knowing what fate may have in store for me, I am writing a little note of farewell to be sent to you in case of my death. I want particularly to ask of you and the family that you will not grieve when our ways are parted for a time, but rather rejoice with me in being accorded from above the greatest honour and privilege of spending my life in the great cause of civilization and right. I can conceive of no higher and nobler use to which my life could have been devoted, and in this I know that you will be the first to agree with me. The day I sailed for France was the very happiest in my life, and it was so in the full realization that I was bound on a mission from which, perchance, there would be no returning. If, therefore, I come to die, I die happy and content and full of thankfulness to God that He should have chosen me to answer this call. To this, I am sure, you will gladly say 'Amen'! In the battlefields of France my grave will be in a very noble company of souls, and I pray that you will not endeavor to single it out, but rather find contentment in the thought that 'Somewhere in France' honourably rest my remains with so many of Canada's and England's best. To Father and to the family one by one I bid a fond adieu, and let my memory to yourself and them be not one of sorrow, but of gladness and anticipation that in the Great Beyond we once again meet. With very much love to you, my dear mother, and to all the others, until the end, your affectionate son."*

Fleming will survive the war (see page 347), but of the 1 million Canadians who will serve in the three armed branches, more than 45,000 will never come home.

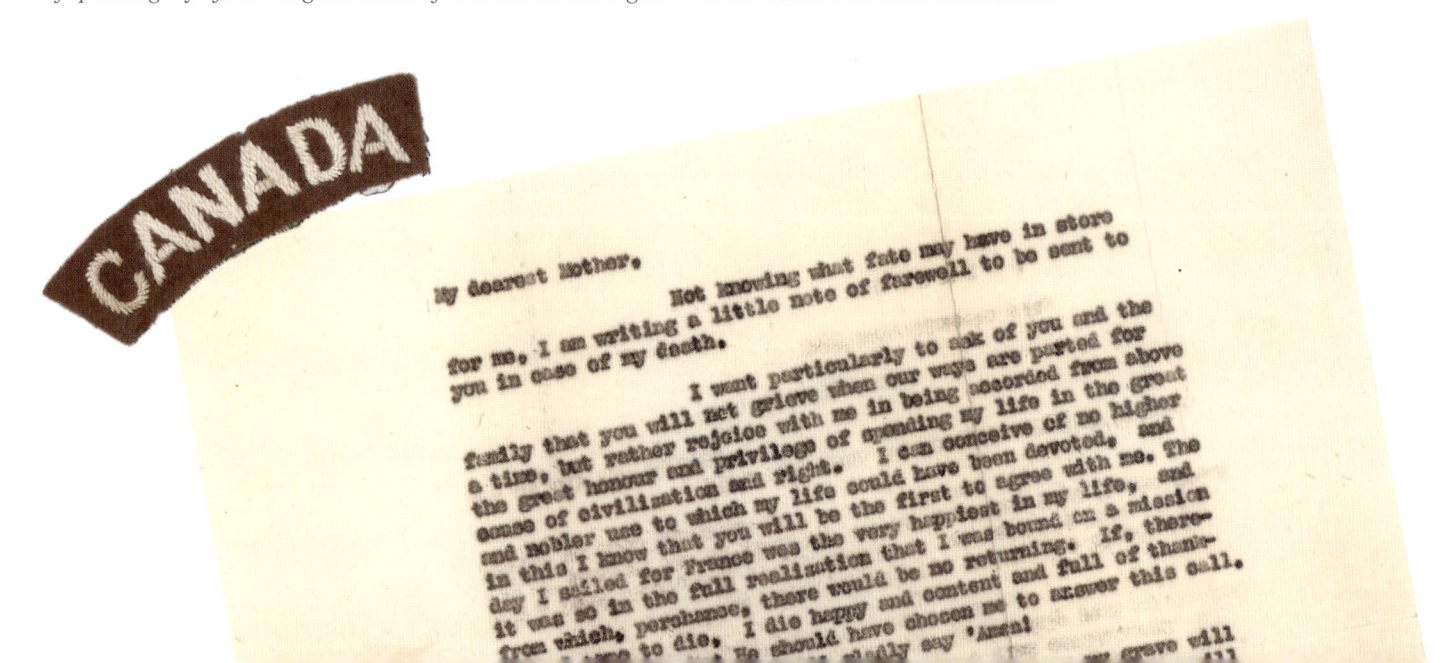

JIM & VERNON MILLER

405 Squadron & 624 Squadron, Royal Canadian Air Force

Jim is a Canadian volunteer of just 18 years old. With his friend Vernon, also in the RCAF (Royal Canadian Air Force), they both have the same young English penfriend from Sheffield, Maisie. A few months after she writes to them, her letters will all be returned to her, marked 'Missing in action'. Jim and Vernon will both be killed aged 19 when their respective bombers crash.

"GETTING MY HANDS ON OLD ADOLF"

James 'Jim' Arthur Miller was born on May 9, 1924, in Mactier, Ontario. Fond of baseball, swimming and football, he works at the Canadian Pacific Railway Company. However, he dreams of leaving his job and joining the Royal Air Force (RAF), despite his mother's disapproval. She has good reason to be concerned about her son: in 1942, only one in five Royal Air Force airmen survived their series of thirty missions, and two series (sixty sorties) must be accomplished before they can be removed from the operations lists. The RAF integrates many foreigners, all volunteers, from occupied countries and dominions of the United Kingdom (Poland, France, Czechoslovakia, New Zealand, Australia...). Indeed, there are so many Canadians that they quickly formed separate squadrons attached to the Royal Canadian Air Force (RCAF).

Jim has a penfriend, a young English woman from Sheffield, called Maisie (who is actually the sister of John Harris, the Canadian tank crewman in training who emigrated to Canada, see previous page). For Jim and many other Canadians, helping to liberate Europe is a duty and he doesn't want to look like a coward to his 15-year-old friend.

Jim and his service number at his enlistment in 1942, and an RCAF badge. He writes to Maisie shortly before: *"You don't need to worry about me letting you down. I'll get into the Air Force if it kills me."*

II - THE COUNTER-ATTACK 1942-1943

JIM AND VERNON MILLER

During his training, Jim meets Vernon Leslie Miller and although they share the same surname, only a deep friendship connects them. Born on January 9, 1924, Vernon is the ninth child of ten Millers in Paris (southern Ontario, Canada). After studying electricity in Brantford and working as a cable installer at the Bell Telephone Company of Canada, he joined the RCAF in April 1942. Like Jim, Vernon writes frequently to Maisie and all three will become very good friends.

When he leaves for Europe, he has a girlfriend waiting for him at home: *"When I started to earn my own living I bought a nice car and got myself a girlfriend. She was the snootiest girl I ever saw and I told her so for which I got my face very soundly slapped in the crowded restaurant. I kept going with this girl and I think she is grand now. She is the only girl I ever had and I do love her very much. She is waiting for me to come back, so she says."* Unfortunately, like Jim, Vernon will never see her or Canada again.

He writes to her in March 1942: *"Maisie, I don't want to disappoint you, and I don't want you to think that I'm afraid and I hate to tell you this but I am not in the Air Force yet. You see I will not be 18 until May 9th, but I told my mother that no matter what happened I was leaving to join the Air Force, Army, or Navy, on the 15th of May. She talked me out of it last time but this time I mean it. I'll try one unit, and if I don't make it I'll try another. But I sure hope I can make the Air Force."* He writes to her again at the beginning of April: *"Well Maisie, it won't be long now before I'll be 18 and I can join up without my mother saying that I can't. When I do get in the Air Force, I hope I can get to England in a hurry and get a crack at a few of those murdering Jerries. And I hope I can get my hands on old Adolf himself. I'll bet he'll never lead a war against freedom-loving people again."*

On July 22, Jim goes to the RCAF Recruitment Center in North Bay, Ontario and officially volunteers: *"I, James Arthur Miller, do solemnly declare that the foregoing particulars are true, and I hereby engage to serve on active service anywhere in Canada, and also beyond Canada and overseas, in the Royal Canadian Air Force for the duration of the present war, and for the period of demobilization thereafter, and in any event for a period of not less than one year, provided His Majesty should so long require my services."*

This RCAF jacket, dated 1942 and manufactured in Montreal, belonged to a radio operator whose bomber apparently flew over Belgium and the Netherlands (see the non-regulatory pins added to the pockets). It has medal ribbons for the 1939-1945 Star, France & Germany Star and the Canadian Volunteer Service Medal.

Jim and Vernon both become air gunners and are made sergeants on December 30. When they arrive together in Britain on February 4, 1943, they seize the opportunity to visit Maisie. Inseparable, the two Millers are still together at the reception center in Bournemouth, then at the air gunnery school from March 3. It is there that they are finally separated on the 17th, at RAF Stormy Down base (Pyle, Bridgend). Jim is assigned to the 23rd Operations Training Unit at RAF Atherstone station (Stratford-upon-Avon) on March 23, while Vernon joins 51 Squadron at RAF Snaith (near Goole, Yorkshire). Vernon writes to Maisie: *"Yes, Jimmie and I got separated and needless to say I have missed him very much. It seems funny not to have him around but in this outfit we get used to separations and saying goodbye, but it is rather disappointing nevertheless."*

In Stratford, Jim takes courses and makes his first bomber flights, but he also discovers the harsh reality of the Air Force: on April 19, one of his friends is killed in a crash, just a week after another plane went down and killed six other men. Jim is designated as pallbearer. He writes to Maisie: *"Another plane crashed Monday afternoon and one of my chums was killed. It sure was a tough break for him. But, that's the Air Force for you. Your life isn't your own after you join this outfit."* In total, Bomber Command will have 8,000 casualties in training, 1/7 of its total losses.

THE LAST FLIGHT

In early June, Jim is assigned to his first bomber crew at 419 Squadron. He is soon transferred to 405 Squadron, whose motto 'Ducimus' ('We lead') refers to the fact that it's the only RCAF recon squadron.

It was also the first bomber squadron created abroad. Flying on Wellington bombers until April 1942, it switched to Halifax bombers and became operational just in time to participate in the historic raid on Cologne, led by 1,000 bombers on May 31, 1942. Jim will only spend a very short time with the unit, as he would be killed one month to the day after joining it.

This tragic August 23, 1943 raid on Berlin is also a major operation: 727 aircraft are to participate (335 Lancasters, 251 Halifaxes, 124 Stirlings, 17 Mosquitoes). That night, Jim is a tail gunner in the Halifax HR918 (code-named 'LQ-G') and he leaves Gransden Lodge base at 8:15 pm for the last time. The resistance from the Flak (German anti-aircraft guns) and night fighters is terrible, and fifty-nine bombers are lost (one in thirteen planes). At 00:18, while en route to its target at the head of the fleet, Jim's Halifax is shot down by the German pilot Franz Laubenheimer (of the Jagdgeschwader 300, a Luftwaffe night fighter unit), at an altitude of 18,000 feet. The bomber crashes in the forest near Dorst, 18 miles northwest of Magdeburg, Germany. Franz Laubenheimer will in turn be killed on March 18, 1944, in the cockpit of his Messerschmitt Bf 109.

None of the crew survive the crash. Jim and his comrades are first buried in Satuelle, then moved to the Berlin War Cemetery, where they still rest today.

Maisie's last letter to Jim, marked 'return to sender, missing'. She had written to him: *"Well James, how is the world treating you? Still alive and kicking, I hope. What have you been doing since I last heard from you? (That's a good while since) [...] It's quite a business writing to you and getting no replies. However, we still keep hoping. [...] Cheerio for now Jim and write when you can. Love, Maisie."*

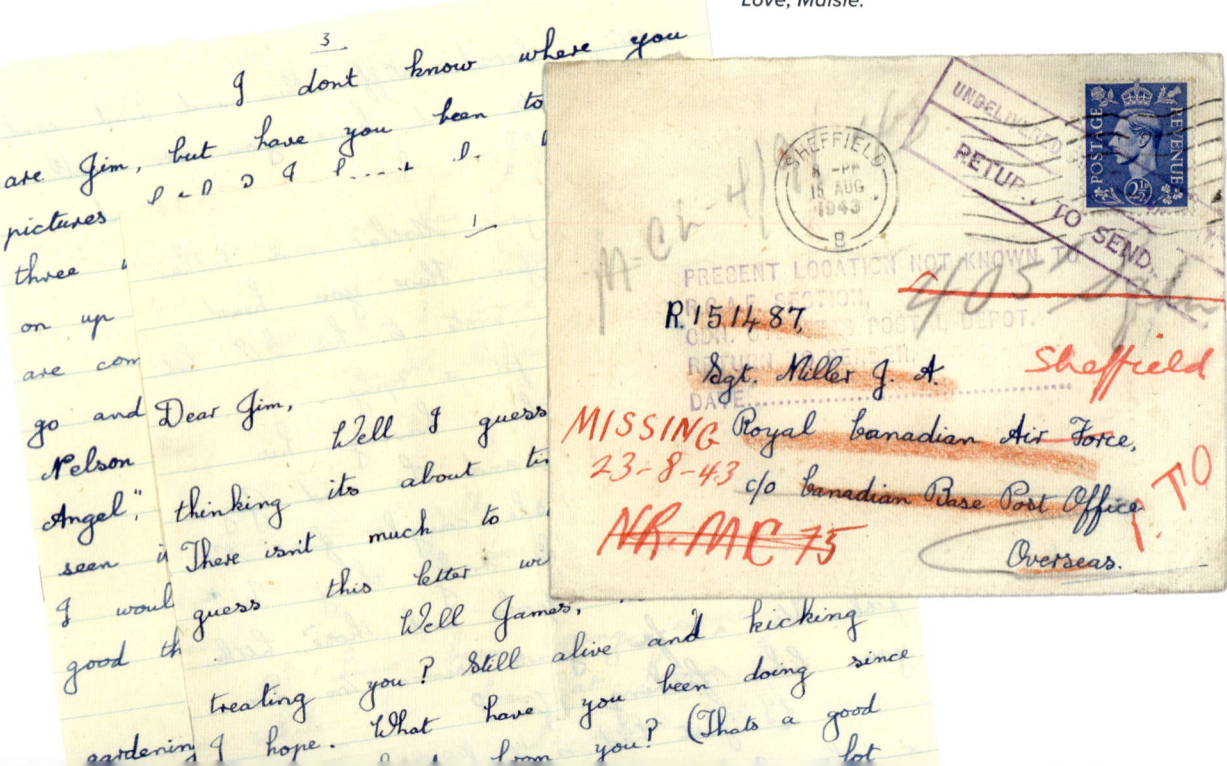

II - THE COUNTER-ATTACK 1942-1943

VERNON AND THE CURSED CREW

In the spring of 1943, Vernon flies as a machine gunner in the Halifax JD299 alongside six other airmen, led by Sgt. Howlett: all are British RAF personnel, Vernon being the only Canadian. Since May 1942 and the first thousand bomber raids, much heavier aircraft have appeared, now guided by Mosquitos as scouts, using a modern navigation system and marking targets with colored flares. This way, the Air Force can both load larger bombs and drop them more accurately.

The first operation in which Vernon participates is consequently the largest bombardment of the war yet, on May 23, 1943. It targets the heart of the German armament industry, right in the center of the Ruhr, in Dortmund. In less than an hour, 826 Lancaster, Halifax, Wellington and Stirling bombers release a 2,000-ton load of high explosive and incendiary bombs that, combined, generate a huge furnace. Thirty-eight Allied bombers are lost during the raid, but the city, which had already been attacked forty-one times, suffers terrifying damage. The head of Bomber Command, Sir Arthur Harris, is proud of the result: *"Congratulations on having delivered the first 100,000 tons of bombs on Germany* [in the last twelve months]. *The next 100,000 [...] will be even bigger and better bombs, delivered even more accurately and in much shorter time"* (the total will amount to 1.59 million tons of American and British bombs in Germany). Vernon tells Maisie three days later: *"I have just finished a 48* [-hour sortie] *after a very shaky operational trip and I spent it in bed sleeping most of the time. We were shot up rather badly so I was kind of shaken myself but I'm all as sound as ever again and ready for another crack at 'his' country. [...] My first raid was on Dortmund the night of the big one of the 23/24 of May. It certainly was a fine show of fireworks and it seemed rather appropriate being Victoria Day."*

Vernon has had no news from Jim, but he has received some about his brother Gordon: he too is in the RCAF, but went missing on May 13. Believing his brother is dead, Vernon writes to Maisie: *"I suppose I shouldn't feel as badly because we all half expect it sooner or later, but just the same it is hard to get used to the idea."* Changing the subject, he adds: *"The news sure is looking much better isn't it? I still have very high hopes of being home for Christmas. I hope so anyway. I don't think Jerry will ever be able to stand more of these heavy air raids. Let's hope not anyway."* In reality, his brother Gordon actually survived. Taken prisoner by the Germans, he will return home at the end of the war, unlike Vernon.

During the twenty-two missions accomplished by Vernon's crew, they almost died nearly every time. On three occasions they even had to evacuate a damaged aircraft. For example, returning from a raid on Gelsenkirchen (Germany) on July 9, 1943, the bomber was hit by Flak while flying over Dieppe. The windshield's cockpit was torn off, but the crew still managed to land the plane in Allied territory in the early morning. The men have proven their worth, and on the 27th, Vernon and all of Sgt Howlett's crew are transferred to RAF Lyneham (Wiltshire) for special operations training. In August 1943 they are attached to 624 Squadron in Blida (Algeria), before leaving for Tunisia and Libya. This unit of the British Royal Air Force generally operates alone behind enemy lines, where it drops SOE agents (Special Operations Executive, a British secret organization specializing in sabotage and support for local resistance groups) or OSS (American agency, ancestor of the CIA). Due to its high-risk operations, it suffers a very high loss rate.

Ignorant of Jim's death, Vernon writes to Maisie in November: *"You have probably noticed by the post mark that I am now in North Africa. I've been here three months and I hate it soundly [...]. We live in tents and eat in tents and when we first came out we were too hot, now it is cold at nights. Some fun eh? I say Maisie do you happen to have any news of Jimmie or his whereabouts? I have lost track of him too."* At last, he leaves the African desert for Brindisi, Italy, on November 21. The Squadron is attached to the 334 (SD) Wing, Mediterranean Allied Air Force, and is to operate in the Balkans and northern Italy. Vernon is also about to take part in his last mission.

Note the 'Air Gunner' badge on Vernon's chest, and the 'poppy' placed on the frame by his family, in tribute to the Commonwealth soldiers who gave their lives for freedom.

During the night of November 30 to December 1, 1943, he takes part in a special SOE mission to Koritza (Albania). The seven crew members are joined by five army officers. Under mysterious circumstances, Vernon's Halifax EB140 explodes in flight and crashes at Karoplesi, near Agrafa, in the mountains of central Greece. The crew and passengers, who cannot be individually identified, are buried in a common grave at Phaleron War Cemetery in Athens, Greece.

BAD NEWS

Maisie had written to Jean, Jim's sister, shortly before her last letter to the airman was readdressed and marked 'Missing in action'. Jim's mother, who had tried in vain to prevent her son from joining the RCAF, writes to Maisie on December 12: *"When your letter arrived for Jean, I opened it as I thought it might contain news of some kind about Jim and Jean is not at home. She is in the Royal Canadian Air Force too [...]. You asked about Jim, well I'm sorry to tell you that he has been missing since the night of August 23-24. He was in a raid over Berlin and 59 planes failed to return, and his was one of them. Up to now we haven't received any word, except that he is 'missing'.*

His Dad and I would like to thank you folks for giving Jim such a nice time when he visited you in Sheffield. He wrote and told us how he enjoyed himself and of how your Father took him around and showed him and told of Sheffield being bombed. We heard about it at the time over the radio. We people over here have no idea just what you English have gone through during those raids, they must be just terrible. I wish you would write again, and tell us just how Jimmy looked, and any news at all that you can tell us about him, the last time you saw him. We are just so hungry for news of him, that anything you might say would be welcome. It is nearly one year now since he left home for overseas. This time last year we were looking forward to him coming for Christmas or New Year's and this year we don't even know where he is. Jean is too far away to come home either, so there will be two empty seats at our Christmas table. [...]

If you happened to get any pictures of Jim while he was visiting you, I would be so grateful if you could get some reprints and send them over. He sent us one of himself in the rear turret of a Wellington, also one of he and his crew. Maybe he gave you one also. If so you may know who the Englishman is in the picture. His name is Sidney Cugley. [...] The rest of the crew are Andy, the pilot missing (Canadian), Collen and Ed (Canadian) believed killed, and Jim missing. The crew were all split up after Andy was missing over Cologne, July 2, and they did want to stay together after training, but I think Jim was the only one of the original crew to go out August 23 and 24. [...] Yours sincerely, Jim's Mom."

As soon as she receives the letter, Maisie is quick to respond: *"Dear Mrs Miller, I am sorry to hear that Jim is still missing, and I hope you will soon have some definite news of him. I hope that it will be good news too. Well, as for telling you how Jim looked when I saw him, I think he looked fine. I have only seen him once and that was when he first came. I think he enjoyed himself and I was glad to see him. I didn't think I should see him so soon after he joined up. However, he seemed in the best of spirits and when he wrote he always sounded cheerful and talked of what he had been doing and what pictures he had seen and when he had been dancing. We both like pictures so it was a thing we both talked a lot of. No, Jim didn't send me any photos of himself and the crew. I haven't heard from him since last May, so with him being moved he maybe didn't get my letters, or if he did he maybe didn't have time to answer them. [...]*

I don't know if Jim ever mentioned his friend Vernon, but they were great pals until they were separated. Vern is in North Africa now. He will be very sorry to hear about Jim. I am enclosing you some photos that we took when Jimmie was here. They were taken in St Paul's Gardens [now called the Peace Gardens] at the side of Sheffield Town Hall. You can see the Town Hall in the background. They were taken on February 18th, the day the boys went back to camp. My friend Joyce and I were taking them to the station, but we changed our minds, and all went to the pictures in town. We took the photos while we were waiting for the pictures to open, then the boys went back on a later train. I am sending an enlarged photo of Jim that I had done for myself. I didn't want to keep you waiting till they were developed again as it takes about three weeks and I wanted you to get them as soon as possible. [...] Let us hope that next year Jimmie will be with you again."

The photo of Jim taken in Sheffield and mentioned in Maisie's letter to his mother.

On January 17, 1944, still unaware of Vernon's death, Maisie sends him a letter with the bad news about Jim (still officially 'missing'): *"Hello Vern, don't drop dead with surprise, I'm really sending you some of those photos. I sent them to be developed as soon as I heard from you, but I thought I would surprise you. I suppose you're wondering where the others are. Here's the story. I had a nice letter from Jimmie's Mother last week. She wrote to tell me that Jim is still missing and they don't know any more. She asked me to tell her all about Jim, when I last saw him and to send some photos if I had any. I had just got them back so I had to decide who was to have them first. Well, I knew you would want Jim's Mum to have them, so I sent all those with Jim on and one of you too. I say Vern, do me a favour and write to her. You saw Jim last and maybe it would cheer her up to hear from you. I'm sure she'd like it. Well, how are things going with you Vern, OK I hope?"*

Maisie's letter to Vernon will also be returned to her in August 1944, covered with inscriptions that are as imprecise (probably because of the secret nature of his last mission) as they are indecipherable. Jim will officially be declared 'killed in action' in July 1944, and Vernon in September of the same year. The two friends were both 19 years old.

Above:
Jim and his sisters Irene (left) and Jean (right), also in the RCAF (colorized by the author).

Right:
The last letter sent to Vernon by Maisie, returned to sender.

It is through this letter above from the Red Cross that Maisie learned Jim was 'presumed dead' in January 1944.

TRAINING

Many young Americans are wearing uniforms for the first time. They will have to comply with army regulations and rigorous training.

The first people to be concerned about the soldiers' situation are, of course, their parents. Hence this letter from a pastor of the 10th Armored Division to a Michigan mother in May 1943: *"Naturally, his training is vigorous and tough, but that fact gives the assurance that the men will be prepared to protect themselves, their 'buddies', and their homes from injury and possible destruction. Major W. H. Lewis is the Commanding Officer of the Battalion and is interested in the well-being of every man. Our Government is leaving no stone unturned to protect the interests, health, and spiritual welfare of the men in the Armored Forces."*

Some brands see it as a promotional opportunity. For example, the beverage brand Pepsi-Cola sends reporters to training camps to record young recruits on 78-rpm records for their families.

Donald Addison's parents receive the following message: "[Host] *Hello Mr. and Mrs. Addison, the Pepsi-Cola Company is happy to bring you the voice of your son Donald, from Pennsylvania, July 17, 1943.* [Donald] *Hello Mom and Dad, let me answer the letter you wrote to me. Now I'm in the best of health, so don't worry about me. I will be leaving this camp soon, I can't say I won't miss it. I wish I had more to tell you. [...] I will survive. May God bless you!"* Donald will become a member of a counter-intelligence service in Normandy.

Despite the reassuring words, however, there is a completely different tone in the letters of other soldiers. In reality, men are not spared and sometimes even lose their lives during their training.

"Through courtesy of Pepsi-Cola, this is a recorded message from your Man in Service!"

II - THE COUNTER-ATTACK 1942-1943

DETAIL ASSEMBLING FOR DRILL

A postcard sent by Gary from Camp Wheeler.

In Camp Wheeler, Georgia (USA), an infantry company learns the basics of the soldier's job in freezing temperatures. Young Gary even saw comrades die of pneumonia as soon as he arrived at the camp: they were all quarantined for two weeks. Gary is very tired from the difficult exercises and night watches. He writes to his sister: *"No I am not dead but if I dropped into a hole I couldn't climb out if I wanted to. It is tough here but we have lots of fun out of it. I am pretty tired but still have to go out on guard after midnight. I won't mind it very much because we are on only one hour so that isn't very long. Two weeks of this kind of training will certainly make us hard, we all look a lot different now, what a mess. [...] Be seeing you in a few weeks, if nothing happens."*

The battalion then carries out a series of maneuvers during which one of Gary's comrades, from the 16th Battalion, is shot and killed in early April 1944. Another friend from the 1st Battalion also dies in the same week, but Gary can't attend his funeral, as it's reserved for the company of the deceased. A few weeks later, Gary will leave for France with the 8th Infantry Division. He will go through the worst battles and come home, but his little brother, Douglas, will not even survive his training. As a pilot of a B-24E Liberator heavy bomber, he will be killed in an accidental crash in the United States in December 1944. Gary will write in the thick of the Battle of the Bulge: *"Dear Sister, when I received the news about Douglas I had to let up writing I just couldn't take it for a few hours but now that I feel better maybe I will be able to write you a line or so. It was the most shocking news because I loved Douglas even more than anyone ever realized. I always tried to hide my feelings and I pray to God Douglas does know how I feel, somehow I have the feeling he does. Albert and I are left and I do want to try and do more than my share if I can. God willing I will be home someday so I can try and make mother and Dad happy and of course my wife and children. Hope you are going to have what you want Sis, let me know all the news and remember I love all of you."*

WELCOME TO THE ARMY

Carl Holmberg arrives at Camp Blanding after two days stuck on a filthy train under a suffocating heat: *"I'm a mighty disheartened kid right now. I'm at Camp Blanding in Florida and in the infantry. I feel just as if my whole world has collapsed all around me. [...] They told us that we're in the infantry and that there is no possibility whatsoever for transfer. We'll get 17 weeks of training and then be shipped overseas. We MIGHT get a furlough unless conditions make it necessary to ship us right over. Whew! The sweat is pouring out of me while I'm writing. Since the war began, I've lived in dread of the day when I'd be in the infantry and now it's here.*

"I've always tried to be a good, clean living kid and now when I so wanted to get in the Navy, this had to happen to me. I guess I'll probably be overseas by Christmas. The fellows here say that it's really hell. The terrific heat has caused more than one casualty in the long hikes. [...] I already hate it and haven't started training yet." His opinion won't change when it starts. More than the hikes in the sand, mud and swamps, above all he hates the rudeness of the drill sergeants shouting at the recruits to push them to their very limits and to resignation. Some of them break down and burst into tears. With their full pack, they crawl from sunrise to sunset and, for a little bit of diversity, they run 4 miles in less than half an hour, sometimes with a gas mask on their faces.

The shooting part of training is no more pleasant: *"The noise makes our ears ring for hours and the kick of the rifle has my face pretty swollen. I haven't been using my glasses for fear the kick would break them. Today, however, we fired from 500 yards and I could hardly see the target so I wore them. No casualties. The real fun is in the target pits. I've worked there three days now, two afternoons and one morning. Those bullets whiz over our heads about a foot at times. Then some wild guy fires in the sand just above the pit and we get showered with sand. Sometimes the bullets ricochet in wild fashion. However, don't worry because it's comparatively safe there. The whole bullet (shell and all) is about 3 or 4 inches long so you can see it's no pea shooter."*

A full 'clip' of eight rounds of ammunition for the M1 Garand rifle (see opposite page). On the right, an empty clip found in Normandy. These are the .30 caliber (7.62 × 63 mm) cartridges Carl mentioned above, and are all dated 1943.

He also discovers other weapons, such as rifle grenades or bazookas, and the cool nights in the wild, sleeping on the ground among snakes. Carl also takes part in maneuvers (combat simulation exercises against other companies), armed with weapons firing blanks. Soon, as the training intensifies, he moves on to village fighting, a life-size, live-ammunition training course: *"One more day here, I'm dying of exhaustion. We do maneuvers and marches all morning, and physical training in the afternoon. The heat here is terrible, some guys get sick and collapse. [...] We were on the range all day today, again, firing the Browning Automatic Rifle. It was 130°F [54°C] on that boiling range. The sand burned right through the soles of our shoes. [...] Boy, those babies can really spit a powerful amount of lead in a very short time. In two weeks we're going to go into village fighting. That's a really tough job. The idea is to run through a village, jump into and out of window buildings, firing and bayoneting as you go. They fire machine guns down the road and anybody who steps into the street goes home in a pine box. They also fire machine guns from rooftops and throw live hand grenades. This war is really a tough item. I'm beginning to think somebody can actually get killed. Tonight our Company is fighting Co. A. in the ring (boxing). I'm going over and watch the boys pound each other's ears off."*

Sometimes, men are given furlough, but the hard combat training and the frustration of life in the garrison lead to dangerous behavior: *"I have to walk guard duty tonight, which really messes up my whole weekend. Most of the boys went out on pass but our platoon pulled guard duty. Such is life! I hope there aren't too many men wandering around the port in high spirits tonight. Sometimes that kind gets hard to handle and they have to be treated rough. An officer was telling us a story about a guy on guard the other day. An officer came up to him in order to inspect him and see that he was on the ball. The guard halted the officer and the officer started to question him. Finally, the officer said to this southern boy: 'What would you have done if I hadn't halted?'. The soldier replied: 'Ah'd have called for an ambulance, suh'.' The officer said: 'What the devil would you call an ambulance for?'. The guard replied: 'To haul yoah daid carcus off in'."*

In mid-December 1944, Carl will leave for Fort Meade with the 8th Regiment of the 4th Infantry Division. He will spend less time on the front line than in training, and even more time in hospital: he will be wounded in Germany in April 1945.

You can follow Carl's story on page 308.

II - THE COUNTER-ATTACK 1942-1943

The M1 Garand rifle is the emblematic weapon of the GI in the Second World War. Created in 1928 by Canadian John Garand, eight years later it became the standard service weapon in the US Army and would also be supplied in large quantities to the United States' allies.

It offers Americans much more firepower than the Germans, who still use old bolt action rifles and needed to eject the cartridge case manually and load a new round into the chamber after each shot. The M1 Garand, on the other hand, is a semi-automatic rifle: it fires clips of eight cartridges very quickly, at each press of the trigger. The empty clip is then automatically ejected, producing a characteristicly metallic sound, and the soldier can then insert a full one from above in a single movement. The Garand is also liked by GIs for its precision, power and reliability.

This rifle will remain the standard weapon of the US Army until 1957, but will still be in use in the 1970s. By the 1980s, more than 6,250,000 M1 Garand rifles had been produced. The one presented here is made by Springfield and dated 1943.

EVERYONE ON THE SAME PAGE

At Camp Crowder, Missouri, Roland trains with a signals unit, which is not a clerical job. He writes to his father on July 2, 1943: *"This is the ending of the second week of basic training and things are starting to get tough. This week we were on scouting patrols, out of the camp area and we had different platoons against each other trying to take positions. Wednesday we went on a hike and walked about six miles with full equipment. The hike was made just like troops would move under war conditions. They had flank guards that would walk about fifty yards from the column in the fields and through woods. I had a crack at it and it was plenty tough because the column was on the roads and could move easily while the flank guards had to go over barbed wire and ditches, you had to do some tall steppin' to keep up. The hike took about an hour and forty minutes and we stopped only once for about ten minutes. About 600 fellows made the little journey, this doesn't include officers and non-coms. And about ten fellows passed out from the heat or exhaustion. Not a bad average.*

We have also been practicing with the rifle, teaching the different positions and how to work the bolt. I was surprised at all the fellows that never shot a rifle before. I guess some of them didn't even know which end the bullet came out. We didn't use any live ammunition yet, that comes next week, and we shoot for record on Wednesday. They hand out medals here and you don't have to buy them, they give them to you if you qualify. To qualify you have to have 134 out of 200 which is 'marksman', 168-177 is 'sharpshooter' and 178 or better is 'expert'. I think I'll get one of those medals but I'm not saying which one. I'm writing this letter while I'm on B.O. (it stands for Barracks Orderly, not Body Odor), it's a soft detail you only have to work in the morning to get ready for inspection. Since I've been here at Crowder I haven't gone to a movie or smoked. Never had the time to get to a movie."

Roland's training will continue until March 1944, when he is sent to Europe. Until then, he will have time to develop new skills. A few weeks after the previous letter, he adds: *"Today we went out on the machine gun range and we shot the Thompson sub-machine gun. I did pretty good in it. My score was 86 out of 100 which qualified me as expert with that gun. In a couple of weeks I'll get a medal for it. Yesterday we were out on a convoy and the roads we went over were rough and I don't mean maybe. We were doing between 25 and 30 mph over them and in a car you would go about 5 mph. I was driving a Diamond-T truck, with air brakes and handling that baby was no picnic. The gross weight of the truck is 13 tons. It has two sets of gears, one for heavy pulls and the high-speed gears. Altogether it has 10 forward and two reverses."*

Even for future Navy sailors, mountain hiking is mandatory. At the US Naval Training Station in Farragut, Idaho, Gordon completed long walks and fired guns just like an infantry recruit. He wouldn't really train for the Navy's daily jobs until a few weeks later, at the US Naval Air Technical Training Center in Chicago, where he writes: *"We had a gas lecture and drill today. They made us take our masks off in a room filled with tear gas, but it wasn't as bad as the one we had at Farragut. We are on the Squadron operations phase of school now and I like it a lot, all we do is take off fuel pumps, carburetor mags, oil lines and so forth. We do that kind of work all morning and in the afternoon we have physical education, signaling and one period of class works."*

In armored troops, the training is also very special, as Eddie writes in April 1943: *"Now I am in a Tank Destroyer Battalion and we destroy all types of different tanks. And then when you happen to know that there is a tank heading our way, we dig ourselves a fox hole, get in, and then let the tank run over the holes, while we're in them."*

TIMBERWOLVES

At last, the training period is coming to an end. Laurence, a non-commissioned officer in the 104th Infantry Division 'Timberwolves', takes part in realistic war games after thirteen weeks of basic training. These maneuvers take place mainly in wooded areas, where the men frequently encounter gray wolves, which will become the emblem of the division. Laurence writes to his mother on October 28, 1943, from the High Lava field near Bend, Oregon: *"We started out in just one helluva snowstorm, marched and rode about 4 hours, bivouacked overnight, crossed a river in the morning. River had a terrific current and our assault boat turned over. We all got a nice drenching but the mythical battle went out.*

A bayonet 'Expert' qualification badge earned by a 45th US Division infantryman.

The top badge changes according to the three qualifications, from which hang one or more bars for the weapons fired in training (pistol, rifle, machine gun, bazooka, flame thrower...).

II - THE COUNTER-ATTACK 1942-1943

Our commanding officer was captured and I took over. He escaped, got back to the company and I took a midnight patrol out and got captured myself. 'D' bar rations were eaten most of the time and in general quite a rat race was had. Now is the break between problems. Our next and last problem of these maneuvers begins this afternoon and then we take a break for a couple weeks and we're off for new fields within the States. I'll let you know the new address as soon as I have it. Yesterday we put on quite a noon chow for the company. Chickens (fried), apple pie, beer... I made the purchases out of company fund and planned it. I'm mess officer and like it a lot. It's a job that's only in addition to my regular duties as platoon leader, 81mm mortar platoon."

In April 1944, Laurence is now in Camp Carson, Colorado. Meanwhile, he had other maneuvers at Camp Hyder (Arizona), then Camp Granite (California), where the 104th Division was the only one to capture the coveted Phelan Pass from the 80th Division. Laurence writes: *"My leave, due to commence May 20, was disapproved today on account I have not yet fired a couple of new-type rifle courses. The deal in this war is a lot different than the last.*

Officers and men must now be POM qualified to get a boat ride, POM standing for 'Preparation for Overseas Movement'. This includes firing a lot of different courses, being fired at by machine guns which are really incapable of hitting you as long as you hug the ground, etc. etc. They're always adding new stuff and it's hard to say at any given moment whether or not you are POM qualified. I'm going to try to fire the courses tomorrow, so I can once more be all set POM and thus eligible for leave."

The commander of Army Ground Forces, Lieutenant-General McNair, will soon review the troops and be impressed by the progress of the regiment's training. The 104th Infantry Division will land in Cherbourg on September 7, 1944 and be assigned to the 1st Canadian Army north of Antwerp. These American soldiers will be surprised to be driven to the front by Polish soldiers, in English vehicles bearing Canadian markings! They will then join the American 1st Army in Aachen and advance to Düren in Germany, when the Battle of the Bulge is in full swing. They will distinguish themselves, with the unit being awarded the prestigious Presidential Unit Citation, while Laurence will receive the Silver Star for bravery in action.

Some men would train for more than two years, a period they would find extremely long. But as the war progresses, bringing with it more killed and wounded, the army will have to provide new soldiers to fill the gaps in the ranks. By 1945, replacements will only be allowed a few weeks of training.

RONALD WHITEHEAD

720th Bomb Squadron, 450th Bomb Group, 15th Air Force

Ronald is undergoing extensive training to become a bomber pilot in the US Army Air Forces, to the great displeasure of his mother, who already wants to see him married and a father. Unfortunately, following a year and a half of hard work to make his dream come true, Ronald will be killed after only one month in Europe.

Ronald R. Whitehead was born on March 10, 1921 in Bethlehem, Pennsylvania, where he lives with his parents and little sister Ileen (whose first name Ronald constantly distorts for fun in his letters). A great ladies' man, he doesn't think much about marriage, and his only dream is to become a pilot in the US Army Air Forces (which will only be renamed 'US Air Force' in 1947). However, just as in the RAF, casualties in the US Army Air Forces are very high: by seeking to accomplish the thirty missions required to return home, the probability of being killed is 71%. Ronald still signs up on March 10, 1942 with the serial number 13054959. His training will be divided into three stages: 'primary', 'basic', and finally 'advanced'.

FIRST STEPS IN THE AIR FORCE

Ronald's training starts in the spring of 1942 at the Air Corps Replacement Training Center in Santa Ana, California. This gigantic base gives future pilots, who have just arrived from civilian life, a basic ground training of nine weeks before they leave for the flying schools. There are nearly 10,000 cadets on the base with Ronald, but in some classes, up to 75% of them will be declared unfit to continue their training. The selection is as rigorous as the dropouts are numerous: many can't withstand the physical training in the heat of the Californian desert, or the spectacular dives in the instructor's plane intended to keep fragile stomachs at bay. The men learn how to fire the famous .45 caliber M1911 pistol, in case they are parachuted into occupied territory, while written tests on subjects such as aircraft identification, Morse code, mathematics and physics, or aircraft engine mechanics and navigation are also very difficult. Yet Ronald gets excellent marks, often the best in the class (92% on average, 70-85% being required to pass, depending on the subject). Like him, every year from 1942 and the inauguration of the training center, 45,000 other cadets will graduate from the pilot school.

In late June, Ronald receives his jacket and cap from the US Army Air Forces and gets to primary training: there he learns the basics of takeoff and landing at the Rankin Aeronautical Academy in Tulare, California. About 500 candidates work with just over 200 aircraft, accompanied by instructors. Ronald writes to his family on the evening of July 2: *"You always worry about my weight more than I do. I weigh about 198 pounds now and am still eating. The food they serve us at this place is the closest thing to your cooking that I [have] ever seen and tasted. We receive hot cakes, Virginia baked ham, sweet potatoes, hot buns, cantaloupe, fruit juices, creamed vegetables, pie, puddings and lots of other d--- good things. [...] Ilean [sic], I will send you a small clipping of my face with my*

II - THE COUNTER-ATTACK 1942-1943

flying goggles and helmet on for your locket. Please wear it when you get married will you. Ha! Ha! I bet Dad loves to hear this teasing. Mom, please don't send any cookies, as I have plenty of these things now. You folks need the sugar and it also costs so much to send them here. I appreciate your thinking of me that way, and hope you will understand what I mean.

Well Dad, your little pilot is doing OK with his flying (I hope). We were doing power on and power off stalls today. Then the instructor put me in a tail spin, we dropped 1,000 feet in no time, this is a great sensation in your ears. I haven't got sick in any of our days of flying so far. We receive 40 to 45 minutes of flying each day. There are so many fellows who are throwing their cookies (getting air sick) every day. I figure anyone who washes out in this flying training is OK, and don't have to feel too bad about it. This flying training is really hard. There are some of the upper-class men who are washing out because they want to. Two fellows washed themselves out yesterday, they even had about 25 hours and were doing fine. When you come down from your 40 minutes you feel so tired and all washed out. Then you have athletics in the afternoon for one hour. The athletics is very hot and dry, yesterday the temperature was 118°F [48°C] in the sun. It is so hot here that we don't have to wear ties and are supposed to wear sun helmets. They also make us wear sun glasses or some fellow almost lost his sight due to the bright sun. I bought myself a pair, they cost me $4.50, they really look like a 75 cents pair, but the lenses are very good and lined up. By the way folks, I am what you call a 'do do'. When I solo, which comes around 10 to 19 hours, I won't be a 'do do' anymore. We had two tests in navigation so far, I made a 100 and a 80, one test in airplane engines, which I made a 96%. Boy, these subjects are hard. I don't know how I made such good marks. I was very much surprised, I won't be one of these wash outs, I am going to keep on the ball. As they say around here, I'm 'cooking with gas'. I really enjoy the flying part. The instructor takes the ship off, and then tells me to take it up to 9,000 feet. I got it up there today, and then he said here we go into a spin. That is a heck of a funny sensation. You dare not get stiff as he can't man the controls. He sits in the front cockpit and me in the back. He has a mirror and can see every movement my face makes. Dad you should be here! [...] Love to all, Pilot Ronald.

On July 16 Ronald is on his own, manning the controls for the very first time: *"Yes sir, yesterday the instructor let me land the plane and take it off by myself. I sure do like to fly this way, no one to yell at you. I mean YELL, these instructors sure are good at it. I passed my solo flight, the instructors say my takeoffs and landings were very good. I did it in about 11 hours. There are fine fellows in my group (my plane). One fellow had about 40 hours before he came here. He soloed first and myself second. The rest tried, but didn't pass."*

By early August Roland is now considered an Upper-class man, superior to the Lower-class men who still lack experience. He now has more than forty hours of flight time and learns his first 'acrobatics'. He will spend more than twenty hours there, since although he has passed all his exams, he needs at least sixty hours to be able to access the next step: basic training with a combat aircraft.

'PILOT RONALD'

Basic training begins on August 28, 1942 at the Basic Flying School in Lemoore, California. Ronald masters night flights, radio communications and meteorology. His flying time count starts back from scratch, but in early September, he is already doing his first solo on a BT-13 training aircraft. It is practiced at a speed of nearly 300 mph, diving from an altitude of 8,000 feet down to only 2,000 feet. On September 22, he successfully passes his first twenty hours of flight testing. Only two other cadets among the fourteen in Ronald's group succeed in doing so. Those who are washed out of the combat pilot school are often offered a second chance as glider pilots, but as the latter only experience one-way flights, never mind safely landing soldiers and equipment on the front line without the slightest chance of taking off again, the job isn't very popular.

Accidents occur frequently during training. On October 23, Ronald tells his family: *"Two planes crashed on the take-off. The one burned and the other was really banged up. It was the cadet's fault. He only had slight cuts in the hand. The other cadet was burned and died in the hospital the next day. This accident happened Wednesday. Today a cadet and an instructor spun in from 2,000 feet and were both killed. This was also an underclassman. Their plane burned and both died immediately. The class before us had a casualty where two cadets were burned to death. We have been lucky so far. That's a pretty bad three days, three cadets and three $25,000 planes."*

Basic training ends that day. After returning his books and flying equipment, Ronald is sent to Williams Field Base in Higley, Arizona, where he is to spend two months of 'advanced' training. During this last stage, he flies up to seven hours a day in the afternoon, in addition to the lessons at the flying school in the morning. He has the opportunity to try different planes, and impresses the instructors as much as ever. In late November he writes: *"I have almost made up my mind as to what I would like to fly. This ship is the B-17-E or B-24, they are four engine heavy bombers. I was talking to my instructor and he said he rode on a B-17. They will do around 350 mph in level flight with no bomb load. When the B-17 goes on a bombing mission it cuts out two engines, and only uses two for power. When it arrives at or near the objective it cuts in the other two engines. They fly at around 30,000 feet for their bombing missions. With two engines, and at this altitude, they can fly at about 200 mph with a 5,000 pounds bomb load. The B-17 doesn't need any pursuit protection, as it is so well armed in itself* [its nickname is 'the Flying Fortress']. [...] *This B-17 that I would like to fly is being used by the US over Africa, Australia, Germany, Alaska, the Pacific Islands, etc. They use this and the B-24 over all the battle fronts. They get right in the thick of it all."*

PROMOTION

Ronald receives a salary of $75 at the time, of which he spends $15 on food, laundry and other miscellaneous expenses. However, a 2nd lieutenant can earn up to $320, so Ronald hopes to be promoted and achieves this on January 3, 1943, when he leaves for Salt Lake City to a B-17, B-24, B-25 and B-26 bomber pilot replacement center. His military serial number now takes the prefix 'O' for 'officer', and becomes O-735848. What's more, he's amused by the fact that everyone must now salute him.

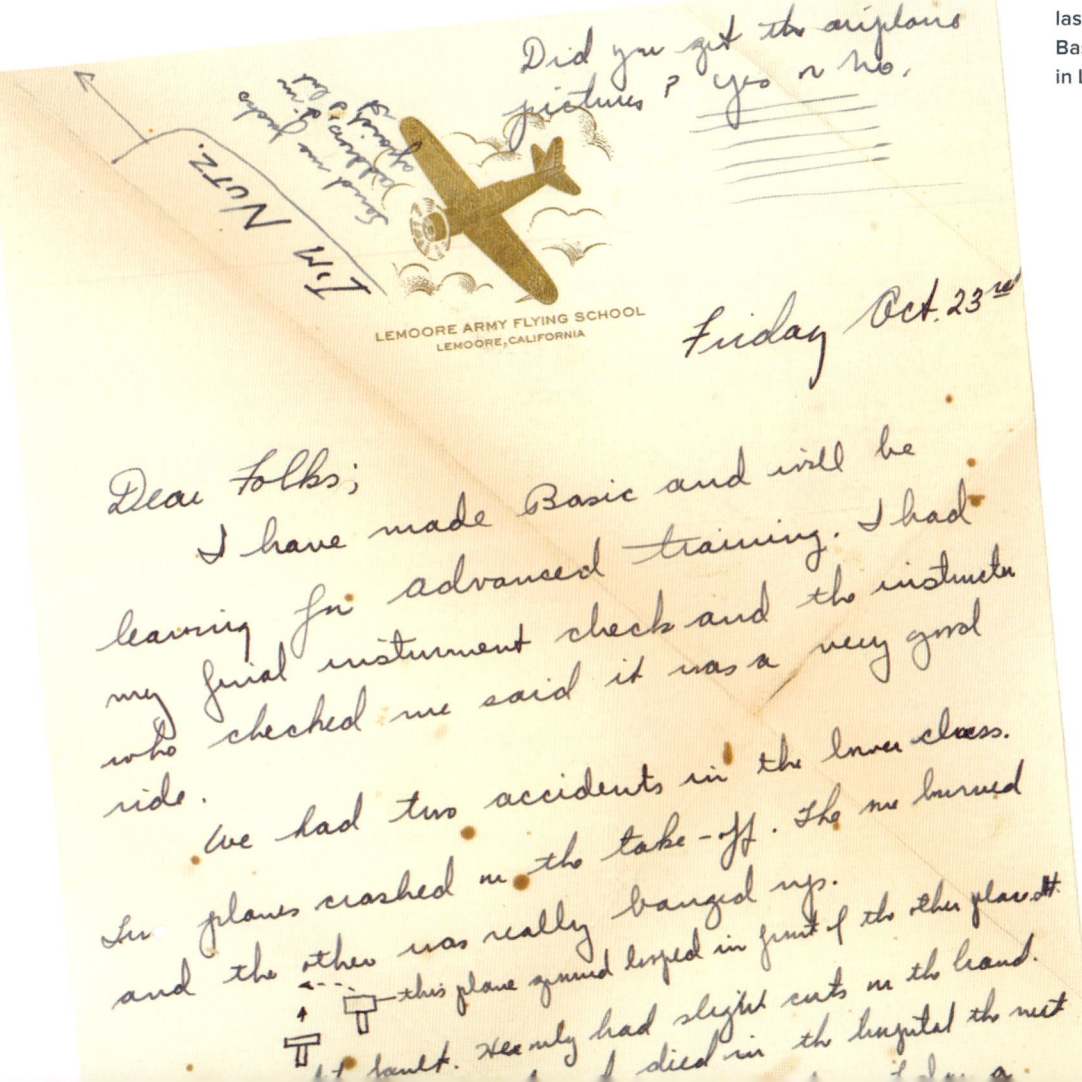

Ronald's last letter from Basic Training in Lemoore.

II - THE COUNTER-ATTACK 1942-1943

Unfortunately, his excitement quickly turns to disappointment, if not pure anger, when he learns that the crews of B-17 and B-24 bombers are all full. In mid-January he's sent to the 77th Observation Group in Alamo Field (San Antonio, Texas), where he trains in taking photographs from a small three-seat reconnaissance aircraft. Then, in late April, he is in charge of the flight schedules for the 95th Infantry Division in training, with the 125th Liaison Squadron. Although he flies very little, he enjoys this experience as an intelligence and operations officer, but he takes advantage of each military maneuver to look for a place on board a heavy bomber. Fortunately, as many crews are sent overseas, Ronald finally seizes an opportunity in May 1943. At Florence Air Force Base in Florence, South Carolina, he is assigned to the 18th Reconnaissance Squadron and to his first B-25 bomber crew.

Ronald during his training in South Carolina, seen here with his sister Ileen.

However, Ronald isn't entirely satisfied. In one of his letters, he states: *"I have to fly with my crew this afternoon. Believe it or not, I'd rather fly pursuits. This B-25 is too slow. The darn thing only cruises at 200 mph. If I can, I would like to fly the P-47. I love them, it's a pilot's dream."*

He still prefers the B-25s to the B-26s: *"Those darn flying coffins (B-26) are no good. They have too small a wing area and can't gain or hold altitude with one engine. If I ever get put in one, that's the day I throw in my wings and transfer to the infantry."* The aircraft's crew is composed of a pilot (most often a captain or 1st lieutenant), a co-pilot (2nd lieutenant), an observer, a machine gunner, a radio operator (who sometimes also becomes a machine gunner), a photographer (also machine gunner, if necessary), and a crew chief. Ronald is the pilot and the only 2nd lieutenant in this position. Before officially assuming this role, he must complete twenty-five hours of flight time as a co-pilot. His objective is achieved on July 7, 1943. Three days later, he is sent to Florida to the B-17 bombers' school with nine of his comrades from the 18th Recon Squadron, including his best friend Don. He then spends several weeks in Hendricks Field before leaving for Clovis, New Mexico, where the final unit is formed. Lieutenant Whitehead is assigned a crew from the 720th Bomb Squadron, 450th Bomb Group, 15th Air Force.

The men finally get their own bomber, a B-24H Liberator, the model Ronald wanted so badly to fly, and are bound for Europe. In November 1943, as they leave the Alamogordo desert, the airmen baptize their aircraft to which they are already strongly attached. Painting a pin-up on its nose, they name their plane *Miss Temptation*.

EUROPE

Ronald and his crew take off on December 7, 1943, but have to make several stops. They spend almost two weeks in Brazil, in Belem and Natal, where they take advantage of the low prices to buy equipment and even a monkey, whom they call Joe. Accompanied by their mascot, they leave South America for Africa and land in Dakar (at the time the capital of the French West African colony). After two days on site, they head for Marrakesh, flying over the Sahara Desert and the Atlas Mountains, where one of the group's planes unfortunately crashes, killing ten of the twelve crew members. After a final stop in Algiers, Ronald and his comrades settle in an air base in Manduria (Italy), about 20 miles from Taranto, where they arrive on December 28. The place is uncomfortable, since the 15th Air Force has lost much of its equipment and must borrow some from the British 8th Army. Indeed, the Luftwaffe bombed the port of Bari three weeks earlier, sinking seventeen Allied ships there. Among the latter, the Liberty Ship SS *John Harvey* secretly carried 1,350 tons of mustard gas bombs, in case the Germans started a chemical war (they won't). The raid killed 2,000 military and civilian personnel (many of them due to the mustard gas).

The full crew of the Miss Temptation – *Standing, from left to right:*
Lt Joseph Brown (navigator), Lt James Pibb (co-pilot), Lt Thomas Lowen (bombardier), Lt Ronald Whitehead (pilot).
Kneeling, front row: S/Sgt Joe Goodman (1st engineer), Sgt Paul Young (engineer), Sgt Chester Kraska (engineer),
Sgt John Sternberg (radio operator), Sgt Don Amundson (gunner), T/Sgt Plentice (flight chief, ground personnel),
Sgt O'Brien (crew chief, ground personnel), Sgt Jack Means (gunner).

Ronald writes in late December: *"This trip sure has shown me how the rest of the world lives and I'm telling you it's terrible. While in West Africa I had a talk with a native man. I couldn't understand him and he couldn't understand me. I got a native lucky charm from him. It's to be worn around the wrist and is supposed to protect the wearer from diseases and harm."* Unfortunately, the charm will have no effect on Ronald, and this will be his last letter home. Less than a month later, he will be killed at the controls of his bomber.

His first overseas mission is to attack facilities in Zara, Yugoslavia. The Allies support Tito's partisans, who would soon total 500,000 men (despite their bad equipment, a year later, these resistance fighters would have rid Yugoslavia of Axis troops, but their leader would go on install a repressive and brutal regime). However, the mission is canceled due to bad weather, although the crew had already crossed the Adriatic. Thereafter, Ronald successfully completes five bombing runs in northern Italy (Pisa, Perugia, Arezzo, and Guidonia).

SACRIFICE

On January 24, 1944, the B-24H *Miss Temptation* (#42-7743) is already on its seventh mission overseas, but this would be its last. It takes off from Manduria airfield at 8 am with thirty-three other American heavy bombers and heads for its objective: a German airfield in Sofia (Bulgaria). As the fleet crosses Albania and enters Yugoslav airspace, it comes under fire from anti-aircraft guns and although Ronald's plane receives some shrapnel, it suffers little damage.

At 12:30 pm, the bombers are suddenly attacked by a dozen German Me-109 and Fw-190 fighters. The escort of American P-38 fighters manages to scare them away temporarily, but the German planes severely damage five bombers and kill a tail gunner. One of the *Miss Temptation*'s engines is lost, and Ronald can no longer maintain enough speed to stay in formation. He becomes separated from the group and is immediately harassed by seven Me-109s.

II - THE COUNTER-ATTACK 1942-1943

The attack lasts about twenty minutes and the bomber, without the support of the rest of the fleet, can do little against the German fighters who manage to evade its fire. *Miss Temptation* is severely damaged, losing a second engine, and gunner Don Amundson is shot in the leg. Ronald searches for cloud cover and succeeds in losing the Luftwaffe fighter planes. The American airmen are in shock, reciting prayers, and unable to understand how the plane could still fly after all the damage it has suffered. Ultimately, the bomber loses power and Ronald orders his crew to bail out. He desperately tries to keep the plane stable and allow his ten comrades to jump at an altitude of about 3,000 feet, which they manage to do over Elbasan, south of Tirana, Albania. Some of the crew are seriously injured, but all will survive, even though they will be captured on the ground by the Germans. Ronald, meanwhile, remains at the controls until the end. Unable to avoid the crash, he is probably killed instantly.

His navigator, Lieutenant Brown, is the last to see the plane disappear into the clouds towards the Adriatic, north of Skopje (capital of North Macedonia). According to a Luftwaffe officer questioning the captured Americans, *Miss Temptation* crashed into the mountains somewhere between Tirana and Elbasan. The Germans will even find a dead body inside a crashed plane near there and although Lieutenant Brown obtains permission to visit the remains and identify the man, the Germans are concerned about Yugoslav partisan activities and so take their prisoners to Belgrade. Lieutenant Brown will never get a chance to see the body.

Later, a well-documentd report from a German anti-aircraft unit will be found, stating that a burning Liberator crashed 30 miles north of Skopje, at around 12:20 pm. However, the plane is never located, and Ronald's remains will never be formally identified, despite numerous searches in Albania and Macedonia. In the crash area, the bodies of four unknown American soldiers will be removed from a mass grave (probably airmen killed in a B-17 crash during the same mission). It's possible that bones from a fifth body, found beside them, may be associated with Lieutenant Whitehead, but the mystery of his disappearance remains.

Ronald's memory is preserved on the wall of the missing at the American cemetery in Florence, Italy, and he would receive the Purple Heart (the American medal for those killed or wounded) posthumously and an Air Medal for his bravery. In his autobiography, one of Ronald's crew members, his gunner and friend, Sgt. Donald R. Amundson, writes: *"In my story, I have tried to show myself as a young airman who tried to do his best. In no way were we heroes. The heroes did not come home. Many were like my pilot, Lt. Whitehead, who lies entombed in our plane on a mountain top somewhere between Albania and Yugoslavia. He stayed at the controls until all crew members had left the plane, for this act he lost his life. May our nation ever be grateful for men like him."*

15th Air Force patch and Ronald's name on the wall of the missing, in Florence, Italy.

THE DIEPPE RAID

Many Canadian infantrymen, volunteers as we have seen, are about to see their first action in France on August 19, 1942. However, this daring operation in Dieppe will turn into a disaster, providing valuable lessons to the Allies for their next landings.

THE PLAN

The exhausted Red Army succeed in repelling the enemy at the gates of Moscow, but the Germans launch a new offensive in the south towards the Caucasus and the city of Stalingrad. Now that the Americans are at war, Stalin expects his new Western partners to open a second front in Europe and although the latter aren't yet ready for a major landing in France, they wish to demonstrate their goodwill towards the Soviets.

Since 1940, the Combined Operations Headquarters, led by Lord Mountbatten, has conducted many commando raids. In Saint-Nazaire, on March 28, 1942, one of the most daring operations was carried out in order to damage the dry dock used to maintain the battleship *Tirpitz*, resulting in British losses of around 60%. Shortly afterwards, Mountbatten planned his biggest coup, to evaluate the effectiveness of the 'Atlantic Wall' that the enemy had been developing since March 1942, by striking quickly and hard. Far from being finished, the German project aims to install bunkers, machine gun nests, artillery guns, anti-tank ditches, barbed wire and other defensive works all along the Atlantic coast from Spain to Norway. Built by the Todt Organisation, which had already built the Westwall in front of the Maginot Line, it bolsters many of the ports along the coast, transforming them into genuine fortresses ('Festungen'). This Atlantikwall must now protect the western front of the Reich, which found itself embroiled with the Soviet Union.

The date chosen by the Allies for this operation in Dieppe, code-named *Jubilee*, is August 19, 1942. The Canadians of the 2nd Infantry Division will make up most of the assault force: 13,000 men, including 6,000 soldiers ready to charge on to the beaches, with 250 ships (including 8 destroyers) and RAF Spitfires protecting them. No massive bombardment will take place beforehand, however, so as to limit civilian casualties and avoid angering the Vichy regime, whose cooperation the Allies believed could be crucial during any future landings in North Africa.

The plan is complex, the timing extremely precise, and the coordination essential: British Commandos Nos. 3 and 4 will land in Berneval, to the north, and Varengeville, to the south, to silence the coastal batteries, while the Canadian infantry will land at Puys (Royal Regiment of Canada) and Pourville (South Saskatchewan Regiment & Cameron Highlanders of Canada) to take the guns aimed at Dieppe. Finally, the Royal Hamilton Light Infantry and the Essex Scottish Regiment will land on Dieppe beach with the support of fifty tanks from the Calgary Regiment, and destroy various targets, including the city's harbor and the German HQ at Arques-la-Bataille. Once these infrastructures are destroyed, the whole group will immediately head back to England. Indeed, civilians are warned: *"People of France, this is a raid and not the invasion. We urge you not to do anything that could lead to retaliation by the enemy. We appeal to your self-control and common sense. When the time comes, we will let you know. Then we will act side by side for our common victory and for your freedom!"*

II - THE COUNTER-ATTACK 1942-1943

THE UNEXPECTED

Although the construction of the Atlantic Wall has only just begun, Dieppe's casino has already been transformed into a bunker, its beaches and accesses covered with barbed wire, ditches and anti-tank walls, and the villas serve as fortified resistance nests. Above all, nature itself plays in favor of the defenders: the 100-foot high cliffs leave only a few entry points to the inland, which are very well defended. Allied Intelligence has also underestimated the number of defenders: the Germans are nearly 1,500 strong, three times what had been estimated! And the enemy, who had already spotted the Allied fleet, is waiting for the Canadians with its finger on the trigger.

No. 3 Commando, heading for Berneval at 4:50 am, is intercepted offshore and a naval battle ensues. Only a handful of commandos manage to land at the planned location, and against all odds advance to the objective. However, they have to retreat against a much larger enemy force. On the other hand, in Varengeville, success is total. Among the men who carry out this mission are fifty American Rangers, a brand-new elite unit modeled on British commandos. One of them, Edward Loustalot, will become the very first GI killed in Europe on that day. Fifteen Free French, Captain Phillipe Kiefer's marine riflemen, are also fighting.

Once their mission is accomplished, the commandos return at 7:30 am, not knowing that for the Canadians, the operation had been a complete disaster.

In Puys, 83% of the Canadians from the Royal Regiment are lost on the shingle beach.

THE CHAOS

In Puys, the Germans hear the shots fired offshore. They're in position, looking down the sights of their machine guns, which are each capable of spitting fifteen bullets per second. Under a terrific barrage of lead and fire, 554 Canadians land in three successive waves and are immediately mowed down in the water and on the shingle. Only a few soldiers manage to leave the beach and take refuge in the woods, where they will surrender to the enemy in the afternoon. Everything is over in just a few minutes: 200 men of the Royal Regiment of Canada lie dead, 289 others are wounded and taken prisoner, and only 65 men are able to return to England.

The fiasco continues in Pourville-sur-Mer, as the boats drift and the Canadians land on the wrong side of the Scie River. They must now cross the only bridge under machine gun fire and anti-tank rockets, and are already suffering heavy casualties. Nevertheless, they courageously reach the other side, despite the dead piling up, but it's all for nothing. At 10 am they are ordered to turn back and follow the same road they took on the way there, still under deadly fire. Only 341 soldiers will reach the landing crafts. In Puys, as in Pourville, the German artillery batteries are still intact, and can fire freely at Dieppe, where the main assault is now taking place.

To make matters worse, the Churchill tanks accompanying the infantry are behind schedule. In any case, they will prove almost useless: their guns aren't powerful enough to penetrate the German defenses, and their tracks don't allow them to progress easily on the pebble seawall, meaning they will all be destroyed or abandoned. The infantry, for its part, simply tries to survive without any artillery support. Above its head, 106 Allied aircraft are destroyed in a fierce air battle against the Luftwaffe (which lost half as many).

Despite the chaos on the beach at Dieppe, masked by the smoke-screen produced by the destroyers, a second wave of landing crafts took the Fusiliers Mont-Royal Regiment into the heart of the inferno. They set off at 7 am and were decimated by shrapnel, bullets, grenades and shells. Only a few men reached the city, but most were trapped under the cliffs. Royal Marines sent as reinforcements were killed or captured.

Dug out of the ground, this helmet most likely belonged to a member of the Fusiliers Mont Royal, 2nd Canadian Infantry Division. Indeed, once cleaned by the author it revealed a blue painted badge typical of this unit, a habit that was mostly abandoned when it landed again in Normandy two years after Dieppe. Once a thick layer of soil and rust had been removed, a manufacturing mark stamped in the steel appeared: the initials 'CL/C' of the Canadian Lamp Company (Windsor), one of three Canadian companies that produced 1.1 million MKII helmets between 1940 and 1943. The first coat of smooth brown paint indicates that it was made before 1942 and was then covered with a second layer of light green camouflage.

Its unfortunate wearer received a large piece of shrapnel that went through the helmet from one side to the other. Sadly, there is no other evidence to identify its owner, and therefore to determine with certainty whether he died in 1942 or when the area was liberated in 1944.

II - THE COUNTER-ATTACK 1942-1943

DOC ALEXANDER'S WORST FIGHT

Facing the beach at Dieppe, Captain Laurence Guy Alexander is a medical officer with the 14th Canadian Army Tank Regiment (The Calgary Regiment). Everyone calls him 'Doc Alexander', or 'Alex' and despite being a veteran of the First World War, he's about to fight his worst battle at Dieppe. His Landing Craft Tank, *LCT 8*, is tasked with landing his ambulance to assist the regiment's Churchill tanks in the attack on the German airfield and HQ. Shortly after 6 am, the unit makes a first attempt in the 'Red' sector, near the pier, but the lead tank becomes stuck in the shingle. Three engineers sent to its rescue are mowed down by machine gun fire, and the ship is ordered to withdraw to find another landing point. His next target is 'White' beach, near the Dieppe casino. It's now about 8:30.

Alex writes in his diary the same day: *"As we drew nearer the beach the second time, Germans could be seen on the shores by the cliffs, and as we drew nearer, we were caught in a terrific hail of fire from Shore Batteries, Field Guns, and a constant hail of Machine Gun fire and bursting shrapnel. The wounded and dead were everywhere. The fire grew worse as we drew nearer the shore – we were called to our stations – the motors of our vehicles were again started, and when we were within fifty yards of shore, all hell broke loose. The call for stretcher bearers was heard in all directions. We left our vehicles and climbed to the upper parts of the boat.*

On reaching the upper part, a shell exploded which knocked me back to the bottom of the boat – but I was unhurt. I climbed to the top again when another shell hit and blew me the opposite direction – right off the boat, but somehow I caught an Engineer's foot – and was pulled back on again. At this time – the ramp on the front of the ship was starting to open as we were approaching the shore – a shell exploded in the front of the ship – breaking the cables and rigging and allowing the door to fall into the sea, forming a brace which kept us from going in further, and a direct hit was registered from the side.

The ship was at a complete standstill, the skipper was wounded and ordered 'abandon ship' then jumped into the water. The call came up from below to reverse the engines and seeing no one on the bridge and discovered no living people left – everywhere were dead bodies – some badly mutilated, some not. I shouted down that there were no living people above deck. I heard a call from the cat walk for help and ran there to find it crowded with dead and dying men – all wounded, not one uninjured man. [...] At this time a little distant from our boat, the sea was dotted with human bodies, held up by Mae West life belts and the Germans were pouring both Machine Gun and shells into their midst."

Captain Laurence Guy Alexander.

A tank that had fallen into the sea sank with its staff before Alex's eyes. A few soldiers managed to escape through the turret and were recovered by a small boat. A few moments later, the latter was hit by direct shell fire, probably killing all its occupants. When the general evacuation begins at 9:40 am, it's carried out in complete confusion, and the last survivors won't leave the beach until 2:00 pm.

LESSONS LEARNED

In his first letter to his family following the raid, Alex writes: *"Now Dieppe is a thing of history, and a memory intermingled with horror and pride at the way in which Canadians can face difficulties. Anything I saw in the whole of the last war – and I saw plenty there – nothing can in the slightest compare with this. A combination of fire from every direction, both sides, in front, behind, above and below, and every conceivable type of weapons pretty well sizes up the situation. The troops were magnificent: the navy and the air force were wonderful but the price which was paid for the results attained was high. I do not know how much I can write due to censorship, so I must not go into details which might be of any benefit to the enemy. You know how we feel. We know how you at home feel, but we also know that things of this nature must be done and to get the results which we must get, we must pay. The paying is cruel to us here, the waiting relatives at home – terrible. If only these things will bring home to those in Canada the fact that this is a war.*

We do need men. We need every effort that man, woman and child can put into this, and we need it now, if not in a voluntary way, the compulsory and rigid at that..."

Alex will receive the military cross for 'devotion to duty'. His citation reads: *"Working under extremely heavy fire to which he was exposed on one occasion while attending to wounded personnel, he was blown overboard by the blast from a shell of heavy caliber. Fortunately, he was not wounded and was able to regain the ship, where he continued to attend the large number of wounded."* In fact, Alex had a wound to his left ankle, a bruised coccyx, and a broken jaw. However, he could consider himself lucky: his Landing Craft left England with 117 soldiers and 13 sailors. Only 33 of the men accompanying him, most of whom were wounded, returned home.

The battle for Dieppe lasted nine hours, and of the 6,086 soldiers who landed on the beaches, about 60% were killed, wounded or captured (68% among Canadians, a very sad record): 1,197 Allied soldiers fell (plus hundreds of pilots and sailors), including 916 Canadian soldiers. Forty-eight French civilians were also killed in the fighting and more than 2,000 men were taken prisoner. The Germans are jubilant, and their propaganda is in full swing.

Vichy also seems to be pleased that the Allies have been thrown back into the sea, while the enemy is rewarding the inhabitants' inaction (not knowing that they have received instructions from the Allies) by releasing 1,500 Dieppe prisoners of war. The Atlantic Wall has proved its worth, and its construction begins once again. On the other hand, the Allies learn valuable lessons from the negligence of the raid and the ensuing disaster: a frontal assault cannot succeed without preliminary aerial bombardment, the support of efficient armored vehicles is essential, reliable intelligence is crucial, and a port is too ambitious an objective.

With the landings in North Africa a few months later, followed by those in Italy and the Pacific, the Allies will perfect their amphibious assault techniques. They will return to France less than two years later, with an even more complex plan, but one that takes advantage of Dieppe's tragic experience: *Operation Overlord*, June 6, 1944. As for the 2nd Canadian Infantry Division, it will take its revenge by liberating the city of Dieppe in September 1944, to the cheers of the inhabitants.

Captain Alexander (under the tank's cannon) and a Matilda tank crew from the Calgary Regiment, in training before the Dieppe Raid.

EL ALAMEIN

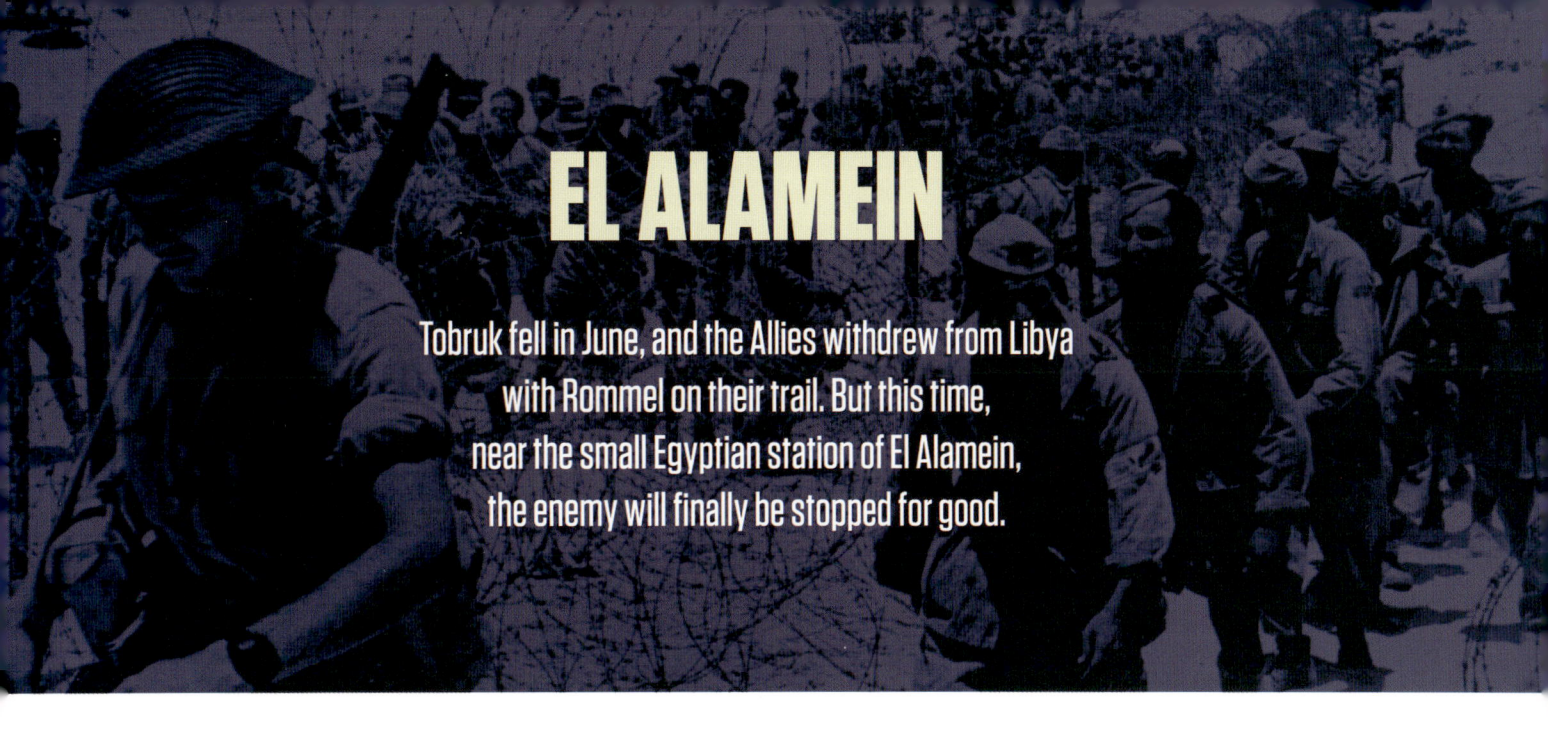

Tobruk fell in June, and the Allies withdrew from Libya with Rommel on their trail. But this time, near the small Egyptian station of El Alamein, the enemy will finally be stopped for good.

THE TURNING POINT

The Afrika Korps has crossed the Gazala Line and Tobruk, entered Egypt and is heading straight for Alexandria and the Suez Canal. It has captured nearly 60,000 British en route and destroyed or took possession of more than 2,000 Allied tanks. However, it was slowed down, notably by the 1st Free French Brigade at Bir Hakeim, thus allowing the 8th Army to retreat on June 30, 1942 to a small railway line by the sea, near El Alamein station. Just like the Battle of Stalingrad on the Eastern Front, which would begin a month later and see the Wehrmacht lose 300,000 men and start a gruesome journey back to the west, the 'First Battle of El Alamein' will mark a turning point in the Second World War. On July 1, 1942, the exhausted Axis troops are pinned down by the 8th Army, only 60 miles west of Alexandria.

Just south of El Alamein is the Qattara depression, a huge area of salt marshes and quicksand impassable for German tanks. Consequently, Rommel is forced to pass via the coast if he wants to seize the rest of Egypt. But once again the supply lines are a problem, despite the fact that the port of Tobruk is in his hands, as three quarters of his supply ships are sunk by the Allies stationed in Malta, and although the Luftwaffe bombed it like never before, the island withstood the attacks.

In late July, El Alamein's defenses are also holding up well. The Axis forces are preparing their defensive lines and filling their ranks. The Italians receive only one unit to reinforce them, but not just any unit: the 185a Divisione Paracadutisti Folgore, an elite parachute unit on which many hopes are based and which will fiercely resist the assaults of the 8th Army a few weeks later.

Montgomery, the new commander of the 8th Army.

Rommel wants to maintain pressure on the Allies and reach the Suez Canal. Informed that the British would receive equipment and reinforcements, he's aware that time is against him. He must attack quickly and rely on the element of surprise. What follows at the Alam el Halfa Ridge, south of the Allied perimeter, will be the last major German offensive in West Africa.

THE BATTLE OF ALAM EL HALFA

Albert is a 24-year-old infantryman from 1/5th Battalion, Queen's Royal Regiment (then attached to the 'Desert Rats' of the 131st Brigade, 7th Armoured Division). His unit has just joined Montgomery's forces to help hold the defensive perimeter of El Alamein. Albert writes to his brother Jim (James) in the 56th (London) Division, still stationed in England. This letter dates from the morning of August 31, 1942, the first day of the Battle of Alam el Halfa, when the Germans have not yet struck his lines: *"Dear Jim, [...] I am getting more used to it here now, but a week ago I was quite bad for a few days with a slight touch of dysentery but I got rid of it and I am none the worse. They don't do much for us when we get that, just a big dose of castor oil and leave the food alone for a couple of days, and nature does the rest!*

I am sorry you have been having trouble over your leave, but as long as you get it in the end, I suppose you don't mind if they put it back a week or two, although it is rather annoying when you have got things all arranged for one particular time. It seems that I will spend the coming Christmas in the desert, but I hope you will get yours at home, as it is certainly the time to be with your own people, so you had better try the coming month [This will not be the case. The 56th Division will soon leave England and be sent to Iraq and Palestine in November 1942. It will fight in Egypt, Libya and Tunisia before experiencing the worst battles of the Italian Campaign]. *I had a letter from John recently, and I was surprised to know he is in that airborne division, but it seems that he is happy there, so I wished him all the best and happy landings!* [Albert refers to the 1st British Airborne Division, established in late 1941, whose paratroopers will serve in France, Norway, Tunisia, Sicily and Italy, before being surrounded and decimated in the Netherlands during *Operation Market Garden*, their last engagement. In May 1943, the 6th Airborne Division will be created from elements of the 1st and parachuted into Normandy on June 6, 1944.] *Give my kindest regards to Mary and all her family, and let's hope it won't be so long before we can have that reunion in peace time! Well Jim, as news is scarce out in this barren old desert, I will bring these few lines to a close for now. So here's wishing you all the best of luck, and keep smiling, from your brother, Bert."*

Albert will be taken prisoner during the ensuing fighting and die in captivity in Italy in late April 1943. He will never see his brother again, nor his wife Mary Margaret and their baby. A few hours, perhaps a few minutes after he wrote these lines, the Germans, who had crossed the minefields, launch their attack at 1 pm.

Montgomery has been waiting for them, as 'Ultra' (the intelligence service in Bletchley Park) has unraveled the mysteries of the German communications encryption machine 'Enigma'.

Letter from Albert on the day of the German attack, and patch of the 7th Armoured Division (in its 1943 version). The latter earned its nickname 'Desert Rats' from the gerbil represented on it.

The 8th Army during an assault at El Alamein.

He knows that Rommel will attack south of El Alamein, so he intentionally left a breach to set a trap for him. A large number of British tanks were deployed on the Alam el Halfa Ridge, about 20 miles back. Albert and his brigade are thus positioned just behind the tanks, on the heights, with artillery guns ready to fire. When the German tanks finally crash into these well-prepared defenses, the Ruweisat Ridge is also attacked, but firmly held by Indian, South African and New Zealand soldiers. The Allied air force wreaks havoc in the Axis ranks, and on September 2, out of gas and realizing that he has lost the momentum, Rommel orders the retreat. Montgomery decides not to push his luck, and continues to concentrate his forces for the attack he would launch later in the fall: the 'Second Battle of El Alamein'.

LIGHTFOOT AND SUPERCHARGE

Rommel returns to Germany, suffering from exhaustion and a liver infection. Montgomery, for his part, is in great shape: he has 195,000 British, New Zealand, South African, Indian, Greek, Polish, Czech and French soldiers in his 8th Army. This is twice the German strength, and the Allies are equipped with 1,100 tanks and 1,000 guns. Montgomery is confident and intends to repel the Axis forces out of Egypt. But before anything can happen, he needs to clear a passage for the tanks: the enemy had laid no less than 500,000 mines on a nearly 6 mile-deep strip between the sea and the Qattara depression. With a typically British wit, the operation will be called *Lightfoot* and was scheduled for October 23, 1942. The main attack will take place in the north, led by X and XXX Corps, while XIII Corps will strike the 21. Panzer-Division and the Italian divisions Brescia and Folgore in the south. Out of the 5,000 Italian paratroopers prepared to fight to the last bullet and grenade, only 32 officers and 262 soldiers, most of them wounded, will survive. In the meantime, de-mining operations are launched. Unfortunately, German defenses are barely scratched and losses are heavy on both sides. Even though the Germans can only field 200 tanks in opposition to the many British tanks, this is the exact number of Allied vehicles they will manage to destroy in just two days. Rommel, recently returned although still in poor health, tries to launch a last-minute counter-attack, but fails. The British get ready for the final blow: 800 tanks, including new American Shermans, attack a very small number of Panzers.

Operation Supercharge starts on November 2. This time it succeeds in breaking through enemy lines and forces Rommel, who now has only about thirty medium tanks of the Italian *Ariete* division at his disposal, to withdraw (despite Hitler's order to hold positions). The Desert Rats suddenly rush into the breach and blow up the surviving Panzers one by one. The 8th Army will pursue the Axis forces from November 5 towards Mersa Matruh, reaching Sallum, at the border, on November 8. On that day, Anglo-American troops will land in North Africa during *Operation Torch*. To Rommel, in full retreat from Libya to Tunisia, this news is catastrophic. Tobruk is at last retaken on November 13, and Benghazi a week later, changing hands for the fifth and final time. Montgomery's offensive led the British to Tripoli, while the Free French liberated the Fezzan region in the south of the country.

Linen flag of the Kingdom of Italy (1861-1946) of King Victor Emmanuel II of Sardinia. The Royalist Army fought with the Germans until the Italian surrender in September 1943, before joining the Allied side (against whom it had lost 161,729 soldiers). This souvenir was brought back from North Africa by a member of the 7th Armoured Division in 1942. A stencil mark on the back of the flag probably links it to the Derbyshire Yeomanry, a volunteer cavalry regiment which deployed a battalion in Alam el Halfa and El Alamein.

On December 27, 1942, a Wellington bomber pilot from 37 Squadron (Royal Air Force) writes about the Second Battle of El Alamein, which he supported from the air: *"Just wait until this war is over, perhaps next Christmas. We seem to lie in a much better position now, all over the world. Out here our boys have done a wonderful job and I do feel proud of having been in it but it won't be known until after the war just what our boys on the ground did and what they went through doing it. They certainly are tough, and I think every captured Jerry will hear me out on that."*

Churchill is a happy man. Not only did he obtain the commitment of the Americans on the European front, but he also realizes that his own troops have saved the day. Although he said *"Now this is not the end; it is not even the beginning of the end. But it is, perhaps, the end of the beginning"*, he will write in his memoirs: *"Before Alamein we never had a victory. After Alamein, we never had a defeat."* English church bells are rung for the first time since Dunkirk. As early as March 1943, Rommel will confide to Colonel von Luck: *"Listen, one day you will remember my words: the war is lost. [...] We must stop what we are doing to the Jews, we must change our minds about religions, and everything else, and ask for an armistice now that it is not too late."*

The *Daily Mirror* of November 5, 1942, spreading the news of *Operation Supercharge*.

OPERATION TORCH

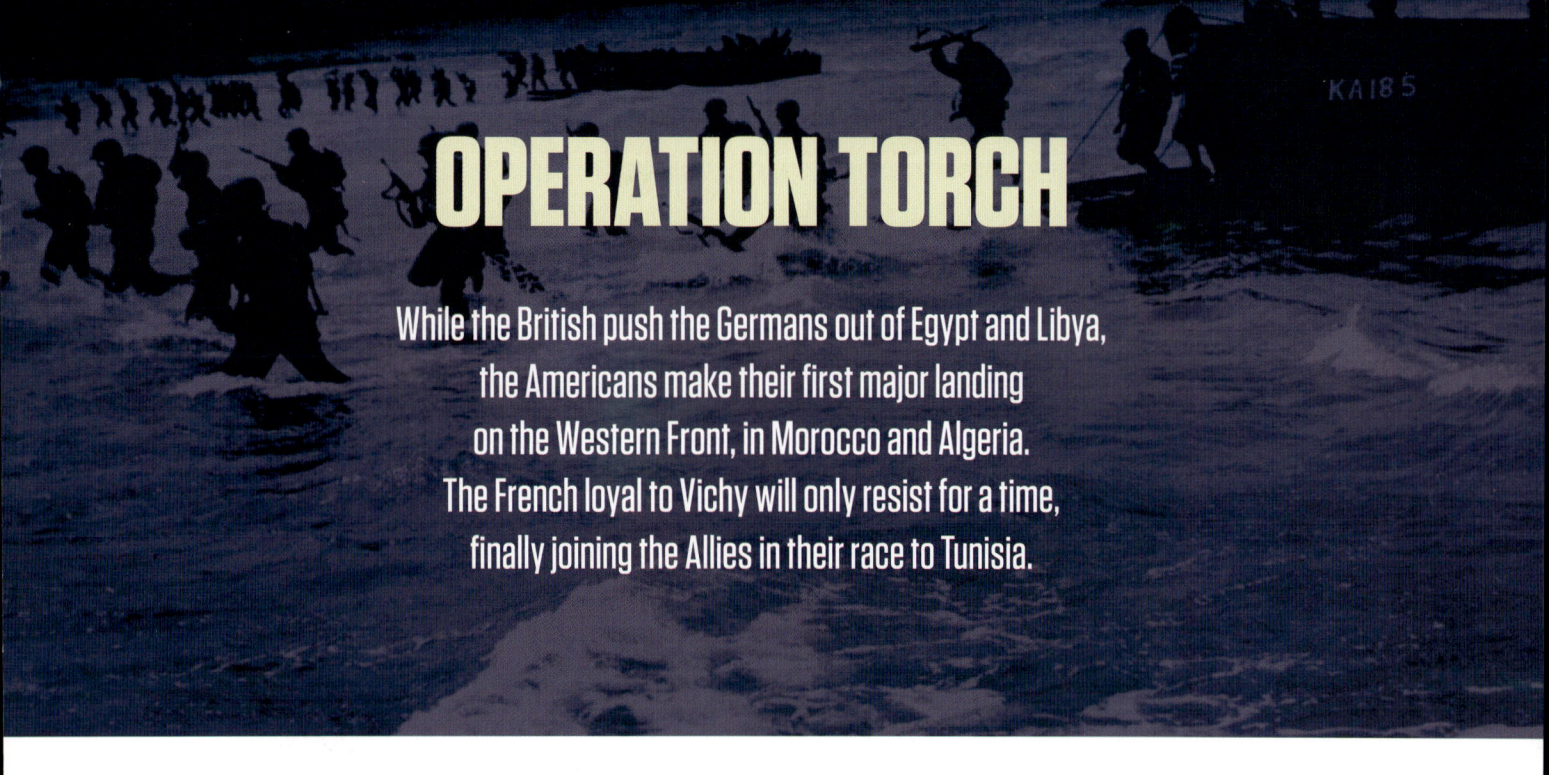

While the British push the Germans out of Egypt and Libya, the Americans make their first major landing on the Western Front, in Morocco and Algeria. The French loyal to Vichy will only resist for a time, finally joining the Allies in their race to Tunisia.

Since the catastrophic Dieppe raid, the Allies sought the ideal place to engage the US Army and honor their promise to Stalin to open a new front in the West. While the Americans wanted to wait until 1943 and attack in France, the British won the debate and planned an allied landing in North Africa. At the time, Morocco, Algeria and Tunisia were French colonies and protectorates, but the Allies believed that the troops loyal to Vichy wouldn't resist. However, some feared a certain resentment from the French Navy, which had been Anglophobic since the attack on Mers el-Kebir in 1940, so the assault would be presented as American, rather than British.

The objective of *Operation Torch* is to take the ports and airfields of the Mediterranean Coast, and then link up with the British, who were giving a hard time to the Axis forces in Libya. The Supreme Allied Commander Dwight D. Eisenhower is in charge of the whole operation from his headquarters in Gibraltar. American General Mark Clark is sent on a secret mission to North Africa to try and persuade Admiral Darlan, Commander of the Vichy Army, to join the Allied cause and not to put up any resistance to the landings. The negotiations are both confusing and difficult. At the same time, Eisenhower has leaflets dropped in French and Arabic, stating: *"The President of the United States has asked me, as Commander-in-Chief of the American Expeditionary Forces, to send the following message to the people of French North Africa: no nation is more closely bound, both by history and by deep friendship, to the people of France and their friends than the United States of America is. The Americans are currently fighting, not only to secure their future, but also to restore the freedom and democratic principles to all those who have lived under the French flag.*

We are here to free you from the invaders who only want to deprive you forever of your sovereign rights, your freedom of worship, your right to live your life in peace. We are only here to destroy your enemies, we don't want to hurt you. We are coming to your land, but we assure you that we will leave as soon as the threat from Germany and Italy has been removed. I appeal to your common sense and idealism. Do not do anything to hinder the achievement of this great purpose. Help us, and the day of universal peace will come closer." The date for *Operation Torch* is set for November 8, 1942.

The Americans, under the command of the 1st British Army (see the patch on the right) of Lt-Gen. Sir Kenneth Anderson, will land in Algeria and Morocco in three Task Forces: West, Centre and East.

THE *BIG RED ONE* IN ALGERIA

The men of the 1st US Infantry Division have been impatiently stomping their feet on the twenty-two ships they have occupied since October 26. The 'Big Red One' (referring to the large red number '1' on its olive-green patch), which left New York on August 2, 1942, feels readier than ever, after numerous amphibious maneuvers in Puerto Rico, Martinique, and Scotland. It will receive a baptism by fire with the Center Task Force in Oran (Algeria).

Three days before landing, Alan Morehouse, an officer in the division, writes to a friend: *"I haven't received a letter from you for a long time, but lately it has been no fault of yours for I have been receiving no mail at all. You see, Mike, we are no longer stationed in Great Britain, but are aboard ships on the high seas – where we're bound for is a military secret. [...] The problem of getting sufficient exercise is acute on board ship. There are quite a number of men & officers in a more or less compact area; but the men do calisthenics for quite some time during each day, and officers either walk around the top deck (a monotonous practice) or throw a medicine ball around. In one respect I was glad to leave our last station – it was beginning to get quite cold and I hate cold weather; where we are now (on the ocean) the weather is lovely. It was like an early June day on deck this afternoon – the sea was calm, there was just a faint trace of a breeze, and the sun was quite warm. I had to take off my field jacket in order to keep from sweating. At night I use only one blanket 'cause it is quite warm although the nights do get a bit chilly. In another respect I hated to leave Great Britain for there is so much of the Kingdom I still want to see. I didn't get half enough time to look around, but I guess sightseeing must wait until the war is over. Haven't been seasick yet, although I came close to it on a couple of rough days, but I'll be glad to set foot on solid ground again."*

Maybe he'll regret it. Landing alongside the 1st US Armored Division and supported by the first American airborne operation in history (led by the 509th Parachute Battalion, as will be seen in the next chapter), his division will quickly realize that the city and port are firmly defended by French troops. Coastal artillery guns and the invasion fleet will fire at each other for two days. While Alan lands on a beach in Arzew (east of Oran), the 26th Regiment of the 'Big Red One', commanded by Brigadier-General Theodore Roosevelt (son of the first President Roosevelt), advances from Les Andalouses beach. The French troops at Oran finally surrender on November 10. Alan will be wounded a few months later in Mateur (Tunisia), but will continue the fight to Sicily, where he will distinguish himself by his courage and leadership. On November 5, 1943, a year to the day after this letter, he will finally return to the Great Britain he had enjoyed so much, to prepare for *Operation Overlord*. Unfortunately, Normandy will be a one-way ticket: in the first hour of June 6, 1944, on Omaha Beach (Easy Red Sector), he will be shot in the head shortly after leaving his landing craft.

To the left of the 'Big Red One', the Eastern Task Force lands in Algiers. The 34th US Infantry Division is accompanied by a brigade from the 78th British Infantry Division and two commando units. They meet no opposition, as the artillery guns were destroyed by the Resistance, and some GIs are even welcomed with open arms by French soldiers. General Juin, who had been captured in 1940 by the Germans and then released to command Vichy troops in Africa, opens the gates of city to the Allied troops at 6 pm. The following year, he will lead the French Expeditionary Force in Italy, alongside the Allies.

Admiral Darlan, a convinced Vichyist at the head of the Navy and the most experienced French officer in North Africa, was in Algiers on the night of the landing. Immediately captured by a pro-Allied group, he receives an offer from Eisenhower: if he orders a ceasefire for the French troops and changes sides, he would be appointed Commander of the French troops in North Africa. He accepts on November 10, but is murdered by a young resistant student six weeks later. Not liking de Gaulle, Roosevelt appoints General Henri Giraud as a replacement. The offer made to Darlan caused a genuine outcry among Gaullists and Allied countries, but it had a further consequence: in retaliation, Hitler ordered the invasion of the South of France that very evening (*Operation Anton*).

There is now no longer a free zone, which pushes many French soldiers to join the Allied cause (among them, General de Lattre de Tassigny, who fled by plane and will later command the 1st French Army). French ships in Toulon are scuttled before the Germans arrive to prevent them from falling into their hands, while in the meantime, the Wehrmacht lands in Tunisia.

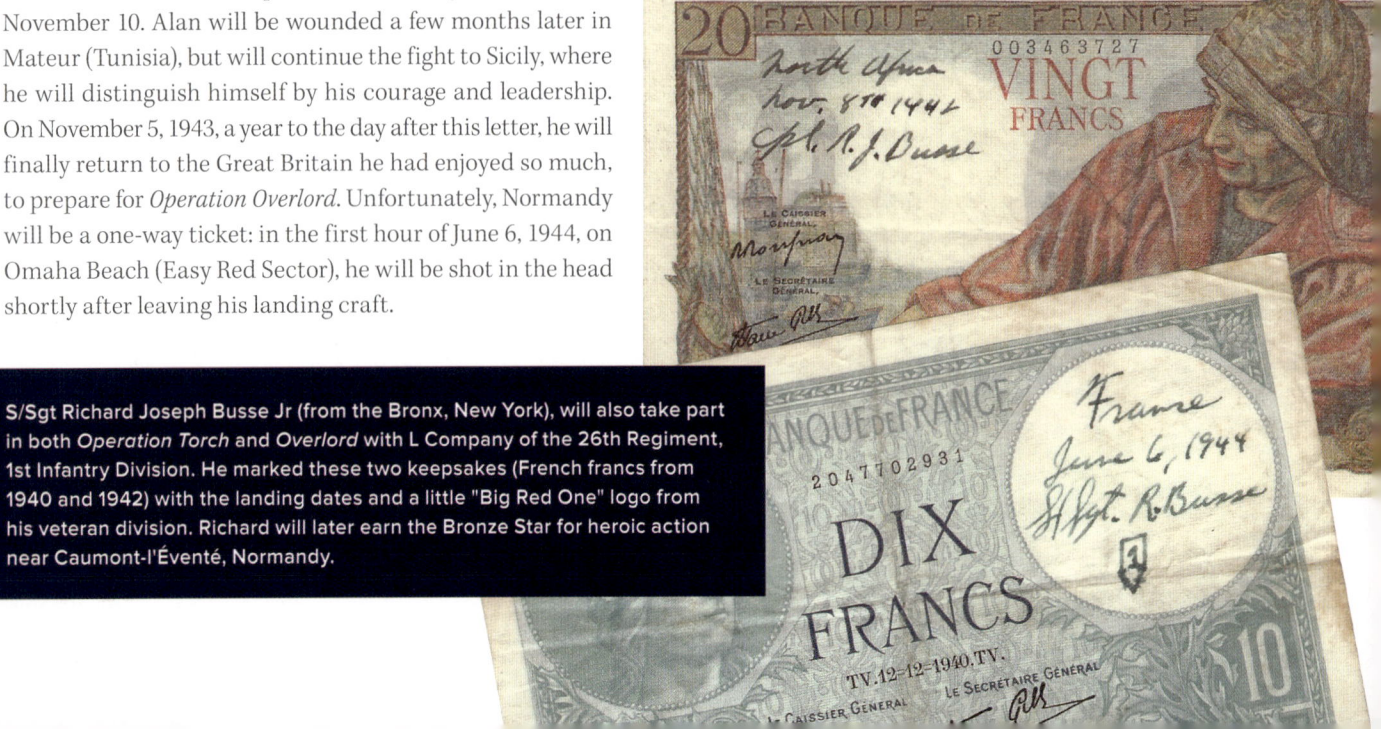

S/Sgt Richard Joseph Busse Jr (from the Bronx, New York), will also take part in both *Operation Torch* and *Overlord* with L Company of the 26th Regiment, 1st Infantry Division. He marked these two keepsakes (French francs from 1940 and 1942) with the landing dates and a little "Big Red One" logo from his veteran division. Richard will later earn the Bronze Star for heroic action near Caumont-l'Éventé, Normandy.

II - THE COUNTER-ATTACK 1942-1943

The GI's uniform differs from that of the British in its very 'sports-like' aspect. The M41 jacket is light and comfortable and will inspire post-war civilian clothing. It's worn over a woolen shirt and pants tucked into canvas leggings (the ones worn here bear the stenciled name of their owner, C. W. Morley).

The new round M1 helmet, here covered with a British small mesh net, consists of a steel shell encircled by an anti-magnetic seam, and a fiber liner at the beginning of the war (as seen here), and then a composite (low or high pressure) one, which was more resistant.

Under his left arm, this soldier wears a gas mask bag in the event of a chemical attack. On his back, the Haversack M1928 contains the GI's toiletries kit, rations and personal effects, but is scorned by the GIs because of its lack of practicality. The shovel is hung directly on the top of the bag and surmounted by the mess kit in a bag. This mess kit bag was marked with the nickname of its owner, 'Tex', near the strap - a Texan?

This 'Yank' pinned an American flag (48 stars at the time) on his sleeve, in the hope of preventing any reaction from the Vichy forces. This way, he will not be mistaken for a British soldier, for whom the French may still feel some resentment following the attack on Mers el-Kebir or the evacuation of the BEF in 1940.

99

HELL ON WHEELS IN MOROCCO

The 2nd Armored Division, nicknamed 'Hell on Wheels', is one of the first American units engaged in the European and Mediterranean theater. It was trained by General George S. Patton, a fearless and impulsive leader with the appearance of a cowboy. His taste for spectacle and thirst for victory would soon make him the most famous general in the US Army. He will teach his men: *"No bastard ever won a war by dying for his country. He won it by making the other poor dumb bastard die for his country."* The division lands as part of the Western Task Force in Morocco, in support of the 3rd and 9th US Infantry Divisions. Vichy's coastal artillery fired first, and the young and green GIs are quickly targeted by French snipers. The latter finally give up later in the day and the last pockets of resistance are cleaned up two days later, allowing the Americans to rush towards Casablanca and start the siege of the city. On November 10, the port is surrounded by Patton's troops (then commander of the Task Force), and the French surrender just before the final assault.

James, a member of the 2nd Armored Division, writes to his fiancée: *"You will probably know by the time you get this letter that I am no longer in the United States but am now in Africa. Here we are allowed one letter a day, and no more. [...] If I answered [all of your questions] I might be helping the enemy, and also endanger myself, as well as millions of lives. I might even lose my job. No joking, I don't answer all of them because I can't. Someday this can all be explained, for I dislike it as much and if not more than you. You and Mom must believe me and try to understand. I have been in the Army now for 10 months and I still don't understand it, so I don't see how you can. [...] It is a very strange place. There is a lot of places of interest here, and the natives here, well they are not what I expected them to be like. Their living conditions are the best that can be expected. Their language – they sound like a bunch of monkeys on the warpath. You probably would like to know about how their homes look, or would you. Well, I can give you a rough idea. Their homes from a distance look very nice, built with stone. They are very clean looking from the outside, of course I have never been in the inside. They are not very large. Most of the homes are white with the exception of a few, which are cream, about the shade of the desert sand. I forgot to tell you further up in this letter about their dress. Well I will add a little more to what I have said. They dress with a long white or gray robe, something like the sisters at the College, with the exception of the stretch band over their heads that the veil covers. The girls just put a white or grey piece of cloth over their head, something like the monks, if you remember your Greek history."*

The Armored Division will be deployed in Beja, Tunisia, in support of the 78th British Division, where it will use the new Sherman M4 tanks for the first time, replacing the old M3 tanks. However, it will spend most of the campaign at rest and training, as it was designated for the next invasion of Sicily. James writes again about Africa: *"Writing another letter I try to translate a multitude of thoughts into a sensible message. It is always the same things of which I think and write of. I miss you so very much, that is always the uppermost thing. Then always there is the hopeful wish that the war will soon end, bringing peace, and most important, [me] home to you. It is incredible how one thinks of home here. No amount of time or no condition can change the firm belief that it is the best. Any unpleasantness immediately prompts a mental comparison of its advantages with those of the moment. Without you it is impossible to think of that heaven. You predominate all my thoughts of it. I picture our home, the things we did, and those we pretend to do. [...]*

Your letters have become to me as important as eating and sleeping darling. It is another harvesting season here again, it is slow and laborious, done by ancient hand methods which have long ago become extinct in our country. In spite of all the difficulty the people do manage to produce large crops, mostly of grain. [...] I'm in the best of health and have grown quite tanned from the sun. Africa's hot, but not nearly as bad as one might expect, and the nights are always delightfully cool. [...] Darling here is something that I think is worth studying, you may call it what you like, but it struck me to be very good. See what you think about it. It is not only houses which are haunted by the ghosts of men. Often men are haunted by the restless phantoms of once familiar homes. It is not that we are homesick, it is only that we are aware of what we have left behind. I doubt if there is one among us who would forsake the battle while America's war frontiers are so far-flung."

Operation Torch killed 500 American and British soldiers, and 1,400 French troops. The attitude of all French forces in North Africa will remain uncertain until November 22, when they will officially side with the Allies. Together, they will move towards their new objective: Tunis. Although the advance in Morocco and Algeria was as fast as it was encouraging for the inexperienced GIs, the Allies acknowledge that the handling of the landings had been catastrophic, and they consider themselves lucky not to have had to face veteran Wehrmacht troops. There is much needed room for improvement before they can hope to set foot in Europe. In the meantime, they will soon meet Hitler's armies in Tunisia. The first German soldiers had landed there as soon as Algiers and Oran fell, in order to reinforce Rommel's Afrika Korps retreating to the north, and they will refuse to leave the Allies a base within Italy's reach.

VOYD TROMBLEE

168th Infantry Regiment, 34th Infantry Division

Voyd is in charge of an infantry company in one of the first American divisions engaged on the Western Front. After Operation Torch, he will lead his company through Tunisia to Bizerte, but not without difficulty.

Voyd is a 32-year-old printer who already has military experience, rising through the ranks to become a 1st lieutenant in the National Guard. In February 1941, his unit was activated and left for Camp Claiborne, Louisiana.

THE 'RED BULL' DIVISION

The 34th Division was formed in 1917 but was sent to France too late to reach the trenches of the First World War. Its shoulder patch, designed by an artist in the unit, is a souvenir of their maneuvers in the New Mexico desert and represents a red bull's skull on a black olla (Mexican jar). Twenty-five years later, the Germans will naturally nickname them the 'Red Bulls'. The 4,508 men of the three infantry regiments (the 133rd, 135th and Voyd's 168th) shipped out of New York in early 1942 for Northern Ireland, where they trained for the invasion of North Africa. There, their commander Major-General Russell Hartle established the first Ranger battalion, an elite unit inspired by British commandos and composed largely of former members of the 34th Division. Hartle placed his aide-de-camp, Captain William Darby, at the head of the Rangers when he left the division to take command of V Corps. For *Operation Torch*, the division is commanded by Major-General Charles Ryder, a veteran of the First World War.

On November 8, 1942, Voyd and the 34th Infantry Division land near Algiers and advance to Tunisia with the 1st British Army, which includes the V and IX British Corps, the XIX French Corps, and the II American Corps. Voyd writes to his girlfriend: *"The Limeys [British] are doing a swell job and saved our shins several times, so are the French. They are sure tired of German domination, you know the way they were set up in Algeria, it amounted to occupation. That's all over and do the French ever appreciate their freedom!"*. He quickly gets used to sleeping in the wadis (dry river beds), even if he can't stand the weather and local wildlife: *"The fleas are eating me alive, Jesus! They have everything over here, snakes, scorpions, fleas, mosquitoes, and buzzards like you never saw before, and also rain and cold and later on 120°F [50°C] in the shade."*

ROMMEL FORCES THE GIs TO WITHDRAW

Voyd leaves B Company (1st Battalion) to be appointed commanding officer of K Company (3rd Battalion), without being promoted to captain. At 32, he looks old among all these young GIs of barely 20 years of age. He's frustrated that these promotions are often given to younger and green soldiers. Incidentally, experience is precisely what the Americans will lack and need as they move eastward.

Indeed, the Allies encounter fierce resistance when taking a succession of mountain passes. At the beginning of 1943, they hold a line stretching from Fondouk to Gafsa, via Faïd. Facing them, driven out of Libya by the 8th Army which had just retaken Tripoli on January 23, the veteran Afrika Korps rushes towards the north of Tunisia (although Rommel left behind some troops on the Mareth Line, built by the French to defend Tunisia). On January 30, the Afrika Korps collides with the lines of the 1st Army advancing from the west. The French cannot contain the 21. Panzer-Division in Faïd, and the 1st US Armored Division doesn't fare any better: each of its objectives is already occupied by German troops who would rather die than let them fall into enemy hands.

Further south, the 1st Battalion of the 168th Regiment succeeds in retaking Sened on February 1, thanks in part to the assault of Captain Bird, commander of Voyd's former B Company. However, this feat of arms costs the battalion more than 200 casualties, including its commander, Lt-Col. John Petty, from a fatal stomach wound. Furthermore, in the days that follow, the 'Red Bulls' would watch helplessly as Allied troops flee backwards, their haggard soldiers crammed into trucks targeted by the Luftwaffe. The GIs would hold the line until February 4, then have no choice but to withdraw. Voyd, sent as reinforcements with his company, has health concerns and is sent to the hospital in Algiers, from where he writes to his future wife: *"The nurse brought me a few books to read and wanted to know if I know Lt. M. who had been with us at Claiborne. It seems they are THAT way about each other and since he is now at the front she is very worried for his safety. I am too, but didn't tell her as Rommel's outfit cut hell out of his Battalion the other day with about 70 medium tanks. The Battalion stopped the tanks and were holding them awaiting reinforcements when we were ordered up to replace them, however I ended up here and the outfit has pulled out for the front now."*

On February 14, the Germans resume the offensive in Sidi Bouzid. In 48 hours, the 1st Armored men will lose two tank battalions and their artillery support. On its own against the 10. and 21. Panzer-Divisions, the infantry alone won't last long. Voyd doesn't yet realize that he's escaped tragedy again, stuck in the hospital, as it's now his 3rd Battalion that is destroyed. After three days of fighting and an armored counter-attack on February 15 that turns into a disaster, the 'Red Bulls' isolated in Jebel Ksaïra have to find a way to get back to the Allied lines. On the morning of the 17th, Colonel Drake tries to evacuate the battalion across the desert, but it's spotted by a German column, opening fire with heavy machine guns. The GIs try a desperate but futile resistance until all their ammunition is exhausted, and the 1,400 survivors are eventually captured. Sentenced to walk with an empty stomach and no water, after three days without food the soldiers that are too weak to advance are shot dead. The others will stop in Sfax, before leaving for the Stalags.

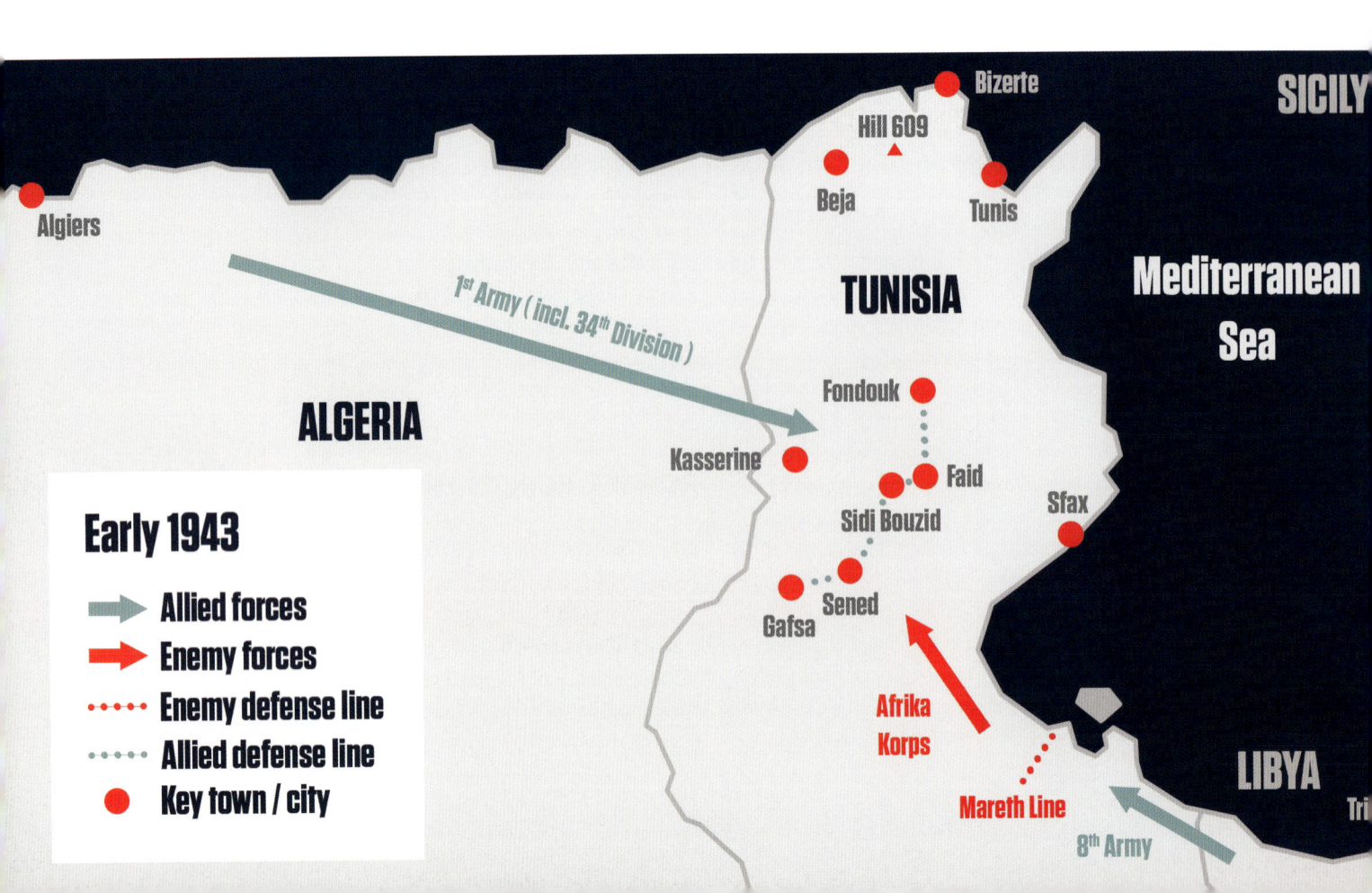

II - THE COUNTER-ATTACK 1942-1943

KASSERINE PASS

Rommel goes westward, as the Allies withdraw to Kasserine Pass, which looks easier to defend. On February 19, the formidable Panzer IV tanks are there. Panic spreads among the GIs, who pull out once again, abandoning their equipment in the field. American counter-attacks are too slow or fail from the get-go, and the Germans wreak havoc in the Allied ranks. If Rommel crosses the pass, he might well send the 1st Army back to Algeria.

Finally, the Allies send reinforcements to Kasserine on the night of the 21st, which the Germans had failed to do and thus exploit their advantage. British and French infantry units, supported by the 9th US Infantry Division's artillery, consolidate the American lines. Faced with this unexpected resistance and fearing for its rear-guard (the 8th Army in Libya was about to cross the Mareth Line), Rommel withdraws to the east. On February 23, the Americans launch a major offensive to regain the lost ground, including Kasserine pass two days later. The ground is covered with hundreds of tanks, burned-out vehicles, and American corpses: Fredendall's II Corps lost more than 6,000 men.

When he joins the regiment, Voyd is worried about two of his friends who stayed in his old company: *"The campaign is going very well now but it is too bad for most of our outfit, still hear nothing from D. and B., apparently they were killed or captured along with the rest that were lost at that time, sure hope not, but may as well be prepared for the worst as they took one hell of a beating and dished out very little. Infantry against tanks don't stand much of a chance unless properly supported by anti-tank weapons and they had very, very few to support them. After the Division received support it really went to town on the Axis. They are still running with the Yanks right behind jabbing them every step of the way."* Voyd will later learn that his two friends are safe.

The sad reality is that no GIs have been trained to use the bazooka, and the most experienced crews have never tested the new Sherman M4 tank before. The Germans fully understand the problem of the US Army in early 1943: despite its advanced equipment, the lack of experience of the 'Yanks' and their commanding officers is a huge disadvantage against the Axis veterans. Indeed, the American replacements have never fired a shot, and are facing an enemy who has been fighting in the desert since 1940. The division therefore plans special training courses to upgrade the troops. In March 1943, Fredendall is replaced by Patton at the head of the II US Corps, taking over his troops with an iron fist. For the Americans, there is no way the Kasserine disaster will happen again.

THE BATTLE OF FONDOUK GAP

Naturally, this setback is a terrible blow to the division's morale, and it will not be the last. On March 27, while the 1st Infantry Division liberates Gafsa and El Guettar, and the 1st Armored has just retaken Sened, the 'Red Bulls' attack Jebel el Haouareb, near Funduq al'Uqbi (Fondouk Gap). They have to drive the enemy out of the mountains and open the way to the Kairouan Plain in the east, in order to cut the Wehrmacht in half and isolate it in the south and north of Tunisia. Attached to the British IX Corps, the 'Red Bulls' fail in their first attempt and suffer hundreds of casualties. Voyd writes: *"Well here it is, about the 14th day of this battle [...]. We have been fighting continuously for a long time now, it seems to be almost finished in the theater now. The going is plenty tough. These S.O.B.s don't know when they are beaten. We are up against troops whose business it was to teach other troops to fight and they are plenty good at fighting themselves. Thank God for the French and Limeys if it hadn't been for them many times we would have had our clocks cleaned."* They will also receive support from the British 6th Armoured Division and French units for a second assault in early April.

Soldiers of the 1st US Division 'Big Red One' in the Kasserine Pass.

On April 12, Voyd recounts the last hours of fighting at Fondouk Gap: *"We were in the line this last time exactly 18 days with some fighting every day and a hell of a lot of fighting a lot of days. One evening I had to make a trip to Division's HQ, it was just turning dark and the road ran parallel to the Schicklgrubers* [the surname of Hitler's father, Alois, Maria Anna Schicklgruber's illegitimate son] *position, over a high hill. He got a peep ahead of mine and proceeded to chase me down the road, dropping shells ahead and behind all the way. We out boxed him by driving fast when a shell hit ahead of us and slow when he hit behind us, a lot of fun as long as he missed us. [...] For three days before they pulled out here we pounded them with artillery constantly, it sounded like a constant rumble of thunder. We reduced several of their positions with infantry at night and then the British cracked through with their armored division and those boys sure know how to fight. They are a little jealous of the 8th Army and wanted to get a little glory for themselves. We took many prisoners and turned them over to the Limeys so they got credit for them too. They really deserve it though as they have done some great work. So did we."* Fondouk Gap is in Allied hands the next day. The division can return to II Corps before undergoing a week of intensive training in Makthar.

The 8th Army finally joins the fight in Tunisia, breaking the Mareth Line in late March 1943 by bypassing it (*Operation Supercharge II*). It lost nearly 4,000 men in the battle, but it convinces Rommel that his own was lost. He returns to Germany to try and persuade Hitler that Tunisia is untenable, and that the Afrika Korps has to be evacuated to Europe. Hitler refuses and Rommel is sidelined. Meanwhile, the traumatized 1st Army and the experienced warriors of the 8th Army link up and join forces on April 7.

However, the enemy now cornered in the north of the country is more dangerous than ever. On April 26, in Beja, where his regiment came to assist the 'Big Red One', Voyd learns of the death of a young friend of his former company, killed by a German artillery shell: *"I feel quite bad over it as he was so full of dreams and plans for the future, and was always so tickled to see me and tell about his baby, which he never got to see!"*

OPERATION VULCAN

The Allies' final objective in North Africa is to capture the ports of Tunis (for the British) and Bizerte (for the Americans), which the Germans use to land equipment and reinforcements from Sicily.

HILL 609, TUNISIA, USED BY NAZIS IN LAST STAND.
US Army Photo 152-9

Unfortunately, blocking their path is Hill 609 (Jabal Tahent, see photo), whose fortified heights control the road from Beja to Mateur and the access to both ports. The mission of taking Hill 609 is assigned to the 34th Division.

The attack begins on the morning of April 29, 1943, when a battalion of the 135th Regiment takes a small village at the foot of the hill. The rest of the division then rushes to the top under heavy enemy fire. The fighting lasts two days, and the 2nd Battalion of the 168th Regiment (to which Voyd, commanding officer of E Company, now belongs) occupies its plateau the next day. On the 31st, the 'Red Bulls' repel a German counter-attack with their devastating firepower, causing the German bastion's fall on May 1, and the collapse of the last enemy defense line. The 34th Division crosses the Chouigui Pass, led by Voyd's company, then advances towards Tébourba. Voyd recounts in detail the engagement in a V-mail of May 5: *"We have cracked through the mountains opening a road to Tebourba for one of our armored divisions. It was tough fighting for four days but I received considerable credit for the excellent operation of 'E' company which I was, should I say, unfortunate enough to command. We took every hill on a thousand yard front clear through to the top of hills that overlooked the road through the pass. The Germans had organized with special crack air corps and infantry troops armed with machine pistols, machine guns or sniper rifles with telescope sights but they admitted the American soldier was too tough for them.*

In the initial attack my company accounted for 45 POWs and over ninety killed. One English speaking Jerry said we had annihilated his entire company in less than two hours after we made first contact. I was pinned in the middle of a large wheat field for two hours laying on a path with Jerry sniping at us every time we stirred a stalk of wheat. Finally passed word back for Major Bird, who is my firm friend as you know, to come up and extricate me. There was myself, my 1st platoon leader and eight men there and my green lovies were afraid to place covering fire on the hill overlooking the wheat field, because there might be

II - THE COUNTER-ATTACK 1942-1943

friendly troops there, but old Birdie slammed the light gun in and covered the hill with machine gun fire and yours truly got up and walked across the field. We bypassed the hill and moved on to our objective killing only a few Jerries and then we went to work on our main objective. That's where we have done the annihilating, we made a 1000-yard salient and made it possible for the rest of the battalion to advance."

END OF THE AFRICAN CAMPAIGN

The 1st Armored Division is now able to chase the Germans to Mateur, then Bizerte, which falls to the 9th US Infantry Division on May 7, 1943. Tunis is taken on the same day by the British V Corps, while the British IX Corps, the French XIX Corps and the 8th Army arriving from the south are clearing out the base at Cap Bon. German troops in Tunisia sign the armistice on May 11, and the North African Campaign officially ends on May 13, 1943.

On May 20, Voyd writes to his girlfriend Mary: *"Just another lazy day here on the shore of the bay of Bizerte, what a lovely place that was! Only shambles, like San Francisco after the big quake, now. If this is only a sample of what we are doing to German cities, they finally know what it is to have their country devastated by shells and bombs. We are resting by acting as subs for the stevedores, the men enjoy it for a change as it gives them a chance to display their frown and muscles, they are pretty husky lads on the average. One of my company's engagements was picked as the most outstanding and decisive in the campaign.*

I didn't realize just how good it was till we had assembled the messages and orders and began to tell the story in continuity instead of by little individual actions, then it began to come clear and it reads just like an Infantry School problem like I used to work at Fort Benning (remember?). The Colonel and General Ryder both were very well pleased and Ryder said it read like something out of the book, and the Colonel said 'No! I don't think any of the officers are good enough authors to have made it up!'. So I guess 'E' don't set all right now! Just a little bragging to which I am entitled as my company is the best in the best battalion in the best Regiment in the best Division.

[This] Undoubtedly means a promotion for me and my junior officers I hope, as least for them. It shows something at least in that I was assigned to 'G' as platoon leader but Major Bird (my old friend) puts me in command of 'E', at this time there were at least six captains available to assume command of 'E' but they put a 1st Lieutenant in to take the company through the hottest battle in the entire campaign, now it's going to be sort of difficult to explain why that 1st Lieutenant isn't due for a promotion. Don't you think so? Or even why for the last 2 years he's been kicked in the **** every time the opportunity presented itself. I've said before I don't particularly care for captains [...]. What I am proud of is that I led my outfit through five days of fighting, lost only 1 officer and 3 men, less than a dozen wounded, none of my men taken prisoner, killed 30 to 1 of [the] enemy, took fifty prisoners, and were going strong when the enemy took to his heels and ran for Tunis failing to reach there because our armored unit went through the pass we opened and caught them on the plains beyond the mountain range we had been fighting for."

For the British soldiers, this was the end of a long, bloody campaign that began in the summer of 1940. In return, they were awarded the Africa Star. This one belonged to a veteran of the 8th Army, as shown by the small bar sewn on to the ribbon.

Around 275,000 German and Italian soldiers were captured at the fall of Bizerte and Tunis. Albert, a lieutenant in the 2639th Quartermaster Truck Battalion, watches the end of the campaign and is impressed by the large number of prisoners his unit has to carry across the desert: *"Dear Jim, received a letter from my father, saying that the local received the Army and Navy Award* [see below]. *Keep up the good work, and it won't be long before we pin back the ears of the Axis. Haven't been so busy since the close of this campaign, with the exception of the first weeks. When we worked day and nights hauling back tens of thousands of prisoners to rear area camps. To hear them talk you'd think we haven't got a chance to win the war. The reason they give you for the fact that their planes have disappeared from the air is that they're being used to bomb New York twice a day. They're all filled up to the ears with absurd propaganda and they're all stupid enough to believe it. Funny thing though the way they up and quit when the going got a little tough. Very strange thing for Supermen to do, don't you think? I picked myself up a German automobile the other day and have been using it for pleasure trips to such historical places as Tunis and Carthage."*

At the beginning of his letter, Albert refers to this 'Army-Navy E Award', which was presented to companies that had contributed to the war effort by achieving 'Excellence in Production' ('E') of war equipment.

Following the African Campaign, the 34th Division doesn't participate in the invasion of Sicily, but instead trains for the future Italian Campaign. Voyd writes: *"We had a picture here the other night called* Random Harvest, *it was very good but made me horribly home sick for you, it was very poor for my morale at least as it clearly showed the attitude of the people when you have been gone two or three years [...]. The day we left Trenton is still as near as yesterday to me with all that's happened in between more or less of a nightmare. We don't expect the people at home to feel quite that way as most people still don't realize what war is, they see a lot of uniforms and damn few soldiers, I believe you still think enough like me to know I mean it takes more than a uniform to make a soldier and more than a few rationings* [sic] *to make people realize what's going on over here."*

Voyd is finally promoted to captain in early August. Two weeks later, he suffers from nasty dysentery in addition to his kidney and back problems, but this doesn't prevent him from training as hard as his comrades for the invasion of mainland Europe. He writes on August 29: *"I guess all the world knows by now that the time for an all-out invasion draws nearer every day. I am a little uneasy myself about the outcome, personally, but it's getting very tiresome just training for one. We are in a good trim for battle as any troops ever were and are anxious to try our mettle again. There's seems to be a general opinion back there that we were a little lacking in courage at Foundouk, expressed by arm chair soldiers never close to an enemy more dangerous than a few bombers. I have utter trust in my own men, my present NCOs were all with me at Eddekhila and Chouigui and I know what they can and will do and my men all seem to be go-getters. This shall be my last campaign regardless if and when it comes, I can feel my grip relaxing and seem to be unable to concentrate my interest in anything military. I have grown to hate the sight on anything in uniform and I shall be glad when it's possible for us to be just plain Mr. Tromblee & wife. I'm not so conceited to think there is no younger healthier man that can take my place, I feel I'm entitled to a damn good rest and chance to rebuild my health but won't do it here and have my friends have reason to say I took the easy way before a fight but God Damn! They better hurry up 'cause I don't believe I got the guts to keep going a hell of a lot longer."*

Voyd's health problems will only get worse in early September, when he'll finally be removed from the lines. He'll leave the division after another stay in hospital, only a few days before the invasion for which he had trained so hard. Upon his release in November, he'll be posted to the US Army Air Forces Air Transport Command, where he'll continue his post-war career. Voyd will finally be able to return to the United States on June 18, 1944 and will marry Mary without further delay.

The 34th Division, for its part, will face heavy fighting in Italy. After 517 days at the front (611 for some of its units), it will count 7,197 dead and missing, 14,165 wounded, 99 Distinguished Service Medals and no less than 11 Medals of Honor (the highest American distinction).

III

THE SOFT UNDERBELLY

From Sicily to Rome

On May 7, 1943, the Royal Navy launches an operation in Malta to prevent the evacuation of German and Italian forces from Tunisia to Sicily. British Admiral Andrew Cunningham names it *Operation Retribution*, in memory of the losses inflicted on its fleet during the battles for Greece and Crete. His order: *"Sink, burn and destroy. Let nothing pass!"* Among the ships taking part in this action is HMS *Exmoor*, which still has Henry on board, the sailor who was learning how to swim (see page 48). He writes to his fiancée: *"We are still giving Jerry a good deal of punishment and I hope we keep it up!"* Confirming that things have been *"lively out here"*, he adds: *"It will soon be over and we should stand a better chance of getting home"*. A total of 897 fugitives are captured by the Allies and although a few hundred manage to escape, many drown while trying to reach Europe by any means possible. Two days after the armistice in Africa, the sea route from Gibraltar to Alexandria is reopened for the first time in two years.

The Allies have taken the decision to attack the Italian peninsula and more particularly Sicily, which seems to be their best gateway to 'Hitler's European Fortress'. As Churchill describes it to Stalin, the Mediterranean looks like the soft underbelly of a crocodile. The island is defended by 230,000 Italians, mainly coastal defense units which aren't considered particularly dangerous (the best soldiers having been lost in Africa) and two German armored divisions. The capture of Sicily would also secure convoys in the Mediterranean and relieve Malta from incessant German air raids.

OPERATION HUSKY

'Husky', like *Operation Overlord* less than a year later, is facilitated by an effective misinformation campaign (*Operation Mincemeat*): a corpse dressed as a Royal Marines officer was voluntarily abandoned on a Spanish beach from a submarine, with false documents detailing an Allied landing in Greece, Sardinia and the Balkans. Hitler fell into the trap and moved troops to defend these coasts to the detriment of Sicily. One of the men behind the plan was Ian Fleming, who would later invent the character of James Bond.

From July 10, 1943, 180,000 soldiers, 600 tanks, and 14,000 vehicles will land on various Sicilian beaches during the first three days. They belong to the new American 7th Army (Patton's old I Armored Corps, renamed the same day) and the British 8th Army (still led by Montgomery). The two armies will be supported by four airborne missions and a naval escort. HMS *Exmoor* was selected in June for the latter and Henry writes to his girlfriend a few weeks later: *"It's only another month now darling before you enter the Land Army [agricultural labor in the UK] and I wish I could get home before you go, but this seems impossible as there is a lot of work for us out here. I put my request in some time this month for my name to on the 'roster'. This is like a waiting list, a long one it is too, you can request for this when you've been away twenty-one months and I have by the twenty-fifth of this month so I'll be staying in, although you must realize darling that this don't mean I'll come home right away as you have to wait your turn."*

HMS *Exmoor* was assigned to the escort convoy 'P' and left Port-Saïd in Egypt on July 5 to protect the assault force towards the beach code-named 'Bark West', at the far southeastern tip of the island. The 1st Canadian Infantry Division has to land there, accompanied by tanks and British commandos. The British 51st (Highland) Division will disembark on its right, opposite Pachino, and further north, the British 5th and 50th Infantry Divisions between Pachino and Syracuse.

1942 Patch of the 51st (Highland) Division.

In a letter dated August 2, 1943, Henry talks about the anxious approach to the Sicilian coast: *"I promised you I'll tell you about our bit in the invasion of Sicily, well darling we escorted the Eighth Army across to Sicily and then we led the way into the beach, we were the first ship in at the port where the Eighth landed. We laid about a mile offshore waiting for the troops and commandos, we have about an hour and half to wait before things started and I can tell you darling I was glad when the first of the invasion crafts began to pass us. If they had been spotted, our job then would have been to lead them right onto the beaches and cover them with our gunfire, but luckily they were not seen. At first while we were waiting right inshore for things to start there was a searchlight that kept just missing us, it's a miracle to me how they never spotted us. Anyhow they gave us a few uncomfortable moments, we were waiting there for over an hour and a half before the landing started. Once the Army got ashore the searchlight soon went out; we stayed there till it got light and then we went along the beach looking for pill-boxes and other targets but there were none left, the Army must have finished them off. Of course there were gun batteries a bit further inshore but they were silenced after a time either by our big ships or else by the Army."*

HMS *Exmoor* mostly defends the beach from the Stukas and Messerschmitt Bf-110s, in addition to enemy ships and submarines, which still remain a constant threat to the invasion fleet. It then quickly bypasses the Pachino peninsula to sail up to Syracuse.

This last port city falls during the day without much resistance. Caught between the paratroopers (who arrived by glider the night before) and the British special forces (the newly created but already feared SAS), the Italians flee north. In their haste, they forget to destroy the port facilities, leaving them intact to the Allies.

ADMIRALS CLASH IN AUGUSTA

Henry's ship sails alongside the fortifications of Syracusa-Augusta, Sicily's largest coastal defense system (twenty-three anti-aircraft and naval batteries, numerous bunkers and minefields and hundreds of machine guns over some 20 miles). Carried away by the prevailing panic, the Italian fascist militia (the 'black shirts') in charge of these positions also left Augusta in the hope of reaching Italy. The fortifications are thus deserted even before they are threatened, to the great despair of Admiral Priamo Leonardi, commander of the area. As the British 5th Infantry Division approached the port of Augusta, reports indicated late at night that the enemy had evacuated it. HMS *Exmoor*, which carries British Admiral Troubridge (transferred from HMS *Eskimo* after it had been damaged by an aerial bomb in front of Syracuse), is therefore sent to the site to verify the information. The destroyer enters a deserted harbor on July 11 at 10:45 am, but is suddenly attacked by a cannon hidden behind trees, prompting it to leave the area.

Letter from Henry about his actions during *Operation Husky*.

III - THE SOFT UNDERBELLY 1943-1944

The *White Ensign*, the Royal Navy's flag.

What has actually happened is rather unusual. HMS *Exmoor* was attacked by Admiral Leonardi himself, who, along with his second in command, aimed at the ship with an abandoned gun. He then manages to assemble a few black shirts to occupy other defenses, and when HMS *Exmoor* returns a few hours later with the Greek destroyer *Kanaris*, they come under direct fire and have to withdraw as well. Finally, under heavy coastal artillery and machine gun fire, the British commandos landing on July 12 are too much for the defenders. The Italians send a battalion of the Naples Division to retake the port, but the British counter-attack in force and liberate Augusta for good on July 13. Syracuse falls on the same day, and soon after, both ports would be operating at full speed for the benefit of the Allies.

Today, the port of Augusta is much more peaceful.

Henry tells his girlfriend about this engagement, in the same letter of August 2, 1943: *"I expect you heard about the ship on the wireless darling that went into Augusta Harbour, sent a party ashore to hoist the White Ensign on the church tower and then waited for the Eighth Army to capture the town, well darling, that was our little ship, it was on the radio so I expect you heard it, I bet you'll be surprised to learn it was us though as they never mentioned the name, they just said 'a destroyer'. We had a pretty warm time of it as we were right behind Jerry's lines and we were engaging his 'tiger tanks'* [the new German Tiger tank, a 56-ton mastodon with thick armor and armed with an 88-mm gun, is the terror of the Allies who see them everywhere. However, Henry might actually have seen a regular 88-mm gun] *and gun batteries which were firing on us from shore, still we came through it all OK so don't get worrying darling and we're alright now. Things are a bit quieter now but we're still busy."*

July 10-13, 1943

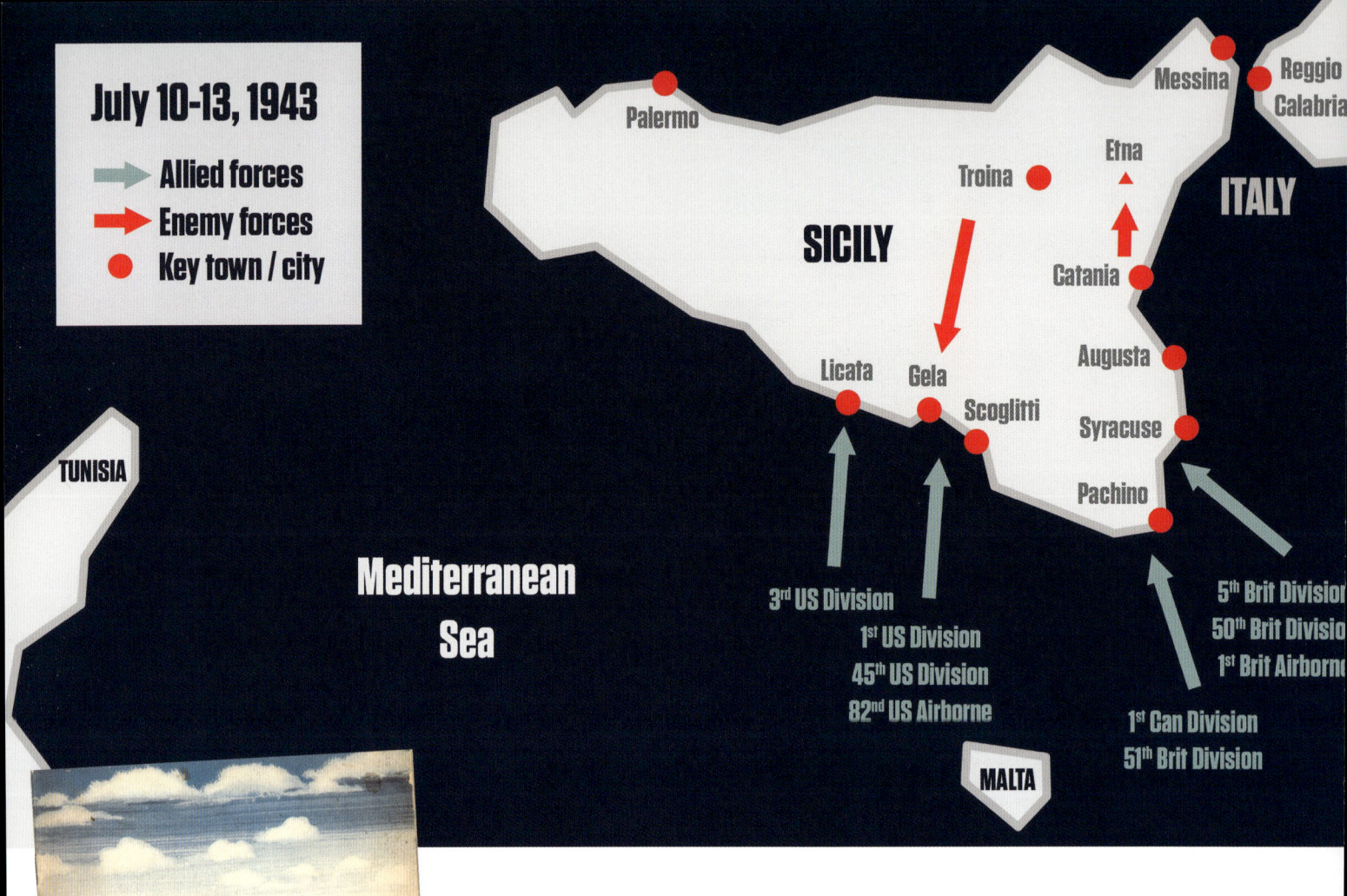

→ Allied forces
→ Enemy forces
● Key town / city

Palermo • Messina • Reggio Calabria
Troina • Etna ▲
SICILY
Catania
Licata • Gela • Scoglitti
Augusta
Syracuse
Pachino
ITALY

TUNISIA

Mediterranean Sea

3rd US Division
1st US Division
45th US Division
82nd US Airborne

5th Brit Division
50th Brit Division
1st Brit Airborne

1st Can Division
51st Brit Division

MALTA

Palermo tourist brochure brought back by a GI.

THE AMERICAN PROGRESSION

On the south coast, the American 7th Army lands on two sectors: to the east in Gela and Scoglitti, the 1st and 45th US Infantry Divisions are supported by the American paratroopers of the 82nd Airborne Division, while to the west, the 3rd US Infantry Division hits the beach at Licata. The Yanks have a successful first day, despite significant German resistance. James' 2nd US Armored Division tanks, which we have followed in North Africa (page 100), arrive in Gela on July 11. They have installed the Scorpion system at the front of their Sherman M4s, which rotate chains that violently whip the ground, exploding possible mines and opening a safe passage for infantry troops. James' battalion is in support of the 1st 'Big Red One' Division, which is supposed to capture the city. The fighting becomes particularly brutal when the 'Hermann Göring' Panzer Division throws its tanks at the bridgehead, before being repelled.

The Americans then head northwest along two parallel roads. General Patton organizes a battle group comprising the 2nd Armored Division, the 3rd US Infantry Division and the 82nd Airborne, with his eyes fixed on Palermo. The Task Force will swallow 100 miles in three days and clean up the whole of western Sicily only two weeks after the landings. Patton thus demonstrates the effectiveness of the cooperation between the infantry and the 2nd Armored tanks he had personally trained. He enters Palermo on July 22 without encountering any resistance. The Germans had fled the city before the Americans arrived, destroying many buildings in their retreat and killing civilians for revenge. The GIs also benefited from the help of the local mafia and the inhabitants, many of whom had family members in the United States.

James has a deep disgust for this island, which he expresses in a V-mail: *"Well to tell you something of this place. No, I wish I could tell you the whole story of this place, but the censor won't allow it. But I will tell you this much, and then you read between the lines. Once an American soldier comes to this island, he will never want to come back. The people here don't live, they only exist. I think that might give you a rough idea of the place. I thought that Africa was hot, but this is twice as bad. I rather not tell you any more of the place, but I think you understand what I am trying to tell you. I made it alright, although it was rough going for a while. I was in the invasion of Sicily and saw a*

III - THE SOFT UNDERBELLY 1943-1944

few things that I was hoping not to have anything to do with, but now that it is all over, I will try and forget it for a while, and think about that little bit of heaven I have back in good old America. [...] Back in America I was used to see nothing but automobiles, but here there is [sic] very few. Their main way of transportation is by horse and buggy. Their buildings are all made of rock and what they do for a living, well I don't think they do more than peddle, some of the girls work in shoe factories, what little they do have, one I believe. Everything is so different, that it will take me a little while longer to get used to it. Although we have been here for a little while I still feel that I am a stranger even in my camp."

THIRTY-NINE DAYS

From July 17, the 8th Army fights the Germans in the Catania Plain, slowly pushing them back towards Mount Etna. The enemy had installed solid defenses on the Etna Line, from Catania and the volcano to the sea in the north. The Anglo-Canadians finally take control of the plain on August 5, having been slowed by much greater opposition than the Americans were facing in the west. They advance with difficulty on both sides of Mount Etna towards Messina, with many men suffering from malaria, before finally joining up with the American forces.

A British captain of a secret Royal Engineers unit specializing in camouflaging troop movements (using mannequins and fake vehicles) writes on August 12: *"My dear Mum, Dad and Sis, I expect you will know now that I am in Sicily? We have not been allowed to mention the fact until yesterday, other than the bare fact we can't say whereabouts or when we arrived. It is a grand change although actually very little different from North Africa. The evening of our landing I unlocked the little chop of Scotch I had saved up and toasted the event of our return to Europe. Well, G. and W. left me behind in this game, but I've stolen a march on them now as I have been the first to set foot upon conquered enemy territory! [...] The lads from the desert complain that it is far hotter than in Libya etc. One of the features of the island of course is the volcano which can be seen from many miles. It is a tremendous mountain rising to 10,600 feet without any companions, which tends to exaggerate its heights. The little towns are incredibly beautiful and are teeming with little kids who all give the 'V' sign and smile at us.*

British newspaper *Sunday Pictorial*, dated July 25, 1943.

The caption next to the woman listening to the radio reads: "'Wonder where Jimmy and the boys are now?' says Ellen Aldritt, as she and her friends at the shell factory listen to the news during the mid-day break. Well, we can show you Ellen – Just where you've put your finger on Sidney Winston's grand map of Sicily. Have another look at the map when you get the news tomorrow, girls. That'll cheer you up!"

Despite the encouraging headlines, the advance in Sicily is as fast as it is deadly.

Everyone seems glad to welcome us but are only too willing to rob us for anything they see. They have had a poor time up till now. I suppose we shall bring a period of prosperity just as we did in North Africa. I am looking forward to a trip to the mainland when the further north we progress will be ever bringing us closer [to] *home. I am quite ready for the war to finish as I guess everyone else is. We are with troops now who have been 'out' for 2 to 3 years and still regard themselves as 'new'! I shall never cease to yearn for the day of 'homeward bound'."* The captain will next serve in Italy with the 101 Royal Tank Regiment, bringing inflatable or wooden tanks to the front line, designed to lure the Luftwaffe.

Patton (left) and an officer of the 3rd US Infantry Division, only 40 miles from Messina.

In early August, the 1st US Infantry Division and two Canadian regiments repel no less than twenty-four different counter-attacks during the Battle of Troina, supported by a formidable and effective Allied artillery. Finally, on the 11th, Axis forces begin to withdraw their troops to Italy and manage to evacuate nearly 117,000 Italian and German soldiers from Messina. The 3rd US Infantry Division enters the port on August 17, a few hours after the last enemy soldier left, officially marking the end of the Sicilian Campaign. A GI from this division then writes: *"Well honey here I am writing to you again. I often wondered if I was ever going to get to write to you again. I am now somewhere in Sicily. I landed on the southern beach of Sicily on July tenth. We had a rough and rugged old go for a number of days, but we fairly knocked down the Germans and Italians. We captured quite a number of prisoners. The civilians (Italians) treated us very nice. They shared with us whatever they had. They really don't have much. They seem to have the money but there just isn't anything to buy. The people here don't think much of the fascist party, they sure hate Mussolini. Honey I received three letters from you, when we reached our objective. Honey you can't imagine how happy that made me feel, especially after going through battle, and not receiving any mail for so long. Thanks very much for the picture, honey. That is the only picture I have of you anymore.*

All our bags were lost when we were committed to the front in Tunisia. I lost everything I had except what I had on me. I even lost the cigarette lighter and case you gave to me for Christmas. I sure hated to lose it! I guess that can be expected in the Army."

CONSEQUENCES

When Palermo falls to the Americans on July 22, Mussolini's opponents try to organize a coup d'état, in the hope of negotiating an armistice with the Allies and continuing the fight alongside them. Indeed, when the war arrives on their territory, the Italians no longer believe in their cause. After more than twenty years in command, Benito Mussolini even has a majority against him in his own fascist Council. He is arrested by the Carabinieri on the orders of King Victor Emmanuel III, and Marshal Pietro Badoglio, appointed in his place to form the new government, signs the Italian surrender on September 3. It must be kept secret until the 12th, but *Radio New York* leaks the news to the public on the 8th. The Allies therefore take the opportunity to land in Italy without delay. From now on, the Italians will continue the fight alongside them (as of October 13), but as 'co-belligerents' and not as 'allies'.

Rescued by a raid of German paratroopers five days after the Italian surrender, Mussolini will create a puppet state in northern Italy, the 'Repubblica Sociale Italiana', and will place his own fascist troops, the national republican army, at the service of the Nazis, which will oppose the co-belligerency army. When he learns of the surrender, a furious Adolf Hitler triggers the *Achse Plan* and deploys sixteen divisions throughout Italy. The Germans disarm their former allies and occupy Rome, which was celebrating what it thought was the end of the war, putting civilians through hell and bombing Italian ships seeking refuge in Malta. Hitler withdrew the 1. SS Panzer-Division from Russia to send it to Italy, a decision that would have a major impact on the outcome of the war: by moving troops from the Eastern Front to defend the West, and by stopping his last-chance operation *Citadel* on Kursk (near the Ukrainian border, where one of the greatest tank fights in history takes place), he allows the Soviets to definitively regain the advantage. After two counter-attacks, during which losses are abominable for both sides, the USSR begins its inexorable advance towards Berlin, crushing the Wehrmacht in battle after battle.

In Sicily, Germans and Italians number 29,000 killed or wounded and 140,000 taken prisoner. The Americans suffered 9,530 casualties (including 2,572 killed), the British 12,843 (including 2,721 killed) and the Canadians 2,410 (including 562 soldiers killed).

THE INVASION OF ITALY

The Allies are finally able to set foot on the European continent.
Within a few days, they will make three landings:
Operations *Baytown* on September 3, and then *Slapstick* and *Avalanche* on September 9.
In the meantime, the Italian Army will surrender.

Robert is a British non-commissioned officer in the Royal Army Medical Corps. The role of his Casualty Clearing Station is to treat the wounded in the field, meaning infantrymen receive first aid there and, once stabilized, are evacuated to General Hospitals in the rear. As a result, the Clearing Station is generally located near the front line, as close to combat and transport routes as possible, while trying to stay out of the range of the enemy's artillery. 'Bob' is in the light section, taking part in operations with the infantry and preparing the ground for the rest of the station, following them with all the heavy equipment.

Bob has seen many countries and a lot of action since his arrival at the front in 1940. As part of the 8th Army, he has traveled several times through Egypt, Tunisia, Tripolitania (a region of Libya at the time of the Second World War), and participated in *Operation Husky* in Sicily, while attached to the 50th (Northumbrian) Infantry Division. He landed there on D-Day in Syracuse, and turned a school into a field hospital. He was also very ill-equipped: the heavy section lost several vehicles, personnel and medical equipment when a transport ship was sunk by the enemy.

BACK ON THE CONTINENT

On September 3, 1943, the day the 'Armistice of Cassibile' (Sicily) is secretly signed, Bob takes part in *Operation Baytown* in Italy with the British 5th Infantry Division, landing alongside Canadians from the 1st Infantry Division and an armored brigade (XIII Corps, 8th Army).

Wearing his full equipment, steel helmet and a red cross armband, Bob crosses the Strait of Messina from Sicily and sets foot near Reggio Calabria, making him one of the first (Allied) men in Italy. The heavy section wouldn't join them until a week later. Covered by heavy artillery fire from Sicily, the British and Canadians encounter very little resistance from the demoralized and poorly armed Italian soldiers, who have been abandoned by their German allies. Indeed, the German commander in charge of the Italian Front, Generalfeldmarschall Albert Kesselring, was convinced that the main landing would take place near Naples, and therefore ordered his troops to retreat north and destroy all bridges and access roads in order to slow down the 8th Army. As the Allies set out on their way, Bob's company moves to Reggio on September 5, where it has 150 hospital beds to work with. On the day he writes this letter to his sister (the 9th), they have already cared for 245 wounded and sick (including civilians) since the landing, 144 of whom have already been evacuated. They have also just learned of the Italian surrender:

"Just a few hurried lines to let you know that I am safe and well in ~~Italy~~ *[poorly censored]. I can't give you any details yet except [our] family was one of the first on the beaches. The news is excellent isn't it, and it will be better as time goes on. Our prisoners danced with joy when they heard the radio about the surrender of Italy. The civilians too give us a good reception wherever we go. The first thing they ask for is food and all seem to be almost starving. [...] I am wanting to get home now and [am] tired of seeing the world although I expect we will see a few more countries yet. We are always on the move and as we go always by road we see quite a lot.*

I went to Suez before Sicily then up the canal to Alexandria again. Then four different places in Egypt. We were in six places in Sicily not forgetting dozens of places in Tripolitania and in Tunisia. Often up to ten miles from Jerry. The Royal Army Medical Corps now do parachute decents with the Airborne troops, storm the beaches with the assault troops and are everywhere wherever there is any fighting. We are always busy fighting typhus, typhoid and malaria, which can do more damage than Tommy guns if let loose. [...] Ted will soon be seeing to Christmas mail again. I am afraid I shall have to be a missing link again. It will be my fifth Christmas away from home. Well dears I have little news as the censor is strict for a while which you can appreciate. So I will say cheerio and do let me hear from you both as often as you can."

Bob will later join the troops landing at Tarento and the V and VIII Corps' battles for the rivers and hills along the Adriatic Coast will rage in the fall, meaning his company will have to deal with a very large number of wounded. On their way northwards they will sometimes treat several hundred British, Canadian and Indian soldiers every day, while still being regularly bombed by the enemy.

(Top) The beach at Gallico Marina, near Reggio Calabria, where Robert landed.

(Below) Robert's letter and Royal Army Medical Corps patch. Note how the word 'Italy' has been poorly erased by the censor.

```
                         N. R.A.M.C.
                         E. C.C.S.
            15.              8TH. ARMY.
                             C.M. FORCE.
                             9/9/43.

DEARS NORAH AND TED.

     JUST A FEW HURRIED LINES TO LET ✓ YOU  KNOW THAT I AM
WELL IN ▓▓▓▓.  I CANT GIVE YOU ANY DETAILS YET EXCEPT
FAMILY WAS ONE OF THE FIRST ON THE BEACHES. THE NEWS
ISNT IT AND IT WILL BE BETTER AS TIME GOES ON. OUR P
DANCED WITH JOY WHEN THEY HEARED THE RADIO ABOUT THE
        THE CIVILIANS TOO GIVE US A GOOD RECEPTION
                     THEY ASK FOR IS FOOD AND ALL SE
                         HAVNT SENT TED ANY MORE S
```

III - **THE SOFT UNDERBELLY** 1943-1944

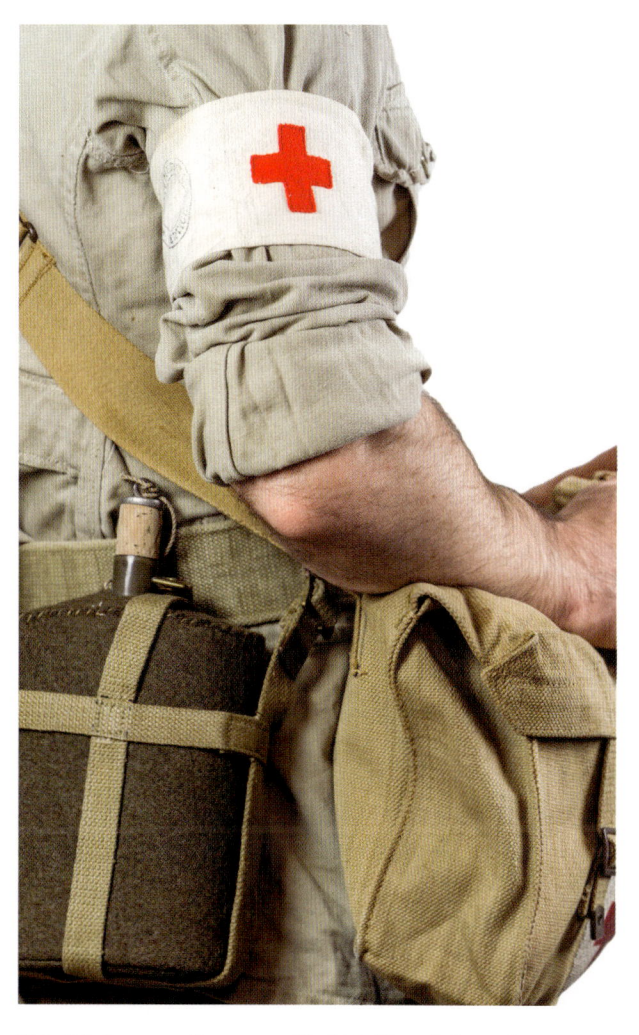

This 8th Army medic wears a Khaki Drill outfit (worn by a soldier named Davies during the war).

Manufactured by J. Compton Sons & Webb Ltd (London) in November 1938, his helmet has been used in many different environments, as indicated by its several coats of paint. Initially conditioned for a desert environment, with a warm sand color, it received a new camouflage with a brush (light green, dark green and brown) in the field for use in Europe.

This medic takes an individual Shell Dressing bandage out of his Royal Army Medical Corps musette bag (dated 1942).

To distinguish himself from the fighting troops, he wears a medical armband with a red cross sewn on it and an 'Army Medical Service' stamp. This armband has a service number handwritten on it and belonged to John Frederick Baker, 5th Battalion, Royal West Kent Regiment (8th Indian Infantry Division).

The division landed at Tarento on September 24, 1943, alongside the 4th Armoured Division and the British 78th Infantry Division (V Corps), reinforcing the ranks of the 8th Army, which was advancing along the Adriatic Coast. In the months that followed, the division crossed rivers in the face of fierce enemy resistance, breaking their lines of defense one by one.

SLAPSTICK AND AVALANCHE

Generalfeldmarschall Kesselring can no longer count on the 3 million Italian soldiers in the hands of the Allies, who can now freely push upwards from the south. On September 9, during *Operation Slapstick*, paratroopers of the British 1st Airborne Division arrive by sea at Tarento to take the 'heel' of the Italian 'boot'. Although they land unopposed, some casualties are reported: HMS *Abdiel* hit a mine and sank, and a few clashes with German paratroopers who were left behind caused around 100 deaths. However, the 1st Airborne makes rapid progress towards Foggia, capturing several intact ports along its route, followed by the British 78th Infantry Division and the Indian 8th Infantry Division. In less than 48 hours, the paratroopers link up with the 1st Canadian Division, leading the 8th Army deployed in Calabria. The parachute division will be removed from the front line a few days later and would have only one battle left: one year after *Slapstick*, the 1st Airborne Division will be decimated at Arnhem during the infamous *Operation Market Garden*, in the Netherlands.

Kesselring was right: a new operation is about to take place near Naples. At the same time as the operations in Taranto, the first wave of the 5th US Army (initially composed of the American 36th 'Texas' Infantry Division, and the British 46th and 56th Infantry Divisions) lands in the Gulf of Salerno: *Operation Avalanche*. Commanded by Lieutenant-General Mark Wayne Clark, the new 5th US Army is less fortunate than the veteran British 8th Army to the south, and German forces are present in large numbers to welcome it. The British divisions in particular encounter violent opposition, and once the troops are on the beach, their positions are quickly threatened by armored counter-attacks. The 16. Panzer-Division in charge of defending the east coast is reinforced by other units and the Allies are clearly outnumbered. However, the latter also receive additional troops, including the American 45th Infantry Division, the British 7th Armoured Division and the American paratroopers of the 82nd Airborne.

The fighting is so chaotic that Clark is very close to evacuating the beachhead on September 14. Fortunately, naval artillery support and Montgomery's 8th Army coming from the south throw Kesselring off balance, who has no choice but to retreat on the 19th. The Americans set out towards Naples, whose inhabitants rise up against the German occupier at the end of the month, routing him even before the Allies arrive on October 1. Among them is the 213th Coast Artillery Regiment, a veteran of *Operation Torch* and the heavy fighting in Tunisia. It landed on September 9 in support of the II Corps, 5th US Army. Randalph is one of its members, telling a friend about his first impressions of Italy: *"The natives are very friendly, which surprised me at first after being at war with them so long. The kids look upon an American soldier as we used to honor a real cowboy back when those 'Shoot'em up Westerners' were famous. Some of the girls are rather cute – yep, we still know how to 'Yi-hoo'. The only obstacle is to know their language, which I've found quite hard to learn, only know a few words."*

A British soldier sent to reinforce the 8th Army has a much darker vision of the 'Sunny Italy' fantasy: *"You will be pleased to know that I have arrived safely in sunny Italy after a rather unpleasant sea journey. [...] I think most of us were very surprised at the condition of the country. It's absolutely terrible. I thought all these articles and pictures were just propaganda but believe me it's true. The people around our camp appear to be nearly on the border of starvation and simply dive on any scraps of food that one left lying about. Also they are very short of clothing. They seem to be in a worse state than the poor old vagrants that used to hang around our place in North Africa. When we marched up to camp after disembarking all the poor kids were tailing alongside asking for biscuits or chocolate and of course, we were not allowed to give them anything. If they survive this war I don't know what they will grow up like but I can quite see why there is so much disease about now. It's hard to realize that four years ago, all these people were just the same as us and I think it would do all the chaps who go out on strike for more money etc. good to come out here and see what a war means. It might change their ideas a little."*

THE CAMPAIGN HAS ONLY JUST BEGUN

The Wehrmacht settles on the Winter Line, a fortification system that includes different lines of defenses, crossing Italy from the west coast (Tyrrhenian Sea) to the east coast (Adriatic Sea). Its main obstacle is the Gustav Line and its two subsidiary lines, Bernhardt and Hitler, which surround the Monte Cassino position overlooking the valley. While the Germans work on the latter stronghold, the Volturno and Barbara lines are supposed to delay the Allies. These man-made barriers all take advantage of the region's rugged terrain: the mountains (the Apennines) and rivers are dotted with minefields, thousands of pillboxes, observation outposts, artillery positions, machine gun nests and anti-tank walls or ditches. To make matters worse, neither the British nor the Americans are trained in mountain fighting. The Allies will have to march on the coastal plains, on either side of the mountainous 'Italian spine' where the Germans are waiting for them with guns at the ready, incapable of bypassing enemy defenses by sea (since landing gear is beginning to be redirected to England for a future landing in France). The extreme weather conditions will also play in the defenders' favor.

III - THE SOFT UNDERBELLY 1943-1944

The two Allied armies facing these lines impress by the multitude of nations that compose them. The American 5th Army in the west obviously includes American divisions, and some units born of segregation (the 92nd African-American Infantry Division, or the 442nd Regiment made of Americans of Japanese descent), but also British, Brazilian, and French divisions (themselves counting Senegalese, Moroccan, and Algerian soldiers). For its part, the British 8th Army to the east has British, Canadians, New Zealanders, South Africans, Australians, Indians, Nepalese (the fearsome Gurkhas), soldiers from Africa, Jews and Arabs from Palestine, as well as exile units (Poles, Greeks, Slovaks, antifascist Italians).

However, these formidable mixtures are a source of logistical problems. The commander of the 5th Army, Mark Clark, said after the war about the sixteen nationalities he had under his command: *"I had with me some who could not eat this, others did not eat that, some did not fight on Fridays or other days of the week. The British had infantry weapons and artillery different of ours. They could not be moved from one front to another easily as the Germans."*

Occupied by fifteen German divisions, the Winter Line will keep Rome out of reach for many months. Although the Canadians will succeed in taking Ortona, at the eastern end of the Gustav Line in December 1943 (page 122), their advance will soon be stopped by the merciless weather. To the west, the Allies will need no less than four costly assaults on the Monte Cassino fortress (page 130) and a diversionary landing at Anzio (page 140) to overcome the German defenses in May 1944. To make matters worse, both Allied armies will see many of their best divisions transferred to Northern Europe in the summer of 1944. Although eclipsed by the Normandy landings and the race to Germany, the war north of Rome will last until May 2, 1945. The total losses will amount to more than 186,000 Allies and 311,000 Axis soldiers, in battles that are not unlike the bloodbaths of the First World War. A very high price to pay for taking Europe's 'soft underbelly'.

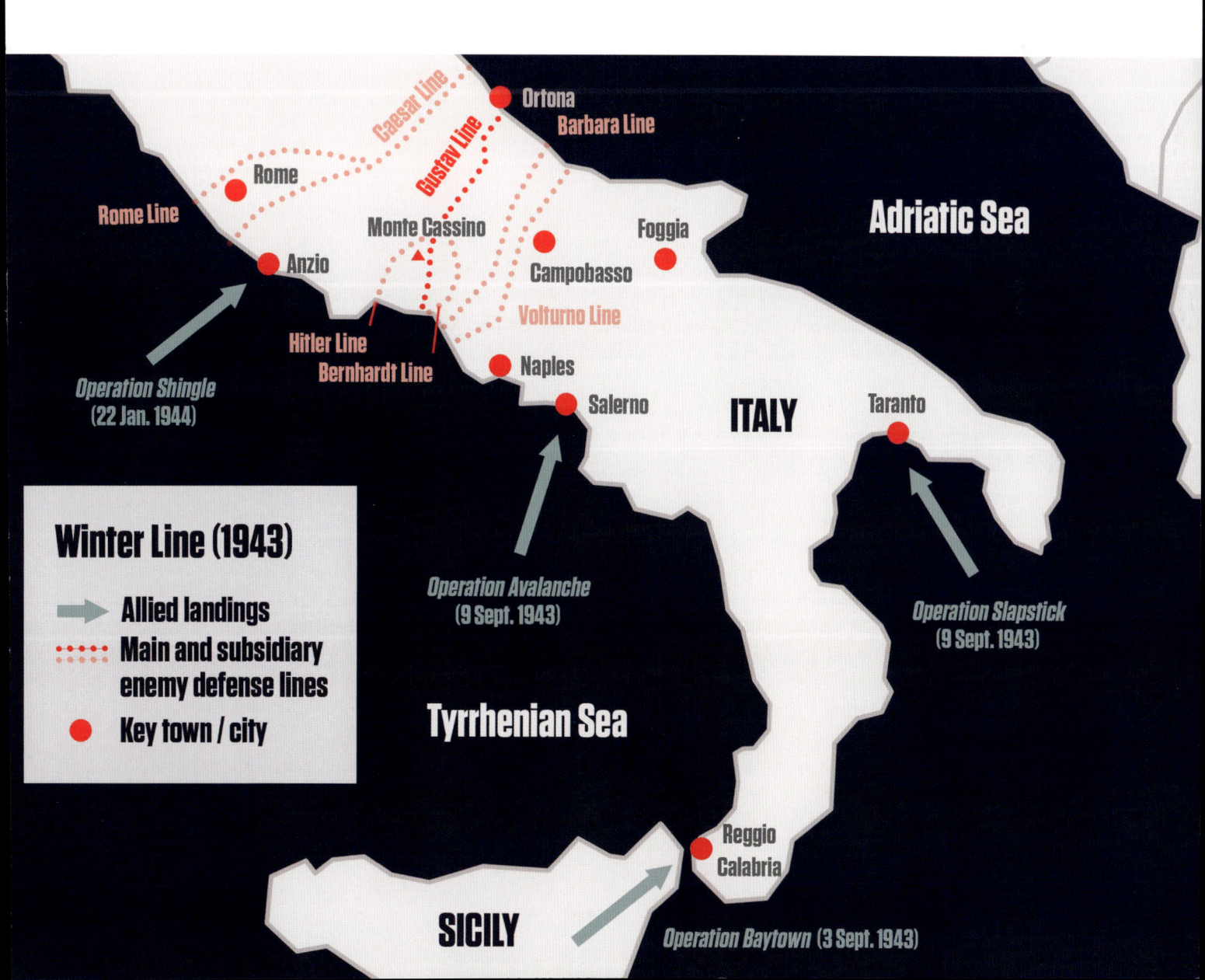

Winter Line (1943)

- → Allied landings
- ⋯ Main and subsidiary enemy defense lines
- ● Key town / city

ERNEST 'BUD' SIEGEL

2nd Battalion, 509th Parachute Infantry Regiment

Ernest is one of the first American paratroopers, who will have a rough start in North Africa. As the Allies invade the Italian peninsula, 'Bud' will find himself isolated behind enemy lines in Salerno. Eventually, he will become a highly respected officer, performing heroic acts in Italy, France and Belgium.

Ernest T. 'Bud' Siegel was born on April 1, 1918. Before the war, Bud was a New York State Trooper, and was drafted in March 1941 in Malone, New York. When he learned that the army was looking for candidates for the officers' school, he immediately volunteered. After basic training at Camp Wolters (Texas), he passed the officers' exam in Fort Benning, Georgia. A brand-new branch, better paid and looking for the elite, was of particular interest to him: the paratroopers.

THE FIRST PARAS

The idea of parachuting combatants into the battlefield dates to the First World War, but the first airborne operation wasn't carried out until 1933, by the Red Army. However, it gave up on it after the disaster of the Battle of the Dnieper in September 1943. In addition, the Soviets were soon surpassed by the Germans, Japanese and Italians, who followed their technological innovations in the 1930s. In 1940 and 1941, the performance of the German *Fallschirmjäger* during the Danish, Norwegian, French and Dutch invasions impressed the Allies. But here too, the heavy losses suffered in Crete led Hitler to reconsider the employment of paratroopers as such, relegating them to a role of elite but conventional infantry. The Allies, on the other hand, will rely heavily on them.

In 1941 and 1943, the British created the 1st and then the 6th Airborne Division. The 1st Airborne had its first parachute drop during *Operation Biting* on February 27, 1942 in Bruneval (France): a company of parachute commandos captured radar equipment and demonstrated the effectiveness of this type of raid. The Americans will be even more ambitious, giving birth to no less than five airborne divisions: the 11th, 13th, 17th, 82nd and 101st Airborne, as well as several small independent units that were created in 1940. Most will serve in the European Theater, except for the 11th Airborne, which will fight in the Pacific.

In the summer of 1942, Bud trained at the Fort Benning Jump School, with the rank of 2nd lieutenant. He joined the third of the four parachute battalions created before the United States entered the war (the 501st, 502nd, 503rd and 504th Parachute Infantry Battalions). These battalions soon became regiments, and Bud was assigned to the Casual Detachment (the reserve meant to replace the men killed or wounded) of the 503rd PIR (Parachute Infantry Regiment) on October 17, 1942. He was about to join the rest of the regiment, which was being trained in Britain by members of the 1st British Airborne Division.

During his crossing of the Atlantic, Bud realized that he had been promoted in an unusual way. At first, he was surprised that he was given the responsibility of 129 replacement soldiers and 12 lieutenants, even though he had only been a 2nd lieutenant himself for three months. He quickly understood that the '2nd' in front of his rank had been forgotten on the list of officers, making him look like a 1st lieutenant in the eyes his superiors. Nevertheless, he will later prove that this accidental promotion was well deserved by becoming an exceptional leader.

On November 2, the 503rd PIR changed its name to the 509th PIR. The day before, Bud wrote this V-mail to a major (now in charge of the Tank Destroyer school) whom he had become friends with while training at Camp Wolters: *"November 1, 1942, somewhere in Britain. Dear Major, well your request for my transfer never came, so we pushed off for Actionland. Much to my surprise at the port of embarkation I met swagger stick and all, Colonel Nielson with the Finance Department. We sailed over together and we chatted about the old outfit. He's temporarily stationed nearby and he asked whether I'd written you recently. How are you and your motorized blitzkrieg outfit doing? From reports you're turning out some crack stuff, more power to you. You sort of get the real feel of things over here, you know there's a war on, the evidence of the Battle of Britain is more than just reading matter. I'm still a 'golden-rod' lieutenant with not too much ambition to go higher, I was in line for a first when I was sent over [so]* it's probably in the mail now. Well it's been a long time since Indian Lake, but I know I'll be back there some day basking in the sun and really appreciating some of the smaller things in life like a warm bed and a full dinner plate. Write me a 'V' mail sir, I sure would like to hear from you. Yours respectfully, Ernie."

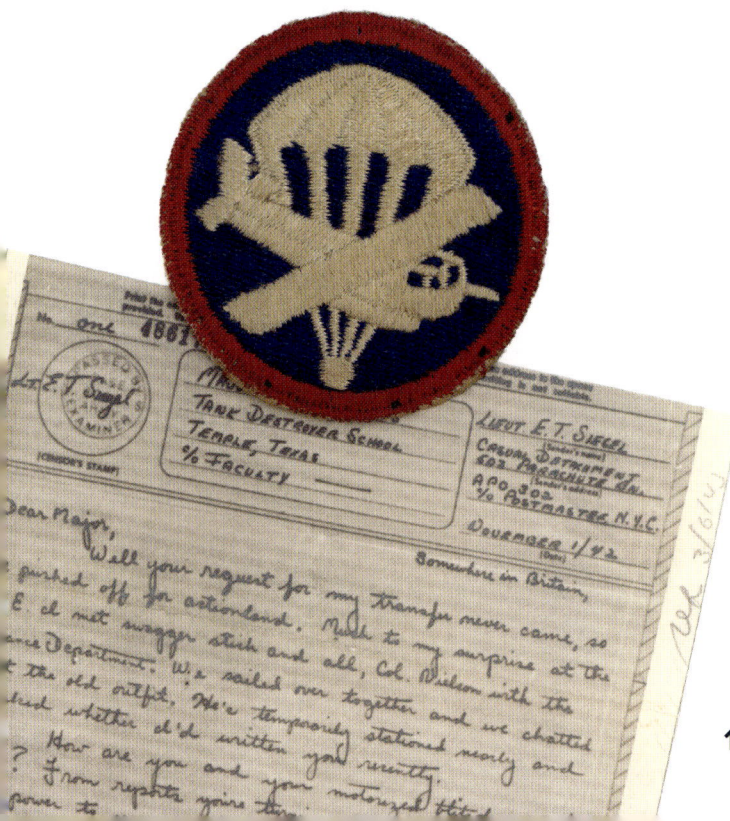

Bud in the United States in May 1942, wearing a paratrooper *Riddell* training helmet.

Less than a week later, 556 paratroopers of the 509th took part in *Operation Torch* and carried out the very first American airborne assault in history. The 509th PIR flew directly from England to jump on Tafraoui and La Sénia, in order to capture the airfields south of Oran, while the infantry landed on the beaches. But the weather, communication and navigation problems had disastrous consequences, and thirty out of the thirty-seven planes failed to reach their objectives, either shot down by flak, ran out of fuel or simply became lost. Bud arrived by boat with the replacements: the losses being very heavy, the Casual Detachment came in to fill the ranks of the 509th PIR. He became platoon leader in the HQ Company of the 2nd Battalion the following month. Unfortunately, he didn't keep this position for long: obtaining a furlough to attend another lieutenant's wedding in Tunis, he stayed longer than he was allowed and forgot to ask for a two-day extension. Bud was then 'AWOL' (Absent Without Leave, considered as a deserter) and upon his return, he was immobilized and degraded to the rank of assistant platoon leader.

The 509th didn't take part in the landing in Sicily and it was Colonel Gavin's 505th Parachute Regimental Combat Team (82nd Airborne Division) that took part in *Operation Husky*, with relative success. Only one paratrooper in six reached the vicinity of his drop zone.

In addition, the Allied anti-aircraft defense, which was inexperienced and terrified by the Luftwaffe, mistakenly targeted its own aircraft and men. The Allied command was almost contemplating the end of airborne operations, but finally learned from previous failures. New measures were being tried out, such as the use of pathfinders (parachute scouts) dropped in advance to mark the drop zones (using 'Krypton' flash lamps and the 'Rebecca/Eureka' radar transponder) or silenced Allied anti-aircraft batteries during operations. These ideas are put to the test under real conditions during *Operation Avalanche* in Italy (September 9, 1943). While German counter-attacks are threatening the landing beaches at Salerno, the 82nd Airborne is sent as reinforcements on September 13, 1943. This time, the parachute drops are a real success.

THE BIG JUMP

Bud makes his first combat jump the next day, September 14, on Avellino (about 16 miles north of Salerno). While the 82nd Airborne jumps right behind the American lines to reinforce them, Bud's 509th PIR parachutes into enemy territory with the mission of cutting German communication lines. The journey from Sicily is hectic and as the operation takes place at night, some transport planes struggle to identify their drop zones. Paratroopers are spread over long distances. Bud is the lead jumper in aircraft #41-7852, coordinating the release of his stick (group) of eighteen men. On the ground, he will only find six of them before attempting to reach the city. Unfortunately, they have an unpleasant surprise: the drop zone is occupied by the entire 6. Panzer-Division, which arrived during the night and against which the small band are unable to make much of an impact. While discreetly asking civilians for directions, the paratroopers are unable to make themselves understood by the Italians, who are kissing the American flags on their sleeves and covering the men with religious medals. As Bud calls Sergeant Barnessi for help, he discovers to his surprise that he actually can't speak Italian. As the city is too far away and the Germans are everywhere, Bud takes the decision to establish a defensive position in a cornfield and wait for more information.

A dusk, a truck full of Germans stops at the nearby farm. Fortunately for Bud and his men, the farmer doesn't reveal the presence of the Americans. However, a German soldier passes by and gets too close for comfort, only a few feet from the paratroopers holding their breath. After what seems like an eternity, he finally walks back to his commander, away from the undetected Americans, shouting *"Nichts zu berichten!"*. ("Nothing to report!") On their own, the paratroopers can only move at nightfall and so rest during the day. They are so invisible that Allied planes, firing at an anti-aircraft position close to their camouflaged foxholes, almost kill them all.

Officers of the 509th PIR in Oran at the beginning of 1943. Bud is in the center (third from left), observing the objective designated by Lt-Colonel Edson D. Raff on a sand table. Just to the left of the latter (second from right), Major Doyle R. Yardley, battalion commander in place of Raff, will be wounded and captured in Avellino and then escape from his Oflag in Poland after sixteen months in captivity.

WESTERN UNION

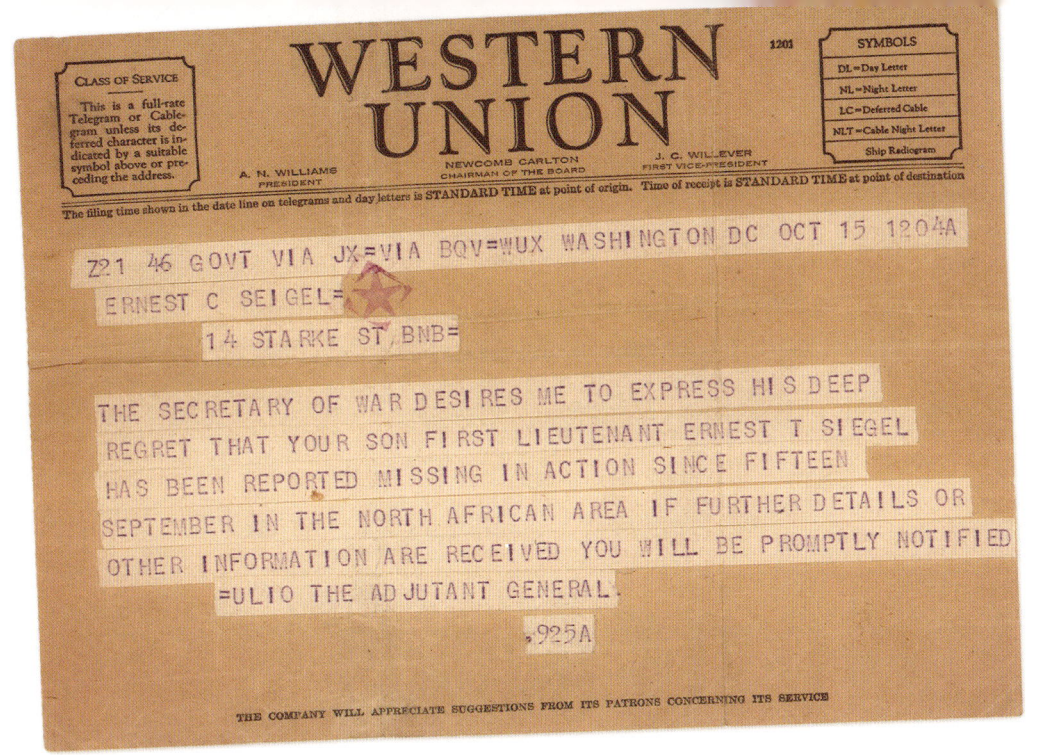

Z21 46 GOVT VIA JX=VIA BQV=WUX WASHINGTON DC OCT 15 1204A
ERNEST C SEIGEL=
14 STARKE ST,BNB=

THE SECRETARY OF WAR DESIRES ME TO EXPRESS HIS DEEP REGRET THAT YOUR SON FIRST LIEUTENANT ERNEST T SIEGEL HAS BEEN REPORTED MISSING IN ACTION SINCE FIFTEEN SEPTEMBER IN THE NORTH AFRICAN AREA IF FURTHER DETAILS OR OTHER INFORMATION ARE RECEIVED YOU WILL BE PROMPTLY NOTIFIED
=ULIO THE ADJUTANT GENERAL.
.925A

The telegram received by Bud's parents saying that he is Missing in Action. A few days later, they will receive reassuring news from their son.

A few days later, Bud and his group find about ten other men from the 509th. They learn that the entire battalion was scattered throughout the area and is now operating in small groups, trying to gather water and food from the civilians. On September 26, their group totals thirty-one soldiers. Forced to maintain a low profile between Avellino and Sarno, they're unable to protect the inhabitants who are being bombed by Allied forces, or even to contact artillery units to stop the unnecessary destruction. The next day, a priest and a young man come to tell Bud that an American truck has been spotted on the other side of the mountain. This might be their chance to stop the futile bombing of the village, as the Germans appeared to have left them alone for a while.

Bud and another officer pick up some civilian clothes and, because they haven't shaved since their jump, have no trouble blending in with the local population. Speaking neither Italian nor German, they have developed a scenario with the young man, just in case they are exposed: they would say they have escaped from an asylum. If the Germans were to be too insistent, Siegel would shout *"Wallyo"*, the boy would throw himself to the ground, and the two Americans would empty their weapons as quickly as possible. Luckily, although their disguises wouldn't fool the Italians, the only small group of Germans they meet, who were dismantling their anti-aircraft gun in order to fall back, completely falls for it.

The small party finally arrives on the other side of the mountain on the 28th, and meets a British lieutenant leading them to Nocera, where the 7th Armoured Division is stationed. Bud details the situation to him using a map, and the British officer has the artillery fire that was pounding Avellino adjusted. He probably saved the lives of many civilians that day.

The majority of the battalion meets on the same day and takes stock of these past two weeks: 123 paratroopers killed or captured, including the commander of the 509th and all his staff. Bud hasn't yet returned from his infiltration into enemy territory, and is reported missing. His parents therefore receive the telegram above, but on October 30, Bud finally writes to his family: *"Sorry to have kept you waiting so long for mail. We haven't devised a system of mail delivery behind the enemy's line yet. We've had a bit of a blow for a fortnight or so and finally came through, nasty but nice. 'Don't worry' seems rather futile but please don't let my whereabouts produce any anxiety. God will take care of me."*

On December 10, the 2nd Battalion, being the only active element of the 509th PIR, will be renamed the 509th Parachute Infantry Battalion, for good. Alongside the 1st Ranger Battalion, the paratroopers will fight in the mountains as elite infantry. Bud will then land in Anzio in January 1944 (and will be wounded there by shrapnel in the testicles).

> You can follow the rest of his journey through Europe in two other chapters of this book, starting with the south of France (where he will again be wounded, see page 231). Narrowly avoiding capture in the Belgian Ardennes, he will end his career with the 509th in a last heroic act (page 279).

LIEUT. ERNEST T. SIEGEL

BEHIND THE LINES AND BACK AGAIN

Lieut. Siegel, Paratrooper, Once On Missing List, Silent On Venture

JOHN LESLIE HARRIS

C Squadron, 11th Canadian Army Tank Regiment (The Ontario Regiment)

John is British by birth, but Canadian by adoption.
He volunteered to liberate Europe and joined an armored regiment.
He will take part in the worst battles of the Canadian Army in Italy,
notably in Ortona on the Gustav Line, before being seriously wounded in action in June 1944.

Born in 1912 in Sheffield, John is the older brother of Maisie, the penfriend of the two young airmen of the Royal Canadian Air Force with a tragic fate (Jim & Vernon Miller, page 70). Leaving school at the age of 13 to work in a coal mine, John dreamed of joining the Royal Navy. Unfortunately, as he was going through the selections, he fell ill and was turned down (according to him, it was the most embarrassing moment of his young life). His two schoolmates, Harry and Chris, were accepted, but had only a short career in the Navy: both went down with HMS *Courageous*, which was torpedoed by a U-Boat off the coast of Ireland on September 17, 1939. It was the first warship to be sunk by the Germans during the Second World War, and resulted in the loss of 519 men.

At the age of 17, John decided to emigrate to Canada in the hope of working on one of his uncles' farms. He arrived in Montreal on the SS *Metagama* on May 20, 1929, leaving his family, including his little sister Maisie, in Sheffield. He worked for many farmers before becoming a lumberjack in 1933, but the strikes in the area the following year left him unemployed and he set off to discover the country: *"That winter I crossed Canada three times riding freight trains, slept in practically every jail house from Halifax to Vancouver, and my experiences were many and varied, looking back I am glad I had the experience. With thirteen dollars in my pocket and no job at the time I got married in March of 1935."* He will spend his life with Fern and although he was already a father of two little girls at the time (and later four), John volunteered for the army at the beginning of the war, like so many other Canadians (see his testimony, page 68).

BACK TO ENGLAND

Even though he'd finally found a job on a farm near Georgetown, John joined the Canadian militia of the Lorne Scots Regiment and stood guard two nights a week. When the war broke out, he wanted to serve overseas: *"I was never really sure whether it was because of itchy feet from my days riding freight trains, the feel of a uniform, patriotism, or the fact that my Father worked at Vickers in England all day, and then was out most nights putting out incendiary bombs with a pail of sand and a small shovel, I have always told myself it was the latter. After a series of fights with Mr. Wright who did not want me to go, and the Military who did not want to take me, because my job was supposedly essential, I finally went active late 1940."*

III - THE SOFT UNDERBELLY 1943-1944

John became a corporal in a tank crew of C Squadron, 11th Canadian Army Tank Regiment (The Ontario Regiment), 1st Canadian Army Tank Brigade, 1st Canadian Infantry Division. This 1st Armoured Brigade also included the Three Rivers Regiment and the Calgary Regiment, which had already served during the murderous Dieppe landing, losing all its tanks and most of its men. John trained at Camp Borden, Ontario, before arriving in his native United Kingdom in July 1941, where the unit was involved in coastal defense. John's role is to load the shells into the tank's gun, while operating the radio. He's the one sending and receiving the messages, a job which he considers to be the second most important one after that of the commander. His crew was first equipped with Matilda tanks and then, in November, with the new Churchill tank: the Ontario Regiment was the first Canadian unit to experiment with it. John wrote: *"The boys of our regiment have received considerable praise for the way they have been handling these big new tanks, which by the way, though not the largest, are the most up-to-date tanks in the world at present and are the biggest of any that are in the Allied armies excepting the Russian. When you get out on a tactical scheme and see these iron, or should I say steel, monsters you are certainly impressed and when Hitler's men see these coming to pay them a social call I have no doubt that they will hurriedly say their prayers."* The Churchill tanks will eventually prove unreliable and be gradually replaced by Canadian Ram tanks, and then by American Shermans in 1943.

John took the time, of course, to visit his family at the first opportunity and to rediscover the country he'd left behind at a very young age. He also wanted to explore the capital and visit Madame Tussaud's museum and the Tower of London. He regularly sent letters to his local Canadian newspaper, the *Markham Economist and Sun*, to let them know about his adventures and have them published. John recounts his experience of England on August 30, 1941: *"When you travel around and get an idea of what some of the people over here have gone through and notice the spirit with which they have gone through these air raids, you feel you have nothing to grumble about. I might also add that my biggest thrill over here was being able to visit Mother and Dad after being away from home for 13 years and I spent a most enjoyable holiday.*

John with his parents and sister Maisie while on leave in England.

While I was home we had the air-raid sirens go around 2 am one morning so promptly went out fire-watching with my father, expecting I was going to experience my first air-raid. However, nothing occurred, as a few planes just went over but dropped no bombs; we later learned that one of them was brought down. I think a great deal of credit should go to these chaps like my father who in most cases are too old to join the active forces, but who go to work all day in munition factories, railroads etc. to see that we chaps get the tools we need, and then they turn out and go fire-watching all night. Of course they arrange a system amongst themselves to do certain nights a week, but in the event of a raid they all turn out, and in my home-town of Sheffield they turned out nearly every night all last winter."

John (left) and his tank crew.

John's unit left the Scottish plains to land in Sicily with the 1st Canadian Army Tank Brigade on July 13, 1943, in support of the XIII British Corps. The Canadians moved rapidly northward to capture their objective: the Strait of Messina. Optimistic, John said in a letter: *"We are on the move once more, so wish us luck and we will be home for Christmas"*. Despite violent engagements, particularly along the Dittaino River in eastern Sicily, the Ontario Regiment had only one casualty and thirteen wounded. On August 26, the 1st Canadian Army Tank Brigade was renamed 1st Armoured Brigade, and its three regiments became the 11th Armoured Regiment (The Ontario Regiment), the 12th Armoured Regiment (Three Rivers Regiment) and the 14th Armoured Regiment (The Calgary Regiment). All were preparing to invade the continent, but in the Ontario Regiment, only B Squadron was involved in *Operation Baytown*.

THE PHANTOM ENEMY

The Anglo-Canadians linked up with advanced elements of the American 36th 'Texas' Infantry Division (who had landed at Salerno) on September 16. Now that the Germans had withdrawn northward, three days later the Ontario Regiment was sent to Praia Mare, on the coast (halfway between Naples and Salerno), which is where John's C Squadron joined them.

John is disappointed to learn that in the two weeks the regiment has been in Italy, he hasn't yet fired a single shot. On the other hand, he appreciates the contact with civilians: *"Our camp is situated in a little town in Italy, the name of which I cannot tell you because I cannot pronounce it as my knowledge of languages is not what it might be. There is a stream running through it, and this is evidently a sort of community washing place where the Italian housewives do their washing. There are no washing machines. Well, here are our boys mucking in among these people, doing their washing, and all having a great time. Old Hitler sure would have gnashed his teeth at this spectacle, for what Jerry told these people the Allies would do to them when they landed is not fit to print. However, we find them quite friendly, and they realize that we have no quarrel with the civilian population. We dicker with them for chickens and beef and various commodities to help out our rations, as we do our own cooking while on operations, the cooks being well behind us; it may be a good place for them – with their bully beef and biscuits."*

Dishwashing chore for John (left) and a friend.

The Germans' Winter Line and its main network of defenses, the Gustav Line, cut Italy in two from the mouth of the Garigliano in the west, to Ortona in the east. The American advance is stopped there to the west on the Garigliano River, opposite Monte Cassino, whose heights control the valley of the Liri River and all access to Rome. To the east, the British push north towards Foggia, facing only little resistance until they cross the Gargano peninsula (the spur of the Italian boot, north of Apulia). The 8th Army is now trying to reach Ortona, Montgomery's objective, which the latter hopes to liberate quickly in order to turn west and take Rome before the Americans. Meanwhile, the Canadian infantry is moving through central Italy towards Potenza and Campobasso, but the Canadian tanks of the 1st Armoured Brigade are asked to reinforce the British on the east coast. John's Ontario Regiment leaves the beautiful Praia Mare beach on September 27 for the Foggia Plains, where it has to engage in a colossal tank battle. However, the Germans have fled the battle before the regiment, frustrated, even reached its destination of Minervino Murge. After various changes of plans, they are sent by sea to Manfredonia (20 miles northeast of Foggia), at the base of the Gargano peninsula. On the boat, John writes this letter to his sister Maisie on October 4 (see opposite):

"Hello Sis. Well suppose you will be thinking it's a long time since I wrote you, well for the past few weeks I have not been in contact with our post office, so have not been able to get any letters away, neither have I had any mail from any place for the past six weeks. Just beginning to hope someone remembered me in their will as just about beginning to think you're all dead. [...] I am fine and have had quite a successful time all through Sicily and up to date in Italy we have had all the best of luck. Have had quite a varied time of it some hard going but also lots of easy going too, have managed quite a lot of swimming in our quieter moments, seen a few of the towns, sampled quite a little Italian wine of various

---

Canadian Soldiers Join in Italian Wash Day

LETTER FROM CPL. JOHN HARRIS, Mediterranean Force, Dated Sept. 21st

Dear Friends:
Well here we are again, still alive and kicking, and in one piece, still trying to catch up with Jerry. Have just received a couple of issues of the Economist, which are really well travelled, having probably gone some seven or eight thousand miles since they went into the post office, as I am at present in Italy; so you see your literary endeav...

III - THE SOFT UNDERBELLY 1943-1944

grades, mostly bad. However I am quite convinced that Italy is a good place for Italians. Me, I'll be glad to say goodbye to it at any time, dirty old Sheffield and such places suit me much better. The boys are all fine [...]. We have a chap with us now who lived quite close to MacTier [Ontario, Canada] and knows Jeannie and Jim Miller real well, said he would have liked to see Jim, maybe you can send his address along in your next letter, have you heard from him lately? [The Jim Miller he asks about is indeed the RCAF aviator, Maisie's friend, who was killed in an air raid a few weeks earlier. When John receives Maisie's answer, he will write, *"Sorry to hear about Jim but guess that's a chance we all must take".*] *Just as I write this I am having a little boat ride moving up once more, don't know just where or when we shall catch up again with Jerry but hope it's soon or will be all browned off again. [...] Well not much other news as there's not much excitement just chasing after Jerry but never seeming to catch up. In this country, it's all hills and one needs to be a mountain goat or something to get around. Well must close now as we are getting close to our destination so for now cheerio and all the best as ever. Your brother Johnnie."*

Once again, the Germans retreat to Campobasso and Termoli (between Foggia in the south and Ortona in the north), when John's squadron must support the advance of the 15th Infantry Brigade (British 5th Infantry Division). The frustration is even more intense, but unbeknownst to him, John is about to take part in battles that will cost Canadians dearly.

In mid-October, his regiment goes west towards Cassino, crossing Campobasso which the Canadians took on the 14th. The region is very mountainous, with some peaks higher than 3,000 feet. Upon reaching the Colle d'Anchise area, the men face the Volturno Line, where the Germans inflict on the Ontario Regiment a barrage of artillery that it had never seen before. Tank and infantry movements are met with a hail of fire and the Canadians repeatedly attempt to cross the Biferno River without success. On top of that, they are even attacked by the US Army Air Forces by mistake. Until the end of the month, they'll fight under increasingly difficult climatic conditions, before being gradually relieved by other units.

The fight resumes in mid-November for John's brigade, sent again to Termoli on the Adriatic Coast to support the crossing of the Sangro River by the British 78th Infantry Division, the 8th Indian Infantry Division and the 2nd New Zealand Infantry Division. The Allies, who now have to deal with snow, have a tough time dislodging the Germans, who take advantage of well-prepared defensive positions in a terrain playing in their favor. Although the 8th Army will eventually manage to break through and repel the enemy to the north, it will soon find itself faced with a similar situation on the Moro River, having to hold on despite numerous counter-attacks, and sometimes forcing Canadians to fight hand-to-hand. Behind the Moro River bed lies their main objective: the medieval city of Ortona, right on the Gustav Line.

FROM THE MORO RIVER TO ORTONA

The heavy rains delay the British troops, leaving the Canadians on their own in front of Ortona. The town is defended by the German paratroopers of the 1. Fallschirmjäger Division, fearsome veteran soldiers who had fought in Africa. With the Americans to the west still blocked near Monte Cassino, Montgomery hopes to win the race to Rome and sends no less than four infantry divisions (the 5th British, 8th Indian, 2nd New Zealand and 1st Canadian, to which John is attached) to attack his objective on December 5 at midnight.

To reach the city, they must cross the Moro River. It will take them three days to do so and cost them dearly. John's tank supports the Seaforth Highlanders of Canada near San Leonardo, but is unable to enter the village until the night of December 8 following the construction of a bridge over the river by the Royal Canadian Engineers. The German forces finally withdraw 3 miles from San Leonardo, behind a ravine 200 feet deep and just as wide, which will be known as 'The Gully'. John's brigade now faces the 90. Panzergrenadier Division and the 1. Fallschirmjäger Division, determined to defend the house adjacent to the road to Ortona. For four days, Canadian assaults on The Gully will fail one after the other. General Vokes (nicknamed 'the butcher' by his men) nevertheless takes the risk to send the 22nd Royal Canadian Regiment west of the objective, to the hamlet of Casa Berardi, in order to take the German paratroopers from behind. The attack starts with an impressive artillery barrage on December 14, with the assistance of the Ontario Regiment tanks.

Four months after the events, John tells his local Canadian newspaper about his experience from the Moro River to Casa Berardi: *"It starts off one afternoon with a terrific artillery barrage, the like of which has to be seen to be believed. We are on a high ridge overlooking the river and previous to the barrage we were being constantly shelled by Jerry, who was on the ridge the other side, roughly a mile away. [...] It seems as though every square foot of the ground must be covered with the bursting shells and flying shrapnel. After several hours of this, we see the infantry moving in, the machine guns begin to chatter, giving covering fire to the others who are advancing; then of course Jerry starts throwing in his mortars and things are plenty hot, but still those lads of the P.B.I. [poor bloody infantry] carry on and finally establish a bridgehead on the other side to which they hang to like a cat to a mouse. Now come the engineers; a crossing must be made and mines cleared so that the tanks can proceed across to give support. Working all through the night this is accomplished and over we go next day, so now we have the tank guns to swell the general chorus.*

Finally, we reach the town at the top of the ridge [San Leonardo] to find old Jerry has had enough of that place and has moved back to the next ridge, the taking of which made history [Casa Berardi]. We move up too, and take a crossroad leading up to this road back of the ridge, which was our immediate objective, as we must refuel and replenish our stock of ammunition. There the weather decided to take a hand. Here we harbor for the night, with our footed friends dug in all around, ready for a counter attack if Jerry should attempt one. Now comes the rain, so we are in for a wet night. [...] We camouflage our tanks with branches of olive trees and with the least movement possible make ourselves inconspicuous. During these couple of days we are kept constantly on the jump with Jerry putting on a general mortaring of the area, with a few stray rifle and machine gun bullets from snipers added for good measure. On one occasion a mortar bomb landed within four feet of the back of my tank while we were eating dinner, wounding two of my buddies, while another chap and I received not a scratch. From then on, I believed in miracles.

John in combat gear, wearing the wool Battledress also worn by the infantry, and a heavy Mark I helmet, specifically made for the Royal Armoured Corps.

The next day it is decided that we will shell the ridge, so my troop moves up into fire position, and await orders. We are here for some little time and then that order was cancelled, but not before a Jerry Observation Post had spotted us and Jerry started to give us the works; his first shot plunged directly under the front of my tank, and you could fair feel her rock as it exploded. The next one was just as close, while a third made a hit on one tank.

III - THE SOFT UNDERBELLY 1943-1944

As we could not see where the stuff was coming from to reply, the old adage 'discretion is the better part of valor' prevailed and we moved back. How the driver of the tank that was hit drove her back I still don't know; put it down to his training that he did it instinctively, as they were all suffering from shock (but all are recovered now). My own tank became mired and it was not long before there were nice little holes in the ground all around us, and I think only darkness coming saved us, as we were away from the rest of the gang, and completely in the open. As there was no hope of getting pulled out, we were up before daylight the next morning and camouflaged her so well that even our friends could hardly find us.

We stayed in this position for four days, living right in the tank and only going out at night for rations, the area being under constant shell fire – but we were never hit. Eventually it cleared up enough for operations and tanks that were not mired proceeded with the infantry to take the ridge and the village beyond that was no doubt the key to the taking of the town that really put the Canadians in the headlines [Ortona]. That turned out to be the acid test for our gang, and they really did a job. We were certainly mauled, but the score in Jerry tanks and guns etc. was easily a good three to our one. At the finish we had a handful of tanks, and the remnants of a well-known infantry company successfully held off Jerry till reinforcements came through. The infantry Major has since been awarded the V. C. [the Victoria Cross, the Commonwealth's highest distinction during the Second World War] for his devotion to duty and great leadership, while our own Major received the Military Cross, for his excellent cooperation to make the show a success."

The 'infantry Major' John writes about is Paul Triquet, head of the 22nd Royal Regiment (nicknamed 'The Van Doos', an anglicized pronunciation of 'vingt-deux', '22' in French). It is a Canadian regiment with a French-speaking majority, based in Quebec City, which also served in Sicily. At 8:30 am on December 14, its C company launched an assault on the Casa Berardi mansion, and was decimated before reaching the objective, despite the support of the Ontario Regiment tanks. With only seventeen infantrymen left and five tanks still in support, Paul Triquet rushed across enemy lines and captured the objective with his men. They held on until the next day against much larger forces (including Panzer IVs arriving as reinforcements), before being relieved by the rest of the battalion.

The Allies won't secure The Gully before December 20, when the German paratroopers fall back to Ortona and order the civilians to evacuate the town (1,300 of them still made the choice to stay and would pay for it with their lives). Buildings are demolished to block Canadian tanks, which will have no choice but to use clear passages that the Germans had conscientiously mined. Every single brick on the ground seems to be connected to an explosive, every corner of the street is watched by a buried Panzer turret, and the snipers have transformed the area into a real 'Italian Stalingrad'. Tired of losing so many men in German traps, the Canadians stay clear of the streets and move on to the terraced houses of Ortona. They soon develop the 'mouse hole' technique: using explosives, they create breaches in the walls to shoot the Germans on the other side, before using the same hole to move into the next house.

On December 28, as the battle seems to drag on, Canadians are surprised to find the streets empty. Although Hitler ordered them to hold the city at all costs, the Germans abandon it for fear of being surrounded by a possible Allied attack from the northwest. While the enemy lost 800 soldiers in the battle, the Canadians suffered about 2,600 casualties (including more than 500 killed), in addition to nearly 4,000 soldiers evacuated for battle exhaustion.

However, these sacrifices still wouldn't allow Montgomery to reach Rome before the US 5th Army.

Major Paul Trinquet, 1944. On his arm is the red rectangular patch of the 1st Canadian Infantry Division, and on his chest the ribbons of the Victoria Cross (left) and of the Canadian Volunteer Medal 39-45 (right).

INJURY

John's unit would participate in so many operations in the following months that by the summer of 1944 they'll be considered as the most experienced armored brigade in Italy. But according to John, these exploits seem to be nothing more than a simple routine. He writes: *"Of engagements there is really nothing in particular to write about – for the most part they are just like schemes back in England, only the targets are real, and one treats the whole thing just as any other day's work. Under fire one does not have time to be scared, the first shell that comes over and rattles the back decks, or blows a pile of earth over the tank, kind of makes your heart miss a beat, and then you hear the tank commander designating the target, giving you the range and fire when ready, the old gun spits out a little calling card and the game is on. So in the reek of cordite fumes you just throw in those old shells as fast as you can and soon get a good sweat worked up. Have had plenty of near misses, but so far have had the luck of the Irish. Have had no spectacular experiences as yet, just straight ordinary slugging tit-for-tat with Jerry, which is just like doing the fall plowing – you eventually finish what you started."*

The 1st Canadian Armoured Brigade is secretly sent west with elements of the 8th Army to assist the 5th US Army, which is still blocked in front of Monte Cassino. In May 1944, they take part in the fourth and final battle for the monastery at its summit (see the following story of Paul Pirat), which the Allies had been trying to capture since January and which had cost them 55,000 killed and wounded. John and his crew have to protect the Allied attackers from armored counter-attacks until the bastion falls on May 18, 1944. A few days later, the Gustav Line is crossed, then the Adolf Hitler Line at the cost of 1,000 casualties for the 1st Canadian Division.

While the majority of the I Canadian Corps goes into reserve, the 1st Canadian Armoured Brigade has to support the British divisions that are pursuing the Germans into northern Italy. The latter need to buy some time to consolidate the last Italian defense system, the Gothic Line, north of Florence. Therefore, two German infantry divisions – the paratroopers of the 1. Fallschirmjäger Division and the formidable Hermann Göring Panzer Division – set up subsidiary defenses near Lake Trasimene, halfway between Rome and Florence, hoping to delay the Allied advance. The Canadians crash into them in mid-June, west of Lake Trasimene.

The assault is launched by the British 4th and 78th Infantry Divisions on June 21, with John's brigade in support. They take the villages of Sanfatucchio and Pucciarelli, losing several tanks in the process, then approach Pescia on the 24th. John and his C Squadron are ordered to help the Royal Irish Fusiliers Regiment of the 78th (Battleaxe) Infantry Division clear the town and a farm named Casa Ranciano. The Germans immediately retaliate with their best tanks. It's here that John will make a name for himself, and receive the prestigious Military Medal. His citation states: *"During the attack by the 1st Battalion, The Royal Irish Fusiliers, on 24th June 1944, Cpl. Harris was detailed to watch the vulnerable left flank. Throughout the advance he led the infantry and was instrumental in getting them on to their objectives. He put out of action one anti-tank gun and three 20 mm dual purpose guns. Later, single handed, he attacked a German Panther tank and succeeded in crippling it sufficiently so that the artillery was able to knock it out. Although his tank was knocked out, and he himself wounded and in great pain, Cpl. Harris insisted on giving information which enabled his officer to locate the Panther. This NCO's courage and complete disregard for his own safety were an inspiration not only to his troop but also to the infantry whom he was supporting."*

John receiving the prestigious Military Medal on September 30, 1944. Note the patch on his arm with the former unit name, 11th Canadian Army Tank Regiment.

III - THE SOFT UNDERBELLY 1943-1944

John's tank was hit by a German Panzer V 'Panther' tank, technically superior to the Sherman used by the Allies, killing John's driver, Tom Huntington Widlake, on the spot. He will later have a street named after him in the suburbs of Winnipeg, his home town. John, on the other hand, had a severely injured left leg and would never be able to serve his country again. However, the enemy tank was destroyed by Allied artillery, thanks to John's information. Two other Panthers were also found out of action at the same location, destroyed by the Canadian crew. One of them even had the barrel of his cannon folded in on itself, *"like a peeled banana"*. Frenchy, the gunner in John's tank, had made an almost impossible shot!

Three German Mark IV tanks were also destroyed near the farm, and the city was secured in a few hours. In four days of fighting, the Ontario Regiment had seven killed and eighteen wounded, including John, who was evacuated. The new commander of the 8th Army, Sir Oliver Leese (replacing Montgomery who had left to prepare for the invasion of Normandy), was so impressed by John's squadron that he sent a message of congratulations to the commander of the Ontario Regiment: *"I send to you and the squadron concerned my warmest congratulations on the fine engagements at Pescia and Ranciano, in which you knocked out a number of Panthers and Mark IV tanks. Please congratulate squadrons concerned."*

John, on the other hand, will be more modest about this heroic act. He will write after the war: *"I wear this medal proudly, not because of any particular bravery on my part, I was just in the right position at the right time. I wear it in trust for the other four members of my tank crew as we were a team, about as closely knit as it is possible for me to be. Tommie Widlake who was killed in this action was my driver, and got us to the objective, Albert (Frenchy) Mageau was my gunner who did all the damage, these two chaps had been my buddies since Camp Borden, and we had gone through many good times and bad together.*

As the strident tones of [the] Last Post ring out on Remembrance Day, the shiver goes down my spine, and I have difficulty in holding back the tears, as I think back almost forty years to Frenchy Mageau, Tommie Widlake, Buddy Miller, Mo Krasusky and of the many others of my acquaintance who put their lives on the line for Canada, and who exemplified the motto of the Ontario Regiment Tank, 'Faithful to the end'".

John Leslie Harris and his medals, from left to right: Military Medal; 1939-1945 Star; Italy Star; Defence Medal; Canadian Volunteer Service Medal and War Medal 1939-1945.

John will be very active at the veterans' club of Markham, Ontario, where he will die on July 6, 2002.

PAUL PIRAT

83e bataillon du Génie, 3e division d'infanterie algérienne

Paul is part of the French Expeditionary Force in Italy. West of the Gustav Line, they'll earn the respect of their American and British allies by playing an important role in the fall of the Monte Cassino bastion. As a motorcycle liaison officer, Paul will receive several decorations for bravery in Italy, France and Germany.

Paul Pirat was born on March 20, 1920 in Tunis (Tunisia), to French parents. At the age of 20, he joined the Youth of the French Empire, a group created by the son of Edouard Daladier (who declared war on Germany after the invasion of Poland). According to its booklet, the idea is not to create a new political party, but to "unite future humanity around the values of justice, fraternity, and peace". It was at one of its reunions that Paul met his future wife, Odile Jourdan. He is deeply in love with the woman he calls "my Dilo", but unfortunately, the couple will have to deal with unexpected events…

THE WAR SEPARATES PAUL AND DILO

As Paul dreamed of becoming an architect and was preparing to go to Oran to study, war broke out. He was called up and incorporated into the 3rd Zouaves Regiment (mostly Algerian soldiers of Kabyle origin) on 16 June 1940, only to be demobilized on 15 October. Two days later he was sent to a Tunisian 'chantier de jeunesse' (youth work camp) and couldn't marry Odile until 29 October 1941.

Paul and « Dilo »

The 1940 armistice having abolished compulsory military service, the chantiers de jeunesse were created for young people from France and North Africa who, from the age of 20, were old enough to perform their military obligations. Loyal to the Vichy regime, this organization teaches its idea of the 'National Revolution' through camps in the heart of nature, supervised by former officers of the French Army. Although the young people mainly perform community service, the leaders of these youth work camps will affirm after the war that they wanted to form a troop which could be mobilized in the event of a resumption of the war with Germany. This is what happened to Paul and his comrades (photo opposite) following *Operation Torch*: recalled and trained, they were incorporated into the French African Army on November 9, 1942. Two months later, Daniel, Paul's first child, was born.

On July 1, 1943, Paul joined the 1st Company of Captain Dumont (a veteran of the French and Tunisian campaigns, where he was wounded by a mine), 83e bataillon du Génie (Engineer Battalion), 3e division d'infanterie algérienne (3e DIA), as a motorcycle liaison officer, or 'dispatch rider'. Among his missions, he has to ride alone on his motorcycle to study enemy activity for command, or to transmit messages and orders to units scattered on the front. The 3e DIA had been created only two months earlier, under the command of General Goislard de Monsabert, from the French Constantine's Division which had helped stop Rommel's Afrika Korps in Tunisia with the XIX French Corps. It totals 16,840 men, about 60% of whom are North Africans and 40% Europeans. In Paul's engineer battalion, however, the proportion of Europeans is higher than in the infantry.

Paul participated in several training exercises near Oran, Algeria, where the division became familiar with the American equipment it was using (only the Adrian helmet, with or without a helmet cover, and a tricolor patch indicated his French nationality). The French soldiers mostly wear the American HBT (Herringbone Twill) uniform and are armed with old US Springfield 1903 bolt action rifles (replaced by the much more effective semi-automatic M1 Garand in the US Army), or the Thompson M1928 machine gun, like Paul. The motorbike he rides is also American: a 1942 Harley Davidson WLA, which Paul names 'Dilo' in honor of the woman who constantly occupies his thoughts. The division was reviewed by General Giraud during a parade on November 13, 1943, headed by engineering troops - Paul was one of two motorcyclists leading the way behind a Dodge truck.

THE FRENCH EXPEDITIONARY FORCE

Paul crosses the Algerian-Tunisian border on December 11 and six days later embarks at Bizerte to liberate Europe. The American ship leaves the harbor a week later on rough seas. Paul sleeps with five comrades in an American GMC truck and spends Christmas Eve in an unusual atmosphere: no lights are allowed, not even that of cigarettes, in order to avoid offering targets to the Luftwaffe. Paul finally arrives in Naples (Italy) on the evening of December 30, 1943. Some French units have already been there since November 19, and have proved their worth by securing Monte Pantano, where the 'Red Bulls' of the 34th US Infantry Division lost 1,500 men without succeeding in capturing the high ground. The Moroccan tirailleurs (infantry) accomplished their mission in two days of violent fighting, and less than two weeks later took Le Mainarde. With the arrival of the 3e DIA, all the French forces, mostly from the African continent, can now be brought together in a single army.

At its head, General Alphonse Juin is considered by his American counterpart Mark Clark as one of the best soldiers he has ever met. In 1940, Juin had fought the German 6. Armee in Belgium with his 15e division d'infanterie motorisée, but was pushed back to Lille where he surrendered on May 30. Held prisoner at Konigstein Castle, he was liberated by Hitler at the request of Weygand and Pétain, who appointed him commander of the French troops in North Africa.

Following *Operation Torch*, French African troops joined the Allied side, and in November 1943, Juin was appointed by de Gaulle as commander of the Free French Forces in Italy. This group of irregular units was initially to be called the '1st French Army', but as it was already under the American command of Clark's 5th Army, it is given the name of 'Army Detachment A' or 'French Expeditionary Force' on January 23, 1944.

This War Office map shows the city of Avezzano (east of Rome, Italy) at a scale of 1/100,000.

Dated 1943 and photolithographed in February 1944 by the US Army, this one was used during the last battles of the French Expeditionary Force by one of its members. Indeed, this map has the particularity of being annotated in pencil by a Muslim soldier: "Finished, Inch'Allah - 25/6/44". It is also stained with Italian mud.

Displayed on the map is an original patch of the French Expeditionary Force in Italy, representing the 'awakening of France'. At its side, an M1938 lensatic compass of the US Army (standard model used during the Second World War) of early manufacture, by W & LE Gurley, Troy (New York).

Paul and his motorcycle, named 'Dilo' after his wife.

The French Expeditionary Force includes four divisions: the 1st Free French Division (Foreign Legion, colonial artillery, marine fusiliers), the 2nd Moroccan Infantry Division (Moroccan tirailleurs and spahis), Paul's 3rd Algerian Infantry Division (Algerian and Tunisian tirailleurs, Algerian reconnaissance spahis), and the 4th Moroccan Mountain Division (Moroccan tirailleurs, mountain artillery). To these are added the Moroccan Goums (groups of 'tabors' or Moroccan battalions, whose 'goumiers' served as replacements in infantry units) and reserve units (African Chasseurs, colonial and Levant artillery). In May 1944, the entire French Expeditionary Force has 112,000 troops.

BAPTISM BY FIRE IN MONTE CASSINO

When Paul arrives in Italy, the Allies are already facing the Gustav Line, whose minefields give his engineer battalion a lot of trouble. At the center of the German defensive system, Monte Cassino is a hill dominating the city of Cassino, between Naples and Rome. Topped by a Benedictine monastery dating back to 529, it's a protected historical site. But to the Germans, it's above all an excellent observation point for their artillery, since its elevation offers a panoramic view of the Rapido, Garigliano and Liri river valleys. The Allies therefore quickly identified Monte Cassino as a priority objective and will turn the beautiful abbey into a pile of ruins after no less than four deadly assaults.

The first plan is to launch the X British Corps and II American Corps at a 20-mile front. Near the coast, to the west, the British 5th, 46th and 56th Infantry Divisions cross the Garigliano on January 19. To their right, the American 36th 'Texas' Infantry Division will launch the main assault the next day on the Rapido, using rubber boats. At the same time, the French Expeditionary Force will advance towards Monte Cairo in the north. Unfortunately, from the very beginning of the attack, the Allies encounter unexpected resistance and this first attempt is a disaster.

The British report more than 4,000 casualties. The French of the 3e DIA manage to take the stronghold of Belvedere, the keystone of the Gustav Line, on February 4, but it costs the 4th Tunisian Infantry Regiment more than 1,500 killed, wounded and missing (two thirds of its strength). Even worse, American regiments of the 36th Division were almost wiped out, with 2,100 casualties. The 34th 'Red Bull' Division attempts another crossing of the flooded Rapido River on January 24, and after eight days of fierce combat finally reaches the peaks north of Cassino. The GIs then move south, making difficult progress on the steep and rocky hills, with the firm intention of seizing the famous monastery held by a German parachute regiment. But just when they are about to reach their objective, they are brutally repelled by machine guns, and on February 11, the 34th Division withdraws from Monte Cassino with nearly 80% casualties in its infantry battalions.

The 3e DIA occupies the Venafro sector, 20 miles east of Cassino, after having relieved the 45th US Infantry Division. Paul carries out more and more reconnaissance missions for his 1st platoon towards Sant'Elia (north of Cassino), either alone by motorcycle, or by Jeep with his captain. His orders are clear: *"Go take a look, and if there are bombs, you come back."* Most of his trips are interrupted by artillery shells. Without really being a believer, he ends up clinging to superstition to carry on. Keeping a medal of Saint Theresa in his pocket, he notices that as soon as he enters an Italian village, the bombs stop falling, and the bombardment always seems to resume as soon as he leaves. He will remain scarred for life by the images of destruction he witnessed in Italy and the innocent victims of the war, especially the horses ripped open by shrapnel on the roadsides, swarming with worms. However, other memories will be even more painful...

MARIE-ALPHONSINE

Occasionally, Paul takes part in mine clearance operations. Early in his deployment, he lost his first friends under the bombs and on the German mines that cover the Cassino area. On his eighteenth day in Italy, he miraculously survived the explosion of his truck, which backed up on a forgotten antitank Tellermine. Paul immediately rescued one of his wounded comrades to evacuate him. He writes in his diary: *"His first words when I took him out of the car were: 'They killed me, the pigs!' Then he repeated several times 'Mom'. I don't think I'll ever forget that one."* Other tragedies will be just as significant. The veteran will keep an article from *The Frying Pan*, the newspaper published by his engineer battalion, whose title refers to the mine detector. Being heavily involved in the paper himself, and having witnessed this scene which he will regularly speak about after the war, it's very likely that Paul was the author of these words:

"February 5, 1944 - The battle is still raging on the Belvedere, which the enemy holds tenaciously. There are many casualties among the tirailleurs and they must be evacuated quickly. Unfortunately, there is only one way to access it: the Terelle-Cassino road through the M'Vila crossroads, so this crossroads is targeted day and night by continuous harassment fire; driving through it is a dangerous feat. The poor female drivers of the Medical Battalion, who go to fetch the wounded at the outposts themselves, are afraid of it, and I am not surprised! To solve this problem, the engineers were asked to open a track that will follow the Rio-Secco bed to reach the Terelle road beyond the crossroads.

Despite the presence of extraordinarily dense minefields and shelling by the enemy, who, from his Sifalco observation post, sees everything that is happening in the valley, the track is finished on February 5 at dawn. With one of my officers, my comrade Cosso, we are removing the last mines when an ambulance, coming down the Belvedere, reaches us. Recognizing sappers (the 3e DIA is a large family where sappers hold a large place), the drivers stop. We know them well and admire the girls' courage. We tell them the good news: they can now take the track we have just finished and bypass the infamous crossroads. Two 'wows' of relief thank us for our efforts. Now some 'advice' on the state of the track: be especially aware of a muddy passage just before the Rio-Secco, after that, you're pretty much safe. The girls thank us again and, after a cheerful 'goodbye', set out to 'inaugurate' our track with their cargo of wounded.

Cosso and I climb a small path on the sides of the Belvedere. With our binoculars, we can soon see our ambualnce down in the valley as it approaches the Rio-Secco, and the muddy passage indicated. I hope it gets through without any trouble. But suddenly, disaster strikes, it's stuck in the mud!!! Despite the driver's efforts, the vehicle sinks deeper and deeper, and what I feared happens: a few shells explode near the ambulance. The Kraut observers on the Sifalco see the scene as well as we do, they certainly noticed the huge red crosses painted on the vehicle, but they continue to direct the fire which is becoming more and more precise. The two girls understood the situation from the first round, and their first reaction is to move their wounded to a half-destroyed house about 30 meters away. Twice, three times, they make the journey, each time supporting an injured soldier, while the shelling continues. Now I see only one girl running towards the vehicle, and suddenly, the tragedy: a shell hits the ambulance, which bursts into flames. I don't see the girl anymore, I hope she wasn't hit.

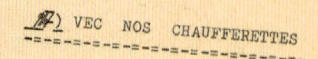

We have all witnessed this helplessly, too far away to help them. But the enemy, probably happy with the result, stopped firing, and already I see some soldiers, who must have been hiding in the Rio-Secco, leaping towards the burning vehicle; they will be able to rescue the drivers. Alas, we were soon to learn that one of them had died devoting herself to saving her wounded men and her vehicle. It was Mrs. Marie Loretti, whose courage and good humor had struck us a few moments before her death. She had wanted to follow her husband, an officer in the 3e DIA, and had joined this magnificent ambulance corps. The spirit of self-sacrifice and bravery shown by all these girls during the hard and exhausting campaigns of the 3e DIA cannot be overemphasized."

Marie-Alphonsine Fifre, wife of NCO Loretti (a tirailleur in the 3e DIA), came from Belfort, France. She arrived in Naples with the women of the 531st Medical Transport Company of the 3rd Medical Battalion, at the same time as Paul. That day, she volunteered with five other girls to pick up wounded tirailleurs at night near the village of Terelle, before being hit by shell fragments on this road, parallel to the 'death road' (at the foot of Monte Cassino), which was littered with destroyed Allied vehicles. The survivors of the group then spent sixteen hours traveling the 25 miles separating them from the medical battalion. Marie-Alphonsine, 28, was the first of five female ambulance drivers killed in Italy, and the first woman in history to receive the Military Medal. It was pinned on her coffin the day after her death by General Juin himself. His comrades will then advance to Germany, where others would lose their lives (such as Lolita Rodriguez, of the same unit, who will die of exhaustion at the wheel while trying to evacuate eight wounded Germans…).

Marie Loretti at work on her ambulance.

'Lorette' still rests in Venafro today, among the 3,400 graves of the largest French military cemetery in Italy.

Top right, Paul (left) and his Jeep.

The next day, in the same place, Paul himself is targeted by the same gun, as he recounts in his diary: *"Departure at 8 am by Jeep with the captain, reconnaissance for mine clearance. On arrival we received three shells, a lieutenant wounded in the buttock. Jeep stuck in the mud, I take it out, park it on the Rio-Secco and take shelter against a wall, shelled for 3/4 of an hour. I go back to get supplies for the 3rd section, then come back to Rio-Secco and I just lie there until 5 pm, hiding, because the shells keep raining".*

TWO MORE FAILURES AT CASSINO

A second operation on Monte Cassino, code-named 'Avenger', is launched. The Americans are replaced by the 2nd New Zealand Infantry Division and the 4th Indian Infantry Division, under the command of Lieutenant-General Freyberg. The idea is to continue the Red Bulls' work by attacking simultaneously from the north of Monte Cassino and the south of the city, but in Freyberg's opinion, the monastery is impregnable in its current state: it has to be blown off the map. On February 15, Paul writes in his diary: *"We are witnessing the bombing of Cassino Abbey by one hundred Flying Fortresses and about fifty Boston bombers. In the afternoon two more waves of twenty aircraft on the abbey."* Indeed, 1,400 tons of explosives fell on the hill, but they only transformed the area into an ideal defensive ground for German paratroopers. It seems that no Germans were even hit by the bombardment! On the other hand, it killed 230 civilians who had taken refuge in the monastery and had not evacuated, despite the Allied warning leaflets dropped the day before. The next three days will also be disastrous. The British Royal Sussex Regiment suffers 50% casualties during its failed attack on 'Snakeshead Ridge', a huge arched path leading to the monastery. The attacks on the latter by the Indian and Nepalese regiments Rajputana Rifles and Gurkha Rifles, although specialists in mountain fighting, are also bitter defeats. To the south, the 28th Maori Battalion of New Zealand fails to defend Cassino station, surprised by a German armored counter-attack for which it was unequipped.

A third attempt by the same New Zealand corps begins on March 15, preceded by another bombardment. Paul writes: *"Around 8:30 am, a first wave of B-17 Flying Fortresses attacks the village of Cassino, then the waves follow one another. One is composed of 116 fortresses. At noon, I count 680 aircraft. In the afternoon, it is the artillery that strikes, plus fighter planes and dive bombers. We can estimate a thousand planes."* However, the 15th Air Force makes a poor demonstration of its precision. American bombs fall on almost every Allied nations' soldiers, up to General Juin's HQ, killing or seriously wounding 475 soldiers and civilians. However, the Indians take several positions in the mountains, and the New Zealanders, this time supported by tanks, finally reach their objectives in town. On March 20, the 78th British Division arrives to reinforce the attackers, but the 1. Fallschirmjäger-Division holds tight and keeps control of the monastery, despite heavy losses. Freyberg's troops, with nearly 5,000 killed, wounded and missing, are again withdrawn from the lines.

ON LEAVE

From March 17, Paul is allowed a few days of rest. He learns Italian and discovers local food while dining with families. He writes in his diary on April 14, 1944: *"I have already noticed and still see that the Italians are naturally whiny. The guy we live with, although quite rich, since he owns several houses, complains all the time. Moreover, they tell us that since Abyssinia* [today's Ethiopia, invaded by Italy]*, they even have restrictions on what they produce. All of them (with more or less sincerity) tell us that they did not like fascism or Mussolini, but that in order to have a job, or even not to starve to death, you had to join or leave* [the country].*"*

Paul explores Naples while on leave: *"The black market is everywhere. You can find everything, but at quite high prices."* Although liberated several months ago, the city is still suffering greatly from the war, and air raid alerts are frequent. Food and water are scarce, and hunger even causes riots. However, a soldier on leave has everything he needs, and Paul visits the ruins of Pompeii, the basilica, attends a performance of *Carmen* in the theater and buys silk stockings for his 'Dilo', and rompers for Daniel. However, he's shocked by the debauchery that reigns in the streets: *"Naples, city of perdition, a vast brothel, I'm being approached from all sides (the French are more esteemed than the Americans)."* He's addressed by an Italian soldier offering him several women and will mention it in a letter to his wife much later, on February 14, 1945, when his unit is in Strasbourg, France: *"In Naples, which was called the Brothel City, morals were very low. A husband gave his wife, a mother her daughter, a brother his sister, when he did not give himself. But all this for money. A night with a woman cost between 1,500 and 2,000 lire* [about $20].*"* Indeed, the Italians lack everything, and in Naples a young girl is often ready to prostitute herself for a simple ration tin, sometimes a few cigarettes.

OPERATION DIADEM

Spring sets in and April's weather conditions are favorable for a new assault on the monastery. *Operation Diadem* brings together no less than half a million men from ten different Allied nations. The plan is as follows: the 5th US Army will attack south between Monte Cassino and the sea, the French Expeditionary Force will cross the Garigliano to clear the Aurunci Mountains, and the XIII British Corps will take care

III - THE SOFT UNDERBELLY 1943-1944

of the Liri Valley. Finally, the Polish II Corps (3rd Carpathian Rifle Division and 5th Kresowa Division), which relieved the British 78th Infantry Division in the mountains north of Cassino, will capture the monastery. The I Canadian Corps will remain in reserve to rush into the breach and head for Anzio and Rome. As they walk to their positions, the Poles pass through Snakeshead Ridge, where the 4th Indian Infantry Division and many others had failed weeks earlier. The traces of these defeats are still very much visible.

Romuald, a Polish soldier from the 12 Podolski Lancers Regiment, recalls: *"The place was a living testimony to what war was like. There wasn't a tree that still had branches. They were just stumps, sticking out here and there. The grass had also disappeared. Bare rocks, covered with dust, unwelcoming, were everywhere. There were other witnesses to the history of the place: corpses. Some were half decomposed, others half covered with dust or all the soil ripped from the surface. Most of the time, they were covered with limestone. They recall the fierce fighting that has taken place here for four months since January, when the 34th and 36th American Divisions made their first assault, crossing the Rapido River to be decimated by the Germans. These two excellent divisions have almost ceased to exist as fighting forces. The complete history of the battle can be read in these bodies. There were corpses of Americans, Germans, Gurkhas, British soldiers, some with their faces half devoured by insects, mice or other animals, blackened by time, with empty eyes, and exposed teeth. The smell of these decomposing bodies was suffocating. They are all silent now, resting in their eternal sleep after their dance of death a few months ago. Every time I looked at them, a sad thought crossed my mind: when will I be one of them? In this situation, I realized that the odds were against me, and that it was only a matter of time before my turn comes, and sooner or later I would be looked at exactly as I looked at those men who were young, bright, full of life and hope for the future. Look at them now... and those flies. They were big, fat, feasting on these rotting bodies. The stench of death was everywhere. So were the rats, and they were huge. I will never forget one of them, sitting on a soldier's half emaciated remains, looking at me. I thought he saw in me his next meal... And there, just below it, was this beautiful valley covered with red poppies. Sometimes the contrast was barely believable: here an atmosphere of death and destruction, and there, beauty, peace and silence. I thought: 'how can these two worlds coexist so close to each other?'"*

The approach of the 50,000 Polish soldiers was screened by a thick smoke covering the valley. The attack is launched at 11 pm on May 11, and once again starts with a massive barrage of almost 1,700 British, American, South African, New Zealand, Polish and French cannons. The most exotic soldier of all serves in the Polish artillery: a Syrian brown bear, named Wojtek, who carries shell boxes on his back for supplies. The animal, whose name means 'enthusiastic warrior', will even be promoted to corporal. On all fronts, the advance is slow but positive, and for the first time at Cassino, the Allies outnumber the Germans three to one. However, the bloody fighting will still last a week. The Poles endure three days of hell on Monte Calvario (Snakeshead Ridge), which will later be taken back by the German paratroopers. The two Polish divisions lose 281 officers and 3,503 soldiers to only 800 enemy paratroopers. Their front line battalions are decimated and have to retreat.

View of Monte Cassino from Snakeshead Ridge. In the foreground is the Polish cemetery, with the re-built abbey on the high ground. Behind it is the city of Cassino.

Above: the kit bag of a sergeant in the 13th Polish Medium Artillery Regiment (II Corps), who took part in the battle.

After Barbarossa (June 22, 1941), the Soviets liberated 75,000 Polish soldiers captured in September 1939. They went on to join the British 8th Army in the Middle East to form the 2nd Polish Corps with the troops evacuated from France in 1940. Its soldiers paid such a heavy price on Monte Cassino that a Polish cemetery with 1,000 graves was built there after the war. In the surrounding valleys there are also many British, New Zealand, Canadian, Indian, Gurkha, Australian, South African, Italian, American and French soldiers, among the 55,000 Allied casualties in this terrible campaign.

It's on the northwest side of Monte Cassino, trapped between rocks, that this MKII helmet shell (British made) was found on May 22, 1976, almost thirty-two years to the day after the last battle for the monastery.

It proudly featured the eagle representing the Polish forces in exile. Painted on the front of the helmet with a stamp or stencil sponge, sometimes with yellow gas detection paint, it's still visible here although strongly degraded by time, the elements and the cleaning of the helmet.

III - THE SOFT UNDERBELLY 1943-1944

On the French side, however, the assault is a success. General Juin opts for an attack in an area north of the Garigliano, where German defenses are not as concentrated, rather than a frontal assault, such as the American one on the Rapido. Used to operating in the mountains, the French Expeditionary Force prepares to capture the Aurunci Mountains. The 3rd section has returned from the Garigliano, where it was fighting when Paul's section was resting. The latter takes over and attacks on May 11. Paul writes: *"At 11 pm the attack is triggered by artillery first, which spits out a terrific barrage (one battery alone fires 2,000 rounds). At 6 am I get up to give a message to the Colonel... I almost didn't sleep a wink last night."* He won't sleep for two days, constantly transmitting messages by motorcycle between the different units involved.

After crossing the river and fighting their way to the high ground, the 3e DIA take Castelforte in less than 48 hours, while the other French units win victory after victory in the other sectors. At night, waves of Goumiers in sandals and striped djellabas jump on the panicked Germans with daggers. They capture Cerasola, San Giogrio, Mount D'Oro, Ausonia and Esperia in a single movement, and their progress is such that some units have to slow down to wait for the 8th Army. The Gustav Line is now broken, and the British 78th Division can at last isolate Monte Cassino on May 15. In the battalion's newspaper, one of Paul's comrades mentions a remark by a German commander in the aftermath of the Garigliano attack: *"The American and British offensives are fairly easy to control, they are methodical. Those of the French, on the other hand, are most often unpredictable and occur, in general, in places considered most impractical to an attack. Beware of the French even where you would think that no one can get through!"*

On May 17, the Poles' second assault on Monte Cassino often results in hand-to-hand combat. Finally, seeing their supply line cut by the British encircling them, the Germans withdraw from the heights and join the next line of defense, the Hitler Line. The fighting for Monte Cassino thus ends on May 18, 1944. The Polish soldiers are so tired that they have great difficulty finding volunteers to climb the few hundred yards that still separate them from the summit. At last, their flag flies over the ruins of the abbey. On the evening of the battle, the song *Red Poppies on Monte Cassino* is sung for the first time in front of the crying survivors. Written on the eve of the final assault by two Polish soldiers, it predicts that the poppies, which have become the symbols of their sacrifice, will always get redder, gorged with the blood spilled on their soil (4,000 killed and wounded during the assault).

The French also played a major role in opening the road to Anzio and the Italian capital, and their fight in the mountains deeply impressed the American command. Yet, on June 5, although Paul is only 10 miles away from Rome (which is celebrating its liberation), he and his men aren't allowed to enter the city: General Mark Clark wants to give this honor to his GIs. After a good night's sleep, Paul cleans his Jeep and learns of the Normandy landings, which will overshadow the recent successes of the French Expeditionary Force and their allies in Italy.

FRANCE

Paul finally enters the outskirts of Rome the next day and on June 9, the 3e DIA is received by the Pope who gives it his blessing in French. On July 3, the French Expeditionary Force liberates Siena and arrives at the gates of Florence: these would be its last days of combat in Italy. Its various units will gradually be withdrawn from the lines and sent to Naples to prepare for the next invasion. On the 16th, in San Juliano, after having completed numerous dispatch missions between Rome and Siena, Paul is decorated by his division (document below): *"Motorcyclist liaison officer who continuously provided front line communication services for three weeks, day and night, sometimes under enemy fire, and with the most complete disregard for danger and fatigue."* He will receive the Croix de Guerre with a bronze star.

From November 1943 to July 1944, the French Expeditionary Force lost no less than 8,665 killed or missing in Italy and 23,506 wounded, out of the 80,000 soldiers deployed on the front line. It will henceforth cease to exist, and its divisions will be absorbed by General de Lattre de Tassigny's Armée B. On August 8, Paul will board an English ship, HMS *Circassia*, in Taranto. He will guess that his next destination will be in the Mediterranean, but will only learn the good news on August 15 at noon, the first day of *Operation Dragoon*: he will help liberate France. The French soldiers will leave the ex-cruise ship on the evening of August 16 in Saint-Tropez, to fight for Toulon and Marseille.

Follow Paul's campaign in France and Germany on p. 299.

JOSEPH NEMEC

HQ Co, 1st Bn, 7th Infantry Regiment, 3rd Infantry Division

'Joe', a radio operator, will participate in his first landing at Anzio, south of Rome. *Operation Shingle* is intended to relieve the Gustav Line front by attracting the Germans northward, allowing a breakthrough at Monte Cassino. However, Anzio's troops will remain trapped near the beaches for four long months, and will only break the encirclement once the Gustav Line is crossed.

Joseph Charles Nemec Jr. was a 19-year-old New Yorker when he arrived in Italy as a replacement. His 7th 'Cottonbalers' Regiment (3rd Infantry Division) is already very experienced, having been among the spearheads of the landings in Africa (November 1942) and Sicily (July 1943). Joe is a radio operator (a job he learned the basics of in high school) and carries the heavy communication equipment on his back, sometimes in the middle of the fighting.

After a stopover in North Africa for a few days, passing through Gibraltar, Bizerte and Malta, the Mediterranean crossing wasn't easy as his convoy was attacked by the Luftwaffe and German submarines. Two Allied ships were sunk, but Joseph's made it out alright, even shooting down two planes during the attack. Joe saw Naples and Mount Vesuvius, but couldn't taste the famous 'pizza pies' he'd heard so much about (and which aren't yet known to many Americans): the Italians no longer make them because flour and oil have become too rare. Joe suffered from dysentery anyway, and was hospitalized for two weeks at the end of 1943. He's sent back to his company on December 28, just in time for his first action. Joe is about to experience his very first amphibious assault on January 22, 1944, in Anzio.

At that time, the Allies hadn't yet succeeded in breaking the defenses of the Gustav Line, and the objective was to land near Rome to bypass the enemy and create a diversion: the maneuver could force some of the German troops stationed at Monte Cassino to move and allow an Allied advance.

OPERATION SHINGLE

Supported by Rangers of the 1st, 3rd and 4th Battalions, who invaded Anzio Harbor, and paratroopers of the 504th and 509th Parachute Infantry Regiments, the 1st British Infantry Division lands on Peter Beach, north of Anzio, while Joe's 3rd US Infantry Division sets foot on X-Ray Beach, east of Nettuno. The surprise is total and the opposition minimal. Of the 36,000 men who land, only 13 soldiers are killed and 97 wounded. But things won't go so well a few days later.

In charge of the beachhead, Major-General John P. Lucas (former commander of the 3rd Infantry Division) receives conflicting advice: General Sir Harold Alexander (commander of the entire 15th Army Group, who would become the Field Marshal responsible for the entire Mediterranean Theater at

III - THE SOFT UNDERBELLY 1943-1944

the end of the year) advocates moving inland, while General Clark suggests not rushing to reinforce his troops before the attack. Lucas chooses to consolidate the front and lands reinforcements for a week without even trying to leave the beaches. The Allies soon gather nearly 70,000 men, but the surprise effect is ruined and the Germans are massed in front of Anzio, on high ground that should already have been taken by the Americans. Joe Nemec and his comrades now face 95,000 Germans who are closing the trap on them. Winston Churchill is mad with rage and says: *"I had hoped we were hurling a wildcat into the shore, but all we got was a stranded whale!"*

In the last days of January, Joe and his division only move 3 miles inland towards Cisterna, but fail to take the city, and the Rangers coming to their rescue face a violent counter-attack from the Hermann Göring Panzer Division. Of the 767 Rangers from the 1st and 3rd Battalions, only 6 men will return behind the Allied lines. The other survivors are taken prisoners and these elite soldiers are exhibited by the Germans on a humiliating parade through the streets of Rome.

BACK IN THE HOSPITAL

On February 1, fighting intensifies in front of Cisterna, and Joe's regiment, alongside the 504th Parachute Infantry Regiment and the 4th Ranger Battalion, launches a failed assault. Joe is shot by a German machine gun through both buttocks. Two days later, he writes to his parents in three different V-mails:

"Dearest Mother & Dad, Well hello there, folks, how are you all? I do hope that you folks are alright and in the best of health and everything is okay at home. I hope you were not worried when you did not hear from me for a couple of weeks. You see I didn't have a chance to write you and tell you that I wouldn't be able to write for a while. You see we had to go on the move again, as you read about the invasion recently made below Rome. Well I can say I saw my first invasion, maybe you wouldn't call it an invasion because we didn't get any German opposition. Although the British took prisoners as you read about it. What did you think when you received the newspapers and read the headlines?

Well I guess I might as well give you a little sad news, because the army will notify you anyway.

I'm in the hospital again, not the dysentery this time. I got hit by a Jerry machine gun bullet. I bet you can't guess where I got it. I got it right plump in the buttock, in other words the priddle, ha ha. But don't go worrying now, it's nothing serious and I'm coming along swell, only I can't sit down. I'll probably be good for a months rest anyway. [...] The bullet hit both cheeks and just sliced it as it passed, it didn't go in. What a feeling it was, as if somebody cracked a whip across my rear end and the first thing I hollered out was 'och, you dirty S.O.B. Nazi!' Well no use wasting paper telling the details I'll tell after the war when I come home. Anyway, here I am back in a nice soft bed again, clean sheets instead of a dirty old slit trench to sleep in with a pack as a pillow. They're giving me a Purple Heart [Medal] for being wounded, but that doesn't do me any good as far as getting home. The only thing that's good for is to stick it in the drawer and keep it as a souvenir after this war. [...]

I'm continuing in letter no. three now. Gee, these 'V' mail are a pain in the neck no kidding. You just about start and then you are ready to sign off again. [...] Boy was I embarrassed last night when the nurse had to dress up my wound on my priddle. And then this morning she came around to wash my legs, feet and back because I couldn't bend down to get at them. Boy what service no kidding. That's something I didn't even let my Mother do, ha ha, I'm only kidding you Ma! [...] Well folks I hope you're all okay, and I probably write tomorrow. Love, Joe."

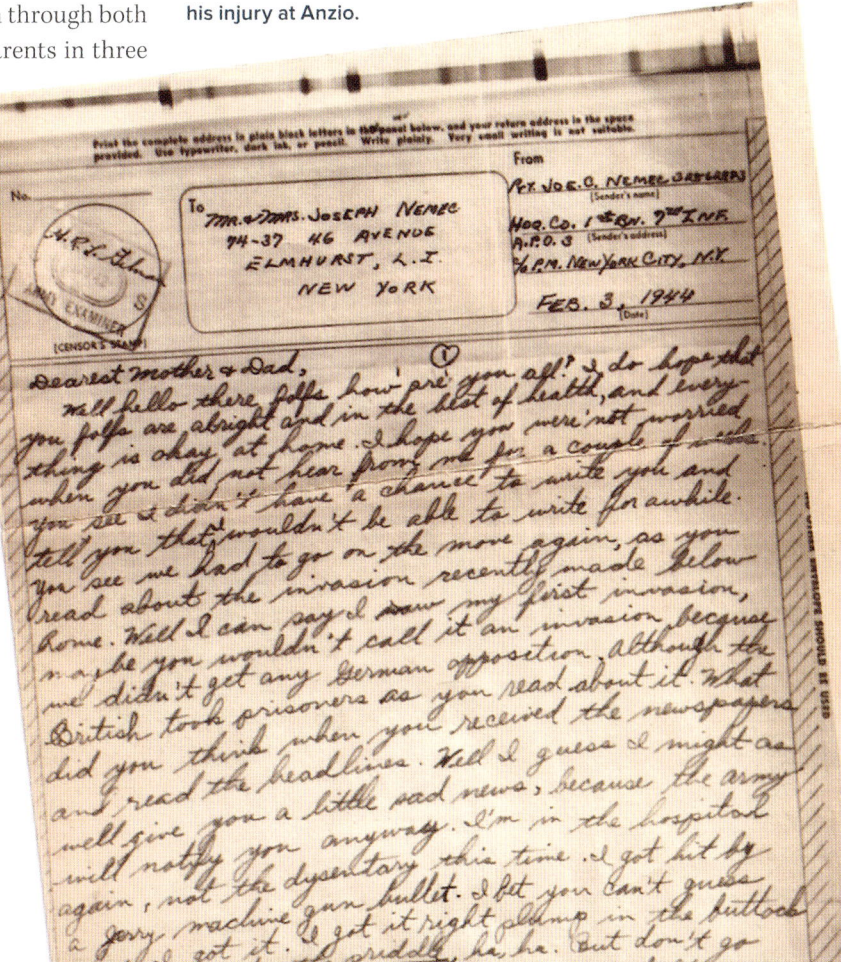

The first of Joe's three V-mails announcing his injury at Anzio.

Joe will spend several more weeks in the hospital. On February 18, he receives his Purple Heart on his hospital bed; he thinks it's a beautiful medal. But he suspects that as soon as his wound has healed, he'll be sent back to the front. His roommate is able return to the United States, but he's no luckier: the poor 19-year-old man was shot by a German sniper who tore off part of his spine, making him lose the use of his legs. For Joe, however, it's always preferable to the horror of combat: *"I'd sure go through what he went through to get to go home. You probably don't agree do you?"* Joe has to go back to the front in March. He then writes in a V-mail to his father: *"Dad you said that they should send the fellows home to recuperate well they do sometimes, if he has a leg or an arm shot off or wounded bad enough. But they try to patch you up as fast as they can and send you back to duty. Just a piece of equipment or machinery. They don't think much of a man's life, as long as they win a battle!"*

Joe in his foxhole at Anzio.

DAILY LIFE AT THE BRIDGEHEAD

While Joe is in the hospital, nothing moves in Anzio, but he writes to his parents: *"What do you think of the Russians killing those 52,000 Nazis and taking 11,000 prisoners? Boy I wish we could move that fast!"* Meanwhile, GIs get bored in their foxholes, occasionally repelling an enemy attack, or undergoing barrages that become almost routine. They do business with Italian families and even produce their own alcohol in makeshift stills. In front of Anzio, Henry, the British sailor on HMS *Exmoor*, writes on March 12, 1944: *"At the present we are in harbour doing a bit of a boiler clean and general straighten up, I think we'll be here four or five days. This place is a lousy hole, all you see ashore is Yanks, they near enough own the place. Still they can have it, it's one of the worst places I've been to and it's not really worth going ashore, I've been once, but I don't think I'll bother to go anymore."*

Leonard is a replacement in the 45th US Infantry Division. His 179th Regiment has endured several German offensives in Anzio and suffered many casualties since its landing. On April 10, Leonard is already a veteran and slowly getting used to his new living conditions (although he's not a big fan of powdered eggs, K rations and dehydrated food). He writes: *"Please excuse the poor handwriting, I'm half sitting and half lying down. I'm in a hole that isn't very big. There's not room enough to sit up in it, and it's more favorable to stay in it than to even stick my head out."* He adds on May 8: *"Italy is nice and green now, it looks like spring is here. Sometimes it's so quiet that you kind of forget there's a war on, then all hell breaks loose. But maybe it won't last too much longer, I sure hope not anyway."*

Others have a harder time acclimatizing. In Joe's 3rd Infantry Division, Savino is a GI of Italian descent who's already experienced combat in Africa, Sicily and southern Italy. At 31, Savino is an exception among the very young American soldiers fighting at Anzio. He's surprised to receive a friendly letter from the wife of a corporal in the 108th Artillery Battalion, defending Anzio from the Luftwaffe's relentless attacks. He replies on April 14, 1944: "[I am] *getting older every day, there's hardly any hair left on my head, the old zip is gone, yes I'm afraid when I get home I'll be a disappointment to many, but as long as I get home and make a few people happy, that's my chief concern. So your husband is here also, well there's no use in telling you anything about this beachhead, really there isn't much to say. I wish him all the luck in the world. [...] I hope for his and your sake that he is not in the infantry. May God protect your loved one from the horrors of war. Arrivederci ['Goodbye' in Italian]."*

Willard Purdy also participates in Anzio's defense with the 895th Anti-Aircraft Artillery Battalion. He writes to his aunt on April 24, 1944: *"Yes we have been through a lot here on the beachhead. We have been through 286 raids night and day and have taken part in bringing down 177 and damaging 117, otherwise it is rather quiet with the exception of a few Screaming Meemies [German rockets] coming over. They have been very scarce the last couple of days. We've had three close calls, the closest, a 500 pound bomb landed 40 yards away from our gun pit, daylight turned to darkness and we all were thrown to the ground and never injuring any of us (16), we certainly were lucky. I lost my best buddy he was on another gun, he was killed by shrapnel February 16, I sure miss him."* On August 15, 1944, Willard will be killed too, in the south of France. He will be one of the very few victims of *Operation Dragoon* (Southern France), when his Landing Craft *LST-282* is hit by a German bomb.

III - THE SOFT UNDERBELLY 1943-1944

The Nazi propaganda minister, Joseph Goebbels, tries to undermine the morale of American and British soldiers by dropping leaflets onto the beaches for the Allies to read: *"Remember the hell of Dunkirk? How great were the hopes of the British Expeditionary Force and how dreadful was the end! Think of the terrible hours when the German broom swept your fellow soldiers, tanks, guns and lorries off the continent. How many ships were sunk then, and how many brave Tommies kicked the bucket! And now, the hell of Nettuno! The American and British divisions that landed at Nettuno met with German soldiers, and not with Italian troops. Since the time of Salerno you know how bloody a landing turns out in the face of German resistance. [...] The beaches at Nettuno are covered in the Dunkirk fashion with debris and dead American and British soldiers crushed by the German military machine. One thing is clear: YOU'll have to bear the brunt of the fighting, just as before."*

German propaganda also strikes on the radio, as one soldier of the 1st Special Service Force (American-Canadian commandos) says in a letter: *"Went over to hear a radio program called 'Jerry's Front', put on by the Germans for propaganda purposes. Dance records for half an hour, with bits of news (all German) to hear them give the news. Of course this is all in English for the benefit of the American soldier. Then for the second half hour a German orchestra murdering American popular tunes, and two commentators, Sally and George, discuss the different fronts, heckle Churchill and Roosevelt. We all get a kick out of it. They read names and addresses of American P.O.W.'s too."*

Soldier of the 3rd Infantry Division, whose three-striped emblem is painted on this helmet found in Italy. Below, some of Joe's souvenirs, including his military dog tags.

JOE'S RETURN

When Joe goes back to his comrades in Anzio, they hadn't moved an inch. The 150,000 Allied soldiers now in the area won't be able to leave the German encirclement until late May 1944, after the crossing of the Gustav Line in the south. Breaking through the pocket won't be without damage, though, and on May 23, the 3rd Division will number 955 casualties in a single day, a sad record for all US Army divisions during the Second World War. Cisterna, the city where Joe was wounded in early February, will finally fall into the hands of his division two days later, where it will destroy the 362. German Division that had refused to surrender. Like tigers kept in cages for too long, the Americans will crush everything in their path. On the same day of the breakthrough, four men of the 3rd Infantry Division will be awarded the Medal of Honor, the highest American military distinction. The division will then reach the outskirts of Rome, and Joe, with his 1st Battalion of the 7th Regiment, will have the honor of being among the first liberators to enter the capital on June 4. However, this is a very small reward for the Cottonbalers, who suffered more than 3,000 casualties during the Anzio-Rome Campaign, including 729 killed, or a complete turnover of the regiment. A total of 7,000 Americans and British died at Anzio and Nettuno, and 36,000 were wounded.

Joe will next serve in Provence and in the Vosges, where he will be wounded again (see page 255).

THE ROAD TO ROME

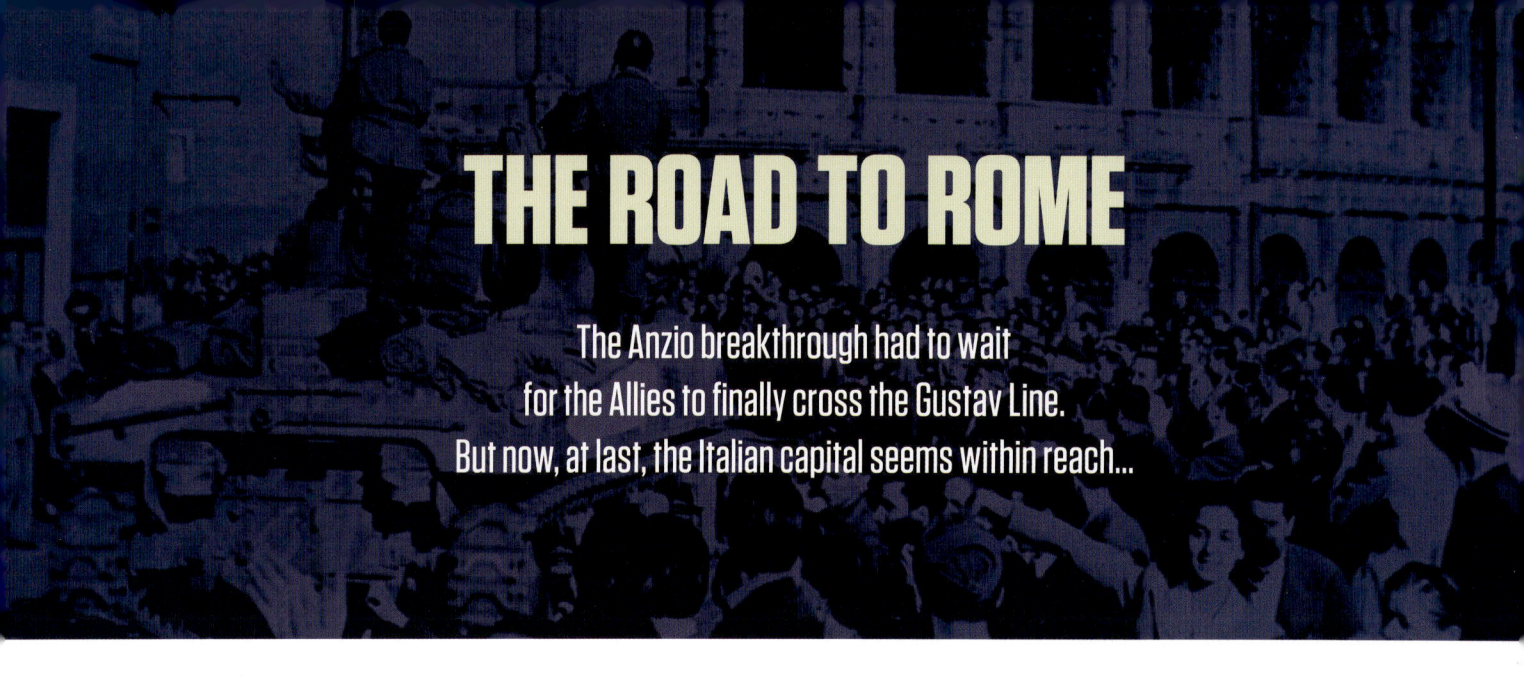

The Anzio breakthrough had to wait
for the Allies to finally cross the Gustav Line.
But now, at last, the Italian capital seems within reach...

The route from Anzio has to follow the plan of General Lucian Truscott (new commander of the VI US Corps), *Operation Buffalo*: while the British 1st and 5th Infantry Divisions will go up the coast to the north, the Americans of the 3rd and 45th Infantry Divisions (supported by the 1st US Armored Division tanks and the 1st Special Service Force commandos) will launch the main assault to the northeast and cut off the German 10. Armee's route, in full retreat from Cassino. If they succeed, the surrounding of the latter could precipitate the end of the Italian Campaign.

However, Clark, preferring *Operation Turtle*, decides to rush towards Rome by bypassing the lake and the Albano hills from the left. Believing that the capital is the main objective and that his troops deserve to enter it first (in fact, the man his officers nicknamed 'Marcus Aurelius Clarkus' was obsessed with the commercial value of capturing Rome), he's ready to let a large part of the 10. Armee escape, even though they're so close to destruction. The latter will settle on the Gothic Line, in front of Florence, on which the Allies will struggle until spring 1945.

For his part, the infantryman is simply happy to leave the foxhole he's occupied for so long. One of them writes to his father in late May: *"Yes dad, have seen dead Germans, and live ones too. Ha! All kinds of Jerry equipment, tanks etc. since you ask, and you will probably continue asking until I tell you. We have, from time to time, been under bombings, artillery fire, strafings etc. Not so much now as when we first arrived. Then too, changes have taken place recently. But it was pretty exciting for quite a period."*

"TOO FAST FOR THE NAZIS"

Andrew 'Andy' Gagalis serves in B Company, 179th Regiment, 45th US Infantry Division. The particularity of this division is that since 1923, it's original emblem was a red square with a yellow swastika. Since its first appearance more than 10,000 years ago, the symbol has had very positive connotations in many cultures. Indeed, for the large Amerindian population in the southwestern United States, it was a sign of good luck. But in order not to confuse the 45th Division with the Nazi swastika, in 1939 the emblem was replaced with another Amerindian symbol that gave its name to the division: the Thunder Bird.

Top:
an original
45th Division patch,
in its 1923
version.

Left:
the one worn by
Andy from Anzio
until his capture.

III - **THE SOFT UNDERBELLY** 1943-1944

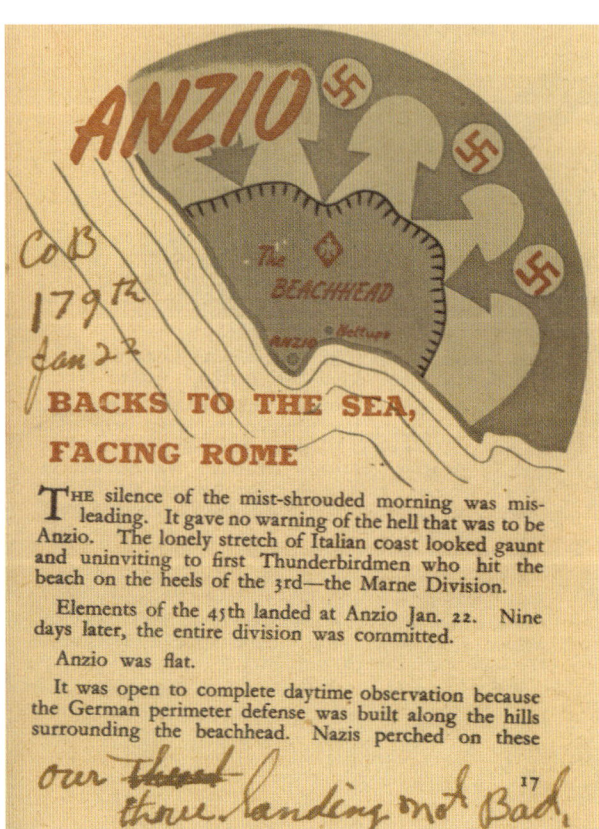

BACKS TO THE SEA, FACING ROME

The silence of the mist-shrouded morning was misleading. It gave no warning of the hell that was to be Anzio. The lonely stretch of Italian coast looked gaunt and uninviting to first Thunderbirdmen who hit the beach on the heels of the 3rd—the Marne Division.

Elements of the 45th landed at Anzio Jan. 22. Nine days later, the entire division was committed.

Anzio was flat.

It was open to complete daytime observation because the German perimeter defense was built along the hills surrounding the beachhead. Nazis perched on these

This article in the *Newburyport Daily News* is titled "Good news from Gagalis beats out bad news from Uncle Sam". Andy's parents haven't yet been informed of his capture near Rome, when he writes to inform them of his escape (see next page).

145

Andy (right) enjoys a beer with a comrade near the end of the war.

The officer with whom he was captured and escaped was Captain James Harmon Cruickshank Jr., of New York. The latter distinguished himself leading B Company in Anzio on February 19, 1944, when he repelled a large enemy force of infantry and tanks. Already a Silver Star recipient (twice), he was promoted to captain after this action. As for Andy, following his escape, he'll manage to return to his unit and land in Provence (Southern France) on August 15, 1944.

Anzio was Andy's third landing. He's already participated in operations *Husky* (in Scoglitti, Sicily) and *Avalanche* (in Paestum, near Salerno). Moving towards the Gustav Line, Andy was wounded for the first time in Longano, 10 miles east of his objective, Venafro, on November 30, 1943. He was by no means the only one to be hit, and the area was even nicknamed 'Purple Heart Alley'. Andy still continued the fight with his unit and took part in *Operation Shingle* in Anzio, landing right after the 3rd US Infantry Division. On May 23, 1944, VI Corps went on the offensive to break through the pocket, with the 45th Division on its left flank. The fighting lasted a week and following Clark's orders, Andy's unit turned northwest towards Rome. But on May 29, in the town of Albano Laziale (a southern suburb of the capital), Andy was taken prisoner with other men from his company. However, the Germans only kept him captive for two weeks.

His mother receives a telegram on June 22, indicating that Andy has been listed as 'MIA' (Missing in Action) since May 30. However, she's not worried, as she received a letter from her son the day before, dated June 14, in which he details his capture and his escape nine days later! A local newspaper on June 23 quotes a long excerpt from his letter, adding as a caption to Andy's photo 'Too fast for the Nazis!': *"It was a tough life living with the Germans. The food was tough because their supplies were knocked out by our air force, so you see we didn't get much to eat. My captain and I were captured the same day. His name is Capt. Cruikshank and he comes from New York. We both planned our getaway. I lived in caves for four days. The Italians took care of us. We ate bread and wine because that's all the people had to give us. We walked through Rome. It's a nice city. The Germans killed the Italians for giving us smokes and things to eat. Tell Jim* [James, his brother] *the Germans have the gun I was going to give him. I can't tell you how many of us were captured. I'm well and don't worry. Might be home soon, I hope. Will write again soon. Keep smiling. Say hello to the gang for me."*

Leonard, who was writing optimistically at Anzio's beachhead, is in the same company as Andy, but was wounded on June 2 in the same area where Andy had been captured a few days earlier. The next day, he writes to his best friend's mother: *"It has been quite a while since I last wrote to you. I'm awfully sorry, but we haven't been able to mail them, even if we got them written. Naomi, I was wounded in action on June 2. I'm not hurt very bad. I got hit in the left leg and left hand. I lost one of my fingers. The one next to the little one. I think they call it the 4th finger. I'm in a General Hospital far back from the front lines. If my address will be different I'll let you know. Well I hope Bob had decided to stay at home. He said in his letter he wished he was over here with me. He wouldn't if he knew how it was. I hope it will be over soon, so he won't get a chance to come. [...] If he really knew how it was going, he would never have said such a thing. I would give anything to be in his shoes."* Leonard's best friend Bob will eventually join the US Navy in September and serve in the Pacific.

While Leonard is in the hospital and Andy is still a prisoner, the 45th Division crosses the Tiber on June 4, 1944, enters Rome alongside other divisions of the VI Corps and is the first to reach the Vatican. However, on June 16, it's withdrawn from the lines to participate in the landings in Provence (*Operation Dragoon*). Like Andy, Leonard will get back to his company just in time to participate, but will be wounded again on the banks of the Moselle River: *"I don't suppose you will be too surprised to hear that I have been wounded again. It's not so bad this time. One of those guys took a few shots at me with a machine gun. I just got grazed across the back and on the right side of my face. Sure hope it won't leave a scar on my face. You can tell Bob that I will have an Oak Leaf Cluster on that Purple Heart now* [rather than receiving a new medal, a soldier who is hit several times pins this little bronze leaf to his Purple Heart for each new wound]. *Write to me at the same address because I will probably be back again soon."*

An American M10 'Tank Destroyer' tank at the Battle of Normandy Museum in Bayeux (France). More powerful than the Sherman's 75 mm gun, which is unable to pierce the frontal armor of German Panther and Tiger tanks, the M10's 76.2 mm gun uses high velocity penetrating shells, effective on most enemy vehicles. Allied tanks are less resistant, but they have the advantage of being far more numerous: in 1944, the Germans produced 24,630 tanks, and the Allies 113,253 (mostly American)!

TANK DESTROYER

Baldwin Chambers is a 30-year-old farmer from Missouri. He serves in B Company, 701st Tank Destroyer Battalion, 1st US Armored Division, with which he landed in North Africa during *Operation Torch*. He fought in Tunisia before landing in Italy on October 28, 1943, where he participated in the Battle of Monte Cassino, supporting the 34th and 36th US Infantry Divisions on the Rapido River. His battalion then landed in Anzio to help the 3rd and 34th Divisions hold their positions. Equipped with the impressive M10 Tank Destroyer, Baldwin's armored battalion specializes in Panzer hunting. Alongside the 45th Division, it actively participated in the breakthrough of Anzio, destroying twenty-two tanks and many guns during the offensive, with very few casualties (five killed and nineteen wounded in one month). A large number of German prisoners captured by the battalion in its advance to Rome are only 15 or 16-year-olds, exhausted and hungry, who begin to doubt a victory for the Reich. Still, the further north the Allies advance, the fiercer the resistance becomes.

The assault on the Italian capital is launched on June 4, but the battalion encounters no more obstacles than a few Germans taking a bath, a handful of guns in the suburbs, destroyed bridges, and a few snipers left behind to cover the Wehrmacht's retreat. Baldwin's company enters the city in the late afternoon and the entire battalion crosses the Tiber the next day. The Americans reach the heights north of the city, where they learn of the Allied landings in Normandy on the radio. Dancing with joy thinking about this new front, which gives them hope for a total victory before the end of the year, they are nevertheless frustrated to realize that this news from France completely eclipses the symbolic capture of Rome.

In any case, the Americans are welcomed as liberators by the Romans, who throw flowers on the tanks rushing into their streets. As he explains in a letter to his parents a few days after the liberation of the capital (he is then near Lake Bracciano on June 13), Baldwin and the 701st TD Battalion didn't take the time to stop in the city, and immediately set off in pursuit of the enemy: *"Just a few lines to let you know I am OK and feeling fine. Received the package with the knife and gum in it. I was in Rome but just for a short time as we were moving so fast we didn't have much time, but I was fortunate enough to get to see most of the city, but may get a chance to see more of it later on, it is the cleanest and most modern city I have seen since I have been overseas. It is a better country where we are now and the weather is very nice."*

Unfortunately, Baldwin won't have the opportunity to return to Rome, as he'll be killed two weeks later. On June 18, the battalion resumes its course towards the Gothic Line, another formidable defensive wall set up in the mountains north of Pisa and Florence. As we saw at the end of John Harris' story (page 122), the enemy needs to buy some time to complete its last real line of defense before Germany, and small groups fight with determination to slow down the Allies around the Trasimene Line (where John Harris is put out of action, between Rome and the Arno River). Not far from there, on July 1, 1944, when it's already more than 125 miles away from Rome, Baldwin's company is ordered to attack the village of Mazzola (halfway between Livorno and Siena). In the course of this action, Baldwin's M10 tank takes a direct hit in its turret and catches fire: the entire crew is killed instantly.

When a tank, vehicle, aircraft or ship is destroyed so violently, most of the time the bodies of the soldiers are unidentifiable. The crew of Baldwin's tank is buried in a single grave (photo above) and then repatriated in 1950 to Jefferson Barracks Military Cemetery in Missouri. Baldwin still rests there today, with his comrades William R. Fulmer, James H. Hallman, and the tank commander, Martin Steffan. Baldwin had been promoted to corporal only a few days before his death.

The fierce fighting for the village and its surroundings, supported by the 'Blue Devils' of the 88th US Infantry Division, would last several days before the enemy pulls back behind the Arno. There, the Germans, now on the Gothic Line, will deny all access to the Po Plain and the German industrial machine for many bloody months. But the world's eyes are now all focused on France, and the forgotten soldiers who will fight in Italy until May 1945 will be unfairly nicknamed the 'D-Day Dodgers' (see page 245).

Rome will become the soldiers' favorite destination for leave. A Canadian soldier shares his impressions with his girlfriend: *"The city was untouched, so you can see we saw everything and nothing was ruined. Everything stands as it always was. As you can imagine, here and there as usual, the dialect changes. The people are more modern and aristocratic. They are friendly and like to talk to us. They have hardly suffered from the effects of war as in other places. Here, of course, they have their food problem which is being looked after but apart from that there are no changes. The people are dressed well, and men conduct themselves as if there wasn't a war on. [...] You could also see the Pope as he holds an audience every morning. The crowd is enormous, and people just go mad trying to get to kiss his ring that is on his hand. He has his guard with him at all times. When we saw him he spoke to all saying he has seen many great warriors and that we all must remember we are small compared to our God. He was really nice to us and spoke wonderful English. In the audience there were Indians, Africans, Australians, Canadians, English and many others of various denominations who considered this occasion a privilege."*

One of Baldwin's last letters, describing his passage through Rome, and original patches of the Tank Destroyer Battalions and of the 1st Armored Division.

IV

OPERATION OVERLORD

The Invasion of Normandy

The largest amphibious invasion in history is being prepared in the United Kingdom, which has been transformed into a gigantic training field: 1,108 camps are scattered throughout the country. The first GIs arrived the month after their entry into the war, on January 26, 1942. In the UK, they have twenty divisions, in addition to fourteen British divisions, three Canadian, one Polish, one French and various small units from Belgium, Australia, New Zealand, Czechoslovakia, Greece, the Netherlands, Norway, and Denmark. Many English villages now have more foreign soldiers than inhabitants.

THE STARTING POINT

Corporal Cole is a member of the 729th Ordinance Light Maintenance Company in the 29th US Infantry Division. With about 100 soldiers, the company must ensure the maintenance of equipment and vehicles in the field. It left New York on September 27, 1942 on board the *Queen Mary*, the famous cruise ship now transformed into a troop ship. Corporal Cole and 10,000 GIs crossed the Atlantic under constant threat from German submarines roaming its depths. Yet it was from the surface that tragedy struck them on October 2, three days before their arrival in Scotland: the large ship rammed into HMS *Curaçao*, a British light cruiser that had come to meet it, and broke it in two. The latter sank in just seven minutes. The Americans who watched helplessly from the *Queen Mary*'s deck were in shock: 332 sailors died in the accident, more than two thirds of the crew. It was one of the Royal Navy's largest accidental losses during the Second World War.

The company has been training for a year and a half with the division in Britain, from where Cole sends the pre-illustrated V-mail shown here, which was very popular among the troops for Christmas 1943. He misses his wife and hopes to return home soon, yet he still knows nothing about what awaits him. His company, which normally has to work in a safe area far behind the lines, will be mixed with the assault troops for D-Day and land right in the middle of Omaha Beach's hell. The 29th Division, which is to endure a baptism by fire, will suffer very heavy casualties on the beach, forever associating its blue and gray patch with sacrifice and heroism.

The V-mail sent by Corporal Cole from Britain and a 29th US Division patch.

Contact between Americans and British civilians is not easy. The English find them *"overpaid* [five times more than British soldiers]*, oversexed, and over here!"* So many young English women will become pregnant by GIs that a British comedian will joke: *"For the next war, just send the uniforms!"*

149

They will have to get used to it, however, because more than 2 million Americans will pass through Britain from April 1942 to June 1944. England is not to the GIs' liking either: everything is rationed, and the blackout has a significant impact on their morale.

Ted, a member of the 735th Tank Battalion, writes to his family shortly after his arrival in England: *"We are quite well situated now, and are getting used to driving on the wrong side of the road, and dealing with Pounds, Pence and Shillings, instead of real money. I have been to most of the large cities here, and a great deal of the countryside. It is very interesting but I'll take Oregon anytime."* He'll probably miss the English countryside a few months later, once he's been deployed in Normandy, in the Saarland, the Ardennes, against the Siegfried Line and across the Rhine. A GI from the 28th Infantry Division writes: *"This place out here will never compare with the US. They're about 50 years behind times. The girls out here, in case you're interested, are not so hot. The American girl has it all over them."* He also complains about the lack of activities and the weather, which is constantly changing from freezing to rainy. He won't experience any better conditions in the hell of the Hürtgen Forest the following winter.

Others, however, appreciate the country, despite the climate. Marshall is a member of the 401st Glider Regiment, the inexperienced but soon-to-be famous 101st Airborne Division. He's just arrived and writes to friends in New York: *"I am here in England now and I like it here, but, the sun doesn't shine very much, rain plenty of it. The nights are very dark. The people have treated us very nice, they will tell us anything we want to know, and how to get around on the buses, when to get off and what to see. Last week I was in London and what a place to see! Owing to the short time, we had to hurry through every building. When we left St. Paul's, we met a Bobby and we asked him the way to Big Ben and he didn't tell us which way to go but took us to it then on to Scotland Yard. The way he showed us fellows around and explaining everything it was very interesting. After two hours with him I laughed, for the way he would tell things you couldn't help it. So, when you want to see London find yourself an old Bobby! Another thing about England it is so clean around the streets and to find paper on the streets is a hard job. The brick homes are also nice looking with plenty of flowers around."* Marshall will land on D-Day and will be decorated for his actions during the Battle of the Bulge.

Some have great respect for the British, and in particular for the women who played an important role in the preparation of *Operation Overlord*, the Allied invasion of Normandy. A captain in the SHAEF (Supreme Headquarters Allied Expeditionary Force) recounts in early 1944 in a V-mail to his brother: *"Most of the personnel on my shift are girls and about half of them are drafted girls. Everybody in England between 18 and 45 is either in the Army or working on an essential war job, and this includes women as well as men. The only ones exempted are mothers with small children. Some of these English girls (ATS) [Auxiliary Territorial Service, the female branch of the British Army] have been in the Army for over five years, and at their last headquarters they we bombed out twice, and yet they are a very pleasant lot and I never hear them complaining. I certainly have changed my mind about the English. I also saw as we came through England the effects of the air blitz and buzz bombs there."*

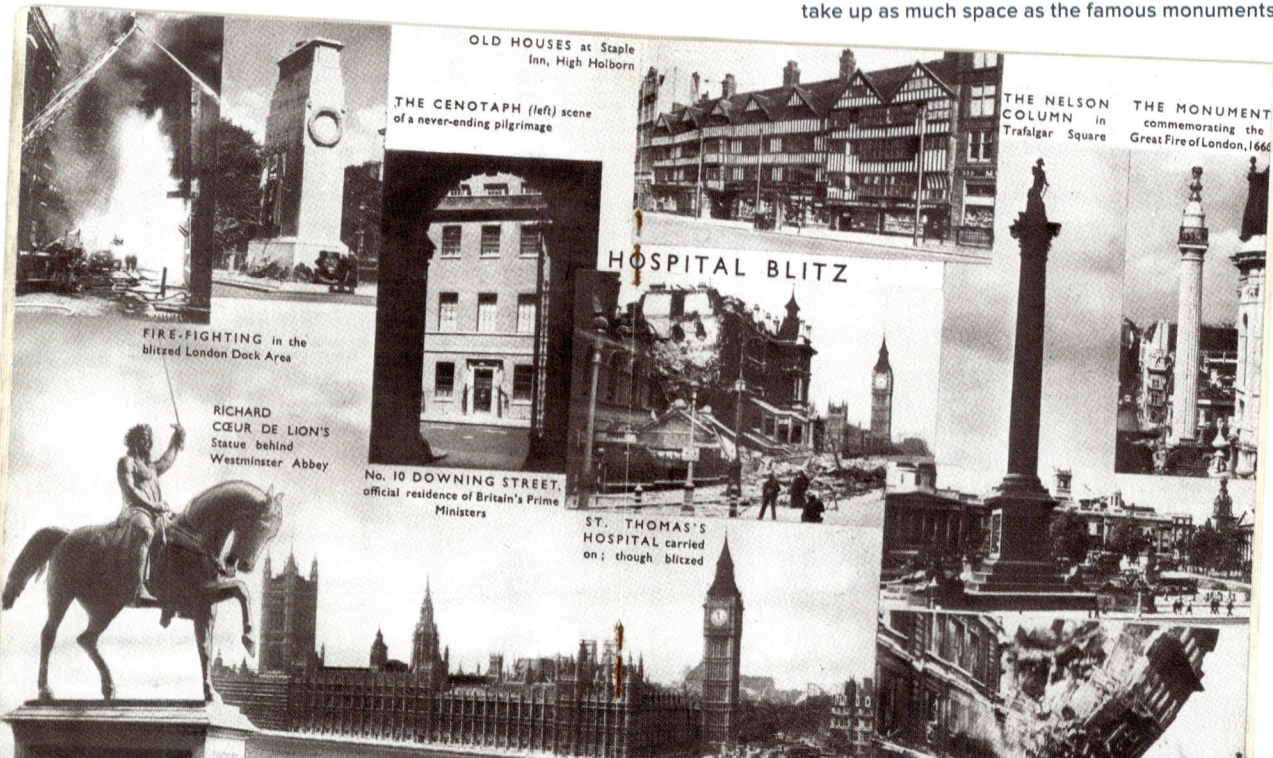

In this London guide for Allied soldiers, the effects of the Blitz take up as much space as the famous monuments.

IV - OVERLORD SUMMER 1944

get plenty to eat, and am happy in my new country. Wish you folks could see what I have seen and I know you would enjoy the wonders of this old world."

THE PLAN

It was at the Casablanca Conference in January 1943 that the idea of a substantial landing in France took shape. *Operation Overlord* was scheduled for the spring of 1944. It was at the Anglo-American summit in Quebec City, in August 1943, that the place was chosen: while the Germans were expecting the Allies in Calais, closer to England, British Prime Minister Winston Churchill and American President Franklin D. Roosevelt chose the Calvados region, where 150,000 men would land on 50 miles of beaches between the Cotentin Peninsula and the Orne River. In December 1943, General Dwight David Eisenhower was chosen to be the Supreme Allied Commander in Europe, with the Americans now representing more than half of his troops. However, the other Allied leaders would be predominantly British: with his deputy, Air Marshal Sir Arthur Tedder, he will have under his authority Admiral Sir Bertram Ramsay (Commander of the Naval Forces), Air Marshal Sir Trafford Leigh-Mallory (Commander of the Air Forces) and at the head of the 21st Army Group, General Sir Bernard Montgomery (Commander of the Ground Forces).

American soldiers visiting Lichfield Cathedral, north of Birmingham.

But above all, the GIs who have just arrived in Europe have only one desire: to kill Hitler. Although still green, they're full of courage and optimism, like Kenneth in October 1943: *"Yes I would have liked to have been home to drive the old Packard down to the country. But I am afraid that there's too much water for me to swim to get back home. Ha! Ha! No joking folks this war I believe will soon be over and I will be home before you can think. I believe by January or February we will have the score settled with Mr. Hitler. Then about another year the little pups will be mopped up. I still have faith in our Army and know they will do this job in record time so we can get back. You only have to be in one of our camps and talk to our boys and you will fully realize that we have plenty of guts and that goes to make up the greatest Army of the world. We must not forget that our noble ally England also has a well-trained Army and Navy, and they are putting up an excellent battle. So we feel proud to fight by their sides. Well folks I must close by saying that I am well and*

This British Pound, dated September 1940, has become a 'short snorter': a tradition for soldiers and airmen to collect their comrades' signatures on local currency before a major crossing, and is also very common among GIs stationed in England before the long-awaited D-Day. This one has at least sixteen signatures, including several lieutenants and captains of the US Army, the US Navy and the Quartermaster Corps.

151

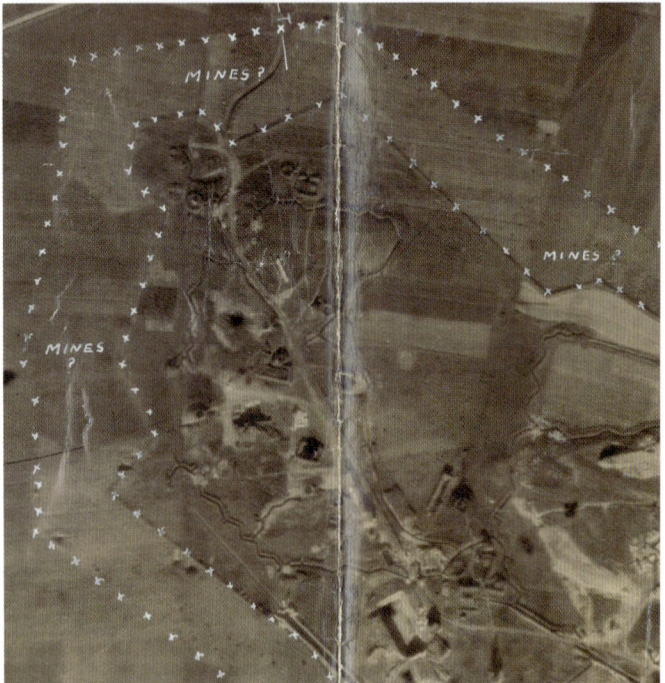

Large aerial reconnaissance photograph, dated January 1944, used for the D-Day planning.

The handwritten note on the reverse side '8th Bde RADAR' was the clue that helped identify the place as the Würzburg radar site (west of Douvres-la-Délivrande), which was the objective of the 8th Brigade, 3rd Canadian Infantry Division (it was kept by an officer of the North Shore Regiment). The photo, handwritten in white ink, shows the assumed positions of minefields and munitions depots. Juno Beach (Nan Red Sector), where the brigade will land, is only 4 miles from the objective.

Since autumn 1943, this important German radar detection site has consisted of five short and long-range devices, protected by numerous bunkers, machine guns, artillery positions and minefields. It's an important part of the Atlantic Wall, which also houses 230 German Luftwaffe soldiers. On June 5, the radar will be jammed by clouds of aluminum strips called 'windows', dropped from Allied aircraft (*Operation Glimmer*). The Canadians will lay siege to these positions for days, with the help of commandos from the Royal Marines and the British 79th Armoured Division. The German garrison won't surrender until June 17.

IV - OVERLORD SUMMER 1944

Fifty-eight German divisions, including six armored ones, are already in France. They are well protected behind more than 3,000 miles of pillboxes, machine gun nests, anti-tank obstacles, mined beaches and artillery positions that form the Atlantic Wall. Reconnaissance photos from 1944 show that this one is much complete than at the time of the Dieppe Raid (although by D-Day, only 3,700 of the 15,000 planned works will be finished). In order not to repeat the tragic mistakes of August 19, 1942, this time, the terrain will be carefully studied. In addition to aerial reconnaissance photos, the British go so far as to ask civilians for their holiday postcards of the French coast. The timing is very precise: the assault must take place at low tide in order to make the obstacles and mines visible, protect the landing crafts and avoid them being stranded with the ebbing tide. On the other hand, the soldiers will consequently be more exposed to enemy fire on a larger beach strip. Naval and aerial bombardments must therefore neutralize enemy defenses and create crater holes in which the attackers can take shelter, before the rising tide pushes them forward. However, Eisenhower doesn't know yet that above Omaha Beach, covered by clouds on the morning of June 6 and thus reducing visibility, the planes coming from England would wait until the last moment to drop their bombs for fear of hitting their allies on the ground. They'll strike the hinterland 4 miles behind the beaches and the assault troops will crash against intact German pillboxes.

The Allies expect strong resistance, but they know that the bulk of German troops are in Northern France. Inland, on the Loire and the Seine rivers, the Allied air force is actively destroying bridges in order to delay enemy reinforcements towards Normandy. At the same time, the secret *Operation Fortitude* aims to make Hitler believe that the landing will take place in Nord-Pas-de-Calais and Norway. In parallel with the disinformation work of the double agents, the Allies even massed an army of inflatable tanks, wooden planes and phantom units in front of Northern France, relaying false communications. This ghost army is even led by the fearsome General Patton himself. This complex and daring scheme will work perfectly and Rommel, now in charge of the defense of the Atlantic Wall and demanding more German divisions in Normandy, will be refused reinforcements by Hitler. Long after the Normandy landings, the Führer would continue to believe that June 6 was only a diversion for a larger operation, and will keep considerable forces in reserve in the Nord-Pas-de-Calais region.

On May 29, 1944, Eisenhower sets the date for D-Day. It will take place on Monday, June 5, although it can be postponed by twenty-four hours depending on the weather conditions. Indeed, a storm is coming, and it's in full swing on June 4!

While many ships have already left the ports of southern England, battered by the waves, Eisenhower decides to set a new date for the landings: June 6, 1944. He now has no choice, because if the weather doesn't improve, a new assault can't take place until the 19th and the Allies could run the risk of having their plans discovered by then. After long discussions between experts all day long, it's on June 5 at around 4 am that Eisenhower takes the decision which will change the fate of millions of men and women: while the rain is beating on the windows of Southwick House, he questions his staff one last time, then says very simply: "OK, let's go".

OK, LET'S GO.

Rommel, the 'Desert Fox' who had distinguished himself in North Africa, is convinced that the terrible weather and the Atlantic Wall would prevent any major Allied operation. He leaves his headquarters in La Roche-Guyon on June 5 to visit his wife and celebrate her birthday in Germany. French resistance fighters, secretly listening to the BBC despite the risks they face, hear the famous coded message announcing the Allied offensive on June 1: the *"Long sobs of autumn violins..."* part tells them that the landing will take place within two weeks, but on the evening of June 5, the radio broadcasts the rest of Paul Verlaine's verses: *"... wound my heart with a monotonous languor"*. The Allies will be there in less than 48 hours, meaning the Resistance must start its sabotage operations, particularly on the railway networks.

A letter from Eisenhower, headed by the SHAEF logo (Supreme Headquarters Allied Expeditionary Force), is distributed to all military personnel. It announces: *"Soldiers, Sailors, and Airmen of the Allied Expeditionary Force: You are about to embark upon the Great Crusade, toward which we have striven these many months. The eyes of the world are upon you. The hopes and prayers of liberty-loving people everywhere march with you. In company with our brave Allies and brothers-in-arms on other Fronts you will bring about the destruction of the German war machine, the elimination of Nazi tyranny over oppressed peoples of Europe, and security for ourselves in a free world. Your task will not be an easy one. Your enemy is well trained, well equipped, and battle-hardened. He will fight savagely. But this is the year 1944. Much has happened since the Nazi triumphs of 1940-41. The United Nations have inflicted upon the Germans great defeats, in open battle, man-to-man. Our air offensive has seriously reduced their strength in the air and their capacity to wage war on the ground. Our Home Fronts have given us an overwhelming superiority in weapons and munitions of war, and placed at our disposal great reserves of trained fighting men. The tide has turned! The free men of the world are marching together to Victory!*

I have full confidence in your courage, devotion to duty, and skill in battle. We will accept nothing less than full Victory! Good Luck! And let us all beseech the blessing of Almighty God upon this great and noble undertaking. Dwight Eisenhower."

Men from the 1st US Army, 2nd British Army, 1st Canadian Army and independent Allied contingents (Polish, French, Czech, Dutch...) are briefed orally. In his memoirs, Leo Brown of the 90th Infantry Division (page 196) recalls the intervention of the 1st US Army Commander: *"General Omar Bradley (four stars) gave us a pep talk and told us how lucky we were to have a front seat to the biggest event in history! He said that we would be in more danger at home driving our cars. He told us that when America landed in North Africa that only seven men per thousand were lost. They didn't expect this one to be any worse. I expected it to be worse than that but wasn't sure how much worse. I lost some respect for General Bradley for telling us that."*

Despite the encouraging speeches, Eisenhower is also very worried. The Allies have no plan B, and if the invasion fails, they'll have to wait at least a year for a possible new attempt. Less known, another letter was written by the Supreme Commander, just in case. It said: *"Our landings in the Cherbourg-Havre area have failed to gain a satisfactory foothold and I have withdrawn the troops. My decision to attack at this time and place was based upon the best information available. The troops, the Air and the Navy did all that Bravery and devotion to duty could do. If any blame or fault attaches to the attempt it is mine alone."* Fortunately, he'll never have to send it. The Germans had four years to prepare their defenses, and the Allies will break through them in a matter of hours.

Paratroopers will be dropped on both ends of the bridgehead to destroy guns and delay reinforcements. The Americans will land on Utah Beach at the base of the Cotentin Peninsula and at Omaha Beach in the Calvados region. At Arromanches-les-Bains, the British 50th (Northumbrian) Infantry Division will attack Gold Beach, with the objective of Bayeux. Another British division, the 3rd Infantry Division, will land at Sword Beach with the mission of taking Caen. They'll be assisted by the Canadians of the 3rd Canadian Infantry Division, landing on Juno Beach, between Gold and Sword. The latter will also have to capture the Carpiquet airfield, west of Caen, and the Oak Line, which runs to the positions of the 50th British Infantry Division to the west. On the evening of June 6, more than 132,000 Allied soldiers will be in France, at the cost of 10,500 killed, wounded, missing and taken prisoner.

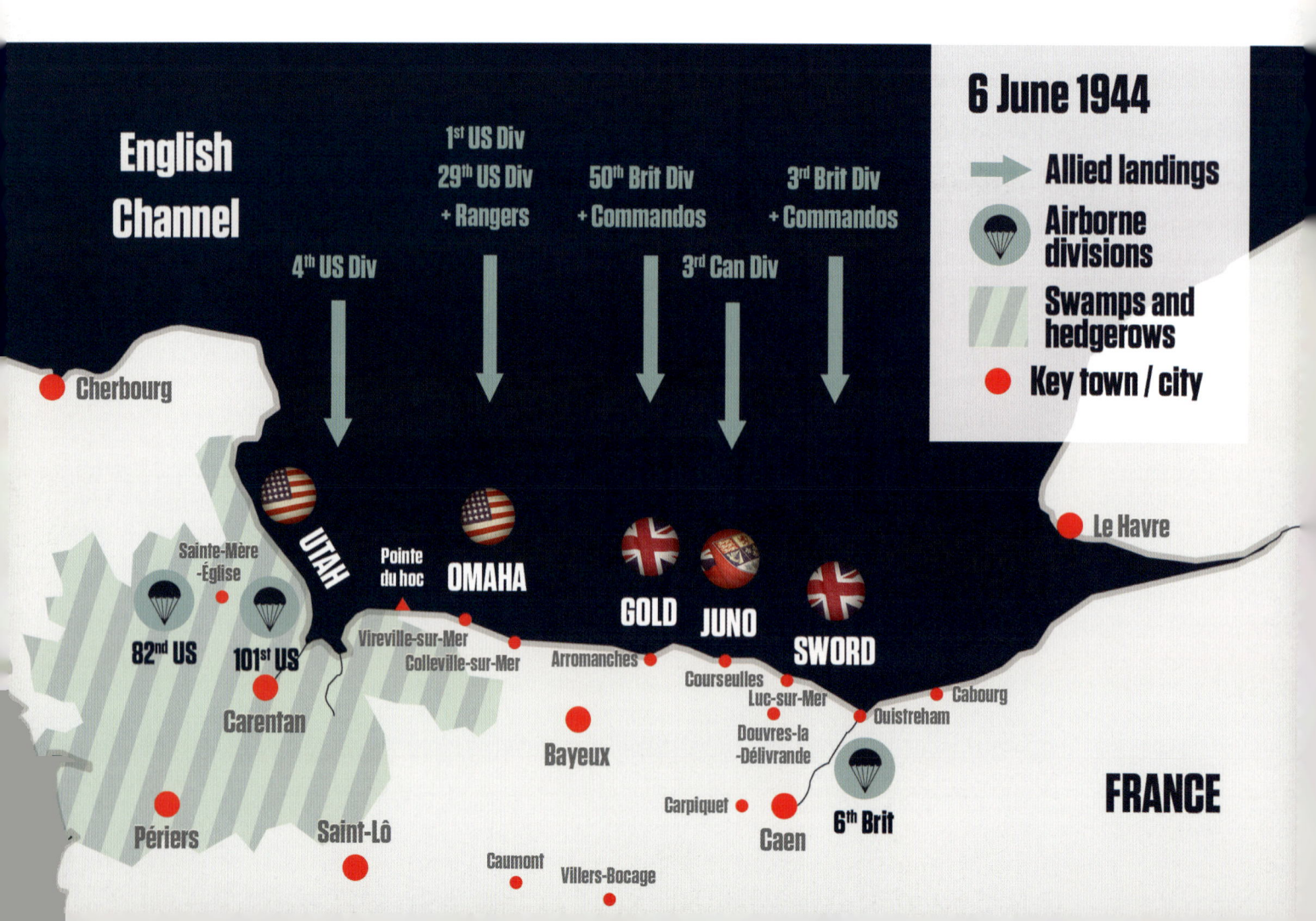

SUPREME HEADQUARTERS
ALLIED EXPEDITIONARY FORCE

Soldiers, Sailors and Airmen of the Allied Expeditionary Force!

You are about to embark upon the Great Crusade, toward which we have striven these many months. The eyes of the world are upon you. The hopes and prayers of liberty-loving people everywhere march with you. In company with our brave Allies and brothers-in-arms on other Fronts, you will bring about the destruction of the German war machine, the elimination of Nazi tyranny over the oppressed peoples of Europe, and security for ourselves in a free world.

Your task will not be an easy one. Your enemy is well trained, well equipped and battle-hardened. He will fight savagely.

But this is the year 1944! Much has happened since the Nazi triumphs of 1940-41. The United Nations have inflicted upon the Germans great defeats, in open battle, man-to-man. Our air offensive has seriously reduced their strength in the air and their capacity to wage war on the ground. Our Home Fronts have given us an overwhelming superiority in weapons and munitions of war, and placed at our disposal great reserves of trained fighting men. The tide has turned! The free men of the world are marching together to Victory!

I have full confidence in your courage, devotion to duty and skill in battle. We will accept nothing less than full Victory!

Good Luck! And let us all beseech the blessing of Almighty God upon this great and noble undertaking.

Dwight D. Eisenhower

This original copy of Eisenhower's letter was kept by a British officer from Kent, who landed with the support units of the 2nd Army (Gen. Dempsey), 21st Army Group. From June 7 he will be in Bayeux, the first liberated city in France. Beside it, two invasion notes (special currency printed for Allied troops), a French phrasebook and a guidebook that belonged to a Canadian veteran.

MICHAEL DAVEY

Royal Marines, Portsmouth Division

The tragedy of the sinking of HMS *Royal Oak* in 1939 had a happy consequence: it helped the young Royal Marine Michael Davey meet an ambulance driver, his future wife Phyllis. Four years later, when the planning for D-Day is in full swing, Michael is secretly in charge of Portsmouth's security, home to the Allied HQ. The correspondence between the two lovers will be filled with mystery and worry, at least for Phyllis.

To understand the relationship between Michael and Phyllis in June 1944, we need to look back at the Marine's exceptional career. Michael Davey was born in Dorset in November 1920. Still a minor, he joined the Portsmouth Division of the Royal Marines on March 7, 1938, in Bristol. The Marines have served as infantry troops for the Royal Navy since 1755 and specialize in being deployed quickly anywhere in the world. They'll be used in almost all operations of the Second World War, including the landings in Norway and Dieppe, fighting in Crete, Malaysia, Madagascar and Singapore, and the campaigns in Tunisia, Sicily, Italy, France, the Netherlands and Germany.

THE SINKING OF HMS *ROYAL OAK*

Michael began his service aboard HMS *Royal Oak* on June 7, 1939, as a simple rifleman. This 600-foot-long warship, weighing more than 30,000 tons, had been one of the Royal Navy's proudest achievements since its launch at the very beginning of the First World War (when it took part in the Battle of Jutland). Michael immediately became friends with two fellow Marines, Frank Brooke and Freddy Senior, and from then on, the three friends were inseparable. At the beginning of the conflict, the ship remained at the Scapa Flow base in the Orkney Archipelago, north of Scotland, to defend it from possible Luftwaffe attacks.

However, the threat really came from the depths: the commander of the Kriegsmarine's submarines, Karl Dönitz, had planned a U-boat raid for the moonless night of October 13-14, 1939. Kapitänleutnant Günther Prien's *U-47* crossed the natural and artificial obstacles of the base without being detected, and at 12:58 am, saw HMS *Royal Oak* 2,5 miles away. The submarine fired three torpedoes, but only one of them hit the bow of the ship six minutes later. Michael and the rest of the crew, awakened by the tremors, didn't realize straight away that they'd been attacked, believing the noise came from the explosion of a flammable product carried on board. The German captain fired three more torpedoes, all of which hit their target at 1:16 am.

HMS *Royal Oak* in 1937.

IV - OVERLORD SUMMER 1944

They opened a large hole in the ship's armored hull, and she began to sink. Michael, Frank, Freddy and the 1,231 other men on board finally understood what was happening to them. Michael watched with horror as a ball of fire rushed down a corridor and ignited men like torches. Frank, who slept in the hammock next to Freddy, managed to reach one of the portholes in complete darkness before it was submerged, and threw himself into the sea. Freddy was not so lucky and would go down with the ship. As for Michael, he also escaped through one of the portholes, sliding on the side of the ship as it turned over. During his descent, he left a large amount of skin on the barnacles attached to the hull.

Frank Brooke (left) and Fred Senior (right).

After several minutes with the stern up at 45°, the *Royal Oak* sank into the icy waters of Scapa Flow, only thirteen minutes after being hit. A total of 834 men, more than two thirds of the crew and soldiers, died that night or as a result of their injuries: 120 sailors were only 14-18 years old. Michael, Frank and those who found themselves in the water still dressed in their pajamas, struggled in a thick layer of oil that made swimming difficult and which they swallowed in large quantities. Some tried to swim the 900 yards to shore, but many drowned. A small boat, the *Daisy*, finally came to the rescue of the survivors and brought 375 men to safety. Among them, Michael, who had spent a quarter of an hour in the cold water, warmed himself up as best he could near the *Daisy*'s engine.

Günther Prien received the nickname 'The Bull of Scapa Flow' and became the first submarine officer to receive the 'Knight's Cross of the Iron Cross' from Hitler's hands. He disappeared in turn with *U-47* on March 7, 1941, sunk by the British destroyer HMS *Wolverine*. As for the survivors of the *Royal Oak*, they were welcomed in villages in the Orkney Archipelago, or rushed to the hospital.

This was the case for Michael, thus separated from his friend Frank Brooke, who will later stay in the Royal Marines as a commando and survive the war. As for Freddy Senior, he still lies today at the bottom of Scapa Flow with many comrades in the wreck of HMS *Royal Oak*, which has been declared a war grave. The ship lies upside down, in water only 90 feet (30 meters) deep.

PHYLLIS

Michael was hospitalized in Torquay, in the southwest of England, and underwent several surgical operations, including skin grafts. He befriended a 22-year-old English woman, Phyllis Mortimore, who drove ambulances for the army. Michael fell in love, but once in better condition, he was to return to duty in January 1940 (on HMS *Victory*, in Portsmouth). The two of them wouldn't see each other for several years, and Phyllis met another young soldier, Edward Palmer, shortly after Michael's departure.

Edward (photo below) was a member of HQ Company, 4th Battalion, Oxfordshire and Buckinghamshire Light Infantry Regiment. Destroyed near Dunkirk in the Battle of France (1940), the battalion was reformed in England, but would never see service as such. Its men would be reassigned to the regiment's other battalions, which will experience heavy fighting in Normandy, some of them as part of the 6th Airborne Division, the first unit in France on D-Day.

As Phyllis was about to marry Edward, his aunt wrote to the young soldier on October 14, 1941, to congratulate him: *"I guess you are very excited about getting married. [...] I wish you both good luck and happiness for the future, when we're done with this damn war. It's quite a mess right now, and I'm afraid we're going to live through difficult times before this is all over. I'm sure you'll be sad to be shipped overseas, but I hope you can spend a few weeks together before."* Unfortunately, only a month later, Edward died in a training accident when approaching a truck to collect his rifle. One of his comrades, freshly equipped with a Thompson machine gun, accidentally fired a burst towards the vehicle while the gun was resting on his lap. Edward was shot twice in the heart, killing him instantly. He was buried on November 8, 1941, with military honors. Although the Thompson gun shouldn't have been loaded and armed during its transport, for some reason it was and all her life Phyllis will remain convinced that it was murder. Phyllis' misfortunes didn't stop there, as her brother Maurice Mortimore, a firefighter from Teignmouth, was fatally injured during a German air raid on the city hall a few months later.

MICHAEL (CONTINUED)

Meanwhile, Michael traveled the world. When the Germans invaded Denmark on April 9, 1940, Churchill launched *Operation Valentine*, which consisted of occupying the Danish Faroe Islands. The next day, Michael was assigned to the *Sandall Force*, which was to land there with 250 Royal Marines on April 12. Apart from a few Luftwaffe attacks, the islands were never invaded, and the Marines were relieved by the Scottish Lovat Scouts Regiment on May 31, 1940. Michael was transferred on December 11 to the battleship HMS *Queen Elizabeth*, which took part in the Battle of Crete to prevent any amphibious landings of German troops on the island. The ship then headed for Egypt, where it was among the victims of the Alexandria harbor raid of 19 December 1941: six Italian divers placed mines under the British ships HMS *Valiant* and HMS *Queen Elizabeth* and under the Norwegian tanker *Sagona*, all of which were sunk. While the *Queen Elizabeth* was refloated and sent for repair in the United States, Michael was stationed on the Nile and served as a driver at a Royal Navy base in Alexandria until January 11, 1944.

He left on the 13th for Colombo in Ceylon (today's Sri Lanka), where he was in charge of the Wrens' security (the female branch of the Royal Navy), who were involved in planning the invasion of Burma. The British had been expelled by the Japanese in the spring of 1942, and had since tried to launch various offensives without any real success. However, they regained the advantage in 1944 by violently repelling the Japanese *U-go* offensive in India from northern Burma. It was during this period, when Michael left for Ceylon aboard the HMS *Kenya*, that Phyllis, who'd taken years to overcome her grief, thought about Michael and decided to write him a letter. She didn't hesitate to ask him if he was married, to which he replied in the negative, since he had never stopped carrying out missions and seeing the world. The two friends, who recalled their nightly meetings at the hospital four years earlier, then engaged in a fiery romantic correspondence. A happy coincidence saw Michael transferred to England on April 3, without him being able to reveal his destination to Phyllis. Indeed, Michael will carry out a mission similar to the one he had in Burma, with the difference that the personnel he will protect are working on the invasion of Normandy: *Operation Overlord*.

NAVAL PARTY 1645

Indeed, Michael is now attached to Naval Party 1645. This coded address is linked to the Allied Naval Combined Expeditionary Force, under the command of Admiral Sir Bertram Ramsay, and redirects mail to Southwick House, near Portsmouth, the headquarters of the main Allied commanders. It's in this residence that Eisenhower will declare his famous *"OK, let's go"* speech and the Normandy landings are planned.

Southwick House.

Ultra-confidential messages are circulating in order to organize all the naval operations of D-Day (*Operation Neptune*). Eisenhower, Montgomery, Ramsay, King George VI and Winston Churchill frequently visit Southwick House to follow the preparations for the invasion. The Wrens, among other tasks, study the weather forecasts to determine the ideal date for an amphibious assault.

IV - OVERLORD SUMMER 1944

Michael is probably among the Royal Marines providing security for the personnel or the surrounding area. Secrecy is therefore essential, and he can't reveal any information about his work to Phyllis (all his letters are strictly censored anyway). The secrecy is such that this period won't even be mentioned in Michael's military file. Only his address on the envelopes exchanged by the couple prove he was with Naval Party 1645.

Phyllis wrote to Michael every day, without exception, in the summer of 1944. With her brother-in-law also deployed on the battlefields of France, the young woman imagines the worst: on June 12, she still hasn't heard from Michael since the beginning of the month. However, she's not surprised, having learned that *"all those who took part in the actual D-day operations are not allowed to write for about 3 or 4 days prior to the attack, so darling I guess I must be patient but it is such an awful anxiety waiting for news, but I'll go on praying you are alright darling, not that praying will help any but somehow I find myself hoping and hoping until I am saying it to myself. [...] Oh! Why didn't I tell you I love you more often than I did then darling, I know I did tell you and meant it from the bottom of my heart but if I'd known you had to go so far away dear I should have said it a lot more times than I did. But I'll make it up to you one day, Michael, I promise you."*

Michael is still in England, however, protecting the offices where landing operations are orchestrated. Although he's far from the front at the moment, he lives under the constant threat of German flying bombs. He finally reassures Phyllis: *"I couldn't stay away from you any longer than I really have to, one of the disadvantages of the services, being away from the person you love so much. There are two things about that though, had I not been into the service I don't suppose I should have ever met you, I'm sure I shouldn't have turned up into a Torquay hospital like I did. I'm glad now I was in the service, and be sent from a ship to hospital, really I hate hospitals but I had no objection to that one after I got to know you so well my dear, [I] have never forgotten your daring night patrol either you know [...] Today I was talking to the CO [Commanding Officer] as regards getting married compassionately, he says it is not granted unless the girl sends a doctor's certificate stating that she is expecting a baby, but somehow darling I don't think that's really the truth, honest I don't. I'm afraid I think a little different to that. I have an idea that I shall be with you the first week of August. Gosh I hope so darling it would be the greatest leave I could ever have! [...]*

The June 6, 1944 edition of the English newspaper *The Star*. Phyllis thinks Michael is involved in the landings, along with the Royal Marines commandos, recognizable by their green berets, landing with the first assault troops. Designed by Churchill to be elite units specially trained to "bring terror to enemy shores", the first army commandos (numbered from 1) were formed in 1940, then the Royal Marines created their own No. 40 to 48 commandos in February 1942. Some, such as No. 10 (inter-Allied) commando, are composed of foreign volunteers (French, Belgian, Norwegian etc.).

Now as to how I got back darling, as you know it poured with rain all the way even this end, well when I got to a certain station I found out that there was a train that would get me back for quicker than I told you. Well I happened to be getting into bed at exactly ten minutes past midnight, to be almost blown out at one o-clock by a flying bomb, to say about having the wind up wasn't in it you would sure have laughed had you seen me get out of those blankets, slide my boots on, grab my overcoat and jump in a slit trench with three feet of water… Well Phyl darling I say you would have laughed, what Hitler was called doesn't matter very much I don't think. Don't think I'm being funny when I say did we laugh about it this morning. After all that I couldn't get to sleep for money, I'll tell you the truth darling, I was thinking so much of you darling, that I just could not. [...] I'm so very sorry to thing you have been so worried darling, believe me Phyl I'm quite alright in every way, hope you won't go worrying yourself too much my darling, nothing whatever has happened to me as you have been thinking, wish I could really tell you exactly what we have been doing the first two weeks or so, but if one day you should ever want to know I'll tell you, which somehow I doubt very much. [...] You will not get any letters from me for Friday + Saturday I was away those two days darling, had I been able to write, you know I would have done darling, afraid I must not give the reason why here but I will tell you some other time. All those hours you were constantly in my thoughts darling, wishing all the time I could let you know what was happening, but you will understand I'm sure. I hope you will my darling."

Phyllis (right) and Michael (left) will manage to get married on leave on August 1, 1944, in Okehampton, Devon. Michael still won't have revealed anything about his activities to Phyllis. Following the landings, the Naval Party 1645 will leave Portsmouth on the 9th, and settle in Granville, southwest of the Cotentin Peninsula. But as the last Wrens abandon Southwick House at the end of the summer, Michael's mission will end. He will be transferred on September 22 to HMS *Frobisher*, which, after being hit by a torpedo in the Bay of the Seine, will be converted into a training ship in England. Michael will be on guard there until January 1946, then leave the Marines on March 15, 1949, eleven years after first joining. He and Phyllis will finally meet again for good and will run a guest house together. Michael passed away in March 1998 in Norfolk and Phyllis in January 2007 in Teignmouth.

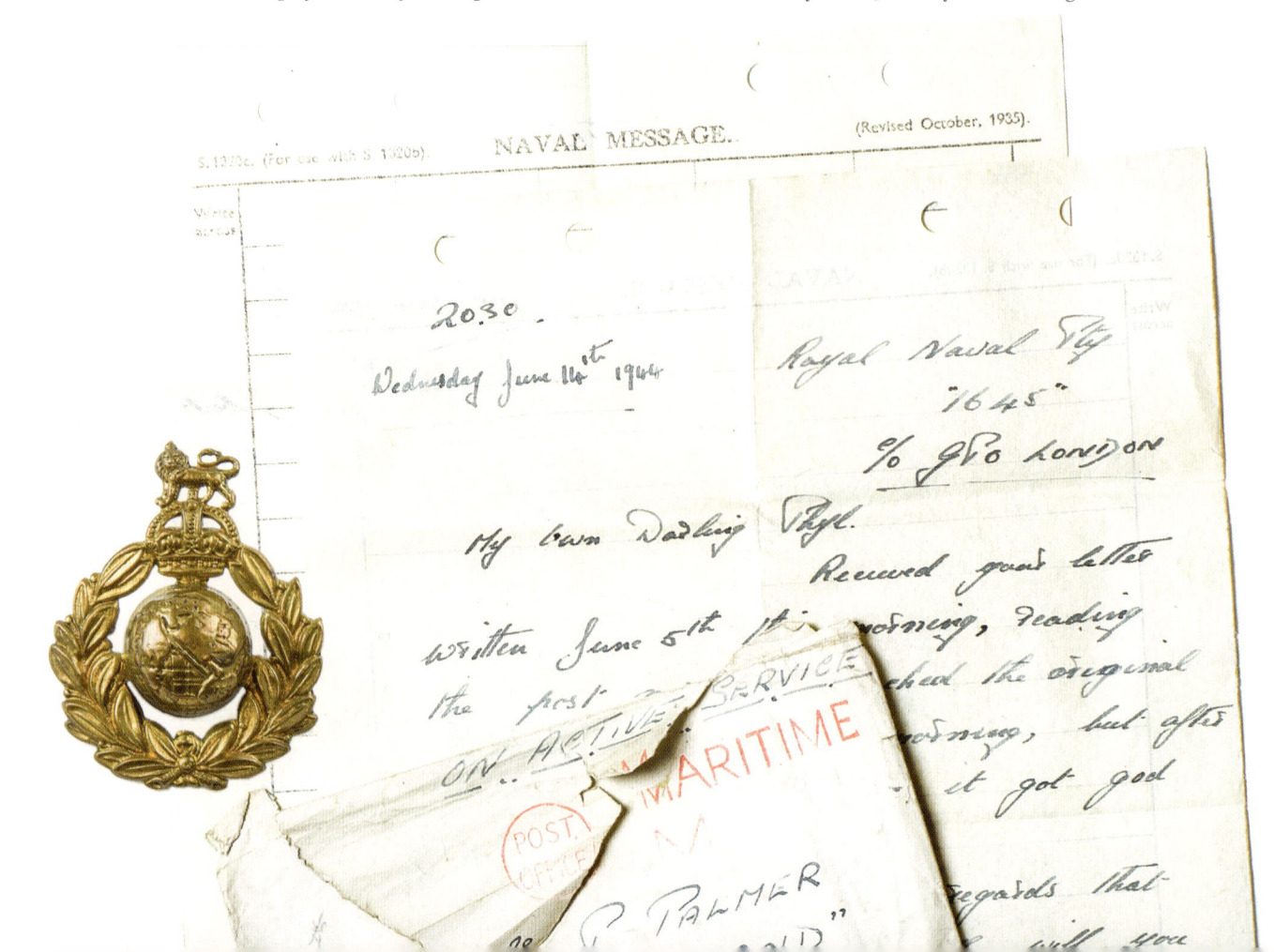

FALLEN FROM THE SKY

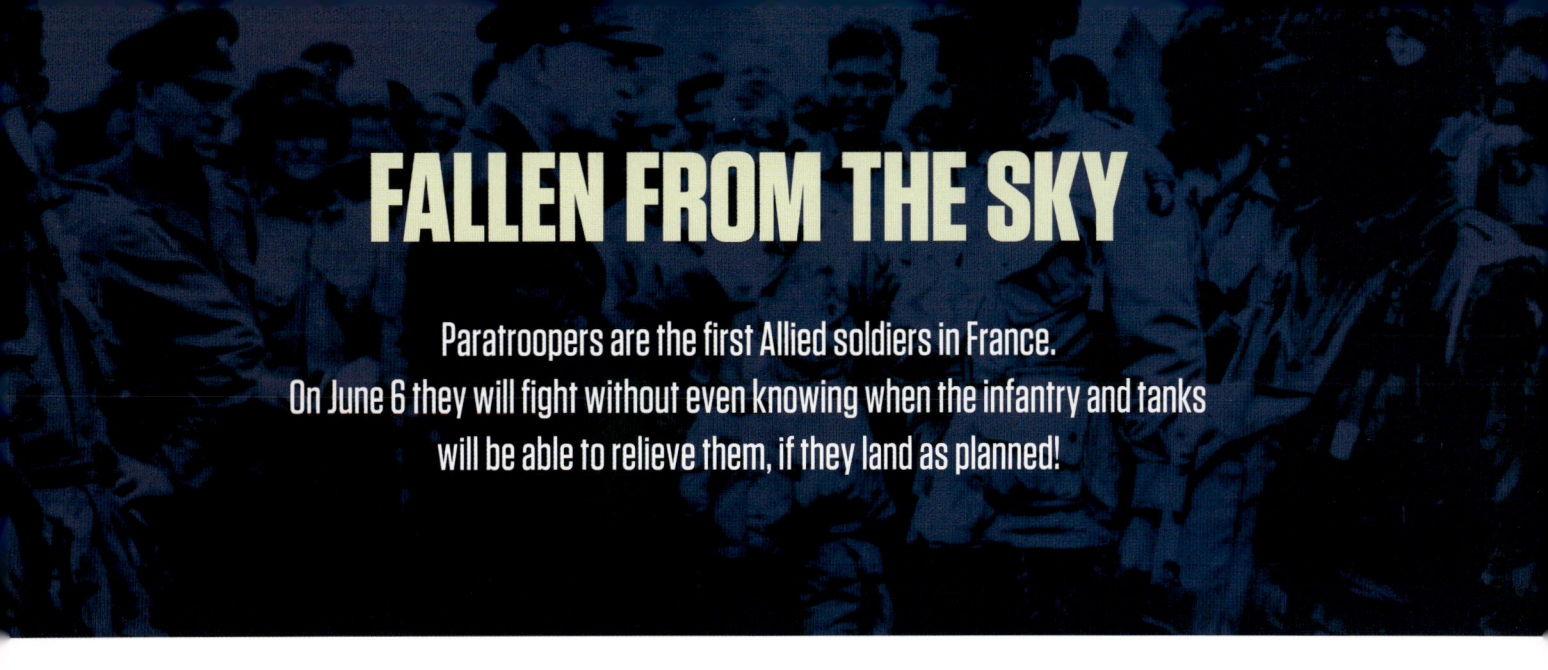

Paratroopers are the first Allied soldiers in France. On June 6 they will fight without even knowing when the infantry and tanks will be able to relieve them, if they land as planned!

ALONE IN HELL

On the evening of June 5, 15,500 American and 7,900 British paratroopers board their planes and gliders. Preceded by 360 pathfinders marking the drop zones, they'll be the very first to touch Norman soil. The veterans of the American 82nd Airborne, like their inexperienced comrades of the 101st Airborne, will have to jump on the Cotentin Peninsula and silence the guns firing on the beaches, while the British 6th Airborne will take the bridges over the Orne to slow down the German reinforcements. The paras are nervous, but so is Eisenhower, as the casualty forecast is as high as 70%. 'Ike' visited the 101st Airborne men who were about to board, and later said *"It's very hard really to look a soldier in the eye when you fear that you may be sending him to his death"*.

The first soldiers to lose their lives in the D-Day landings are indeed paratroopers. Lieutenant Den Brotheridge and Corporal Fred Greenhalgh of the Oxfordshire & Buckinghamshire Light Infantry Regiment (British 6th Airborne Division) are killed in action at 12:22 am, when the Bénouville Bridge is attacked on the Orne Canal (quickly nicknamed 'Pegasus Bridge', after the Pegasus horse featured on their patch). Their comrades, however, will quickly take the objective and hold it until a hypothetical relief, alone behind enemy lines. Almost simultaneously, in Plumelec (Brittany), the first Frenchman from *Overlord* is also shot dead during *Operation Dingson*: Corporal Émile Bouétard, a 29-year-old Breton, had just jumped on the Morbihan département with the 4th Free French Battalion of the SAS (Special Air Service, the British special forces that had incorporated thirty-six Free French). Unfortunately, his small group was spotted and while in charge of defending the radio team, Corporal Bouétard is surrounded, wounded and executed by the Germans with a machine gun burst to the head. In the Cotentin region, American paratroopers also experience the terrifying solitude found in the middle of occupied territory. The diary kept by Staff Sergeant Murray Goldman of the 3rd Medical Battalion, 505th Parachute Infantry Regiment (82nd Airborne) is an impressive testimony to the anguish felt by the first men on the ground:

"June 5 – Left Cottesmore about eleven. Flew all over England then over Channel, came in France at 0200. Nice and quiet and lots of smoke, commented that this was easy. Suddenly tracer & flak, red and green. Plane started violent evasive action. Green light and went – plane was on its side and low, about 150 [meters]. Terrific tracer coming up into chutes. Slipped away for all I was worth. One man screaming in [erased word]. Landed easy and stayed flat... reason... grazing fire... terribly scared. Crawled into hole and took off equipment. Lots of firing. C47s still coming, men still jumping into hell. One plane burning, but men bail out. Met two jumpers and joined. Met 8 more, met 20 more, feel good now. All kinds of weapons. Now we seek trouble: tore down telephone wires. No Germans.

June 6, next morning – Joined a mixed group of 502nd, 506th, 508th, 505th men and came to farmhouse, produced map and French man showed Ste-Mère-Église to us. Occasional sniper fire but inaccurate. Reached Ste-Mère-Église about noon and found that Co. H had town taken. Moved into a big building and set up hospital. Gliders had taken a hell of a beating, crashed all over countryside. Wounded pouring in now. Companies set up town defence and prepare to hold town at all costs as ordered. Already we are surrounded and fighting. Town being shelled and mortared. Eighty-eight artillery tearing hell out of us. Wounded pouring in. Hospital hit repeatedly. Germans want that town. Getting dark now, this night will be pure hell 'cause we are all alone and cut off. The boys are fighting like cornered lions."

They fight hard all night around the town as the hospital overflows with dying soldiers, desperately waiting for the arrival of the reinforcements who had landed on the beaches: *"Violent enemy artillery and infiltrating attacks. Some Germans enter town. They don't leave it again, they are dead. Tanks knocked out just outside of town by GIs with grenades. Our guys are strictly mean now. They are fighting mad. Morning and we still hold town, but what a price!"*

The 4th Infantry Division doesn't arrive from Utah Beach until the afternoon of June 7, but now that the town is in Allied hands for good, the Americans control the road to Cherbourg.

Later, in the Ardennes, a GI will write about the 82nd Airborne paratroopers (original patch below): *"They sure are a tough bunch of guys. Killing means nothing to them as they've seen so much of it!"*

Below: American paratroopers complete a last-minute check of their parachutes before boarding the C-47 planes that will take them across the English Channel. The planes all bear three white stripes and the big Allied star to facilitate their identification on the ground.

MASSACRE IN GRAIGNES

Focused mainly on Sainte-Mère-Église and the Merderet River to the west, the 82nd Airborne generally performed better than its green sister division, the 101st Airborne, deployed near Utah Beach in Sainte-Marie-du-Mont and Saint-Côme-du-Mont. However, the lack of visibility and the violence of the anti-aircraft fire scattered the men, who often dropped far from the drop zones or directly into the flooded marshes, causing several of them to drown.

On June 6, at about 2 am, twelve gliders carrying the 3rd Battalion, 507th Parachute Regiment (82nd Airborne) are flown to Amfreville, west of Sainte-Mère-Église. On the ground, the pathfinders are responsible for setting the Eureka beacons guiding the C-47s, but they have a hard time accomplishing their mission in the dark night. Moreover, the C-47s have to go through a powerful anti-aircraft barrage over the Cotentin Peninsula, disorienting and destabilizing the pilots, who end up dispersing their men more than 12 miles south of the drop zone: the worst parachute drop of D-Day. Once on the ground, the Americans regroup as best they can in the Graignes village cemetery and set up an observation post for their mortars in the church tower. Isolated in enemy territory, Major Charles D. Johnston's 181 paratroopers are ordered to hold the position. Civilians, with the support of the mayor, organize food for their liberators, despite the dangerous risks they face so far behind the German lines. Fortunately, except for a few shots fired, the village of Graignes won't really be threatened until June 11. But on that day, as paratroopers and civilians are gathering in the church to attend Sunday mass, the Germans launch an initial assault on Graignes, which is easily repelled by the Americans.

Fragment of a camouflaged main parachute (worn on the back) and a white parachute (probably a reserve, worn on the belly), with buckles and harness parts.

Despite efforts to equip each man with a camouflaged parachute, only half of them were able to have one. The others jumped with a white canopy, offering a perfect target to the German shooters in the dark night. Once on the ground, the soldiers quickly abandoned or buried their parachutes before trying to find their unit.

Rain and ploughing brought these D-Day relics to the surface in 2017 in a field in Sainte-Mère-Église, on one of the 82nd Airborne's drop zones.

A few hours later, the 17. SS Panzergrenadier Division 'Götz von Berlichingen' repeats the offensive with overwhelming odds: ten Germans to one American.

The SS are supported by intensive mortar fire, inflicting heavy casualties on the paratroopers. But it seems obvious to the latter that the main attack will occur at night, after an 88 mm shell fired from Thieuville destroys the church tower (as well as the observation post essential to the village's defense), killing Major Johnston. Captain Brummitt immediately takes command of the few remaining American strongholds scattered throughout the village and often out of ammunition. The SS initiate the final assault on Graignes in the evening, forcing the disorganized Americans to abandon their positions and try to rally their comrades in Carentan or Sainte-Mère-Église.

On the evening of June 11, the SS enter the church where the American aid post is located and execute the wounded soldiers and two priests for revenge. Seven captured paratroopers are taken to the nearby village to dig their own graves, before being shot by the Nazis. While searching the houses, they then shoot and kill two young girls (aged 18 and 8) in their beds. Accused of collaborating with the enemy by the Germans, civilians are subjected to violent interrogation, sometimes with tragic results. Graignes is almost entirely burned to the ground in retaliation. The SS are furious at its inhabitants for helping the Americans, as some of them went hunting for abandoned ammunition in the surrounding marshes to support the besieged GIs. Nevertheless, this handful of men who have fallen from the sky inflicted severe damage to the German ranks (about 300 men).

Above all, they've considerably delayed the advance of the 17. SS Panzergrenadier Division to the town of Carentan, helping their comrades in the 101st Airborne take the latter on June 12. With no reinforcements arriving in time, the Germans will withdraw from Carentan and a beachhead will be consolidated between Utah Beach in the Cotentin Peninsula and Omaha Beach in the Calvados region.

The church tower at Graignes was rebuilt after the war in the cemetery which still bears the marks of the fighting. It's all that remains of the small village, now completely rebuilt nearby.

The two priests shot on June 12 are buried in the center of the tower, where there's also a memorial listing the thirty-two civilian martyrs and fifty paratroopers killed.

RAY ALM

B Company, 2nd Ranger Battalion

Ray is a member of the Rangers, the elite American commandos whose new 2nd Battalion will see its first action in Normandy. Ray will land in the early morning of June 6, 1944, in the midst of the chaos on Omaha Beach, and will be one of the very few of the original company to reach Germany.

TRAINING

Raymond Francis Alm was born on November 12, 1921, in Chicago. After working for a few years as a carpenter, he joined the US Army on September 30, 1942. During his classes at Fort Dix, his dream was to join the Rangers, whose 1st Battalion, led by William Darby, had distinguished itself particularly well in North Africa. Ray therefore tried to get in the new 2nd Ranger Battalion, formed on March 11, 1943 in Camp Forrest (Tennessee). The selection of volunteers and the merciless training were so difficult that among the soldiers picked for their performance in already prestigious units, few actually became Rangers. On top of that, their missions are so dangerous that the unit refused to incorporate married men. Ray managed to be accepted on the condition that he received written permission from Audrey, his high school sweetheart, whom he'd married at the age of 20. The latter agreed to sign the document, mistakenly thinking that Ray would become some kind of Forest Ranger.

A few months later, the 2nd and 5th Rangers Battalions left Camp Forrest and embarked for England, before moving to Braunton Camp, Devon. The place looked like Normandy: its beach was similar to Omaha Beach, its cliffs almost identical to those that the Rangers will have to climb at Pointe du Hoc, and the landscape reminiscent of the Norman bocage.

Ray and Audrey at Fort Dix in April 1943.

IV - OVERLORD SUMMER 1944

Ray and his comrades trained daily on the cliffs, trying to reach the summit, while carrying their heavy equipment under machine gun fire. They also participated in amphibious exercises, long hikes and live ammunition shooting. Their training was exhausting and both their muscles and morale were strained. Ray wrote to Audrey: *"I've never been so lonesome or homesick as much as this in my life. And it gets worse as each day goes by. When work is done each day I sit in my hut and write or read until bed time. Same thing, day after day. I haven't been to town in weeks. Not even a movie. Just want to be alone with my memories of you and the fun we used to have before all this came along. Sometimes I wonder just what we're fighting for? But as far as I'm concerned you're the only thing I am fighting for."*

At the same time, and not far from here, some men were faring much worse. On April 28, 1944, on the beach of Slapton Sands (Devon), the Navy, combat engineers and the 4th Infantry Division simulated the landing on Utah Beach under realistic conditions. Named *Operation Tiger*, the dress rehearsal turned into a disaster when an attack by infiltrated German speedboats killed 946 soldiers.

Ray is a staff sergeant in charge of a 60 mm mortar platoon, whose role is essential for the Rangers company. Mortars are short and easily transportable guns, firing bombs at high angles and perfect for supporting the infantry during an attack or withdrawal, or for destroying an enemy defensive position. Ray's second son, Donald, will remember an anecdote from his father proving how effective this support weapon is: in reconnaissance with a handful of other soldiers in a village, Ray will be attacked by a rather nervous German sniper, pinning them down to the ground. Ray will call for a mortar fire on the sniper's position and won't wait long before the German waves a white flag. Ray's very small group will thus take about sixty prisoners. In May 1944, the men were already well trained on it and have been able to test their mortars and explosives on replica German bunkers.

Between exercises, the Rangers managed to relax by playing baseball, Ray's favorite sport (he dreamed of becoming a professional player). They were all impatiently waiting for D-Day and knew it was finally coming close when they were sent to Swanage, Dorset, in early May. A few days before the operation, the men customized their equipment and worked on their warrior looks. Some drew pin-ups on their combat jackets, while others had a Mohawk haircut to intimidate the enemy. A friend of Ray's, Charles 'Jack' Bramkamp, even became the battalion's official hairdresser and had his picture taken several times. Ray is so close to him that he frequently writes to Jack's mother Margaret, affectionately calling her 'Mom'. Jack will unfortunately be killed on Omaha Beach in the first few minutes of the landing. Men also painted their girlfriends' names on their guns, and Ray's bazooka was no exception: 'Audrey' was written on its tube and 'Muzz' (the nickname he gives his wife) its handle. Unfortunately, Ray would lose it in the Channel during the chaos of the landing.

Jack cutting fellow Ranger Elmer Olander's hair. The latter will also be killed on the morning of D-Day: Elmer's arm will be torn off by a machine gun burst as he comes out of the water, running towards the cliff alongside a comrade, who was also shot dead. The tourniquet applied during the battle will not succeed in stopping the bleeding.

D-DAY

On June 1, the Rangers embarked on the British ship HMS *Prince Charles* in Weymouth, where they would spend the next five days. Ray's battalion includes six companies of sixty-eight men each, from A (Able) to F (Fox) - Ray belongs to B Company (Baker). Dog, Easy and Fox, commanded by Lieutenant-Colonel James Rudder, will have to climb the cliffs of Pointe du Hoc and silence six old and powerful French guns captured by the Germans, who have an unobstructed view of Utah Beach. Of the 255 men who'll hit the beach, 190 will manage to leave it, and after two days of German counter-offensives on top of the cliffs, only ninety Rangers will still be standing. Meanwhile, Charlie Company will land alongside the 5th Ranger Battalion, to support the 1st 'Big Red One' Infantry Division and the inexperienced 29th Infantry Division on Omaha Beach. On June 6, they reach the Dog Green Sector at 6:33 am, with the first waves of the 29th Division's 116th Regiment, which suffer terrible losses.

Between the actions of the 8th Air Force bombers and the guns of USS *Texas*, the Pointe du Hoc received more than 10,000 tons of highly explosive shells, almost the equivalent in power of the Hiroshima bomb. As soon as the shelling was over, Lieutenant-Colonel James E. Rudder's Rangers landed on the thin strip of sand and climbed the vertical cliffs with grapples and ropes soaked with seawater, while still under heavy enemy fire. A Navy officer studying the plans said, *"It's impossible! Three old women with brooms could keep the Rangers from climbing that cliff!"* Yet most of them reached the top and neutralized the bunkers. Their mission was to destroy guns pointed at Omaha and Utah beaches, and they were surprised to discover that they had been replaced by telegraph poles. The Germans lost a cannon in the bombardments and tried to protect the other five: the Rangers would find them by chance 1 mile inland and destroy them immediately. Thanks to their actions, many lives were saved on the beaches, but having already suffered heavy casualties themselves and their ammunition running out very quickly, the cut off Rangers were on the verge of being thrown back into the sea. However, they were to hold out until the morning of June 8, on their own, despite several German counter-attacks. The site is now preserved as it was in 1944, with craters and bullet-ridden walls testifying to the violence of the fighting.

IV - OVERLORD SUMMER 1944

Able and Ray's Baker companies must remain on standby until 7 am. They are waiting for the coded signal, 'Tilt', to reinforce either their comrades at Pointe du Hoc or those on Omaha Beach, depending on the objectives achieved. On HMS *Prince Charles*, Ray at last boards his assault barge using huge nets hanging from the sides of the ship. As news from the other Rangers companies is scarce (the situation being critical and radio contact difficult), Lt. Col. Max Schneider chooses plan B and directs his troops towards Omaha Beach. The 5-mile-long beach is divided into eight sectors. At 7:40 am, Ray's company is heading towards the western sector of Dog Green (near the exit to Vierville), the most violent and well defended of all of the sectors. At the last minute, seeing the infantrymen of the 29th Division being decimated in the water and on the sand, Schneider decides to divert his men to Dog White on his left, hoping for more favorable conditions.

Ray carries a heavy load: a Colt .45 pistol, a bazooka and anti-tank rockets. While the men all suffer from seasickness, their assault boat tossed around by the raging waves, they are briefed: *"We are all going to die anyway, so just go and get it over with!"* The landing craft is flooded and so the men must bail the water out with their helmets to keep it from sinking. According to Lieutenant Fitzsimmons, Ray does a particularly good job of it, but they are only 200 feet from the beach when a German mine or 88 mm shell hits the landing craft, ripping off the ramp and killing or wounding several men, including two of Ray's best friends who are stood right in front of him. Ray and the surviving Rangers quickly jump overboard to avoid the MG42 machine gun fire, which spits twenty bullets per second, all of them concentrated inside the barge. The men sink under the weight of their equipment in the icy waters of the English Channel, nearly 12 feet deep. Ray manages to free himself from his pack and weapons, keeping only the rockets. He advances slowly underwater and when his helmet finally emerges from the surface, he's in hell: the beach is covered with the smoke of burning landing crafts, bullets whistle in all directions, the sand is strewn with corpses, and the water in which he floats is already red with the blood of the 116th Regiment soldiers who landed before him. In spite of everything, Ray decides to swim to Dog Green.

'BLOODY OMAHA'

When he emerges from the water, the only cover Ray can find are the metal 'Czech hedgehogs' laid by the Germans to pierce the hulls of the landing crafts. He picks up an abandoned rifle and rushes behind one of these obstacles to protect himself, where he's soon joined by two other GIs. As a German machine gun sprays the area, Ray decides to abandon his position and run to the base of a cliff, about 300 feet from the water's edge. He leaves just in time: when he looks back, the two soldiers who had taken shelter with him are both dead, having been shot in the head. The Americans are all pinned down, caught under the crossfire of several German fortifications, including a machine gun nest at the entrance of Vierville, which sweeps the whole beach from the side with an unobstructed view.

View from the exact spot where Ray set foot on Omaha Beach on June 6, 1944 (with the same weather and tidal conditions). Note the distance to the cliffs. The German defenses were positioned at the top of the hills facing him, almost invisible, and placed in such a way as to provide cross-fire both along the entire length of the beach and hillsides.
On the right of the photo, overlooking the large villa (present in 1944), was WN70, an important German fortified stronghold that the Rangers took at around 8:30 am. Jack Bramkamp, the 'hairdresser', was killed as he climbed these hills.

Ray suddenly feels a sharp pain in his back, but when one of his fellow Rangers lifts his bag to examine his wound, he only finds a bullet lodged in the TNT block that Ray was carrying. Fortunately, Ray had removed the detonator and put it in his pocket as he'd been taught, which saved his life and that of the men around him. A few moments later, he also receives a piece of shrapnel in his arm, which will earn him a Purple Heart but won't stop him from continuing the fight. Men still drop like flies under the shells or bullets of machine guns and snipers' nests. Private Robert R. Whitehead, a very close friend of Ray's, is killed in front of him by a sniper bullet in the back. Ray will write to Audrey a week later: *"I hate to say it dear, but that dinner that we were planning for three will have to be cut to two. My buddy Whitey got it on the beach and died from loss of blood. He was real pale and I won't forget him."*

Armed with a Thompson M1A1 machine gun, widely used by elite troops who appreciated both its precision and powerful automatic fire, this Ranger goes on to attack the hills. He has already abandoned his cumbersome lifebuoy and will soon part with the waterproof bag for the M5 assault gas mask attached to his chest. On his belt he carries a Colt .45 pistol in its leather holster, a General-Purpose musette bag for his ammunition and grenades, a compass in his pouch and magazines for his handgun.

For a moment, General Bradley, who was watching the scene from the sea, thinks about abandoning Omaha Beach, but the US Navy takes the initiative to approach the coast and pound the German defenses, despite the risks to its fleet, and manages to save the day. Colonel Schneider of the Rangers requests artillery support from the battleship USS *Texas*, which would fire all day long at the enemy with the support of two other destroyers, eventually allowing the Americans to get off the beach later in the morning. Other initiatives will also help unblock the situation. Sheltered behind an anti-tank obstacle, Ray witnesses a scene that will go down in history: a big man is walking calmly and fearlessly through explosions and bullets, waving his Colt .45 in the air. Norman Cota, chief of staff of the 29th Division, seeing his own terrified troops unable to advance, noticed the presence of the Rangers and gives them an order that remains the unit's official motto today: *"Rangers, lead the way!"* Ray and two other comrades, mixed with men from the 5th Ranger Battalion, jump off the beach and cross the road to Vierville, before attacking the hills overlooking Omaha. It's at this precise moment that Ray's friend, Charles 'Jack' Bramkamp, is killed by a German sniper. When Ray is asked decades later how he found the strength to get through all this, he'll say, *"You know you've got a job to do. Ours was to cross the beach and get to the base of the cliff, then join up with some other companies. You keep your focus on that task."*

In the early afternoon, the Americans gradually take control of the hills and clear the German pillboxes one by one. However, at the end of the day, of the sixty-eight men from Ray's B Company, only eight are left. Even by regrouping the survivors of Able, Baker and Charlie companies, the Rangers barely form a complete company. After a busy night in Vierville, they set off for the Pointe du Hoc to relieve their isolated comrades, who are still being harassed by the Germans. They are supported by tanks of the 743rd Tank Destroyer Battalion, the 5th Ranger Battalion and elements of the 29th Infantry Division. Together, they experience heavy fighting in Saint-Pierre-du-Mont and secure the Pointe de la Percée on June 8. Meanwhile, members of the 5th Rangers and 116th Regiment join forces with the few survivors of Dog, Easy and Fox companies of the 2nd Rangers at the Pointe du Hoc.

IV - OVERLORD SUMMER 1944

Estimates of the losses on Omaha Beach range from 2,000 to 4,500 killed, wounded and missing. In certain places, the soldiers had to cross 300 yards of sand without cover, a pebble wall and dunes topped with barbed wire, a minefield and marshes before climbing steep 100 feet-high slopes. It took them all day to silence the twelve fortified strongholds that dominated Omaha Beach and advance inland.

Fox and Easy sectors allocated to the 1st Infantry Division (in front of Colleville and Saint-Laurent-sur-Mer, above) and Dog and Charlie sectors of the 29th Infantry Division (Vierville-sur-Mer) were covered with destroyed equipment, shell craters and corpses, but were already receiving endless waves of reinforcements who began their journey towards Germany.

Today, tourists have replaced the dead and wounded, and the seaside has regained its calm. Few bunkers have been preserved, while villas and monuments have multiplied, but there are still a few rare traces of the events that took place there, such as this bullet-ridden 'dead-end' road sign at the exit of Les Moulins (Dog Red Sector).

Other traces are invisible to the naked eye. Shown here is a section of barbed wire found on Omaha Beach in the 1990s and a piece of shrapnel collected in 2017 above WN65 (Le Ruquet), while this small pile of sand from the Dog White Sector contains microscopic fragments of history. Studies on the sand at Omaha Beach have shown that where the fighting had been most violent, nearly 4% of it is still composed of tiny shrapnel fragments (mostly less than a millimeter in size), pieces of molten iron, and even glass formed by the heat of the explosions decades earlier!

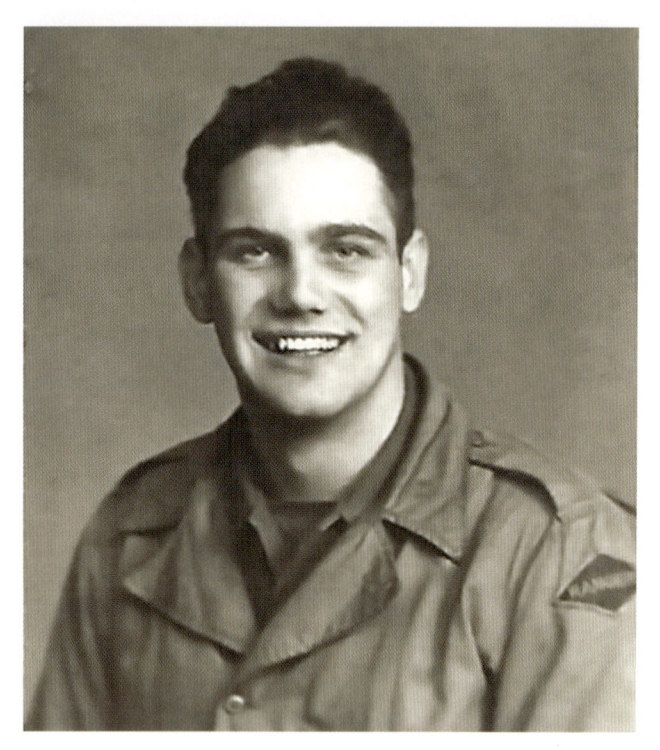

Ray in 1944, wearing the Rangers' patch on his M-41 jacket.

IN NORMANDY

On the evening of June 11, the 2nd Battalion finally gets some rest. The men settle in Molay Woods, and for the first time since D-Day, Ray has the opportunity to write home: *"Well Audrey, I imagine you have been pretty worried since the invasion started. But everything is OK and I'm alright. Thank God. It's been damn close at times, too close, but so far my prayers have been answered. I pray that they will continue to be answered. I can't tell you a great deal dear because of censorship, but I'll have plenty to tell you when I get back. So just be patient and pray hard darling as I've been doing. But believe me when I say this. That Sherman wasn't half right when he said 'War is hell'. It's more like a nightmare or a bad dream."*

Two days later, Ray finally writes in detail about his landing: *"Well Audrey dearest, I've just finished washing, shaving, and changing clothes for the first time in over a week and it sure feels good to be clean again. We've been having a well-deserved rest the past few days and to sort of get our nerves back together. [You don't know what] snipers and machine guns firing at you can do to you until you actually face it. It is like a horrible nightmare. As long as I live, I'll never forget that hour of crawling over the beach after swimming the last 50 yards into shore after the front of our landing craft was blown off by a direct hit of an artillery shell. And then, seeing your buddies fall all around you. My pack saved my life coming across the beach, as it stopped a bullet from going through my back. God was really with me."*

The shrapnel wound Ray received in the arm eventually becomes infected and he's taken to a field hospital. He writes to Audrey: *"No mail today. And I probably won't be getting any for a few days either as I won't be with the outfit for a few days. I am getting a few days rest in a field hospital as a result of a little infection from a shrapnel wound on my left wrist. But it isn't anything for you to worry about and I'll be back with the rest of the boys in a few days. Meanwhile I'll have a good rest and can catch up on my reading and letter writing. And there are sure a lot of pretty nurses around. Especially the one in our tent, boy it's a good thing I love my wife so much. Are you jealous? Good! But don't worry darling, you're the only girl for me first, last and always, and I love you with all my heart and always will."* Enclosed with the letter is a poem he wrote to his wife, a habit he'll maintain throughout the war, even in the most difficult situations.

Ray leaves the hospital in August 1944, but not before a young Red Cross volunteer, Elizabeth Black, draws his portrait. This rising artist from Pittsburgh will spend two years traveling throughout Europe during the war. She started by serving coffee and donuts to the troops, before drawing them with charcoal and will eventually produce 1,000 portraits, about a dozen a day, and then send them to worried families in the United States.

Ray's portrait by Elizabeth Black, August 19, 1944.

IV - OVERLORD SUMMER 1944

THE WAR CONTINUES

During Ray's convalescence, the Rangers guard prisoners of war in the Cotentin Peninsula and secure bridges on the Mayenne River, before taking part in their first real battle since D-Day on August 25: the capture of Brest, two weeks after the beginning of the battle for this port city transformed it into a real fortress. Ray will join his company on the Brest – Le Conquet front line, supported by the French Forces of the Interior (FFI) and former Russian prisoners eager for revenge. They'll enter the town of Locmaria-Plouzané in late August, where Ray's mortar team will drop a hailstorm of bombs on two approaching patrols: those not killed on the spot will be captured by the Rangers. The latter will have great difficulty preventing the FFIs, screaming and wielding their weapons in the air, from executing the terrified Germans. Le Conquet will eventually fall on September 10 after long and heavy fighting, with Ray's men taking 814 prisoners.

They won't see the end of the Battle of Brest on September 19, as the Rangers will take a train to Belgium where a short training period awaits them. Ray will then experience dark hours during the battle for Hill 400 in Bergstein (Germany), not far from the infamous Hürtgen Forest. The German counter-offensive in the Ardennes in December will bring the Rangers back into battle with the 78th Infantry Division, before they can advance, at last, towards the Ruhr pocket. On April 2, 1945, they'll stop for a while in Fritzlar, the town's airport having been taken the day before by an American armored division. Indeed, many bodies of German soldiers will still be lying where they fell only a few hours earlier.

There, on April 8, Ray will write this letter to Margaret, the mother of his friend Jack who died on Omaha Beach:

"Dear Mom Bramkamp, I received your nice letter of March 6th this afternoon and was very glad to hear from you again and I hope my letter finds you in the best of health. I am feeling fine and everything is OK with Jim and the rest of the boys. Jim received your package alright and the address was correct. Thank you for sending me Shirley's address. I'll be very glad to drop her a few lines. We haven't heard from Chris Mohr in over 6 months. I guess he's forgotten us all. He was hurt D+1 when either his gun or one of the fellows close by accidentally went off and he got shot in the back of the leg below the knee cap. We never really got the whole story on that.

Pfc. Christian J. Mohr, from Kenosha, Wisconsin, photographed on the plane that evacuated him to Scotland. He received the Purple Heart for his injury.

Ray's letter from Fritzlar to Margaret Bramkamp, the mother of Jack, Ray's friend killed on D-Day.

Following the death of her son, she was so close to Jack's friends that she was soon called 'Mom' by the men in 2nd Rangers. The treats she regularly sent were an invaluable source of comfort to the soldiers.

Yes it would be grand if Jack was still here with us. We all miss him a lot. He was a real buddy and we won't forget him. As you say it was the will of God that he was taken from you. That's the only [missing word?] it can be figured. The reason Jack didn't carry a rifle was that he carried the 60 mm mortar which weights 42 lbs and a rifle would have been too much of a load. He also carried a pistol which was enough protection as he had 5 other men to protect him when we were in position. We just never got a chance to get into position. I asked our CO about whether or not I could tell you where Jack was buried but all I can say is that he's buried in a National Cemetery for Allied soldiers in France. He also said that after the war the War Department would give you all that information. I saw where he was buried and it was a very nice spot near the ocean. He is among some other Rangers and buddies of ours."

Jack must have first been buried on the edge of Omaha Beach, facing the Dog White Sector, where a remembrance stone is still present today, marking the location of the first Allied cemetery in Normandy. The 457 graves were, however, quickly moved for reasons of hygiene and morale for the troops who subsequently landed there. When this letter was written, Jack was probably in a temporary cemetery of 3,808 graves in Saint-Laurent-sur-Mer, behind the cliffs east of Le Ruquet. Once it was closed on September 17, 1944, those coffins not repatriated to the United States at the request of the families were added to the large, and now famous, American Cemetery in Colleville, where ten temporary burial sites were regrouped. However, Jack's body has returned home and rests today at the Vine Street Hill Cemetery in Cincinnati, Ohio.

Ray will close his letter as follows: *"There are about 100 of the boys that Jack knew left. Yes the Rangers in the Philippines did a wonderful job* [the 6th Rangers, the last of the six battalions raised, is the only one to serve in the Pacific. On January 30, 1945, they'll help 511 Allied prisoners of war escape in a raid north of Manila, killing 523 Japanese at the cost of only 2 casualties. This is the event Ray is talking about]. *Since you need a request to send things and had to use one of Bus's I'll ask for some cookies and candy. And thanks a lot mom. I'll have to close now as I have to get a guard list ready for tonight. So take care of yourself mom and God bless you. Give my best to Bus and I'm going to write to Shirley tonight. Your loving 'Son', Ray."*

The Rangers will leave Fritzlar the day after, attached to the 2nd Infantry Division to push into the heart of Germany. They'll reach Czechoslovakia on May 7 and learn of the end of the war in the Czech city of Newberg. Ray will correspond with Margaret for many years to come, and his sons will often hear about his friend Jack.

'Mrs. B.' will even often come by the house and will be like a third grandmother to the young boys. Her other, natural, son, Louis (104th Infantry Division 'Timberwolves') will be wounded twice during the war.

The blue and yellow diamond patch is worn by all Ranger battalions. But, inspired by the 1st Battalion, which had a special 'scroll' patch bearing its name, the men of the 2nd Rangers had one of their members (whose father worked in the textile industry) make this additional patch, which was worn later in the war above the 'Rangers' diamond.

AFTER THE WAR

Ironically, although Ray will go through a great deal in Europe, his worst injury will come while waiting for the ship due to bring him back to his wife. He'll break his leg during a baseball game with his brothers-in-arms and consequently delay his departure for six long weeks. Ray and Audrey will still talk about it long after the war, but even after his return from Europe, Ray won't get tired of baseball and will even play a season with the Chicago White Sox in 1947.

Ray in his baseball uniform, marked 'Rangers'.

He'll resume his carpentry job and have two sons, Rick and Donald. In the 1970s, Ray and Audrey will visit Rick, stationed in Worms (Germany) with the US Army, and together they

IV - OVERLORD SUMMER 1944

will travel to Normandy. Ray and his son will walk on Omaha Beach, the Pointe du Hoc and visit the impressive Colleville-sur-Mer American Cemetery. Rick will see his father burst into tears over the graves of his fallen comrades: their memory will never leave the former Ranger.

Ray at the Pointe du Hoc in 1972.

Many years after landing on Omaha Beach, in July 1998 Ray will relive the events he has never been able to forget, when Steven Spielberg's movie *Saving Private Ryan* is released in American theaters. The opening scenes recreate the assault on Dog Green in a brutal way, told from the point of view of Rangers from Ray's unit. The film is so realistic that Ray will recognize some of his former comrades and see in Captain Miller (played by Tom Hanks) his former commander, Captain Sidney Salomon. The latter took charge of B Company just after the landings. In the *Chicago Tribune*'s article about him in July 1998, Ray will say of his captain: *"He was the kind of commander who wouldn't ask you to do anything he wouldn't do himself. If he had asked me to jump off a building, I would have done it."* As his wife Audrey reacts to his words, he adds: *"I still would"*.

For one of the first times in cinema, war is shown in its most raw and bloodiest form. Many shocked spectators will leave the Chicago Ridge Theater, but Ray won't be able to turn his eyes away from the screen. He doesn't want to miss a thing: the scene is identical to what he experienced on June 6, 1944. For Audrey, his wife, it'll be a traumatic experience and she'll have to leave her seat and go out into the hallway to get some fresh air. Until that moment, she'd never realized what her husband had been through.

Ray will die a month later, at the age of 76, of a brain hemorrhage on September 1, 1998 in Oak Lawn, Illinois. As for Audrey, she will live to be 85 years old and pass away on December 22, 2007.

Colleville-sur-Mer American Cemetery, overlooking the Easy Red Sector of Omaha Beach where the 1st Infantry Division made its breakthrough inland. Today, more than 9,000 American soldiers are buried there, including many of Ray's comrades.
"Soldiers' graves are the greatest preachers of peace" (Albert Schweitzer).

JAMES P. C. MACPHERSON

Cameron Highlanders of Ottawa (Machine Gun), 3rd Canadian Infantry Division

East of Omaha, on Juno Beach, Canadians suffer the second highest Allied casualty rate on D-Day.
After this first terrifying experience, James will face young SS fanatics determined to push him back into the sea.
His company will lose its officers in action, encouraging James to take command:
his excellent initiative will earn him the Military Cross.

James Pennington Carlyle Macpherson was born in England on June 13, 1916, while his father was in the French trenches with the Canadian Expeditionary Force. 'Jim' returned to Canada on board the *Olympic* ten months later. Coming from a long line of renowned officers, it was only natural for him to join the Canadian armed forces and on July 9, 1940, he arrived in Reykjavik (Iceland) with the Cameron Highlanders of Ottawa (Duke of Edinburgh's Own) as part of the Z force intended to occupy the country. He was appointed 2nd lieutenant on November 22 and left for the United Kingdom on July 21, 1941.

James in Iceland, 1940. On the left, he's seen wearing the infantry combat uniform and above, his Service Dress uniform. His regiment continues the military traditions of the Highlands, with its members wearing Scottish kilts in a tartan unique to the Canadian and British Cameron Highlanders. They also wear a Balmoral cap, on which are attached the regiment's tartan and metal badge.

174

James was one of 100,000 soldiers in the 1st Canadian Army (representing a quarter of all Canadian volunteers) destined to liberate Northwest Europe. As the Cameron Highlanders were training for D-Day in Scotland, James met his future wife, Elizabeth Taylor, a young Scottish member of the Auxiliary Territorial Service (ATS), at a dance. Without delay, the couple married in Edinburgh on April 17, 1943.

JUNO BEACH

On June 5, 1944, James embarks from Southampton to the sound of bagpipes, his LCT loaded with Jeeps and tanks. Its destination: Juno Beach. The Canadians' objective is a long strip of sand dunes and coastal villas, stretching 5 miles from Graye-sur-Mer to Saint-Aubin-sur-Mer, passing through Bernières-sur-Mer and Courseulles-sur-Mer. The 1st Battalion of the Cameron Highlanders of Ottawa consists of three companies of machine gunners (A, B and James' C) and one mortar (D Company). When needed, they're attached to other regiments of the 3rd Canadian Infantry Division, each platoon supporting the advance of an infantry battalion with .303 Vickers machine guns from the First World War. James lands in the late morning of June 6 with reinforcements from 9th Brigade to help the vehicles progress inland. Hitting the beach under heavy fire, the 7th and 8th Brigades that formed the initial assault wave suffered heavy casualties on Juno: the 3rd Canadian Infantry Division had 355 men killed, 574 wounded and 47 prisoners, and their British allies 243 killed and wounded.

James shares his memories of D-Day: *"Soon little assault craft were scurrying into the beach with their groups of thirty infantrymen, armed to the teeth and tense, as they approached the battle for which we had all waited so long. Naval rocket ships put down their terrific barrage ahead of the approaching craft and over our heads could be heard the screaming of huge naval shells from our battleships, some so far away they could not be seen. And in the sky, our fastest fighters swooped back and forth, undisputed masters. Soon, splashes, in and around our circling landing craft, indicated that the enemy had found our range and the fight was on.*

After a couple of hours, we intercepted the message on my wireless set that our infantry had cleared the beach, and that it was time for us (the first wave of vehicles) to go ashore. [...] We were in Normandy – in enemy-occupied country. 'The rest is up to you' shouted the Naval Officers from the bridge of our LCT. As we endeavoured to drive as quickly as possible off the beach, I saw a few wounded being attended by a medical orderly, then I saw a few badly battered German prisoners in their field grey uniforms and looking out on the other side of my truck, I saw my first dead man – a Canadian by his shoulder badges. His head was blown off.

The slow-moving column of vehicles came to a halt in a little French village, just off the beach, and I saw an old, old man scraping in the ruins of what had been a pretty little house. [...] I saw a French woman with her little girl, gazing with shocked and saddened eyes at what had once been their home. The little girl was crying with fright. Suddenly she stopped crying, and ran laughing, and pointing to a single huge pink rose, which somehow had escaped destruction, and clung precariously to a shattered piece of fencing - all that was left of a once beautiful garden. And then the guns started, a whistle blew, and the column moved on. [...] In those first hours of the invasion we were initiated in a little of all that was to follow - the noise, the suffering, the prisoners, the violent deaths, the futility, the sacrifice, the destruction - and even the rare moments of beauty which come when the best in men instead of the worst is brought to the fore. And the sum of all these is War."

James writes to his parents three weeks after D-Day: *"Everything about this operation has been beautifully planned. Now I can tell you something about the many full-dress rehearsals we have had during the past two years. I tell you we just couldn't miss – not a detail was overlooked, and we could have done our landing with our eyes closed, almost from memory. The last exercise we did in England was a landing on a very similar piece of coastline. Every man was briefed several times and knew everything that was to happen over the whole beachhead."*

AGAINST HITLER'S YOUTH

By the evening of D-Day, 14,000 Canadians have landed and are heading for the Oak Line and the Carpiquet airfield. However, Caen was not taken by the British and the 12. SS Panzer-Division called in to counter-attack is now heading straight for the 3rd Canadian Division. SS-Standartenführer Kurt Meyer, head of SS-Panzergrenadier Regiment 25, taught his very young fanatical recruits: *"Never forget that the last bullet in your magazine is for you."* The Sherbrooke Rifles and the North Nova Scotia Highlanders, supported by James' company, quickly nicknamed these SS the 'Baby Division', as their age rarely exceeds 18 years. They'll soon rename them the 'Murder Division'.

On June 7, James approaches Villons-les-Buissons, northwest of Buron and Authie. The picturesque little village is captured by the Canadians at 9:30 am, despite sporadic sniper and mortar fire. But in the early afternoon, the Canadians are engaged on all fronts by Meyer's tanks, who'd established his headquarters nearby at the Abbaye d'Ardenne (Authie). Without support and outnumbered, Canadians are forced to withdraw or surrender to the ruthless Hitler Youth soldiers. In Authie, Buron and the surrounding villages, Allied prisoners are executed on the street. Unarmed and with their helmets removed, they're shot in the back of the head then horribly mutilated, while others are lined up on the road to be crushed by the Panzers' tracks. In one day, the Canadians lose 422 men (110 dead), while still inflicting 300 killed and 15 tanks destroyed on the German SS. The battle for Caen has only just begun.

A Canadian soldier supported by James' company recalls the fanaticism of their enemies from his hospital bed a few weeks later: *"I've seen a lot over in France in a short while, chums killed in front of you, dead Jerries blown apart, legs here and there. Not a house that a bomb hadn't hit. I guess you've read the papers about the Canadians fighting in Carpiquet, taking a large airfield, fighting in Gruchy and a village called Authie, our regiment sure gave the Jerries hell in there, and I'm proud to say as we advanced through the grain fields to our objectives, I done a lot of praying. I seemed to run a little way with my Bren gun and go down and let out a burst, then start to pray and get up and change my spot. We sure gave the Germans hell in all these places. They were a bunch of kids 14 and 15 and felt sorry for some of them when they surrendered until one of the rats in a hole shot one of our boys in the back as we were leading his Heinie pal away, so from then on we made a vow amongst us: no more sympathy and no more prisoners."*

On D+2, James particularly distinguishes himself in this region during one of the three actions that would earn him the Military Cross: *"On 8 June 44 at Les Buissons, when his company commander and one platoon commander had been killed in action, and another was missing, Capt. MacPherson assumed command of the company and re-organized it under fire. His fine leadership enabled the company to support successfully the attack of the 9th Brigade in that area."*

Nevertheless, the SS are determined to push the Canadians back into the sea and will hold their positions firmly for a month. James writes on June 21: *"Dearest Mother & Dad, […] you say you find it difficult for you to picture my surroundings at any time.*

Well how's this – just think of a scene from 'Journey's End'. I've moved into an old barn rather the worse for wear, but it's dry. I am writing this from candle-light. The candle is stuck in an old wine bottle. The rough table is stained with chicken blood, there is the remains of a bottle of whisky, an empty jam tin and a couple of pieces of hard tack, an army mug and curiously enough Betty's pictures propped up against another empty wine bottle in which my batman has placed 3 very big, very pink roses – Dad will recall many such a familiar scene! Things are comparatively quiet for the present.

The first days were hectic. By now you will have heard the news of Charlie Hills and Joe Courtright's death, both the same day. I didn't want to tell you about it until I had written their next-of-kins, but now that I have taken care of everything like that, I can tell you. Thank God, I had so much to do taking over the company that I have not been able to think too much about the loss of my three friends (Jack Couper is missing too). [Major Charles Christie Hill, commander of C Company, and Captain Joseph William Courtright died on June 9. Lieutenant John Stanley Couper was killed the day before by a mortar shell in Authie, although he was still missing at the time James wrote this letter.] *Hal has been wounded and has gone back to England, he's quite OK I'm glad to say (he's not in my company). I don't mind saying I've been scared sometimes, but I am getting to be a veteran very quickly. Being an officer is a great help, you have so many other things to worry about and so many other people, you can generally forget all about your own troubles. I have been lucky I suppose, but I have a strong feeling that I am going on that way, so please try not to worry too much. I am as fit as a fiddle, I have a fine, fine body of men – they can't be beaten anywhere, and that goes for the whole battalion. Everyone has a good word for us and the work we've done so far. It's my job to carry on Joe's, Jack's and Charlie's work as well as my own but with God's help, I am going to do it."*

The Canadians now have to wait for *Operation Charnwood* on July 8 and its massive bombardment to be able to resume their assault on Buron. The town is liberated the next day, after a tough and often hand-to-hand fight.

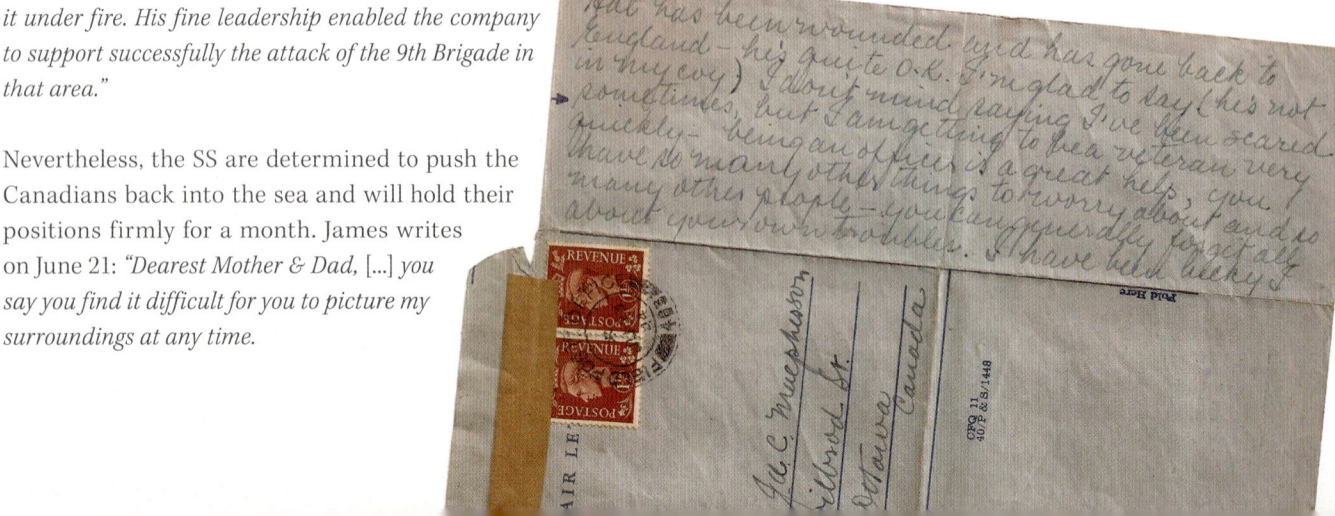

IV - **OVERLORD** SUMMER 1944

MILITARY CROSS

James is again mentioned for his bravery: *"During operations on 8 July '44 and in particular the attack of the 9th Canadian Infantry Brigade on Cruchy and Buron, he handled his company of medium machine gunners in outstanding manner, making his reconnaissance under fire, and personally leading two of his platoons into their fire position under heavy enemy fire. His action contributed in no small degree to the successful support of the infantry on to their objective."*

Finally, on July 25, 1944, a third mention supports his recommendation for the Military Cross: *"During the attack on Tilly-la-Campagne, the company commander of C Company was wounded and a platoon commander killed. Capt. MacPherson again assumed command and under difficult circumstances steadied the company, and by his coolness and example contributed in no small measure to the successful action of the company in support of the 9th Canadian Infantry Brigade on that occasion. His coolness under fire, disregard of personal safety and good example are in the highest traditions of the service."*

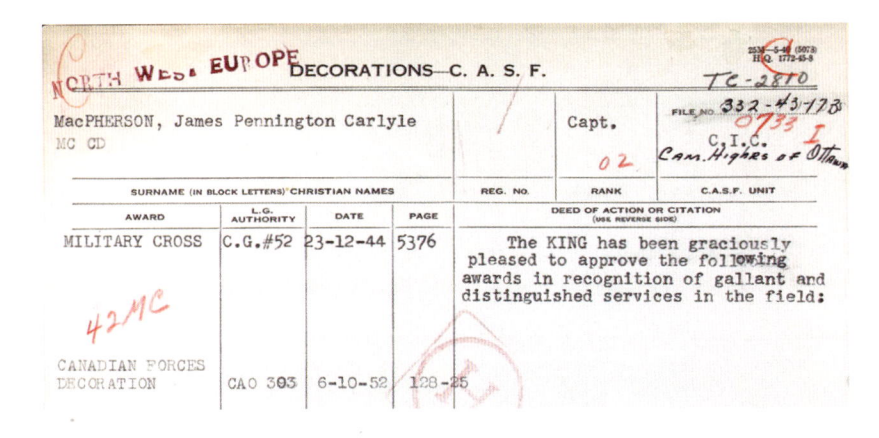

James will be involved in all Canadian battles in France, Belgium, the Netherlands and Germany, before his return home on June 29, 1945. He'll end his military career as a lieutenant-colonel at the head of the Royal Montreal Regiment, and afterwards begin a successful career at the Bank of Montreal until his retirement in 1981.

James died on January 17, 1998 and now rests in Kingston, Ontario.

Two soldiers from the Cameron Highlanders of Ottawa at the end of the Battle of Normandy. They've just taken their revenge and proudly display this Nazi flag captured from the enemy in a quarry south of Hautmesnil (August 10, 1944).

GEORGE E. E. ROSS

B Company, 2nd Battalion Warwickshire Regiment, 3rd (Iron) Infantry Division

Montgomery had promised the 3rd Division, the last to leave Dunkirk in 1940, that it would be the first to return to France. Major George E. E. Ross will lead B Company, 2nd Battalion, Warwickshire Regiment from Sword Beach to its D-Day objective: Caen. However, George's advance will be slowed down for weeks and he'll be wounded on July 20, 1944, not long after Caen finally falls.

George Edward Edgar Ross was born on April 25, 1910, near Birmingham (Warwickshire, England). His father was a former soldier of the Black Watch (Royal Highlanders), and married to Gabrielle Huchin, a French woman from Boulogne-sur-Mer. His origins will make the landing in France particularly moving for his family.

George and his younger brother Reginald already have several years of service behind them, and are both majors in the Warwickshire Regiment. George is in the 2nd Battalion, while Reginald is in the 9th, which will never be used in combat. At the end of 1940, George married Renee: she is pregnant with their first child when he leaves for Normandy.

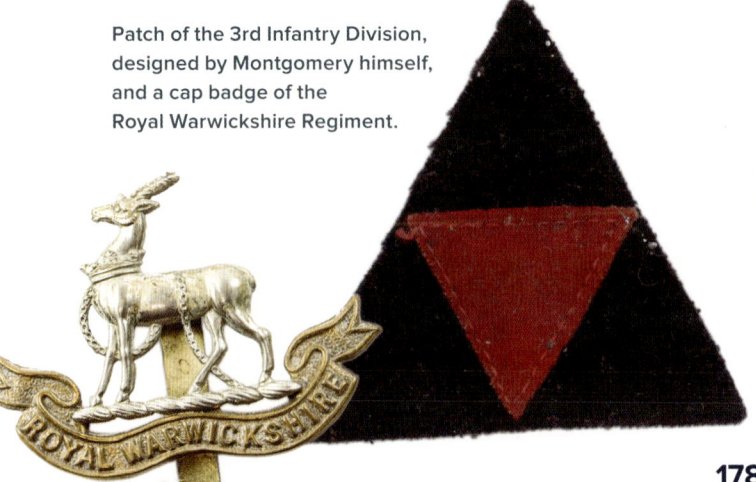

Patch of the 3rd Infantry Division, designed by Montgomery himself, and a cap badge of the Royal Warwickshire Regiment.

SWORD BEACH

On June 4, 1944, the men of the '2nd Warwicks' are getting ready to take part in Overlord. The regiment is composed of A, B, C and D companies, plus S Company (anti-tank and mortar units), HQ Company (supply, medical units and chaplain), Battalion HQ, and finally a forward observation officer for the artillery. It sets sail at 9 pm and heads for the easternmost beach of the whole operation.

The battalion's mission is to land on the Queen White Sector of Sword Beach, reserved for the British 3rd Infantry Division, then to advance as quickly as possible inland and take Caen on the evening of June 6. On its right flank, the 3rd Canadian Infantry Division would set foot on Juno Beach and on its left, on the other side of the canal going all the way to Caen, British and Canadian paratroopers from the 6th Airborne would have to take the bridges over the Orne River and contain enemy reinforcements. Alongside the 2nd Warwicks, three infantry brigades of the 3rd British Division would land, supported by an armored brigade, artillery guns and engineers, as well as the 1st and 4th Special Service Brigades (commandos and Royal Marines). Among the latter are Captain Phillipe Kiefer's 177 Free French commandos, who would capture the port of Ouistreham.

Queen White Sector, where George landed on June 6.

As the news of D-Day spreads like wildfire, Reginald thinks of his older brother George. On June 6, he writes from Humbleton Camp (Barnard Castle, Durham, England): *"Dear Mother, just a very short line to say how much my thoughts are with you and Dad and George. Every moment, at this eventful time. It seems to me – and it is only my own idea – that all our forces are not yet committed, and other landings remain to be made. In that case George MIGHT not be involved at the moment, though I do not think it is very likely. Our duty is now to have complete confidence Mother, and pray. We all have a duty to be courageous in our thoughts, even more than in our actions. How must the people of France feel! If ever there was a Crusade, then this must be it. I do not think the Germans will fight for long. They are being defeated at this very moment on three big fronts, and in their own country."*

In fact, George is just about to land. On the ship taking him to Sword Beach, he writes: *"5th June 44 – My dear Mother & Dad, just a little line on the boat before the big show. It is just to tell you I am quite cheerful and happy and in good company. Do not worry yourselves, all will be alright, and I'll be home again. By the time you get this you will see everything in the papers."* (Letter photographed below.)

In command of B Company, George is assisted by Captain J. F. K. Jerram, and three platoon commanders: lieutenants Allan Dockerty, Dennis Field and Ord Roberts. The men are split into three LCI (Landing Craft Infantry) ships, much larger than the LCA (Landing Craft Assault) vehicles, which can only carry thirty-six men. The LCI can land 200 soldiers directly on the beaches from two footbridges on both sides of the bow.

D-DAY, H-HOUR

George's ship approaches the village of Lion-sur-Mer and finally reaches land at 9:55 am. The 8th Brigade and the men who landed an hour and a half earlier are already working to clean up the beach exits at the cost of several lives. The area is still under continuous mortar and small arms fire, swept by machine guns and snipers installed in the houses along the promenade. George's LCI receives three shells which destroy the landing ramps. The Tommies have to use another ship from 8th Brigade stranded beside them in order to get off their landing craft. Confusion reigns on the beach and some casualties are suffered, but at 11:30 am all of the companies are gathered 800 yards south of Lion-sur-Mer.

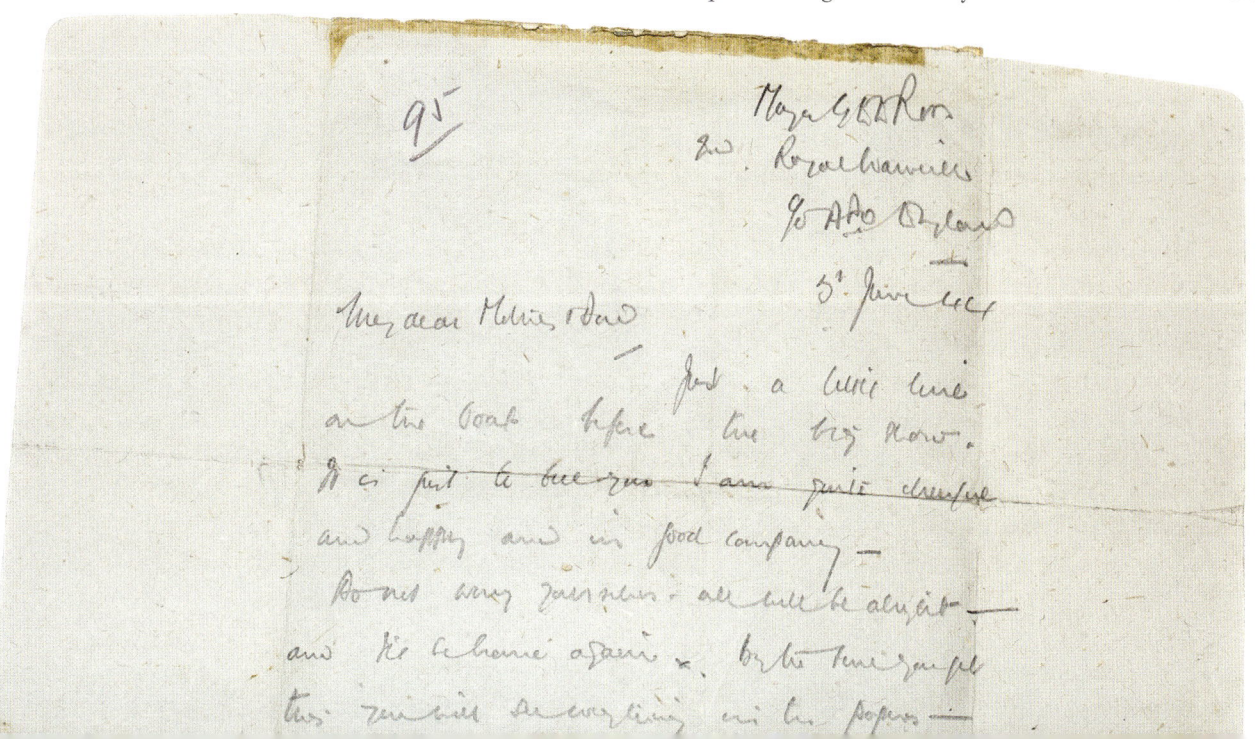

British soldiers of the 3rd Infantry Division moving out of Sword Beach on June 6, 1944. Many are equipped with bicycles in order to progress quickly and silently inland. Opposite, a relic of a military bicycle tyre, made by Avon Avebury (War Grade), found during excavations in the area.

George will write to his parents three months later: *"We sailed all night, which is where I wrote my letters. It was just like an exercise – no aircraft, submarines, or anything. When we got near the coast, we heard firing. We put on our equipment and suddenly found ourselves in the war. The landing was not as bad as I expected, though exciting enough. The gangways (down the front – I expect you have seen pictures) were blown off. The ship was hit once by a shell but no casualties. To get off we had to climb into a ship alongside which was sinking and then into another on the other side and go ashore. We were being sniped from houses and there was some mortar fire, but we got off well and lightly."*

As they leave the village of Hermanville-sur-Mer, A and C companies lose a few more men in combat inside the Lion-sur-Mer cemetery, shot at by snipers and machine guns from Cresserons on their right flank. The pillboxes of Colleville-sur-Orne are still resisting the assaults of the King's Shropshire Light Infantry and the Royal Norfolk Regiment. These German strongholds won't be completely silenced until 6:30 pm, when George's battalion crosses Colleville-sur-Orne and Saint-Aubin-d'Arquenay. There they're ordered to attack Bénouville at 7 pm and link up with the 6th Airborne paratroopers who had captured its bridge (soon to be nicknamed Pegasus Bridge) during the night. As George's men move into position before the assault, they see several waves of British gliders landing airborne troops as reinforcements, crashing down all around them. One of the aircraft even lands on two radio operators of the 2nd Battalion, killing them instantly as they couldn't hear the warnings shouts from their comrades.

Suddenly, the German flak opens fire on the paras falling from the sky, revealing its position to the 2nd Warwicks, who set out on a hunt led by George's B Company. The fighting is violent, rapid and at very close range. Even after the German anti-aircraft positions are cleared, the British are still harassed by snipers, who must be flushed out one by one. Once the area is finally secured, D Company remains on site to relieve the 6th Airborne and hold the bridges, while the rest of the battalion follows the canal to Blainville. As soon as they move out of Bénouville, the men are attacked by heavy machine guns and anti-tank fire. Two British tanks are immediately taken out, one of them having its turret torn off by the force of the explosion.

'Pegasus Bridge' in Bénouville.
Note the 6th Airborne Division gliders crashed behind the trees.

IV - OVERLORD SUMMER 1944

But it's a victory for the British and the 2nd Warwicks stop for the night northeast of Blainville, after having established a defensive perimeter. They counted four dead and thirty-five wounded during the day: a relatively small figure compared to the 683 Germans killed by the Allies around Sword Beach (against 630 killed, wounded and missing among the British).

LEBISEY WOODS

According to the plans, Caen should have already been in Allied hands. On the morning of June 7, 185th Brigade launches its first attack on Lebisey Woods, overlooking the north of the city. Unfortunately, the German tanks of the 21. Panzerdivision and the Hitler Youth fanatics of the 12. SS Hitlerjugend had jumped into position during the night to stop the Anglo-Canadian advance. The members of the Hitlerjugend are so loyal to their Führer and his ideology that their captured wounded are known to refuse transfusions, preferring death to the risk of being infected with non-Aryan blood. George's company is the first to go in, crossing the corn fields and climbing the hill leading to the edge of the woods.

They're supposed to be supported by artillery fire from the 3rd Division's batteries and offshore warships, but at 8:45 am, the attack is postponed, unbeknownst to the 2nd Warwicks, who had communication problems, meaning the battalion is heading straight for disaster, without any real support. It quickly finds itself in trouble, unable to progress in the face of fierce resistance, and can't move until nightfall, when it has no choice but to withdraw. George has lost several soldiers that day, including his battalion commander (Lieutenant-Colonel Hugh Herdon, killed by a machine gun burst to the head) and his best platoon commander, Lieutenant Alan Dockerty. The British remain stuck in the area for a month, near Beuville and Bréville, under constant artillery fire. Their daily routine is punctuated by patrols, bombs and the arrival of replacements. Without really attacking, the 2nd Warwicks and the Germans nearby will do everything in their power to make each other's lives as unpleasant as possible. On June 27, George Ross writes the following long letter: *"My Dear Mother, I seem to have been trying hard the last few days to get a letter to you, without success. I have received your little parcel last night – thank you very much indeed. I have had the soap too. I do not need any more soap, thank you Mother dear, we have really plenty, and tooth paste too. Renee has also sent me a terrific box. Well, I am hoarding it and keeping it in my Bren Carrier [British infantry tracked vehicle]. I have eaten the chocolate biscuits already and we are sitting in a stable, which is my Company HQ, about to eat the chocolates. We have tried again to get a bottle of wine without success. The papers giving pictures of buying champagne and pastries etc. in Bayeux really make me laugh. I haven't been in a pub or a shop now since the Monday following my last weekend at home, and we have been in the line continuously since we landed. Of course, one doesn't fight continuously in the line, but it is nearly always noisy and tense by day and night.*

Typical items the English soldier has in his foxhole, found during excavations in Normandy: candy box (a), S.J. Moreland and Sons matches (b), iron cup impacted with a bullet (c), charred biscuits (d), pocket knife or 'Jack Knife' (e), and can opener (f).

British folding marker used to indicate mines: an invisible enemy at the beach exits.

Mom, for the benefit of Dad, I can tell you a bit of past history, as within limits I am allowed to talk about actions over a fortnight old. As you know we landed on D-Day in the morning. Our craft was hit twice but no one was hurt, only it made it more awkward to land. We came under fire, mortars and snipers almost immediately, but my company was again very fortunate. Some houses were burning but the people were not very dismayed. I spoke with my first French early on, asking if the enemy had laid any mines anywhere, and all were very helpful. We moved that day steadily inland on our two legs, having slight skirmishes and taking some prisoners. It is all a confused memory to me. I saw too much ever to remember it all – blazing houses and tanks, noise, guns, snipers all the time, the wonderful sight of our grand airborne forces coming in in the evening, the plane fights in the skies, and the big guns on the ships firing overhead... and always on we marched, sometimes ducking, crawling, or running, but God was kind to my little company and very few indeed fell by the wayside.

We marched all through the next night until we made contact again with the enemy. It came quite suddenly out of the darkness. A tank was hit and some fire came from a house into the darkness. The old company soon made short work of the house with fire and grenades and five prisoners soon popped out. Anyhow we had gone far enough so we dug ourselves in in a wood and waited for an attack by the enemy at dawn which never came.

So we moved again next morning, early, through another village where all were glad to see us. All company commanders were then sent for and I got my orders for an attack on a nearby hill. Our first attack, and rather a perplexing prospect in the early morning. My company led the attack at 9:45 in the morning, reached the objective, but could get no further as the enemy were strongly defending the woods – snipers were in the trees and machine guns were further back. We were reinforced by each company in turn till all the battalion was engaged, then after that by another battalion. Late in the day enemy tanks appeared and owing to the nature of the country, ours could not come up. We fought all day until 10 o'clock in the evening, then we were ordered to withdraw, my company being one of the last two from the battalion left on the hill. It's a thing which I shall never understand, and why the Boche never made full use of his temporary advantage I don't know, but I withdrew my company (always a risky operation) without a single casualty. That refers of course only to the withdrawal, and not to the previous fighting. I cannot give you numbers of casualties, but taking it all round we were again very fortunate indeed for such a day [the casualties actually totaled 10 officers and 144 soldiers].

The edge of Lebisey Wood, where George launched his first assault.

I shall never forget that heavy march back a mile or two. I was allocated a position by a blazing farmhouse where a couple of snipers were being taken out. That night we dug again, on the old principle of 'dig or die'. You must always get below ground. But we were not attacked in the morning. Old Jerry had probably had enough too. I was moved forward again to take up a new position as soon as it was light – we dug again – had some food and slept. Since landing I had had no sleep and two bars of chocolate and a pint of water – my whisky flask had again been smashed, and we had had our equipment dumped before the attack. The next day Dennis Field (Dad knows him) took out a patrol to get our kit back – he found five Germans about to rifle it. He shot them up and took some prisoners and brought all our stuff back – a good show! But my little pack and pipe and cigarettes had been taken already.

It has not since ever been as bad as those early days, and I feel well, and get a certain amount of sleep. I am very fit, and quite an old soldier. Don't worry about me, I am as you know very resilient and just the same, though perhaps ever more grateful for my home and comforts. [...] I have written to Reg. Tell him to take it easy and wait on to go with his battalion. He is a fool to worry. Just take things as they come and NEVER VOLUNTEER. Since I seem to be sermonizing, I would like to say that my chaps were fine – no grumbles, no shirking, no indiscipline, still just grand and I am a proud man to be in such company. For myself I have done nothing brave or distinguished as did some of my brother officers in the battalion. I was just there. The men are singing outside the farmhouse and beating on their mess tins as I write. R. is having his tea, the artillery is still firing, soon at dusk. I shall go round the trenches to see all is in order for the night, see if they are OK and have a little joke with them. One thing is certain. England is free for my generation and France will soon be again. We have the men, we have the equipment. The Hun is good, but not near good enough. The end is in sight."

THE CAPTURE OF CAEN

Since D-Day, the German presence in Caen has prevented the Allies from accessing the port of Le Havre, the flat ground inland suitable for aerodromes, as well as Paris and the missile bases in the Pas-de-Calais region. Realizing that a frontal attack on Caen was impossible, Montgomery tries to bypass the city and launch several operations that would prove to be very costly.

Firstly, *Operation Perch* (June 7-15), is stopped in the west by the German Panzers and supply problems. *Operation Epsom* (June 25-July 1), which intended to take the city from the south across the Odon, is also blocked by SS armored divisions. However, Hill 112, a strategic high ground between the Orne and the Odon, is captured and held by the 11th Armoured Division with the support of the 15th (Scottish) Division, the English 43rd (Wessex) Division, and the 53rd (Welsh) Division. But Montgomery is slow to exploit this advantage and a brutal counter-attack forces the British to retreat. The fighting to retake the hill and its surroundings (*Operation Jupiter*) would last until August 4 and result in the loss of thousands of men. Finally, *Operation Windsor* (July 4-5) is launched on Carpiquet, but without succeeding in taking the aerodrome from the Germans.

Montgomery therefore changes his strategy and decides to try a frontal attack again, and *Operation Charnwood* thus starts on the night of July 7, with a long and violent bombardment by the Royal Air Force.

The 2nd Warwickshire Regiment crossing a wheat field during *Operation Charnwood*, July 8, 1944. Montgomery would say of the battalion that there were *"no better soldiers"*, helping the 2nd Warwicks justify its motto: *"Seek glory"*.

In the early morning, as the Canadians push the SS out of Buron and Authie, George's company is back in Lebisey Wood and its village. The Germans had meanwhile received reinforcements from the 16. Feld-Division, who set up its command post in Lebisey, strengthening the lines and camouflaging its Panzers in the forest. However, the RAF bombardments had pulverized its defenses and the enemy, disorganized, is forced to withdraw. George's men, supported by the 2nd King's Shropshire Light Infantry and Staffordshire Yeomanry tanks, enter Lebisey at 4:30 am.

As the King's Shropshire soldiers are clearing the woods, the Royal Warwickshire men capture the small village. This time, they manage to do so despite heavy machine gun and 'Nebelwerfer' fire (a German rocket launching battery making a terrifying sound) and the area is secured by 11 am. The English still had 26 killed, 102 wounded and 25 missing in the process, but they helped the Canadian and British forces launch a coordinated assault on Caen and enter the city that same evening. It will be completely liberated the next day. George will write to his mother: *"You may remember a letter I wrote to you on the 8th early in the morning. Well, you may or may not have guessed we were due to attack at dawn. I lost two of my officers that day. The battalion and the Company did very well indeed, and the Commanding Officer told me confidentially that he has put me in for a 'Mention in Dispatches' for what I did, though it wasn't much except being in the right place at the right time..."* In another letter, he adds: *"My company's particular task was to secure the right flank, and it was done properly and well. We killed many Germans and took a lot more prisoners. If you see a large-scale map you can see the wood dominates Caen, and was the keystone of that front. The British and Canadians attacked all along the front later that day and Caen had fallen by the evening, the Royal Ulster Rifles passing through us found resistance and were the first troops to enter that bitterly contested town."*

A soldier from the Stormont Dundas and Glengarry Highlanders (3rd Canadian Infantry Division) recounts his entry into Caen at 1 pm on July 9: *"It's the size of Toronto, split up in the center by the river Orne and the Odon, we had one half under control except for a few snipers but the other half was still in the Germans' hands, but not for long. With the support of thousands of bombers, we advanced cleaning up village after village, we were itchy on the trigger as we went and ready to shoot anything that moved in front of us. A pal of mine saw a curtain move and let go a burst and over toppled a cat, we all started to laugh. We went about five miles on the other side of Caen to some small village where we had a little battle, Germans were giving themselves up by the hundreds. There was a lot of Ukrainians & Poles who said they were forced to fight."*

Canadian soldiers from the Stormont Dundas and Glengarry Highlanders at Caen's main train station. This unit also claims to have been the first to enter the city.

OUT OF ACTION

After a short rest, on July 18, George's 2nd Warwicks take part in Montgomery's new plan to liberate the second half of the city (*Operation Atlantic*), and then *Operation Goodwood*, designed to push the Germans south. The battalion is engaged in a diversionary operation east of Caen, tasked with capturing Emiéville. As the battle rages, led by the King's Own Light Infantry and the Norfolk Regiment, George's company remains in reserve on the morning of the 19th, near the village. George is at the battalion's headquarters when a mortar shell falls on his position, killing two of his officers and throwing him to the ground, completely stunned. Having received only a piece of shrapnel in his arm, he decides to continue the fight. With a simple bandage, without realizing that he's actually weakened from loss of blood, he participates in a new assault on the village at 4 am.

In Emiéville, the British endure some intense sniper fire and a counter-attack by two fearsome Tiger tanks. As they cross an open field, they find themselves under heavy fire and sustain heavy casualties. George's company is the target of a machine gun killing several men at close range. Corporal Millard crawls towards the latter with his Bren machine gun, then stands up to charge the position while firing from the hip. He manages to kill two enemies but ends up being mortally wounded. He is one of 34 killed and 202 wounded in one week.

IV - OVERLORD SUMMER 1944

On July 20, the Allies push 7 miles south of Caen before they are stopped on Bourguébus Ridge. As *Operation Goodwood* comes to an end, George is ordered to go back to the rear for treatment. When he puts his company into the trusted hands of Lieutenant Dennis Field, only one sergeant and eight soldiers are left who were there on Sword Beach a month and a half earlier. Dennis Field, promoted to captain, will be wounded a few days later near Bas Perrier (east of Vire) in a brutal engagement against the 9. SS Division. The casualties in the battalion will then be such that it will be reorganized around three companies, with George's B Company ceasing to exist.

George writes to his mother on July 22: *"When I last wrote I said I was going to a rest camp for a day or two. Well, it didn't quite work out that way and I have been pretty busy. Anyhow I am alive and well. I got a very small shrapnel wound in the arm which did not interfere at all with my duties. I am now really resting in a back area. The Commanding Officer has been very kind and says I have done well but I do not think I shall have to command a rifle company again, as I am pretty well worn out. Anyhow my duty is mostly all over as nearly all the chaps have changed. The luck I have had is amazing. […] I do not think somehow I shall be employed much as a fighting soldier again but there is no doubt that wherever fighting men drink their beer after this is over, I shall feel entitled to have a little say myself."*

He gives more details to his parents in September, when he is definitely removed from the lines: *"We took part in Monty's 'left hook' which started on 18 July. I was wounded slightly just as we captured Emiéville. A heavy shell landed just in front of me, killing two of my Company HQ. I was blown over and completely blacked out for a second or two. I thought I was finished, but I only had a small shell splinter in the arm, right in a bit of good old tough muscle, so there was little harm done and I was able to carry on OK. We were again successful. I must have been more shaken than I thought, because when I received orders for a further attack at 4 the following morning, I had to be assisted to get to Battalion HQ. Anyway, I called in at the First Aid Post, had my hand dressed, had a cup of tea and a reviver tablet, and put in another attack. We ran into a much larger force of Germans than what was left of my company, and though we killed several with light casualties to ourselves, we were forced to withdraw back into the village again. I stayed another 48 hours and the CO ordered me back to rest. He was right. I was then hardly fit to command a girls' school. My eyes could not stand the light, I could hardly hold a cigarette. The CO was being nice and fatherly, too fatherly in fact and I cried like a baby and felt much better for it. I think I had perhaps done my share. Now I know I was a pig-headed fool. I should have gone to hospital. I have seen chaps much better than I was go to hospital for exhaustion (the new word for shell shock)* [now called Post-Traumatic Stress Disorder or PTSD].

They gave me new clothes (I didn't mind, I had fallen into a sewer!) and the very best food they could find. Gallons of fresh sweet tea. Rum! They found a bed for me in a local house. They found me gin and cigarettes. They were very kind indeed and seemed so pleased to see me alive. Of course, rumours get round and I had been reported killed at least twice."

The day George was evacuated, Caen was finally free, although there wasn't much left of it. It was supposed to have been taken on D-Day, a month and a half earlier. Montgomery defended himself by saying that he wanted above all to draw the German tanks there in order to facilitate General Bradley's breakthrough in the Cotentin Peninsula. In any case, Caen will be remembered as a martyred city: nearly 2,000 civilians lost their lives in the fighting and the bombardments. More than 600,000 shells fell in 78 days amid the ruins. In the end, the Allied strategy of bombing the main roads to prevent any enemy reinforcements would cost the lives of nearly 20,000 Normans, despite the leaflets that had been dropped to warn the population.

After recovering from his physical and psychological wounds, George will return to England in early 1945 and be fortunate enough to attend the birth of his son. As for his battalion, in mid-September 1944 it will move to the Netherlands, cross the Rhine and then participate in the fall of the city of Bremen at the end of the war. George Ross died in Birmingham in June 1971.

Letter from the War Office to George's parents, dated August 7, 1944, confirming the major's wound.

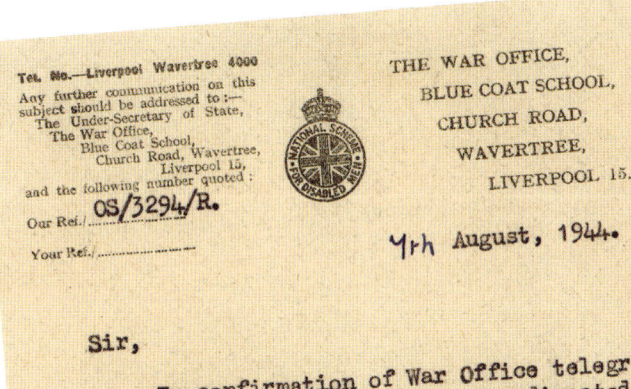

LEONARD WOOD

D Company, 1/5th Battalion, Queen's Royal Regiment (West Surrey), 7th Armoured Division

Leonard will land on Gold Beach with reinforcements and immediately progress inland. But when the British reach Villers-Bocage, a German armored counter-attack will take them by surprise and Leonard will be killed by a shell, only a week after his arrival in France.

In early summer 1944, Leonard was a 21-year-old Londoner who had just married his girlfriend, Sheila. She is serving in the ATS, the female branch of the British Army, in an anti-aircraft battery protecting Lepe Farm camp in Exbury (Southampton). Leonard joined the 1/5th Battalion of the Queen's Royal Regiment (West Surrey) on January 29, 1942. This unit, which had experienced the Battle of France with the BEF, was later attached to the 7th Armoured Division. After North Africa, it landed in Salerno, Italy, on September 15, 1943, shortly after *Operation Avalanche*. Following the crossing of the Volturno River, it was withdrawn from the lines at Montgomery's request and sent back to Britain with other experienced units such as the 50th (Northumbrian) and 51st (Highland) Infantry Divisions, in order to prepare for the invasion of Normandy.

JUNE 8: GOLD BEACH

The regiment left Italy at the end of December 1943 and arrived in Glasgow (Scotland) in early January 1944. Leonard's division was equipped with the new Cromwell tank and was to be the only British unit to use it as its main tank, accompanied by Fireflies (a version of the Sherman tank equipped with the powerful 17-pounder gun). The 'Desert Rats' spent months training near Norwich for amphibious assaults and perfecting different tactics every day, such as street fighting, maneuvering with tanks, and attacking and defending a position. At the beginning of May, the exercises were completed and the vehicles prepared for their journey across the Channel. The division then consisted of the 22nd Armoured Brigade and the 131st Infantry Brigade, with three of its five battalions belonging to the Queen's Royal Regiment. The men boarded the Liberty Ship *MT24* and the *Leopoldville* on June 4 at Tilbury Docks, east of London. Protected by a smoke screen, the convoy managed to cross the English Channel without incident, despite coming under fire from German coastal batteries.

Leonard lands with the reinforcements on Gold Beach at noon on June 8, surrounded by prisoners of war from the German 716. Division, then walks 7 miles to be stationed near Bayeux. The day before, other units of the 7th Armoured Division had already progressed inland towards their objective, Caen (*Operation Perch*).

JUNE 12: OBJECTIVE TILLY-SUR-SEULLES

On June 9, the German 352. Division is pushed back from Omaha Beach by the 1st US Infantry Division and withdraws to Saint-Lô, thus creating a gaping hole in the German lines. The British must seize this opportunity to rush into the breach.

IV - OVERLORD SUMMER 1944

The next day, three regiments of the 7th Armoured Division have landed and are ordered to move through the 50th British Division towards Tilly-sur-Seulles (between Bayeux and Villers-Bocage) and take Caen. Unfortunately, opposition in the village is severe and the formidable Panzer Lehr Division is determined not to give up an inch of land. At 6 am on Sunday, June 11, Leonard's battalion, called in as reinforcements, sets off for Tilly-sur-Seulles. When the Queen's link up with the division the next day, the advance is very slow. On the 12th, they settle at the Pont de la Guillette, between Tilly and Bucéels. A, B and Leonard's D companies advance southward, west of the village, but are stopped in the morning by a machine gun nest.

Meanwhile, the 1st US Infantry Division had informed the British that it'd received only slight resistance on its way to Caumont. The 7th Armoured Division therefore decides to bypass Tilly on the right and resume its march to Villers-Bocage around noon, in order to take the Panzer Lehr Division from behind, passing through Saint-Paul-du-Vernay, Livry and Briquessard, with the 22nd Brigade in the lead. Leonard's 1/5th Queen's, still fighting in the forest alongside the 1st Royal Tank Regiment, would join them as soon as it can disengage – it will only succeed at nightfall. That evening, Leonard writes for the last time in his diary: *"Spent day wood clearing. Met some Jerry machine guns, got hold up. No meal for over 24 hours. Letter No 4."*

The letter in question is the one presented below: it will be the last one he would ever write to his wife, as he will be fatally wounded only a few hours later.

THE LAST LETTER

"Monday 12th June, Letter no 4. To My Darling Wife,

Just a few lines to let you know I am safe and well, hoping you are the same my Darling. I expect you have guessed where I am now Fairy and I don't like it here at all sweetheart. I hope you have received my other letters that I wrote before this one and they are not taking too long to reach you my Darling. I have not received any mail for over a fortnight now Fairy, I shall be very glad when I do my Darling and get some news. I keep thinking about you and wondering what you are doing with yourself sweetheart. I['ve] no need to tell you how I feel about being out here again Darling. I keep thinking about the time we had together and wishing we could have it over again sweetheart. I hope everything is alright at your place Fairy. I hope you got settled up with Grace now Fairy. Also you have to answer all the questions I ask you in my letter my Darling and I will answer your questions in [case] you have written them in one of your letters Darling.

Well my Darling I am sorry this is only a short letter but I will make up for it later on sweetheart. So look after yourself my Darling. I am always thinking about you Darling, longing for the time we shall be together for good Fairy, I miss you so much my Darling I love you Darling. God bless you Darling. With lots and lots of love from your own Darling Husband, Len."

Occupied with the fighting and the movements of his unit, Len won't have time to post this letter and it'll still be in his bag at the time of his death, before later being sent back to England with his personal belongings.

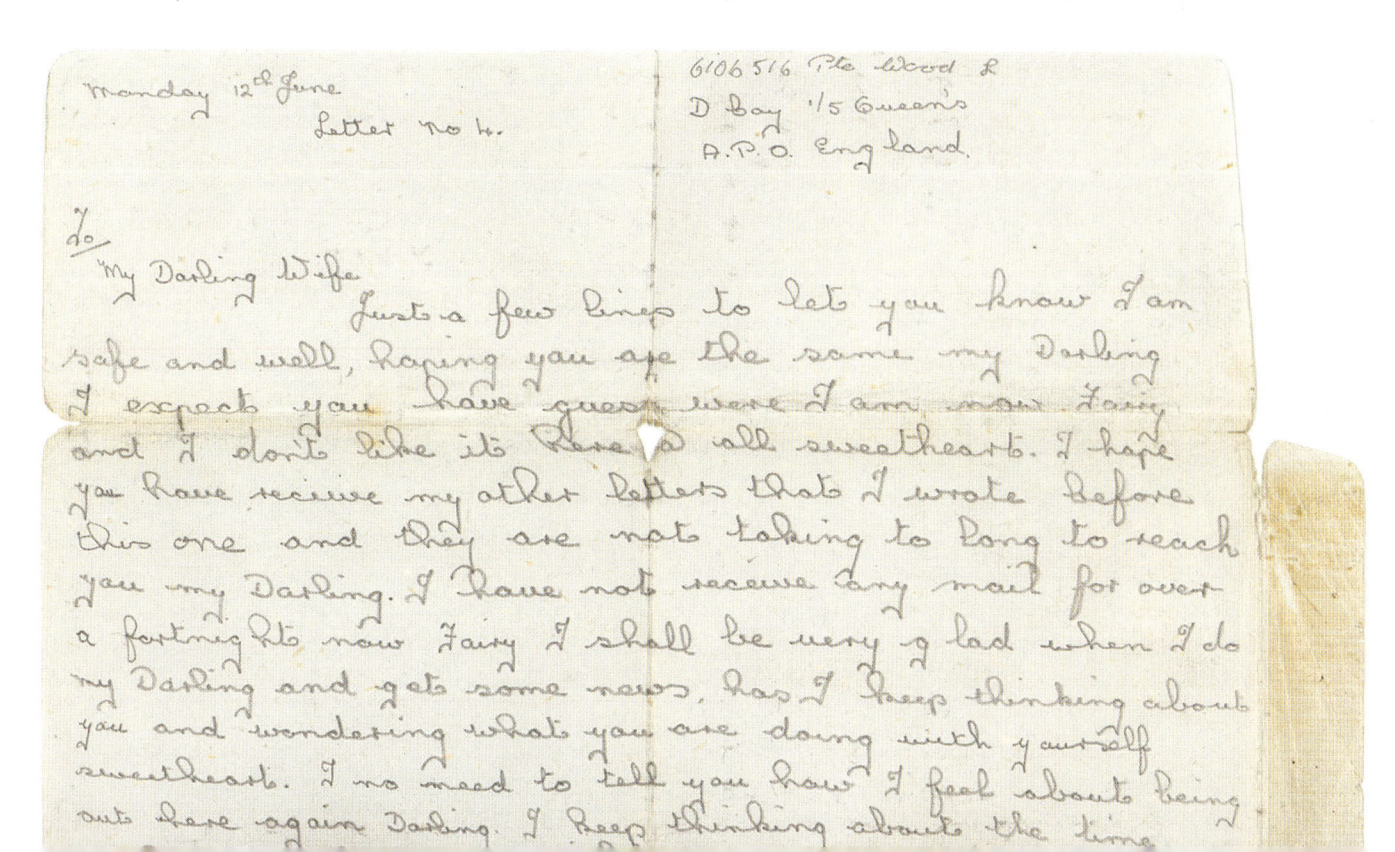

JUNE 13: VILLERS-BOCAGE

On the morning of June 13, 22nd Brigade, led by the 4th County of London Yeomanry, enters Villers-Bocage by the Caumont road (recently taken by the Americans), and is welcomed by the cheers of the population. Suddenly, however, a group of German Tiger tanks appears south of the Caen road, blasting away at the British vehicles, which immediately catch fire. These enemy tanks belong to the Schwere SS-Panzer Abteilung 101 (101st SS Heavy Armored Battalion), commanded by Captain Michael Wittman (a Tiger 'ace' from the Eastern Front, with 119 tanks destroyed), and had been specifically dispatched from Beauvais to fill the gap in the German lines. At 9 am, with the help of three other Tigers, Wittman destroys twelve British tanks, two anti-tank guns and thirteen transport vehicles in less than fifteen minutes.

The Allied forward units are isolated as all hell breaks loose east of the village. German machine guns fire from the windows at the disorganized British, while Tiger tanks invade the streets, hitting their targets one after the other. The 1/7th Queen's, the twin battalion to Leonard's, arrives as reinforcements to repel an armored and infantry attack in the heart of the village. It would resist until the evening, succeeding in slowing the Germans down with anti-tank weapons and destroying nine Panzers. But in a few hours, Villers-Bocage would become a graveyard for tanks and charred vehicles. The 4th County of London Yeomanry in particular, which had been welcomed in such a festive atmosphere, had lost its entire regimental headquarters and A Squadron, several senior officers, 76 missing soldiers, 27 tanks and many vehicles destroyed during the day. As for the 1/7th Queen's, it suffered 128 casualties, including 8 officers.

Meanwhile, Leonard's 1/5th Queen's bypasses Tilly to the west, then digs in in Saint-Germain (between Amayé-sur-Seulles and Tracy-Bocage), only 2 miles west of Villers-Bocage. As the 7th Armoured units stuck in the village gradually withdraw and take refuge behind the hill occupied by Leonard's battalion, the division is now able to focus on its line of defense, receiving support from the American artillery of the 1st Infantry Division, stationed nearby, to repel the first German attacks. However, the 'Desert Rats' are cut off, deep inland, and are unable to count on the support of the 50th British Division, which is still blocked by the Panzer Lehr Division in Tilly. For the time being, Leonard's battalion has only six wounded men in its ranks, but the toll will increase in the following hours.

In this small area, a fierce fight will go down in the history of the division as the 'Battle of the Brigade Box'.

JUNE 14: THE BATTLE OF THE BRIGADE BOX

Widely used by the division during its desert campaign, the 'box' strategy aims to concentrate several units in a small area so that they can provide covering fire for each other. As a result, the 1st Rifle Brigade, 5th Royal Horse Artillery, 11th Hussars, 5th Royal Tank Regiment, 4th County of London Yeomanry and the HQ of the 22nd Brigade are gathered just south of Amayé-sur-Seulles, while the Queen's are in the front line, on the edge of the perimeter. The 1/6th Queen's guards the road to Livry at the rear, the 1/7th Queen's is located southwest of Saint-Germain and Leonard's 1/5th Queen's are at the southeastern edge of the box, at La Bruyère. To his left, he has the 8th Hussars in sight and to his right, the 5th Royal Tank Regiment. The night before, patrols had met with strong opposition and the men of the 1/5th Queen's quickly realize that they're in contact with the enemy on all fronts. In fact, the Germans launch small reconnaissance attacks on all sides of the box in the early hours of the day, making the British expect a massive attack imminently. Although visibility is reduced, the area is relatively easy to defend.

At 4:40 pm on June 14, Leonard and his comrades are signaled that the enemy is moving towards their position. Two hours later, they bear the full brunt of the attack from elements of the 2. Panzer-Division, Panzer Lehr, and about ten surviving Tiger tanks from Wittmann's battalion (together representing the equivalent of two battalions and about thirty tanks). The British call in the American guns for help, resulting in the largest concentration of heavy artillery seen in Normandy to date. All guns within range, including American and Navy guns, thus open fire at their 'Yoke' target.

IV - OVERLORD SUMMER 1944

Despite the heavy artillery fire, the fighting lasts for hours and the Germans even manage to penetrate as far as Brigade Headquarters in the heart of the box. However, the British hold their positions and at 10:15 pm, the attack is finally repelled. Nevertheless, shortly after midnight and covered by a Royal Air Force bombardment, the British soldiers withdraw near Briquessard, where they would spend the rest of the month. The enemy is too exhausted to run after them. During its attack on June 14 the Germans had suffered 1,000 killed or wounded and lost nearly 20 tanks (in comparison, only three Cromwell tanks were destroyed on the Allied side). It was a sad day for the 1/5th Queen's as well: six dead, plus two officers and thirty-six other ranks wounded – the heaviest toll of the entire month of June.

LEONARD'S DEATH

Leonard is one of the seriously injured. During the German assault on the box, his company was the victim of 'friendly fire': at 9:26 pm, a salvo from the Royal Artillery was too short and fell on the British positions, inflicting Allied casualties. One of the British shells fell into the slit trench Leonard was occupying with Private Knight, who was killed on the spot. According to the diary of stretcher-bearer Robert Wiley, Leonard was evacuated to the nearest hospital with a shrapnel wound to the head and left shoulder. According to one of his friends, Leonard was smiling on the stretcher, convinced he would now return to his beloved wife. Two days later, on June 16, 1944, Leonard would die of his wounds at the age of 21.

A 1944 photo of Leonard's temporary grave in Normandy, and the notification letter informing Sheila of her husband's death.

An ATS colleague writes to Sheila: *"I am so very sorry to hear that your husband has been killed in action and would ask you to accept my deepest sympathy. I do hope that the fact that he has given his life unselfishly in fighting for his country may help to console you, although it is very hard for us to understand. These are very worrying times for us all, as there are really very few people without their families, sweethearts or friends, connected with the fighting. I hope that you will soon be able to return to your work and I would like to take the opportunity of thanking you for the excellent part you are playing in the war. No large part of machinery can work satisfactorily unless each little part of that machinery is doing its job. We are all those very minute but necessary parts."*

Villers-Bocage will at last be liberated by the 1st Battalion of the Dorset Regiment, 50th (Northumbrian) Infantry Division, on August 4, 1944, after two massive bombings. After the disaster that took place there, and both the campaigns in Africa and Italy, the 7th Armoured Division will show clear signs of exhaustion. However, it'll continue to fight in Normandy, Belgium (liberating Ghent on 6 September) and the Netherlands, where it'll help secure the Meuse River. In January 1945, it'll take part in *Operation Blackcock* in the Roer Triangle, then in the Rhine crossing (*Operation Plunder*) between Xanten and Wesel, before heading for Hamburg.

No. Cas/19/1925
(If replying, please quote above No.)

Army Form B. 104—82.

Infantry Record Office,
ASHFORD, Middlesex.

14th July 1944.

Madam,

It is my painful duty to inform you that a report has been received from the War Office notifying the death of:—

(No.) 6106516 (Rank) Private
(Name) Leonard Thomas WOOD
(Regiment) The Queen's Royal Regiment
which occurred in the North West Europe Theatre of War
on the 16th June, 1944

The report is to the effect that he Died of Wounds

I am to express the sympathy and regret of the Army Council.
I am to add that any information that may be received as to the soldier's burial will be communicated to you in due course.

I am,

No. W/27367 Pte. S. WOOD
A.T.S.
OFC. W 67/M Hy.A.A.Battery R.A
Lepe Farm, Exbury, Nr. SOUTHAMPTON.

Madam,
Your obedient Servant,

for Officer in Charge of Records.

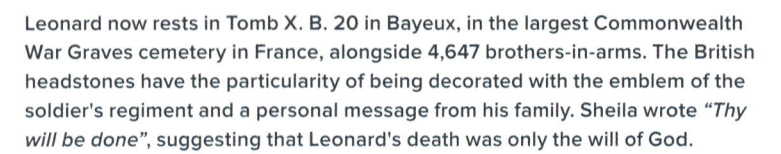

Leonard now rests in Tomb X. B. 20 in Bayeux, in the largest Commonwealth War Graves cemetery in France, alongside 4,647 brothers-in-arms. The British headstones have the particularity of being decorated with the emblem of the soldier's regiment and a personal message from his family. Sheila wrote *"Thy will be done"*, suggesting that Leonard's death was only the will of God.

CAPTURING A PORT

The beachhead is now established, but the Allies must land as many soldiers and equipment as soon as possible to reinforce the existing troops and advance. To do this, the capture of a major port is essential, and Cherbourg therefore becomes a key objective. But the city, like many other ports, had been transformed into a genuine fortress.

As Anzio had proven, the first few hours after an amphibious assault are crucial. It's important to move inland quickly, while concentrating forces and supplies on the beachhead. Around 132,000 men have already set foot in Normandy by the evening of June 6, and 2,744,000 others are waiting their turn in the UK! Half of them will land before the end of July, along with the various cargoes of equipment, petrol, ammunition and rations that must be transported to the front lines. Each Tommy receives more than 20 pounds of supplies each day, while the GI gets 30.

THE BEACH GROUPS IN ACTION

A British soldier, unfortunately anonymous but whom we will call 'John', records his first days in France in his diary. According to his notes, he must be an engineer in a Port Operating Company, part of the 7th or 8th Beach Group: his job is to unload Allied cargo ships on the Norman beaches and ports. Originally from Hull (England), which is also a port city, John is probably a stevedore in civilian life. A veteran of North Africa, he returned to England in February 1944 and was reunited at last with his family: *"Waited for this for 18 months. [...] Had my first good look at Michael. Hard to realize he is our baby. Thrilled at the prospect of 14 days leave. Good to be home again!"* However, the days went by very quickly and he finally returned to his unit in Scotland, taking part in maneuvers to prepare for D-Day: he received his first course on amphibious assaults in North Berwick and practised unloading barges in DUKWs (amphibious vehicles). After its training, his unit arrived in Purfleet (east of London) on May 26, when John noticed that he was surrounded by military police.

Soon, boredom settled in and the excitement at the idea of participating in the biggest landing of all time quickly gave way to frustration. John went from base to base, which he called *"concentration camps"*, under well-armed guard: *"Prisoners in England, disgusting. Worse than* [a] *Stalag, live confined indefinitely. Lying about doing very little. Weather very hot."* When he finally embarks with 850 other men at the West India Docks on the Thames aboard the MT5 *Samzona* (an American Liberty Ship steamer given to the British), his situation does not change much: *"Still waiting off Southend. Water alive with shipping. Browned off waiting for this invasion."*

On June 6 at noon, the ship finally sets sail: *"Shore batteries open fire, score direct hit on MT12. Burned out in 15 minutes. Strait of Dover."* The *Samzona* belongs to the 'ETM 1' convoy of fourteen cargo ships and four escorts, including the Liberty Ship *Sambut* (MT12), which is indeed sunk in front of the Pas-de-Calais region by a German coastal artillery battery. It was carrying troops and their vehicles to Juno Beach, where John is about to land.

Other Port Operating Companies have landed with the first waves and are already at work. These Royal Engineers weren't spared from chaos and death, as 122 of John's comrades lost their lives on June 6 (10% of the total British killed in action), and were actually the British units which sustained the most fatalities that day after the paratroopers (189 killed).

Remains of a ring bearing the Royal Engineers' emblem, found during excavations in Normandy.

However, the enemy isn't their main concern: the sand, tides, beach congestion and several other issues have caused many logistical problems in the past, but in Normandy, however, the Engineers have come up with a very ingenious temporary solution.

THE MULBERRIES

Thanks to the Dieppe disaster in 1942, the Allies understood that they couldn't take a port without bombing it first, thus rendering it unusable. This meant that if they were unable to capture functional infrastructure in the early hours of D-Day, then they'll cross the Atlantic with their own ports!

The artificial 'Mulberry' harbors arrive in Normandy as early as June 6. These steel roadways floating on pontoons, rising and falling with the tide (thus allowing continuous unloading day and night) run for miles all the way to the beach. All around them, sunken 'Phoenix' caissons (200-foot-long, 50-foot-high concrete blocks weighing 6,000 tons each when filled with water) form an arc to protect the harbor from the waves. Two structures are installed, each representing the size of the port of Dover: Mulberry A (for 'American') at Omaha Beach (Vierville-sur-Mer) and Mulberry B (for 'British') at Gold Beach (Arromanches).

On June 19, Mulberry A is destroyed by the worst storm to hit the coast in forty years. A few miles away, John is unable to unload anything for three days, and writes on June 21: *"No decrease in gale. Getting browned off."* Mulberry A is quickly repaired, but the incident proves that it's becoming urgent to seize a real port. Mulberry B at Gold Beach will continue to operate throughout the war, landing about 2.5 million men, 500,000 vehicles and 4 million tons of equipment. But obviously, despite the ingenuity of the system, the Mulberries will become less popular when the port of Antwerp is up and running six months after D-Day.

John writes in his diary:
[June 7] *"Arrived off French coast somewhere near Caen. Hundreds of ships. Troops go in. Navy pounding shores. No air opposition. Commenced discharging 6 pm* [at sea, from a Navy ship to an amphibious vehicle]. *Terrific shelling."*
[June 8] *"Finished discharging 8 pm. Disembarked 8:30 on landing craft. Ran up on beach, waded through 3 feet of water. Battered to pieces this village. Dead on beach. Jerry evacuated quickly. Slept under hedge."*
[June 9] *"Jerry over night and morning strafing beach. Moved into evacuated houses in village of Graye-sur-Mer, 20 km from Caen."*
[June 10] *"Getting dug in. Went out to discharge ship. Slept aboard. Navy still shelling Caen. Main beachhead held. Heavy tank battles near Caen."*

John will spend most of the summer unloading equipment from American, Canadian and British ships onto the beaches, including a total of nearly 10,000 jeeps, trucks and tanks. The work will be made particularly difficult by the German bombardments, particularly on June 12, 22 (when John escapes near death, a shell falling only a few yards from him), June 30 (*"terrific barrage"*) and August 14 to 17, when the Germans harass them with long-range guns every 15 minutes.

Remains of Phoenix caissons at Mulberry B in the port of Arromanches.

IV - OVERLORD SUMMER 1944

Mulberry pontoon at the exit of Omaha, Vierville-sur-Mer.

Other great ideas make the soldiers' lives a little bit easier. For instance, a pipeline under the sea ('PLUTO') supplies their vehicles with petrol directly from England. This flexible hose, several miles long, brings them more than 1 million tons of petrol per day, all the way from pumping stations disguised as shops or other establishments on the British coast. And yet, despite the logistical feat, the operation manages to satisfy only 0.16% of the total Allied consumption. Once again, a genuine port is needed.

Dog tags of sailor Joseph Francis Cawley, US Navy. On D-Day, he was aboard LST 312. The ship landed men and equipment on Gold Beach on June 6 and Omaha Beach on June 7.

LEAVING THE BEACHES

On Utah Beach, the men of the 4th US Infantry Division are the first seaborne infantrymen of *Operation Neptune*. With the first wave lands Theodore Roosevelt Jr., the son of President Teddy Roosevelt. The losses on Utah (only 197 soldiers) are much lower than on Omaha Beach, thanks to the bombers and paratroopers' actions. Strong currents have also caused the assault troops to drift into a less defended area, allowing them to rapidly advance into the marshes beyond the sand dunes. However, this part will prove to be much more difficult and the division will lose nearly 5,000 men in the Cotentin Peninsula. But many other units follow them closely, including the 90th Infantry Division, which will split the Cotentin in two, and the 9th and 79th Infantry Divisions, which will help the 4th Division take Cherbourg.

Despite the terrific bombardments along the French coast before the summer of 1944, the Allies are greeted with immense joy by the Normans, who have just emerged from four years of German occupation. Disregarding danger, they throw themselves into the arms of their liberators, offering them flowers and drinks. Yet, although history has kept these scenes of intense happiness in mind, not everyone seems to be happy with the arrival of the Allies. An English tank crewman writes home: *"A number of French girls married Jerries and when our lads landed, they were sniped by such women."*

Indeed, Montgomery himself mentions these female snipers in a letter he writes to General Simpson on June 8: *"Snipering in beach areas has been very troublesome [...]. The roads have been far from safe and we have lost several good officers. I have been all right myself, though I have toured the area all day. There have been women snipers, presumably wives of German soldiers, the Canadians shot 4 women snipers."*

CHERBOURG

The port city was to be captured on D+15, in order to facilitate the landing of reinforcements directly from the United States and improve the Mulberries' situation. On June 18, the GIs face their objective, which the Germans have transformed into a *Festung* (fortress). On Hitler's orders, like many Atlantic ports, it must be held until the last man and the last bullet. While the 4th and 9th US Infantry Divisions methodically clear the bunkers held by tired German troops, and a British commando attacks Octeville under a naval bombardment, the 79th US Division experiences violent clashes around Fort du Roule. Dominating the city, the fall of this strategic position on June 26 puts the German resistance at an end and Generalleutnant Karl-Wilhelm von Schlieben, who led the Cherbourg garrison, is captured. The last enemy pockets surrender on July 1. This is the first real harbor taken by the Allies, with more than 25,000 prisoners in American hands.

A GI in an artillery unit, in charge of defending the port, writes to his father: *"You should see the West Wall the Germans put up. It really is something to see. [...] One thing to me seems so ironical. The French tried to hide behind a wall of steel and concrete and the Germans broke through it. Then the Germans made their big mistake. Instead of invading England they sat down and built a wall of their own. They tried the same thing the French did and they themselves proved that it cannot be done. The Germans pay a big price for their wars but every time they learn a little more and I am afraid that someday they will have learned enough to see their plan through.*

The Germans know now that they should have attacked England. The next time they will. I hope it soon ends so that we all can get home again. [...] They had fine weapons and plenty of ammunition. They left them both behind when they fled. The German soldier seems to have been well equipped. [...] From a few letters I have found it would seem that the German soldier is no different from ourselves. They write of the same things as we do, of home, of shows they have seen, of concerts they have heard, of women, and politics."

John Irvine, commander of an infantry company in the 4th US Division, writes on July 18: *"We are back in a rest area at present and believe me we need a rest. This is the first time in over a month that I've been out of German artillery range and it's nice not to have to stay in a hole every night. I had a hot shower today. I took every piece of clothes I had on and threw them away – they were too filthy even to wash. We are hoping for a nice long rest. I expect this war to be over in a month or so and believe me I'll really be glad. I'm not allowed to tell you anything about our operations until two weeks after it's happened, but you probably read about it in the papers anyway. We captured a German PX [army store] and pay roll before we took Tourlaville [east of Cherbourg] and I was a rich man for a little while but turned the money in because it's used to pay the French underground. I'm still using German shaving kits and towels etc. The Germans are very clean. We have run into SS troops and parachutists' troops recently – they're tougher than the first ones we met but not too tough. We've been using them for litter-bearers occasionally. We really had a rat race going into Cherbourg, they threw everything but the kitchen sink at us, but our outfit doesn't quit once it starts moving. I personally made a victorious entry on all fours – it was really rugged. The infantry is really the cream of the crop over here. When we march back from the front all the rear echelon boys rush out to give us water and candy and try to buy our German pistols etc. They all say nothing's too good for the infantry – and of course, we lord it over them plenty."* John will be wounded in early August during the breakthrough out of Normandy (page 202), before being killed in the Hürtgen Forest.

IV - OVERLORD SUMMER 1944

The American 79th Infantry Division started using the Lorraine Cross as its emblem after its battles in eastern France during the First World War. Three decades later, the soldier shown here wears an early model of the HBT jacket with the 79th Division's patch (original to the jacket). It belonged to an officer called Olin Miller, who wrote his name in the flap of the collar. The HBT or 'Herringbone Twill' was the very first tear-resistant fabric. First used by the Rangers in Dieppe in 1942 and the paratroopers in training, it's welcomed for its robustness, wide pockets (which will grow even larger later) and comfort. This soldier has added a wide mesh net to his M1 helmet. Although mainly used to hide vehicles, it can provide great camouflage when adding branches and vegetation, rendering the soldier invisible in the 'bocage'. After he had to endure the hard fighting in the impenetrable hedges of the Cotentin, he finds solace in the Norman population, who offer him flowers and 'calva' (Calvados). The bottle photographed here is certainly from the period, and its producer used to bury his bottles to hide them from the Germans – this one has never been cleaned since.

As the 79th Division marches through the peninsula and sinks into the Norman hedgerows, it loses more than 1,500 men in La-Haye-du-Puits and its surroundings in early July. It'll only reach Lessay, less than 7 miles to the south, at the end of the month. But the price paid for each yard of terrain feels lighter when the soldiers see the smiles on the inhabitants' faces, as one GI writes from La-Haye-du-Puits in July 1944: *"Have been getting acquainted with a few of the Frenchmen. They really have gone through a lot of hell but take it all with a smile. A guy feels that all this fighting is not in vain when confronting the French and seeing how happy they are about their liberation. Each family has about a dozen 500-gallon barrels of cider and as we pass by, they pass it out along with flowers. Good thing they have sufficient supply because you know how thirsty a GI is all the time, ey! Most of them wear very heavy wooden shoes (Dutch style) and the women carry buckets of water with some sort of wooden contraption over their shoulders, like we have read about the Dutch."*

195

LEO BROWN

F Company, 359th Infantry Regiment, 90th Infantry Division

Leo survives the sinking of his ship before landing on Utah Beach, but his experience of Normandy will only get worse when he fights through the Cotentin's bocage and then takes part in the great offensive on Mont Castre, being wounded on the first day of the attack.

FROM TEXAS TO 'UTAH'

Born in Oklahoma in 1918, Leo H. Brown was a farmer in New Mexico when he joined the US Army on April 1, 1942, in Fort Bliss, Texas. He was naturally assigned to the 90th Infantry Division 'Texas & Oklahoma', whose two initials on its patch will give its men the nickname 'Tough Ombres' (the use of Spanish resulting from the State's proximity to Mexico). After a long training period in Texas, Louisiana and California, Leo left for Europe from Fort Dix, New Jersey. He was to land on Utah Beach on June 7, 1944, on D+1, with the reinforcements. But his ship, the *Susan B. Anthony*, hit a mine offshore that morning and sank in two hours, fortunately without causing any casualties. Leo was picked up by a British ship and tasted English tea for the first time in his life.

Patch of the 90th Division. Note the letters T and O for 'Texas & Oklahoma'.

When he finally lands on Utah Beach, he's mixed with men from other units and has no equipment, as everything was lost in the sinking. To Leo's dismay, the soldiers are given weapons looted from the Germans. Despite a sniper threatening the GIs in the orchard nearby, he takes the risk of venturing alone into the field where crashed American gliders lie. An injured American paratrooper gives him his weapon and ammunition, and Leo will find an M1 helmet, various equipment and precious rations in one of the gliders' frame. When Leo returns to his company, he's at last ready to go to war. The division's mission (attached to the 1st US Army) is to cut across the Merderet River in a westward march, through the Cotentin Peninsula, while other units move up to Cherbourg.

THE HELL OF THE BOCAGE

The Americans discover a terrain as inhospitable as it was unexpected. The Norman bocage consists of an infinite succession of parcels of land, ranging from a few hundred square yards to several hectares. These are surrounded by centuries-old hedges that are so high, thick and deep-rooted that the US Army will have to develop new additions for its tanks to help create breaches and facilitate the advance of infantrymen. The bocage also includes 3-foot high banks, which are just as thick, and topped by dense vegetation at

IV - OVERLORD SUMMER 1944

least 10 feet high. The Germans had dug in and organized solid defenses where snipers, camouflaged Panzers, ambush squads and 88 mm guns provide covering fire for each other. The simple act of progressing through the natural defenses of the bocage is already a real challenge for the Americans, but to top it all off, it has to be done under heavy rain, making the swampy terrain and visibility even worse. A soldier in the 563rd Signal Air Warning Battalion writes to his father in July: *"They have made every hedge and bank a place of danger. For camouflage they used the earth itself. They lived in dugouts. They had fine systems of trenches dug so they could retreat from field to field without ever exposing themselves to enemy fire."*

The enemy has set up many traps, sometimes in the shape of a simple wire stretched between two bushes, decapitating Jeep drivers as they pass by. The shell holes in front of the machine gun positions are full of mines, unseen by the terrified GIs who are looking for some cover. The Germans have also prepared small openings at the base of the hedges in order to shoot while taking advantage of the invisibility and protection offered by the terrain. Sometimes, one of them would come out with his hands in the air, pretending to surrender, before throwing himself to the ground at the last moment to let the camouflaged MG42s mow down the GIs who came out of their holes to take a prisoner. American morale falls to a very low point, nerves give way and evacuations for 'battle fatigue' become more and more numerous (30,000 psychological losses, for the 1st US Army alone). On a good day, the US Army manages to capture one hedge, while losing a man for every yard of land conquered.

Leo soon watches his first friends fall and by June 9, his company already has only forty-two men left, even though they've only been in France for two days. He writes on the 26th: *"Here I am in a foxhole in France. I can't tell you what day I landed but I can tell you that there weren't very many who landed ahead of us. We have spent nearly all our time on the front lines. I lost my gunner the first day in combat. A sniper got him. I think he will live O.K. [...] He is a really swell boy, but that is the way with war."*

Quinn Buffington, whom Leo lived with every day and night for two years, was shot in the stomach while trying to bring ammunition to G Company. Leo brought him to the aid station just in time and he'll survive the war. However, he'd spend the next two years in hospital and never really recover. At the aid station, Leo sees rows of dead American soldiers lying on their backs, perfectly aligned. The sight is particularly difficult for him as he'd become very close to many of them during his two years of training.

The MKII (American) fragmentation grenade is the GIs best ally in the Normandy hedgerows: when exploding, it breaks up into many fragments, becoming a terrific threat to a dug-in enemy. This grenade was found during excavations in Cormolain (Calvados).

HILL 122

At the beginning of July, as the Cotentin Peninsula is partially liberated after the fall of Cherbourg, the Allies head south. They are seeking to clear access to Périers and Coutances, but will still have to cross miles of impenetrable and firmly defended hedgerows before reaching these cities. An elite regiment of the 5. Fallschirmjäger-Division (a German airborne division) was deployed to block their route, taking up position on the Mahlman Line, which extends from the west coast south of La-Haye-du-Puits, to the marshy area in the center of the peninsula, in Beau-Coudray. Dominating the line, Hill 122 must be taken by the Allies, whatever the cost. With a panoramic view of the whole Cotentin region, and occupied by an enemy determined to fight to the death, its artillery guns cover all angles. At its foot, the forest of Mont Castre is the 90th Division's objective. The 'Tough Ombres' are in charge of the line's eastern sector, starting from the village of Prétot, while the 79th Division is to take La-Haye-du-Puits in the west, with the paratroopers of the 82nd Airborne in between. The latter have already lost half their headcount since D-Day, but will soon be relieved by the newly arrived 8th Infantry Division.

The attack is launched at 5:30 am on July 3. Leo's regiment takes the division's right flank and his battalion advances through a constant barrage of artillery. At noon, German resistance becomes fierce as the battalion crosses a road south of Prétot. The enemy shoots at wounded Americans from the trees, while the artillery fires at will from the heights of Mont Castre. Lying in a field, Leo can hear machine gun bullets mowing the wheat spikes above his head. On its first day, the division has progressed less than a mile on average and Leo has only reached the edge of Sainte-Suzanne, but the Germans pull back a few hundred yards and the village is secured by 9 pm. Despite their heavy losses, the GIs have taken dozens of prisoners, including Russians and Poles, whom the Germans had left behind to buy themselves some time.

That day, Leo meets his future commander. He'll write in his memoirs: *"There was a German tank that kept shooting into the big ridge of dirt that we had driven the Germans out of. I don't know why it was shooting; the ridge was 15 feet thick. Anyway, we got two new second lieutenants. I liked the looks of one of them. They were just standing around as they hadn't been assigned. One of them just walked out beyond the ridge of dirt, and the tank shot him with the big gun. After that, we only had one new second lieutenant. His name was Lesser. Not long after that, on the 26th of July, the company commander was killed. Lieutenant Lesser took over the company and was made captain and was our commander for the rest of the war. He was a good officer."* Among the casualties of the day, Leo's friend Odell Sullivan was shot in the wrist. Leo will never see him again as Odell will be killed in a car accident on his return to the United States. For the moment, Leo doesn't know that he too will be injured a few hours later…

The offensive resumes at 6 am on the next day (July 4), from Sainte-Suzanne towards the eastern edge of the Mont Castre Forest. The GIs manage to reach the road leading to La-Haye-du-Puits, but incessant German counter-attacks and accurate artillery fire make the advance slow and costly. The battalion is forced to withdraw to its former positions at Sainte-Suzanne, where it'll push back several assaults until late in the afternoon. Leo is given the task of bringing a mortar to the front of the lines to destroy a machine gun nest, even though the enemy is only 100 yards from the GIs, while the minimum range of the gun is four times that distance. Be that as it may, Leo runs back to his platoon, only to find out that they'd already used all their ammunition, despite the fact that they hadn't received any firing instructions. The commander therefore orders Leo to take a few men with him and go in search of anything the Americans could throw at the Germans.

WOUNDED

With five of his comrades, Leo finds a 12-foot deep depression, at the bottom of which is an American tank facing the German lines. Next to it, a Jeep had just dropped all kinds of ammunition. As Leo approaches the pile, the tank receives the order to move, which always tends to attract the attention of the enemy's artillery. Thus, as the men hurry to fill their bags with ammunition, they're shaken by a sudden and deafening explosion above their heads as the German guns fire as expected. One of the soldiers is killed on the spot by a piece of shrapnel to the head, two are seriously wounded and two slightly injured, including Leo.

He receives a fragment the size of a thumb below his right knee, but doesn't really suffer, even though the piece of shrapnel is white hot (which at least has the merit of stopping the bleeding). Leo manages to walk half a mile to the aid station, where he's taken care of by a medical officer offering him a dose of morphine. As Leo says, *"If it's all the same to you, I am not hurting that much and I don't think I need morphine"*, the captain replies: *"I have a policy: I give everyone a shot because a lot of people are in shock and don't know they are hurting."* Shortly after, Leo is evacuated by Jeep to a field hospital and then repatriated to England.

He writes on July 19 from his hospital bed: *"I am back in England now in a G.I. hospital. I got a small piece of German 88 shell in my right leg. The place where it went in has healed up. They say it won't bother me to leave it in, but I sure want it taken out! I can walk O.K. but I have to walk on the ball of my right foot. It seems that muscles are too short to set my heel down. It doesn't hurt at all now. It was just about O.K. before I came back to England. It sure does seem quiet over here to compare with France. There is a PX where we can get our rations (3 bars of candy, 3 packages of cookies, and a pack of gum + 2 Cokes) per week. I never have money to get a Coke, yet, I have had one pop since I have been gone from the States – it was a Dr. Pepper, just before I went to France, in an American Red Cross.*

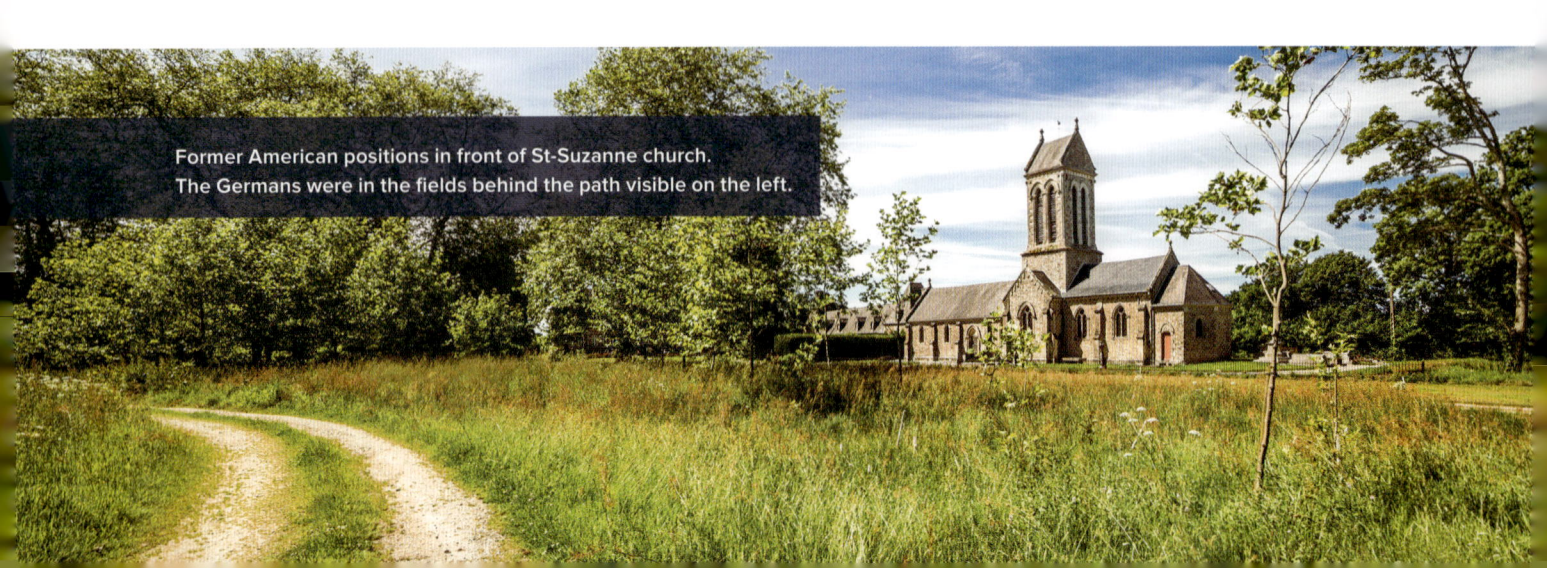

Former American positions in front of St-Suzanne church. The Germans were in the fields behind the path visible on the left.

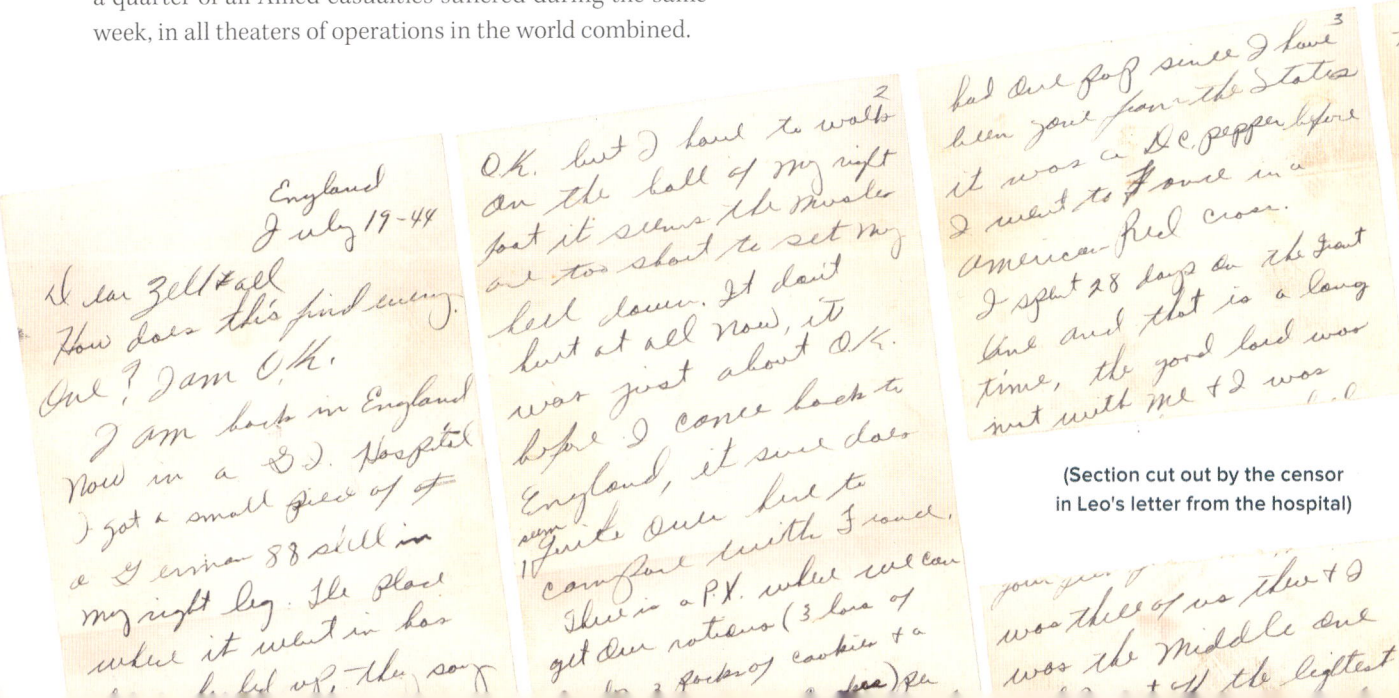

The depression where Leo and three of his comrades were wounded and a fifth soldier killed instantly by a German 88 mm shell.

I spent 28 days on the front line and that is a long time [when he landed, Leo weighed 174 pounds but by the time he reaches the hospital he's only 132]. *The good Lord was with me and I was* [censored segment]. *There were three of us there and I was in the middle one and I got off the lightest and that is too much to just be called luck. I came back to England in the transport plane. It was a real nice ride and just a matter of minutes by air. I rode on one American ship, a British ship, and a landing barge going over there. They really take good care of the wounded. The doctors and nurses are O.K. and my hat is off to those first aid boys on the front lines. They are on the ball."*

The medics will have a lot of work to do in the coming days. The 'Tough Ombres' wouldn't reach Mont Castre until the evening of July 5 and four more days would be needed to dislodge the German paratroopers clinging to its heights. Counter-attacks would multiply and all available men, from engineers to cooks, would be sent into battle to support the American infantry. They'll only arrive in the village of Plessis-Lastelle, only 3 miles from their starting point, on July 12 at the cost of 5,000 losses. The killed, wounded and missing of the 90th Infantry Division alone would represent more than a quarter of all Allied casualties suffered during the same week, in all theaters of operations in the world combined.

ONLY THE BEGINNING

The 'Tough Ombres' will continue their advance without respite towards Coutances. An assault on the 'island of Saint-Germain-sur-Sèves' (so called because of the many rivers surrounding the village) would fail on July 23, forcing the division to bypass it and take Périers four days later. July 26 will be a tragic day for Leo's former company, which will lose more than 100 men out of 186 in total. Yet it will manage to break out of Normandy to cross the Mayenne and Sarthe rivers, before turning northward to help close the Falaise Pocket, the last battle of the campaign.

After recovering from his injuries, Leo will return to his unit in November, while the division is on the Saar River, and will participate in the Moselle crossing, fighting for an additional 161 days. The engagements in January 1945 will cost him many friends, as well as part of his hearing ability when a shell once again explodes nearby, piercing his eardrum. He'll see the end of the war in Czechoslovakia, then return to New Mexico at the end of October 1945 to resume his peaceful farming activities. Leo passed away on August 30, 2006.

(Section cut out by the censor in Leo's letter from the hospital)

THE BREAKTHROUGH

In mid-July, the GIs are still blocked in front of Saint-Lô, and the Anglo-Canadians around Caen. *Operation Cobra* finally helps the Americans leave the Cotentin Peninsula, before a final German counter-attack fails near Mortain. The Allies will then surround the enemy near Falaise, where the Battle of Normandy will come to an end.

Since the capture of Cherbourg, the liberations of many small villages have required plenty of sacrifices. In places such as Sainteny, between Carentan and Périers, 7,000 GIs were killed and wounded, and in La-Haye-du-Puits and Lessay, another 10,000 Americans were lost. In spite of it all, the Germans are still clinging to their positions and Saint-Lô remains out of reach.

Patch of the
9th Infantry Division.

SAINT-LÔ

On July 9, while the British and Canadians have just launched their own assault on Caen (*Operation Charnwood*, in which Major Ross was involved, page 178), US General Bradley gathers his troops south of Carentan for a major offensive towards Saint-Lô. Among the units taking part in the operation is the 9th Infantry Division, a veteran of Africa and Sicily.

Since its landing on Utah Beach, the division has already lost more than 300 killed and almost 2,000 wounded men. On the other hand, it's managed to capture 18,490 Germans and a large quantity of weapons, food and vehicles. Attending the Cotentin fighting and then the fall of Cherbourg, the famous reporter Ernie Pyle (who would die eight months later while covering the American invasion of Okinawa in the Pacific) writes in his book, *Brave Men*: *"The 9th [Division] was good. In the Cherbourg campaign, it performed like a beautiful machine. Its previous battles paid off. Not only in the individual fighting, but in the perfect way the whole organization clicked. [...] The Ninth did something in that campaign that we hadn't always done in the past. It kept tenaciously on the enemy's neck. When the Germans would withdraw a little, the Ninth was right on top of them."*

Cortland Kester is a 19-year-old soldier from New York. Called up in September 1943, he serves in the 60th Regiment of the 9th Infantry Division, nicknamed the 'Go Devils'. As the rest of the division entered Cherbourg, Cortland and his regiment advanced to Jobourg (Cap de la Hague), securing bunkers, trenches and minefields. They finished their work on July 30, then left for a week's rest in the village of Les Pieux, before the start of the great offensive towards Saint-Lô. Without knowing it, Cortland is now living his final days.

On July 2 he writes one of his last two letters to his mother: *"My Dearest Mother, we just pulled in for a 5-day rest. So while I did have the time I thought I'd write. We do have very little time to write here. The only time we can write is when we're in rest. I really wish I could write you a letter a day. But here I'm lucky if I can write 3 letters a month. I'm in the very best of health. And I'm tan as a beet. I'm terribly homesick mother, I miss you terribly, I can't wait till the day we'll be together again. I love you dearly Mother. Your mail doesn't come here to me so hot. It's been almost a month since I've received a letter from you. It's time for chow so I'll have to close now. Forever your loving Son, Cortland."*

IV - OVERLORD SUMMER 1944

Photos of Les Pieux taken by Cortland Kester and sent with one of his last letters. Next to them are photos of the same places today. Below, a picture of Cortland sent to his mother.

CORTLAND'S FINAL FIGHT

His battalion arrives west of Saint-Jean-de-Daye in the afternoon of July 9. It reinforces the right flank of the 30th Infantry Division, which is aimed at a ridge northwest of Pont-Hébert, from where the Germans have an unobstructed view of the area. Cortland writes his very last letter to his mother that day: *"In every letter you write me you say you worry so much about me. Why, tell me. I'm in better care over here than I was in the States. So please don't worry so much about me, I'm far from any danger."* This, sadly, is not the case. At the same moment, the enemy counter-attacks on the positions of the 30th Infantry and 3rd Armored Divisions to the south, between Le Dézert and Pont-Hébert. Elements of the SS Panzer-Division 'Das Reich' are repelled by the American artillery in a grueling fight. Further west, other units of the 30th Division are holding their positions, facing the approaching Panzer Lehr, which, although exhausted after a month of combat in the British sector, is still one of the most feared and best equipped units of the German Army. It approached Hommet Woods, in order to join other German units in their attack from the south towards Saint-Jean-de-Daye. Cortland and the 9th Division come into action on July 10, with the mission of stopping the Panzers from breaking through the Allied lines on the road to Graignes, a martyred village (page 162) that had just been liberated. The Panzer Lehr finally attacks at night, advancing a mile into the American lines between the 47th and 39th Regiments. The 60th Regiment, which was further north near Graignes, is ordered to help contain the German breakthrough. Cortland and his company are tasked with attacking a machine gun position threatening the north/south road, 'Les Landes'. The fighting is extremely violent and lasts all morning. The Americans eventually manage to take the position in the early afternoon, but Cortland had to pay the price for it: wounded in the German attack, he dies of his wounds on July 11, 1944, aged only 19.

201

The 'Les Landes' road, where Cortland was killed. Today's landscape is still typical of the Norman bocage of the time, with its farms, hedges and narrow roads.

Pfc. Kester

Eighteen days later, his mother will receive a telegram stating that Cortland had been *"slightly wounded in action"*. Initially buried in a temporary cemetery in Blosville, his body is later repatriated to the United States and now rests at the Woodlawn National Cemetery in Elmira, New York. Cortland Kester is one of 2,500 killed and wounded in the 9th Infantry Division between July 10 and 20, 1944.

Thanks to the support of the American air force and artillery, the Panzer Lehr counter-attack is halted by 4 pm. The latter has lost at least half of its personnel in the battle and is no longer able to carry out any major offensives. The Allies resume their advance all along the front line, although progress will remain slow. The 4th and 83rd Divisions, for example, would advance only a few hundred yards a day, facing an enemy determined not to leave his fortress of vegetation. Saint-Lô is finally taken on July 19, when units from the 29th and 35th Divisions enter the ruined city after heavy fighting, inch after inch. The liberated city is 95% destroyed and a sergeant in the 1709th Signal Service Battalion writes to his brother in the Navy: *"St. Lo was just a mass of rubble, and there are many more like it. All along the road we pass wrecked German equipment."*

One of the last letters from Cortland, written on a V-mail form.

Nearly 5,000 more soldiers are lost in the offensive on Saint-Lô, but the toll could have been even higher. Following the liberation of Caen on July 20, the Germans established a new line of defense south of the latter, and *Operation Goodwood*, designed to destroy it, prevented enemy reinforcements from being sent to the American front. Nevertheless, although it would go down in history as the largest tank battle in Normandy (involving 1,100 British tanks), *Goodwood* was canceled after three days, stopping the Anglo-Canadians in front of Verrières Ridge. Its failure thus motivates the creation of an American Army Group, the 12th Army Group, which would from then on compete with Montgomery's 21st Army Group. General Omar Bradley, former commander of the 1st US Army, takes command of the Group, which will eventually include 43 divisions and 1.3 million men. On August 1, it incorporates the newly created 3rd Army of General Patton, who had been sidelined for a while after slapping a shell-shocked soldier in the face whilst in Sicily.

In the meantime, the Germans still have to be pushed out of the Cotentin Peninsula. John Irvine of the 4th Infantry Division (page 194) sums up the situation in a letter to his wife on July 23, not far from Périers: *"The weather has been not so good but I think it's going to clear up today. We have a radio in the area today and we're all listening to the news – sounds like Germany is about ready to quit. Sure wish I could be home when the baby is born but guess there isn't much I could do anyway. We're pretty lucky anyway. There is so much misery over here you realize how fortunate we are in the US. Normandy is very pretty but I'll be glad to get out of these hedgerows and into open country. This is practically like jungle fighting and it's very difficult for our tanks to operate. I threw all my clothes away and bought all new ODs* ['Olive Drab' colored combat uniform] *so I'm all set for a while. If it would just stop raining so I could get my blankets dry, I'd be happy."* His jaw will be broken in an explosion in Mortain two weeks later, but he'll return to his company afterwards. However, he'd never have the chance to meet his daughter as he'll be killed in the Hürtgen Forest in November 1944 (page 266).

OPERATION COBRA

Preceded by a massive air bombardment between Saint-Lô and Périers, *Operation Cobra* is launched on July 25 to put an end to the hedgerow warfare and finally enter Brittany. The remnants of the elite Panzer Lehr Division are cut to pieces by the American bombs, but the latter would cause further and unintended casualties. The US Army Air Forces had loaded 500-pound shells in their bombers, much more powerful than the 100-pound shells originally chosen, without warning ground commanders.

This error, in addition to the terrible weather, would cause nearly 900 killed and wounded among the Allies. One of them is Lieutenant-General Lesley McNair, the most senior officer killed in the European Theater. General Bradley, who was a close friend, remembers in his autobiography, *A General's Life*: *"A bomb landed squarely on McNair in a slit trench and threw his body 60 feet and mangled it beyond recognition except for the three stars on his collar"*. His death is hidden from the public, however, since he was playing an important role in *Operation Quicksilver*, part of the *Fortitude* deception plan. He'd just replaced Patton at the head of a fictional army preparing for the 'real' D-Day that Hitler is still waiting for in the Pas-de-Calais region.

Nevertheless, the violence of the raid opened a breach in which the infantry quickly rushes into, led by the 9th Infantry Division (to which Cortland belonged) still supported by the 30th Infantry Division and soon followed many others. On July 28, the 4th Armored Division, which had just arrived on the front, seizes Coutances. Although the Germans attempt various desperate counter-attacks, most of their units are destroyed, including the famous Panzer Lehr. When Generalfeldmarschall Günther von Kluge, who is in charge of the Western Front, calls his HQ to report this *"Riesensauerei"* (complete mess) and is asked about the status of the German defenses, he replies: *"Defenses? Where do you live? On the moon?"*

A US Army medic, not far from Saint-Lô, writes about the bombings: *"Well now that I have finished the battle of St-Lô, maybe I can get this letter finished. You know that was our first baptism of fire. We could not write about it at the time. The bitterest battle of the early invasion days was there. For days on end it see-sawed back and forth until 3,000 planes came over the town and blasted it off the map. That marked the end of German resistance in Normandy. Then we moved on and stayed as close as possible for a general hospital to the front lines. Sometimes I figured too danged close. Ha! Ha! One time close enough that the vibration from the guns caused some windows to fall out of our mess hall."*

This 'British Made' American canteen cover (made by the British in exchange for the 1941 lend-lease) was found in a Cotentin barn in the 1990s.

It belonged to Sgt. Corbett Clyde Vandyke, a member of the 50th Field Artillery Battalion, 5th US Infantry Division. Equipped with eighteen 105 mm Howitzers guns, his unit fought in the bocage in support of the 2nd Regiment. With the 3rd Army, they went through Avranches and headed for Nantes. On August 7, they took Angers and the bridges on the Loire River before experiencing heavy fighting in Metz and then in Germany. Although he'd abandoned his canteen in the field, Corbett survived and returned to the United States in July 1945.

BREAKTHROUGH IN AVRANCHES

Avranches (at the base of the Cotentin Peninsular) is reached on July 31. After four hours of fighting, Patton's tanks and the 4th Infantry Division enter the city. They capture the Pontaubault bridge intact and within a few days, Patton would lead twelve divisions out of Normandy in pursuit of the Germans in Mayenne and Brittany. Melvin Berg, a New Yorker of Swedish origin, is serving in the 4th Quartermaster Company, 4th Infantry Division. At almost 35 years of age, he is much older than the 20-year-old infantrymen he lives with.

203

However, although its primary role is the management of rations, ammunition and equipment, rather than combat, the 4th QM Company endures the same difficult daily routine as the infantry: digging their foxholes and washing in their combat helmets whilst under artillery fire.

Quartermaster Corps badge.

When Melvin writes the following letter, the 4th Division is pushing the Germans towards Mortain, where they're caught between Patton's 3rd Army and the British 2nd Army. Montgomery has just launched *Operation Bluecoat* in order to build on the Americans' success while protecting Bradley's left flank, and take Mont Pinçon, the highest feature in the Calvados region. The fighting rages between Avranches and Vire, as well as on the banks of the Sée River. The day after this letter, the 4th US Division will take Saint-Pois, before the enemy's very last counter-offensive in Normandy.

Melvin's letter is sent to a friend, also of Swedish origin, whom he met in high school while acting in a play: *"France, Thursday August 3, 1944. Dear Regna, [...] You have probably heard many of the details of my sojourn in England so won't go into them too much again. However, my stay in dear old England will always remain one of the pleasanter memories of my life in spite of (shall I say?) the auspices of the army. It was all topped of course by my 7-day furlough in London. I met some grand people both in and out of the theater and they were all swell to me. In addition to that I managed to see a goodly share of the current productions as well as a certain amount of the sights. And then we had the Spring in England which in itself was worth-while. It was one of the most beautiful Springs I have ever known except for the fact that I was away from those who mean much to me. Someday when the world is again at peace, I should certainly like to go back to England and wander around as I please. There are so many things I should have liked to have done which were impossible. Time certainly flies, and especially so since D-day. It is over a year now since I was last home, and in many ways it doesn't seem possible. The days now are fuller than ever which is one reason no doubt why the days fly by so fast, and in many ways, I am thankful that they do fly by because then you don't have too much time to reminisce. At night, though, lying in your slit trench trying to get to sleep, you can't help thinking back over your life, and sometimes some of the memories seem almost as though they must have occurred in another incarnation, they seem so far removed from the present. It's a strange thing sometimes. You lie there, and you begin thinking, and then you say to yourself 'to hell with it' and you try to keep your thoughts from crowding in on your consciousness but somehow or other it doesn't seem to work out. One thing pushes out another until a particular line of thoughts has run its course. And so it goes. There isn't much of France for obvious reasons so far that I want to keep in my memories. Pictures of utter devastation somehow have never even touched what we have experienced in actuality. Some of the towns we have been through are almost completely gone, and it is a pitiful sight to see the civilians returning to what was once their homes with what personal effects they were able to take with them when they left them. Occasionally you see horse drawn carts piled high and then more often you see just the peasants carrying what they can on foot. Yet, they are seemingly glad to see the Americans and very friendly. We have bivouacked a great many times in the numerous apple orchards, the trees of which are usually overrun with mistletoe, and the apple trees, as ancient, I guess, as the ruined buildings they adjoin are one of the things I think I shall always remember.*

Forgotten in a Mayenne field by American soldiers and recovered just after the fighting, this French phonograph, probably 'borrowed' from an abandoned house, represents a rare distraction for the GIs. Next to it were various jazz records and hits of the time, including Ella Logan's vinyl, *The Hut Sut Song* **(1941).**

```
T/5 Melvin E. Berg, 32380681
4th Q.M. Company
A.P.O. #4, c/o Postmaster
New York, New York
```

IV - OVERLORD SUMMER 1944

When we landed, the trees were just losing the apple blossoms and now they are filled with a tremendous crop of good-sized green apples which, when they drop in the dead of night on your slit trench roof, inevitably startle you. Hope that by the time the crop is ready to harvest the war will be over, and we can begin to think of going home again."

THE GERMAN COUNTER-ATTACK

Shortly after this letter, the Americans are hit hard by *Operation Lüttich*, von Kluge's counter-attack. Moving up along the Sée River from Mortain to Avranches with several armored divisions, the Generalfeldmarschall hopes to cut the Allied positions in half. However, his officers are well aware that Normandy is lost, and some are already waiting for the negotiations with the Allies. Indeed, following the American breakthrough, and according to all military logic, the Germans should already have withdrawn. But this stubborn idea to remain doesn't really come from von Kluge, but rather Hitler, who's still sure he can push the Allies back to the sea. The latter has lost all confidence in his staff, and for good reason.

On June 22, 1944, *Operation Bagration* began on the Eastern Front. Three years to the day after *Barbarossa*, the Red Army launched an unprecedented attack, throwing more than 1,670,000 men supported by 6,000 tanks, 30,000 cannons and 7,500 aircraft at a 600-mile long front from the Baltic Sea to Romania. In less than three weeks, twenty-eight German divisions were destroyed in Belarus. When the operation ends in mid-August, the Wehrmacht has lost 589,425 men, as the Red Army reaches Warsaw. German morale is at its lowest and some officers are even joining the 'Nationalkomitee Freies Deutschland' (anti-Nazi Germans in the Soviet Union). On July 20, 1944, as the Russians approached East Prussia, Hitler was the victim of an attack in one of his command bunkers in Rastenburg, but the bomb placed under a table by German Colonel Claus von Stauffenberg only slightly wounded the Führer, and his miraculous survival convinced him that divine intervention encouraged him to continue the war. A British soldier wrote two days later: *"A great pity Hitler didn't get bumped off the other day. The revolution would most likely have been on now if he had been killed."*

The failure of this assassination attempt had immediate repercussions: more than 7,000 people were arrested by the Gestapo (the Reich's Secret Police) and many of them were executed. Rommel himself was now suspected by Hitler of having encouraged this attack, since he'd expressed his disillusionment with the outcome of the war.

But in memory of his exploits in North Africa, Hitler gives the marshal the opportunity to commit suicide. However, his injuries received on July 17 by a British aircraft's strafing run would become the official reason for his death and he would be buried with full military honors. Rommel died on October 14, 1944 and the real cause of his death (cyanide) wouldn't be known until after the war.

Above all, the attack had a strong impact on German military strategy. It made Hitler realize that his ultra-secure bunkers are useless if the threat comes from within. Consequently, the Nazi salute with the famous 'Heil Hitler' is therefore extended to all branches of the armed forces in replacement of the military salute, so that every German can prove his loyalty to Hitler. This is a real blow for the soldiers of the Wehrmacht and particularly the Kriegsmarine, few of whom are convinced Nazis (unlike the SS units). The Führer also took the decision to assume full command of operations on the Western Front, without even listening to his men on the ground. All this led to his order to counter-attack towards Avranches, without realizing that the advanced units would be dangerously exposed and would risk being surrounded and destroyed. Von Kluge, himself accused of having participated in the July 20 plot, wants to free himself from suspicion and therefore follows Hitler's instructions blindly.

Admittedly, the powerful offensive that takes place during the night of August 6 to 7 doesn't surprise the Allies, who knew all about the plan well before its launch: the tired units had been replaced and were arranged to contain the German attack. But the damage is still significant and the 30th Division, which had relieved the 1st Division in Mortain, suffers the most casualties (about 2,000 men). Placed in reserve, Melvin's 4th Division has to be taken as quickly as possible in front of the corridors used by the 2. Panzer and 2. SS Panzer Divisions, so that its artillery can provide vital support to the 30th Division (patch below), whose regiment is surrounded on Hill 314, near Mortain. The 12th Regiment of the 4th Division, sent as reinforcements, experiences the most difficult battle in its history under a deluge of mortar and artillery shells. However, the Germans are soon halted as Allied Mustang, Typhoon and Thunderbolt aircraft invade the skies of Mortain, silencing the Luftwaffe. The 35th Division in turn comes to assist their comrades surrounded by SS tanks and on August 12, the Americans even manage to push the Germans back.

This bitter failure won't help von Kluge redeem himself in Hitler's eyes and on August 18, he's replaced by Walter Model, another veteran of the Eastern Front. The next day, von Kluge is summoned to Berlin to explain himself, but he commits suicide on the way by swallowing a cyanide pill. He leaves a letter to Hitler, suggesting that he surrenders to the Allies and shows *"the greatness necessary to put an end to this desperate struggle."*

THE FALAISE POCKET

In the Mayenne region, an officer of the 5th US Armored Division is in pursuit of the enemy as it retreats to Falaise. He writes to his wife on August 14: *"First chance I have had for a few days to write and let you know I am in France and doing very little actual fighting, by that as you know I mean actual shooting... I have my hands full directing fire of the platoons. The horror of this war and the killing that is going on 24 hours a day cannot be described... I often wondered how I would feel when I saw my first killed or mangled body... Well that didn't affect me at all. Then how would I feel when I killed my first enemy, the other day I got my first. I was standing along a road walking* [along] *a ditch and I thought I saw something move. I kept a watch on it and soon it moved again. So I took a good bead on the spot and kaputt. One more dead Jerry... I guess it wasn't in my mind at all. All I thought of was that I had to clean my rifle again. They are not very good shots as they have had plenty of chances, and some have darn close calls. The main things to watch for are snipers and ambushes. An artillery or bombing just comes and you hope you are not where it lands. We have had some men killed in our battalion, but for 12 days of continuous fighting and darn near 24 hours each day the number is very small. I lost one man in my company, a ricochet hit. He did not suffer... One thing I can't say is where in France we are or when we fight. So far I have not yet got any souvenirs. I would like a German Luger* [Parabellum pistol 1908] *but the way we travel so fast we don't bother to stop and look around. I may get one later... Our planes sure rain hell over the Germans every day."* This officer will be killed a few months later in the Hürtgen Forest.

Found in a farm in Pré-en-pail (Mayenne), this Jerrycan was used by Patton's 3rd Army. Marked G for 'Gasoline', it's just one of the 19 million units that powered Allied vehicles in Europe until May 1945.

While the Americans drive to the south, between Flers and Argentan, the 1st Canadian Army (still south of Caen) tries to reach Falaise to cut off the German retreat into the 'gap'. *Operation Spring* in late July fails to capture the Verrières Ridge, which cost the Canadians 2,800 killed and wounded. But from August 7 to 14, operations *Totalize* and then *Tractable* finally allow a significant advance, even though the three Canadian divisions, the British 49th (West Riding) and 51st (Highland) Divisions and the 1st Polish Armored Division face fierce resistance. In the race to Falaise, the Canadians pay the highest price with more than 18,000 casualties.

Between these two fronts, the British 2nd Army pushes the enemy into the Falaise trap from Vire and Flers. Raymond Edwards belongs to one of its English armored regiments, the 4th/7th Dragoon Guards, then attached to the 50th (Northumbrian) Infantry Division. In mid-August, Raymond writes: *"The weather is very hot here but we only know it means clouds of dust on the roads and makes the infantry and us very tired. The infantry are great and like to see us around and we like to see plenty of them moving with the tanks.* [...] *The news is good just now and if we don't spend our time 'mopping up', should push right on when Jerry cracks. We are not counting on it being too soon, the papers will tell you that they fight to the last and very bitterly.* [...] *We've a hell of a lot to wipe out yet, the gap couldn't be closed soon enough, but the boys did wonders."*

The Allies can now throw 37 divisions, including 11 armored ones (representing more than 600,000 men and 3,500 tanks) at the Germans. The latter are exhausted by the two months of fighting in Normandy, and in particular by Mortain's recent counter-attack attempt. The Wehrmacht now only has debris left from 18 infantry divisions and 10 armored divisions, representing no more than 250,000 men and 250 tanks. Allied superiority is overwhelming, and many German soldiers feel that Falaise could be their last battle. Moreover, unlike the Norman bocage, the large open fields of the region aren't conducive to defensive action. On August 15, upon learning of the catastrophic situation in Normandy and of another Allied landing in Provence that same day, Adolf Hitler tells his officers *"today was the most horrific day of my life"*, before ordering further impossible counter-attacks and eventually giving the order to retreat on August 17.

It's now time for the Allies, who were a bit slow to react, to entrap as many enemies as possible near Falaise and close the gap. But time is running out...

IV - OVERLORD SUMMER 1944

Left, a British helmet found in a home north of Falaise, bearing the remains of a possible 53rd (Welsh) Infantry Division emblem. Its owner seems to have received a piece of shrapnel that damaged the stainless-steel rim.

This German helmet (1940 model) for the Wehrmacht (right), including remnants of the silver emblem with the black eagle, was found during excavations in the Falaise Pocket. The rear of the helmet has cracked either due to an explosion, the passage of a tank during the fighting, or a post-war tractor.

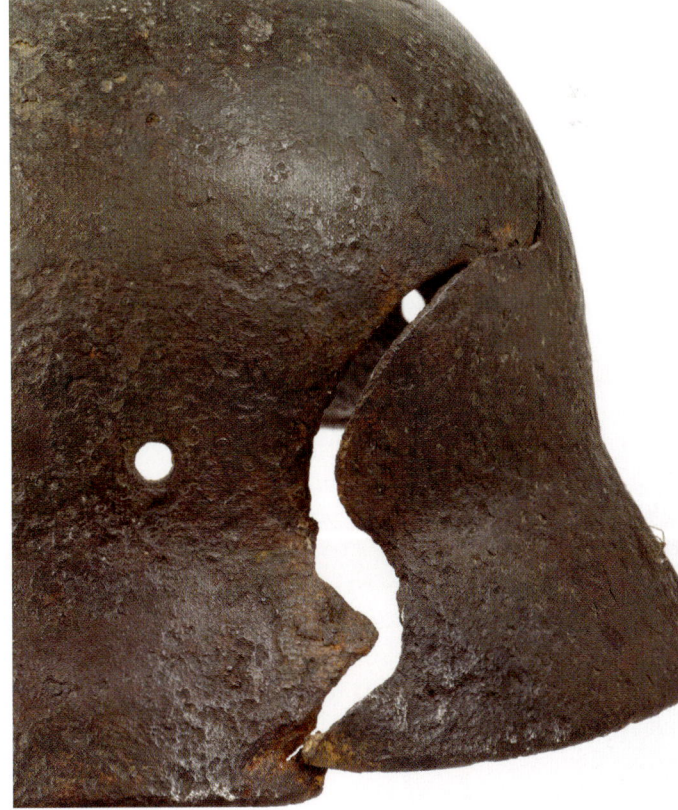

207

This piece of gutter torn by bullets and shrapnel, found in Saint-Lambert-sur-Dive, bears witness to the violence of the fighting in the 'corridor of death'. Above, a photo of Lt. Donald Grant shows his cameraman Jack Stollery (left) in the same village, immortalizing a German surrender to the Canadians. On August 18, Major David Currie's (holding the pistol) men closed one of the last gaps in the Falaise Pocket in this location.

Many had already managed to take refuge behind the Seine River, but on the evening of August 17, 100,000 Germans are caught in the pocket. The narrow passage that forms between the Anglo-Canadians in the north and Americans in the south, near Trun and Chambois, is now known as the 'corridor of death'. On August 19, after a bloody fight, the Polish Armored Division takes Hill 262 at Mont-Ormel, a strategic feature that dominates the entire area. They then head for Chambois to close the gap definitively. This is also the objective of the French 2e division blindée, which landed in early August, and the 90th US Infantry Division advancing from the south. They link up at the end of the afternoon. German Marshal Model tries a last desperate counter-offensive on Mont-Ormel, believing the Polish defenses to be very weak. The Poles who remained on Hill 262 are in turn surrounded, but resist heroically for two days at the cost of 1,500 casualties. A few thousand Germans manage to get out of the pocket but on August 21, those who couldn't escape are forced to surrender, leaving the Allies free to head for Paris.

There are no precise figures for the losses sustained by the Germans in the pocket, but they're estimated at 10,000 dead, 50,000 prisoners, and 40,000 escapees. Eisenhower will visit the battlefield and write: *"It was literally possible to walk for hundreds of yards at a time, stepping on nothing but dead and decaying flesh"*. The battle marks the end of the Normandy Campaign, which cost the Allies 209,672 casualties (39,976 killed), and the Germans 450,000 (240,000 killed and wounded, plus prisoners). Out of the 1,500 German Panzers engaged in the region, only 26 were able to cross the Seine. The tides of war seem to have turned, and the French welcome their liberators with open arms. Shortly after the Battle of Falaise, British tank driver Raymond Edwards writes: *"It is quite a sight to see the people of towns and villages a few hours or even days after Jerry has left. They line the roads all smiles and wave and throw flowers. Just like it was in Italy. I suppose everyone at home is thinking it will soon be over. I'm not banking on it being just yet."* Indeed, Raymond will be killed a month later (page 239).

V
VICTORY BY CHRISTMAS?
Facing the Gates of the Reich

The Allies have finally broken out of Normandy and are now rushing to the north of France and the German border. On the way, the French 2e division blindée (armored) will liberate Paris, while the British and Americans are welcomed as heroes in the countless villages deserted by the fleeing enemy. On August 15, 1944, the 7th US Army and the 1re Armée française will land in the Provence region during *Operation Dragoon*, and reach eastern France in record time. They'll then face the Siegfried Line, a huge network of fortifications protecting the Reich.

Montgomery will try to precipitate victory by launching an ambitious armored and airborne operation in the Netherlands, *Market Garden*, and bypass this line. However, although the end of the war would never seem so close, the troops cut off in Arnhem will suffer a stunning failure, while the Anglo-Canadians in the west will struggle to capture heavily defended ports. In Italy, meanwhile, the 'D-Day Dodgers' will be mired in deadly fighting on the Gothic Line. The chances of seeing the war end in 1944 are becoming slimmer and slimmer...

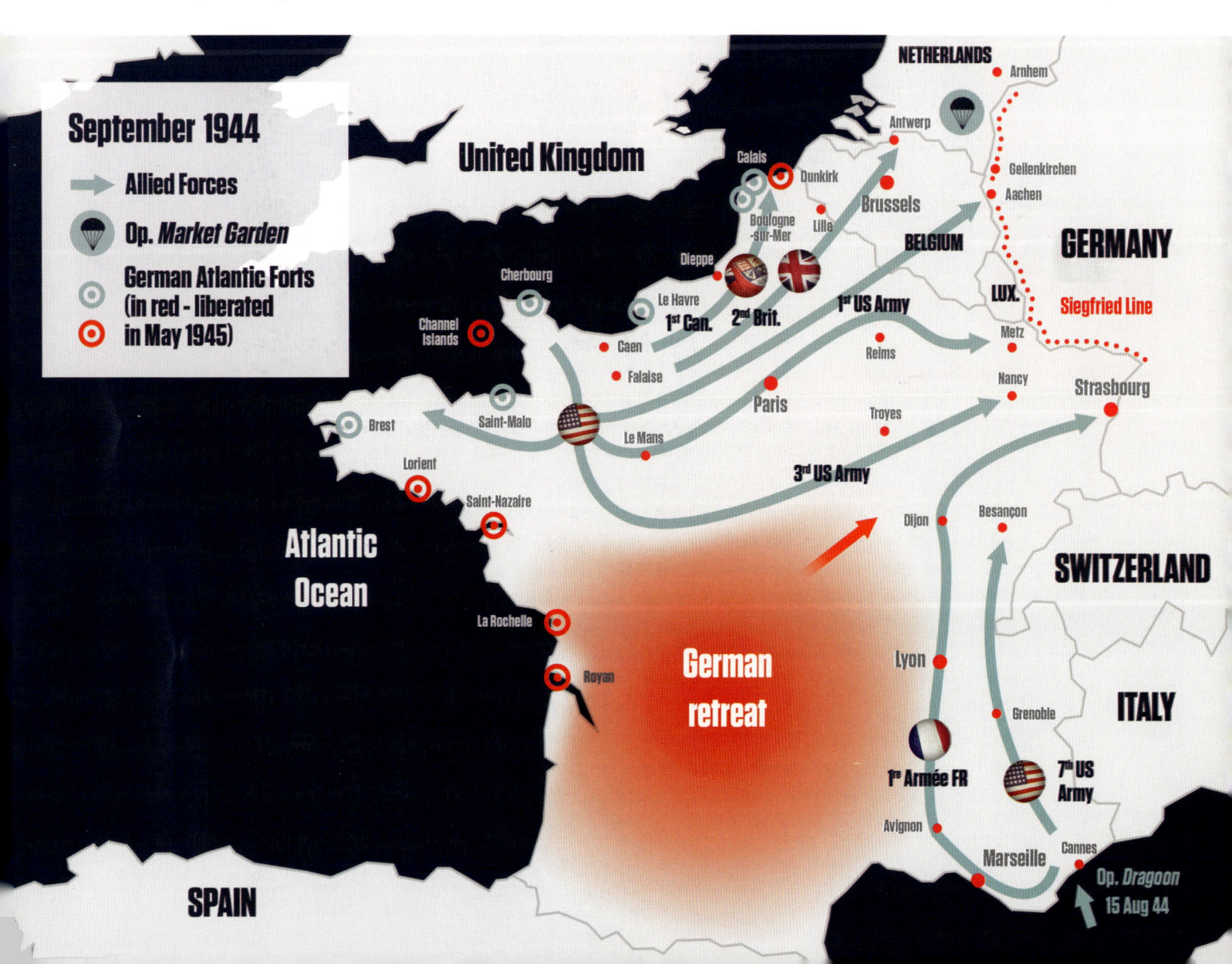

ANDRÉ BONNAFOUS

12e régiment de cuirassiers, French 2e division blindée (armored)

André is a lieutenant in the only French division in Normandy, the 2e DB (2e division blindée) 'Leclerc'.
After helping to close the Falaise gap, the division will enter Paris and then Strasbourg.
In letters sent to the English family who'd welcomed him before the invasion,
André will share the emotions he feels whilst liberating his own country.

THE ORIGINS OF THE 2e DB

When General de Gaulle announced that he wanted to continue the fight from England in June 1940, he initially received very few volunteers. One of the first to join him, however, was a captain named Philippe de Hauteclocque, a veteran of the Battle of France and an escaped prisoner, who would soon become known by the war name 'Leclerc'. Brazzaville, in French Equatorial Africa, became the capital of Free France before the new government moved to Algiers in 1943. African colonial troops (mainly Chadians and Cameroonians) formed the core of his army, led by former metropolitan officers rallied to de Gaulle. Of these African soldiers, 90% of them were rural people who'd never seen a white man before, not to mention never having heard of tanks or even been in a truck. However, they learned quickly and became excellent soldiers. Their baptism of fire began in mid-February 1941 in Koufra, Libya. Leclerc, promoted to colonel, led nearly 400 men (295 Africans and 101 Europeans) from Chad to a stronghold held by the Italians. After ten days of siege, the latter surrendered to Leclerc, giving birth to the myth of the Free French Forces. On March 2, 1941, Colonel Leclerc took the 'Oath of Kufra': *"Swear not to lay down arms until our colors [flag], our beautiful colors, fly over Strasbourg Cathedral."*

On August 1, 1943, in Algiers, General de Gaulle and General Giraud (commander of the African Army, formerly loyal to Vichy) decided to join forces and form the 'French Liberation Army'. The expression 'Free France' then disappeared in favor of 'Fighting France' and new units were created. On the 24th, the former 'Leclerc Armored Column' thus became the 2e division blindée (2nd Armored Division) in Morocco. It included twice as many elements from the African Army as former Free French Forces, but was still commanded by Leclerc, who was now promoted to major general. The history of the '2e DB' reads: *"Never has there been such a mosaic of peoples, races, religions, political convictions, as there were in this division of French citizens, early Free French Forces, coming from Syria, young people who had escaped through Spain, men from Chad, Senegal, Guinea, Lebanon, Tunisia, Algeria and Morocco, blacks from French Equatorial Africa, Indians, foreigners in the service of France, as well as Catholics, Protestants, Jews, Muslims, free thinkers and Quakers, but ALL volunteers and all united in the desire to free France from the occupier."*

In November 1942, André Bonnafous was a married man who'd just turned 40. However, he didn't hesitate to leave his native Tarn region and join the Liberation Army as soon as German troops invaded the free zone. André managed to flee through Spain in January 1943 and found General de Gaulle's army in

V - VICTORY BY CHRISTMAS? LATE 1944

Algeria just in time to be considered a member of the Free French Forces (male or female volunteers, under the command of General de Gaulle from June 18, 1940 to July 31, 1943). Just like André, more than 120,000 French people (mostly in 1943) tried to cross the Pyrenees mountains with the firm intention of returning to liberate France. But only one in three would succeed. Many were handed over by the Spaniards to Vichy, or captured and deported by the Germans. In Morocco, André joined the 2e DB where he met General Leclerc, who was his instructor at the Cavalry School in Saumur. On March 26, 1943, André was assigned to the staff of a very old regiment, the 12th Cuirassiers, commanded by Lieutenant-Colonel Warabiot. It was created by King Louis XIV on March 24, 1668, to protect his son, the 'Dauphin' of France (Dauphin is the French name given to the next in line to the throne. However, it also means 'dolphin', which consequently became the unit's emblem). Thereafter, the regiment would participate in any war in which France was involved (even today). Composed of various infantry, armored and artillery units, plus engineers, logistics, maintenance and medical companies, it represents more than 14,000 men.

All are very proud to belong to the Liberation Army, but there are often disagreements between the former Free French Forces and the African soldiers over who was their true leader. Thus, on January 25, 1944, in the Temara Forest (south of Rabat) where the division is stationed, General Leclerc's aide-de-camp wrote in his diary (*War Diary 1939-1944*, Christian Girard, Editions L'Harmattan, Paris, 2002): *"Lieutenant Bonnafous, of the 12th Cuirassiers, went a few days ago to Person's tent* [Jean-Marie de Person, commander of the regiment who would lose his life on April 15, 1945, in the fighting for the Royan Pocket] *and asked him for a photograph of General Giraud, to the astonishment of Person and the officers in his company. Bonnafous explained that at his regimental mess, he placed a photograph of General de Gaulle on the chimney that was built under the mess tent. Commander N... described his act as unacceptable idolatry and asked him to remove the photograph. Certain officers pointed out that for three years everyone had been forced to put portraits of Marshal Pétain everywhere and that there was no reason not to put the photograph of General de Gaulle in his place today. N... ended up giving in on the condition that Giraud's would be there as well. Today, General de Lattre came to inspect us. When he entered the mess tent of the 12th Cuirassiers, he saw the two photos which the General had told him about in the car... He approached the chimney. Silence - then he turned around smiling: 'Alright... the sacred union'* [a reference to the movement of reconciliation that united the French of all political and religious orientations at the outbreak of the First World War]."

THE FRENCH IN NORMANDY

In 1940, the regiment received the most modern equipment in the entire French Army, but three years later, to replace their heterogeneous armament and clothing, the men received American uniforms and weaponry. Leclerc's crews were also equipped with the new Sherman and Stuart tanks, which they named after major French cities: the 1st squadron painted names of southern cities on the hulls of its tanks, the 2nd chose cities in Normandy, Île-de-France and Brittany, the 3rd in the Loire, Garonne and Limousin, the 4th cities in northern and eastern regions, while the support units chose ones in North Africa and Corsica. André's M2 Half-Track vehicle was thus named 'La Rochelle'. In February 1944, the 2e DB made a strong impression on the Franco-American Commission, which decided that the division was ready to fight. Detached from the B Army that remained in Africa for a future landing in the Mediterranean, it would leave for England and be the only French division in Normandy (in addition to the 177 French commandos who would land on Sword Beach on June 6).

A letter from André bearing the emblem of the 12th Cuirassiers and its motto 'In danger, my pleasure'. As the 2e DB is under the command of the United States, note the 'US Army' address and the American stamps.

After a final training session, General de Gaulle himself arrived on April 7 to talk to André and his comrades about the situation in France and the role they would play in its liberation. Two days later, the first units left Africa via Casablanca. Lieutenant Bonnafous' Landing Ship Tank (LST) weighed anchor at 4 pm on April 11 and arrived in Swansea (Wales) eleven days later. André was staying in Hull (Yorkshire) with Norah, a woman whose husband had gone to war. The French felt extremely welcome, and André and a few others would maintain regular correspondence with Norah. A few months after the invasion, he would write to her in French: *"Your wishes for the fate of my country and the success of the Allied armies have touched me deeply; it is more and more important that our two countries come closer together, the cruel hours they have gone through must help them to do so, and it is only in the tightening of this cooperation that we can hope to prevail in peace as we did in war. [...] You see, I felt so much affection or simply fraternal friendship in Yorkshire that everything which comes from this region, everything that allows me to relive such good memories, is very dear to me."*

The division landed on Utah Beach on August 1 and joined Patton's new 3rd US Army. André had left his mortar platoon a few days earlier, on July 27, to become a liaison officer. After crossing Sainte-Mère-Église, Saint-Sauveur-le-Vicomte and La-Haye-du-Puits, the regiment spent their first night in France bivouacking in a field in Gerville, surrounded by German corpses and rotting animals, abandoned American foxholes and ruined buildings. The division was finally ready to go on August 5 and had set off for Avranches when von Kluge launched his counter-attack from Mortain.

Patch for General Patton's 3rd US Army.

The 2e DB lost its first soldiers there, before heading for Le Mans, which it reached on August 9. They'd progressed more than 120 miles without sleep when the race to Falaise began. The 2e DB was ordered to turn north and attack Alençon (an important supply center for the German 7. Armee) to the delight of Leclerc, who was born there. It liberated the city on the 12th alongside the 90th US Infantry Division, facing the 9. Panzer-Division which had been dispatched from the south to block its way. As they left the city, certain units of the 2e DB destroyed the remains of the 2nd Panzer SS Division 'Das Reich', infamous for its involvement in the civilian massacres at Tulle, Argenton-sur-Creuse and the tragically famous town of Oradour-sur-Glane. The 2e DB then methodically cleaned the area between Écouché, the south of Argentan, Sées and Carrouges, before joining up with the Poles near Chambois on August 9 and definitively closing the Falaise gap. During the battle, the division inflicted at least 4,500 killed and wounded on the Germans, destroyed 117 tanks, 104 guns and more than 700 vehicles, as well as taking nearly 9,000 prisoners.

The Sherman tank 'Normandy' of the 2e DB in front of Saint-Martin-de-Varreville beach (Utah Beach), where Leclerc and his men landed. The base on which it rests bears the division's emblem, the Cross of Lorraine.

V - VICTORY BY CHRISTMAS? LATE 1944

THE PARISIAN UPRISING

More than 20,000 Germans are now defending Paris, with about ten tanks and many guns. Inspired by the Warsaw Uprising at the same time with the Red Army at its doorstep, the Parisians want to drive the occupier out before the Allies arrive. The French don't know yet that in Poland, Hitler would crush the insurgency under bombs without any intervention from the Soviets (who despised the Poles just as much): the *Armia Krajowa* (or 'Home Army') would consequently be defeated and more than 200,000 civilians massacred by the SS. In the same way, the Führer is determined to leave Paris in ruins for the Americans, while the Parisians dream of retaking possession of their city. In August 1944, the French capital is completely paralyzed by the lack of supplies, gas and electricity cuts, and strikes that follow one after another: railway workers first, then the police, the post office, nurses, etc. The Germans would respond by shooting many resistance fighters, police officers and employees. On August 18, Colonel Henri Rol-Tanguy, a communist militant, veteran of the Spanish War and head of the French Forces of the Interior (FFI) in Île-de-France, calls for a 'general mobilization', and since the Allies aren't far away, all Parisians are called upon to join the movement.

Indeed, on the same day, advanced elements of the 79th US Infantry Division, under Patton's command, are crossing the Seine River in Mantes-la-Jolie. The next day, the Parisian insurrection begins from the police prefecture, now transformed into a stronghold. One by one, suburban town halls fall under FFI control, while shootings break out in the streets of the capital. In total, there are nearly 25,000 Parisian fighters, the majority of whom are police officers, all wearing a blue-white-red Cross of Lorraine armband. They arm themselves as best they can, collecting rifles from German bodies, but ammunition is quickly running out. As the occupying forces' tanks are now beginning to join the fight, the Parisians improvise barricades to slow them down.

Le Populaire is a socialist newspaper that went underground. From the summer of 1944 onwards it became one of the main daily newspapers in Paris. This issue, dated August 23, 1944, was published the day before the first Allies entered Paris, and encouraged the population to rise up against the occupier. Note the handwritten inscription at the top declaring "do not throw away".

Charles de Gaulle sends units of Leclerc's 2e division blindée in reconnaissance near Versailles, without even obtaining the agreement of the American command, who are furious at this insubordination. In reality, the Allies had planned to bypass the capital (which had no real tactical value), but Eisenhower eventually gives in. Leclerc's 4,000 vehicles leave Argentan on August 23 at 6:30 am. The 12th Cuirassiers has to drive through the Rambouillet Forest and reach the west of Versailles. The division encounters several pockets of resistance between Trappes and Villeneuve-le-Roi, but manages to overcome them with the help of the FFI. At 9:22 pm on August 24, Captain Dronne, accompanied by a few tanks, arrives at the city hall's square to inform the underground that the 2e DB would arrive in the morning. On Friday, August 25, at 9:15 am, Colonel Noiret of the 12th Cuirassiers receives his orders from Leclerc: *"After passing through the Porte d'Orléans, behind the Rouvillois task force responsible for attacking towards Montparnasse station and La Concorde, you will turn left, via the external boulevards, and drive up along the left bank of the Seine to Champ-de-Mars. Once you arrive at Champ-de-Mars, you will take care of possible resistance at the Military Academy and reach Montparnasse Station immediately, which will be the division's headquarters."* The French soldiers cry with joy when learning that they are going to take back the Eiffel Tower from the Germans, and there's no better symbol, nor better visual cue for these men who are only used to navigating with a compass.

This armband, marked with the Cross of Lorraine stamp of the FFIs of the Western Paris sector, was worn during the liberation of the capital by Jacques Hennel, from August 20, 1944 onwards, as he indicated on the back of it in pencil.

FIGHTING IN PARIS

However, the soldiers must hurry up: Hitler had placed several tons of explosives under the Eiffel Tower, Notre-Dame Cathedral and the Louvre Museum, while many other buildings and bridges are mined and ready to be destroyed. The 12th Cuirassiers enters through the Porte d'Orléans at 10:58 am and arrives at the Eiffel Tower exactly one hour later. After raising the French flag on its top, the tank crews clean up the Champ-de-Mars and attack the military school, which is occupied by more than 200 Germans firing from the windows. The inside of the building is soon secured with handguns and grenades. All afternoon, fighting rages at the Invalides, in the Luxembourg Gardens, in front of the City Hall, the Quai d'Orsay and the burning Chamber of Deputies. A tank duel takes place in a street west of the Senate and the sound of automatic weapons resonates on the boulevard Saint-Michel, around the Lycée Montaigne and the School of Pharmacy.

Jean Denise (right) was 20 years old when he was recruited with his friend René (left) by the FFIs to help liberate Paris. Among other tasks, he received the dangerous mission of stealing Italian (and unstable) grenades from the Hotel des Monnaies. This photo was taken soon after nearby, on the Quay de Conti, in front of the Institut de France. Jean was awarded a medal for his actions and joined the 1st French Army in the Jura region one month later (see page 282). He wouldn't see Paris again until September 1946.

As the fighting continues, the 2e DB succeeds in capturing the German commander Dietrich von Choltitz, who surrenders his garrison. The ceasefire is signed in the late afternoon at Montparnasse Station and gradually, the various enemy troops start to raise their white flags. The 12th Cuirassiers alone killed 150 Germans and took more than 600 prisoners, including 10 officers. On the other hand, it lost 9 men, 36 wounded and 5 tanks destroyed and damaged on August 25 alone. The FFIs and communist partisans lost 910 killed and 1,500 wounded. As for the 2e DB as a whole, it had 78 killed and 300 wounded.

Two months after the events, André recounts in French his experience of the liberation of Paris in a letter to Norah:
"The emotion you felt when we announced our entry into Paris comes as no surprise to me, I know too well as I have had the good fortune to experience it, like the affectionate sympathy you have shown to our country. For this I thank you again and rest assured that as far as I am concerned, I remain a fervent admirer of the hospitality and generosity of your dear Country.

As for us, what we experienced when we entered Paris is truly untranslatable. Just know that when I left the suburbs where we had fought the day before, I was very cold and firmly determined to ensure the safety of my men by all means. That's the way it happened and thank God, we had no problems. But, around Val-de-Grâce (which is, as you may not know, a large military hospital), a lady walked up to my Jeep that I had parked on the sidewalk and with tears in her eyes told me with all her heart and both hands outstretched, these simple words: 'Thank you, Lieutenant! We've been waiting so long for this day!' I took off my helmet, and unable to speak, I kissed her, then I started to cry like a baby... Don't laugh! Because this is the most accurate truth.

V - VICTORY BY CHRISTMAS? LATE 1944

During the battles for the liberation of Paris, a regimental tank was at the entrance to Place de la Concorde opposite the Hotel Crillon, one of Paris' famous monuments. The fighting had this particularity, that the Parisian population was willing to help us and was working hard to inform our cuirassiers as best as possible. As machine gun bursts hit our tank, an old gentleman, perhaps a former officer, caught the gunner's attention by telling him something like this: 'Oh, my young friend, you see, it's that Fifth Column again!' I think you know what the Fifth Column is, which was so fatal to our armies in 1940: they are actually enemy units disguised in more or less civilian attire. The tank commander, at these words, takes a quick look at the Hotel Crillon, carefully inspects each of the columns decorating the facade, then suddenly turns towards the shooter: 'At my command, in front of us, a hotel, on the facade, columns, fifth from the right – 1, 2, 3, 4, 5, FIRE!' That's how a 75 mm gun demolished the fifth column of the Hotel Crillon, which, thank God, had nothing to do with the Fifth Column. Tell me in a future letter if you have understood correctly. [...] Keep doing well, have fun, smoke a little, drink as well when you have the opportunity, it doesn't shock me in any way. Write to me as often as possible and if fate is good to me, I will be happy to see you again, I will be happy to part with my many friends to answer all your questions and make you laugh, since IT IS NECESSARY."

To de Gaulle, who wished to restore France's image after the dark Vichy episode, this triumphant entry into the capital is a strong symbol. On August 25 he declares at the City Hall: "Paris! Paris outraged! Paris broken! Paris martyred! But Paris liberated! Liberated by itself, liberated by its people with the help of the French armies, with the support and of the help of all France, of the France that fights, of the only France, of the real France, of the eternal France." The next day, the 12th Cuirassiers will parade on the Place de la Concorde. Hitler, meanwhile, would leave a final message to the Parisian population, with 108 bombers raiding the city on the night of August 26 to 27, killing 189 people and injuring 890 more. In ten days of fighting, 582 civilians lost their lives. The 2e DB must now prevent a possible German counter-attack on Paris, so André's regiment leaves the capital through the Porte de la Villette to seize Le Bourget airfield. The latter is captured quickly, but the old village of Blanc-Ménil is taken on the 27th after bitter fighting. Around Le Bourget, as more and more American units move north, the regiment takes some time to refurbish its equipment, receive replacements and reorganize itself.

If the liberation of Paris is, above all, symbolic for the Allies, for the Germans it's a bad blow to morale as the end of August brings other bad news... As the last shots ring out in the French capital, to the east, Romania switches sides and engages the fourth largest contingent (after the USSR, the United States and the United Kingdom) against Germany and Hungary. Similarly, in northern Europe, Finland (an ally of Germany, although it doesn't share its ideology), is invaded by the Red Army and begins to negotiate an armistice that it would soon sign with the USSR, before in turn fighting against the Third Reich.

The 2e DB cheered by the crowd on the Champs-Élysées.

THE OATH OF KOUFRA IS FULFILLED IN STRASBOURG

André will be transferred to the regiment's support units, replacing Lieutenant Libersart, on September 7, 1944. Following the fighting in Normandy and Paris, the 2e DB will incorporate many FFIs, including two of Leclerc's sons. It will rush towards Épinal and make its junction with the 1re division de marche d'infanterie (former 1st Free French division), which had landed in Provence with Leclerc's competitor, de Lattre. With the help of Resistance fighters, it will liberate many cities in the Vosges region. Strasbourg, Leclerc's obsession for three and a half years, will then be the French's next objective. André will write to Norah on October 15: *"Since [Paris] we have kept on moving and we are now in a region where everything is gray, raining, and muddy! This is hard for our vehicles and our march is therefore slowed down. Nevertheless, the Krauts are still being hustled and the news is like our morale: excellent."* André will play a significant role in keeping the regiment in a good mood: in late September he'll return from a long journey through the recently liberated central regions and bring back the 12th Cuirassiers' ensign, which had been hidden there since 1942.

On the morning of November 22, 1944, André's regiment will set off into the Alsace plain and reach Dettwiller. The next day, continuing its momentum, the 12th Cuirassiers will be the first unit to enter Strasbourg at 10 am, secure the Kehl bridge, and fly their flag (handmade at the last minute from pieces of cloth) over the city on November 23. Leclerc's men will be welcomed as heroes by the inhabitants of the Alsatian capital, which had been annexed by the Third Reich in 1940. The Americans will award the 2e DB the prestigious Presidential Unit Citation for its actions in the city. André will write to Norah two weeks later: *"I imagine you must be very happy with your husband's return, and despite the demands of the service that prevented you from having him as often as you would like, that you are satisfied with your fate. As for us, life goes on, hectic and erratic. It has been so long since then that it seems difficult to me to go back to a normal and calm existence. This is quite bad, actually... Events continue to look good and despite all their cruelty and evil genius, the Krauts are getting closer to the end every day. You must have learned of the brilliant successes of our division in the liberation of Strasbourg. General Leclerc once again distinguished himself and later our grandchildren will know what a great French General he was."*

But this doesn't mean everything is now over. The Germans will organize themselves and prepare the defense of their territory. The Colmar Pocket will be the scene of a fierce battle, and during the major enemy counter-attack in the Ardennes in December 1944, Strasbourg will once again be threatened. Under the command of General de Lattre de Tassigny's 1re Armée française, the division will fight bitter battles until the total liberation of the Alsace region on February 12, 1945. At that time, André Bonnafous will leave to join a regiment of Spahis in Morocco. He'll remain there until August 1946, then be appointed to go to French Indochina, shortly after General Leclerc's support to have Vietnam's independence recognized. In the spring of 1945, after a period of rest in the Loire Valley, the 12th Cuirassiers will be tasked with destroying German pockets of resistance on the Atlantic Coast, particularly in Royan and in the port of Bordeaux. As for the rest of the 2e DB, it will advance into Germany and be among those units who'll claim to be the first to enter Hitler's 'Eagle's Nest', perched on a peak in the Bavarian Alps.

A total of 1,687 soldiers from the division will give their lives in the liberation of their country, in addition to 3,300 wounded. André will be rewarded for his service during the Second World War and on August 13, 1947, will be made a Knight of the Legion of Honor as captain of the 12th Cuirassiers, for exceptional war service. After his retirement as a senior officer, André will settle in Strasbourg, the symbolic city he had helped to liberate, and will die there on October 15, 1967.

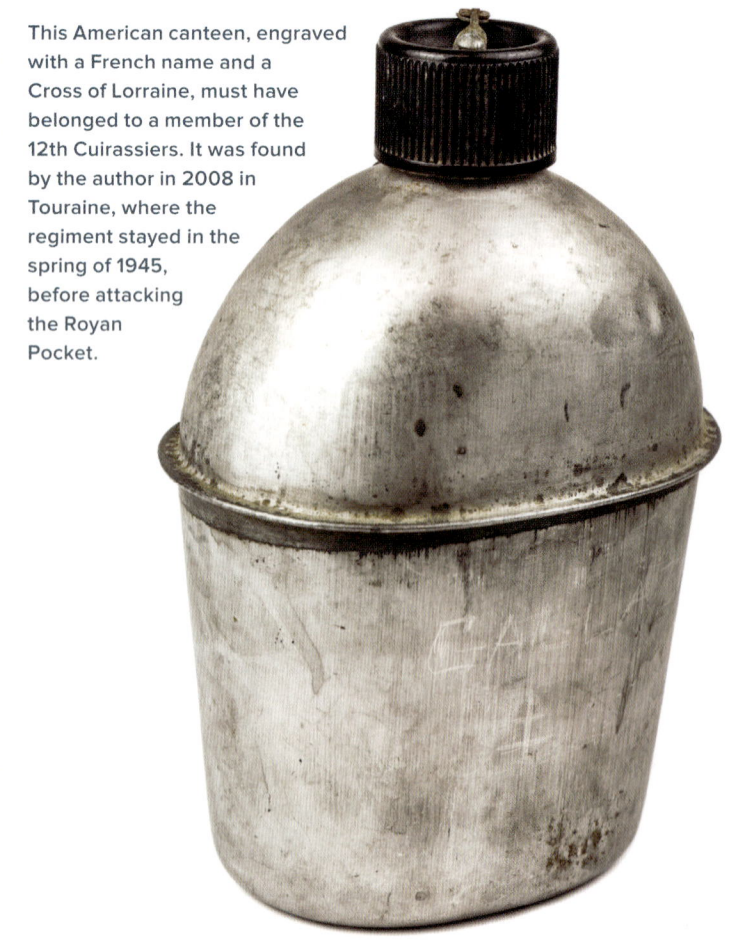

This American canteen, engraved with a French name and a Cross of Lorraine, must have belonged to a member of the 12th Cuirassiers. It was found by the author in 2008 in Touraine, where the regiment stayed in the spring of 1945, before attacking the Royan Pocket.

THE RACE TO ANTWERP

The Allies dream of capturing the second largest European port, but first they'll have to fight for the Atlantic fortresses, enter Belgium, survive the traps of the Scheldt and avoid the new V2 flying bombs…

As the British rush towards Belgium and the Americans hit the old Maginot Line, a large majority of the French population enjoys its freedom again. However, the war in France isn't over yet, and many Atlantic and Channel ports necessary for the resupply of Allied troops still remain in German hands. As the GIs drive quickly across the country, they soon run out of fuel, thus allowing the enemy to organize around its borders. To overcome the lack of railroads (destroyed by their own bombardments), the Allies must establish supply lines by road, such as the famous Red Ball Express. This marked route, closed to civilian traffic, is used by 6,000 priority trucks (marked with a red circle) every day, carrying more than 12,000 tons of ammunition, rations, equipment and fuel from the beaches to the front. However, it's no longer enough to supply the tanks as they progress deeper inland at full speed, without encountering much resistance. A new port must be seized closer to the new front line – a mission which falls on the Anglo-Canadians' shoulders. Unfortunately, following the Allied bombardments and the sabotages undertaken by the Germans in their retreat, they'll often sweat and bleed for unusable infrastructures.

FESTUNGEN

Among these harbors, the one in Boulogne-sur-Mer has already taken quite a beating, having been continuously pounded by both sides since March 1940 (from that time until its liberation, the city would sustain nearly 500 bombardments). Just like Cherbourg, now far from the front, its port was declared a *Festung* ('Fortress') by Hitler in March 1944, meaning it must be held whatever the cost. This is also the case for other Festungen on the Atlantic Wall, such as Dunkirk, Calais, Le Havre and Dieppe. The one in Saint-Malo was cleared at a high price in August and by the beginning of September 1944, the one in Brest had been resisting for more than a month. The human cost of its capture on the 19th gives rise to a new strategy: from now on, the Allies would simply encircle the fortresses, without launching any unnecessary assault, and at the first signs of enemy resistance, the besieged ports would henceforth be 'forgotten', for the most part, until the German capitulation of May 1945 (as would be the case in Lorient, Saint-Nazaire, Royan, etc.). The port of Boulogne is guarded by more than 10,000 men from the Wehrmacht, the Kriegsmarine and the Luftwaffe's anti-aircraft units, under the command of Generalleutnant Ferdinand Heim.

On September 1, as the 3rd Canadian Infantry Division advances towards Boulogne, its compatriot from the 2nd Infantry Division enters Dieppe, from where it had been thrown back into the sea two years earlier. This time, it meets almost no resistance and the French give the Canadian soldiers a wild reception. Two days later, an engineer attached to the Canadian infantry writes in his diary: *"Moved off 3 pm in convoy bound for Dieppe. Passed through Caen. Never seen such devastation. Lisieux completely wiped out."*
[Sept. 4] *"Crossed the Seine 2:30 am. Passed through Rouen at 4 am, badly battered. Arrived Dieppe 2 pm. Plenty of damage. Allotted billets on the sea front in a hotel."*
[Sept. 5] *"Dieppe docks badly bombed, unworkable, except for coasters. Repairing quay today."*
[Sept. 6] *"Carrying out repairs preparatory to coasters arriving."* The latter would arrive with ammunition and gasoline two days later. The soldiers feel welcome and frequently dine with the inhabitants. On September 14 the engineer writes: *"This place livening up again. Evacuees return, business starts booming."*

Five days after the liberation of Dieppe, the Canadians move on to Dunkirk, another symbol of an earlier Allied defeat. In the suburbs, where the fighting ended tragically in 1940, they face a stubborn opposition, immobilizing them for several days. Dunkirk is consequently bypassed as Montgomery sets his sights on the port of Boulogne-sur-Mer. *Operation Wellhit* is to involve the 3rd Canadian Infantry Division and various British armored and artillery units. But in order to invade Boulogne, the troops engaged in the capture of Le Havre (*Operation Astonia*) need to be redeployed. On September 10, the British 49th (West Riding) and 51st (Highland) Infantry Divisions had spearheaded the assault and secured Le Havre and its port in just three days, for only minor losses. In contrast, Allied bombardments, while greatly facilitating operations, destroyed more than 15,000 buildings and killed many civilians.

Metal cap badge of the British Seaforth Highlanders Regiment. Within the 152nd Brigade, 51st (Highland) Division, its 2nd and 5th battalions participated in the night assault on Le Havre on the evening of September 10, where they took 1,000 prisoners.

BOULOGNE-SUR-MER FALLS

Waiting for the green light, the 3rd Canadian Infantry Division stands in front of Boulogne, continuously bombarding the city. During the siege, between September 2 and 16, 1944, the enemy took the time to destroy all of the harbor facilities in order to prevent any future use by the Allies. From the 11th to the 13th, the Germans evacuated nearly 8,000 inhabitants, including Marie and Jules (see page 31), who must once again leave their house once under force.

On the morning of September 17, 700 British Lancaster and Halifax bombers drop several thousand tons of bombs on the German pillboxes at Mont Lambert, which would fall the next day, while the infantry advances to the east. The Canadians take possession of the port and the northern part of the city on September 21. On the 22nd, the Fort de la Crèche is in Allied hands, as well as the small town of Wimereux. It's all too much for Generalleutnant Heim, who surrenders at last to the Canadians. The city is 85% destroyed, with only one house in twenty still habitable, the railroads are also destroyed and there is almost nothing left of the port. However, British engineers quickly set about restoring the latter, which would be operational again by October 12, 1944.

Marie and Jules, French cousins of Major George Ross of the 3rd British Infantry Division (page 178), write in French to his mother, who was born in Boulogne before she emigrated to England: *"If I may, I will first tell you about a letter we received from Georgie. He told us that he landed in Normandy on D-Day and that he has been slightly wounded during the fighting the heroic English and Canadians had to do to overcome the Boche resistance. He added that he has now completely recovered and that he will soon be a father. [...] My dear Gabrielle, you don't need to worry too much about our fate. Admittedly, for the time being, supplies are a real issue, but a large part of the population is going through the same thing. During the Boche occupation, we had severe restrictions, but we were still able to find – but at what cost? - a few supplements to the daily menu. However, the destruction of the road network that preceded our liberation, and which greatly facilitated it, and the raids the Germans carried out before their retreat, made the 'black market' disappear or at least considerably reduced it. For several weeks now, our meat ration has been down to 75 grams per person per week, the butter ration has been 100 grams per month… In short, the regulatory rations are barely enough to ensure survival. Obviously, things will get better in a while, but everything is currently lacking. No potatoes, little coal, no soap, no cloth, well, we are like all the people who moaned for four years under Hitler's boot, having almost nothing. But still, I would like to insist on this to calm your anxiety, thanks to Mary's ingenuity, we are among the privileged, that is, among those who eat properly. The fine Lance/Corporal Ord, who was often in the kitchen when we had dinner, did find our evening meal very lean, which usually consists of soup, potatoes, bread, a cooked apple and a cup of bad malt. But in times of war, you have to be happy with what little you have; the most important thing is to get rid of the Boches. And actually, Mary manages to cook us a small dessert on Sundays. Did she tell you that for Christmas, she made us some pudding without tallow, candied fruit, raisins, or many other ingredients, and yet it tasted excellent to us!*

So you are reassured about our fate. Don't worry either for the money situation. Believe me, from a financial point of view, everything is fine. But we should have thanked you earlier for the solicitude you showed us in May 1940, when you sent us £5, which arrived in the small village of the Loire-Inférieure where we had taken refuge. We didn't have to use it, because I was able to take a few million francs with me, which allowed us to survive until our return in August 1940. During the four years of occupation, the £5, as well as your letter and Reggie's photograph, remained hidden in our bed frame. Indeed, we had to beware of the Boches who, under the slightest pretext, carried out meticulous searches in the houses. [...]

You can stay with us as long as you want, and Mary, believe it or not, will make sure you don't starve. It is surely with emotion that you will go back to Boulogne, so terribly affected by the four years of war. It is the city that has experienced the most aerial bombardments. Those of May and June 15, 1944 were appalling. Entire streets were destroyed by torpedoes and incendiary bombs. And the fighting that preceded our liberation considerably multiplied the ruins. In the cemeteries, whether in the east, Capécure or Saint-Pierre, the graves of the victims of raids are numerous. Sure, we paid our toll in the war, but most of the people of Boulogne, while mourning the dead, still love the British, and the Boches know it well. What a painful sight to watch the German air formations in September and October 1940 that were going to pound London, Coventry, Birmingham... But the old England, while everything was crumbling around it, resisted splendidly, and it is, in large part, thanks to its indomitable courage that we are free. And it is in all sincerity that we shout: 'England for ever!'

As soon as we were free, our English friends cleared our streets of rubble, repaired the sewers, and restored the port. It will take years to rebuild Boulogne, but life is already picking up again. Our population, which at the time of the siege had fallen to only a few thousand, is now back to 18,000 people. The British military authorities will return the harbor to civilian activity, and soon, I hope, trade with England will resume. At first, business will be slow, as the Germans blew up a large part of the docks and destroyed the cranes and most port facilities. I was talking to you earlier about Lance/Corporal Ord. As we say in French, he is 'brave', but his education has been somewhat neglected. He began his military career at the age of 12, and has since lived among soldiers. Without being impolite, he is 'informal', and has certain sense of humor. He was in the 8th Army of Marshal Montgomery, and it was hard for him to leave Boulogne. I will give the pen to Mary, I apologize for being so talkative, but I took such pleasure in writing to you, I hope you will forgive me. [...] Jules.

My dear Gaby, Georgie, in his last letter, told me about himself what you had already told me. He still misses being with his boys at the front, but he has done his part and must now dedicate himself to helping his country in a completely different role. He was kind enough to add a small photo to remind us of his friendly face. However, I think he looks tired. The hard work in the months following the D-Day invasion left its mark on him. To all these valiant warriors we must wish an early end to this horrible war, so that they can find in a calm and peaceful life the desire to live and a well-earned rest. [...] We still need many things, but we manage to take advantage of everything and survive with ingenuity. When after four years, some gray coats really become too worn out, we turn them over and have a brand-new gray tartan one, a little light perhaps, but still very presentable. Another old coat was used to make comfortable slippers for each family member, which are much more durable than the ones that can be obtained commercially. Underwear is no longer 'inviting' so wives who have fickle husbands can sleep soundly as these gentlemen would not dare to take off their clothes. Where are the silk pajamas of yesteryear? Joking aside, we will be happy to find a few meters of flannel one day, and some good soap to wash them. [...]

Yes Gaby, we would certainly have found great comfort in you, and our life would have been easier, but it seems to me that our duty was to remain in our invaded country and suffer with our own to deserve our liberation. It has now been done and we must regain courage and work hard to earn that peace. The horrible Boches, who martyred so many men and women, gouging their eyes out, tearing their nails out, mutilating them, burying them alive, were indeed of the same race as those of 1914. They massacred entire villages in France these thugs!

Jeanne is working for the Davignons again. Mr. Davignon, the only survivor of the truck, is a frightening sight to see. His wife and daughter were burned alive in a truck hit by phosphorus shells; what a tragedy for this poor man. Jeanne says he looks like a skinned rabbit. He no longer has eyelids, eyelashes or hair; he was given grafts to restore a human face. My aunt Adele is still in Campagne-lès-Hesdin, but she should come back soon. I wonder how she will be able to live in her damaged house... Fernand was also the victim of a Boche and his mother could not bear her misfortune. That's very sad! The house they had built is safe though. [...] Mary."

On July 10, 1947, the city of Boulogne-sur-Mer will be awarded the Legion of Honor for the suffering it endured throughout the Second World War.

THE BRITISH LIBERATE THE NORTH

Allied soldiers enjoy a warm welcome in the villages they pass through, including Alan, a British Trooper in the 49th Royal Tank Regiment. Attached to the 79th Armoured Division, his regiment specializes in night combat, having fixed very powerful lights (called 'artificial moonlight') on the turrets of their Grant tanks. In September 1944, Alan has only been in France for three weeks, but he seems to feel at home in this country. He writes to a friend: *"Glad you offer condolences on the terrible state of the beer supplies here. It is pretty grim. All we can get is some weird concoction they call Cognac, but isn't. As it is, they charge exorbitant prices and issue about a thimble full. The first time I got the stuff I was rather amazed, and, murmuring 'here's how' to Ted, I quaffed it back. I regretted it. It was like sulfuric acid. My throat felt as if I'd swallowed a coal and I thought I'd never be able to get the old vocal chords to function again. The top of my head lifted a good three inches. My!! Never again!! Water with it after that. The stuff they sell at the* George & Gloucester *under the misleading appellation of whisky has nothing on it. [...]*

Actually, these 'little Mademoiselles' you mention seem rather elusive; they exist all right, in places, but having tackled one I became rather chary of repeating the performance. I stooged along to H...t [self-censored] for Len (you know, the bloke who's engaged to A. A.?) and between us we produced some rather passable French. Len's French consists of 'Voulez-vous promenade [sic] avec moi ce soir Mam'selle?' which he repeated at convenient intervals. And mine, oh I just say 'je ne comprends pas' and between us we get on all right. The men aren't so bad, but the girls, oh my!! They can't get the words out fast enough. I just look intelligent and say 'oui, oui'; That sort of diplomacy has its points. Other blokes think actions speak louder than words."

Cecil Newton is an English tank crewman in B Squadron, 4th/7th Royal Dragoon Guards. His Sherman tank was one of the first on Gold Beach, before it crossed through Normandy to Flers. He experienced violent battles in Verrières and Tilly-sur-Seulles, before crossing the Seine on August 27, attached to the 43rd (Wessex) Division. Their advance is now so fast that the troopers joke the initials BLA, standing for 'British Liberation Army', actually mean 'Burma Looms Ahead'.

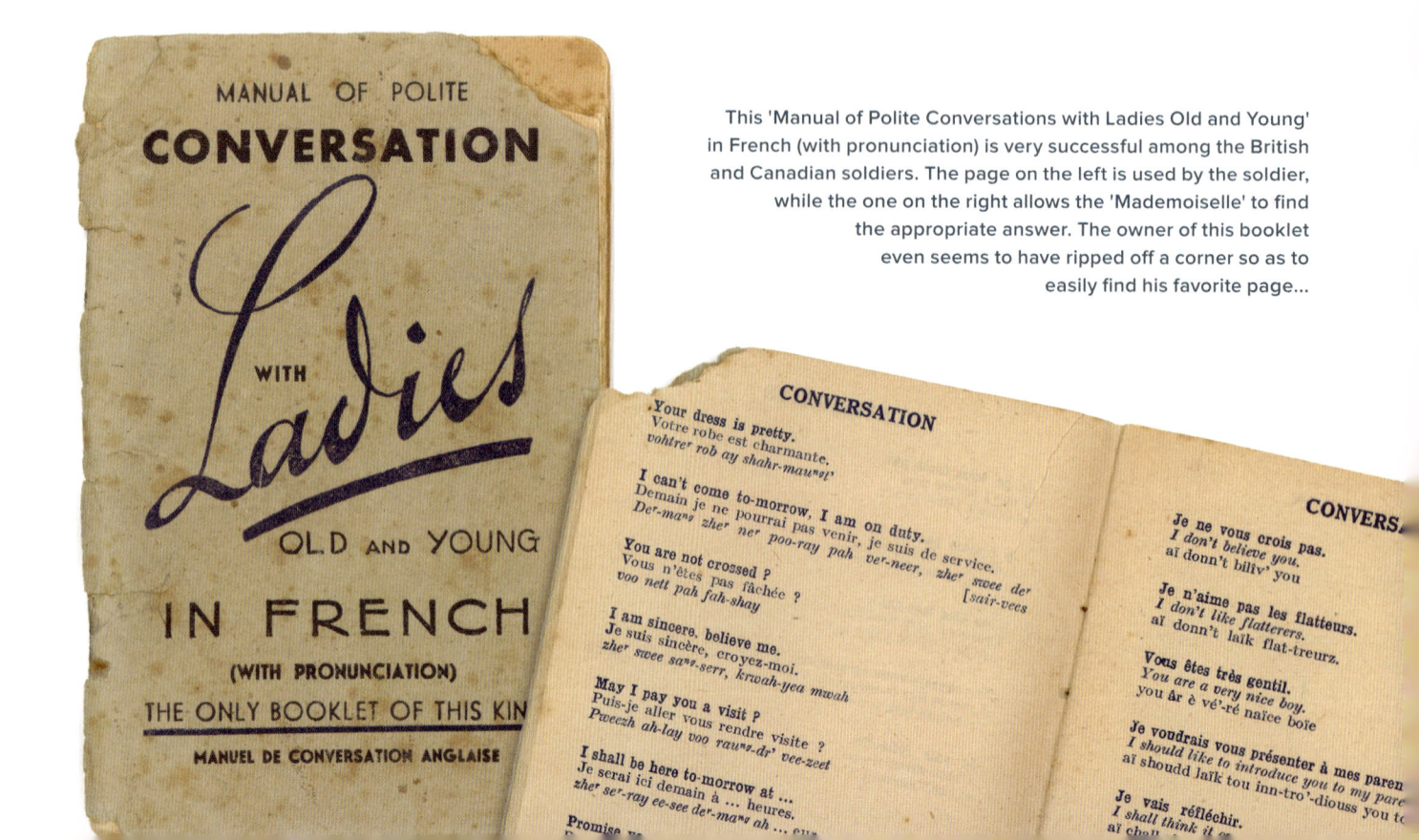

This 'Manual of Polite Conversations with Ladies Old and Young' in French (with pronunciation) is very successful among the British and Canadian soldiers. The page on the left is used by the soldier, while the one on the right allows the 'Mademoiselle' to find the appropriate answer. The owner of this booklet even seems to have ripped off a corner so as to easily find his favorite page...

V - VICTORY BY CHRISTMAS? LATE 1944

On September 2, Cecil is at the gates of Lille. He writes home: *"At the moment of writing I am in an orchard enjoying a spot of rest and sunshine. Since I last wrote to you the welcome we have been having has been very warm and sincere. The people wave their flags, which seem to have been brought out from the blue. They have most likely been made and hidden for the great day. It is a common sight to see people weeping and singing their National Anthem on top of their voices. If we stop food and flowers appear from everywhere, much to our delight. In one small village the female population mobbed us and insisted on kissing the whole crew including the commander. In another place an old lady had tea already waiting for us and I had my photo taken with her pouring out a cup with the majority of the small place clustered around. We were lucky this morning; we stopped by a house for the night and lo-and-behold a cup of coffee was awaiting us when we woke up, then eggs – fifteen of them – were brought and bread and butter for our breakfast. More coffee mid-day then a terrific plate of chips to help our lunch along."*

The next day, Cecil's Sherman tank is the very first to enter Lille. As the houses' windows open wide, the inhabitants take to the streets to greet the tanks with their handkerchiefs.

When the column of tanks stops on the main square, in front of the City Hall, the crowd goes wild. The young girls bring bottles of wine and champagne to the crews, while members of the underground climb on the tanks, emptying their weapons into the air. But the Germans aren't far away and without infantry to support them, Cecil and his comrades have no choice but to withdraw for the night. The next morning, his Sherman is ordered to carry out a reconnaissance to the south-east of Lille, in search of retreating German units.

Cecil's tank, the first to enter Lille, and the French crowd waving flags.

This French flag, hastily sewn together for the liberation, was simply nailed to a wooden rod.

In the main square outside Lille City Hall. Cecil is indicated by the small white arrow. According to him, the civilian standing next to Cecil was "having his own private disco".

In his memoirs *A Trooper's Tale*, Cecil tells a funny anecdote about this morning: *"Whilst we were stationary, unknown to me, two French refugees were engaged in conversation with the Troop Leader who was speaking to them from his position in the turret hatchway. Later I learnt that they told him that the farm buildings at the other end of the track were occupied by a platoon of German infantry. With time to spare and as I wanted to relieve myself, I peed into an empty wine bottle already part full from previous use, replaced the cork and opened the small hatch which was in the turret wall behind the gunner/operators seat, to push it out. Instead of falling to the ground it was gently taken from my grasp. I was indeed surprised and looking out of the periscope, saw the two refugees walking down the lane, one of them showing to his admiring comrade the present the British had given him for the information he had told the tank commander!"*

Lille is completely liberated on September 4. Cecil and his unit will continue to advance northward and participate in *Operation Market Garden*, in Holland. In November, near a farm in Tripsrath (Germany), his Sherman will be struck by an anti-tank weapon, wounding Cecil in the left leg. Trying to escape through the hatch, he'll then be shot in the back by a German soldier. Recovered by a comrade at the foot of the burning tank, Cecil would hold out all day, defended by the British infantry keeping the enemy at bay.

Cecil will survive the war, but will lose many friends. His brother will be shot dead on April 9, 1945 by two SS soldiers pretending to surrender, as he leaves his reconnaissance vehicle to take them prisoners.

Patch of the 43rd (Wessex) British Division to which the 4th/7th Dragoon Guards was then attached.

Cecil Newton's crew at Brunssum (Netherlands), ready to enter Germany, just before Cecil's injury in Tripsrath.

From left to right, Cecil and Ted Hoare in the foreground, Arthur Kingsbury and Ken Knowles on the tank, which will be destroyed shortly afterwards. Note its camouflage to blend in with the forest.

THE PROBLEM OF ANTWERP

On September 2, the 1st US Army enters Belgium near Chimay and drives rapidly towards Liege. The British liberate Brussels without much difficulty the next evening, with the help of Belgian soldiers from the Piron Brigade. On September 4, Antwerp is the Allies' next objective. Europe's second largest harbor could finally solve the issue of the long supply line that still runs from Normandy to Germany's borders. Thanks to the actions of the Belgian Resistance's Witte Brigade, the port facilities aren't destroyed by the Germans and 5,000 enemy soldiers are also captured there, held in the city's zoo as the Allies don't know where to keep them.

Harold Major is a Squadron Quartermaster Sergeant (SQMS) in the Royal Electrical and Mechanical Engineers, in a workshop of the British 11th Armoured Division. He is hailed as a hero in Antwerp, after a 350-mile drive in six days. He most likely took the photographs on the right himself, capturing on film the warm welcome given to the British tanks and soldiers in the city. Unfortunately, two days later, the enemy resistance would be too strong and the 11th Armoured would fail in its attempt to create a bridgehead on the Albert Canal. The area will finally be secured on September 12.

A selection of Harold Major's belongings, including a picture of him in England, his paycheck, two fiber identity discs (British dog tags, different from the American stainless steel and rectangular ones), a memo with some practical sentences in French, and at the bottom right an un-stitched badge of the 11th Armoured Division.

However, the Allies will soon realize that Antwerp is of no use until the whole Scheldt Estuary is under their control. The Germans have dug in along the banks and are monitoring all maritime accesses west of Antwerp from the Beveland Peninsula north of the Scheldt, the Breskens Pocket to the south, and the surrounding islands. Unfortunately for Antwerp, the Allies want to get to Berlin as soon as possible, and *Operation Market Garden* is therefore launched in the Netherlands in mid-September. According to Montgomery, the harbors of Dieppe, Boulogne and Calais should be enough to supply the troops. Meanwhile, the Germans would consolidate their defenses in the Scheldt and flood the estuary.

When *Market Garden* eventually turns out to be a failure, the Allies will finally understand, albeit too late, the importance of clearing the estuary to make the port of Antwerp operational. Once again, the Allies rely on the Canadians to fulfill this mission: the 3rd Infantry Division will take charge of the Breskens Pocket to the south (*Operation Switchback*), while to the north, the 2nd Infantry Division will clear the Beveland Peninsula (*Operation Vitality*), supported to the east by the 4th Armoured Division driving north towards Holland. Finally, the 2nd Division will invade Walcheren Island, crossing east from Beveland, while the commandos of the 4th Special Service Brigade and British soldiers of the 52nd (Lowland) Division will land south and west of the island, at Flushing and Westkapelle (*Operation Infatuate*).

After the heavy losses sustained in Normandy, the state of the remaining Canadian troops is alarming. Their promise only to send volunteers overseas weighs heavily on units that have no choice but to give their cooks a rifle and take them to the front line. From October 2, amphibious assaults and open ground charges multiply on the various small 'islands' that appeared in the flooded areas. The Germans gradually withdraw, covered by snipers and pre-set artillery barrages on the few roads which are still passable. They leave behind a large number of land and sea mines for the Canadians, slugging forward inch by inch under heavy rain. Every landing, every canal crossing, every attack across the fields results in terrific casualties. With their mud-soaked clothes literally rotting on their bruised bodies, the Canadians are truly exhausted.

BLACK FRIDAY

Established in 1862, the Black Watch is the oldest regiment in the Highlands of Canada. It mobilized only one battalion on September 1, 1939, participating with the 2nd Canadian Infantry Division in the Dieppe Raid, with the result we now know. Tragedy struck its members even before the operation, as a grenade accident aboard HMS *Duke of Wellington* had already claimed several lives en route to the coast. The misfortune continued in Normandy, with the 1st Battalion of the Black Watch holding the sad record for the highest number of casualties of any Canadian infantry battalion in Europe. During the battle of Verrières Ridge on July 25, the Waffen SS reduced a Black Watch attack force to almost nothing: of the 325 men that charged the Germans, only 15 returned. On October 13, 1944, in the battle for the Scheldt Estuary, the Black Watch will experience another terrible day, which will go down in history as 'Black Friday'.

The 2nd Division is ordered to clean up the north of Antwerp and fight their way to the Beveland Peninsula. On October 8, a German counter-attack is repelled by Canadians determined not to give up their hard-won ground, forcing the enemy to take refuge on a railway line over an embankment, the track of which links the mainland and the Beveland Peninsula to Walcheren Island. Eager to put this battle to an end, and without waiting for the expected reinforcements from the British 52nd (Lowland) Division and the American 104th Infantry Division (then under Canadian command), Montgomery launches *Operation Angus* with tired infantry battalions, supported by armored and artillery units lacking ammunition.

The Black Watch is tasked with capturing Korteven (south of Bergen-op-Zoom), thus isolating the Beveland isthmus from the continent. Ironically for this battalion, which already has a reputation for being cursed, the area is nicknamed 'the coffin' due to its appearance on topographic maps. At 6:15 am, the Black Watch sets off, marching through a mile of open beet fields to attack the German position. From the top of its embankment, the enemy immediately slaughters the Canadians below. The first two waves are decimated and only the third, in the afternoon, reaches its objective thanks to the support of Wasp Flame-Thrower Carriers. The losses are heavy. A lieutenant writes to his father from the hospital: *"We formed up behind a dike and advanced over open ground. When we got practically to our objective – 600 yards away – the machine-guns and mortars became too hot and we began to drop right and left. Somehow a few managed to get to the objective. Those of us who were hit lay out in an open field with no cover... The battalion seems to have horrible shows periodically and this was one of them."* The Allies will have to evacuate the wounded at night, instead of consolidating the captured objectives.

V - VICTORY BY CHRISTMAS? LATE 1944

This officer of the Black Watch (Royal Highland Regiment) of Canada at rest in the fall of 1944 wears a heavy Canadian wool coat and a traditional Glengarry bonnet.

The Glengarry is worn in regiments originating from Scotland and the Highlands (a mountainous region geographically and historically separated from the rest of the country). For the Black Watch regiment, the bonnet is a very dark shade of blue, with a small red toorie and black ribbons hanging down behind. On the left side is attached the metal badge of the regiment.

From 1939 onwards, the Tam O'Shanters and Balmorals are generally worn with the field uniform, but Glengarries are still used for parades and rest. Those who wish to wear it on the field must pay for it themselves, but it's still highly appreciated by officers, certain units, and Pipers (bagpipe players).

225

Light Pack belonging to a Canadian soldier named Bailey, of the Calgary Highlanders (who closely followed the Black Watch on 'Black Friday'), and an MKII helmet with its original net.

Shortly after midnight, the Black Watch is ordered to retreat. *Operation Angus* is a failure. The battalion has lost its four company commanders, all experienced and well respected, who were killed along with fifty-six other men. Twenty-seven Canadians were taken prisoner and eighty-nine others wounded. One of the 90-man companies now has only four able-bodied men left.

Combat in the area would last for several more days, until the reinforcements expected by Montgomery finally arrive. Despite its condition, the Black Watch would still fight with the 2nd Infantry Division through South Beveland, and even launch the first assault on Walcheren Island on October 31. However, it'll be brutally pushed back when trying to cross the causeway. Once the Breskens Pocket to the south was liberated for the most part, the 155th British Brigade (composed of battalions from the King's Own Scottish Borderers and the Royal Scots) will land at Vlissingen, while the British, Belgian and Norwegian commandos will take Westkapelle on the morning of November 1 after violent street fighting. The island's capital, Middelburg, will fall on November 6. In six weeks, the Allies would report 12,873 killed, wounded and missing, half of whom are Canadian. It would take an additional three weeks to clear the estuary and port of the mines left by the Germans, before the first Allied ship can at last unload its precious cargo in Antwerp on November 29, 1944. However, the area still wouldn't be safe...

V-1 flying bomb in the London skies, 1944.

FLYING BOMBS

The first cruise missile in history is catapulted from launch ramps, flies on autopilot at high speed, then crashes on its target once the fuel is cut off. Since June 13, 1944 and its first hit on London, the formidable German V1 rocket has been fired at a rate of about 100 per day from the Dutch and northern French coasts. It takes its name from *Vergeltungswaffe 1*, or 'Revenge Weapon 1', and represents the last hope of the German soldiers who die while waiting for the Führer's new weapons to bring them victory. When not intercepted by experienced pilots, these 'flying bombs' cause frightening damage. An English family, who'd just learned of the death of their son Sidney in the war, writes in July 1944: *"It's too dangerous here, with all these bombs flying about, the damage is terrible. I've seen forty houses destroyed by one bomb, I was there in two minutes after it had happened rendering what assistance I could."* From October onwards, the Germans would use V1 rockets on Antwerp and the rest of Belgium.

However, Germany has now developed an even more destructive bomb and on September 8, 1944, it launches its first V2 rocket. This is the first long-range guided missile in history, and the first rocket to ever reach the limit between the Earth's atmosphere and space. Flying at the impressive speed of 3,580 mph, it's impossible to shoot down. This 45-foot long missile will cause more than 9,000 deaths, mainly in London (which will receive 1,350 of these bombs), Liege and Antwerp. The latter, whose harbor has just resumed its activity, is naturally a prime target for the enemy and 561 soldiers and civilians would die there on December 16, 1944, when a V2 rocket hits a cinema.

V - VICTORY BY CHRISTMAS? LATE 1944

An American in a railway transport battalion, bringing equipment from the harbor to the front lines, writes from Antwerp to a former co-worker. He's already experienced the terrible V1 flying bombs (also known as 'Buzz Bombs' and 'Robot Bombs') in France, Belgium and Luxembourg, and has since witnessed the ghastly aftermath of the V2s: *"Men of your type are what the countries over here could use after this war is ended. They will need men that can perform miracles to reconstruct the ruins caused by war. Some cities are completely demolished, others partially, and still others untouched. I have seen the German robot bombs doing their dirty work and also aerial bombs. They are both plenty nasty and destructive. The worst bomb they have seems to be the V2 which is also the flying type that you most likely have read about. There is no warning of its coming whatsoever. The only thing that can be heard is the whistling of its descent and if a person hears that, it is too bad as it is too late to get out of its way. The concussion of this bomb is terrific and carries for many blocks. One happened to hit around four blocks from us one night and it not only blew all the windows out of the place but rocked the whole building. Old Adolph doesn't spare the TNT in those babies."*

Nevertheless, the V1 and V2, as well as the Me262 jet aircraft and the new XXI and XXIII submarines won't change the course of the war. Although these 'miracle weapons' would come too late to save the Reich, 2,448 V1 bombs will still strike Antwerp before the Allies take possession of the last launch site in the Netherlands, in late March 1945. Hundreds of Nazi scientists who worked on the V2 rockets would be captured a few weeks later before being taken to the United States in order to develop new inter-continental weapons, as well as the American space program (*Operation Paperclip*). The Red Army will also employ former Nazi technicians with the same goal (*Operation Osoaviakhim*).

A British tank crewman writes in September 1944: *"The buzz bombs must have stopped altogether now that we have taken possession of the French coast. Good job isn't it? Wonder what the Germans are going to use for propaganda now. We came across a terrific amount of their leaflets. Probably think they can break our morale. What a hope. One of his leaflets is headed 'Where will Russia stop!' and we all laugh at that one cause we sorta think he would like to know the answer to that one. It certainly worries him more than it does us. We find that this stuff makes excellent toilet paper."*

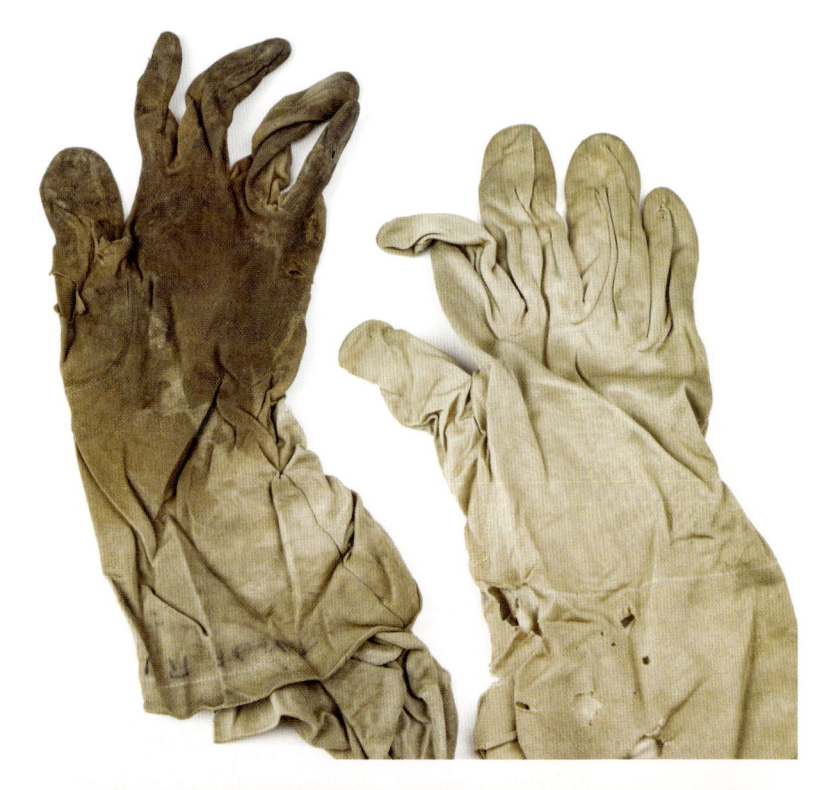

Gloves belonging to Royal Air Force Sergeant Ronald James Taylor. Originally from Durham, UK, he was a member of the Volunteer Reserve and joined 467 Squadron as a flight engineer. Its crew was mainly Australian.

On Friday, July 7, 1944, his Avro Lancaster type I took part in its fourth mission: the bombing of a V1 flying bomb storage site in Saint-Leu-d'Esserent (Oise). In total, 208 Lancasters and 13 Mosquitos from 13 different squadrons were to destroy the tunnel entrances, which before the war had been used to grow mushrooms. The attack was successful: all of the tunnel entrances were blocked due to the landslide caused by the bombardment and the missiles were therefore inaccessible. However, German night fighters shot down twenty-nine Lancasters and two Mosquitos, including Sergeant Taylor's plane, which crashed at Le Grand Montagny in Saint-Germer-de-Fly (12 miles west of Beauvais). Of the eight crew members, only two were able to bail out and escape. Sergeant Taylor is now buried in the French national cemetery of Beauvais-Marissel with the other airmen killed that night. These gloves were sent back to his family after his death. At 20, Ronald was the youngest member of his bomber crew.

OPERATION DRAGOON

As the Normandy front collapses, the 7th US Army leaves the Italian Front to land in Provence, alongside the 1st French Army. They would soon drive up the Rhone Valley, in hot pursuit of the German 19. Armee seeking refuge behind the Siegfried Line.

This second landing in France falls on General Patch's shoulders, commander of the 7th US Army, composed of experienced units which had just been withdrawn from Italy. Eleven divisions are to take part, more than half of which are French. Initially supposed to take place at the same time as *Operation Overlord*, *Operation Anvil* was postponed due to the lack of landing craft. The operation is eventually named *Dragoon*, and is scheduled for August 15, 1944, in Provence (South of France). However, preliminary operations actually begin the day before. French troops of the African commandos, assisted by American special forces, are ordered to neutralize the coastal batteries at Cap Nègre, Canadel Beach and Pointe de l'Escquillon. At the same time, American paratroopers (codenamed 'Rugby Force') are dropped inland to prevent any German reinforcements. Meanwhile, the US VI Corps ('Kodak Force') is on its way to the beaches…

THE LANDING

Joe is a New Yorker of Italian origin serving in the 179th Regiment, 45th Infantry Division (the regiment's actions at Anzio can be seen on page 140), and lands in Provence on D-Day, with the first wave. As part of 'Delta Force', the 45th Division sets foot on La Nartelle Beach at Sainte-Maxime, between the American 3rd Infantry Division ('Alpha Force') on its left at Cavalaire and Saint-Tropez, and the 36th Infantry Division ('Camel Force') on its right at Saint-Raphaël. This is now its fourth amphibious operation and it's a great success: losses are very low and the weak enemy opposition is quickly wiped out by the US Navy's guns. All in all, the Allies sustain only 95 killed and 400 wounded. The men rapidly advance inland to capture the Maures Plains and link up with the 1st Special Service Force.

The next day, the French ('Garbo Force') finally arrive on their own soil. General de Lattre de Tassigny's Armée B has just merged with the former French Expeditionary Force in Italy (Armée A) to become the 1re Armée française, with 256,000 men. From D+1 to D+9, 65,000 of them and nearly 10,000 vehicles will land in two waves, gradually reinforced by large numbers of available reserve and numerous French Forces of the Interior (FFI). While the Americans progress towards Avignon and Grenoble, French forces liberate the ports of Toulon on August 24 and Marseille on August 28, a month ahead of schedule. These cities cost the French 5,000 men, but are essential for the landing of new troops and equipment. The German divisions of Heeresgruppe G, which are understaffed and had come to the South to recover from the heavy fighting in Normandy, are taken by surprise and quickly withdraw to the northeast. Joe's 45th US Division pushes in a northwest direction from Barjols, crosses the Durance River, and branches off towards Sisteron and Gap. On August 23, it enters Grenoble, already empty of any enemy occupation. The French underground had carried out high quality harassment work and so the German retreat allowed an unexpected advance with minimal losses. Indeed, Grenoble had been a D+90 objective, but is occupied by the Americans barely a week after *Dragoon*. The warm welcome from the French and an easy drive north would lead to the nickname 'the champagne campaign', as fighting is relatively rare and the celebrations are omnipresent.

V - VICTORY BY CHRISTMAS? LATE 1944

M1 helmet dated autumn 1943 and found in Saint-Paulien (near Le Puy-en-Velay) in August 1944, after the passage of American GMC trucks. It has since spent sixty-five years in an attic. The liner, normally present inside the steel shell, is unfortunately absent here.

Although the region was liberated by the 1st French Armoured Division and the Resistance, this helmet seems to have belonged to a GI: the laundry number (first letter of the soldier's name and four last digits of his serial number) painted inside the shell is a typically American practice. Unfortunately, it's not enough to properly identify its owner.

Joe is the first GI to arrive at a small village north of Grenoble. He writes to his uncle and aunt on August 29, 1944: *"I'm now somewhere in France. The people are nice to us and the underground has helped us a great deal. I really have seen a good part of the world so far. My buddy and I were the first soldiers to enter a small town here in France. The people came running and cheering us. They said we are the first Americans to enter the town and the first American soldiers they saw. We had a big dinner and wine. Boy the girls are really OK here. I'll tell Mom all that I can about it and she will tell you. Yes Mom is doing all she can toward the war effort! [...] Give my Love to everyone at home and I miss everyone very much. [...] Joe."*

On September 12, in Dijon, they will join forces with the American 3rd Army, coming all the way from Brittany. They will then head for Belfort and take the well-defended city of Epinal on the 24th. There, Joe and his fellow GIs would read a painted sign on a bridge, pointing in two opposite directions: *"St. Tropez, 430 miles; Berlin, 430 miles"*. In only a month, *Operation Dragoon* would liberate half of France and trap 150,000 Germans.

THE BLACK DEVILS

William, from Los Angeles, has been a member of the elite 1st Special Service Force since its formation in 1942. A bi-national unit composed of American and Canadian commandos, the names of the two countries appear on the patch, representing the red tip of a spear. They're the forefathers of today's special forces, trained in jumping from planes and fighting on skis... Despite being only 1,800 men strong, the unit would kill and wound more than 12,000 Germans and take 7,000 prisoners. William and his comrades have already proved their worth in Italy alongside the 36th 'Texas' Division, seizing the mountains of La Difensa and La Remetanea (protecting the Gustav Line) in December 1943, which cost them 77% of their men. In Anzio, they fought for ninety-nine consecutive days, terrorizing the Germans: the commandos darkened their faces for their night operations, earning themselves the nickname, the 'Black Devils'. As they then had a reputation to maintain, they carried stickers representing their patch and the warning *"The worst is still to come"* (in German), to stick on their victims' foreheads.

On August 14, 1944, the Black Devils land on the islands of Port-Cros and Le Levant, between Toulon and Saint-Tropez, and take the forts occupied by the Germans in just two days. On the 22nd, they are attached to the 1st Airborne Task Force, created for *Operation Dragoon*, and move up the French Riviera with the paratroopers to the Italian border (while the rest of the 7th US Army pushes northward). The 1st Special Service Force will liberate Menton on September 8, after violent engagements alongside the French Resistance.

William writes to his parents on September 5: *"Don't imagine you are a bit surprised to find me in France, as you know the Force couldn't stay out of this, the largest show. [...] The change from Italy to France was and is very favorable. The country here is beautiful. Even in so short a time, have seen many beautiful sights, and many places which I had always wanted and hoped I would be able to visit. This country is so much cleaner than Italy, and the people are so friendly, and so happy to see, finally, the arrival of the American troops. So all in all, it is very pleasant. Our bivouac area is the nicest we have ever had. Once again indoors and more than comfortable. I have a cot with a nice thick mattress, sleeping among beautiful flowers. We are keeping busy and are allowed little time for scouting around, although I imagine soon they will be more generous with the pass privileges. Seems that there is a different attitude on the part of the Allied Governments concerning the French than the Italians, which can be understood, as the French are a liberated people, the Italians a conquered people. They seem to want to keep the majority of American Military off the streets, so they will do as little damage as possible. Not that they go around wrecking everything, but you can imagine the number of troops that could be let wander through these beautiful towns all at once. Maybe they learned a lesson in Italy. As I say, they may let things cool down a bit before they become any more generous with the pass privileges. It was a joyous welcome we had in all our trips through this section. From our several bits of conversation with the people here – they have been waiting for a long long time for the present situation. The Maquis – The Free French* [the 'Maquis' or underground, is actually made of FFIs, not Free French Forces] *really did a job, and no doubt made it possible for the rapid advance which the troops have made. Have had several good talks with a member of the Maquis and have learned much about the events leading up to all this."*

The Black Devils will occupy defensive positions in front of the Italian border for a few weeks. On November 23, 1944, the 1st Airborne Task Force will be disbanded and its commander, Major-General Robert T. Frederick (who had also led the 1st Special Service Force), will be asked to head the 45th Infantry Division. He'll be wounded nine times during the war! Having lost too many men, the 1st Special Service Force will also be broken up on December 5, 1944 and its members sent as elite replacements to American or Canadian Airborne units or to the Rangers. An American member of the 1st SSF remembers the end of it: *"This was the day I saw some of the toughest S.O.B.s ever break down in tears. As the Canadians pulled out, some of us Americans ran alongside and behind the trucks for a mile with tears in our eyes."*

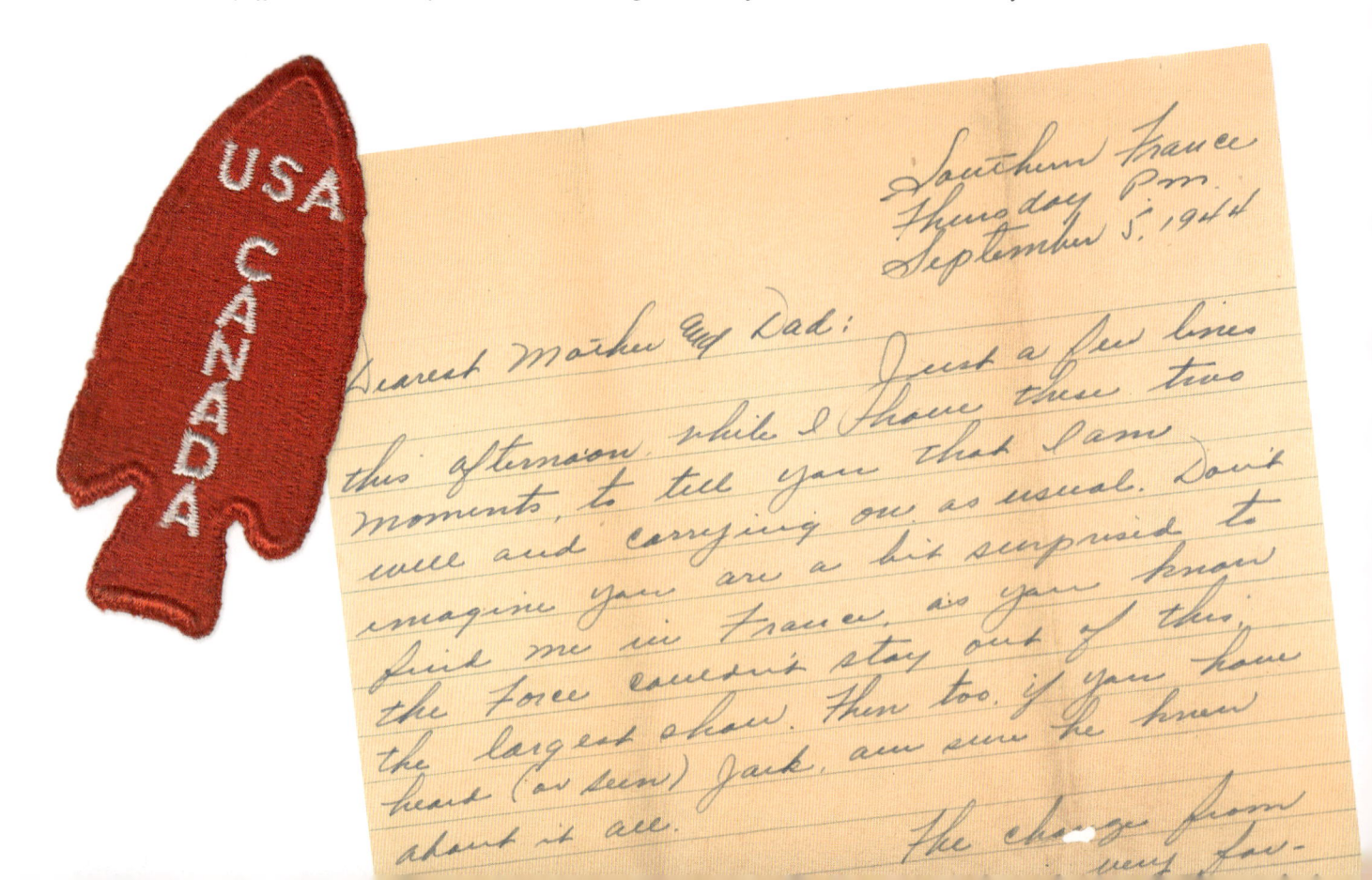

V - VICTORY BY CHRISTMAS? LATE 1944

A booklet published in London to inform English-speaking soldiers and civilians about the actions of the underground in support of Allied operations. Its cover features the Cross of Lorraine and the order "Forward Maquis!". The Maquis were particularly active in Provence and were responsible for ambushing the fleeing Germans and holding the bridges to facilitate the Allied advance.

'BUD' JUMPS ON PROVENCE

We last read about Ernest 'Bud' Siegel and the 509th Parachute Infantry Battalion when they were in Italy, on a mission behind enemy lines (page 118). On July 27, 1944, Bud was promoted to Captain and put in command of A Company. On August 15, Bud is jumpmaster in the very first plane of the main assault on Drop Zone C, with Le Muy as his objective. He would recount his mission many years later: *"This was my first combat mission as A Company C.O. and I wanted our company to do a job we could be proud of. This mission had better planning than any mission since the initial invasion of North Africa by our battalion. The battalion mission was to secure the area to facilitate the seaborne forces and the glider wave coming in the next morning. Since A Company was chosen to lead the invasion, I had my headquarters section with communications in the lead plane. I wanted to be the first to jump and that was the way the jump came out. We were taking off from a field near Grosseto [Follonica, Tuscany], Italy. I spoke to Colonel Schmidt who was to be the lead plane pilot. He assured me he would land me next to the woodshed I was planning to make our first headquarters. There was no discernible flak or ground fire when we went out the door. A short drop and I hung up in a tree about twenty feet from the ground. I was able to bounce myself down to a stand-up landing and proceeded to pick up our stick. We were able to regroup within the first half hour and I was waiting for Edward F. Wojick to bring up the large radio which would connect us with battalion HQ and the other companies. Wojick said he could not find the equipment canister with the big radio. I was unhappy and told him not to come back until he found it. Little did I know that I wouldn't see him for over three weeks.*

Bud (left), checking the parachute of one of his men before the jump on August 15. They are about to board the C-47 in the background. Note the helmets and jump jackets are camouflaged with paint, the rubber band around the helmet instead of the usual net, the 'Mae West' life jackets in case of landing on water and the American flag sewn to the sleeve.

By dawn we were on top of a high hill overlooking Le Muy. We had advanced some patrols on the road into Le Muy, we had secured the bridge which was part of our mission. I was feeling pretty smug about securing the bridge and having patrols on their way to Le Muy when Colonel Yarborough came up behind me. He formally asked 'Captain, what are your plans to attack?' My plans were nebulous since I had no idea whether there were Jerries in Le Muy or not. The question answered itself when the patrol sent into Le Muy reported on the walkie talkie that there was a formation of Germans marching northward into Le Muy. We decided we were in an excellent position to trap them. Lt. Kenneth Shaker sent a patrol to the north end of the town. They had set up an O.P. in a small farmhouse a few hundred yards from the one road going through the village. We had bad communications with them and we were using runners as messengers. Lt. Hoyt Livingston told me he would get Lt. Sol Weber's communication section to string wire. I suggested that he tap into the local phone wire and put a hand set with our forward Observation Post. He was able to accomplish this within a half hour.

All this time a column of German infantry and horse drawn equipment was marching through Le Muy and turning past our forward command post. The light machine guns and mortars were deployed where they could rake the road. We issued orders to all units to hold fire until ordered. Our northern patrol was along the road waiting for the columns to reach them. The Germans became suspicious and opened fire into the woods. The order was given to open fire and all hell broke loose. The German column broke up.

Some ran to a marshy area forward of our position and another group took up a position in a farmhouse near our O.P. and set up a machine gun in the attic. The German group in the tall grass started to fire over our heads. I turned around to yell at the guys behind me to keep their heads down. Behind me were Colonel Yaarborough and Maj. Gen. Walker. I learned that he had elements of the 45th Division ready as soon as we had secured Le Muy. We captured the remaining column and they were marched to the rear. We moved into Le Muy and the 45th Division went forward. We regrouped and set up a field camp on the outskirts. It was early nightfall by that time. Rumors were that Capt. Miller's whole lead plane had jumped over the water near the beach and none had been heard of."

A few days later, at 8 pm on August 21, he'll set out to attack the San Peyre hill southwest of Cannes. He'll pass through the castle of La Napoule in reconnaissance with Lieutenant Fraizer and sustain two heavy artillery shellings. Bud will be wounded again (he was hit by a shell fragment in the "family jewels" at the Anzio Beachhead), this time by shrapnel in the shoulder, and will have no choice but to be evacuated and taken to the hospital. However, the paratroopers will still manage to return to the Allied lines at 11 pm, and allow the assault to be launched the next day at 6 am. Siegel's A Company will take the hill an hour and a half later, and continue the fight towards Cannes.

Bud will return to his company again for one last heroic action... To be continued on page 279.

Bud, shortly after being wounded in Provence, and his sister, a nurse in the US Army in England.

His cap bears the captain bars, and his M-42 paratrooper jacket still has the holes caused by the shrapnel received in the shoulder near Cannes, Southern France.

The tear is visible on his right shoulder, just above the patch on his sister's sleeve.

PAUL L. WILLIAMS

General, IX Troop Carrier Command

General Paul Williams organizes the transport of paratroopers to the front.
He's been in charge of logistics for all the airborne invasions thus far, and the one in Southern France is a real success.
He'll next work on a new large-scale mission, *Operation Market Garden*, in the Netherlands.
Here's a look back at his extraordinary career...

Born in Detroit on April 16, 1894, Paul Langdon Williams will become one of the greatest airborne troop transport tacticians in the US Air Force, where he'll serve for more than thirty-three years. After a short career in the Infantry Reserve during the First World War, he joined the United States Army Air Service in 1918. He flew for many years and became an instructor in 1927, then Director of Flying Training at various air bases. In June 1937 he graduated from the Air Corps Tactical School at Maxwell Air Force Base in Maxwell, Alabama. He took command of the 90th Attack Squadron of the 3rd Attack Group, then the 3rd Bombardment Group, and finally the 27th Bombardment Group in 1941.

AIRBORNE OPERATIONS

In May 1942, Paul arrived in England and was one of the very first members of the 8th Air Force, the soon to be famous 'Mighty Eighth', where he helped prepare the strategic bombing campaign on German industrial targets. At the same time, as a colonel, he began to manage the transport of troops by air for the various Allied invasions. He then took command of the 51st Troop Carrier Wing and the 60th, 62nd, and 64th Troop Carrier Groups. He thus enabled 531 men from Bud Siegel's unit to participate in North Africa in the first American airborne operation in history, which unfortunately was not a great success. A few days later, on November 28, Williams led 44 Douglas C-47s from the 62nd and 64th Troop Carrier Groups, carrying 530 British parachutists. With more than 8,000 hours of flying in his career, he personally flew Lieutenant-Colonel John Dutton Frost's lead aircraft with ease to the objective: Depiennne airfield in Tunisia. The parachute drop was a success, and Paul Williams received his first Distinguished Flying Cross, which was presented to him a few months later by Major General James H. Doolittle. However, once on the ground, Frost and his paratroopers went through hell, half of them being killed or captured trying to return to the Allied lines. History would repeat itself two years later, when General Williams would drop John Frost and his 1st British Airborne near Arnhem (in the Netherlands).

In January 1943, Paul Williams was promoted commander of the XII Air Support Command, and then became brigadier general on March 18. For the invasion of Sicily, he personally flew one of the lead planes dropping paratroopers on the island. Once again, the result was more than disappointing: only 12 of the 144 British gliders landed in the right place, and many paratroopers were lost at sea. When the Allies doubted the efficiency of the airborne divisions, Williams remained hopeful and called for their continuation.

It was he who ordered the Troop Carrier Wings to train with the 82nd Airborne, using pathfinders and innovative communication technology. The parachute drops of *Operation Avalanche* were indeed much more successful, but the general narrowly escaped death when flying one of the C-47s to Italy. During the flight, the plane's door was suddenly torn off and struck the tail of the aircraft. It plunged to just 100 feet above ground before Williams and his co-pilot were able to regain control at the last moment. They struggled for the rest of the trip to avoid a fatal spin and managed to bring the C-47 back to its base in Sicily, more than 300 miles away!

"ON TOP OF THE WORLD"

On February 25, 1944, when the general staff was planning *Overlord*, Paul Williams took over the IX Troop Carrier Command, which now included the 50th, 52nd and 53rd Troop Carrier Wings (the latter unit was assigned the new 101st Airborne Division), for a total of fourteen Carrier Groups. In his letters to his wife, Bird, he gave no indication of what was about to happen. Williams, however, led an armada of more than 1,000 C-47s and 900 Waco gliders to Normandy during the night of June 5 to 6, 1944. Only 41 planes and 9 gliders were lost. Airborne operations, now under control, then became an essential phase in any Allied invasion.

On June 8, Paul met the men of the 82nd and 101st Airborne Divisions, whose training he'd supervised, on the ground in Normandy. He then wrote to his brother, from *"just another battlefield"*: *"I always felt optimistic about things and knew we would get a good break and have the necessary amount of luck. We did and in addition to a swell job were miraculously fortunate in suffering much fewer losses than anticipated. Of course, we are still busy and will be, but the pressure is off and I feel a new man. My team is on top of the world and all chomping at the bit for 'more worlds to conquer!'"*. He then left France for Italy to meet the next wave of assault on Fortress Europe.

On July 13, General Williams (head of the Provisional Troop Carrier Air Division) and Brigadier General Robert T. Frederick (commander of the 1st Airborne Task Force) worked on a new operation, called *Rugby*, the airborne part of *Operation Dragoon*. Williams recommended a parachute drop during daylight, just before the landings, so that the Germans wouldn't have time to prepare a counter-attack on the beaches. Eventually, one part would be dropped early in the morning, the other around 6 pm providing reinforcements. In total, 6,488 paratroopers and 2,611 soldiers brought by gliders prevent the Germans from reaching the coast, with the help of the FFI. Les Arcs, Le Muy, La Motte, Draguignan and all the other objectives are taken in less than forty-eight hours with very few losses (mainly missing paratroopers, probably lost at sea).

Extracted from a film of June 5, 1944, shot on a take-off runway in North Witham (England), this image shows Paul L. Williams offering a cigar to a paratrooper about to board for D-Day. The paratrooper is Captain Frank L. Lillyman, a pathfinder in the 502nd Parachute Infantry Regiment, who'd promised his men he'd jump with a cigar. Lillyman will be able to celebrate the fact that he's the first American paratrooper to touch down in France at 00:16.

V - VICTORY BY CHRISTMAS? LATE 1944

A 'Mae West' Life Preserver (B-4), dated May 1943, found in a barn near Les Arcs-sur-Argens (Var, Southern France).
Worn around the neck, it was used by aviators and paratroopers to prevent them from drowning if they landed in flooded areas.
It takes its name from an actress and sex symbol of the time, Mae West, famous for her ample bosom.
Les Arcs was one of the Drop Zones assigned to the 517th PIR, where the 1st Battalion paratroopers fought a ferocious battle, surrounded and harassed for two days. This relic must have belonged to one of them.

In the letter below, written by Paul Williams to his older brother Eugene and his wife the day after *Operation Dragoon*, he expresses his pride at having set up the operation and praises the capabilities of the airborne troops: *"Another 'D' day for us. You know now why I have been here. It was a great achievement to move down and put on such a show. You can be sure it was better than ever. We are really getting good. My outfit is the world's best and is tremendous and as you can see eminently strategical. I am relaxing and hope to get a few visits in. Hope to see Capri and Palermo again before moving back. Had a private audience with Pope Pius XII the other day. It was a great honor and a memorable occasion in the magnificent Sistine Chapel where Michael Angelo's [sic] greatest paintings, sculptures and mosaics are. He blessed me and the family. I picked up a pipe in Rome for you. Sent it with some other things to Bird, also a blessed rosary for Gretchen. Wish I could see you and talk things over but am still nervous as a wet hen."*

He leaves Italy and returns to France where, on August 26, he's promoted to major general. His IX Troop Carrier Command now belongs to the 1st Allied Airborne Army, and is getting ready to participate in a new large-scale operation: *Market Garden*.

OPERATION MARKET GARDEN

Montgomery thinks Germany is nearly finished, having already lost half a million men in Normandy, 43 divisions and 2,000 tanks. In the East, the Red Army is advancing at lightning speed and the British leader, who's just lost part of his command to the Americans, intends to be the first to reach Berlin. Optimistic and trying to return to being front of stage, he develops a risky operation: while the American troops of Hodges (1st Army) and Simpson (9th Army) create a diversion by attacking towards the Rhine in Cologne, the British would bypass the Siegfried Line in the north of the Netherlands, cross the Rhine near Arnhem, push further to cut off the country, then drive towards Germany. They would encircle the Ruhr, the German industrial heartland, before launching a final assault on Berlin. Montgomery's plan would bring the Reich to its knees and everyone thus hopes to see the end of the war by Christmas. The tanks of XXX Corps (British 2nd Army) are assigned this ambitious mission. However, they wouldn't be alone... For the first time, paratroopers would no longer be used as a tactical help, but would play a major role: they would pave the way for XXX Corps, capturing the bridges while keeping the corridor open.

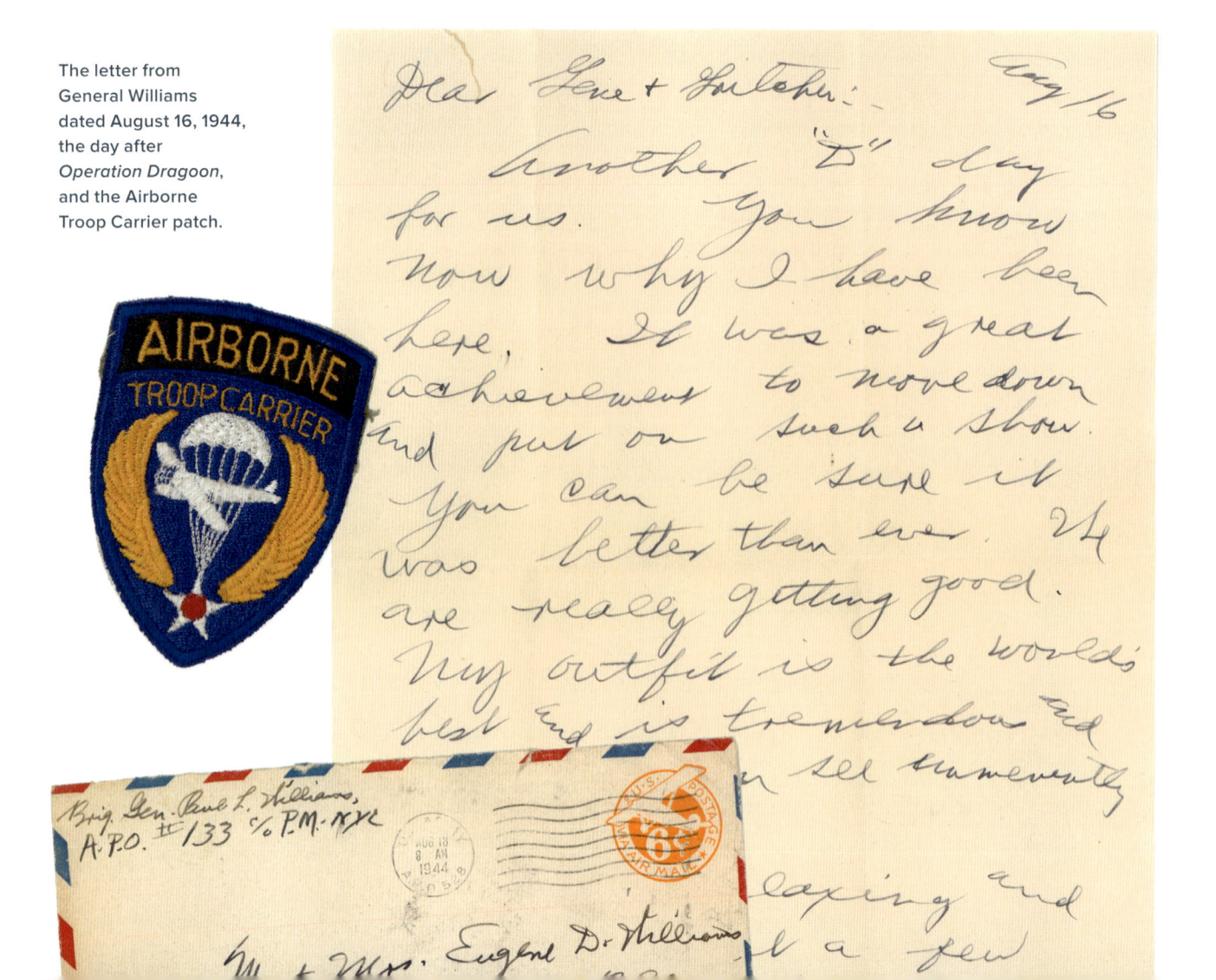

The letter from General Williams dated August 16, 1944, the day after *Operation Dragoon*, and the Airborne Troop Carrier patch.

Color photograph of General Williams' men in training above a base in France. Douglas C-47s from IX Troop Carrier Command are dropping paratroopers in preparation for *Operation Market Garden*.

Lewis H. Brereton, commanding the new 1st Allied Airborne Army, briefs Paul Williams on September 10, leaving him the choice between two routes: one to the north (shorter and passing through the occupied Netherlands), and one to the south (safer, near Belgium). General Williams chooses both. At the northern end of the Siegfried Line, the 1st Airborne Division (British) will take Arnhem and its bridges over the Nederrijn (Lower Rhine), assisted by a Polish parachute brigade. Further south, American paratroopers from the 82nd and 101st Airborne Divisions will capture various bridges near Nijmegen and Eindhoven and hold them at all costs until the arrival of the British tanks. A single failure in one of these three zones would jeopardize the entire plan. Airborne operations will be coded as 'Market' and ground operations as 'Garden'. It's a high-risk plan as not only would the long armored column advancing northward be vulnerable on its flanks, but above all, while waiting for reinforcements the paratroopers would be alone for two days, 100 miles behind enemy lines. Moreover, when the American and Canadian offensives on the other fronts are stalled, Montgomery (promoted to marshal) is slow to act, and the Germans, who can see the blow coming, have plenty of time to set up their defenses.

'Market' is finally launched on September 17, 1944 and is the largest airborne operation ever yet carried out. In two days, more than 34,600 men are dropped by around 1,400 American and 480 British aircraft, or land in 2,400 gliders. If the Allies had more, they would have been able to put everyone on the ground at the same time. A new troop transport technique is tested: each C-47 now tows a glider (42% of the men will hit the ground in the latter). Paul Williams' Troop Carrier Command also sends more than 1,500 tons of equipment by plane and 1,200 tons by glider to the Arnhem area, in addition to what paratroopers carry with them, jumping with the equivalent of their own bodyweight on their backs.

Once again, General Williams is personally involved in the operations and is in one of the lead planes during the first assault on Arnhem, the northernmost target. He'll receive a second Distinguished Flying Cross for this action. An embedded journalist recounts the operation: *"I watched Troop Carrier Command, one of the units of Lieutenant General Lewis H. Brereton's air army, drop thousands of parachutists from hundreds of C-47 Douglas transports. The multicolored parachutes glittered gaily in the bright noon-day sun as they fluttered to the earth with men, arms and supplies for the latest blow at the Reich. General Brereton and Major General Paul L. Williams of Los Angeles, commander of the Troop Carrier Command, flew with the spearheads of the First Allied Airborne Army for personal observation of their plans for the operation. Flying in tight, low formations, these sky-trains slipped over the coast of Holland from the North Sea and reached the drop area before the Nazis, caught flatfooted, manned their anti-aircraft guns. By the time the second and third formations of C-47s began dropping, light flak was shooting up into the sky fleets. One burst raised the Flying Fortress in which I was riding as an observation plane, leaving one small hole in the tail. Another piece missed our wing. I saw only one C-47 go down and it appeared to be under control.*

We did not see a single German fighter and the only airfield I saw was so pockmarked with bomb craters it was unusable. Hundreds of fighters circled around our long sky train, which extended for miles in straight lines of troop transports, tow-planes and gliders."

The aircraft loss ratio is actually equivalent to that of airborne operations in Normandy: ninety-one aircraft and twenty-five crews are lost, but overall, the September 17 drops are a success. Everything seems to be going according to plan, and Williams writes to his brother on the 26th: *"Just a note to let you know I am OK and rested a little now. Just sweated out another Big One last week, as you may have read about. It was probably the best and will have a major influence on things. Still busy, as usual. My gang were very efficient. We lost few, far fewer than anticipated, but I am unhappy over those that have gone. On top of everything my driver was killed in London. [...] What is next? Good luck was with us."*

EVENTUALLY PROVEN RIGHT

On the ground, however, losses are extremely heavy, and the 'Garden' part of the operation will be a fiasco (as will be seen in the following pages). While General Williams is criticized for his inflexibility in his choice to spread the drops over several days, and in areas so far away from the objectives, he regrets that the public only sees the failure of the operation as a whole and forgets the success of the bold initial assault. To him, airborne operations have a genuine future and will prove crucial when the Reich falls. Parachuting men with this effectiveness among the Germans, who may lead a guerrilla war in the mountains after the fall of Hitler's armies, could be a vital asset. Also, these operations can still get better and better and take on an even greater dimension. What will happen next will prove him right.

On March 24, 1945, *Operation Varsity* will involve 14,365 men from the British 6th Airborne and American 17th Airborne Divisions, dropped on the Rhine. The lessons of *Market Garden* have been learned and this time the C-47s will drag two gliders each, which will land directly on their targets. This gigantic fleet will extend over 200 miles of sky and be watched for more than two and a half hours by the amazed ground troops. It's the largest single-day parachute drop in history, perfectly planned by Paul L. Williams. Despite the loss of fifty-three aircraft, not a single pilot will miss his objective.

Following this success, General Williams will return to the United States in July 1945. Between 1946 and his retirement on April 30, 1950, he'll command the 3rd, 9th, 2nd and then 10th Air Forces, before dying on March 3, 1968 in Riverside, California. He received numerous medals, including the Distinguished Service Medal for leading the airborne troop transport operations in Normandy and the Netherlands, two Distinguished Flying Crosses for his direct involvement in the invasion of North Africa and the assault on Arnhem, the Legion of Merit, the French Legion of Honor, and the British Order of the Bath title.

Paul L. Williams decorated by Lt. Gen. Lewis H Brereton in England on August 26, 1944.

RAYMOND EDWARDS

C Squadron, 4th/7th Dragoon Guards

Raymond is a tank driver. Even though he's optimistic about the outcome of the war, in August 1944 he wrote near Falaise: *"I suppose everyone at home is thinking it will soon be over. I'm not banking on it being just yet"* (page 208). One month later, he would lose his life in the Netherlands during *Operation Market Garden*. Riding with XXX Corps, his tank will be destroyed only a few miles from his objective: Arnhem.

Born on November 24, 1919, in Cheshire, Raymond was destined to be a chemist, inspired by his father, a pharmacist. But being fond of reading old war stories, when war broke out he was thirsty for adventure and wanted to do what he thought was his duty. Although he could have avoided the army, handicapped by his poor eyesight, Raymond decided to volunteer.

Raymond in 1935, captivated by the adventures of the famous British officer Lawrence of Arabia.

He joined the 4th/7th Dragoon Guards, the same unit as Cecil Newton (who liberated Lille, page 220). On his last leave in England, Raymond somehow knew what fate was awaiting him, telling his family that he thought he'd never return home and would be killed in action. Yet he didn't back down, and his prediction will prove to be correct. His final days are detailed by a member of his tank crew: *"In the morning the CO briefed the officers for Operation 'Market Garden'. [...] XXX Corps was to push right up to the Zuyder Zee and, turning East, straight into Germany, outflanking the Siegfried Line. The vital road bridges along the route were being seized by airborne troops – those across the Maas at Grave and the Waal at Nijmegen by the American 82nd and 101st Airborne Divisions* [American]*, and that across the Neder Rijn at Arnhem by the British 1st Airborne Division. We had already seen some of the huge fleet of transport planes going over. The advance had already been started by the Guards Armoured Division, supported by a 'cab-rank' of Typhoons. The 43rd Division* [British]*, plus 8th Armoured Brigade, was to follow up and take over from the Guards beyond Nijmegen. It sounded like a fairly good thing. I suppose the thought of the Airborne ahead of us at every stage made it seem easier, and although Duggie told us that Holland was stiff with 88s, he said that they were mostly Flak-type, with sights unsuitable for anti-tank work. That afternoon the regiment moved off. The advance, of course, was to be only one-road wide again. The flanks were completely unguarded."* With the Guards in the lead, the armored column leaves Belgium in the early afternoon of September 17, but falls into an ambush right after the border: the convoy, which has less than two days to reach Arnhem, is already late.

XXX Corps patch and beret badge of the 4th/7th Dragoon Guards.

Raymond's squadron crosses Oosterhout in flames, a fate that seems common to all of the villages surrounding the Allies. This corridor will soon go down in history as 'Hell's Highway'. The British tanks stop in an orchard on the edge of Elst. On September 23, while B Squadron heads to Driel to assist the Polish paratroopers, C Squadron is about to attack Elst alongside the 1st Worcestershire Regiment. Raymond's comrade recounts: *"Numbers of infantry were passing up the road towards Driel, some marching and some in Ducks [armored vehicles]. Odds and ends of people were coming back in the opposite direction – including a shot-down RAF crew, who looked pretty shaken up. It seemed to us that salvoes often coincided with the appearance of Ducks, and it looked rather likely that Jerry had the road under direct observation. The infantry had some casualties, and the unnerving cry of 'Stretcher bearers!' was frequent. Our crew made a sort of dinner of K rations, lying under the tank, and afterwards I got inside the turret and lay on the floor to have a read in comparative safety, as I thought. [Raymond] Edwards climbed into the driving compartment to do the same. I didn't even bother to close the turret flaps, as it seemed so unlikely that a shell would just happen to drop through a hole only about three feet across.*

The next morning, the column arrives in Eindhoven, where the 101st US Airborne paratroopers already seem *"to be making themselves at home"* after taking the bridges north of the city. But this initial success would be short-lived, as the 101st Airborne would fail to seize crucial bridges in Zon and Best, just north of Eindhoven, meaning XXX Corps engineers therefore have to build an artificial bridge over the Wilhelmina Canal in Zon, before the tanks can cross the Veghel bridge and try to catch up. In the afternoon of the 19th, they reach Grave, under the control of the 82nd Airborne. The latter, overwhelmed, has taken all its bridges except the most important one, in Nijmegen. When the Guards' tanks arrive on September 20, they're forced to fight hard for the town, which should have already been in Allied hands. American paratroopers bravely attack across the Waal in small rubber boats, before running through an immense open field under terrific fire and capturing the northern part of the bridge at the cost of heavy losses. Unfortunately, the British Sherman tanks are unable to take advantage of this opportunity, as the majority of them are engaged in a fierce battle for the city of Nijmegen. Those crossing the bridge are blocked shortly afterwards by an anti-tank gun, and the British therefore decide to stop their advance for the night, even though they're only about 6 miles from Arnhem. The English and Polish paratroopers there are still holding on, but time and ammunition are running out.

To make matters worse, the men of the 4th/7th Dragoon Guards encounter strong resistance south of the city of Elst, on the 'island' bordered by the Waal and the Lower Rhine, halfway between Nijmegen and Arnhem. While A Squadron, assisted by the 7th Somerset Light Infantry, looks for another way to Arnhem, the rest of the armored regiment awaits orders near Nijmegen. On the other side of the Waal River, the area is extremely hostile and once back on the road,

> This 4th/7th Dragoon Guards tank crewman, wearing a black beret with the regimental badge on it, has put on his suit and communication equipment. Peeking out of his pocket is a tobacco box bartered from an American paratrooper.

V - VICTORY BY CHRISTMAS? LATE 1944

Looking through a periscope after a while I saw several shells burst very near. One landed right beside Ron Walker's tank, which stood next to ours, and Ron and his crew, who were lying underneath it, had a very lucky escape. A squadron of American Thunderbolt fighters, with gaily painted names and black and white chequer-board markings, came over very low and started to shoot up something a mile or two away. They buzzed around for about a quarter of an hour and while they were there the shelling stopped. I hoped they had knocked out the guns, but the shells began to come again as soon as they had gone.

It must have been around five o'clock when the order to prepare to move finally came through and all the crews mounted. Le Maitre closed down the turret flaps as soon as he got in, I switched the wireless and we were ready to go. I certainly wasn't sorry to be moving. Getting out of the orchard would require a good deal of manoeuvering, difficult for a driver closed down, so Edwards opened his hatch and stuck his head out, in spite of protests from Le Maitre, who said: 'Close down Edwards! You're no ----- hero!'. Ron Walker climbed up on the front of his tank with some message for Edwards, which of course I couldn't hear, and then jumped down again.

At that moment there came a blinding yellow flash from down in the driving compartment, and there was the most shattering explosion I have ever heard – it seemed as though a bomb had gone off in each of my ears. The concussion was so tremendous that I was almost unconscious for a few seconds. By the time I had collected myself the turret was filled with thick brown smoke and reeking of cordite. My ears were ringing furiously but I could distantly hear a few faint moans dying away into silence, then Bill Dawson's voice, very shaky and as if from the end of a long tunnel, saying 'is everybody OK?'. I said I was.

The smoke in the turret began to thin and I could see that the flaps were wide open and that Le Maitre had gone. There seemed to be no sign of fire and I could hear shells bursting all round outside, so I sat where I was for a minute or so. It seemed the best thing to do. Then there came a lull and Bill climbed out. Before I followed him, I peered through into the driving compartment [where Raymond was]. There was still a good deal of smoke in there and I couldn't see very clearly. There was what looked like chunks of raw meat splattered all round it. I joined Bill and Le Maitre, who were crouching under the back of the tank. I told them that I was sure that both the others had had it [Raymond and his best friend, Robert Armstrong]. The idea took some getting used to. Duggie and Ron Walker came round to us. Ron was nearly as lucky to be alive as we were. He had only just jumped to the ground when the shell hit, and his back had been peppered with tiny splinters, which had buried themselves in his leather jerkin.

Raymond in training with the Royal Armoured Corps.

I had some difficulty in hearing what was said, as the ringing in my ears seemed to be getting worse. An infantry padre came up and said something to us, but I couldn't make out what it was. Anyway, Duggie said that he would take us down the road to HHQ in his tank, so we all climbed in. It was a bit of a crush, with me sitting on the gear box and Bill and Le Maitre on the turret floor. Another salvo landed just as we got in and Duggie closed down. Bill Mumford, Duggie's gunner, had taken a look in the front of our tank and the sight had shaken him considerably. The shell must have burst right on the rim of Edward's hatch, and most of the blast and fragments had gone inside. How we came to be unharmed in the turret is something I have never understood. Incidentally, the moaning I mentioned had been heard by Bill Dawson as well. It must have come from Armstrong – obviously it couldn't have been Edwards."

Raymond's temporary grave, just after the war, at Arnhem Oosterbeek Cemetery, where he's still buried.

DISASTER AT ARNHEM

In and around Arnhem, the 10,095 men of the 1st British Airborne still await the arrival of XXX Corps. They're completely cut off and face the unexpected and devastating opposition of two SS armored divisions. The outcome will be catastrophic, and *Operation Market Garden* a resounding failure.

HOLDING ON...

From day one, the situation on the ground looks very bad. Most paratroopers are stranded on the outskirts of the city, near Oosterbeek, with the exception of a small group led by Lt. Col. John Dutton Frost, who manages to reach the bridge on the main road in Arnhem. They must now hold their position until the tanks arrive. In the initial plans for *Market Garden*, 3,000 paratroopers were to hold the bridge for two days, which was already a challenge, but in reality, only 740 men would endure a real siege for three and a half days. In Oosterbeek, the fighting will last no less than eight days and nine nights. The 'Red Devils' are surrounded, with no ammunition or food, battling sustained close-range German Panzer attacks without even being able to retaliate.

However, they refuse to surrender, expecting to see XXX Corps tanks arrive at any moment. Some survivors who haven't yet been taken prisoner, and with no anti-tank ammunition, continue fighting the infantry with their daggers, inflicting a 50% casualty rate on the German troops attacking them. The last radio message from the Arnhem bridge, *"Out of ammo, God save the King"*, was only heard by German operators intercepting the signal.

Captain Basil Anthony Bethune Taylor commands an anti-aircraft artillery battery from the 2nd Airlanding Light Battery, in support of the 1st Airborne Division. The unit already has combat experience, having fought in Normandy alongside the 6th Airborne. Basil recounts his Arnhem experience upon his return to the *Daily Mail*, in the special edition for the armed forces on September 28, 1944 (opposite): *"Most of the division dropped on Sunday* [September 17].

I – a gunner – dropped on Monday. It was easy. A bit of flak hit our glider, but we landed west of Oosterbeek and took up positions. There were odd snipers, but they did not cause much trouble, and we started moving towards the bridge. One brigade began to move down the railway lines. It ran into the first tough opposition. Eighty-eight-millimeter guns were at the road and rail crossing and they forced this section back. That was the beginning of the fireworks.

V - VICTORY BY CHRISTMAS? LATE 1944

The next day the situation began to deteriorate. We were forced to take up new positions. We scooped out some earth in a cabbage patch and got our guns going. We took a bit of a bashing that day – from 88 mms, from tanks, and machine-guns. We were told to withdraw, and at nightfall we did so, with tanks following us up. We then got into a field in the middle of a wood. The German tactics were to send in tanks followed by infantry. The tanks fired then turned away, leaving the infantry. We usually managed to clean up the infantry, who were not too good. But then the Germans brought in flame-throwers and self-propelling guns. They gave us more than we gave them. They also sent over fierce fire from mortars. [...] Shelling became more intense as the enemy moved up artillery round the perimeter which had been formed round our gun positions. On Thursday the Germans overran one of our gun positions with tanks. We were using American-type 77mm cannon. At one moment two tanks were being held off by one man with one gun – all the others of the crew had been killed. The tanks bashed at houses, knocking them down like packs of cards. So troublesome were the panzers that a Major went out with a PIAT ['Projector, Infantry, Anti-Tank', an individual rocket launcher] *and took two on. He nosed round the corner of a house. Every time his head appeared the German tanks fired. But he got his PIAT in position and bagged one of the tanks. The other moved off and we started stalking it with PIATs until nightfall. The hide-and-seek chase for enemy tanks became the sole object in life of the gunners in the perimeter. Whenever a tank was signaled they limbered a gun to a jeep and went in pursuit."*

OPERATION BERLIN

Despite the paratroopers' courage, XXX Corps arrives too late. Of the 10,095 men from the 1st Airborne Division deployed in Oosterbeek, fewer than 2,500 are still standing, cornered in the villas turned into fortresses or aid stations, surviving on the rusty water collected from the radiators. The efforts of the Polish parachute brigade and the 43rd (Wessex) Division (who finally arrived on the 22nd) to cross the river and rescue them ends in failure. On September 25, there is genuine urgency as the Germans, receiving reinforcements from the east, launch a violent assault on the shrinking defensive perimeter with their mighty Tiger tanks. *Operation Berlin* is underway: under artillery cover from XXX Corps, those paratroopers still able to move are evacuated during the night in small boats across the Rhine to the village of Driel, held by the Poles. But first, they have to cross the woods at night, following white ribbons hung on the trees by scouts.

Correspondent Alan Wood (*Combined Press*), reports on the evacuation of the Red Devils: *"We were told the password - 'John Bull'. If we became separated, each man was to make his way by compass due south until he reached the river. Our Major is an old hand. He led the way and linked our party together by getting everyone to hold the tail of the parachutist's smock of the man in front of him, so our infiltrating column had an absurd resemblance to some children's game. It was half-light, with the glow of fires from burning houses around, when we set out. We were lucky; we went through a reputed enemy pocket without hearing a shot except for a stray sniper's bullet. Another group met a machine-gun with a fixed line of fire across their path. Another had to silence a bunch of Germans with a burst of Sten fire and hand grenades. Another had to pause while a German finished his evening stroll across their pathway.*

In Oosterbeek on September 20, a battery of the 1st Airlanding Light Regiment has dug a firing position for its 75 mm Howitzer. Opposite: "Pegasus" shoulder patch of the Airborne Divisions.

But we all got through without the enemy realizing that we were doing anything more than normal night patrolling. The worst part was waiting two hours by the riverside till our turn came for assault boats to ferry us across. The Germans, if not yet definitely suspicious, were inquisitive; they kept on sending up flares and it was vital to lie flat and motionless. In our boat queue we lay flat and shivering on a soaking field with cold rain drizzling down. Occasionally machine-guns spattered out and bullets tweaked through the grass."

Fortunately, their crossing is relatively quiet. But nearly 300 unarmed and wounded men are left behind in the hope that the Germans would provide them with the medical assistance they need. On the 26th, enemy units from both sides of the perimeter link up and realize that the British have evacuated Arnhem. The wounded are captured, as are the men in the aid stations and the few pockets of resistance still active. Without radio contact, they hadn't even received the order to fall back. The British lost around 8,000 men at Arnhem, including 1,500 killed. To this must be added just as many casualties among American paratroopers and in the British 2nd Army along 'Hell's Highway'. The Allies withdraw between Arnhem on the Lower Rhine and Nijmegen on the Waal, in a large area that was partially flooded and mostly evacuated by its inhabitants, known as 'The Island'. This blurred area between Allied and enemy territory wouldn't be definitively cleared until April 1945 during *Operation Destroyer*. *Market Garden* will at least have the merit of advancing the front line by nearly 60 miles and making the Allies cross two major rivers. They must now focus on consolidating the Nijmegen bridgehead in order to prepare for the future breakthrough through the Reichswald Forest: their gateway to Germany.

These British paratroopers, most of them wounded, would end the war in captivity. Still, some of them are unable to hide their joy of seeing these "230 hours of hell" come to an end.

Found by the Canadian soldiers liberating Arnhem in April 1945, this cross bears the inscription in German "unknown English soldier". On top of it hangs the parachutist's helmet, pierced by shrapnel.

In the newly liberated region, the Dutch willingly welcome GIs and Tommies into their homes, grateful for their freedom. The canals, windmills and green meadows almost make them forget the horrors of war. An American gunner writes home at the end of September: *"(Somewhere in Holland) Well, at last I can put something besides 'France' up in the corner [of the V-mail]. Uncle Joe is sure letting me see Europe but I'm ready to stop and come home if he is, but he isn't. In my opinion, the people are cleaner and the houses are more modern and beautiful by all means. [...] I guess there isn't any place besides the US that can compare with France when it comes to women but they aren't too bad here. I guess we're in the most beautiful apple orchard I've ever been in or even will get in. The trees are in straight rows in every direction, the branches are held high with poles and the limbs are loaded with nice red juicy apples. They are just a little green but they are sure getting good. The ground is covered with green grass and it could be cut with a lawn mower."*

It's clear that the war won't be over by Christmas. But could the success of *Operation Market Garden* really have shortened the war by six long months, saved millions of lives, and allowed the Western Allies to reach Berlin before the Soviets?

The world we know today would certainly have been very different.

THE D-DAY DODGERS

While the eyes of the world are on Northwest Europe, the fighting in Italy is still raging. Misinformed parents write to their sons: "*We are so happy that you are in Italy, and not in combat in France!*". In reality, however, after the fall of the Gustav Line, the 'D-Day Dodgers' would experience their worst battles in front of the Gothic Line. Indeed, Allied casualties in September and October 1944 will actually be the highest in the entire Italian Campaign – the forgotten war.

Under construction by the Todt Organization (who also built the Atlantic Wall) since 1943, the Gothic Line extends from the south of La Spezia, on the Tyrrhenian Sea, to Pesaro, on the Adriatic Sea. It stretches 200 miles across the Apennines, dotted with thousands of pillboxes, communication trenches, minefields, anti-tank defenses, machine gun nests, artillery guns, all of which are camouflaged in the mountains with clear fields of fire onto the valleys below. In the summer of 1944, the Allies crossed the Arno Line on the Arno River, near Pisa and Florence. Wishing to preserve the architectural treasures and works of art he'd fallen in love with while visiting Tuscany, Generalfeldmarschall Kesselring had evacuated his troops from these cities on July 23, while ordering them to delay the Allies as much as possible. The Germans settled on the Gothic Line, which has to be kept at all costs: it's their last defense before Northern Italy and the industrial power of the Reich installed there. Kesselring asked them to hold on until winter arrives, after which *"the climate would take care of the rest"*.

Taking these defenses wouldn't be an easy task, especially since at that time, many Allied units had been removed from the lines to land in Southern France. This included three experienced American divisions, a third of their artillery battalions, and particularly the French mountain troops who could have been very useful in crossing the Gothic Line. Although they were replaced, in particular by the 1st Brazilian Infantry Division and the 92nd African-American Infantry Division 'Buffalo Soldiers', these units have never been in combat before and are insufficient to compensate for the loss of troops. From June to August, the Americans went from 231,000 to 147,000 men, and the British from 44,000 to 16,000. Infantry units, such as the 85th US Infantry Division, were therefore hastily trained in mountain combat and mule transportation, the only way to move supplies and ammunition through mountainous terrain. The Allies wouldn't receive the support of the American 10th Mountain Division, specialized and composed of top athletes, until months later. In the meantime, the Americans have to improvise using every means at their disposal: the partisans (underground fighters) and Italian troops as mountain guides, tanks as artillery guns, and artillerymen as infantry troops.

Newly arrived, the 91st Infantry Division reached the Arno River on July 18, 1944. A sergeant in its 362nd Regiment writes to his fiancée: *"Just a short note to let you know that I'm in actual combat now and that I'm in as good a shape as when I left. What's more I intend to stay that way. [...] So far I haven't had much actual fighting but I sweated out an artillery barrage that I thought, for a while, had my name on it. I guess I'm either too lucky or else my guardian angel is on the beam. Once in a while we'd have a little trouble with a sniper that was tired of living and wanted to stick his neck out just to get it clipped off. If I'm lucky, we can have that date in 1945. I sincerely believe that I will come back, and I am only very rarely wrong (I think)."* A few weeks later, the situation will be quite different. His men will have to cross endless minefields, before taking on pillboxes, one by one, with grenades. The campaign will be slow, bloody and costly. Nevertheless, the division will succeed in breaching the Gothic Line at Futa Pass on September 22, but the weather, as predicted by the German commander, will stop its advance.

Remains of the Gothic Line can still be seen today, such as this pillbox facing the sea on the edge of a charming village of the Cinque Terre (left), or this anti-tank wall in Borgo a Mozzano (below). The latter was liberated by the FEB (Força Expedicionária Brasileira or Brazilian Expeditionary Force). The authoritarian Getúlio Dorneles Vargas regime in Brazil had broken its neutrality following the attack by German submarines on its rubber convoys to the United States, but was reluctant to fully engage in the Allied war effort. A popular saying was born in 1943: *"It's more likely to see a snake smoking a pipe, than to see the FEB at the front and fight."* The expression *"when the snake smokes"* (similar to the saying *"When pigs fly"*) was used so often that the shoulder patch worn by the Brazilian soldiers represents a snake smoking a pipe.

V - VICTORY BY CHRISTMAS? LATE 1944

BUFFALO SOLDIERS AND NISEI

African-Americans have long suffered from segregation in the United States, both as civilians and in the military, regardless of the branch. According to American officers and politicians of the time, they lacked intelligence and courage, and were only to be used in support units. General George S. Patton Jr. wrote in a letter to his wife: *"A colored soldier cannot think fast enough to fight in armor"*. In France, the 'Black Panthers' he reluctantly welcomed into his 3rd Army would prove him wrong. In the summer of 1940, the American Congress passed the Selective Training and Service Act, stating that *"in the selection and training of men, [...] there shall be no discrimination against any person on account of race or color"*. Still, a few weeks later, the White House added that *"the services of Negroes will be utilized on a fair and equitable basis"*, and segregation in the armed forces would continue: African-Americans would be assigned to 'All-Blacks' units for the duration of the war.

In 1942, African-American soldier Jim Dansby described his experience at Camp Shelby, Mississippi, in a letter to his girl-friend: *"The colored here in camp seem to be neglected to a certain extent. We are poorly organized, and I am pretty much disgusted. I don't think they're treating us right. Honey I am telling you I'll be glad when I get away from this place. A* [colored] *soldier got killed in town last nite,* [sic] *also the nite* [sic] *before. The one that was killed the nite* [sic] *before was found by the railroad tracks with his head cut and arm almost cut off. These soldiers down here are really bad... so anything liable to happen."* Only a few African-Americans were actually serving at the beginning of the war, including sailors in the US Navy (often simple cooks), or the 445 'Tuskegee Airmen' of the 332nd Fighter Group in North Africa (the only black unit of the US Army Air Forces). It was only after a strong need to replace casualties that the 92nd and 93rd Infantry Divisions, composed mainly of African-Americans, were raised and sent into battle (in Italy and the Pacific, respectively). In the field, the situation would not improve. In France, according to a report by the G-2 (Intelligence) Normandy Base Section, the 'Negroes' are accused of most cases of rape, murder and looting. Black American soldiers are hanged in village squares, in front of officials and the population, in order to *"create a better feeling toward the American forces"*.

Despite the racism to which they are subjected, many men of the 92nd Division, nicknamed 'Buffalo Soldiers' in reference to their shoulder patch, would fight valiantly, to the point of earning the highest military distinction of the US Army: the Medal of Honor. Thus, in the western part of the Gothic Line (Aghinolfi Castle, north of Viareggio), Lieutenant Vernon Joseph Baker, a 25-year-old African-American, takes a machine gun nest on his own, two observation posts, two bunkers (killing all its occupants) and destroys a network of German telephone lines. However, he wouldn't receive the recognition he deserves right away, as black soldiers would sometimes have to wait more than fifty years to receive their medals. In January 1997, six African-American soldiers would finally be awarded the Medal of Honor posthumously, in addition to Vernon Baker, the only surviving recipient.

Among them is Lieutenant John Robert Fox, a 29-year-old Buffalo Soldier and a forward observer in the 598th Field Artillery Battalion. On December 26, 1944, his comrades of the 366th Regiment, overwhelmed by the Germans, have to evacuate the small village of Sommocolonia, not far from the Gothic Line. The enemy had infiltrated the city in civilian attire on Christmas Eve and launched an organized attack at 8 am. John volunteers to stay and cover the American retreat with a small group of eight Italian soldiers. It will cost him his life.

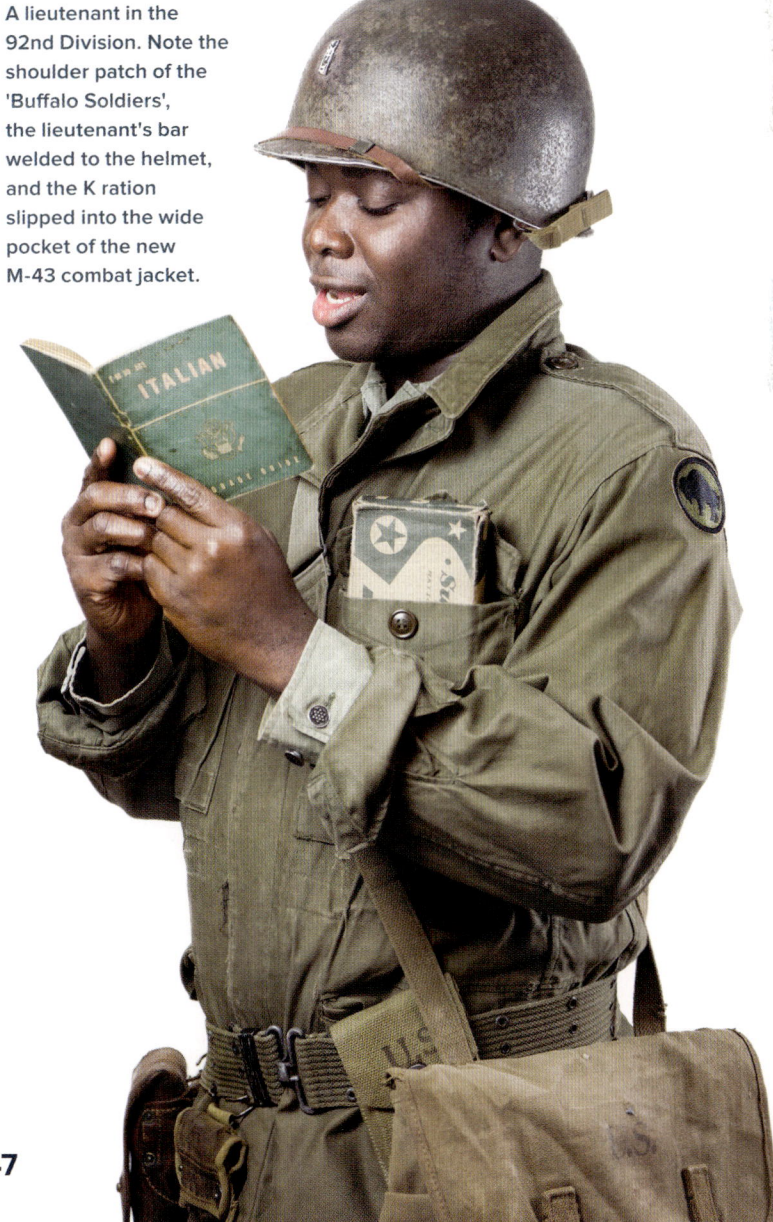

A lieutenant in the 92nd Division. Note the shoulder patch of the 'Buffalo Soldiers', the lieutenant's bar welded to the helmet, and the K ration slipped into the wide pocket of the new M-43 combat jacket.

247

As the Germans arrive in large numbers at John Fox's position, the lieutenant gives orders to the artillery guns by radio from the second floor of a house. Surrounded by Wehrmacht soldiers who are getting closer and closer, American shell bursts also land dangerously closer to John. Giving his own coordinates, he tells the gunners: *"That last round was just where I wanted it, bring it in 60 yards more!"* At the other end of the line, the operator asked for confirmation, explaining that John wouldn't survive a 75 heavy caliber gun strike on his position. Lieutenant Fox's last words are: *"There's more of them than there is of us. Fire it!"* A few seconds later, hundreds of shells hit the house. His sacrifice would allow the Americans to regroup and take back the village. When they arrive on the scene, they find John's body among 100 German corpses. His widow will receive his Medal of Honor from President Bill Clinton at the White House on January 13, 1997. After liberating Lucca, the 92nd Division will follow the Ligurian Coast to Genoa, where it'll enter the city on 27 April 1945. In just a few months, it'll have lost 3,200 men.

In total, more than 1 million African-Americans would serve in the US military during the Second World War, alongside 51,000 Puerto Ricans, 44,000 Native Americans, 20,000 Japanese, 13,000 Chinese, 11,000 Filipinos and 1,000 Hawaiians. All would seek to gain the respect of their white counterparts through multiple acts of bravery. The most determined would be the second-generation Japanese-American soldiers, known as 'Nisei'. Indeed, following Pearl Harbor, doubting their loyalty and thinking they might be spies in the service of Japan, the American government had classified them in category 4-C ('enemy aliens'). Around 110,000 Americans of Japanese origin, three-quarters of whom were born in the United States, were consequently expelled from their homes and held in US internment camps to prevent any 'terrorist attacks'.

Finally, in May 1942, General George C. Marshall formed a battalion of Nisei volunteers from Hawaii: the 100th Battalion. Deployed in Oran (Algeria), it was attached to the 34th US Infantry Division. The number of volunteers was such that on February 1, 1943, President Roosevelt announced the creation of the 442nd Regimental Combat Team, an autonomous regiment of 4,500 Nisei that would absorb the 100th Battalion. To combat the suspicious and sometimes hateful looks of the white soldiers (some of whom had lost brothers and friends in the Pacific to the Japanese Imperial Army), the Nisei showed exemplary courage and distinguished themselves during brutal battles in Italy, such as at Monte Marano and Monte Cassino. On June 26, 1944, the 100th Battalion / 442nd RCT headed for Belvedere, where it fought hard for rivers, high ground and villages along the Gothic Line.

However, it wouldn't see the end of this campaign, since the regiment was among the units bound for Southern France. Engaged in the Vosges Mountains in Bruyères, it loses 1,200 men when taking the city on October 19 and 20, before rescuing the 'lost battalion' of the 36th 'Texas' Division (also a veteran of Italy) surrounded by the Germans. They lose another 863 men in this feat of arms, but in this month of combat alone, the regiment would receive no less than five Presidential Unit Citations, eventually becoming the most decorated unit of its size in the entire US Army!

The 100th Battalion would also acquire the nickname the 'Purple Heart Battalion', since each of its members received at least one medal for injury or death in action. They earned the respect of the men in the 34th 'Red Bull' Division, who remained in Italy without their best element. Their war diary says, *"As men of the 34th observed the battle conduct of the Nisei, they grew to resent the treatment accorded the parents and relatives of these little, brown American Fighters. They resented the confiscation of their property and the herding of their families into concentration camps at home, while their sons were dying by the hundreds in the cause of human liberty. They determined then to raise their voices in protest and to demand justice and recompense for the wrongs inflicted upon these people. The Nisei became true buddies of the 34th."*

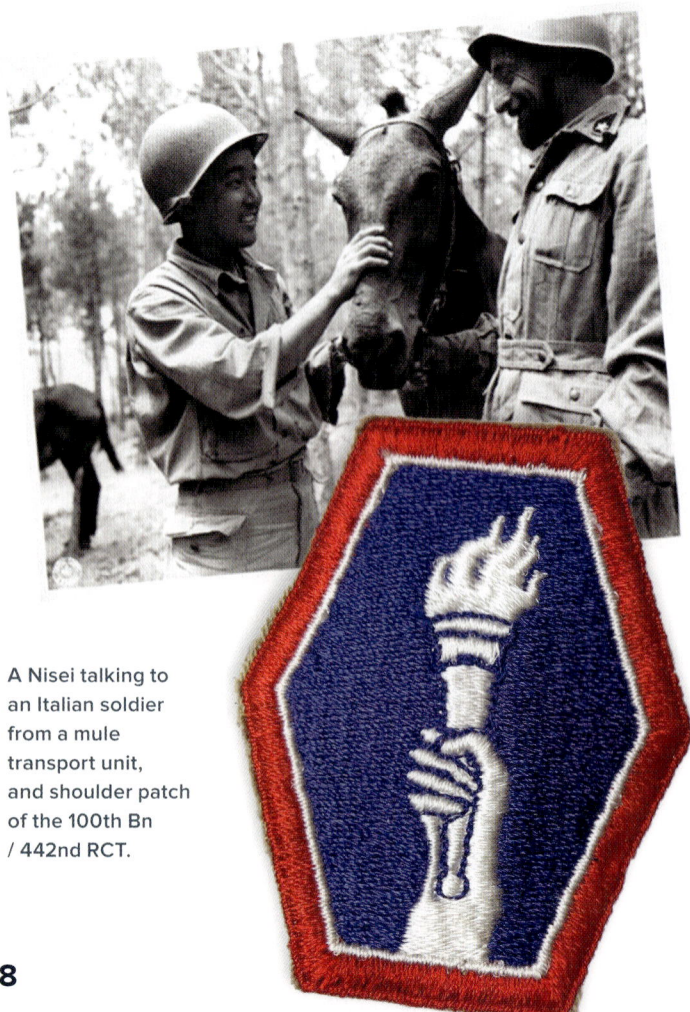

A Nisei talking to an Italian soldier from a mule transport unit, and shoulder patch of the 100th Bn / 442nd RCT.

V - VICTORY BY CHRISTMAS? LATE 1944

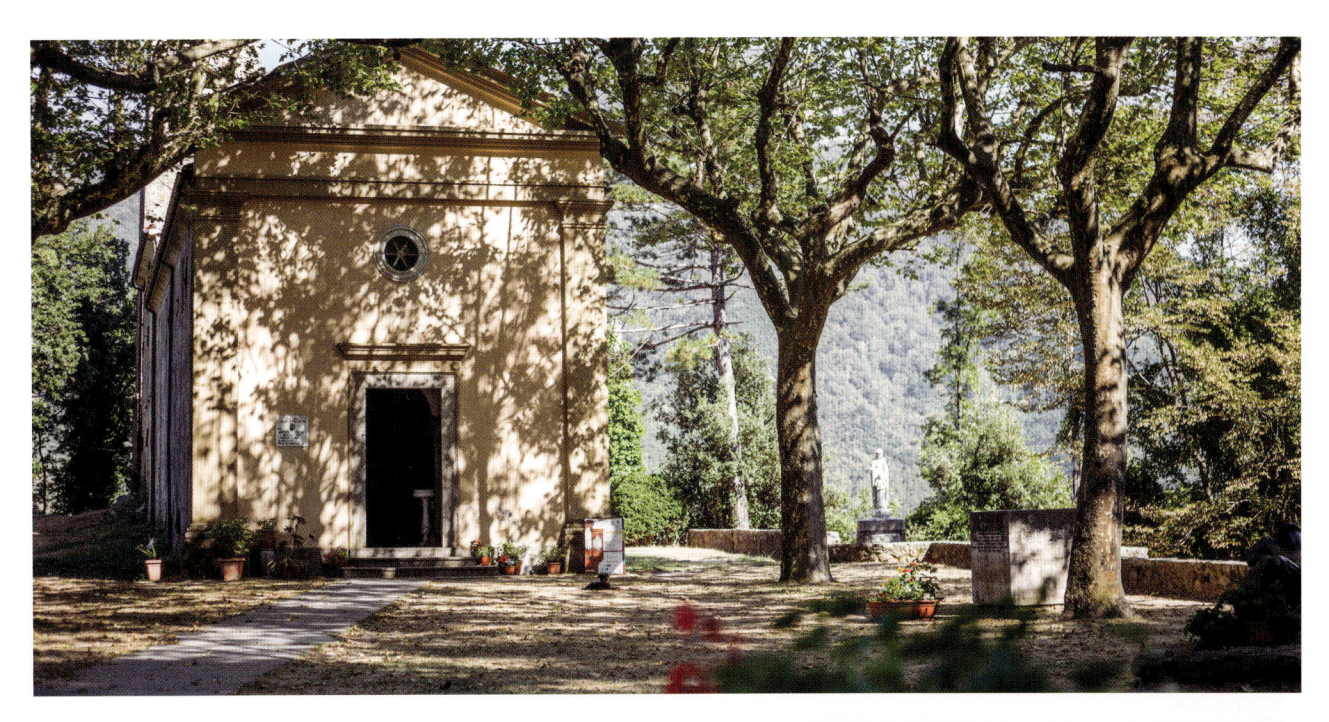

Hitler ordered that for every German soldier killed in Europe by the underground, an entire village must be massacred. In France, 16,000 innocent men, women and children were murdered in retaliation for the Resistance's actions, such as in Oradour-sur-Glane (642 victims, June 10, 1944) or Maillé (124 victims, August 25, 1944). The Waffen-SS sadistically abided by the order all the way to Russia, and Italian civilians were treated in the same manner. As the Allies progressed northward, Partisan activity intensified in the mountains, harassing German troops day and night. The sixty or so inhabitants of the small village of Sant'Anna di Stazzema, isolated in the hills of the Gothic Line, thus faced a tragic fate.

The village was home to many refugees who'd fled the fighting and believed they were safe there. But on the morning of August 12, 1944, soldiers from the 16. SS Panzergrenadier-Division 'Reichsführer-SS' entered Sant'Anna and gathered around 100 inhabitants and refugees in the small church square (above), before executing them with heavy machine guns and shooting the priest at close range. The other civilians were locked in the village houses, which were burned and destroyed with grenades and flame throwers, leaving no survivors (photo below, and right).

More than 560 civilians were killed on that day, including at least 107 children (the youngest being only 20 days old). The barbarity of the SS is limitless: of the eight pregnant women who lost their lives in Sant'Anna, one was disemboweled with a bayonet, and her baby ripped out and killed before her eyes. The memorial at the top of Sant'Anna is dedicated to her (right). The massacre lasted for three hours, after which the bodies were burned in the church and the SS contemplated their macabre work while eating their lunch.

With the exception of the division commander, no one was prosecuted until 2004, when some of the ex-soldiers were sentenced to prison. A few weeks after Sant'Anna, a unit of the same division was responsible for the largest massacre of civilians committed in Western Europe by the Waffen SS. South of Bologna, at least 770 inhabitants of Marzabotto were executed for their support for the local partisans. Some historians estimate that there were, in fact, as many as 1,830 victims, more than 250 of whom were under 16 years of age.

249

THE BLUE DEVILS

Italy has had the 'Red Devils' of the 1st British Airborne, the 'Black Devils' of the 1st Special Service Force, and now the Gothic Line would have the 'Blue Devils' from the American 88th Infantry Division. They've already distinguished themselves on the Gustav Line and in the race to Rome, but since the Normandy landings, these men attached to the 5th US Army (just like their comrades in the British 8th Army) feel like they've been forgotten by the public. A member of the British parliament, calling the soldiers in Italy 'D-Day Dodgers', enraged the bitter veteran soldiers on the Italian Front, who sarcastically sing: *"We're the D-Day Dodgers out in Italy - Always on the vino, always on the spree - Eighth Army scroungers and their tanks - We live in Rome, among the Yanks [...] On our way to Florence we had a lovely time - We ran a bus to Rimini right through the Gothic Line - On to Bologna we did go - Then we went bathing in the Po - For we are the D-Day Dodgers, over here in Italy."*

Joe Marchlinski, son of Polish immigrants from Connecticut, serves in the 349th 'Kraut Killer' Regiment of the 88th Infantry Division and seems to be having fun with the fact that the public thinks they're on holiday. In this pre-filled V-mail *"Greetings from Italy!"*, sent to his future wife on July 6, 1944, there's no indication of the extent of the fighting carried out by his company. The checked lines even suggest that he's having a good time: "Dear _friend_ / How are you? I am _fine_ / Wish I had _more to write_ / Doing lots of _work_ / Hope you have _everything you want_ and have _been having fun_ / Italy is _sunny_ and _beautiful_ / The food is _good_ / Are you _happy_? / Rest camp is _swell_ / Will be _writing you again_ / I have seen _GI Army – USO Shows, historical spots, interesting places_ / Yours _Sincerely_ / Name: _Joe_."

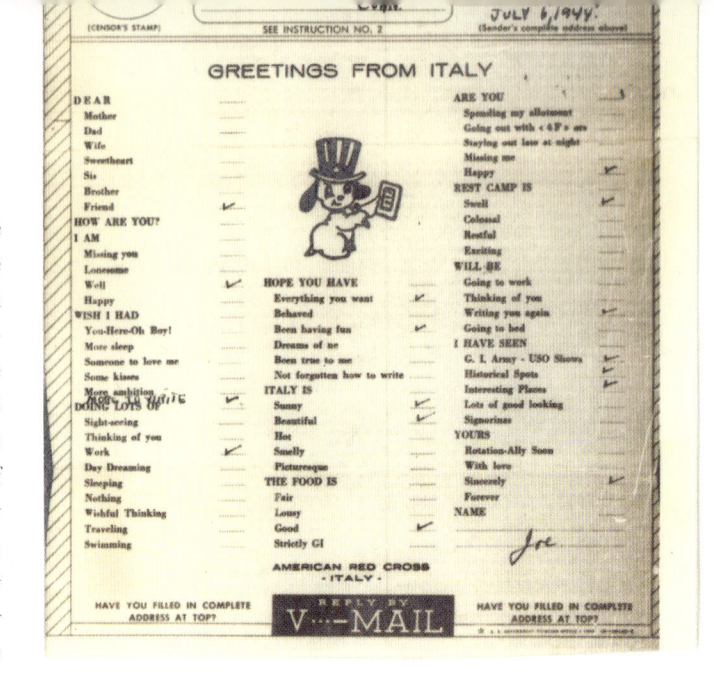

In reality, the day before, Joe's regiment relieved the 1st US Armored Division as it moved towards the Arno River. The Germans are now clinging to every inch of ground, but it's nothing compared to the fighting he would see a week later on the very well-defended hills 184 and 188, near Villamagna, which the regiment would rename the 'Bloody Ridge'. After specialized river crossing training, the division returns to the front at the end of August to support the Nisei of the 100th Battalion / 442nd RCT, who are in contact with the enemy near Florence, and then joins the 34th, 85th and 91st Divisions in their major offensive towards Bologna.

88th Infantry Division patch and Joe's letters.

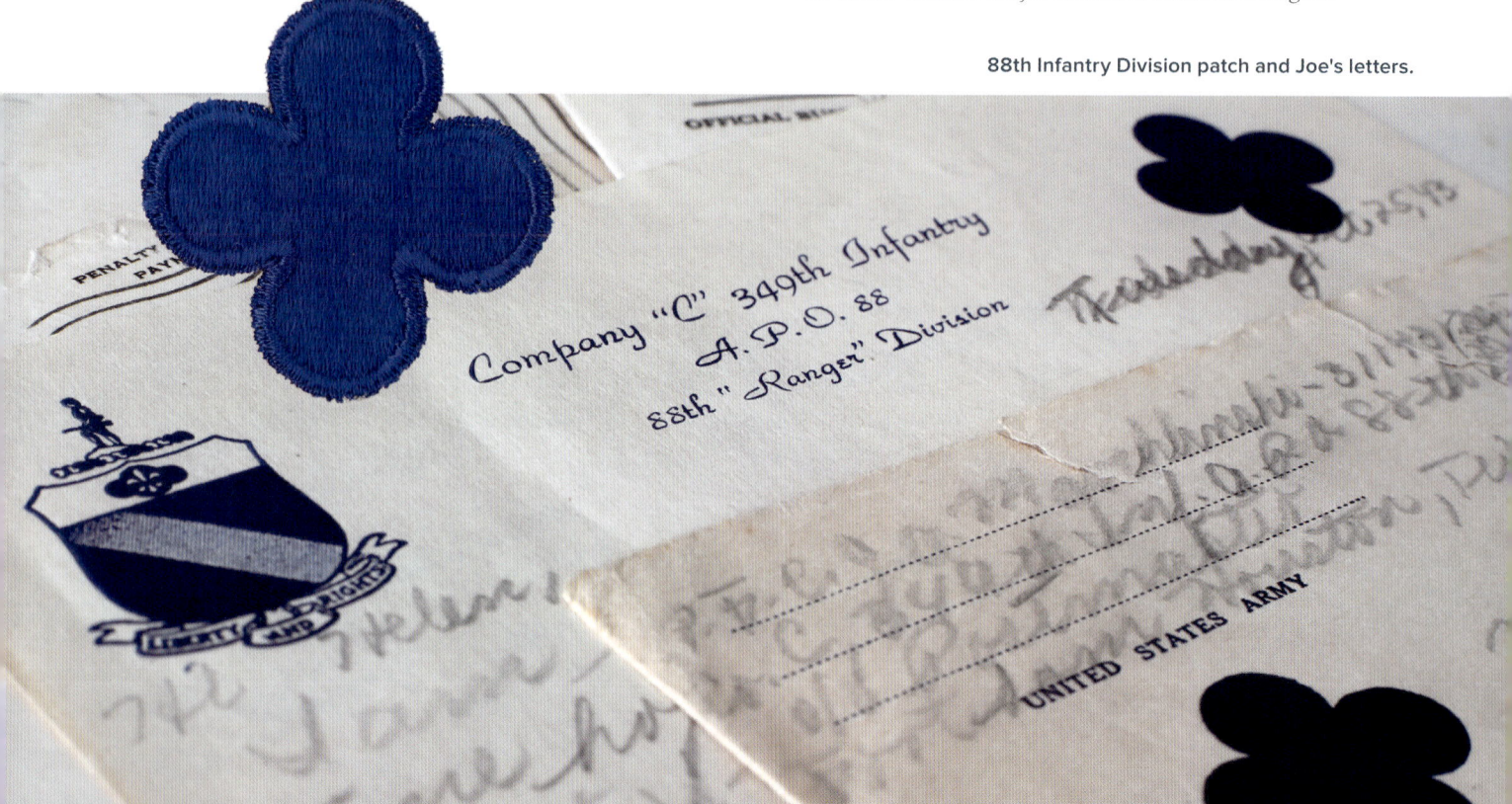

Joe and his comrades are on the Gothic Line in mid-September, pushing northeast of Florence towards Castel del Rio, capturing firmly-defended heights in the process. During their difficult march in early October to Monte Grande, which dominates the Imola-Bologna road, Joe's unit dislodges the Germans from the small town of Belvedere. A captured German officer would later say: *"In nine years of service, I fought in Poland, Russia and Italy. I've never seen such a spirit before. I would have been the proudest man in the world if I could have commanded a unit like the one that took Belvedere."* In the battles around this crucial objective, Joe receives a German bullet in the ankle. However, he won't write a word about his actual situation in Italy, even if it means perpetuating the myth of the D-Day Dodger. Most soldiers try to preserve their loved ones, already terribly worried about them, from the horrors of combat.

Roy is a sergeant in the 350th Regiment, 88th Infantry Division. When the Blue Devils were the first to enter Rome (the 'Eternal City') after hard fighting in the suburbs, two of his buddies, Elmer Duncan and Earnest Hill, had already been killed in action. Not wanting to alarm the young woman he'd just married, he kept the bad news to himself, although rumors and the press leaked the information anyway. Consequently, he had to explain himself in a letter dated July 10 (photographed below): *"Honey I didn't want you to know about Duncan but I guess you know about it now. Why Dottie told you I don't know. She knew Duncan and Hill both are in my company and what happened to them I didn't want you to know about it. But don't worry about me honey for it don't help any and it was no good for you. Honey tell Mom not to worry for I'm always okay and hope to be home soon and help her. I'll never forget the fun we had when we were in Kansas. I dream of those times now. Hope it won't be long before we can be together again."*

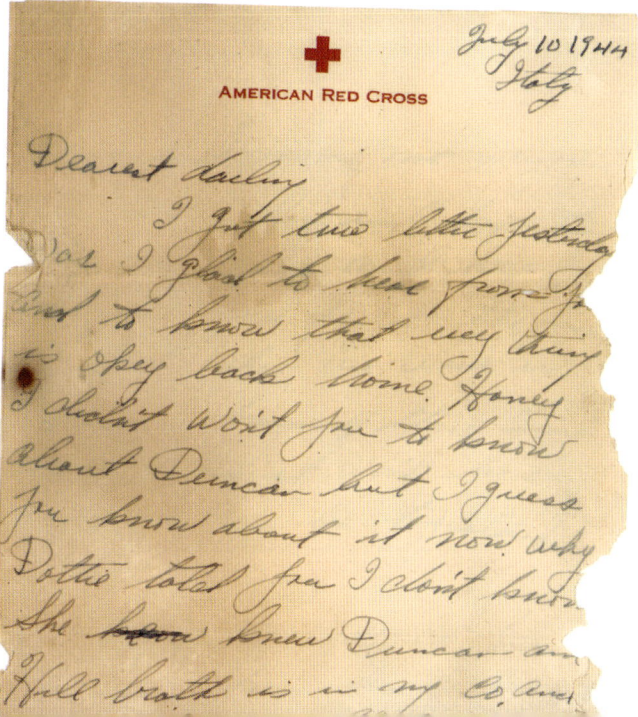

Photographs of Italy sent home by Roy: his Jeep in front of a peaceful panorama, and with friends on an Italian café terrace.

MONTE BATTAGLIA

Roy and his regiment are about to experience their worst battle yet, in the cold and mud of the Gothic Line. On September 27, Roy's battalion is to take and hold Monte Battaglia, a strategic summit north of the Apennines, whose control could open up the way to Imola and Bologna for the Americans. Its summit is quickly seized on the 28th, but the same day, Generalfeldmarschall Albert Kesselring launches a surprise counter-attack, throwing elements from no less than four divisions at Roy and his comrades. For seven days, the latter would repel attack after attack. Preceded by a deluge of artillery and mortars, German offensives start with flame-throwers and often end up in hand-to-hand bayonet combat. The weather conditions on Monte Battaglia (named 'Battle Mount' by the GIs) make the situation even worse. Stretcher-bearers have to evacuate the wounded on muddy slopes, under pouring rain and shells falling from all sides. As resupplying soldiers on these heights can only be done with mules, ammunition runs out quickly and, on several occasions, the Blue Devils are literally forced to throw stones at the Germans!

On the very first day of the battle, Captain Robert E. Roeder (commander of Roy's company) is involved in an action that would earn him the Medal of Honor.

Taking advantage of the fog, the Germans make their way through the American lines with flame-throwers and the company is soon engaged in close combat. Under his command, it inflicts heavy casualties on the enemy, but Captain Roeder is seriously wounded by a shell burst. When he eventually regains consciousness at the command post, he refuses any medical assistance, crawls to the exit, picks up a gun and leans against the door while shouting orders and encouraging his men. After shooting two German soldiers, he's killed instantly by a shell.

After a week of such fierce fighting, the 350th Regiment finally manages to keep control of Monte Battaglia, and the 2nd Battalion would receive a Distinguished Unit Citation for its relentless resistance. However, it has suffered terribly: nearly half of the men have been killed, wounded or reported missing. Still, they have to carry on, despite the fact that their losses can't be replaced quickly enough. On October 18, still in the Apennines, Roy writes to his mother: *"Yes Mom, it is tough going over here and this war can't end too quick for it's getting cold and raining every day and sleeping on the ground is no fun. But it can't last forever, I hope. [...] I am sorry that I don't have more time to write. Honest Mom I am going all the time and I know you folks won't know me when I get back. But don't worry about me for I am doing okay so far, someday Mom I will tell you all about sunny Italy, okay?"*

After forty-four days on the Gothic Line, the division has lost 6,000 killed, wounded and missing. In November, the Blue Devils halt their advance because of the weather conditions. Kesselring has won his bet. Roy, like his counterparts fighting in Northern Europe, realizes that the war would continue into 1945.

Greetings card sent by Roy in 1944 and bearing the emblem of the 5th US Army.

He still tries to reassure his wife in early December: *"Darling quit worry[ing] about me and forget about everything. I am alright, and I don't worry and I see why you do. I think everyone is stupid for doing it. It's a job we all got to do, and I am glad that I am one of those who is well and strong enough to do my part. This war can't last forever and, in my opinion, it is almost over now. It won't be long before we all will be back to stay and then we can start life like we want it."*

The division will occupy various defensive positions until the final assault across the Po Valley in April 1945, before chasing the Germans into the Austrian Alps. While the division occupies Trieste after the end of the war, Roy will leave the army in November 1945.

PADDY, THE EYES OF THE GUNNERS

Frank, nicknamed 'Paddy', is an artillery forward observer in the British 4th Infantry Division (8th Army). His role is to progress with the infantry and transmit the enemy's target coordinates via radio to the artillerymen in the rear. He must also assess the effects of the bombardment and adjust the coordinates, if necessary, until the firing mission is complete. In a way, he's the eyes of the artillerymen, who themselves are miles from the front. When not working from a camouflaged position, he travels in armored transports that act as mobile observation posts.

Frank has already served in Africa and at Monte Cassino, where he attacked the Gari River with the 8th Indian Division to his left and the Polish Corps to his right. The British had been surrounded, but the artillery support called in by Frank stopped several counter-offensives, including at least two armored ones. He then wrote to his girlfriend: *"You have read all about crossing the Gustav Line and Cassino, well darling you will be proud to hear your own Paddy was with the leading infantry in both places. I was quite pleased with myself when it was all over but believe me dearest while it was on I certainly kept down as far as I could but with a Bren Carrier, the driver has to look over the top and that's not so good. Anyway the push is on and we had the honour to start it and now we hope to get a decent rest for a change!"*

In June 1944, Frank's brigade crossed the Hitler Line and moved along the Tiber to the Trasimene Line, where it discovered a new kind of war against German rearguard units entrenched in the hills. The terrain was becoming increasingly mountainous, causing real trouble for the vehicles. Artillery observers were therefore forced to walk with the infantry and carry their heavy radio equipment on foot for miles.

V - VICTORY BY CHRISTMAS? LATE 1944

Shoulder patch of the British 4th Infantry Division.

Frank described his daily missions as an artillery observer in a letter dated July 12 while he was near Arezzo, targeting the German positions in Civitella (which would fall into the hands of the British 6th Armoured Division three days later): *"I hope you will not mind the pencil & paper, but under the circumstances I guess this is the best I can do. Three days ago I started an air letter to you, but was called away to the infantry lines almost immediately. I guess they cannot do without me. Anyway I have been waiting to finish that letter but at present it is miles away so I shall try and make up for it by writing this. The paper came out of the Italian house we are in which has only newly been captured, it certainly is in a mess. We are using it as an observation post so I guess this will be slightly disjointed because I have to keep looking out to see what the Boche are doing.*

There are several milling around the skyline by one of their dugouts and when I find the rest they are going to get an awfully big dose of shell fire. I am getting awfully fed up with those Boche, they certainly have caused me some worries and now I am in the position of being able to say 'Fire' to the guns and a ton or so of High Explosives will land right amongst them. That will probably give them something to worry about. [...] The last two nights have been really painful but laughable. Owing to the proximity of the enemy lines we have had to spend the last forty-eight hours in a small trench big enough for a small-sized dog and I have aches and pains all over. [...] Anyway, we are in a house for a little while and I am sitting on a real mattress, when it is my turn off duty I shall have to see just how soft it is. At present the officer and I are doing six hours on and six off. We are living on a half beer, half a loaf of bread and a tin of salmon per day but I hope this will improve. The trouble is we are fighting in some hilly country again and the transport trouble has occurred. Still when we get him out of the hills things should improve. By the way angel we are with the forward company of the most northernly troops in Italy, that's what you call front line (modest guy huh!)"

Embedded with the 2nd Battalion of the Bedfordshire and Hertfordshire Regiment, Frank follows the Arno River to the northwest. On July 17, 10 miles west of Arezzo, he writes to his girlfriend: *"Good to hear that you are fighting with us or at least taking an active interest in our whereabouts. Most people have forgotten Italy.*

Our latest push was not too bad after about three weeks in the hills. I hope to have a rest in Florence, it is not so far now in fact I should think we shall have it before you receive this. It is still really tropical out here and the only time we can be comfortable is in the cool of the evening." On top of this, the terrain is still mountainous, each peak topped by a church, whose bell tower serves as an observation post for the enemy.

Frank's division plays a major role in the approach to Florence, allowing the South Africans, followed by the New Zealanders, to enter the city on August 4, which the Germans had evacuated a week earlier. The Allies thus safely cross Ponte Vecchio, the only bridge over the Arno River still standing, which Hitler himself chose to save. From the city center, they gaze with apprehension at the intimidating mountains looming on the horizon. The Gothic Line awaits them.

This artillery forward observer is equipped with a map, binoculars and a radio to transmit coordinates. To blend into the landscape, he's covered his helmet with a large mesh net (Indian-made), wrapped his individual camouflage net around his neck, and smeared his pouches and straps with 'blanco' and green paint (this original kit was actually used by a soldier in Normandy, but the practice is common on all fronts).

OPERATION OLIVE

On August 18, while the men are enjoying a well-deserved rest in Assisi (southeast of Perugia), the divisional artillery is ordered to move towards the Adriatic Coast and passes under the command of the I Canadian Corps, along with the 2nd New Zealand Division. In fact, the entire 8th Army in Florence has to leave for the East Coast (and join V Corps, which it had left in April to help capture Monte Cassino). On the evening of August 25, 1944, the Allies launch a massive offensive on the Gothic Line: *Operation Olive*. The I Canadian Corps is to attack in the center, with the II Polish Corps on its right (on the coast) and on its left, along the Apennines, the V British Corps. The mission is to take Coriano Ridge (east of the State of San Marino), establish a bridgehead on the Marano River, capture Rimini, and finally hurl the British tanks into the Po Plains. While the 8th Army draws the Germans' attention on its eastern flank, the 5th Army has to crack the Gothic Line north of Florence and rush towards Bologna. The latter would attack the mountains on September 12 (as seen on page 251), three weeks after the start of *Operation Olive*.

Commonwealth troops face a less rugged terrain than their American allies, but they must cross a succession of rivers and face an equally determined enemy. Near Coriano, no fewer than twelve assaults are necessary to take Gemmano from the Germans (the 4th Indian Division would finally succeed on September 15), and the capture of Croce by the British 56th Division is a five-day struggle, only moving forward inch by inch. The 8th Army will lose hundreds of men every day on the Gothic Line. On September 11, Frank helps the Canadians take Coriano Ridge and cross the Marano River. On the 17th, the 4th Indian Division smashes the German lines in the neutral state of San Marino after three days of intense fighting, and the Canadians cross the Marecchia River, forcing the enemy to withdraw.

British crewmen of a 155 mm artillery gun fire at a German position on the Gothic Line on September 13, 1944, during *Olive*.

On the same day (September 17), the Americans in the west take Monte Altuzzo and Monte Pratone, before capturing Il Giogo Pass on the 22nd, which opens the way to Bologna. However, instead they decide to turn east towards Imola in an attempt to encircle the German 10. Armee facing the British. On the 8th Army front, on the morning of September 21, the Greek 3rd Mountain Brigade enters Rimini with the help of New Zealand tanks. Eighty per cent of the city is destroyed, after no less than 11,510 air missions, resulting in the deaths of thousands of civilians.

The 8th Army is finally racing into the region of Emilia-Romagna, but as Kesselring had predicted, torrential rains fall on Frank and the troops, turning the terrain into a real logistical nightmare and halting their advance. Back in early September, Frank's battery had taken twelve hours to move its guns up a muddy slope. On the night of September 21-22, the downpour is such that the regiment's headquarters, located on the side of a river bed, is drowned in the sudden rise of water. As Frank's battery's Command Post is threatened by the same fate, the men try to contain 5 feet of water with an improvised dam. Unfortunately, it would soon give in, swallowing up their equipment.

Frank's morale falls to its lowest point as he writes on the 29th: *"I am so miserable that I have decided to let you share some of my concerns. I am not feeling at all well my sweet and coupled with that the weather is terrible. It has been raining for nearly three days now and there is stacks of mud. Gosh what a terrible life, but still I guess I have at least a silver lining to my cloud, the thought of being able to see you sometime in the future is something that would cheer me up however bad things are. Last time I wrote we were up in the combat zone but I am back at the gun and now things are pretty quiet. [...] Too bad about the airmail service, I hope it will improve. Yours took nine days to get here but of course, the transport problem with all this mud is just nobody's business. It does seem peculiar the way we are always put into the thick of the fighting. Evidently, they cannot do without our Division, when Jerry has to be pushed back. Incidentally, we have had all sorts of congratulations from Army Commanders and even Winston [Churchill] himself. [...]*

Glad to hear your mother is so optimistic, but I guess we shall be fighting through most of this Italian winter. I wonder why the British Army does not make use of Italian houses. The Boche always does but I guess we have to be content with the muddy hills and valleys."

His girlfriend, however, seems to think that Frank is luckier than the soldiers operating in Northern Europe, although she's impressed by the Allied advance from Normandy. Frank's sarcastic and bitter tone in his reply is quite revealing of the D-Day Dodger's state of mind, after fighting all the way from North Africa and struggling with the Gothic Line for weeks: *"Sorry for the blot on this page that comes of writing with a crowd milling around. As you see I am once more back at the gun position. We had rather an exciting time getting back, because we had to pass within 300 yards of a Spandau machine-gun nest which commanded the whole road. I drove the truck as quietly as possible until we turned on to the road and then we fairly flew down the road, but the Boche only sent a short burst in our direction as it was rather dark at the time and he could not see us. It is these little things which make life a little more exciting than it should be. I am longing for the peace and quiet of civilian life after the war, I am going to have at least two months rest before plunging into work. [...]*

I am sorry about the newspaper cutting, I did not send it out of conceit, you say you want to know how we live, and it is quite a truthful account, so you can see why I am getting a bit fed up with war. Must be nice for these Canadian Air Force boys to have tea in a flat with lovely English girls floating around, all we get are shabby signoritas [sic] *in a broken-down house and usually they are only too glad to eat our meagre rations for us. I really am envious of them. Nowhere near Venice yet, we manage to push on about five hundred yards a day up to our knees in mud, it's great fun. [...] Sure, I heard all about the latest fighting round Arnhem, somebody high up has made another mistake, I guess. It must be pretty tough for these poor guys in France, fancy having to fight after spending such a long time in England having a good time. Of course, as you say it's easier out here. All we have to do is sit out somewhere in the middle of no man's land in a small slit trench, amidst torrential rain and fathoms of mud. Of course, there are mortars and nebelwerfers* [rockets] *and stray bullets and shells falling here and there but after all we have only done it for eight months, so it should be easier than France. Anyway, they have my sympathies and you have all my love forever."*

Frank will later express regret for the tone of his letter: *"I must apologize for my last letter, I was awfully sarcastic about your feelings about the invasion armies but you know darling if you were in my position you would feel differently I'm sure. Because after all the Boche has been told that the British shoot all prisoners and this is firmly fixed in his head when he fights out here. In fact, one which we captured was offered a cheese sandwich, and he would not take it because he believed it was poisoned. When we convinced him that it was perfectly OK, he ate it and was so overcome, he burst into tears. But really, my sweet, war is never easy and lately with all this rain, it has been really disheartening."*

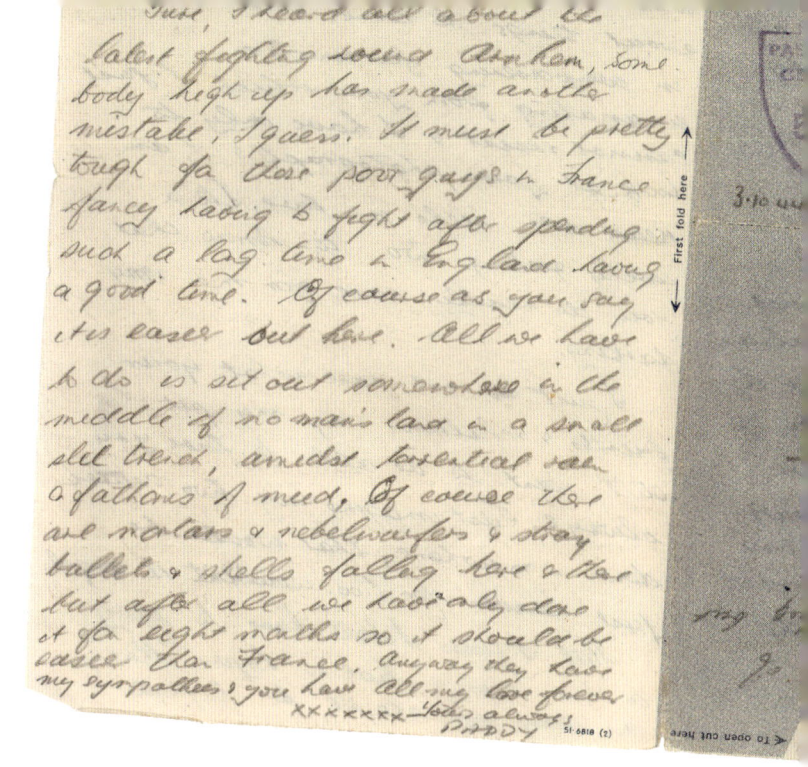

FINAL ATTEMPTS

The 8th Army reaches the Rubicon River, which the Indian 10th Division crosses on October 5, forcing the German 10. Armee to retreat to Bologna. On the same day, the American II Corps in the west launches a new offensive towards the city. Despite the terrible weather, the 8th Army continues its advance on Route 9 along the East Coast, and crosses river after river until the Ronco, the final barrier before Forlì (between Rimini and Bologna). On the morning of October 25, Frank's small group of five men, led by Captain Hannam-Clark, is embedded with the 2nd Battalion of the Duke of Cornwall's Light Infantry Regiment in their attack on Forlì. They advance rapidly until engaged by the enemy in Selbagnone. After a short battle, won mainly thanks to the artillery support from Frank's group, the Germans are pushed back across the Ronco River. The British infantry, in turn, crosses during the night, taking up positions in two barns that have been cleared of any enemy presence.

However, the Germans immediately counter-attack, destroying the lead tank of the 51st (Leeds Rifles) Royal Tank Regiment, whose burning carcass now blocks the progress of the others. The British infantry is therefore condemned to fight without armored support. To make matters worse, during the night a rainstorm prevents the men from digging fire positions, and they've no choice but to hold the houses, all the while being attacked from all sides. At least two Tiger tanks suddenly appear, firing at the buildings occupied by Frank and his men. Initially aiming at the corners of the first floor so that the roof would collapse on the soldiers inside, they then fire at the ground floor to prevent any exit.

As an explosion makes the barn shake from top to bottom, Captain Hannam-Clark is hit on the head by a roof beam, but is fortunately protected by his steel helmet. However, as he removes it to get the dust out of his eyes, a shower of bricks and tiles injures both his head and hands, as well as destroying his radio set. Now surrounded and unable to communicate with the rear, the British have no choice but to turn back and cross the flooding river. The captain and Frank manage to swim to the other side and call for a smoke screen to cover the retreat of about 80 soldiers of the 2nd DCLI, but 120 other infantrymen and 4 officers arrive too late in front of the flooded Ronco, and fall into the hands of the Germans. In Frank's small team, Lance Bombardier Pollard (wounded in the battle) and gunners Hardman and Davis are taken prisoner.

Frank writes in early November: *"Our party of five has now been reduced to two, the Captain wounded and myself OK. The other poor fellows are missing, believed either prisoners or killed. Bit of a blow but thank God I am still alive and well. It was at a river crossing, but things did not turn out at all well when Tiger tanks counterattacked. It was back across the river or nothing and the three signalers just didn't make it. Easy to tell but I guess it means heartbreak in at least three homes. [...] Please do not get worried about me getting soaked, it is the thought that I am helping to enable people at home to lead a more comfortable life, that makes one want to carry on. If I knew that solely by my actions in the Army, you could have a comfortable bed and a fire, well darling then I would stay in the Army for life!"*

He adds on the 4th: *"Have not received a letter from you for nearly a week, but there is probably one waiting for me when I return to the gun position, I hope so anyway. We have been up with the infantry for four days now and I shall be glad when we return, the weather is pretty foul, lots of rain and the mud is getting pretty bad again and that rather hampers operations. Have been shelled pretty regularly and the number of machine gun bullets which pass this way is just nobody's business, but as you see I am still alive and kicking. I really am getting fed up with this d-----d war and the prospect of spending winter in Italy does not appeal to me whatsoever. Maybe they will let us out of the line for a couple of months, if so I hope we go to Egypt for a rest, it is still sunny out there I guess, but I suppose that is just wishful thinking again. Since our last catastrophe the Captain has gone on leave and I am out with a Lieutenant who is a pretty good fellow. Anyway, he is learning fast under my 'expert guidance'. By the way I have not heard any further news about the three boys, so I guess and hope that they are all prisoners."*

A new crossing takes place on November 1, and the fighting around the Ronco would last several days, with German artillery, mines, snipers, machine guns and Tiger tanks still present. The Germans would finally withdraw north of Forlì on the night of November 8. The British would only cross the Cosina River on November 23 and the Lamone on December 17 (leading to the liberation of Faenza) and will have covered only 30 miles in over a month. Bologna, keystone of the entire Italian front, is closer than ever, but as winter sets in, the weather deteriorates.

THE WINTER TRUCE

The Americans, short of personnel and ammunition, halt their advance south of Bologna. After a final assault on October 16, which allows the 88th US Division to seize Monte Grande (on the 20th) and the 78th British Division to take Monte Spaduro (on the 23rd), the 5th US Army's march comes to an end. Although only about 60 miles away from Bologna in the northwest and Imola in the east, the men are exhausted and can no longer replenish their losses. The American 34th, 85th, 88th and 91st Infantry Divisions have lost 15,716 soldiers since September 10. As it moves to attack the Senio River, behind which the 10. Armee has settled comfortably, the 8th Army also interrupts its operations, discouraged by the first snows. Since the beginning of *Operation Olive*, it has lost more than 14,000 men and its artillery has fired no less than 1,470,000 shells, almost as many as the Second Battle of El Alamein and Monte Cassino combined. It had been a close call, but Kesselring has got what he was hoping for. Although some minor breakthroughs were made, the fighting on the Gothic Line was extremely violent and no sufficient progress was made to break it. The Allies therefore take the decision to hold 'offensive defense' positions until the spring.

Frank won't see the end of the Italian Campaign as his regiment will be withdrawn from the lines on November 27, before being re-equipped and sent to Greece in mid-December to deal with a civil war. The Greek resistance, financed by certain communist countries such as President Tito's Yugoslavia, had formed the Democratic Army of Greece (the military wing of the Greek Communist Party) and now sought to replace the Greek government, supported by the British and Americans after the country's liberation. On December 3, 1944, a demonstration in Athens by the National Liberation Front (close to the Democratic Army) will turn into a fight with the Greek police and British soldiers. The incident will soon grow into a real conflict with the involvement of Albania, Yugoslavia and Bulgaria on the one hand, and the increase of the Anglo-American support on the other. This will be the very first conflict of the Cold War, long before the end of the Second World War.

V - VICTORY BY CHRISTMAS? LATE 1944

The 4th Division will thus leave Italy with the British 46th Division, the Indian 4th Division, the Greek 3rd Mountain Brigade and various armored and parachute units. Frank will remain in Greece until 1946, and then transfer to the army reserve in July 1947. But the Greek Civil War would not end until 1948, when the growing American involvement, the inability of the Democratic Army to attract enough recruits and the side effects of the tensions between Tito and Stalin (who wants to make Yugoslavia a satellite country of the Soviet Union), leads to the defeat of the communists in Greece. The country will then join NATO.

Just like the units withdrawn from the front to be sent to Greece, the British 5th Division and the entire I Canadian Corps will leave for the Netherlands in February 1945. The Allies in Italy will therefore once again see their strength considerably reduced, although the war on this front will still be far from being won. Gerald, a gunner in a Sherman M4 tank belonging to the 2nd Lothians and Border Horse (British 6th Armoured Division), lost his tank and half of his unit at Monte Cassino. In January 1945, he'll be fighting in the (snowy) hills of the Apennines as an infantryman and write: *"None of the chaps in the office have been called up since I left but there seems to be a great deal of anxiety regarding this new call up. Quite a lot of the chaps are around the age of thirty and they don't fancy being called up for the services. I wouldn't mind seeing some of them called up and put in our place out here. It would do them good. Did I tell you that I shall probably be resting for some considerable time now? [...] Old Joe [Stalin] is going to finish the war off while we are still thinking about it. I hope he can make the grade before my rest is finished because I'm not so keen as I used to be. [...] Lady Astor in the House referred to the lads in Italy as D-Day Dodgers. Nice sort of person isn't she. I'd like her to have seen some of the sights I saw a week ago at the front. She might have changed her ideas. 'Nough of her."* His new tank will be hit by a shell in Bondeno during the spring 1945 offensive on Bologna, and he will be killed on April 22, at the age of 22.

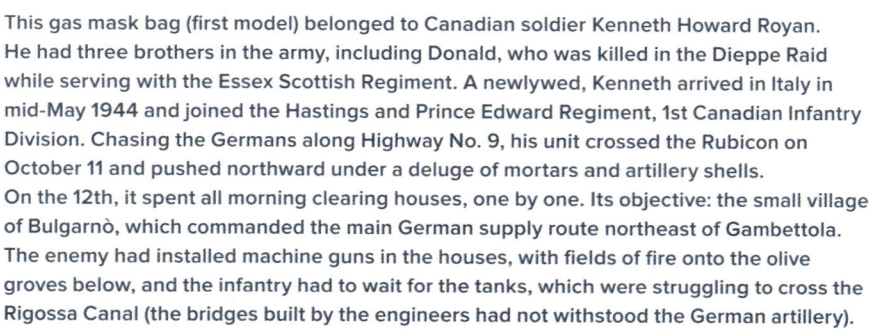

This gas mask bag (first model) belonged to Canadian soldier Kenneth Howard Royan. He had three brothers in the army, including Donald, who was killed in the Dieppe Raid while serving with the Essex Scottish Regiment. A newlywed, Kenneth arrived in Italy in mid-May 1944 and joined the Hastings and Prince Edward Regiment, 1st Canadian Infantry Division. Chasing the Germans along Highway No. 9, his unit crossed the Rubicon on October 11 and pushed northward under a deluge of mortars and artillery shells.
On the 12th, it spent all morning clearing houses, one by one. Its objective: the small village of Bulgarnò, which commanded the main German supply route northeast of Gambettola. The enemy had installed machine guns in the houses, with fields of fire onto the olive groves below, and the infantry had to wait for the tanks, which were struggling to cross the Rigossa Canal (the bridges built by the engineers had not withstood the German artillery).
On October 14, tanks and soldiers worked together for more than seven hours and while the infantry protected the tanks from the formidable 'Panzerfaust' bazookas, the tanks fired piercing shells into the walls before firing a second high-explosive shell to kill the defenders. Bulgarnò fell at 4:30 pm, but Kenneth was killed in the fighting and is now buried in the Cesena War Cemetery in Italy.

As is often the case in the army, his equipment had a second and even a third life. The bag was reused by a British major, then sent to Denmark to be refurbished and used by the Civil Forsvaret (Civil Defence). It was finally found by the author in 2008 in a Danish surplus store in Copenhagen. The bag still bears the name of the young Canadian who died in October 1944, handwritten in white paint. The gas mask, dated 1943, may also have belonged to him.

Italy is home to two large American cemeteries (the Commonwealth dead rest in over fifty-four cemeteries, including civilian ones). The one in Florence has 4,398 graves and the names of 1,409 missing soldiers, most of whom fought on the formidable Gothic Line.
Two of the crosses have gold inscriptions and are for the recipients of the Medal of Honor, the highest American military distinction: Sergeant Roy Harmon (362nd Regiment, 91st Division), killed on July 12, 1944 while single-handedly destroying two German positions in Casaglia, and George Dennis Keathley (338th Regiment, 85th Division).

On September 14, 1944, on the second day of *Operation Olive*, George's B Company was fighting for Mount Altuzzo. All the officers were killed or seriously wounded in three German counter-attacks, all of which were repelled, and the men ran out of ammunition. Sergeant Keathley therefore took command of the twenty survivors and volunteered to crawl from corpse to corpse, under enemy fire, to collect ammunition for his men and medical supplies for the wounded. The Germans suddenly launched their final counter-attack from three sides at a time, using grenades and machine guns and supported by a terrifying mortar burst. George was shouting his orders with precision and his men obeyed with great efficiency. A grenade exploded near George, opening his left side, but rather than stop the bleeding, he stood up and, removing his left hand from his gaping wound, grabbed his gun to kill several Germans converging on his position.

He continued to fight for fifteen long minutes, until an Allied artillery fire suddenly put an end to the firefight, forcing the Germans to withdraw. A few minutes later, George died in the arms of his friend, Charles Dozier. His last words were: *"Please write my wife a letter and tell her I love her, and I did everything I could for her and my country. So long, Dozier. Give'em hell for me. I'm done for."* Even if not all of the graves are covered in gold, each of these names and crosses hides a story, a shattered family, and a life cut short in its prime.

VI
THE LONGEST WINTER
The Allies in White Hell

As the first snowflakes fall in France, the Allied advance is at a standstill. The 7th US Army, which had landed in Provence, has difficulty crossing the Vosges mountains, Patton's 3rd US Army is stuck in Alsace-Lorraine, and to the north, the 1st and 9th US Army face the well-defended city of Aachen and the Hürtgen Forest. The enemy is entrenched only a few miles from his homeland but, unlike the Allies, his supply lines have never been so short, and those who didn't want to die for the Reich's victories are now ready to defend their *Vaterland* ('Fatherland') at whatever cost.

THE 3rd DIVISION IN THE VOSGES

Joseph Nemec, whom we last heard about near Anzio (page 140), landed in Provence on August 15, 1944. His division drove up along the Durance and then the Rhône rivers, in pursuit of the retreating Germans on their way to Belfort. It reached Montélimar in late August, where it took nearly 2,000 prisoners, killed hundreds of Germans and destroyed or captured more than 3,000 vehicles and heavy weapons. On September 1, it advanced at high speed from Montélimar to Leyment, bypassing Lyon from the east, before crossing Lons-le-Saunier and then Besançon on September 5. It was here the Germans decided to halt and occupy the old forts to hold the city. But the 7th Regiment, which gave them little time to organize, took the city after three days of fierce fighting.

Approaching the Moselle River on September 24 under enemy fire, the division liberates Vagney and Sapois in early October. Combat conditions in the Vosges are abominable. Joseph writes: *"The weather over here is still pretty bad, as it is over a week now of rain and cold, which doesn't help matters any. The poor visibility up in the wooded area limits our fighting and prevents us from moving ahead very fast. We are all hoping for the war to be over soon, but the way things are going we'll probably be here another winter. Gosh I hope not, I sure dread another winter over here in combat..."*

In mid-October, Joe completes four days of training in Eloyes, where his unit receives replacements to fill the gaps in the ranks. He takes this opportunity to write to his parents again on the 17th: *"About another week and I'll be with this outfit one year; gosh did that time go by fast. I'm the third oldest man in the radio section, so I can call myself an old man in the company. Because a few went home on rotation and some was [sic] killed or wounded. Naturally that dwindles them down to us year olders. I sure would like to go home with this outfit, because I'm pretty proud of this division. I suppose though when we do come home the civilians will praise and cheer us, but shortly afterwards those who fought overseas will be forgotten; just like in the last world war. Half of them should come over here and just see what really is going on, and what we are going through to get this war over with."*

Despite the fatigue, by October 20 Joe has to return to the front lines. The regiment leaves Grandvilliers for the Col du Haut Jacques, west of Saint-Dié: a strategic crossroads for both sides, which the Germans really don't want to let go. The American assault, part of *Operation Dogface*, is intended to help the VI US Corps break through the Vosges to Strasbourg. Men often fight at close range in difficult weather conditions and with almost no visibility. Joe, who carries the radio for Major Benjamin C. Boyd (the battalion commander), would play a crucial role in the battle, as communications are essential for the troops' progress in the rugged terrain of the Vosges.

The American EE-8 field telephone and its TS-9 handset. Working with batteries, it kept the front-line GIs in constant contact with the rear.

As night attacks are common, good coordination between units is necessary to avoid the many traps laid by the Germans: 120 mm mortars, artillery, 88 mm guns, camouflaged machine gun nests, anti-tank and anti-personnel mines, booby traps (explosive devices often triggered by an invisible wire), roadblocks and ambushes, all lie in wait for the Allied forces. Joseph is wounded again in the first days of the attack, somewhere between Les Rouges-Eaux and the Col du Haut Jacques. Sheltering in a small barn, his small group of radio operators is about to cook a pasta meal when, suddenly, the German artillery scores a direct hit. A fragment of the wall fractures Joe's cheekbone and damages his right eye. On October 29, as the fighting in the mountains continues (Le Haut Jacques wouldn't be secured until November 4), his sergeant writes to Joe's parents: *"I suppose you have heard by now that Joe was hit again. He will be OK but I sure miss him. He was one of my best radio operators and as a soldier he couldn't be best* [sic]. *That son of yours was the coolest kid I ever saw. He never got excited. One day he ran into some Jerries. He pulled out his .45 and shot him out of things. When he came back he wasn't excited at all. All he said was 'You should have been with me!'"*

Joe also announces the sad news to his parents on November 8: *"I'm afraid I won't be too pretty a sight to look at when you do see me, as I got it pretty bad this time. This makes it nine times I've been hit and remember the old saying a cat has nine lives. I'll have a pretty bad scar on my right cheek and I'll probably lose the sight of my right eye and hearing of my right ear. Otherwise everything else will be okay. I was one of six that was wounded and I was hit the worse. Two of the other men that was* [sic] *hit were radio operators. I was lucky I didn't get it sooner as we had some days that were pretty hot. You'll notice the 'Sgt.' up there in front of my name. Yes, I made T4 the same day I was hit. I met Major Boyd, my Battalion Commander, here in the same hospital. I was lying in bed and he comes walking up to me and he sure was surprised to see me here. He's really a swell man to know; I was with him quite often, as I carried the radio for him."*

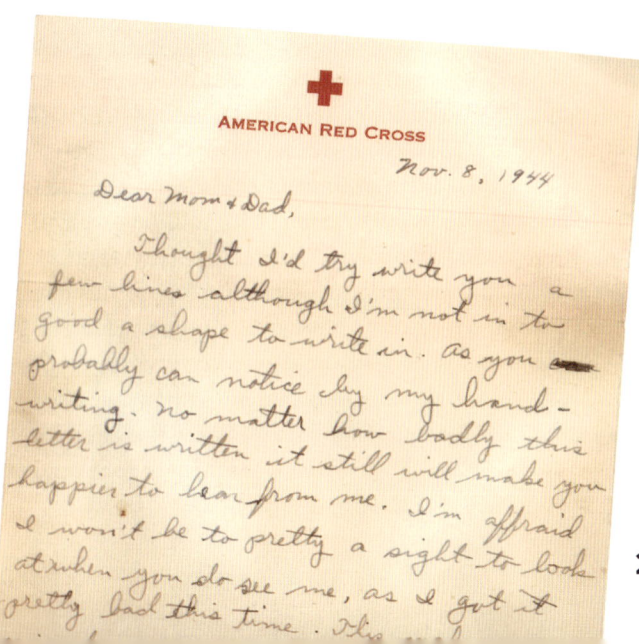

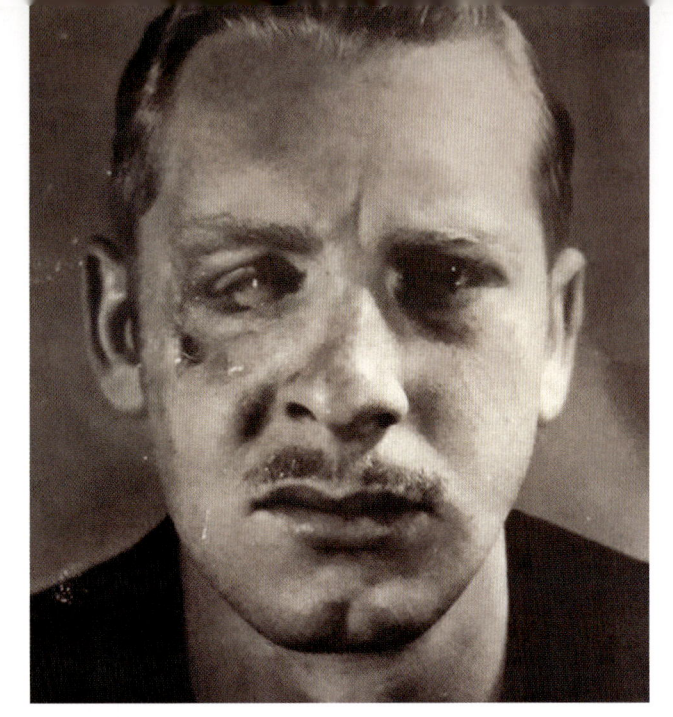

Joe Nemec was disfigured when he returned from the front. You can see in his eyes the sadness, bitterness and anger of a man who lost the best years of his life in the war.

Major Boyd was also wounded in the face a few days after Joe, during a heroic action on the second day of the battle for Le Haut Jacques, on October 31. When the assault was launched at 8 am, C Company suffered seventeen casualties in only one minute of climbing the pass under a shower of mortar shells, throwing their burning metal fragments and splinters from blasted trees in all directions. Seeing A Company pinned down by continuous machine gun fire, Boyd left his command post and crawled more than 600 yards amidst whistling bullets and crashing bombs to join the foxhole of a group of GIs, who'd been exposed and discouraged by the violence of the enemy fire. He managed to galvanize the troops, and the previously silent American positions suddenly opened fire with all their might, supported by Major Boyd, who'd borrowed a sergeant's rifle. Boyd even killed a German sniper, about 100 yards away, who'd caused several casualties among the Americans. At that very moment, a bullet hit him in the face, creating a gaping wound in his right cheek and resulting in a great loss of blood. However, the major refused to be evacuated and continued the fight for an hour, shouting at his men to *"give the Krauts hell"* and never let up. They finally repelled the enemy, before Boyd joined Joseph Nemec in the hospital. For this action, Boyd received the Silver Star.

The regiment will later manage to destroy the German units sheltered in the Vosges mountains completely. A major offensive launched on November 14 would made it possible to reach the Rhine on November 19, liberate Mulhouse the next day and then Belfort on November 25. As for Joseph, he'll leave his hospital bed in early 1945 and be sent back to the United States with his Purple Heart (with oak leaf cluster).

VI - THE LONGEST WINTER WINTER 44-45

While undergoing months of rehabilitation at William Beaumont Hospital in El Paso (Texas), he'll meet his future wife, Alice, who was a secretary in the hospital. They'll have three daughters and live in Elmhurst, New York, but Joe's life will never be the same again. Mutilated, and suffering from post-traumatic stress disorder and alcoholism, he'll no longer be the funny young man he was before the war. These issues will cost him his marriage, and Joe will be in pain for a long time. The loss of his eye (replaced by a glass one), will prevent him from working as an engineer, as he had always wanted to. He'll become a repairman instead, and the asbestos contained in the appliances he services will lead to cancer that will take him away on October 28, 2009. Joe rests today at the Long Island National Cemetery in New York.

ALSACE-LORRAINE

When the 3rd US Army knocks on Germany's door in early September, they were out of gas. At that time, not all of the ports in Northern France had been liberated by the British, the Scheldt Estuary prevented any use of Antwerp's harbor, and *Operation Market Garden* had monopolized most of the resources. The 'Red Ball Express' (the famous truck convoy system that supplied Allied forces as they advanced through Europe following the Normandy Invasion) was no longer sufficient and Patton's tanks really needed their 350,000 gallons of gasoline per day in order to face the German soldiers cornered at the Reich's borders who were fighting for their lives. On top of this, the terrain was perfect for the defenders: the dense forests, the driving rain that flooded the Moselle River and drowned the GIs in mud, as well as the cold that was beginning to set in, all conspired to make the fortified hills very costly objectives. The crossing of the river on September 5 was a disaster, and a second attempt five days later, although it helped the Americans surround Nancy, was met with a violent armored counter-attack. Saarland and Frankfurt now seem out of reach for Patton's men, who've lost the initiative...

Dog tags belonging to Chester Gill, 134th Regiment (35th Division), and shoulder patch. Promoted to sergeant in Saint-Lô on July 20, this GI was wounded with 14 other men on November 15 in Morhange (east of Metz and Nancy). His division liberated 124 cities, including Nancy.

For the Germans, keeping the 3rd US Army at bay was an absolute priority. Only 40 miles from the Siegfried Line, the Germans were occupying a series of thirty-five nineteenth-century forts, built on the Moselle around Metz and Thionville. At the beginning of September, the city of Metz was even declared 'Fortress of the Reich' and received new elite troops to defend it. The 3rd Army, which had just liberated Nancy on September 15, was stopped in front of the city gates.

Wendell Follansbee (pictured below behind his truck) serves in its 10th Armored Division (21st Tank Battalion, HQ Company). He landed in Cherbourg on September 23 and by October 31 has reached the woods on the western outskirts of Metz.

The 10th Armored Division is then engaged in the fighting for the city's liberation, alongside the 5th and 95th US Infantry Divisions. In the forest, Wendell and his men experience their very first bombardment: several soldiers of HQ Company are wounded and a young French boy is killed near the HQ. The Germans hold former French positions on the Maginot Line, which they'd taken four years earlier, and just behind is the Siegfried Line. On November 10, the battalion arrives near the Luxembourg border, northwest of Thionville, as war rages on in Metz. The final assault on the city is launched three days later, before finally falling on November 22. However, certain forts west and south of Metz are still occupied by the Germans, who refuse to surrender, despite the bombs and the use of napalm. When the 95th Infantry Division withdraws after an excellent fight, the 5th besieges the remaining positions. The last of them, Fort Jeanne d'Arc, wouldn't surrender until December 13, after three months of stubborn resistance. Wendell and his comrades enjoy their Thanksgiving meal on the Franco-German border and four days later settle in Eft, where they're subjected to heavy artillery fire.

It's there, on November 28, that Wendell writes this letter: *"Dear Mom, [...] things are quiet here right now, but of course, we are a little way behind the front, so I don't know what is doing up there. I pulled shift on the radio this morning from 2 till 5 o'clock. Instead of going to bed then I went down and started the stove and prepared breakfast for the rest of our gang. I found some potatoes and fresh eggs in the barn. Besides that, we had fried bacon, jam (from the cellar), coffee, toast and cocoa. We eat like kings. They have a new ration that contains 3 complete meals for 10 men ready to cook. Cigarettes, candy, gum and other accessories come with this ration. We found a cellar full of preserves yesterday. The boys take turns cooking the meals. After breakfast, I relieved another operator for chow. I watched the medics bring in the wounded from the front. It's almost a blessing for some of them to get back to the hospital where they can rest and be warm. A few prisoners were brought in on jeeps. They all looked like old men. Our artillery gave them hell last night, but it has quieted from somewhat today. I haven't been way up to the front lines yet and I hope I don't. At 10 o'clock I left the set and went up the street to where the tank section are staying. They have a beautiful setup, only 10 men, and they have 6 rooms with a kitchen, beds with mattresses and a bath. The kitchen has a cooking stove... The radio gang were up there but they made us move down where the officers were, so now we have no beds to sleep on. We really take over these houses. They put all the 15 civilians in the place into one house and placed a guard over them. I am picking up souvenirs here and there, the Krauts leave their equipment everyplace. Well I am going to make coffee. If I had flour, I would bake a cake. We have a nice cook stove here. Keep the letters and packages coming. Love, Wendell."*

K 'Supper' ration and an inner waxed cardboard box (in this case, a 'breakfast' example). Although not very popular with soldiers, these rations made up the bulk of their meals on the front, despite being designed for emergency situations (ration C, which is more substantial, contains three to four different preserves). Depending on their version – breakfast, lunch or dinner – K rations contained canned meat and cheese, cookies, fruit pastes or chocolate bars, and a variety of other items, such as water purification tablets, toilet paper, cigarettes and matches, chewing gum or caramels, sugar, salt, and coffee or powdered drinks. A resting GI watching infantrymen coming back from the front wrote to his family: *"Was wondering what for a Sunday you had back home and too whether you are eating K-rations. Ha! Ha! I hope not. Well anyway we are fortunate, when you see some of the fellows I have seen I'll eat my K-rations and like them and not say a word."*

THE 3ᴿᴰ ARMY IN THE SAARLAND

When Metz is finally in Allied hands, Patton moves towards the Siegfried Line. Among the units in his already famous 3rd Army, the 6th Armored Division 'Super Sixth' has already distinguished itself in Normandy and Brittany. Having raced across France, it reaches Saarland in November between Nancy and Metz. It crosses the Nied River on the 11th, facing strong German opposition, and advances alongside the 35th and 80th US Infantry Divisions. The division is on the Reich's border on 6 December and consolidates defensive positions not far from Saarbrücken. Carl, a member of a US armored infantry battalion attached to the 6th Armored Division, describes his daily life on the front of Eastern France in a letter to his parents on December 18: *"I'm not living out on the ground all the time. Usually two or three days is the longest I have to stay out and then it's mighty rough generally. Besides being shot at there is seldom cover to get in and out of the rain and cold. There are many small towns and villages all over France and when we're not actually in contact with the Jerries we sleep in houses. As for sleep that isn't hard to do. Usually I'm so tired I can go to sleep standing up. Sometimes the situation doesn't permit sleep for a couple of days but as soon as things quiet down you move into a house or barn and sleep all you want except for pulling guard. As far as the noise of gunfire is concerned you get used to it and I generally don't wake up till Jerry throws in a barrage pretty close. Probably the reason very few soldiers get the flu etc. is because there's no rapid temperature change. You get cold and you stay that way. I don't have to carry all my equipment on my back. Being in the armored infantry practically all moving is done in our half-tracks. We carry all our personal belongings with us, besides our rations, etc. I always carry my stationary in my shirt, that's the reason the stuff always looks beat up. Generally my shirt pockets are the only ones that are dry. You get pretty well soaked if you lay in a ditch with several inches of ice water in it for any length of time. We feed from a field kitchen and get hot meals if we're not in too much fire. The rest of the time we either cook our own meals with 10 in 1 rations or eat field rations – C or K.*

Quartermaster supplies us with everything. We don't pay for anything. If you need or want an extra article all you have to do is open your mouth. Every five days we are issued clean heavy wool socks. Combat troops are well supplied at all times. [...] I've pulled my guard for tonight and since I haven't slept for the past 40 odd hours I think I'll hit the hay."

Operations in Saarland will still be ongoing when the Germans launch their last major offensive in the Ardennes in mid-December, and on December 23, Carl's division will be dispatched north of Metz to help contain the enemy assault and hold the south of the region. Alongside the 4th Armored Division, a few days later it will rescue the American paratroopers cut off in Bastogne, before pushing the enemy back across the Our River. The movement of the 3rd Army to the southern flank of the Battle of the Bulge will mark the end of the first phase of the Lorraine Campaign. General Patch's 7th US Army will take over in January 1945, and the region will be liberated two months later after bloody clashes in Forbach and Bitche. In Saint-Avold, between Metz in France and Saarbrücken in Germany, the largest American cemetery in Europe contains the graves of 10,489 GIs who died in the Battle of Lorraine.

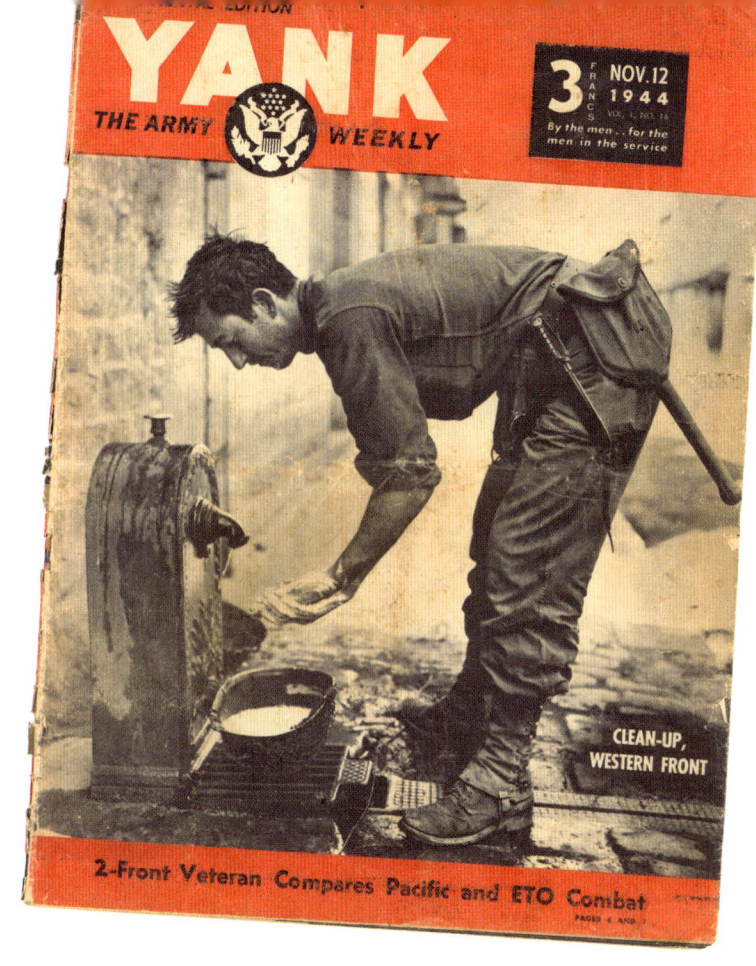

Private Schronce, a member of an anti-tank unit, appears on the cover of *Yank*, a popular weekly magazine for GIs (November 12, 1944). He's seen taking a break in the village of Villedieu to wash in his helmet.

This shirt and pants set belonged to a medic in the Medical Detachment, 50th Armored Infantry Battalion (6th Armored Division), who took part in the Battle of Lorraine. Carl, who was in the same division, wrote: *"As for Daniel I would like to see him be put in the Army as a medic. They don't carry weapons, so he wouldn't be killing anyone, but in about five minutes under fire he'd probably wish he could. The medics have it just as rough as the Infantry soldier. I've helped fix up wounded men and it's sure no fun, especially when you're being shot at at the same time."* Another GI said: *"Had a letter from a fellow who I took basic with in Texas. He is a combat medic up in Germany and he said he has seen enough for him for the rest of his life. He has the toughest medic assignment in the Army."*

A staff sergeant in the 110th Regiment, 28th Infantry Division, enjoying a moment of relaxation in a liberated village. His victorious march will be short-lived as his unit will go through hell once the Siegfried Line is reached.

He wears an officer's shirt made by a local tailor or purchased with his own money in an army store to replace his standard uniform. On this original shirt are sewn the staff sergeant's stripes and the division's 'Bloody Bucket'. The laundry number B-9447 (first letter of the soldier's name and the last four digits of his service number) is stamped in the shirt. Unfortunately, its owner has not been identified to date.

When liberating Europe, the Americans brought with them 'The American Way of Life': Jazz music, chewing gum, nylon stockings, blond cigarettes, 'aviator' glasses, blue jeans, milk chocolate, disposable razors, cereals, soluble coffee and Coca-Cola, which the company provided abundantly to the US Army. This bottle is dated March 1944 and was found during excavations on a former US Army camp in Normandy.

VI - THE LONGEST WINTER WINTER 44-45

THE 'BLOODY BUCKET' DIVISION

The US 28th Infantry Division, born from units of the Pennsylvania National Guard and a descendant of Benjamin Franklin's battalion The Pennsylvania Associators (1747-1777), is the oldest division of the US Army and is known as the 'Keystone' division in reference to the shape of the Pennsylvania state on the unit's shoulder patch. The Germans, however, would soon rename it the 'Bloody Bucket', both for its ferocity in the Normandy Campaign and for its heavy losses on the Siegfried Line. The 1st Battalion of the 110th Regiment had the honor of parading on the Champs-Élysées on August 29, 1944, immortalized by the press around the world, with the Arc de Triomphe in the background (below). William joined the battalion as a replacement when it started its push to the North. He was about to take part in some of the most violent engagements of the war, but the advance was initially extremely fast. William wrote: *"Well here I am still some place in France and still in the best of health. I am now near a town and we are one of the first Americans to get here. So yesterday I got a pass to go out and I went to town with a couple of buddies of mine and all the people would run up to us and shake our hands even the little kids. It kind of gave us a funny feeling. We met up with a couple of Free French boys and we went out and painted the town red. We were drinking champagne and red wine and beer. Boy we had a swell time!"*

The 28th Infantry Division was progressing at a rate of nearly 20 miles a day, driving through Compiègne, La Fère, Saint-Quentin, Laon, Rethel, Sedan and Charleville-Mézières, before crossing the Meuse and entering Belgium. The division liberated Arlon, then entered Luxembourg in early September. Only a few days had passed since the parade in Paris, but it didn't take long before the boys hit the Siegfried Line. Officially called 'Westwall', but nicknamed by the British in 1939, it extends over nearly 400 miles (opposite the Maginot Line) and is equipped with more than 18,000 pillboxes connected by tunnels. To stop the tanks, several rows of 3 to 6-foot high reinforced concrete 'dragon teeth', whose interstices are covered with barbed wire and mines, were built. On September 11, the division is one of the first to set foot on German soil and enemy resistance become fierce.

William writes again to his girlfriend a week after the previous letter, and his tone is no longer so cheerful: *"Hello Honey, well here I am someplace in Germany. You will have to excuse the writing as I am up in the front lines and I have nothing to lean on except my lap. [...] I sure would like to see you. It seems like I have been over here for years. Boy will I be glad to see that day when I sail back past the old statue of liberty, and march down old Broadway. I hope that day isn't too far away. It sounds like fourth of July over here every day, only all day and night."* As they approach the Siegfried Line, the men of the 28th Infantry Division capture no less than 153 pillboxes and clear the Monschau Forest of any German presence: *"I guess I told you I have been in combat. I just hope and pray that this war is over soon. I guess all the prayers from home have kept me alive all this time. I have some great stories to tell you when I get back home. I'll tell you what it is like living in a foxhole."* The Bloody Bucket's wild race will be slowed down when they enter the Hürtgen Forest on November 2, 1944, before experiencing bitter struggles for Vossenack, Kommerscheidt and Schmidt. William will be wounded in the leg at the beginning of the battle.

'HELL WITH ICICLES'

Just behind the Belgian border is Aachen, the first major German city reached by the Western Allies on September 16. A symbolic place for the Germans, who saw all their emperors crowned there, Hitler ordered the city to be defended at all costs. The region is also of strategic importance, allowing control of the Roer River dam (which the enemy wants to use to flood the area and slow down the Allies) and because they plan to launch their next counter-offensive in the Ardennes. After breaking through the Siegfried Line, the 1st and 30th Infantry Divisions enter Aachen in early October, facing a garrison of 5,000 men determined not to give up an inch of ground. Street fighting claims many victims, forcing the Allies to send the 29th Division as reinforcements. As with the Canadians in Ortona (Italy), the GIs blast their way from house to house with bazookas to avoid the deadly streets. The capture of Aachen and its suburbs will take a total of six weeks, costing each side more than 5,000 killed and wounded.

Two GIs watching a section of the Siegfried Line, including its anti-tank obstacles called 'dragon teeth'.

The 1st US Army, in charge of supporting the 9th US Army in the capture of the city, enters further south into a dense and dark conifer wood with steep peaks and plunging valleys. Covering nearly 80 square miles, the Hürtgen Forest extends from Malmedy (Belgium) to the south of Aachen and to the west of Düren (Germany). Among the elements of this 1st Army, the 9th Infantry Division is sent there first on September 19 with the mission of taking the town of Hürtgen. The town would only fall at the end of November, and to dislodge the Germans from the surrounding woods, the Allies would send the 1st, 4th, 8th, 28th, 83rd and 104th Infantry Divisions, plus the 2nd Rangers Battalion and elements of the 5th Armored Division in support, nothing less…

The terrain of the Hürtgen Forest is very hostile: the lack of roads prevents any armored support and the bad weather keeps the air forces grounded. The numerical superiority of the Americans, who sometimes fight five to one, actually works against them as they're facing experts in camouflage in an area that the latter had taken the time to know and prepare. Each trail is barricaded and booby-trapped, and its coordinates already registered by the German artillery guns, which stand by ready to fire. The forest is dotted with mines, including the undetectable wooden 'Schu-mine', and the 'S-mine', which explodes 3 feet off the ground while throwing metal balls in all directions. When the latter doesn't kill, the terrifying 'Bouncing Betty', also known as the 'Debollocker', inflicts the painful wound that all men fear the most… Hidden pillboxes and invisible machine gun nests take the GIs by surprise at the bend of every path; the density of the pine trees and lack of visibility make orientation difficult, and some units get lost far behind enemy lines. Shivering in the snow and icy rain, the men are physically and mentally exhausted after a few days in the forest. It doesn't take long before the many green replacements who joined the Allied ranks break down, and cases of desertion, self-mutilation and suicide increase at an alarming rate. Those who are lucky enough to survive nickname the Hürtgen Forest 'Hell with icicles'. The battle itself wouldn't end until February 1945, officially becoming the longest in the history of the US Army.

The 28th 'Bloody Bucket' Division, one of the first to enter, relieves the 9th Division in Vossenack. In an attempt to contain an enemy attack without armored support, a number of the division's units are decimated after finding themselves in the middle of a minefield and being pounded by German artillery. Frank is a corporal in the 109th Field Artillery Battalion and was with the division in all its battles. He writes to his little sister: *"This war out here is no good, there is a lot of stuff our here that isn't so pleasant to look at, and the stink makes you pretty sick at times. I wish this darn mess was all over. […] Haven't seen a movie in a long time – and do I miss them – gets your mind off a lot of things. […] Things out here were rough for a while. Now the weather here is pretty nice and not too cold, but I guess it won't be long and it will probably snow again. When you said I'm getting old you weren't kidding I feel old. I'll bet I aged about 10 years since I've been here. Well it's bound to be over one of these days. I hope. […] I've seen a lot of young boys get killed for no good reason at all."* With the Battle of the Bulge that follows, the 28th Division will suffer more than 15,000 casualties and will have to be removed from the lines to recover. Nevertheless, it'll return to the front line in January 1945, assisting the 1st French Army in the liberation of Colmar.

John Irvine (4th Infantry Division), who's just returned from the hospital after being wounded in Normandy, writes in late October: *"Belgium is a very uninteresting country. Looks about like Iowa and the people are all in rags and starving. The women all run after the train and fight over the biscuits the soldiers throw away. It's been raining all the time and we had to put up tents in about four inches of mud – everything gets covered with it. We have good meals here, except your mess kits get full of rain before you finish eating. I expect to be back with my outfit in a day or two, and hope we get some decent weather before that. Even snow would be better than this."* On November 12, on his way back to H Company, John helps the battalion's officers get the men of the 12th Regiment in position near Germeter, southwest of Hürtgen. The group then suddenly receives a violent artillery barrage, before watching with horror as the enemy overwhelms F and G companies, who've been cut off at the flanks.

VI - THE LONGEST WINTER WINTER 44-45

THE RANGERS IN HÜRTGEN

Kenneth Young is a sergeant in B Company, 2nd Ranger Battalion, to which Ray Alm still belongs (page 164) and who also experienced the horror of Omaha Beach. On November 3, 1944, the Rangers are moved to Neudorf (Belgium) and advance in mid-November to the vicinity of Vossenack in order to relieve the exhausted 28th Division. Kenneth is wounded with three other Rangers on the morning of November 22, near Germeter. After having just set up a command post in an abandoned German dugout, the men are being briefed by Captain Solomon when a German shell suddenly scores a 'direct hit'. Kenneth is evacuated on a stretcher to Germeter, where he's treated at the aid station and then taken by ambulance to the wounded collection point before being repatriated to England for hospitalization. We'll return to his story in a short while.

Soon after Kenneth's evacuation, the 2nd Ranger Battalion leaves the heart of the forest with great relief, but has no idea that it would next take part in one of their most terrible battles of the war: the capture of Hill 400 at Bergstein, on the edge of the Hürtgen Forest. The Germans had established an observation post there preventing any breakthroughs by the 8th, 28th and 45th US Divisions towards Cologne. Reducing Hill 400 to silence is therefore a priority mission for D, E and F companies, while Ray Alm's (and formerly Kenneth's) B Company would hold the town of Bergstein, below. When they arrive on site on December 6, the Rangers pass by the carcasses of American tanks and corpses of elements of the 5th US Armored Division who'd taken Bergstein and lost half their men and vehicles in the process.

Ray and his comrades set up their mortars in a field on the right-hand side of the hill and are soon engaged by German anti-tank guns firing on their position. As Ray acts as a forward observer, his men fire as many mortar shells as fast as they can. But the news from D, E and F companies is bad and although they finally take the hill on December 7, killing more than 500 Germans in the process, only a handful of survivors are left in each Rangers' company, having repelled no less than five counter-attacks in forty hours. The next day, Ray's company fends off another German offensive, before being relieved by the 8th Division.

Ray and his comrades will enjoy a few days rest in Belgium, but their recovery would soon be interrupted by the surprise major counter-attack of almost thirty German divisions in the Ardennes, on December 16 (see following pages). The enemy is targeting Antwerp and Aachen, which Goebbels (Reich Minister of Propaganda) had promised as a Christmas gift to Hitler.

John immediately volunteers to bring them ammunition, making his way through mines and explosions, while organizing the American line of defense. On his second trip, he's hit in the back by shrapnel and dies quickly from his injuries, as the first snowflakes fall on the Hürtgen Forest. He played a decisive role in maintaining the Allied lines while waiting for the 1st Battalion to come to their rescue. For his last action, John Irvine would posthumously receive the Silver Star.

LIEUT. JACK IRVINE Of Denver, who gave his life to help the Twelfth infantry, Fourth division, to victory in the Huertgen forest. With all but a single, dangerous route cut off, he volunteered to get supplies thru to embattled Twelfth troops. He fell after his second trip, but he had saved the units. The Silver Star was awarded posthumously.

A soldier in the 8th Infantry Division writes in his regiment's history: *"It was not a pretty sight. Bodies were lying all over the woods. I didn't mind seeing dead Germans but the sight of the 4th, 28th, and 8th patches on the shoulders of those dead men made me gulp. It was a madhouse of confusion. There was every kind of weapon, German or American, one could think of. In one day, I fired a BAR, a light machine gun, a German machine gun, a machine pistol, a carbine, and an M-1. I stuck to the M-1. It had saved my life many times. Besides, the others drew too much return fire."* Despite the fall of Aachen on October 22, the chaos in Hürtgen drags on.

Gary is still among the men of the 8th Division (we followed his training in the United States, see page 77), and is already suffering from the cold. In the early morning of November 28, his battalion takes part in the attack on the town of Hürtgen. Supported by tanks pounding every house in their way, the GIs face a tenacious enemy entrenched in the cellars and ruined buildings. The town falls at 5:30 pm, although the forest is still far from secure, and the regiment moves on to its next objective: Obermaubach, to the east. The weather conditions are appalling, as one of Gary's comrades writes: *"Our machine gun section supported the attack of Company C into Obermaubach. That was a cold, bitter day (December 22). I'll always remember it because the only way we could keep our guns from freezing was to warm the barrels with fire from lighted K ration cartons."* On December 1, Gary writes to his sister after a silence of more than two weeks: *"Gosh, bet you think I am a swell brother seeing as I haven't sent you a letter for quite a while but you can believe me when I say we have been busy and really didn't have any time for writing so hope you will believe me and forgive me too. Being somewhere in Germany isn't just the best place to be in this large world and have been here some time. This is one war the German people will never forget and hope they will never be able to start another."*

267

The Rangers would thus return to the cursed woods of Hürtgen to support the 78th US Infantry Division, at Simmerath. At the same time, on the other side of the Belgian border, the 9th US Infantry Division are fighting near Malmédy. Pushed by the German breakthrough to the other end of the Hürtgen Forest, where it fought for more than three long months, it will have a hard time reclaiming all the ground it had lost in just a few days.

Among the 9th Division men, Vernon is a childhood friend of Kenneth Young, the Ranger wounded by a shell a few weeks earlier. Vernon is responsible for keeping records of American casualties, and from his deployment in the area in September to the early days of 1945, his division has lost more than 16,000 men, including nearly 900 killed. Many were lost to diseases, such as 'trench foot' caused by cold and humidity, or exhaustion. Vernon writes to Kenneth on February 13: *"Hi Ken ole boy! Thought it was about time I inquired as to how things are going with you. Sure hope your wounds are healing well and that you will be around before long. Of course, Mother has been worried about you so please don't forget to drop her and Audrie a line and let them also know of your condition. Afraid I cannot say that much has been happening around the western front since you have been gone and we are still anxiously awaiting for something to crack in order to finish this darn war. The Russians have slowed down considerably, and it looks as though we are in for a longer siege than everyone predicts. The weather around this 1st Army front is still bogging down our troops with mud and rain and the action has turned into a tit for tat battle with slow but sure gains. Things have been going well with us in our present area, which is not too far from the spot where you were hit. I have been fairly busy with my casualty work although many times it becomes so monotonous and then my thoughts turn to home and all the good things we are missing. [...] Guess things are fairly pleasant for you back there in England and the thought of war must be far from your mind. Bet laying around becomes very boring also, doesn't it? Too much time to think of home and those future married plans I hear you are thinking about. Marriage is wonderful, Ken, so don't let anyone kid you about it. I for one have been very happy and I'm sure you too can find it the same. I only hope your present casualty status will not interfere with your plans. As you already know, a soldier's life is uninteresting and things rarely change except to bitch and wonder when we are going to get home. That's the extent of my life from month to month so I'm sorry to say that I can't supply you with any interesting news. Again let me wish you a speedy recovery Ken. [...] Lots of luck!"* Ken will pass away in 1983, and Vernon in 2006.

The last battles of the Hürtgen Campaign will blend with what will become known as the 'Battle of the Bulge'. As detailed in the following pages, the Germans will reach the Meuse River before finally being pushed back in January 1945. The Americans will launch their final assault through Hürtgen in early February and take the coveted Roer Dam on the 9th. However, the Germans will open it as planned, flooding the valley and forcing the GIs to wait until February 23 to cross the Roer. The 9th Division will only leave the Hürtgen Forest at this time, after almost six months spent in its deep and sinister woods. The 1st Army will lose more than 47,000 men in Hürtgen (7,000 killed, 35,000 wounded, and 5,000 missing and captured), to which must be added 51,000 men evacuated for illness or fatigue. As for the 9th US Army, near Aachen, it will count more than 30,000 casualties, with the Germans suffering almost as many. In fact, both sides have exhausted each other, with neither gaining enough ground to make a difference. Although the Battle of Hürtgen did divert some German units from Aachen, the sacrifice of experienced units was soon found to be completely unnecessary. As Major-General James Gavin said, *"For us, the Hürtgen was one of the most costly, most unproductive, and most ill-advised battles that our army has ever fought"*.

GIs searching a captured German machine gun nest in the Hürtgen Forest. Note the MG42s and equipment camouflaged by the branches.

GORDON PIERSON

155th Anti-Tank / Anti-Aircraft Battalion, 17th Airborne Division

Gordon met his future wife during his training, but was sent to England shortly after. While eagerly awaiting New Year's Eve, he predicts that the German resistance will end on December 15, 1944. In fact, the next day, von Kluge will make a crashing breakthrough across the Ardennes, where Gordon will be sent to try to contain the 'bulge' in the Allied lines.

LOVE STRIKES WITHOUT WARNING

Gordon Wesley Pierson was born on May 29, 1916 in Saint Paul, Minnesota, and enlisted on March 31, 1941. He trained at the Airborne School in Fort Benning, Georgia, completing the five required jumps in different configurations before obtaining his 'wings' (the parachutist's license, representing a silver parachute with wings, which the paratroopers proudly wear on their jackets). He first joined the 80th Airborne Anti-Aircraft Battalion of the already prestigious 82nd Airborne Division, then HQ Battery, 155th Anti-tank / Anti-Aircraft Battalion of the 17th Airborne Division.

His battalion plays an artillery role and is specially trained in landing with gliders, with their heavy guns towed by Jeeps. It's about 500 men-strong, divided into six batteries, headed by an HQ battery to which Gordon belongs. A, B and C batteries (anti-tank) each have eight squads equipped with 57 mm British guns, while D, E and F batteries (anti-aircraft) each have twelve squads in as many Jeeps, towing .50 caliber machine guns aimed at the skies. Each of these units can be attached to other regiments to support them when required. It was during a training maneuver in February 1944 that Gordon met Myrtle and fell in love. Unfortunately, he had to leave the USA after a few months spent at Camp Forrest in Tennessee (where Myrtle was born). Gordon arrived in England on August 26, 1944, narrowly escaping the *Market Garden* disaster as the division didn't have time to train for the operation.

THE ENEMY STRIKES WITHOUT WARNING

Gordon has no idea that in a few hours, the Germans will launch a major counter-offensive in Belgium during the century's harshest winter. For the Americans, it'll be one of the most famous and bloodiest battles of the Second World War. Just three days before the beginning of the Battle of the Bulge, Gordon writes to Myrtle: *"Happy Holidays dear, the way the mails* [sic] *been running I imagine the above greeting will arrive as late as 30 days, right? We're planning quite a party for Xmas Eve, and Xmas day, but I'm sure we'll be occupied in mind, but not spirit. Our memories will look back thousands of miles to our families, and my 'blonde bomber' with only one thought 'Oh, that I were there'. I'm getting kind of used to being away from home, or maybe I should say weathered, but just haven't got used to being away from Myrtle for so long. I doubt if I ever will. If we didn't see each other every night, it was every noon hour, which is rather a tough proposition, when relations of such a sweet person are cut out completely, just can't get used to it.*

Gordon in the history book of the battalion and 17th Airborne shoulder patch cut from an M42 jump jacket sleeve.

Seems like we've been gone a good year already. Seventeen more days and I'll have three and three quarter years in the service. Putting both foreign service and regular service together, the time sometimes seems it should be doubled, all in all makes a lot of Army life, I'm thinkin'. Come to think of it, I did just what I planned on never doing, and that was falling in love with a girl, when I'd have to leave the US, and then be heart sick and forlorn all the time I was abroad. I avoided girls, I broke relations with I don't know how many, always expecting a love call, and then a shipment out of the country. This went on and on for 3 years, and I used to say, kiddingly, I'll bet just before I really do ship out, I'll find my one and only, and I'll be a sad sack all the time I'm across. Well dear, I don't think and I also hope I'm really not a sad sack over here, but I do know that I miss you a hell of a lot, which at present times makes me very itchy to get moving, to rush this thing along so we can get home as soon as possible. Several months ago I set a date in my mind, being the 15th of December, as the day the German resistance would cease, but it looks like I missed the date by quite a little.

Men are fighting hard and moving slow over there, and the Germans are putting up a losing but unheard-of battle. I also said I never thought the war would actually be over until I and many more men were actually engaged, fighting, to see that, and help such a thing become a reality. Maybe they won't wait for us over there, after all, but if they are, well, I hope they don't have to wait too long. Sweetheart I hope you and the family are in good health, and again I wish you all a Merry Xmas and a Happy New Year. Guess what, I'm really putting on some weight, guess I'll have a fatty New Year. Maybe someday I really will fill out to the proportion I've always wanted. No fat, but a husky 165 lbs, OK? Tell Dot and Pat I'll drink a toast to them New Years of a moderate dry champagne 'French' 8-year-old, as well as to you dear. My wish will be to be with you as soon as possible forever and always. I love you dear, in case you weren't sure, or I hadn't mentioned this before, thought maybe you'd like to hear it some more, huh? Good night lovely, Gordy."

Gordon isn't the only one who doesn't see the last great German attack of the war coming. On the morning of December 16, Eisenhower is receiving his fifth star as a General and attending his driver's wedding, while Montgomery is playing golf while awaiting his Christmas leave in England. At the time, Allied units are scattered along more than 1,200 miles of borders, one of the least defended of which is, as in 1940, the Ardennes Forest. Enemy communications are intercepted by the Allies, but they don't pay them any heed. For Hitler, who'd already taken advantage of this route four years ago when the Allies considered the area impassable, the opportunity is too good to miss. What if the Allies hadn't learned from the past?

Prepared in the greatest secrecy, the German operation *Wacht am Rhein* ('Watch on the Rhine') plans to take elite SS armored units and Hitler's best troops across the dense forest in Belgium and Luxembourg all the way to Antwerp, cut the front from east to west, deprive the Allies of their main source of supply and force them to negotiate a separate peace. Nearly 450,000 men from 14 infantry divisions and 9 armored divisions (1,500 tanks and mobile guns), including many Waffen-SS units, supported by more than 4,000 pieces of artillery, would strike on the morning of December 16, taking the sometimes inexperienced American troops responsible for defending the line completely by surprise.

The offensive is of a speed and brutality reminiscent of that of May 1940. The 28th Infantry Division, which had been badly mauled in the Hürtgen Forest a few weeks earlier, takes the full force of the attack by the 5. Panzer-Armee in northern Luxembourg. Here, the Germans manage to advance 55 miles behind the American lines, reaching the outskirts of Dinant (Belgium) on December 25.

VI - THE LONGEST WINTER WINTER 44-45

On the maps that make the front pages of newspapers around the world, the dent in the lines is clearly visible and will give its name to the 'Battle of the Bulge'. Now the Allies must do everything they can to contain and reduce it but, for the time being at least, confusion and chaos reign supreme and a significant fog prevents any intervention by the Air Forces. Moreover, a special English-speaking German brigade disguised as GIs spread rumors and paranoia in the ranks, not to mention reversing the road signs. Military Police must now set up roadblocks and question every man about the geography of the United States or baseball, while Allied convoys are retreating in disaster.

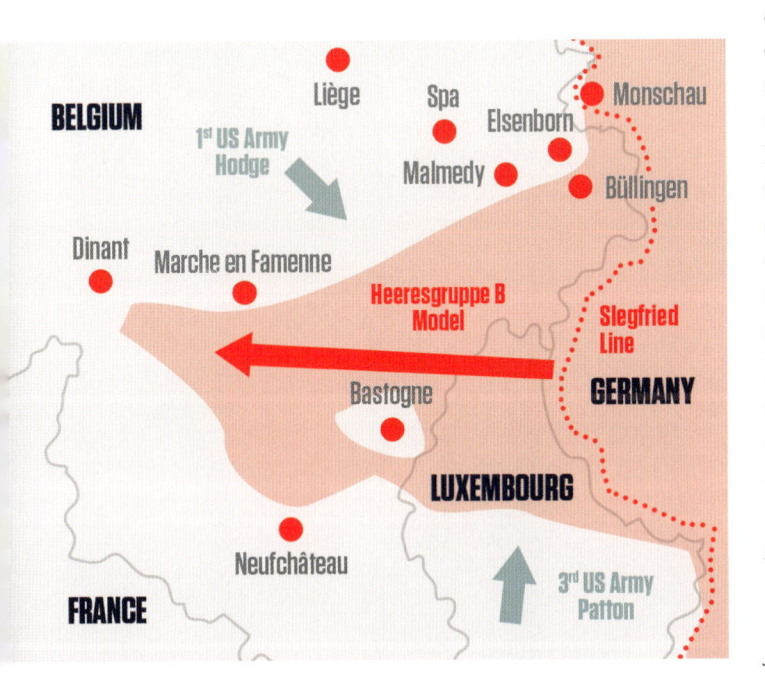

"NUTS!"

In response, Eisenhower only has two divisions in reserve, the 82nd and 101st Airborne Divisions, which are both at rest in Reims after *Market Garden*. Unlike its airborne counterparts already stationed in France, the 17th Airborne doesn't arrive at the front until December 23, as bad weather limited air transport from England. While Gordon and his comrades occupy a defensive line near Charleville, the 82nd Airborne is tasked with protecting Spa, while the 'Screaming Eagles' of the 101st Airborne protect a road junction of strategic importance in the small town of Bastogne. Their resistance is so fierce in the woods around Noville, Foy and Bastogne itself that the Germans, believing the area is defended by a much larger force, prefer to continue their advance westward, while at the same time surrounding the town for good measure. On December 20, 1944, the siege of Bastogne begins.

Duette Mills, originally from California, joined A Company, 401st Glider Infantry Regiment (GIR), 101st Airborne Division after Normandy. Taken by truck to the snow-covered forests of Bastogne to help defend it, he's in such a hurry that he's still wearing the summer clothes he'd received for *Market Garden*. Worse still, some paratroopers have gone up to the line without ammunition and are recovering what they can from the American infantrymen who are retreating. The 401st GIR sets up positions in the southern sector and soon fends off attack after attack alongside its colleagues from the 327th GIR. On Christmas Eve, in the same area, the Germans offer the paratroopers a chance to surrender when General von Lüttwitz sends the following letter: *"To the U.S.A. Commander of the encircled town of Bastogne. There is only one possibility to save the encircled U.S.A. troops from total annihilation: that is the honorable surrender of the encircled town. In order to think it over a term of two hours will be granted beginning with the presentation of this note. If this proposal should be rejected one German Artillery Corps and six heavy A. A. Battalions are ready to annihilate the U.S.A. troops in and near Bastogne. The order for firing will be given immediately after this two hour term. All the serious civilian losses caused by this artillery fire would not correspond with the well-known American humanity. The German Commander."* General McAuliffe, commander of the division, replied in the negative, with a word that will remain famous: *"To the German commander. NUTS! The American commander."*

On Christmas Eve, the paratroopers are huddled in their foxholes, shivering with cold, and waiting for the artillery that pulverizes the trees into thousands of deadly shards projected in all directions to finally stop.

This American paratrooper from the 101st Airborne Division has finally received his heavy coat and woollen scarf and is trying to get warm by wearing an anti-gas hood under his M1 helmet. However, frostbite and hypothermia are still a threat.

Having lost his jump jacket to the new standard M43 uniform he wears under his coat, nothing distinguishes him from a regular infantryman, although the division's screaming eagle can easily be recognized on his shoulder patch.

Attached to his Garand M1 rifle ammo belt, in addition to a bayonet and an individual first aid kit, he always keeps his M-1943 folding shovel close at hand. It can be used as a pickaxe and is an essential tool for a GI's survival in the Ardennes Forest as he would need it to dig foxholes there.

VI - THE LONGEST WINTER WINTER 44-45

Duette Mills, of the 401st Glider Regiment (101st Airborne), is surrounded in Bastogne. His wife, whom he married before leaving for Europe, writes to him every day. On December 25, she receives the card opposite for her family, without knowing under what conditions Duette is spending Christmas Eve. After receiving shrapnel in his legs during the violent German bombardments, his wounds will prevent him from staying with his division and he'll be assigned to an administrative unit (pictured above in Paris, July 1945).

In quieter moments, Duette and the men of the 101st Airborne can hear the Germans sing *Stille Nacht* (Silent Night), just a few hundred yards from their foxholes. On December 24, the night is indeed milder and the cloud cover is finally dissipating. This is bad news for the Germans, because in addition to the food, ammunition and medical equipment needed by the 101st Airborne, gliders loaded with artillery and nurses are also dropped. On December 26, Patton's 3rd Army tanks break the encirclement after a week-long siege, supported by the US Army Air Forces, who are once more masters of the sky. Wounded and exhausted, Duette is evacuated from Bastogne after the division's relief on January 18 and taken to a General Hospital. In a V-mail he'll send in September 1945 to his girlfriend's sister, he'll write that he hopes to be home by Christmas 1945, stating that for Christmas 1944 the menu had been *"grenade salad, shrapnel pudding, fragment desert, small arms steak, songs by Screaming Meamies* [rockets]*, and music by the German 88-piece band* [referring to the 88 mm artillery guns]*."*

DEAD MAN'S RIDGE

Gordon arrives in Bastogne on January 1, where the fighting is still fierce. For its first engagement, the battalion's various batteries are attached to the 193rd and 194th Glider Infantry Regiments, as well as the 507th and 513th Parachute Infantry Regiments of the 17th Airborne Division. At 8:15 am on January 4, the 17th Airborne launches its counter-offensive in the middle of a snowstorm, alongside the 101st Airborne and 87th Infantry Divisions. Their objective is a ridge a few miles northwest of Bastogne, along the highway leading to Marche-en-Famenne. The Germans had withdrawn to this position using their tanks to repel the parachutists' attacks. In just three days, the 17th Airborne would suffer more than 1,000 casualties. Camouflaging their helmets and uniforms with white sheets found in abandoned houses, the inexperienced GIs cling to their positions, even though falling back seems the most reasonable option given the catastrophic losses and the violence of the attack. This episode will be remembered as the 'Battle of Dead Man's Ridge'. On January 7, not far from the town of Flamierge, Gordon writes to Myrtle with a reassuring tone: *"The maneuvering we did around your place, you know when, it is almost an exact duplicate here, only a little colder and this time it's not just a simulation. We asked for it, and we're satisfied to be here, and soon you'll hear of our accomplishments, I hope."*

These 82nd Airborne paratroopers, now masters in the art of camouflage, have made a sled to carry their heavy equipment across snow-covered Belgium.

On the same day, the division leaves its foxholes to finally gain some ground, but of the 130 men from a company in the 193rd Glider Infantry Regiment who attack, only 16 would return. However, little by little, villages are falling, even if it sometimes ends in hand-to-hand combat. The 17th Airborne will capture Flamierge, lose it, and then capture it again, with the Battle of Dead Man's Ridge finally concluding on January 9, 1945. In the course of the month it would clear the Ardennes of the remaining German troops before chasing them to the banks of the Our. It will then link up with the British 51st (Highland) Division in late January, before testing the defenses of the Siegfried Line, which the Allies now encounter again, attacking it near Dasburg several times. Gordon and the 17th Airborne will finally be relieved by the 6th US Armored Division on February 10.

On March 24, 1945, Gordon will take part in *Operation Varsity* (supporting the Allied crossing of the Rhine), the last and largest airborne operation of the war to take place in a single day. Even before the operation begins, he would narrowly escape death, but fate chooses to spare him. When the glider he's supposed to board is full, he's asked to wait for the next one, only for the original plane to crash during the assault, killing all of its passengers. The 155th Battalion will suffer more than 30% casualties in the first two hours of the operation and, according to Gordon, five out of eight officers will be lost during the fighting that would follow the crossing of the river. Nevertheless, his troops will secure the area and destroy several German artillery guns and tanks.

Gordon will be promoted to captain and return to the 82nd Airborne Division, with which he would finish the war and occupy Berlin. Although as an officer he'd have the option to return home on a plane, on his way back to the United States in November 1945 he'd decide to take a boat in order to stay with his men.

Gordon in service uniform at the end of the war. Note the 82nd Airborne patch, the silver jump wings, the captain's rank on the shoulders and the artillery badges (two crossing guns) on his collar.

He'll regret this choice as when he calls his parents from New York to let them know he's coming home, he's told that his father, John Pierson, had just died of a heart attack. A veteran of the First World War who'd served in France in a combat engineer unit, it was he who'd inspired Gordon to join the army. In his letters, Gordon wrote how he dreamed of spending his life with Myrtle and his wish is granted when they marry on February 6, 1946. Five days later, Gordon will leave the army and pass away on March 22, 1987, in Florida.

RAYMOND HURD

HQ Company, 2nd Battalion, 18th Regiment, 1st Infantry Division

Called up at the age of 30, Raymond served in Sicily and Normandy with the 'Big Red One' and is now headed for Belgium. One of his most sinister jobs will be to pick up dead GIs in the snow of the Ardennes after the hard fighting to reduce the salient in December 1944.

Born on December 10, 1912 in Gloversville, New York, Raymond grew up with eight brothers and sisters. Some of his siblings are in the services, including his younger brother Donald, who took part in the terrible battles of Guadalcanal and Peleliu in the Pacific serving with the 1st Marine Division. Raymond was called up on October 23, 1942 in Utica (New York) with fifty-one other men, ten of whom didn't pass the selection tests. Shortly after, he joined the HQ company of the 2nd Battalion, 18th Regiment, 1st Infantry Division as a replacement during the Tunisian Campaign.

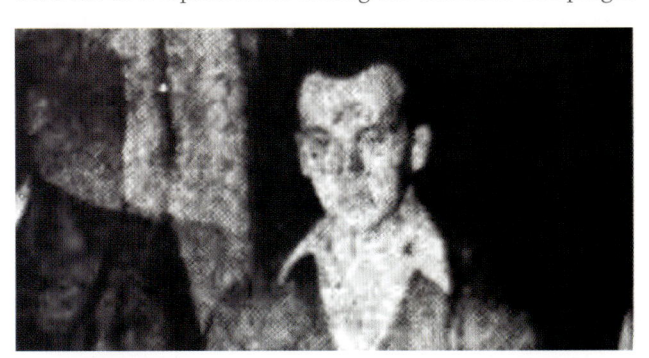

Photograph of Raymond from the local newspaper. Taken on October 23, 1942, the day of his departure for the army, it reveals in spite of its bad quality the state of mind of Ray, as if he knew what was coming... His brother would write to him three years later: *"How are your nerves holding out these days? Has the long rest after V-E Day given you any relief from war fatigue? Don't let things get you down [page 370]."*

TWO PURPLE HEARTS ALREADY

In Sicily, Raymond experienced bloody encounters in Gela and especially in Troina, a mountain village located on the German Etna Line west of the volcano. In one week, some Big Red One units lost nearly half their men there, but the village eventually fell on August 6. Following the capture of Monte Pellegrino (which dominated the area) by Raymond's regiment, the Germans withdrew to the new Hube Line that had been hastily built on the slopes of Etna. Moving towards Cesaro to the northeast, Raymond was wounded on August 8 by a shell burst during a night attack. The Fulton newspaper published a month later: *"Private Raymond L. Hurd, US Army [...] has been awarded the Purple Heart for wounds received in action in the Sicilian campaign. The information was contained in a letter just forwarded to his parents. Private Hurd's letter gave no details as to what his wounds consist of, where they were suffered or when. The letter is in his own handwriting which brings comfort to the family since it is assurance that he is not critically hurt and apparently on the road to recovery. He merely stated that he is now confined to a base hospital. Private Hurd was in the campaign in Tunisia before the troops made the jump into Sicily and cleaned it up in a whirlwind three weeks' campaign."* Ray spent four months in the hospital, while his brothers in arms returned to England to prepare for D-Day. He returned to them just in time and landed on June 6, 1944 on 'Bloody Omaha'.

The 2nd Battalion, which set foot on Easy Red Sector at 10 am, was the first to leave Omaha Beach just before noon. Raymond then liberated many villages, including Caumont and Marigny, before chasing the Germans all the way to the Siegfried Line in September. The 'Big Red One' then had the dangerous task of capturing the first German city reached by the Allies: Aachen. During the vicious street fighting there, Raymond was again wounded on October 9, but was able to stay with his unit. Shortly afterwards, he battled in the Hürtgen Forest before finally reaching the Roer Rver.

On December 11, 1944, after the terrible casualties suffered by the 18th Regiment and the rest of the 1st Infantry Division in Hürtgen, Raymond is sent to a rest camp east of Liège, Belgium. On that day, he writes to his older brother, Samuel 'Ed' Edwin: *"You say in your letter of November 26 which I received yesterday that you hope I will soon be out of the fighting for a rest. Well we are out for a rest now but I don't know for how long. I don't know if it is for good though, it's still a long way to Berlin."* This respite will indeed be brief, as five days later, the Germans launch their surprise attack through the Ardennes.

THE 'BIG RED ONE' AT ELSENBORN RIDGE

In the first days of the offensive, the German Panzers smash everything in their way, but in some areas, despite many Allied casualties, they're still unable to break through the American lines. This is the case on Elsenborn Ridge, east of Malmédy, which is held by veterans of the 2nd Infantry Division and inexperienced troops of the 99th Infantry Division, who were originally placed there because of the low probability of an attack in that sector. Yet in Spa, a few miles behind them, are the 1st US Army HQ and a large quantity of equipment and petrol, while Liège is one of the largest American supply centers in Europe. Fortunately, the US infantrymen would bravely hold their ground against the tides of German tanks from the 6. Panzer-Armee, and although it loses a fifth of its strength in the initial shock, the 99th Division would inflict a ratio of eighteen German casualties to one American, despite fighting against an enemy with five times its numbers.

The 'Big Red One' is quickly deployed to help contain the enemy assault from December 19, alongside another experienced unit, the 9th Infantry Division. To Raymond's right and left, the two other regiments of the 1st Infantry Division (the 16th and 26th) hold the line from Waimes to Büllingen. It's a tough fight in terrible conditions, but Raymond reassures his family about the fact that his regiment wasn't present during the initial breakthrough and that the worst is now behind them. In reality, his 18th Regiment is facing elements of the dreadful 1. and 12. SS-Panzer-Divisions. These fanatical units had recently committed several massacres of American prisoners in Büllingen, opposite the Elsenborn Ridge, and at the Baugnez Crossroads, southeast of Malmédy. The men under SS-Obersturmbannführer Joachim Peiper, whose 1. SS-Panzer-Division Leibstandarte SS 'Adolf Hitler' is at the core of the 6. Panzer-Armee, executed around 100 unarmed GIs, who as prisoners of war were theoretically protected by the Geneva Convention, before abandoning their bodies in the snow.

A GI inspects the body of one of the victims of the 'Malmédy massacre'. Opposite, a metal tag, formerly nailed to a white wooden cross in a temporary Belgian cemetery, identifying an unknown American soldier killed during the Battle of the Bulge. As no dog tags or personal effects were found on his body, the poor man will forever be known as 'X-207'. He was later moved to the Ardennes American Military Cemetery, his new cross bearing the inscription *"Here rests in honored glory a comrade in arms known but to God"*.

On December 23, Raymond writes to his brother: *"I have been pretty busy moving around so I haven't been writing lately. I guess you have read the news about what has been going on over here, in the last few days. Things looked pretty bad for a while but I guess they have things pretty well in hand now. It's still pretty hot around here. We would have been back for a rest over Xmas if this hadn't come up."* Raymond's other brother Donald will be lucky enough to be able to return to the United States for Christmas, although like many Marines returning from the unhealthy jungles of the Pacific, he's suffering from malaria. Raymond is familiar with the disease as many 'Big Red One' men have been sent home because of (or thanks to) it, after contracting it in North Africa and Sicily.

The Germans would keep on pounding the American positions for several days with their best armored units, personally selected by Hitler. Still, each assault is repelled with a barrage of artillery and anti-tank weapons. Around December 26, the fierce resistance in Elsenborn forces the enemy to turn southwards, toward Saint-Vith, where the Allied opposition is considered weaker. But the 6. Panzer-Armee, which has already lost its best units, is now almost out of gas. Continuously harassed by the Americans, it realizes that taking the roads to open the way to Antwerp is no longer possible. It's time for the Allies to take the upper hand and push the Germans back behind the Siegfried Line. Raymond writes on January 4, 1945: *"If it keeps on snowing like it has since last night, Uncle Sam is going to have to give us snow shoes. We have about a foot so far, and it don't look like it's going to stop just yet. [...] You ask how the Artillery is making out. Those boys on those guns are OK, there's none better. They can sure throw the stuff over when they have to. If you don't believe it just ask Fritz!"*

The famous 'Big Red One', shoulder patch of the 1st Infantry Division.

WHITE HELL

Raymond receives a sinister new assignment: to recover the frozen bodies of GIs who have fallen in action. He writes on January 7: *"I am afraid you got the wrong idea about my job. I don't exactly assist the Chaplain. There are five of us here. All we do is go up front and pick up the dead after there has been a battle. Outside of that I have nothing to do with the Chaplain. That letter I wrote Ma, saying I was waiting for the Chaplain to come back and see if he had any work for us, was written while there was a fight going on and the Chaplain had a call from up front. We were waiting to see if we had to go up, but we didn't go until the next day. We aren't exactly out of danger, we take a lot of chances. But we do get out of staying up there in a foxhole. It isn't a nice job but it's better than being up there in a hole. Well we are getting a little more snow today. It has been cloudy and foggy for the last three days and nights. I wish it could clear up, the Air Force don't come out on days like this. I guess by now Don is back in camp. I hope he gets to stay in the States for a while. Have you heard more from Roland? I hope I don't run across that kid over here. This outfit has got a lot of new men. I don't know hardly anyone anymore. I was lucky to get transferred just as I did. Well I guess I will say so long for now and try to get off a letter to Ma. It's sure hard to write her a letter."*

Roland is Raymond's nephew and as a sergeant in the 424th Regiment of the 106th Infantry Division, he's indeed nearby, on the German Schnee Eifel mountain range, near the Belgian border (south-east of Saint-Vith). The division took the December 16 attack head-on, while the other two regiments of the division, the 422nd and 423rd, were surrounded at Schonberg and forced to give up the fight three days later. With 6,000 GIs captured, it was the largest American surrender in Europe, but Roland and the 424th (the last regiment of the 106th Division) were able to retreat to Saint-Vith and then Manhay and, once again, courageously resist alongside the 7th US Armored Division. Roland will stay with his unit until the end of the war.

American prisoners in the Ardennes, December 1944.

Although the Germans are now turning back, the advance towards the Bucholz Forest is very slow. In mid-January, the 1st Division still manages to destroy forty-one German tanks in just two days and fend off the infantry units rushed to reinforce the SS armored divisions. Raymond is still doing his macabre work, in the fields that his older brother may have marched through twenty-seven years earlier with the 52nd Pioneer Infantry Regiment. He writes to him on January 25: *"Well it looks like this war will last through the rest of January, but I am very hopeful that it will end sometime next month, if the Russians keep up the way they are going* [in January, the Red Army takes advantage of the frozen land to push from the Vistula to the Oder, about 60 miles from Berlin!]. *Boy they really go places when they get started. Have been doing a little traveling ourselves lately. It won't be long before we will be back in Germany. We go by yards and the Russians go by miles. Gosh they must have a lot of fight in them. [...] I believe you said in your letter of December 31st that you picked flowers over here in March 1919. From the looks of things now, we won't pick any before July. We got plenty of snow now. The men who work the roads work days and nights to keep them open. They are doing a swell job too. It will be tough if we get another blizzard like we had a week or so ago. Have you had to do any shoveling yet?*

You know, you think these Jeeps are good. You should see these Jeeps with treads on. I guess they call them 'Weasles'. Boy, they go anywhere. We had one this morning take us about a mile across a field so we could pick up some dead GIs. The snow was over your knees, but we went through it just as though it wasn't there. Went through wire fences and everything. It sure saved us a lot of hard work."

In February, the advance suddenly accelerates and the 'Big Red One' rushes towards the German city of Bonn. Raymond writes on February 1: *"Well Ed, if this rain keeps up, we may be picking those flowers you wrote about long before March. It has rained for a couple days and the snow is going fast. I bet it will turn off cold again and snow for a week. The roads are a mess. It takes all day for a convoy to go three or four miles. We have been moving a lot lately. I hope the next move we make will be toward the beach. Things are looking pretty darn good over here. I hope the Jerries haven't got another trick up their sleeves. The fellows seem to think the war will end in a few days. I hope it does. It may even end before you get this letter."*

It won't. South of Bonn, his regiment will cross the Rhine at the famous Remagen bridge, and then participate in the clearing of the Ruhr pocket. They will then drive across Germany, clean up the Harz mountains, and by the end of April 1945 will be at the Czech border alongside the 97th Division. Traumatized by his experiences of the war, Raymond will leave the army at the end of September 1945 and pass away fifty years later on September 25, 1995, leaving no family behind.

On February 15, 1945, a 'Half-Track' truck of the 1st Infantry Division crosses the Hürtgen Forest. As the snow melted, the roads were turned into rivers of icy mud.

THE TABLES ARE TURNED

The German operations 'Wacht am Rhein' and 'Nordwind' are the last breaths of a dying beast. Although they have lost more than 80,000 GIs in the Ardennes, making January 1945 the costliest month for the US Army in Europe, the Allies take the upper hand and cross the Siegfried Line for the second time. Some of them will even enjoy a little rest before the final push into the heart of the Reich.

THE ALLIES REGAIN THE ADVANTAGE

Now that the weather has cleared up, the US Army Air Forces dominate the skies over the Ardennes, supported by anti-aircraft artillery units, which fire relentlessly. A corporal in the 116th Anti-Aircraft Battalion writes, *"I see you hope we don't have many more busy times. I hope we do. It may sound funny, but it's fun to make targets out of those rats. If we don't get a break soon we never will get enough paint to get caught up on the black crosses. [...] I see you wonder how things are going here and I don't blame you, because the papers think the war is over one minute and we've lost it the next. I just wish I could see a few of those guys around here for a while."*

Paul is a gunner in the 264th Field Artillery Battalion, 1st US Army. In the last days of the Battle of the Bulge, he fires 200-pound shells continuously at the enemy from 16-ton, 8-inch Howitzer guns. On February 6, in Belgium, Paul writes to his aunt: *"Everything over here at the present time isn't too bad. It's not too cold, the war is progressing a bit, and outside of being pretty darned lonesome at times I'm quite well. For a while things weren't too good as you probably read in the papers. I was pretty lucky and wasn't unfortunate enough to be caught in the big offensive of the Germans; although later I did see some of the things the Germans did. For instance, the mass murder of innocent civilians. In one small town in Belgium, I saw an entire family that had been murdered in cold blood just because they happened to be in the way. After seeing a few such things a person begins to realize just why he is fighting. [...] It's raining now so I don't suppose that it will be long before the place where I am living will be like a lake. Perhaps I had better quit and see what I can do to prevent the ceiling from leaking. I don't imagine there is much that I can do since the roof of the house has been bombed and shelled so much. I think the people over here instead of rebuilding some of these towns should just start building another in some other place. Perhaps they will do that."*

Not all American units have done as well, and some have even ceased to exist. This is the case of Ernest 'Bud' Siegel's 509th Parachute Infantry Battalion (pages 118 and 231). Recently returned from the hospital after his injuries in Southern France, he'll fight his last battle on December 24 in the snow-covered forests of Malempré (Belgium). Shortly after midnight, his Jeep is escorting a supply truck to the 509th PIB's position, north of La Baraque de Fraiture. Unbeknownst to him, he's heading straight for a position occupied by the 2. SS Panzer Division. Bud recalls: *"A machine gun opened up about 20 feet in front of the jeep. Bullets came through the windshield."* The driver manages to jump from his seat and escape, while Bud falls violently out of the vehicle. A third soldier, Henry Eliszewski, having trapped the leg of his pants in the gearshift, gets out just before a Panzerfaust (German bazooka) blows up the vehicle. As the SS soldiers approach Bud, he shouts *"Ich bin ein Hauptmann!"* (*"I am a captain!"*).

After confiscating Bud's M1 carbine and Colt 45, the SS officer gives his squad an order that Bud understands perfectly: *"Get rid of them"*. As the Americans are taken to a field for their execution, realizing that he only has a few seconds left to live, Bud comes up with a plan: he'd offer one of his cigarettes (which hadn't been confiscated) to his executioner and when he lights it, he'd knock him out with a right hook, before taking out the Beretta pistol hidden in his second pair of pants. As Bud opens his mouth to formulate his offer, he's thrown to the ground by one of the Germans as an allied Sherman tank, alerted by the shooting, suddenly appears.

GIs of the 75th Infantry Division in a snow-covered forest in Belgium.

But the enemy is spotted and the firefight is now in full swing. The Sherman is immobilized but can still fire. Bud remembers: *"The tank commander was shot in the finger and the tank thought we were Jerries and fired his .30 caliber machine gun at us. They couldn't depress enough to hit us. Then the cannon was fired with the same results – the cannon round couldn't explode because of the deep snow."* Bud tries to make the tank commander understand that they're actually Americans by shouting names of local sportsmen and actors, to which the commander only responds with insults. Bud tells Henry to hold his hand: *"When I pull your hand, run for it. We can get behind the tank in ten steps."* As the Sherman reloads, they make a break and reveal their identity through the hatch in the back of the tank. Bud then helps the gunner hit his targets, forcing the enemy to retreat, unable to compete against a tank. The Germans leave an injured soldier behind, who just happens to be the one who had captured Bud. The SS man begs him: *"I didn't kill you, don't let them kill me!"* The tank commander exits through his turret, furious at having lost two fingers in the attack, and approaches the German to finish him off with the butt of his Thompson machine gun. Bud stops him: *"I've had enough! Look, the German tells me he knows where the mines are, don't kill him! He can show you the mines!"*

Bud will receive the Bronze Star (photo below) for his bravery in this action. With the situation under control, he returns to his unit and goes to bed, exhausted. When he wakes up, he finds out he has a piece of shrapnel sticking out of his leg, a bullet lodged in the brass whistle hanging around his neck, and another that had smashed into a .45 clip on his belt. He'd narrowly escaped death, coming away with only a few broken ribs. On Christmas Day 1944, Bud returns to his blown-up Jeep and notices American medics treating a man on the ground: the German soldier he spared the day before. He greets Bud warmly with tears in his eyes and will go on to survive the war. On the other hand, by late January 1945, near Saint-Vith, the 509th PIB would cease to exist. Badly hit during the Battle of the Bulge, the unit has only 50 able-bodied men left of the 700 that had originally been deployed. The battalion is disbanded and its survivors assigned to the 82nd Airborne Division.

As for Bud, his latest injuries are enough to prevent him from returning to the front. After leaving the 106th General Hospital on January 22, 1945, he becomes an investigating officer on General Courts-Martial. The shell fragments he received throughout the war would sometimes reappear under his skin before they are later removed by a local doctor. However, the wounds that cause him to suffer the most are the memories of those comrades who were never able to go home. Bud will return to New York where he'll eventually become a Police Inspector with the Suffolk County Police Department; his leadership and humor leaving a great mark on his colleagues. Ernest 'Bud' Siegel passed away on October 4, 2013.

During the Battle of the Bulge, the Americans lost 77,000 men and 700 tanks, but the Germans, in this last-ditch effort, lost 90,000 soldiers and 600 armored vehicles. Both were difficult to replace and such forces would've been useful in defending the German border.

OPERATION NORDWIND

The 44th US Infantry Division arrived on the front lines on October 18, relieving the 79th Division in the Parroy Forest, near Lunéville. It then joined the 7th US Army, with the mission of securing several passes in the Vosges. Progressing with difficulty and stopping multiple attacks, it finally reached Strasbourg in mid-November, helping liberate the city alongside the French 2e division blindée. In December, it attacked the Maginot Line (in German hands) at Bitche. Fort Simserhof fell on December 19, after which the division occupied defensive positions east of Sarreguemines.

Taking the Allies by surprise on December 16, the Germans built on their initial successes by launching *Operation Nordwind* further south. The objective is to support the German troops involved in the Battle of the Bulge, retake Strasbourg and the industrial area of Haguenau, and then to destroy the 7th US Army, which had relieved Patton's Army. Heeresgruppe G, under the command of Reichsführer-SS Heinrich Himmler, is ordered to fight to the last man and smash everything in its path. On the evening of December 31, the German attack is once again unexpected, taking place only thirty minutes before the New Year. Nine German divisions in white camouflage and several others in reserve (including two armored divisions) throw themselves at 25 miles of lines held by only two American units, the 44th and 100th Infantry Divisions. Despite their widespread defensive positions, the understaffed GIs hold their ground and inflict heavy losses on the attackers. The 44th Division fends off three attempts to cross the Blies River, and some of its units are surrounded several times. Individual acts of courage make the difference, such as at Wœlfling-lès-Sarreguemines, where Sergeant Charles MacGillivary (71st Regiment, 44th Division) is awarded the Medal of Honor on January 1. On his own initiative, he single-handedly destroys four nests of MG42 machine guns from the 17. SS-Panzergrenadier-Division, killing all of their occupants with his M1 Garand rifle, but losing his own arm in the action. The Germans have by now thrown their last remaining forces into the battle and from January 3 onwards, their attacks are losing their intensity. On the 6th, the 44th Division even launches a major assault, but encounters strong enemy resistance. The lines then stabilize for good, and the two armies would hold their positions until March 1945.

VI - THE LONGEST WINTER WINTER 44-45

Norman is a lieutenant in the 44th Infantry Division. When the Germans attacked, his battalion was the northernmost in the division, near Sarreguemines, facing the Blies. On January 16, as a period of static warfare begins east of the city after many weeks of unrelenting fighting, he writes to his parents in Florida: *"This morning I had my first shower in over 2 months. After the weeks and weeks of no baths at all or of washing out of buckets, etc., a good hot soaking shower was a real treat. A change of clean clothes was an added luxury too. The snow-covered hills of Germany are little different than those of Eastern France, and the villages are no different either. The people on both sides of the border are German speaking, so that there is no abrupt change when you pass from one country to the other. Christmas packages are still drifting in, so that [al]most every day someone has fruit cake or candy to pass around. One of my crew is an ex-cook, and an excellent baker, so that as often as we can chisel lard, flour, and sugar, we have pie or doughnuts. Last night there were 3 big cherry pies, enough for 2 pieces per man for 10 hungry soldiers. Combat isn't all shooting by any means and sometimes we hole up in one spot for days at a time, just waiting for things to start rolling. If we are fortunate, we get a good warm thick-walled stone house, complete with beds, stoves and kitchen utensils, and maybe some homemade wine and schnapps to boot. There is no use being any more miserable than you have to. [...] Some of those Florida grapefruit and oranges would certainly taste good. It has been quite a while since we have seen either. The nearest things to the real stuff are grapefruit juice and orange marmalade. Some enterprising orange grower must have thought up a way to dispose of surplus orange peels – make marmalade out of them and sell the stuff to the army. We get it by the gallon."* Norman will go on to earn the Bronze Star for his actions during the fighting in the region. He'll survive the war and later serve in Korea as a captain.

Patch of the 42nd Division, created from units from each of the American states, covering the country "like a rainbow". However, its emblem was reduced to a quarter circle in memory of its colossal losses (about half of its strength) during the First World War.

Near Strasbourg, the newly arrived 42nd 'Rainbow' Division relieves the 36th 'Texas' Division on Christmas Eve and must hold a 30-mile-long line north and south of Strasbourg, along the Rhine. It repels several attacks, such as at Hatten and Rittershoffen, two villages that had been liberated without a shot being fired three weeks earlier. This time, however, the terrible tank battles kill more than 2,500 people between January 8 and 20, and the Americans are forced to pull back to the Moder River in Haguenau as the Germans reclaim the forest on the edge of the city and several other surrounding villages. All hell breaks loose, including within Haguenau itself, which is stormed by the tanks of the XXXIX. German Panzerkorps (supported by the first jet aircraft in history). GIs and Germans clash inside the houses, often in hand-to-hand combat, and on the banks of the Moder River that flows through the city center.

Operation Nordwind is finally aborted when the Allies receive reinforcements from the Ardennes. Yet the Germans are still determined to hold on to the north of the Alsace region, which is far from being secure despite the 1re Armée française capturing Colmar on February 2. Haguenau is bombed by the enemy every day for weeks, while 7,000 inhabitants are still trapped in its cellars. On February 14, the 42nd Division sets up defensive positions in the Hardt Forest, north of Haguenau, which are frequently bombed and shelled. Between patrols, the Americans' raids are feared by the Germans, who call the Rainbow Division 'Roosevelt's SS'.

George is a 19-year-old infantryman from Maryland, who belongs to the 232nd Regiment, 42nd Infantry Division. He writes from his foxhole on March 8: *"Damn the rain, if it wasn't for that I'd feel happy. The war news is good and I'm well. [...] You know I think I've cracked up. Since none of our Co. K boys are fighting this week, the war seems terrifically amusing. [...]*

It seems so silly sitting out in an observation post midway between the lines reporting rifle fire to the left or right once or twice a night that you can't help but call in stuff like 'Hey, Joe, Joe' - old Joe back in the command post thinks something bit like a Jerry patrol is up and gets all excited and says 'yeah' breathlessly – then you say 'does your cigarette taste different lately?' or 'Joe, call for artillery quick, I haven't heard a sound for two hours and I'm going nuts'. Such is life on the front. We don't mind Jerry blowing the roof off our heads half as much as we do a --- striker back in the States. I know if I had a choice between shooting one or the other, I think I'd favor Jerry. Some Jerries are forced to fight, strikers are voluntary. But of course, out here it's you or Jerry so we have to shoot the bastards."

George's daily routine will take a different turn when the Allies launch the counter-offensive *Operation Undertone* on March 15. His unit will attack northward through the Hardt Forest and breach the defenses of the Siegfried Line once more, before cleaning up the area around Dahn and Busenberg. The Alsace and Lorraine regions (annexed by Germany in 1940) are now liberated at last, and Strasbourg retained – the firm stand taken by General de Gaulle and Churchill, opposing the strategic withdrawal suggested by Eisenhower, made it possible to maintain the 1re Armée française there throughout *Operation Nordwind*.

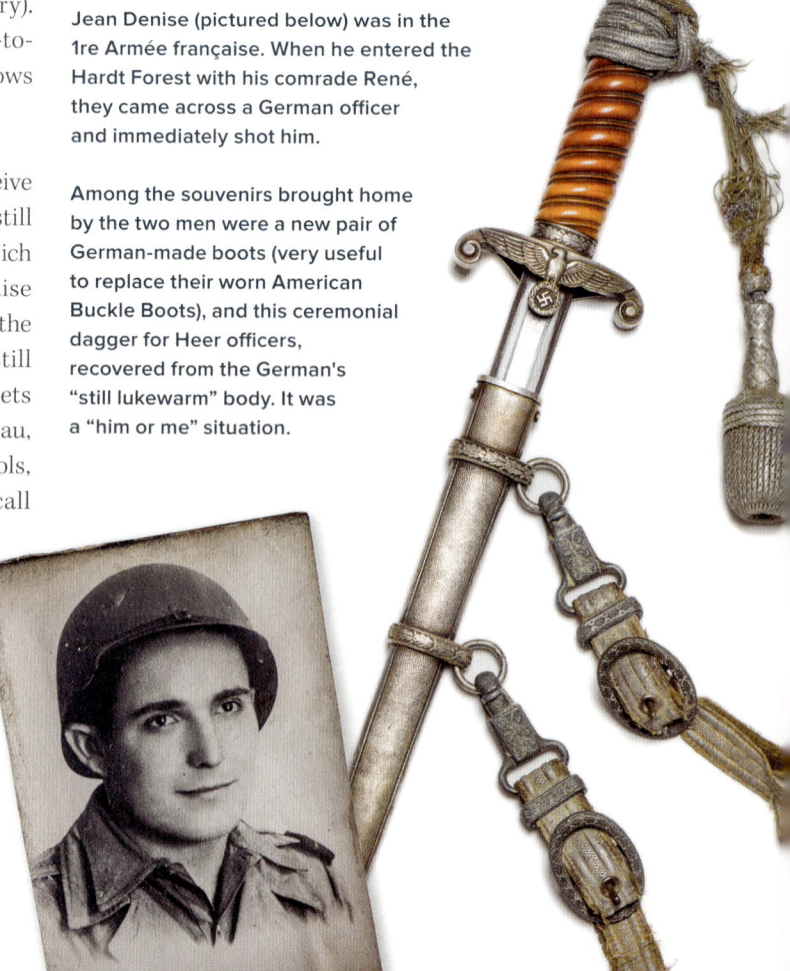

Jean Denise (pictured below) was in the 1re Armée française. When he entered the Hardt Forest with his comrade René, they came across a German officer and immediately shot him.

Among the souvenirs brought home by the two men were a new pair of German-made boots (very useful to replace their worn American Buckle Boots), and this ceremonial dagger for Heer officers, recovered from the German's "still lukewarm" body. It was a "him or me" situation.

After the liberation of the Colmar Pocket on February 9, French soldiers and GIs share sweets and cigarettes.

This map of Brussels showing the billets of a 2nd British Army soldier on leave includes the following: *"Do not talk about where your unit is or what it is. Do not discuss equipment, losses or battle experiences. The people of Brussels are very hospitable and will do all they can to make your leave enjoyable. Enjoy yourselves with them but do not tell them anything."*

ON FURLOUGH

While waiting for the last push into the heart of the Reich, the soldiers rest, train, and for the lucky ones, enjoy a bit of tourism. Everyone dreams of a leave in Paris, Brussels or London. One American soldier is surprised at the large number of British soldiers in Brussels and the fact that he's one of the few 'Yankees' around: in reality, the Belgian capital is home to the British Army Headquarters and Paris to the US Army Headquarters. But what strikes him the most are the girls who throw themselves into the arms of the soldiers, a scene he's often witnessed in Paris.

On March 23, on his return from leave in Brussels, he writes: *"If you walk down some of the side streets the gals call to you from the windows or they come up alongside of you and practically tear your arm out of its socket trying to get you inside some joint, but it's a good thing I was with all respectable married men (ahem!). Seriously tho' Honey, it's really something the way they come after you. I guess they've had to develop such forwardness to entice these 'Tommies' or 'Limeys'* [nicknames for the British soldiers] *who are so slow. [...] As you pass some of the joints you can see these guys back from the front really having it up with a dame or two or three. In a way I guess you can't blame them after all the hell they've been through, and if you talk to them, they'll tell you they're having their fun while they can, as they expect to get humped off anyway. Funny, how they use the same guys over and over again in these campaigns. I saw one guy with 7 battle stars. He told me he was just lucky. Very few of his original buddies are still with him. And they won't let him go home on account of his experience. Just occasional passes to some big town and so they go all out. It's really a shame. Clean cut young fellows who just don't give a damn anymore. [...] I hope this mess is all over soon and it has good promises of being so. The sooner the better."*

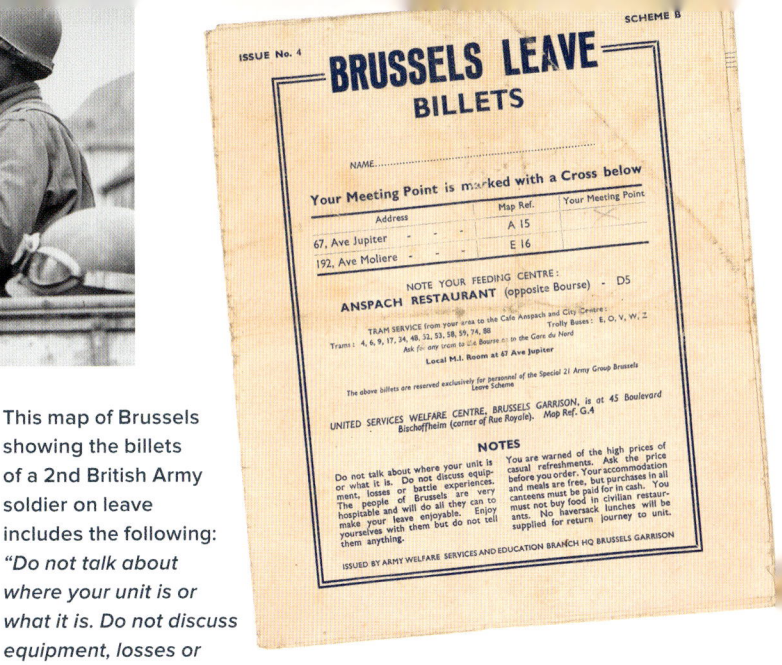

For the British, leave can be pretty special, as some have the opportunity to return home to see their families. Charles is a Scottish tank crewman with the 107th Armoured Regiment 'King's Own Royal Regiment (Lancaster)'. His unit landed with the 34th Independent Armoured Brigade in Normandy on July 3, attached to different Allied divisions as required. Unfortunately for 'Charlie', who hopes to see his wife again soon, the armored units are in high demand. After taking part in the battles for Caen, Falaise, Le Havre, Eindhoven and Venlo, he supported the British 6th Airborne in the Ardennes. Paratroopers and tankers fought fiercely for the city of Bure, which changed hands several times in just a few days.

By January 27, 1945, Trooper Charlie is exhausted and only wants one thing; the furlough that every soldier dreams of: *"Dear Sweetheart, I have quite a few things for a change to write about tonight. The first thing is leave. Well it has not been put up yet, the list I mean, but someone who* [has] *seen it today was letting us know about it. I don't appear to be in the first 80, at least, that's the amount that goes in February. Actually, it was Captain Well, my tank commander, he mentioned that both Edgar and our operator were in that lot. They come out one after the other, so I think had I been in it he would have noticed though he just got a glance at it. He was kidding about 2 of the crew being on leave at the same time. We have been waiting all day for it to reach the squadron. He* [has] *seen it at the regimental headquarters. They expected it at dinner time but it had not come by tea time, so I can't post this till I get to know something definite. I know I am not the last on the list, we know who that is. I will go over and listen to the news at 9 o'clock perhaps we will know something by then. It is just 7 o'clock now. [...] I heard a bit of the news at 6 o'clock and everything was going well.*

Someone since then has come to us with the news that [the Russians] are only 100 miles from Berlin. That may be so but at dinner time the nearest they were was 140 miles. [...] If I'm not on the March list I think the war may be over by then and that will be almost as good as leave!

[Sunday] YES!!!!! Well Darling I have seen the list this afternoon. My number is 100, so I reckon I should be home at the end of February. There is no use saving a date, but it will certainly be the end of the month so that's great isn't it? Edgar met me to tell me as I came out of church this morning so that's 3 of us this month in our troop, all in our tank and well the others are all well behind up to 500 and 600, so that means probably July or August. So you can imagine how happy I feel today after hearing the good news. [...] This is certainly the most exciting letter I have written for a long time, so it won't be so long darling, 4 weeks or so. [...] You have something to smile for now. Charlie."

But Charlie may have rejoiced a little too soon: a week after writing this letter, his unit will attack the Rhine Valley, attached to the British 51st (Highland) Infantry Division.

FROM THE NETHERLANDS TO GERMANY

The winter of 1944-45 is one of the coldest in the century. Rifleman Norman Woodley, of the Queen's Own Rifles of Canada (3rd Canadian Infantry Division) is from Toronto, known for its extreme temperatures. Yet, he writes in late January 1945: *"I am not missing snow by being away from the city of Toronto. Oh no, on the contrary. I wish I was fighting in the tropics where there is no snow and a fellow can keep warm. This is the toughest winter I've ever been put in, in my life, and I'll sure be glad when spring comes even if it does mean mud and more mud. I never knew Holland had snow like we're getting. It makes things very uncomfortable for the troops and I wish there hadn't have been any at all. [...] Well I am glad another Xmas is over and we're into a new year with spring and summer coming up. By next Xmas the war might be over and some of us back in good old Canada and living once again."*

He won't have the chance. Less than a month later, on February 26, Norman will be killed in a night assault on Mooshof farm, near Uedem (Germany). His D Company will be practically destroyed, with only 36 able-bodied men left at the end of the day, out of 115. His superior, Sergeant Aubrey Cosens, will also be shot dead by a sniper shortly after taking the three barns on his own against a much larger force of German paratroopers from the 6th Fallschirmjager Division (he would receive a posthumous Victoria Cross). The Germans are determined the Allies won't cross the Rhine.

Badge of the Argyll & Sutherland Highlanders of Canada.

Lieutenant Eugene Boyd 'Duke' Cleroux is a former member of the 1st Canadian Parachute Battalion, 6th British Airborne, who was unable to take part in *Operation Overlord* due to illness. Transferred to the infantry, he joined the Argyll & Sutherland Highlanders of Canada (4th Canadian Armoured Division) at the end of October 1944. After entering Belgium on September 6 and liberating the former battlegrounds of the First World War such as Ypres and Passchendaele, the division found itself blocked by the Germans on the banks of the Scheldt. Eugene wrote to a friend: *"I'm a platoon commander in a rifle company. Sorta gives me a chance to get a close look at things – at times. Very interesting occupation, may I point out. I have a fine bunch of lads right now. Worst part of it all is that I lose main cogs every now and then. Sorta breaks up good fighting teams, although we're now seeing many wounded lads return to us from hospitalization and convalescence depots."*

To the northwest of 's-Hertogenbosch is a small island on the Meuse River, near the small port of Kapelsche Veer. Gathered here are several German units determined to hold the ground in case Hitler's counter-offensive in the Ardennes was successful. After two failed attacks by the Poles, then two more by the 47th Royal Marines Commando, Eugene's regiment launches its assault in support of the Lincoln and Welland Regiment in late January. This major operation (*Elephant*), using heavy artillery barrages and tanks, would last for an extremely intense five days. This time, all enemy presence is destroyed south of the Meuse, but Eugene is wounded in action. A few days later, he contemplates the irony of his fate from the hospital: *"Only the other day, it seems, I wrote to our mutual friend Daisy telling her that, so far, I'd managed to dodge all the big chunks – well, it looks as though I spoke in haste, for here I am in hospital with a machine gun slug in my shoulder. Not painful, mind you, but awkward. I'll not bore you*

VI - THE LONGEST WINTER WINTER 44-45

with the gory details, however, let me assure you that it was a singularly bloody assault for a man of my quiet temperament. The news is particularly encouraging this morning – looks as though the end might be just around the corner – again! Just give me a baseball bat and turn me loose in Germany! I'll be very glad to get back to my unit which by now has most likely passed on into Germany. Incidentally, I was wounded in dear old Holland. Boy! They can have this watery country for keeps."

Indeed, the British have finally crossed the border. *Operation Veritable*, launched on February 8 (in conjunction with the American *Operation Grenade* to cross the Roer River to the south), aims to break the Siegfried Line in the Reichswald Forest, east of Nijmegen, and move south between the Meuse and the Rhine. General Harry Crerar's 1st Canadian Army gathers an unprecedented force: in addition to the Canadian divisions, it includes nine British divisions, as well as Belgian, Dutch, Polish and American units supported by 1,000 artillery guns. Although the Canadians pound the Siegfried Line with one of the most formidable artillery barrages of the war, Hitler refuses to allow Feldmarschall Gerd von Rundstedt (who had just pulled his divisions out of the Ardennes) to take refuge behind the Rhine. Taking advantage of the melting snow that had caused the rivers to swell, the Germans open the dams upstream and flood the valley to delay the Allied advance. As a result, the Americans are forced to postpone *Operation Grenade*. However, the Anglo-Canadians actually benefit from the flood, as the water neutralizes the German minefields and defenses, not to mention isolating the enemy on several small 'islands'. The Allies are easily able to take care of them with their amphibious 'Buffalo' vehicles and their 'Churchill Crocodile' flame-throwing tanks.

Eugene leaves the hospital and returns to his unit in Germany in time for *Operation Blockbuster*, launched on February 25. His mission is to break the last German line of defense west of the Rhine: the Schlieffen Line in the Hochwald Forest (near Uedem). Intense short-range combat in the cold, rain and fog makes *Blockbuster* a costlier operation than anticipated. The Germans' relentless resistance in Hochwald would result in 5,304 Canadian casualties and continue until March 4, when the Anglo-Canadians move on to their next objective: the small town of Veen, southeast of the forest. On the 6th, a German anti-tank gun camouflaged in a barn destroys Eugene's 'Kangaroo' vehicle. He's killed instantly. Veen wouldn't be liberated until March 9, and Eugene is now buried in Groesbeek Cemetery in the Netherlands.

One main objective remains to be taken: the city of Xanten, located on the Rhine. A platoon commander of the South Saskatchewan Regiment (2nd Canadian Infantry Division) and *Blockbuster* veteran writes on March 7, the day before the attack: *"Just now I'm sitting amongst the straw in a deep root cellar at the end of a long barn. We're getting the old stonk dropping down on us occasionally. The rest of my lads who aren't on guard are sleeping around me. We just took this place over yesterday afternoon. Just a little skirmish although I felt sure that some Joe had his eye directly on me the way lead kept pecking around. Lovely linen sheets and mattresses used in cow stalls. Eating delicious preserves and from beautiful china and crystal ware and the next minute diving flat on our faces in the duckpond dodging moaning minnies [German rockets from the Nebelwerfer]. At that it's a nice break from roaming around through those damn forests continually digging holes and living in them and then picking up and going on. One of my lads was picked up by the Jerries when he wandered too far astray and shot them a smooth line in German, which he could speak fluently, and they let him go. Evidently, he had really piled it on because when we made a patrol over to that area the next night, we discovered they had pulled stakes. Not many civilians, although at one place I found about 35 living in a barn away from the shelling. Some old women and five of the cutest little girls I've ever seen."*

The next day, this platoon commander would participate in the assault on Xanten, whose capture is essential for the imminent crossing of the Rhine. The fighting against the German paratroopers defending the city would last more than two days, with 85% of Xanten being destroyed.

This soldier of the 2nd British Army follows the progress of the 9th US Army and 1st Canadian Army troops beyond the Roer from his foxhole. He's wearing his rain cape and a 'cap comforter' (foldable scarf) under his helmet to protect himself from the cold and wet.

This British REME (Royal Electrical and Mechanical Engineers) engineer belongs to the 21st Army Group. Specializing in repairing destroyed and abandoned vehicles and weapons, these technicians play an essential role: 70% of the tanks recovered from the field have only a broken track or engine and can be returned to their crews within 48 hours, the more serious cases being broken down into spare parts. During *Market Garden*, which required significant armored resources, the REME men were sometimes able to send back about ten tanks a day!

For operations *Grenade* and *Veritable*, the 21st Army Group, now including the 9th US Army, had a huge number of vehicles to manage. In early 1945, the REMEs carried out several modifications on Allied vehicles at the request of units entering Germany, in particular on Buffalos and Kangaroos. These engineers also played a major role in *Operation Plunder* and the push towards the heart of the Reich, with their bulldozers clearing the roads of enemy vehicles destroyed by the RAF. Around 59,000 engineers will participate in the Rhine crossing operations.

This non-commissioned officer wears the 1940 Battledress jacket, which belonged to Sergeant R. Robinson of the REMEs, attached to the 21st Army Group. The blue and red crest is that of the General HQ of the 21st Army Group (1943). On the jacket is Sergeant Robinson's dog tag, made in the same year. Sergeant Robinson had his jacket modified with an open collar in order to reveal his tie. His service number (10,590,084) indicates that he originally enlisted in the Royal Army Ordnance Corps. Three ribbons for the following medals are present: the 1939-1945 Star, the France and Germany Star, and finally the United Kingdom Defence Medal. The wrench shown here comes from the field and has the date 1944 on its handle.

This Purple Heart medal and ribbon belonged to Frederick Sanders, from Maine. He joined the 3rd US Army in January 1945 as a replacement. Only two months later, he was wounded in Germany and evacuated. This superb medal is awarded to all Americans who were wounded and killed in action, and was produced in such large quantities in anticipation of the fierce resistance of the last few months that those medals dated 1945 are still being distributed at the beginning of the 21st century.

DAS VATERLAND

Now that the Siegfried Line is broken for good, everyone knows that the Third Reich will lose the war. For the Allies, who no longer refrain from thinking about home as the day of their return finally seems to be getting closer, each new casualty is an unbearable and unnecessary tragedy. All ask themselves: *"But why don't the Krauts give up?"* While the Canadians and British have great trouble filling their depleted ranks, the Americans send unlimited waves of fresh troops to the front. However, they still fall by the thousands alongside the veteran soldiers as the Germans remain determined to defend their 'Vaterland'.

Bill serves in the 15th Regiment, 3rd US Infantry Division. Having arrived in North Africa in early 1943 with the same group of replacements as Audie Murphy (the most decorated GI of the Second World War, who would play himself in the movie *To Hell and Back*), Bill fought in Sicily, Italy, France and Germany. He was wounded in the leg on the Volturno River (Italy) in November 1943 and then again on Anzio's beachhead in February 1944. A year later, almost to the day, after helping to clean up the Colmar Pocket, Bill is finally fighting on German soil. He's seriously wounded by shrapnel in the chest, and writes to his wife on February 23: *"How are you today, darling? I am getting around pretty good now. I've improved quite a little in the last week. The doctor took out some of my stitches yesterday. He left three big ones in. It sure is nice out again today. It's even kind of warm out. I received my Oak Leaf Cluster for the third time wounded in action. I certainly hope this has to be the last time. They had better send me home pretty soon or else I'll be a total wreck or else won't get home at all. I'm really sweating it out. I'm thinking of going home every day. Wouldn't that be nice if I could be back home with you, honey? Of course, don't be thinking too much of me coming home or you might be disappointed. All we can do is hope and pray for the best."* Two months later, Bill would learn that he's finally withdrawn from the front for good – but he'll never fully recover from his injuries due to the damage caused to some of the nerves.

Philip belongs to the 255th Regiment, 63rd Infantry Division. After passing through through Saarland on February 17, 1945 and cleaning up the Mülhen Forest, he experiences fierce clashes in Güdingen in early March. Battle casualties are heavy, but the cold and insanitary conditions cause almost as many losses as the bullets and shells. On the 5th, Philip falls ill and is evacuated to France. He writes in his letter: *"I'm back in the hospital again. This time however, it is a much larger one and quite a bit farther back. They have it set up in a convent and it seems every bit as nice as a lot back home. In fact, to us it is luxury of the highest degree. They are doing a lot of surgery here at the present. I rode back in an ambulance with a lot of wounded and it was quite an experience. You find it hard to believe that a person can take so much. I held a cigarette for one and talked to him a lot and he had what it takes... like all the rest. It makes you feel rather small in a way to be sent back with a bunch who are worse than sick. But I'm damned glad I'm no worse than sick."*

Patch of the American 63rd 'Blood & Fire' Infantry Division. Spreading 'fire and blood' on its way from Sarreguemines to Landsberg, it also suffered heavy losses due to the fierce resistance of the last German pockets.

MELVYN ROAT

A Company, 405th Regiment, 102nd Infantry Division

Melvyn, a talented young student, had been enrolled in a specialized program to become an officer. Unfortunately, the losses in Europe are such that he's transferred to the infantry as a simple replacement. He will be killed in Germany on February 25, 1945, during *Operation Grenade*.

FROM UNIVERSITY TO THE INFANTRY

Born in Ohio in 1923, Melvyn enlisted in Cincinnati on February 22, 1943, almost two years to the day before his death. A serious student wishing to pursue a career in medicine, he attended the Army Specialized Training Program (ASTP), which aims to train junior officers in technical skills related to languages, medicine or engineering. The selection is rigorous: candidates must obtain very good results on an IQ test, the army officers' exam, and then reach the end of the thirteen weeks of basic training to be sent to a university campus. It was at the University of Heidelberg (Ohio) that Melvyn met his girlfriend Maythorne.

Melvyn began training with the US Army Air Forces at Sheppard Field, Texas. In a letter written in April 1943, he told his aunt: *"The other day we were out on a thirty-mile road march with full equipment in the mud and a driving rain. We were up near the Oklahoma border. Yesterday we were on another road run. Those are really nice things to go on. Last night I was on guard duty. I could go on forever telling you about these things, but it would be rather monotonous. At least, you have an idea of what we do. We, also, have Commando training. You have seen pictures of Commandoes in action, so I presume you know how hard it is."*

Melvyn proudly posing in uniform in his garden, a year before his death.

Training intensified, but Melvyn did very well and in May, he was sent to Camp Sibert (Alabama). He wrote: *"Eight of us boys were shipped out of Sheppard together to get this training. I am in a thirteen-week Non-Commissioned Officer school course. I now have two weeks of that course behind me. Whoopee! I am a corporal now, having been made one after only 9 weeks of training or as my record shows after 48 days of training. The best part about this thing is that I am still in basic training but receiving the pay of a corporal. The first nine weeks of this course is basic training in chemical warfare and the last four weeks is our NCO course. That is when I will actually handle gas. Right now, there are about 200 of us Army Air Forces men down here to get this training. We are very much disliked by all the other soldiers, but we more or less expected that."* By the end of 1943, 140,000 students were following the ASTP program, but with the upcoming invasion of France, the US Army needed infantrymen trained and ready to deploy.

VI - THE LONGEST WINTER WINTER 44-45

In February 1944, 110,000 of them were transferred to the infantry, whether they had completed the program or not, and dispatched to 35 divisions. Melvyn was, unfortunately, one of these men and even lost his rank of corporal in the transfer. He became a private in A Company, 405th Infantry Regiment, 102nd Infantry Division. The latter bears the nickname 'Ozark' in reference to the native Americans discovered by French explorers in the mountains of Arkansas and Missouri, at the time of the Wild West. Attacked by Indian archers, the French nicknamed the region 'Terre aux Arcs', which led to the Americanized name, 'Ozark'.

102nd Infantry Division patch.

Family photo before leaving for war: Melvyn (second from left), his brother Kenneth, who was in the US Army Air Forces (to his right), and two cousins.

Melvyn wrote to his aunt: *"I guess Mother has already told you that the Army has moved most of us AST boys out of college and back to the Army. We are all going to combat divisions in the infantry. The division that I'm in is supposed to be hot so I don't know how soon we will be going over. This is really a drastic change, but one never knows what the Army is going to do next. [...] We are located about 35 miles outside of Austin right in the middle of a desert. We will be restricted pretty much because our training is being rushed [...]. All of my buddies from Heidelberg are here with me but are in another regiment, the 406th. We are all getting a rough deal considering the fact that a lot of us know little about the infantry and also despise it, but it is rougher still when you think that it won't be long before we'll be ready. What a life! There are not so many good things to talk about now."*

He complained again a few days later: *"What times these are! I wish this war were over. All I'm doing now is wasting my time. Really, I haven't strained my brain once since I've been down here."*

Melvyn finished his training at Camp Swift (Texas) and sailed for France in September 1944. Just before his departure for the front, he married his girlfriend Maythorne on August 21. It was the last time they would ever see each other.

OPERATION GRENADE

His unit landed in Cherbourg on September 23 and after a short training period in Valognes, it left for Germany to defend the Wurm-Waurichen Line (between Roermond in the Netherlands and Aachen). On November 19, Melvyn wrote to his aunt, who had learned about his recent marriage: *"Thanks loads for the congratulations! I'm very satisfied Aunt Gail. I have the best little wife I could possibly want. I love her terribly. I guess Mother has told you about my movements over here. Since being in France I've been in Belgium, Holland, and now Germany. I've been seeing lots of action here in Germany. I hope the Germans realize soon that they are beaten. I'm dying to get back to Maythorne. Life isn't much without her. The weather in France was rainy and the going was muddy. Their weather here is rainy and much colder. Sometimes it even sleets and snows. [...] I picked myself up a pair of combat boots and three pairs of socks in a town near here so I'm getting pretty well ready for Old Man Winter."*

Ten days later, they attacked eastwards towards the Roer, and took Geilenkirchen, Welz, Flossdorf and Linnich, from where they would later cross the river. They patrolled for weeks along the banks, making contact with the enemy, while training for the approaching amphibious operation. On January 15, 1945, Melvyn writes: *"You talk so much about the weather we have to fight in. We have loads of snow on the ground with plenty of cold weather to go with it. I have been seeing plenty of action, but nothing heavy. I hear that my little brother is directly supporting me. The plant where he works is turning out casings. [...] I wish I could say that I can see the end of the war here in the ETO [European Theater of Operations] but I can't. It might drag on for quite a while yet. I have my ETO ribbon now. Great honor!"*

While the 1st US Army rushes towards Cologne, the 9th US Army, to which the 102nd Division is attached, is ordered capture Düsseldorf. The assault across the Roer is scheduled for February 10, 1945, during *Operation Grenade*, under the command of Montgomery and his 21st Army Group. The Americans needed to link up with the 1st Canadian Army pushing down from Nijmegen (*Operation Veritable*), but as we have seen in the previous pages, the flooded Roer delays the American operation. The GIs are therefore forced to wait.

Melvyn writes his last letter to his aunt on February 20, just five days before his death: *"I've been taking things easy during the past few days. Living conditions have been good. I only hope that they continue that way. We've been running into a lot of bad weather lately; rain and mud dominates. Have you been reading anything about us? I feel so good this morning. Believe it or not we had fried eggs for breakfast. The first we've had since we left the States. They tasted so delicious!"*

Nearly 4,000 miles away, Maythorne worries, and despite their regular exchange of passionate letters, she misses Melvyn terribly. When her husband is about to cross the Roer, she spends the weekend with his parents. Melvyn would never read the account of this family reunion, nor even receive the card his wife sent him for Valentine's Day: it will be returned to her with the note *"deceased"* (below).

Maythorne (left) and Melvyn's mother support each other during Melvyn's absence.

The Americans finally launch their *Operation Grenade* on February 23 at 2:45 am. It's preceded by their most powerful artillery barrage, fired by 2,000 guns, which would last for three-quarters of an hour. The first waves cross with amphibious tracked vehicles equipped with machine guns, the 'Alligators', under German mortar and artillery shells. Melvyn and his regiment attack between Flossdorf and Ruhrdorf. The losses are heavy, but the floating bridges are installed quickly and by 2 pm, all 102nd Division units are on the other side, making it the first complete American division to cross the river. It then establishes a bridgehead near Linnich, almost halfway between Aachen and Düsseldorf, and begins its progression towards Krefeld. Soon, Melvyn and his regiment face counter-attacks from the 363. Volksgrenadier-Division and German Panzers at Boslar, where they must protect the right flank of the rest of the 102nd Division (south of Erkelenz). The latter has advanced fewer than 6 miles northeast from the Roer when Melvyn is killed in action on February 25, in the heart of the small village of Titz.

MEMORY

To the general public, *Operation Grenade* goes almost unnoticed, as on the day of the assault on the Roer, the American flag is hoisted on Iwo Jima's Mount Suribachi. The newspapers focus on these Marines fighting the Japanese on this small Pacific volcanic island, where the Americans lost nearly 7,000 killed and 19,000 wounded. On March 4, not knowing her husband's fate, Maythorne goes to the cinema to watch *Music for Millions*: *"Hearing José Sturbi play the piano makes me homesick,"* she writes. *"It was an awfully sad picture, a story about a girl and her husband overseas."* Coming home from the movies, she writes a passionate love letter to Melvyn, which she won't have time to post after receiving the telegram informing her of her young husband's death. She'll keep her letter in a scrapbook with an article announcing the sad news. The latter never had the opportunity to read the previous letters either, many of which were sent back to his wife with the same black 'return to sender' stamp.

Many 'ASTPers' like Melvyn will act as infantrymen to reinforce decimated regiments. Just out of school and trained mostly on the job, these green replacements arrive in units where they don't know anyone, and where few give them respect. The rare veterans, who've been promoted and hope to return home in one piece after going through so many battles, no longer take as many risks so close to the end. The replacements are thrown into the heat of the action and killed by the thousands in Germany, some having known only a few hours of combat. The GIs would finally make their junction with the British during *Operation Veritable* in Geldern on March 4. In this campaign, the Americans lost around 7,300 killed and wounded, and the British 15,600. The Germans would flee in panic behind the Rhine, blowing up the last bridge at Wesel, and leaving over 90,000 killed and wounded behind, in addition to 230,000 prisoners.

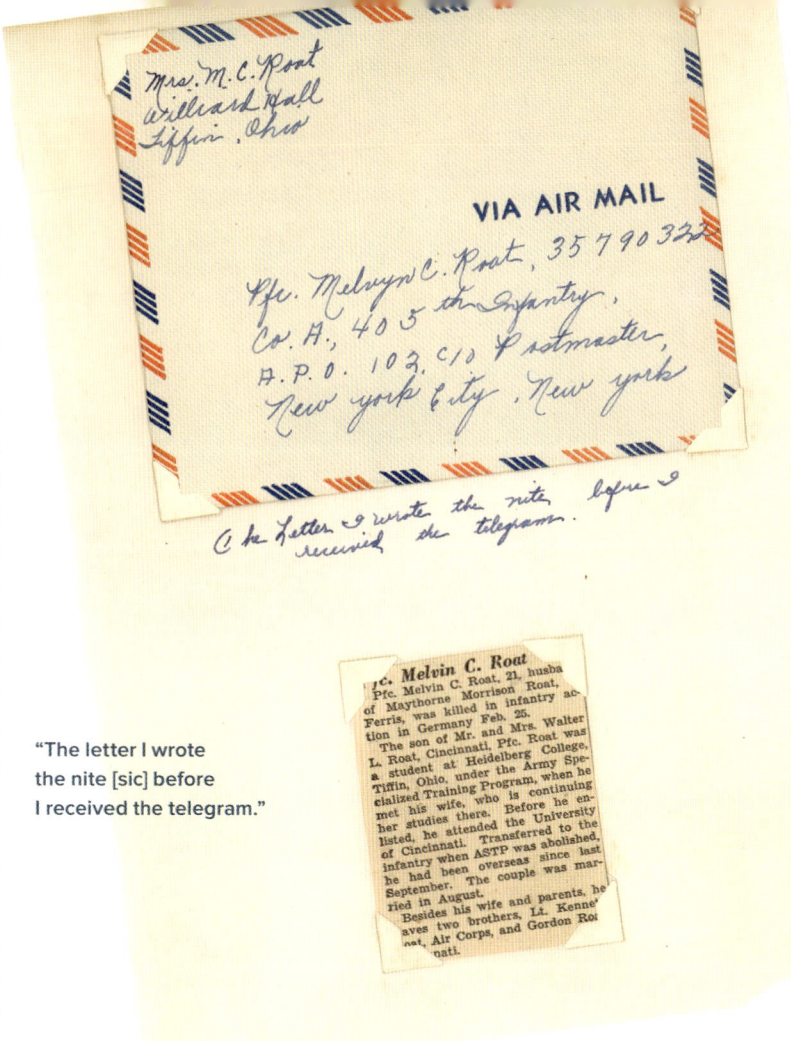

"The letter I wrote the nite [sic] before I received the telegram."

Melvyn is buried at the American cemetery in Margraten, in the south of the Netherlands (east of Maastricht). A young Dutchwoman from Eys-Wittem, Menny, tends to his grave there. Like many of her fellow citizens, she places flowers there for free as a tribute to the soldiers who liberated her country. Her village saw its first Americans on September 19, 1944, and across the country, every GI found a new family in every home.

Menny met Melvyn around Christmas while he was on leave near her home. In September 1945, Melvyn's parents will be surprised to receive the following letter (pictured left): *"Dear family, with this letter a Dutsh [sic] girl will write some few lines to you. The reason to writing is this. Just I have been on the American Cementary [sic] here in Holland a few miles from my home. I did ask to this soldiers graf [grave] because I did hear from a other soldier Melvin [sic] was killed. I don't know who I got his address, maybe I saw him here in Holland or in Brussels. I have many address[es] from us liberators I had it from Melvin too. So I go to this Cementary did ask to his grave and got his home address too. I lett [sic] you know that I take care for his grave, so long is [sic] I can. The next time I go I take a picture from it Cementary and some of Melvin grave too, and soon as I can will I send it too [sic] you.*

On this Cementary are 18,000 American soldiers and 1,300 Germany soldiers too. But the graves from us liberators are nice, but no body care for the Germany's graves. Well, family I'll close this letter. Hoping to hear real soon from you. Take much greets [sic] from all of my family, but the most from a 18 years old Dutsh girl that take care for it grave from Melvin. Menny. P.S. Please excuse me for all the mistake in this letter. I did lern [sic] only from the soldiers this little English."

Menny will correspond with Maythorne and Melvyn's parents for several years, putting flowers his grave on each anniversary of his death and returning regularly to take photos. She will write to Melvyn's mother: *"We never can give you as much as you and your son did for us. Please don't write any more some thing [sic] about trouble, I tell you again, nothing will be to [sic] much for me."* However, Melvyn's body will be repatriated three years later and he is now buried at Greenlawn Cemetery in Milford, Ohio. Maythorne would move back to New York and eventually remarry.

Menny placing flowers on Melvyn's grave.

KENNETH GLEMBY

514th Squadron, 406th Fighter Group, 9th Air Force

As the pilot of a P-47 fighter aircraft escorting bombers, Kenneth played an important role in the liberation of Bastogne. He's now supporting the troops advancing towards the Rhine and will witness the destruction of Cologne, one of the first major German cities to fall into Allied hands.

Lieutenant Kenneth Lane Glemby enlisted on December 7, 1942, one year to the day after Pearl Harbor. Fighter pilots must be volunteers, as the role requires great courage and a certain talent, which Ken doesn't lack: according to him, he'll be among those to fly their aircraft between the columns of the Arc de Triomphe in Paris. Ken arrived in the ETO at the end of September 1944 and had a choice between the 8th or 9th Air Force. Feeling that he'd a better chance of seeing action with the 9th, he joined the 406th Fighter Group in France on November 4. This group of fighters is composed of three Squadrons (512th, 513th and Ken's 514th), with about twenty pilots each, plus their support staff. Kenneth named his plane *Paula*, after his wife, with whom he fell in love at a summer camp when he was 9 years old. They married three months before he left for Europe.

HERO OF BASTOGNE

Kenneth was stationed in Mourmelon-le-Grand, sharing his camp with the paratroopers of the 101st Airborne. During the worst days of the Battle of the Bulge, grounded by bad weather, he had to wait until the conditions improved after Christmas to help free the Bastogne Pocket, where his camp neighbors were surrounded. Out of bombs, with only his machine guns left to cover the ground troops, Ken took a chance: dropping his fuel tank over a group of Panzers, he then fired on it to blow it up in the air. His improvised bomb was a success and he renewed the experience once again.

He also tried to destroy the German anti-aircraft guns: *"I was flying over and around Bastogne, suppressing flak and doing ground attack and here comes a whole group of these C-47s. There had to be hundreds of them, as far as you can see, coming in a narrow line. And as they got over Bastogne, guys were kicking supplies out the door down into the besieged area. The Germans were surrounding Bastogne and were pretty well concealed; they were dug in during the daylight hours. From their positions they were able to knock these planes out of the sky readily. So the guys behind would see these planes flaming up and falling to the ground and they still kept coming. Nobody ever turned back. They had no self-sealing tanks, no guns, no armor. No way of protecting themselves, just nothing between them and the bullets. And they kept coming and that was the most courageous thing I ever saw in my life. I was almost crying as I saw this. As soon as we saw gunfire or flak coming up we would attack, but there were just too many Germans, and too many positions, too well concealed. Couldn't save them all."*

During the siege, Ken took part in several missions every day and lost many friends. Patton himself congratulated the fighters with crates of Calvados.

Kenneth wearing the leather jacket typical of US Army Air Forces pilots.

Kenneth was eager to take on a German fighter. On December 29 he wrote to his friend Milt Goldstein, a 2nd lieutenant in the 716th Bomber Squadron (449th Bomber Group): *"I don't have to bullshit you about the war – you've no doubt lost the same illusions I have. I'm in the 9th Tactical Air Force. I'm flying Thunderbolts in direct support of Patton's 3rd Army. We do a lot of Flak busting, strafing of all sorts of targets, low level, dive and skip bombing and once and a while we even find some Heinies to fight. I missed the best chance I'll probably ever have just the other day. Our flight was bounced by a whole flock of Jerries as we came off a strafing run. Not one of my guns had fired on the run and just before the fight started I broke for home. The other guys pulled up into a stiff dogfight and beat the hell out of the Heinies. I found out that there'd been a fight only after I landed. The only other scrap I've had with Heinie planes was when an Me109 blundered into another of our strafing patterns. I was closest to him and I chased his butt on a tree top level fight 30 miles into Germany. I had buck-fever and fired too soon and out of range and hence burned my guns up before getting into effective range. When at last I was sitting on his tail my fire was wild and erratic – burned out barrels. I scored hits on him and must have scared the s--- out of him but that was all. He never got to fire at me – all he wanted to do was go home. He was a good pilot though and flew like a madman – tho' who wouldn't with tracers whipping by your ears. Congrats on your promotion – Pauly sent me word of it. Here's hoping your next step up will come just as quick. I hope to hear from you soon – in the meantime be careful and fly low and slow so you don't get hurt."*

Unfortunately, Kenneth's friend will never receive this letter. His bomber had, in fact, been shot down two days earlier. It'll be returned to Ken at the end of January with the note "missing in action". He'd keep the letter sealed for seventy years.

COLOGNE IN RUINS

After Metz, Kenneth is stationed in Asch (Belgium) when *Operation Lumberjack* begins. Launched on March 1, it should enable the 12th Army Group to secure the region of Koblenz and the western bank of the Rhine. The 1st US Army crosses the Eft River, enters Euskirchen on March 4, and then Cologne the following day. Heavy tank fighting takes place on the outskirts of the city, but it's cleared on the 6th. Meanwhile, Patton's 3rd Army is advancing rapidly from the Eifel to the Rhine. Kenneth visits Cologne on March 18, 1945. Since its first bombardment by the RAF on May 12, 1940, no less than 262 different air raids have dropped 34,711 tons of bombs there. The most famous one had taken place on the night of May 30-31, 1942, in which an armada of 1,000 bombers took part. In 1945, photographs from the Signal Corps and the embedded reporters show a field of rubble, from which the dark and majestic Cologne Cathedral rises, apparently spared by the bombs.

Kenneth describes the scene in a letter home: *"Yesterday I and some friends 'jeeped' into Cologne – which as you know is on the Rhine river. We went on a sightseeing tour, souvenirs gathering and general curiosity cruise. Fighter pilots seldom get a chance to see the front unless they're flying over it in a plane. From the air there isn't much to be seen. As much of Germany as we saw is torn clean to hell. Cities and towns are torn down until they are not recognizable as such. In front of one such town there was a sign in German & English quoting Adolph Hitler: 'Give me 5 years and you shall not recognize Germany again'. His words were prophetic – no Heinie would recognize the place now. Cologne itself is ruined completely. Just about every house is ruined. The walls of some are standing – but the floors have all collapsed leaving only hollow shells. Very few places are habitable and the remaining Heinies have difficulty finding a place to stay. They stared at me as if they'd like to kill me and we returned the look and desire with interest. Shells were landing in the city for the Heinies were only a few hundred feet away across the river. We managed to procure a few furnishings for our tent – rugs and radios, but most of the stuff had been picked and sorted over by the infantry. Many beautiful things were left behind by the fleeing Germans. Cologne was a rich city with beautiful homes. It's all wreckage now but if a person cared to they could procure millions of dollars' worth of furniture etc. The Heinie couldn't take it with them. Germans are not handled with kid gloves. What they've got is taken from them by any GI that happens to want it, and they don't get thanked either. It was a fine trip – if a cold one in our open Jeep. I passed several towns that had been targets for our bombs. I'm happy to report that we didn't miss. There isn't a German house or building anywhere that hasn't been clobbered. Most of the Germany I've seen looks like something out of a bad dream. I hope the rest of Germany gets the same nightmarish treatment. If any justification was needed for what's happening to Germany now one only has to travel around in the countries formerly occupied by Germans. They set the pattern – now they're suffering for it."*

Kenneth will finish the war between Handorf and Nordholz, Germany, in August 1945. He'll be deeply marked for the rest of his life by his wartime experiences, and in his spare time will not only build models, but real planes! He'll also apply for a new pilot's license forty years after the war.

He'd tell his children very little about his time in Europe, but at the end of his life he'd feel the need to tell his story and would publish his autobiography *Flyboy: Memoirs of a P-47 Pilot*. Kenneth died on August 26, 2015, at the age of 92.

Letter about Cologne and patch of the 9th Air Force. Above, a GI reads a sign next to a destroyed German tank in front of Cologne Cathedral: *"Sightseers, keep out! Beyond this point you draw fire on our fighting men."* **Indeed, the Germans are just on the other side of the Rhine.**

21 ARMY GROUP

PERSONAL MESSAGE FROM THE C-IN-C

(To be read out to all Troops)

1. On the 7th February I told you we were going into the ring for the final and last round; there would be no time limit: we would continue fighting until our opponent was knocked out. The last round is going very well on both sides of the ring—and overhead.

2. In the WEST, the enemy has lost the Rhineland, and with it the flower of at least four armies—the Parachute Army, Fifth Panzer Army, Fifteenth Army, and Seventh Army; the First Army, further to the south, is now being added to the list.

   In the Rhineland battles, the enemy has lost about 150,000 prisoners, and there are many more to come; his total casualties amount to about 250,000 since 8th February.

3. In the EAST, the enemy has lost all POMERANIA east of the ODER, an area as large as the Rhineland; and three more German armies have been routed. The Russian armies are within about 35 miles of BERLIN.

4. Overhead, the Allied Air Forces are pounding Germany day and night. It will be interesting to see how much longer the Germans can stand it.

5. The enemy has in fact been driven into a corner, and he cannot escape.

   Events are moving rapidly.

   The complete and decisive defeat of the Germans is certain; there is no possibility of doubt on this matter.

6. 21 ARMY GROUP WILL NOW CROSS THE RHINE.

   The enemy possibly thinks he is safe behind this great river obstacle. We all agree that it is a great obstacle; but we will show the enemy that he is far from safe behind it. This great Allied fighting machine, composed of integrated land and air forces, will deal with the problem in no uncertain manner.

7. And having crossed the RHINE, we will crack about in the plains of Northern Germany, chasing the enemy from pillar to post. The swifter and the more energetic our action the sooner the war will be over, and that is what we all desire: to get on with the job and finish off the German war as soon as possible.

8. Over the RHINE, then, let us go. And good hunting to you all on the other side.

9. May "the Lord mighty in battle" give us the victory in this our latest undertaking, as He has done in all our battles since we landed in Normandy on D-day.

B. L. Montgomery

Germany,
March, 1945.

Field-Marshal,
C.-in-C.,
21 Army Group.

VII
INTO THE REICH
The Last Weeks of the Nazi Regime

OPERATION PLUNDER

By March 22, 1945, there are no German soldiers left fighting on the west bank of the Rhine. The Americans had already crossed the river on March 7 almost by accident. Indeed, the Germans had blown up all the bridges during their retreat, except one, the Ludendorff Bridge at Remagen, which was only left because the enemy is now short of everything, including good-quality explosives. A Task Force of the 9th Armored Division thus risked crossing the railway bridge despite sniper and machine gun fire, not to mention the threat of the bridge exploding at any moment. However, American engineers succeeded in preventing its demolition despite the enemy's efforts. The first Allied troops crossed the Rhine, leading Eisenhower to change his plans and stake everything on this opportunity. For the next ten days, the Germans tried to destroy this access to the Ruhr by any means possible: Hitler sent no less than eleven new V2 missiles and his best aircraft, but the Americans gathered the largest concentration of anti-aircraft weapons of the war in order to keep the Luftwaffe at bay.

The Ludendorff Bridge eventually collapses on its own at 3 pm on March 17, after being battered by weeks of bombing. Six divisions and more than 25,000 men had time to cross to the other side of the Rhine several days before *Operation Plunder*, which is to accomplish the same goal. Montgomery is once again being robbed of the spotlight by his allies.

The Rhine is indeed the most important symbolic objective after Berlin. As a result, Winston Churchill takes great pleasure in urinating in the river at the first opportunity, just like many soldiers and officers. Patton does the same, going as far as to be photographed while doing so to let the world know about it. As he closes his pants, he proudly says *"I have been looking forward to this for a long time. I didn't even piss this morning when I got up so I would have a really full load. Yes, sir, the pause that refreshes."* The race with the British is won, yet he also makes his 3rd Army cross the Rhine again at Nierstein (southwest of Frankfurt) the day before *Plunder*. Still, Field Marshal Montgomery launches his operation as planned on March 23, 1945, to move his 21st Army Group to the other side of the river.

On March 11, units from 1st US Army cross the Remagen bridge (visible in the background).

Operation Plunder's preparations are hidden by the largest smoke screen ever created. After a four-hour artillery bombardment by more than 4,000 Allied guns and bombing raids on the town of Wesel, the first troops set off on the Rhine. In Rees, on the evening of March 23, the 7th Battalion of the British Black Watch Regiment (not to be confused with its Canadian namesake), attached to the highly experienced 51st (Highland) Infantry Division, takes the lead at 9 pm, soon followed by the 7th Argyll and Sutherland Highlanders.

Two miles west of their objective, the British commandos grouped in the 1st Commando Brigade are ordered to capture Wesel, a communications center housing a large German garrison (*Operation Widgeon*). Under heavy fire, and with the assistance of No. 3, 6 and 45 Commandos, No. 46 (Royal Marines) Commando moves through the minefields and enters the city, already destroyed by another raid of 250 Lancaster bombers. Clearing the streets one by one, the brigade fends off many German counter-attacks, including two with Panzers. As No. 45 Commando pushes northward, the other three drive the last German defenders into a pocket south of the city. At 2 am, the 15th (Scottish) Infantry Division lands between Wesel and Rees, while the American 30th and 79th Infantry Divisions reach the east bank to the south of the city. On the morning of March 24, the 1st Cheshire Regiment crosses the Rhine near a destroyed railway bridge and helps the commandos take the south of Wesel. There are few casualties, mainly due to the fact that the German defenses had been destroyed by the huge Allied artillery barrage.

Two months after *Operation Plunder*, engineers built two bridges at Wesel, on either side of the original, which had collapsed into the Rhine.

Operation Varsity starts shortly afterwards, at 10 am. Led by 14,365 British 6th Airborne and 17th US Airborne paratroopers, it's the largest airborne operation ever conducted in a single day. In order not to repeat the mistakes made at Arnhem, the paratroopers hit the ground as close as possible to their objectives, right in the middle of the German artillery batteries pointed at the Rhine. However, this means the enemy guns were therefore ready to retaliate and scored direct hits on the gliders coming down from the sky (see Gordon Pierson, page 269). The paratroopers would nevertheless succeed in their mission and damage enemy communications.

Although resistance is tough in several places, the Allies are superior in numbers and soon establish a wide and solid bridgehead. In the panic, the 1. Fallschirm-Armee (paratroopers) withdraws to the northeast, leaving a big hole in the German defensive line. It's a perfect opportunity for the Allies to rush towards the Ruhr's industrial center and encircle the 15. Armee. The days of the Third Reich are now numbered...

British commandos in the suburbs of Wesel, and patch of the 46th Royal Marine Commando.

Paul Pirat (crouched down on the left) and his fellow soldiers in the Vosges, late 1944. Opposite, a 'France' American-made patch produced during the war for French troops.

THE 3ᵉ DIA IN SPEYER

On page 130, we followed the reconnaissance missions of motorcyclist Paul Pirat from the French Expeditionary Force in Italy. As the latter no longer exists, the 3e division d'infanterie algérienne (3e DIA) is now part of General de Lattre de Tassigny's II Corps, 1re Armée française. Paul and his comrades had landed in Provence and liberated Toulon and Marseille, before fighting on the Doubs River and at the foot of the Vosges Mountains, alongside the Americans. Along the Swiss border, Paul's company was travelling up the Rhone Valley at high speed. The entire division was engaged in the surrounding forests and plains, already covered in snow. The weather was so cold that Paul lined his jacket with newspapers to get warmer on his motorcycle. In his diary, on Tuesday, October 24, he talked of carrying out missions under a deluge of shells. In fact, he'd just completed a liaison mission that earned him a new star on his Croix de Guerre medal in early 1945: *"As a Motorcyclist liaison officer who had already distinguished himself by his composure and courage, he crossed without hesitation an intense artillery barrage at Vagney on 24 October 1944 to ensure an urgent liaison."* When the 3e DIA defended the Strasbourg area in January, Paul hoped to meet his brother, who was stationed in the city with the 5e division blindée (armored), but was unsuccessful. On the evening of January 26, he went on a reconnaissance trip along the Rhine in a Jeep with Colonel Caminade.

In March 1945, Paul and his battalion train in amphibious assaults on the Doubs River with storm boats, and practice building *Treadway* (a floating bridge) and *Bailey* bridges (stronger, prefabricated portable structures, widely used by Americans, British and Canadians). The big day is coming up...

Paul writes in his diary in March:

[Wed. 7] *"I am still in the asylum for the insane, or officers' school, or the asylum for officers or school for the insane. Breach crossing."*

[Sunday 11] *"Breach crossing exercise by Treadway and Bailey Bridge. In the evening I am a taxi driver and accompany a colonel to Mulhouse (tip 20 francs)."*

[Thursday 15] *"At noon, all the students in the 3e DIA left school (why?). I witnessed a shooting over students crawling. I think the 3e DIA is leaving for an attack on the front."*

[Friday 16] *"A reporter comes for the demonstrations, I am photographed."*

[Saturday 17] *"Great visit of General de Lattre de Tassigny."*

[Monday 19] *"Breach crossing on Treadway and Bailey. The 3e DIA enters Germany."* (This is no longer an exercise: Paul and his fellow engineers built the Bailey Bridge and allowed the first elements of the division to cross the Rhine. The next day, Paul would celebrate his twenty-fifth birthday on German soil.)

[Friday 23] *"I find the battalion near Niederroederern by asking for information twenty times. The battalion had many casualties. Arrived at 23:30 with the captain* [and] *enter Germany, then into the Siegfried Line. Visited a casemate in the middle of the night. The progression begins."*

[Saturday 24] *"In the morning, routine patrol on the front: everything is quiet. In the evening, on the frontline again in a house. We go in, it's empty. The captain sets an example by breaking a chandelier with his pistol, and in turn we break everything that breaks. Then we go to Hagenbach: there, we receive a shell barrage fifty meters away. We get in a Jeep and receive another shelling less than thirty meters from us. Everything is shattered around us. Shells keep falling, but the Jeep goes for it. We then visit an unexplored casemate, and bring back cans, a Red Cross kit, a bandoneon and a rangefinder, and then we go home. Dubois was in a motorcycle accident. We defuse a system designed to blow up a bridge."*

> de Nuderneodern en demandant 20 fois
> des renseignement. le bataillon a eu
> beaucoup de pertes. arrivé à 11h ½ à
> 10h du soir avec Capitaine je rentre en Allemag-
> nes dans la ligne Siegfried. Visite
> casemate en plein nuit la progression
> commence
> Samedi 24. matin façon de route
> sur le front : tout est tranquille. le soir
> de nouveau sur le front dans une maison
> nous entrons elle est vide. le Capitain
> nous donne l'exemple en cassant tout
> avec revolver et nous cassons tout ce
> qui se casse. Puis nous allons
> à Hayembach là nous recevons

In the northern part of the Rhine, *Operation Plunder* is in full swing, but further south, between Mannheim and the French border, the bulk of General de Lattre's troops have yet to break through. On the night of March 30-31, Paul's Sapper Battalion is tasked with helping the 3e DIA and then the entire 1re Armée to cross the river. According to Paul, his company is the one ensuring the first passage of troops at Speyer. The engineers are desperately short of equipment, as the M2 boats and floats had been made available to other engineering units, who had to make another crossing to Germersheim, further south. Still, Paul's 83e Bataillon is speeding them up with the only pneumatic float it has. The first battle group crosses at midnight, without alerting the Germans. Six other floats arrive as reinforcements around 5 am and the pace then accelerates. By the time the enemy notices the maneuver, it's already too late: two companies have crossed and are retaliating. The Germans have no choice but to pull back.

Despite the artillery and the intense firefight, the French have no casualties, and the engineers of the 83e Bataillon are the first Frenchmen to cross the Rhine. The next day, Paul works tirelessly: up at 5:30 am, he carries out missions under heavy shelling from 7 am to 2:30 am the following morning, at which time he can finally eat and wash. Paul's actions that day would earn him another bronze star: *"As a conscientious, dedicated and admirably zealous sapper [...] he distinguished himself particularly on April 1, 1945, during the Rhine crossing at Speyer, by providing an urgent liaison, despite the strong reactions of the enemy artillery."* In April, German cities will fall one after the other in the path of the 3e DIA: Guglingen, Maulbronn, and then the suburbs of Stuttgart, where the division will take more than 18,000 prisoners.

Paul will see the end of the war there. The 3e DIA, which would be the most decorated French division in the war, would by then have suffered 3,078 killed (one man in five), two thirds of them being North Africans. Seventy-five men of Paul's battalion will have been killed in action. On June 15, Paul will return to Tunis and reunite with his wife Dilo, before being demobilized on September 13, 1945. In 1957, the couple and their three children will move to France, near Le Havre, but Paul will be deeply traumatized by the war for the rest of his life. Hospitalized for a heart attack, he'll die on February 10, 1976, as a result of a medical error.

Paul (right) and his motorcycle in Germany.

NON-FRATERNIZATION

While his troops are on the Rhine, Field-Marshal Bernard Montgomery sends a message to all soldiers and officers in the 21st Army Group:

"Twenty-seven years ago the Allies occupied Germany: but Germany has been at war ever since. Our Army took no revenge in 1918; it was more than considerate, and before a few weeks had passed many soldiers were adopted into German households. The enemy worked hard at being amiable. [...] To evade the Armistice terms, they had to find sympathisers, and 'organising sympathy' became a German industry. So accommodating were

the occupying forces that the Germans came to believe we would never fight them again in any cause. [...] This time the Nazis have added to the experience of the last occupation; they have learned from the resistance movements of France, Belgium, Holland, and Norway. These are the type of instructions they are likely to give to their underground workers: 'Give the impression of submitting. Say you never liked the Nazis; they were the people responsible for the war. Argue that Germany has never had a fair chance. Get the soldiers arguing; they are not trained for it, and you are. Use old folks, girls, and children, and 'play up' every case of devastation or poverty. Ask the troops to your homes: sabotage or steal equipment, petrol or rations. Get troops to sell these things, if you can. Spread stories about Americans and Russians in the British zone, and about the British to other Allies.'

Because of these facts, I want every soldier to be clear about 'non-fraternisation'. Peace does not exist merely because of a surrender. The Nazi influence penetrates everywhere, even into children's schools and churches. Our occupation of Germany is an act of war of which the first object is to destroy the Nazi system. There are Allied organisations whose work it is to single out, separate and destroy the dangerous elements in German life. It is too soon for you to distinguish between 'good' and 'bad' Germans: you have a positive part to play in winning the peace by a definite code of behaviour. In streets, houses, cafés, cinemas, etc, you must keep clear of Germans, man, woman and child, unless you meet them in the course of duty. You must not walk out with them, or shake hands, or visit their homes, or make them gifts, or take gifts from them. You must not play games with them or share any social event with them. In short, you must not fraternise with Germans at all.

To refrain from fraternisation is not easy. It requires self-discipline. But in Germany you will have to remember that laughing and eating and dancing with Germans would be bitterly resented by your own families, by millions of people who have suffered under the Gestapo and under the Luftwaffe's bombs, and by every Ally that Britain possesses. You will have to remember that these are the same Germans who, a short while ago, were drunk with victory, who were boasting what they as the Master Race would do to you as their slaves, who were applauding the utter disregard by their leaders of any form of decency or of honourable dealings: the same Germans whose brothers, sons and fathers were carrying out a system of mass murder and torture of defenceless civilians. You will have to remember that these same Germans are planning to make fools of you again and to escape the loathing which their actions deserve. [...] Any slackness will be the cue for the resistance movements to intensify their efforts. Be just; be firm; be correct; give orders, and don't argue. Last time we won the war and let the peace slip out of our hands. This time we must not ease off – we must win both the war and the peace."

Montgomery's letter No. 3 will finally allow the Allies to speak to German adults... on July 14, 1945!

It's very difficult, however, to curb the enthusiasm of young Allied conquerors, as they enter a country almost devoid of men. Everything is therefore done to dissuade soldiers from 'fraternizing' with young German women, such as a prevention campaign against sexually transmitted diseases (the treatment of which would only delay their return home) and, above all, a significant fine. Reported cases of sexual assault are punished very severely by the authorities. This American soldier writes home: *"It shouldn't be too hard for most fellows to stay clean, altho' these German gals really stack up and are very enticing – but don't get caught or you'll pay a $65 fine* [more than $930 nowadays] *or should she prefer 'charges' it might mean prison or death. These gals will do anything to get you in trouble and are very tricky. They'll invite you in for a good time, then squeal on you claiming rape. So we are told and read in the papers."* For the Red Army soldiers, on the other hand, who'll reach Berlin in the east, rape is an efficient way of spreading fear and revenge, affecting more than 2 million German women. Soviet war correspondent Natalya Gesse writes: *"The Russian soldiers were raping every German female from eight to eighty. It was an army of rapists. Not only because they were crazed with lust, this was also a form of vengeance."*

GERMAN CIVILIANS

Henry Crookhorn is a reservist who'd worked for the New York Telephone Company for fourteen years. Called up for duty in May 1943, he naturally joined a communications unit: the 303rd Signal Operations Battalion. After serving in Normandy and the Ardennes, he took his first steps in Germany after crossing the Remagen bridge in March 1945. He watches German civilians with great curiosity: *"What surprised me most, was to see how well off these people are. More so than either the Belgians or French. They are more robust, especially the women with emphasis on the 'bust' part of that word, robust (don't worry Darling, we are not allowed to fraternize). They are strong, healthy-looking people and try very hard to be friendly to us, but we just give them that stiff upper lip and poker face treatment. It's tough, but those are the orders. They are all very well-clothed too. The girls all wear stockings (silk or nylon) and I have yet to see any going bare-legged, a common sight in France and Belgium. Yesterday was probably 'First Communion Day' as all the girls were running around in 'White' from top to bottom with a sort of wreath on their heads. They seem to be very religious around these parts. Here and there along the road you'll see a great big crucifix sit in open fields. It's all very unusual. [...] The German equipment is more like ours and far ahead of other European countries. That goes for their electrical fixtures, sanitary set-up, home lay-out, dress and so forth. They seem to be very clean too. They are our enemies, by deed and act, but you must give credit where credit is due. [...] It sure is one beautiful country. I can't for the life of me see why the Germans should be interested in anyone else's land when they have the best set-up right here at home. They are a good-looking people, and well-built, and are the nearest thing to the Americans in both their customs and habits. Of course, we are forbidden to 'fraternize' with them. We hence must give them the cold shoulder so to speak which makes it hard on everybody, but that is the only way to make them understand and respect us, and at the same time protect ourselves. I have been into many abandoned homes and have picked up quite a few souvenirs which I will send home as soon as I get around to it and have them approved. Some of the boys have been quite lucky and picked up some valuable cameras and watches. [...]*

I am now in a town in Germany called Bad Neuenahr, about four miles from the Rhine and about six miles from that now famous Remagen bridgehead, the Ludendorff Bridge where the US forces first crossed the Rhine river. [...] Went on a little sight-seeing trip today with Lt. Dick. It was his day off and so he invited me along for the ride. Saw the Rhine river again and also the beautiful surrounding country. We went to a big lake and hung around there awhile snapping pictures in color. All these villages are so cute. You ride up a long hill and come to the top of it where you can look down and see a small group of houses nestled in a valley so pretty-like and then you ride down and up to the next hill and see the same thing repeated again. Of course the bigger towns took a terrific beating and are leveled to the ground, but the little villages in between stand there as tho' they never saw a war. Along the roads you see plenty of burned-out German vehicles but very little of ours."

Most of the cities around the Rhine were destroyed by Allied bombardments and street fighting. Once out of the countryside, Henry witnesses scenes of desolation surpassing anything he'd ever seen in France, and other very grim sights: *"The business about the German atrocities is true and not so much propaganda. These Germans are a hard-tough people. The other day I saw the remains of a little girl splashed all over the side of a house and on the walk-in front thereof, as a result of her playing with an unexploded shell she found somewhere. The woman living in the house just nonchalantly came out with a whish broom and swept off the window sills and sidewalk as tho' she was cleaning up her front parlor with not even an expression of sorrow or regret. The average woman would hardly have the courage to go within sight of the scene. I usually can stand such sights but this one turned my stomach, so I couldn't eat supper that night. Apparently, they (these Germans) are used to such things and it pleases them none. So believe what you hear about the way our 'boys' have been treated. I've seen it, believe me."*

Henry's brother, Edmund Crookhorn, is also on the Rhine, but 100 miles further south. With the 759th MP Battalion (military police), he traveled through Europe all the way from Oran (Algeria). Finally entering Germany on April 1, 1945, he writes: *"Moved from Haguenau to Landau, Germany. This is probably the most important move in my army career, because it stands out as the primary cause of my being a soldier. We came over the border at exactly 9:17 AM, Easter Sunday to do duty in the German town of Landau. It was quite a thrill to go through the Siegfried Line and one could notice the work put in this defense. [...] The houses of brick construction are similar to the houses built in Brooklyn about 1900. The houses are massive, but well-built. The people are well-dressed but walk around with a defeated look. We are not allowed to talk to them, nor do we hand out candy like we did in Africa, Italy and France."* Two days later, Edmund will be placed in charge of controlling traffic on a floating bridge over the Rhine.

The non-fraternization policy will gradually be lifted. This US Army German dictionary was apparently used as an exercise notebook by a German child who was learning to write the name of his new American friend.

GUENTHER AHLF

F Company, 378th Regiment, 95th Infantry Division

Despite being a German immigrant, 'Gunner' managed to win the respect of his fellow GIs in the tough battle for Metz. A few weeks later, he enters the country he was born in, and his chats with the locals reveal the grim reality of civilians caught in the crossfire.

William Carl Guenther 'Gunner' Ahlf was born in Hamburg, Germany, on February 1, 1922. His father, a former German soldier in the First World War, emigrated with his family to Illinois (United States) two years later, and the whole family obtained American citizenship in 1930.

However, Gunner, who signed up on August 29, 1942 after leaving high school, had great difficulty finding his place in the armed forces because of his origins, and was initially refused by the Air Force, which he'd dreamed of joining. He was then given an opportunity to become a spy, but unfortunately, his American accent was considered too strong. The army therefore gave him a rifle and sent him to the infantry, where he joined F Company of the 378th Regiment (95th Infantry Division). He'd eventually use his origins to his advantage, later serving as an interpreter and participating in the interrogation of prisoners and communicating with the German population. In Germany, he'll even give language courses to 190 American soldiers.

Shortly before leaving the United States for the European front, Gunner married his girlfriend, Elizabeth (Betty) Locke, on October 16, 1943 in Elmhurst, Illinois. After a short stay in England, he arrived in France on September 15, 1944.

Betty and Gunner on their wedding day.

"PLEASE, DON'T BE ALARMED!"

The separation was hard for the young couple, especially since Gunner was quickly thrown into battle. His baptism of fire took place in November 1944 in Metz, a city in which the Americans had been struggling for several weeks. He wrote from there after a tough day of combat: *"I just finished re-reading about twenty of your old letters. I'll keep three or four of them for a while and destroy the rest of them. It really hurts to destroy those wonderful letters of yours, but we're not supposed to carry them at all. I usually carry them until I've read them five or six times. I never get tired of reading all about you – what you're doing, how much you love me and how much you miss me. I hope you never get tired of telling me you're in love with me. [...] I realize that it must be rough on you, honey, in some ways rougher than it is on myself. You have no way of knowing whether or not I'm OK. I can tell you not to worry, but I know you will anyway. [...] I could tell you that I'm not actually in combat, but I think it's better to stick to the truth. All I can say, honey, is to keep faith and hope and pray that everything will turn out the way we want it to. You know that the one thing I'm concerned with is coming back to you and I'm going to be as careful as possible and always remember that I've got the most wonderful wife in the world."*

Gunner took part in the battles of Task Force Bacon, which earned his 2nd Battalion a Distinguished Unit Citation: from November 11-15, they crossed the Moselle under enemy fire and seized Fort Yutz and then that of Illange, allowing the creation of a bridgehead in Thionville, which was essential to the capture of Metz. On the Moselle, Gunner was hit by a shell fragment that slightly cut his face only 1 inch from his eye. He was extremely lucky. The doctor put a bandage on him, gave him an aspirin and Gunner immediately returned to combat. Although he received a Purple Heart for his injury, Gunner avoided the subject in his letters so as not to worry his wife, but a fellow soldier on leave called Betty and leaked the information: *"Don't worry, he's fine, it's just a little cut!"* Gunner waited two weeks to confess to Betty in a letter: *"I'm sending home a Purple Heart medal that they gave me. Please, don't be alarmed! I got it for a little scratch. You know they give it for almost anything. I just walked around with a bandage for a while. I wasn't even bad enough to be evacuated for. I don't think I'd even tell the folks about it if I were you. They'd only think it was something serious. I promise you I won't get any more."*

Not being able to tell about his recent exploits in Metz, Gunner wrote on November 20: *"I have a few moments to spare and I want you to know that I'm still OK. We've been terribly busy the past ten days, so you'll have to excuse me. I consider myself extremely fortunate that I'm able to write at all.*

Someday I'll be able to tell you about everything we've done, but that's impossible now. I've certainly learned plenty the past few days. I've never been keen on the infantry before but I've found out that they have the bravest men in the world. I wish I'd have the 'guts' some of them have. Don't ever let anyone fool you – there's only one outfit that'll win this war and that's the infantry. [...] Don't worry about me too much because I'm coming back to you. Pray for me. I've prayed more the past few days than I ever have and it helps."

Shoulder patch of the 95th Division. Its men were nicknamed 'The Iron Men of Metz' after their actions in the French city.

BACK TO GERMANY

The 95th Division then moved on to Saarland, and Gunner returned to his country of birth on November 28, taking part in the hard fighting in Saarlautern (Saarlouis) at the beginning of December. Gunner wrote: *"We've been plenty busy pushing these Germans back. I only hope we can keep pushing them. I want to come back to you, but fast. Our battalion and our company are making quite a name for themselves. We have the best men and officers in the whole army I believe. My German has come in quite handy on many occasions. I've questioned a lot of the Germans we've captured and it helps when we need anything from the civilians. The Germans are pretty tired of this damn war, especially now that it's been fought on their own soil. Those that we capture are glad that the war is all over for them. The SS and party men in Germany are the only ones that are keeping this war going. They won't keep it going for long tho'. I'm feeling fine. I need a bath and a shave and some clean clothes and I'll be like new. [...] See if you can't send me a batch of chocolate bars. It's pretty hard to get stuff like that up at the front. There's [sic] more important things to haul first. We are getting fed well. They try to bring up at least two hot meals to us every day and they usually do."*

The bridgehead over Saarland was only secured on December 19 and shortly afterwards, Gunner's unit was decorated with the CIB (Combat Infantry Badge), which was received with the greatest joy since it offered a salary increase.

VII - INTO THE REICH SPRING 1945

A few days later, Gunner carried out a new reconnaissance mission with the lieutenant in the same area. In the woods, they asked a German civilian for directions and started a long conversation: *"He told us how both of his sons were gone. One was killed in Russia and the other was wounded and released from the hospital too early, and consequently died of his wounds. Not only did he lose his two sons, but his home was bombed too. I told him I was from Hamburg, and he said what everyone else has said, that Hamburg has been almost completely demolished. In one week 500,000 persons were killed by air raids in Hamburg."*

On January 21, he added: *"Someone just mentioned that today is Sunday. I've spent pleasanter ones, but I thank God that I'm spending them at all. Over here Sunday is no different from any other day – except that the Germans seem to take great pleasure in throwing more shells on it. […] I questioned a Jerry we captured today and he gave me the usual story. They are all anxious for the war to end. When I told him the Russians were in Germany he actually seemed happy about it. There was one Jerry 36 years old who's been in the Army for four years and he's still a private. […] They claim that the Germans are beginning to force 50 and 60-year-old men to fight. I can see why the Germans hope the war ends soon – we're in a town where our Air Corps raised considerable hell and you could go on for blocks and blocks and not find a house or building that hasn't been blown to hell. You couldn't even find a whole window. The town is almost completely destroyed and this place hasn't been bombed half as much as most of the larger cities."*

While the fighting moved north of the Ardennes, Gunner remained in his native country. At the beginning of January, he told his wife Betty a rather original war story: *"Lt. Ingersoll and I went on a little reconnaissance trip in a jeep. We went through an old trail in the woods and half the time the jeep was on a 45° angle. We got to the top of a mountain (there was a beautiful view up there – you would look down into the snow-covered valley and small villages below) and when we got up there, we had to go down into the village below. There was no trail so we started making one. We got most of the way down and then the Lt. got out and the hill got steeper. About 100 feet from the bottom we started sliding and the driver lost control and jumped out. I like a damn fool stayed in. It was something like Riverview Park. The jeep stayed on its wheels and ended up in a little creek. All I got out of it was a helluva jolt when it hit the bottom. We got the jeep stuck in a creek and a civilian helped us get it out. The fact is, he darn near lifted it out by himself.*

We finally proceeded through a pretty fair-sized town which is full of civilians. We were snowed under here. There is [sic] a million kids in that town and I'll bet every one of them threw at least two snowballs at us. When I got back I was covered with snow. At one spot we got a pretty heavy barrage so we stopped the jeep and got out and started throwing them back. This was a mistake. As soon as we started throwing kids came swarming in from every angle. We never had a chance. The people think we're nuts, I guess. The kids know darn well we don't do anything to them. I can imagine what'd happen to them if they threw snowballs at a German officer. I know darn well he wouldn't get out and throw them back."

THE CAPTURE OF DORTMUND

The Iron Men were moved to Belgium and then to the Netherlands. Stationed near Maastricht, they relieved British units in Meerselo in mid-February 1945. For Gunner, who'd just lost a tooth after biting a bland Ration C biscuit, the war seemed to drag on forever. He wrote: *"I see by the* Stars & Stripes *where Roosevelt says the war here MAY end in 1945. I remember when Walter Winchell, Drew Pearson and Gen. Marshall said it'd end in October 1944 – and everyone else said it'd certainly be over by Christmas. I guess my dad is the only one who didn't think it'd end over here in a short time. I hope and pray it'll end before summer. It'll take a few miracles, but they've happened before."*

Gunner even bet twenty dollars with his comrades that the war wouldn't end before May 21. He'll eventually lose by a narrow margin. In fact, the men are mainly concerned with being deployed to the Pacific or the CBI (China, Burma, India) once the German problem is solved. As he is friends with his censor (the lieutenant of the snowball episode), Gunner openly expresses his opinions in his letters.

The lieutenant simply signs the envelope before Gunner even starts writing (see bottom left corner of the envelope below)! In reality, the officer is overwhelmed by the number of letters written by his men, who've so many opinions to share about Germany. The lieutenant even asks them to write less: *"The censor has been raising hell because the boys are writing too much. He told me he was going to send me on a ten-mile road march during the day and a night problem at night to keep me busy. He was joking (I hope)."*

At the beginning of March, Gunner is back in Germany and helps destroy a German resistance pocket near the Adolf-Hitler bridge (now the Krefeld-Uerdingen bridge), before crossing the Rhine. The cities then fall one after the other: Neuss, Beckum, Hamm, Kamen, Werl, Unna... Other pockets are being cleaned up north of the Ruhr. On April 12, Gunner faces the large city of Dortmund. Two days later, he describes its capture in the following letter: *"My Darling, this has been an important day for our outfit. Today our Battalion – led by F Company – walked in and took the city of Dortmund without having a shot fired. We had a few skirmishes in some of the suburbs and had a little trouble with mines, but all in all the battle for Dortmund wasn't rough. The city is 'kaput'. You can walk for miles and you won't see a building that isn't in ruins. You can see that at one time it was a very beautiful city.*

The Air Corps really did a beautiful job on it. The boys were unhappy when they saw that the famous breweries were destroyed also. The original population was 600,000. It now has a population of 300,000 and every one of them was on the street. We marched into town early in the morning and the town seemed deserted. An hour later the streets were packed. They came out of their cellars and bunkers and could hardly believe their eyes. The first thing they ask is whether we are English or Americans. We tell them we are Americans and their faces brighten. They fear the English because they believe the English hate them more than we do because of the blitz and the V-bombs. One or two small sections of the city haven't been damaged too bad because there are no big factories near it. There certainly are some big steel mills here – the largest I've ever seen. And they're blown to hell too. It'd take two days to go through one of those things. The people here were really glad to see us – they can sleep peacefully for the first time in over two years. No more bombings to sweat out for them. The women had tears in their eyes and the men were getting drunk. The kids were begging for chocolate and chewing gum and the girls were flirting with every GI that was on the street. I got two more pistols. I now have a Luger, P-38, 32 special, and another kind of 32. If I brought them home now I could easily get $400 for the lot of them [about $5,750 nowadays]. [...] Keep on praying for me and it may not be so very long until I'll be home. I want to come home to you. All my love, Gunner."

Gunner's letter is dated March 14, although it was written the day after Dortmund was captured on April 14, 1945. The postmark of the armies' post office on the envelope clearly indicates the date of April 15.

This mistake is very common in letters from the front and reveals the fatigue of soldiers who were trapped in a boring and stressful routine. On the eve of June 6, 1944, Eisenhower himself had dated his letter written in case of failure "July 5" (page 154).

A mortar platoon from the 95th Division entering the ruins of Dortmund on April 12, 1945.

After the liberation of Dortmund, Gunner occupies its suburbs, staying in the inhabitants' homes evacuated by the division. He writes to his wife about the coffin of a child, who'd died the day before, being still in the house where he's staying. Shortly afterwards, he takes to the road again and gets as close as 80 miles from his hometown. On the way, Gunner passes through the cities of Münster and Osnabrück, now reduced to ghost towns: *"The RAF did quite a bit of work on the last two. They must enjoy avenging the bombings of England."* As he approaches Bremen, waiting for the city to fall before settling there, he writes on April 23: *"The English are bombing Bremen again. I can feel the earth shake and the windows are rattling. Planes are flying back and forth all day. Bremen will fall in two or three days. Berlin will have fallen by the time you get this letter."*

Indeed, the British 2nd Army will take Bremen at the very end of the month. Refusing to surrender, the city held by young SS soldiers in training will be besieged for two weeks by the 43rd (Wessex) Division in the north, the 52nd (Lowland) Division in the northeast, the 51st (Highland) Division in the west, and the 3rd (Iron) Division in the south. Gunner's second prediction will prove to be correct: Betty will open his letter on May 7, 1945. When the war ends, Gunner won't have enough points to go home, despite the Bronze Star he received for bravery in battle. The 95th Division will return to the United States on June 29, 1945 and begin training right away to be deployed to the Pacific. However, the atomic bomb will change their plans, and Gunner's unit will thus stay in the United States. After 151 days of fighting it will have lost nearly 10,000 killed, wounded and missing. Gunner will leave the army on November 21, 1945 and return to university. He'll have a successful career as vice-president of an insurance company and pass away on June 14, 2005, in Scottsdale, Arizona.

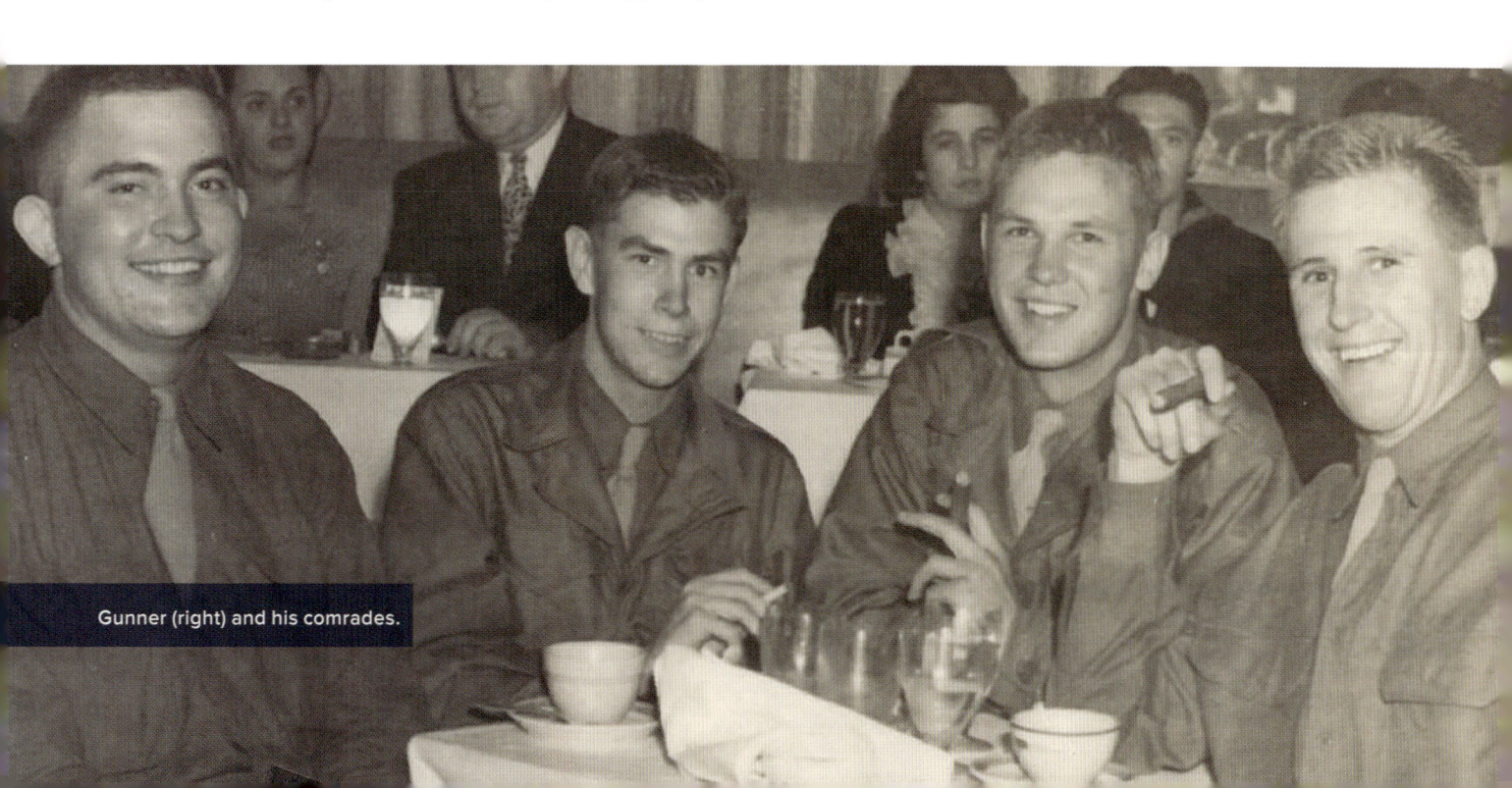

Gunner (right) and his comrades.

CARL HOLMBERG

F Company, 8th Regiment, 4th Infantry Division

Carl is one of the many replacements who have to experience their baptism of fire in enemy territory. The resistance is stiff and will put an end to Carl's dreams of one day becoming a recognized baseball player, after being wounded only two weeks before the end of the war.

Carl Norman Holmberg was born on June 12, 1923 in New Britain, Connecticut. He studied engineering at university, which meant he initially avoided the army as young people who wished to complete their studies were able to do so without being called up for military service. In 1944, however, due to significant losses on the various fronts, this system was suspended and Carl was enlisted on July 14, 1944. He hoped to join the Navy, but ended up in the infantry. In his letters, he told his parents about his disappointment and his difficult training (page 77).

On December 14, 1944, Carl was at the replacement depot of Fort George Meade (Maryland): *"A fellow says that they told him at the Orderly Room that 114 of us were on a shipping list coming out. That probably means we'll be leaving over the weekend sometime. I'd give my right eye to get home just once more. One guy has been held here for two weeks while all his buddies shipped. He got home two weekends. Some guys are lucky. He's sick of it and wants to ship. We're just hanging around now so they probably won't hold us long. I'm telling you these physicals are strictly a joke. I had a tougher physical for baseball at college than the army or induction center ever gave. Monday we had a physical that lasted all of a minute and a half. Not undressed, a dentist opened my mouth and picked me out of the chain with the same motion, short arm [inspection of soldiers' penises], turned around once before an M.D. - all thru. A guy could have one and pass I believe. I don't know what to do with all this underwear I brought. We only can take 2 pair of cottons (GI) and 2 woolens. I haven't any way of shipping the rest home or my furlough bag either. I don't know if I can take my scarf, gloves or anything else that I got. They'll probably confiscate it all. I can't get a box big enough but I'm going to try. […]*

I certainly hope H. doesn't have to get into this thing. He and Hulda [his aunt] can joke about it but, when the time draws near to leave, it won't be any picnic. The guy in the next bunk to me has five children, three of them before Pearl Harbor. That's mighty tough to take. It doesn't make much difference anymore – married or single I guess. I'd say that perhaps the majority now are married, possibly even fathers. […] Boy, would I like to be stationed in a place like this, passes every night and weekends, good food and barracks. But then everybody can't expect those things. A great many of these men have been overseas and in combat."

Shortly before Christmas, Carl finally left the United States to join F Company, 8th 'Fighting Eagles' Regiment, 4th 'Ivy' Infantry Division, which had been fighting in Europe since June 6, when it landed on Utah Beach.

VII - INTO THE REICH SPRING 1945

199 DAYS

Carl arrived in France at the beginning of January 1945 and joined his unit in Luxembourg. On January 21, in the middle of a snowstorm, he attacked the wooded heights of the Shnee Eifel, on the Belgian-German border (from where the Ardennes offensive had started), clearing the bunkers and fortified gun nests of the Siegfried Line the Americans had already taken in September 1944. He was due to cross the Prüm River on February 9, but the division encountered strong German resistance and stopped its advance. The next day, Carl wrote to his family for the first time since his arrival in Europe: *"I've been in Scotland, England, France, Luxemburg, Belgium and lastly, Germany. You can gather your own conclusions from that. I've only had fleeting glimpses of all, however. Please note my new and permanent address and inform everyone of it. I can't write to all because it's impossible. It's really miserable living in watery foxholes, getting little or no sleep and being cold and wet most of the time. Why supposedly civilized people can desire this sort of thing every twenty years is beyond human conception."*

The town of Prüm fell on February 12 and the 4th Division occupied defensive positions west of the river of the same name, while waiting for other units to catch up before resuming its progress. Carl wrote to his mother on the 24th: *"You wrote in one letter about Bill having written from a foxhole by the light of a bonfire. He's lucky to be in the Field Artillery where he can light a fire. Where I've been, a man doesn't dare light a cigarette in his foxhole after dark for fear that some Heinie will shoot his ears off. [...] Yeah, Mom, it's a rough, tough, dirty job that has to be done. We can only hope and pray that kids like John and his playmates will never have to do the job again. Dad fought the last one with the same hope. Let's have faith that our leaders have profited by the 1918-19 mistakes."*

Carl crossed the Prüm River at Hermespand on February 28, charged with the mission of taking the large hill to the east of the town and Weisheim. Despite a major counter-attack, the area was secured on March 1 and the division crossed the Kyll River a week later. It then headed northeast, ending its frantic run at Adenau and Reifferscheid. Carl is particularly proud of his unit and attaches a flattering article from the *Stars & Stripes* about the 'Ivy Leaf Division' (the emblem of the 4th Division) to a letter: *"Naturally, I haven't been with the Division all this time covered by the clipping but have taken part in some of it."* This official US Army newspaper may not be the most objective source, which is why Carl relativizes his comments: *"I know the news headlines at home are very optimistic now. I've seen in* Stars & Stripes *where the headlines scream that the final phase has begun. I certainly hope the American people won't make the mistake of slackening up on the war effort because every mile of the way forward is paid for dearly in American sweat, blood and suffering. The people at home can't let the fighting men down no matter how optimistic the headlines."*

Written shortly after crossing the Plüm River, this letter evokes the omnipresent mud, which still stains its envelope seventy-five years later: *"March 2, 1945. Dear Mom, I'm writing this letter in a cellar by the light of a gas flame. I'm somewhere in Germany. It's starting to snow again here which will only help to increase the mud. I never thought any place could be so muddy."* He also attaches an article from the *Stars & Stripes* about his division: *"Ivy Leaf Division, first unit on German soil, closes 199-day contact with Wehrmacht in Rhine chase."*

The American soldiers are certainly being realistic. Not only do the Germans defend their territory fiercely, but the GIs have no illusions about the outcome of the war for them: *"If the war ends soon over here, many of us will carry on the fight in China, Burma or India. Not too pleasant an outlook but then, one never knows what's going on anyway. We've got a job to finish over here in Europe first so I guess we'll sweat that out before worrying about what comes after."* Carl doesn't yet know that he himself will pay the price of the Allied advance to the heart of the Reich.

Carl in his service uniform, before leaving the United States.

WOUNDED

On March 10, 1945, the 4th Division leaves Patton's army to join the 7th Army of General Patch, 190 miles to the south. Before returning to combat, the division is put at rest for a short while in eastern France and Carl takes the opportunity to send more news to his family: *"I guess Rudy had to take you all out to dinner because he lost that bet on when the war would be over. This war is something that a person can't make predictions or bet on. A great many have already made fools of themselves by predicting the end of it. The last few days have been really fine. The weather has been rather warm and best of all, the sun has been shining. Our bombers have been continually in the air and you can bet your boots that somebody is catching the vent of their fury. I wish they could drop so many eggs that nothing but a large crater would remain of Germany. [...] Three of our boys received Bronze Stars yesterday for exemplary courage and actions in the line of duty. One of your letters which I received today was written around Jan. 3. It stated that Dad was all set to enlist in the Infantry. I certainly hope he doesn't get any more such crazy ideas. It's bad enough that you have a son in this mess, Mom, without Dad getting into it too. If it lasts much longer, he'll probably get drafted despite his age. You can't imagine how many fathers there are over here. Men with four and five children too. [...] It would break your heart Mom to see some of these little tots, Martha's age and even younger, out asking us soldiers for candy and gum. Yesterday I'll bet there were twenty tiny kids around our mess area. After we all ate, the mess Sgt. gave them mess kits and fed them. Now they're there every meal. We had chocolate pudding yesterday and those kids were chocolate from ear to ear. All I could think of was Martha. You have to see things like that to appreciate America."*

The 4th Infantry Division crosses the Rhine at Worms on March 29, and while the Germans are surrounded in the Ruhr, it continues its advance into the heart of Germany, towards Würzburg. On April 3, it establishes a bridgehead on the Main River in Ochsenfurt, before rushing through Bavaria – but the German Army doesn't give up the fight. Carl is wounded on April 17, 1945, only two weeks before the end of the war, about 12 miles from Ochsenfurt (south of Würzburg and west of Nuremberg). Pieces of shrapnel went through his neck, left arm, left leg and knee, although to him, they're just *"a few nice scars to remind me of Hitler and his bloodthirsty henchmen."*

He waits several days before telling his parents the bad news, thinking it's better for them to hear it directly from the army. He finally writes to them: *"I guess you know by now that those Heinie son's o' guns (we have lots more emphatic names for them) knocked me out of the fight a few days ago. We're all laying in bed here in England, awaiting the signal that will mean the end of the war in Europe: it can't be too far off now, as the commentators keep repeating that it should only be a matter of hours. Believe me, Dad, it can't happen too soon for me, nor for all you folks back home either, I reckon."* In reality, Carl's parents haven't yet received the telegram informing them of their son's injury, and they're very concerned. Carl answers them two days after the victory to reassure them: *"I received the letter today which you, Dad and Betty wrote the day you found out about my being wounded. I really thought the war department telegram would get to you first. I'm coming along OK, so don't worry. Dad said he was so nervous he couldn't write. I guess that's any parent's reaction to news of that kind. However, tell him to keep smiling [...]. Hulda says she's going to spit on all Germans she meets. She's really a card. Except for a few repairs, I'm doing fine. As yet, I have not received any of your packages, but we were moving so fast at times that mail service was impossible. The plane ride I had was a thrill in that it was my first. However, it doesn't float as smoothly as one would imagine. Sometimes the plane pitched like a ship on a choppy sea or a jeep on a bumpy road. Some got sick but I didn't."*

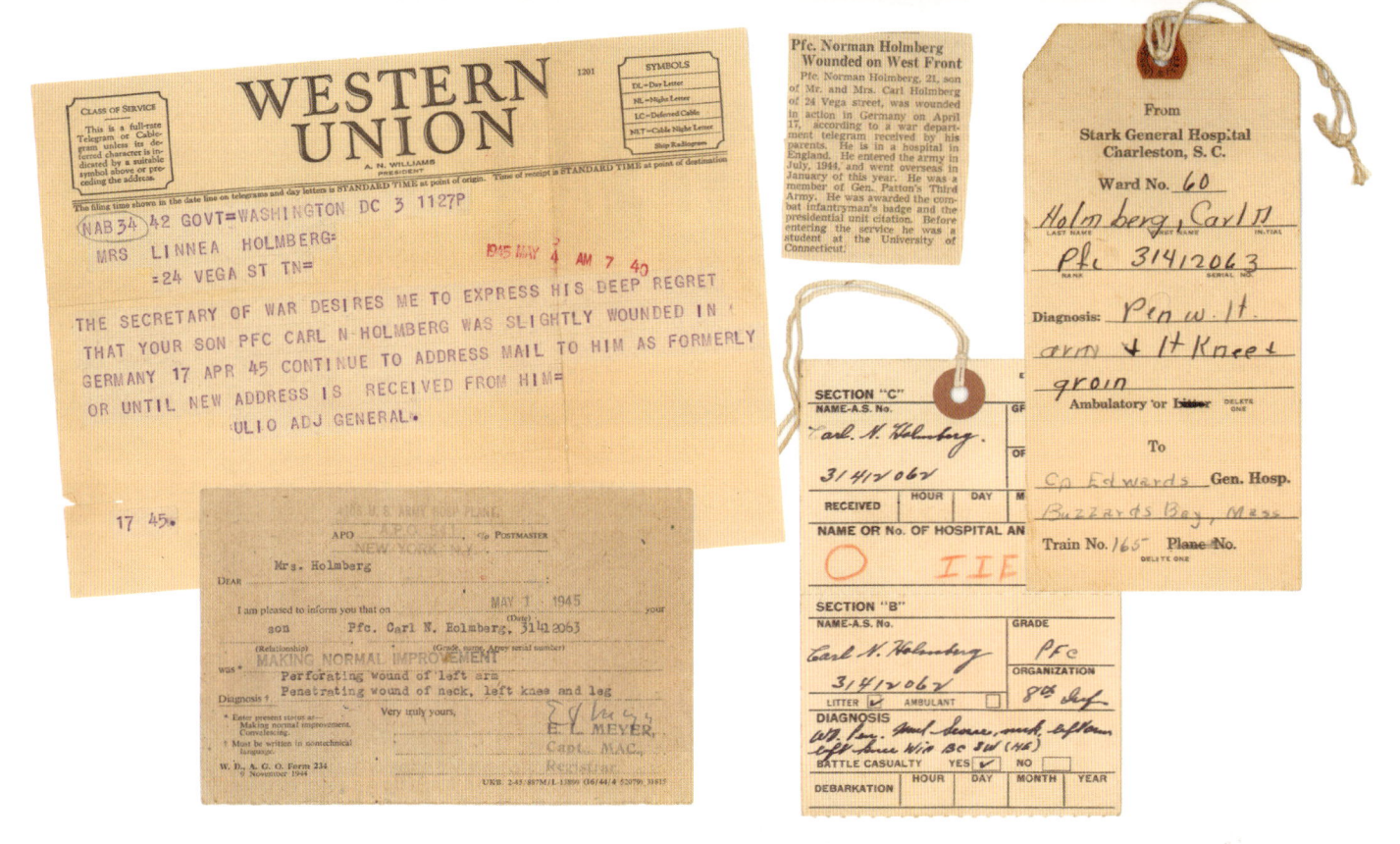

The telegram that arrived too late, an article about Carl's injury, and two rare toe-tags. These tags hung from his feet in the hospital so that the medical staff could identify him.

Carl will spend five months in hospitals, in Germany, England and then finally the United States, where he'll receive his Purple Heart. He'll also earn the Bronze Star for his actions during his last days in combat. He'll spend his days in England waiting for news from his loved ones, playing card games and listening to news of the war. He's impressed by the morale of the American soldiers, who always keep their sense of humor, no matter how serious their injuries. For his part, he's eager to get home. In late July, he'll write: *"I am walking now and am confident that it won't be too long before I see a certain lady of whom I've been dreaming lately – 'the Statue of Liberty'. It's an awful sensation to pull out of New York and watch her majestic lines grow dimmer and dimmer. All the time wondering silently 'will I even see it again?' But, after you see what's going on in European cities and happening to European cities, a guy is thankful that it hasn't happened at home."*

At the end of August 1945, Carl will finally be repatriated to the United States, although he still won't have fully recovered from his injuries, which would unfortunately prevent him from playing baseball again. However, he'll return to the University of Connecticut and graduate in 1948, before starting a long career as an engineer. He'll die in his county of birth on June 29, 2010 and be buried with military honors.

Carl receiving his Bronze Star towards the end of his life.

THE END OF AN ERA

The balance of power has changed considerably: the Allies have 94 divisions against 65 under-equipped German divisions. Most of the latter will be destroyed in the Ruhr Pocket, while the race to Berlin is underway. At the same time, however, the Americans will lose their president.

THE RUHR POCKET

In February 1945, the American 8th Infantry Division and others received specific training in river crossing, combined armored and infantry combat, street fighting and open ground assaults, even in the use of enemy anti-tank weapons. These skills will now be useful, as two American armies converge on the industrial sector of the Ruhr, formerly the heart of the German war machine. For Dwane and his Signal Battalion in the 8th Division, walking by charred German tanks hit by Allied artillery, the dreaded fierce enemy resistance encountered once the Rhine was crossed in Bonn (on March 28) is actually weaker than anticipated. While the 3rd US Army continues on its way to eastern Germany, the 1st US Army, to which the 8th Division belongs, stops its advance in the Ruhr region to encircle it from the south. The 9th US Army, now separated from the British 21st Army Group (which is headed to the Baltic Sea), is responsible for the northern side of the Ruhr.

Stuck between the 1st and 9th US Armies, only 430,000 men of Walter Model's Heeresgruppe B remain. Among them are the remnants of the Wehrmacht (twenty-one exhausted divisions), a few SS units still in training, a militia of elderly men (the 'Volkssturm') and Hitler Youth boys, whose youngest members are no more than 12 years old. The pocket extends from the Rhine to the west, the Ruhr River in the north and the Sieg River to the south. Bonn, Düsseldorf, Essen, Dortmund and Hamm are in it, imprisoning millions of civilians. The pocket is completely closed by April 4 and two days later, the 8th Division, in position towards Siegen (which it'd taken a few days earlier), is ordered to attack the pocket from the south and split it up as it moves northwest towards Essen. Dwane's unit is the spearhead of the XVIII Airborne Corps.

Shoulder patch of The XVIII Airborne Corps, that no longer consists exclusively of airborne units. For the Rhine crossing and the battle for the Ruhr Pocket, it holds the 8th, 86th, and 97th Infantry Divisions, as well as the 13th Armored Division.

As small towns fall, the pocket shrinks at high speed. It's even becoming difficult for Dwane and his fellow signalmen to keep up with the rapid advance of the infantry companies. On April 12, the 1st and 9th Armies join forces, splitting the pocket in two, with the eastern part surrendering the next day. Meanwhile, the western part fights on against both the Allies and the German Underground, which can finally take action against the Nazis in broad daylight. Resistance fighters try to secure Düsseldorf in order to spare civilians, but the Gestapo and SS units massacre the anti-Nazi groups of 'Aktion Rheinland'. However, the courage of the latter would lead to the cancellation of a new wave of Allied bombardments and the city is finally taken by the Americans on April 17, marking the end of the fighting for the pocket.

The GIs lost 1,000 men killed in action and more than 3,000 wounded. Small enemy groups continue fighting a desperate battle for a few more days, but even Generalfeldmarschall Walter Model, who'd promised Hitler to fight to the death, eventually surrenders. He commits suicide in a forest south of Duisburg, at the far northwest of the pocket. The 325,000 surviving German soldiers, most of whom are wounded, are taken prisoner (including 30 generals) and interned in temporary camps near Remagen (the 'Rheinwiesenlager').

Germany, spring 1945

→ Allied Advance

▨ Ruhr Pocket

⋯☭ Soviet 'Red Army' and positions on May 7

● Key town / city

In reality, these 'Rhine Prairie Camps' (see photo next page) are much less pleasant than their name suggests, as German soldiers are camped outdoors without having the advantages known to the protégés of the Geneva Convention. Eisenhower took care to classify them as 'unarmed enemy forces' instead of 'prisoners of war', in order to feed his own troops and the many refugees first. Many German soldiers will consequently die of hunger and dehydration.

This 2nd lieutenant of the 28th Regiment, 8th Infantry Division at rest is wearing an 'Ike' jacket dated June 9, 1944, and holds his helmet's fiber liner, decorated with the divisional emblem; an 8 crossed by the golden arrow to which Dwane would refer in the letter to follow. Note the 'garrison cap', whose top is more pointed than regularly observed, and the blue bar for the Presidential Unit Citation above the right pocket. This uniform belonged to a GI occupying Germany at the end of the war.

Near Remagen, an MP (military police) guards a Rheinwiesenlager. German prisoners are visible as far as the eye can see.

Dwane writes to his sister: *"We have finally come to a slight halt in the completion of this job over here so will take a few minutes to send home a V-mail... We are moving so rapidly that it is difficult for mail to catch up with us so if you don't hear from me too regularly, please don't worry because that is the reason. The battle of the 'Ruhr pocket' is over and the great industrial center of Germany is back in operation once again: only this time for the allied cause. Yes, it is over and considered just another job well done. However, it holds a significant meaning to us. The 'Golden Arrow' that represents our division was a mighty wedge that completely split the pocket in half and resulted in the reduction of 'Supermen'* [nickname given to the Nazis by the Americans, in reference to the German word 'Übermensch': a philosophical concept developed by Nietzsche in 1883 that made the Übermensch an ideal to be achieved for all humanity, used by the Nazis to describe the Aryan race] *as well as the great material value of the Ruhr. And now we are moving on to the other pockets, all that remains of the once mighty Deutschland.*

The news this morning indicates that the remaining Germans are attempting a last-minute crawl to their holes. But there seems to be a Yank [American], *Tommy* [British], *or Ivan* [Russian] *there blocking the way. They really are throwing in the towel when they start putting out 'peace feelers' with the hope that perhaps at home and on the front, confusion will exist giving them a little more time. But I know for sure that there is no let up over here and their attempts have been in vain. [...] The situation here is definitely under control and as the news indicates, we are really rolling through Germany. At the moment, I am situated in a German office of some kind complete with desks, paper clips, desk lamps, and the whole works including this typewriter. As I look out the window, there does not appear the usual picture – shell craters and bombed and wrecked buildings – no, on the contrary – that explains the swiftness of the 'big drive'. I very well remember how rapidly we came through France, but this beats anything yet. German equipment wrecked and scattered everywhere. That's where the Tank-Infantry combination comes into play and works so beautifully. Yes, Dotty, it is a glorious picture and with God's help may V-day be a possibility and not a thought for the future. The roads are lined with happy, smiling, French PW's – heading 'HOME'! And in seeing them, it is a glorious feeling that after all, not all of this has been fought in vain. Then of course, there are the refugees from Poland, Holland, and all the rest of the enslaved countries of Europe – at last out of the grip of Nazi dominated Europe."*

A dentist in a medical unit cannot believe the news he receives about the number of Germans captured (the 3rd Army alone has 300,000 "in the bag"): *"This town is quite destroyed, and upon investigation of the ruins, there proves to be nothing there. Obviously, the people left with everything of value. Cellars are all connected from house to house. German soldiers could easily escape or sneak up that way in safety. Each home has sand boxes and sacks of sand all about for incendiaries. Many buildings have been burned out too. Each cellar is fixed up in one place for bomb shelter, with reinforced doors, rooms for things of value, even pianos, and aid kits. Gas masks are in every home for civilians. [...] I read in the Army newspaper that we have taken so many prisoners they have no room for the Volksturmers and are turning them loose to go home, believing they had no heart for the fight anyway, and will remain peaceful. Hope so."*

Top of the next page, the dentist's medical unit in Magdeburg, the last city reached by the Americans before meeting with the Red Army.

VII - INTO THE REICH SPRING 1945

"THE PRESIDENT IS DEAD"

However, this important victory in the Ruhr is tarnished by the death of Franklin Roosevelt. At the Yalta Conference in the Crimea at the beginning of February, a sick, tired and thin American president came to Churchill and Stalin to discuss the future of Europe. The following days in the White House were extremely difficult for him, and as he prepared to attend the first meeting to create what would become the 'United Nations Organization', overwork forced him to take a few days off in late March at the Little White House in Warm Springs, Georgia. On the afternoon of April 12, while having his portrait painted, Roosevelt complains: *"I have a terrific pain in the back of my head"* before collapsing on his chair, unconscious. At 3:35 pm, the doctor declares him dead, having suffered a brain hemorrhage. On the same day, the Secretary of the Navy sends the following telegram to all Navy troops: *"I have the sad duty of announcing to the Naval Service the death of Franklin Delano Roosevelt, the President of the United States, which occurred on twelve April. The world has lost a champion of democracy [...]. Colors shall be displayed at half-mast for thirty days beginning 0800 thirteen April west longitude date insofar as war operations permit. Memorial services shall be held on the day of the funeral to be announced later at all yards and stations on board all vessels of the Navy, war operations permitting. Wearing of mourning badges and firing of salutes will be dispensed with in view of war conditions. Signed James Forrestall."*

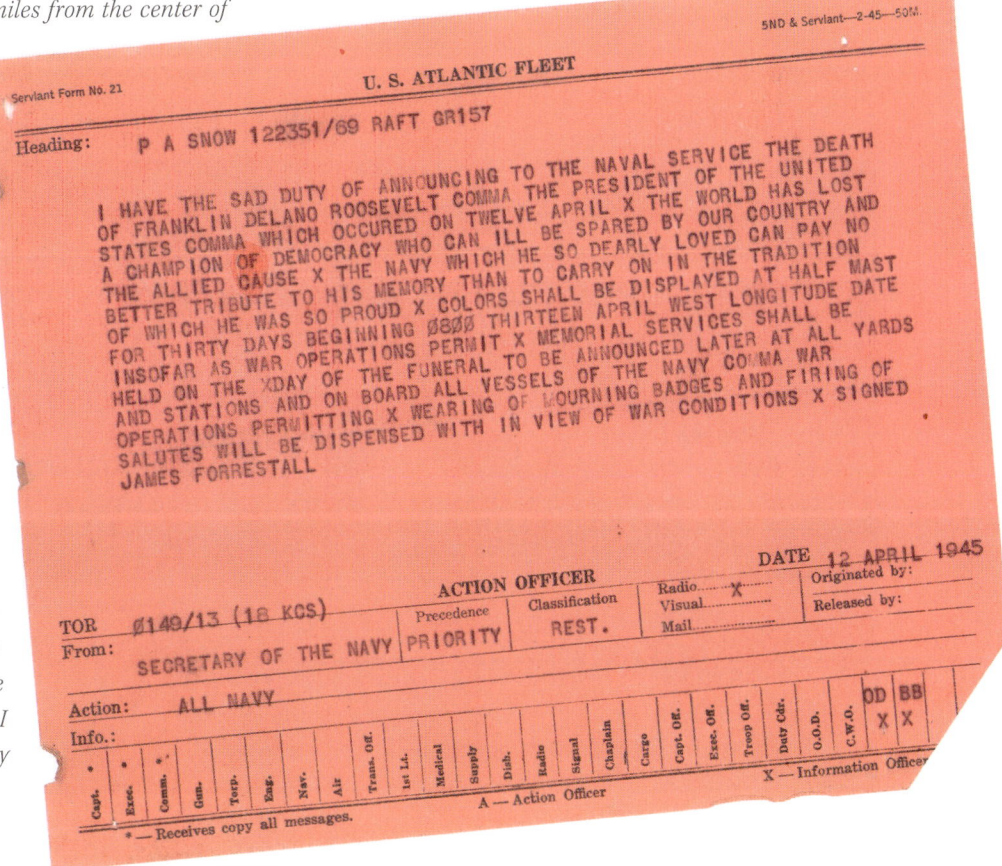

A number of these prisoners are sent to the United States – Edward guards some of them at Camp Au Train, a place lost between the great lakes of Michigan. Americans maintain relatively good relations with their detainees, and sometimes even take pity on the fate of their enemies. On April 22, 1945, Edward writes to his wife, at home in Kansas: *"I just listened to the news and it appears that the Reds have Berlin about encircled and are about 2 or 3 miles from the center of the city. My guess is that Berlin is probably about 25 miles across, so they must really have gone into it. [...] My prisoner of war friend rode to town with me the other day and mentioned how or why the war in Germany has continued for the last 2 or 3 months. His home is in Koblenz and while he has not heard from his folks since mid-January, he says he know his 2 children and parents have been killed. That town is on the Rhine and of course was taken some time ago. I just thought when he mentioned it to me how very very awful and dreadful it must be to realize one's loved ones are in such circumstances and he is here absolutely helpless to aid them, even though he couldn't do much if he were there but it would be horrible and then I thought how fortunate I was to know my loved ones were in safety."*

The President's bad health had been kept secret and the news therefore comes as a shock to American citizens, Democrats and Republicans alike. On April 12, just as the two American armies have split the Ruhr Pocket in two, the information starts to leak. An American MP writes to his wife on April 13, 1945: *"'The President of the United States is dead' – a sudden and untimely message that all radio stations carried this evening and night. [...] Even though the man's political views and activities were not to everyone's likings* [sic] *he will without a doubt go down as one of America's greatest presidents. His passing was untimely first because it is undesirable to have such an occurrence during a time of strife as now exists but mainly for the reason that such an undesirable and undoubtedly incompetent man was elevated to that most responsible position* [Harry Truman]. *In my meager opinion I believe that the president died at the zenith of his career or perhaps a bit on the decline of his climax for unlike Wilson who lived to attempt a lasting peace program and failed, this man will be remembered for his peace theories only, which some* [sound] *noble but which too may fail or result unworkable."*

Another GI in Germany writes the day after Roosevelt's death: *"Have just come from a memorial service to former President Roosevelt. Our chaplain gave a rather appropriate sermon in memory of the man. It was a tremendous shock to all of us when we heard the news. In the previous issue of the* Stars & Stripes *there had not even been a paragraph that the President was in Warm Springs. I fully realize that we will win the war, but I'm quite worried about the peace that is to follow. Roosevelt had many faults, but I sincerely wish that he could have finished the present term."*

Guenther 'Gunner' Ahlf, 95th Infantry Division, also gives his point of view: *"We heard the sad news of the President's death today. I say 'sad' not because I'm a Roosevelt man, but because Truman is now president. That's the worst thing that could happen to the US. It won't affect the progress of the war, but it can affect the peace. Stalin and Churchill trusted and respected Roosevelt and nobody can deny that FDR was a good diplomat. Now everyone wished they had voted for Dewey."*

THE LAST RAMPART

Stalin wants to be the first to capture the 'fascist beast's den' and get his hands on Berlin's uranium for his nuclear research project, *Borodino*. Officially, he says he deserves to see the red flag fly on the Reichstag, given what his country has endured. Eisenhower knows that the Red Army will have Berlin, which will in any case be divided into four zones of occupation, but doesn't really want to become involved in costly street fighting, and every GI agrees. If the Russians want to die for the capital, let them have it! Eisenhower's sole objective is to end the war as soon as possible, reaching the Elbe River and destroying the divisions massed in Bavaria and Austria before they settle in the 'Fortress of the Alps', which was seen as a last resort by Himmler.

An officer in the 83rd Infantry Division, and a veteran of Normandy, approaches the town of Barby on the banks of the Elbe River, only 60 miles from Berlin. He writes on April 12: *"We are now billeted in a Lutheran Rectors home, and it is a very nice old building. Like a lot of these old homes in the States it is*

President Roosevelt's funeral procession in Washington on April 14, 1945, which was attended by more than 300,000 American citizens.

2nd Lieutenant William Robertson (US Army) and Lt. Alexander Sylvashko (Red Army), in front of a sign 'East meets West' in Torgau.

full of furniture to overflowing. And the pictures on the wall show individual good taste but not, taken as a whole, do they fit in. I wish that looting was in order. Boy all the nice things I could have in my home. There is a nice set of silver candle sticks in the building the Command Post is in, here there is a nice silver ship, in one place there is a beautiful set of silver goblets with gold inlaid inside. But we are not supposed to loot! Then there is so much nice Dresden china and such beautiful cut crystal that would look good in my future home. And I certainly can rationalize myself into the right! I think of the three years nearly totally wasted that I could have been spending in school and getting this sort of stuff for myself. [...] We certainly are leading this race! If it means winning the war, I would be glad to let anyone beat us to Berlin, even the Russians!" The next day, the 83rd Division will take the town of Barby and establish a bridgehead on the Elbe, thanks to the work of the combat engineers, whose experience means they're now building bridges at record speed.

During the night of April 12-13 in Westerhusen, James, from the 17th Engineer Armored Battalion (2nd Armored Division), builds a floating bridge over the Elbe in complete darkness. Along with his colleagues, he sustains heavy German artillery fire despite the smoke screens that are supposed to hide them. As the casualties mount, they're ordered to abandon the bridge. James will tell his girlfriend about this event after censorship has been lifted: *"Well to tell you the truth that is just another one of the many bridges that E Co. put up. That river was the hardest that we have ever tried to bridge. If anything was a death trap, that certainly was [...]. Remember when the 9th Army was pushing so fast and so far? When we were up to the Elbe and crossed to the other side, and then pushed back again? The 2nd Armored was leading the way and the 17th Engineer was in the front. Yes, in the front of everything. We hit the Elbe hard, we fought hard, and so did the Germans, and I mean that they gave us everything they had. We almost completed the bridge when an artillery blast came in all around us, then at last it made a direct hit on the bridge. We patched it up and then started to extend the bridge again but without any success, so there is but one thing left for us to do, and that we did, give it up. Yes, it had us beat. Our division, the 2nd Armored Division had to back up. That hurt many of us old fellows, because we have never backed up any at all since we hit the continent."*

James and his men start building another bridge at Magdeburg on April 17, and this time complete it despite German attacks and a Luftwaffe raid. A week later, Americans and Russians would shake hands there, but their first junction would be further south in Strehla and Torgau on Elbe Day, April 25, 1945. That first meeting between the men of the 69th US Infantry Division and of the 58th Guards Rifle Division (USSR) will seal Germany's fate.

"HELL ON WHEELS" April 29, 1945

Somewhere in Germany

My Dear Maxine;
Well you did write me a long letter, diden't you, but I bet that I won't get another for a long, long time now.

ARCHIBALD SAYCE

L Company, 8th Regiment, 4th Infantry Division

Assigned to the same regiment as Carl Holmberg, Archibald is one of the few left in the unit who landed on Utah Beach on D-Day. However, his luck sadly won't last and he'll die only three days before the end of the war, aged 20.

Archibald Holton Sayce Jr. was born on October 6, 1924, in Chicago. Just out of Deerfield Academy, Massachusetts, where he played several sports and enjoyed great popularity, he volunteered for the US Army on August 9, 1943, aged just 18. After training in different camps, he joined a machine gun and mortar platoon in L Company, 8th Regiment, 4th Infantry Division in May 1944. He landed on Utah Beach on June 6 and fought in Normandy, on the Siegfried Line, and in the forests of Hürtgen and the Ardennes, before rushing across Germany. He already knows Europe, which he had visited with his family in 1937 and 1938, but since then, the landscape has changed a great deal...

THE GERMAN CAMPAIGN

The 4th Infantry Division, which has recently joined Patch's 7th Army, has just returned from a well-deserved rest in France. Two days before crossing the Rhine near Worms on March 29, the men settle in a German house. The owners had been drafted in the Volkssturm, an armed militia created in the last months of the war to defend the Reich's territory. Officially made up of men between 16 and 60 years of age, it is composed mainly of children and elderly men. Archibald writes: *"It is without doubt the most modernistic building we have come in contact with since arriving in the ETO. The plumbing, furniture, interior decorating, etc. would be on par with any house in the States. At present two middle aged ladies are residing in the building. It seems the gentlemen of the household have recently been drafted into the Volkssturm. If the electricity was functioning the lights and several radios would add to the conveniences we already have. There are several scrumptious beds about so tonight should be long remembered."*

Among the items of comfort discovered in the house occupied by the GIs before they crossed the Rhine, Archibald got his hands on a typewriter. He'd spend most of his scarce free time in Germany recounting his impressions of the country.

As for the German people they still have the same stolid expression on their faces. As we go by the inhabitants stand sullenly in the shadows and watch the convoys go by. Up to this point I have seen very little fraternization. I just hope this policy keeps up as I believe so much depends on how we treat the civilians. Was surprised to see a few boys of over fourteen on the streets today. The Wehrmacht left in such a hurry I suppose they overlooked a few. Read in a Time *magazine recently that the German Army was playing for time in hopes that by Spring they could call to the colors the seventeen-year-olds and thereby form a few new divisions. That is all bunk as every seventeen-year[-old], sixteen-year-old, and I believe fifteen-year[-old] is in the Army. [...] Yesterday afternoon the Red Cross girls came around to hand us out a few doughnuts. The last time we laid eyes on them was before Paris. Last evening another songfest was in session. A couple of French girls joined in to make the evening more interesting.*

[The next day, March 28] *Have just had breakfast and we are now in the process of cleaning up our room. The people left quite a bit of trash about so the room is in quite a chaotic condition. Naturally, as soon as the boys had deposited their things in the room, they immediately turned the place upside down looking to see what they could find – that is of military value. An order came out we can only confiscate such things, but we just think everything is of military value and let it go at that. The troops have been quite good at not looting and only in an abandoned house will take such. A rather dull gray day out. I suppose now that we are in the Third Reich the weather will be as disagreeable as ever. In this sector the buds are beginning to pop out and the cherry trees are in full bloom. From where I'm sitting, I can see for miles around. Every now and then a figure is seen in the distance tending his vines. Cattle can be seen plowing, taking the places of horses as the latter has [sic] all been commandeered into the Army. A few hundred yards down the road, where our kitchen is set up, is a large brewery. Thereunder the order of Berlin they turn out the wine. Naturally it is strictly rationed and up until recently a Gestapo agent was in charge of the establishment. It's a mystery to me what the people eat as I have seen no vegetable gardens – just vineyards. The people do look more prosperous than the French and most of the buildings are fairly good looking. All seem to have red tiled roofs and it's quite a pretty sight observing the clusters of buildings off in the distance."*

On April 3, 1945, when the division had just taken Würzburg (between Frankfurt and Nuremberg) and crossed the Main River in Ochsenfurt, Archibald writes: *"The last few days' events have been moving rapidly. As one moves forward group after group of former prisoners of war passes you by. Russians, Poles, Jews, Slovaks, French, and practically every other segregated race in Europe are on their way to the rear – and home.*

Many wear some sort of uniform, often German and one never knows for sure if he is a captured German or not, as many of the latter are on their way back without guard. Surprised that none of the former P.W.'s pillage and plunder the countryside as they are on their own. Thought they would unquestionably hate the German civilians, but such doesn't seem to be the case: often one sees them conversing with the civilians in the friendliest of terms. Maybe it was the Army who treated them so bad. Thought I might go through Grandfather's old university town. Missed it though, and I am well beyond. Countryside is really beautiful, yet we are not in the most scenic section of Germany. We as a family, never passed through this section. Only a few of the towns have been devastated and only in isolated places. The streets are rather clean and buildings rather good looking for Europe. One sees an occasional chalet on a hillside, which reminds me of Switzerland or Bavaria. Yesterday, for the first time, a couple of former Hitler Youths asked me for chocolate and cigarettes. These people over here are beyond me."

"DEUTSCHLAND KAPUTT"

Although the fighting continues, living conditions are more pleasant for the GIs. Archibald spends the night in a hotel above a brewery and its hosts go to great lengths to make the Americans feel at home. Hot showers, cold beers and real eggs make the soldiers happy. Three days after the previous letter, Archibald writes: *"Asked repeatedly on different occasions concerning the 'Volkssturm'. Many of the old timers were members of it but as soon as the American forces neared the city the organization quickly dissolved. Have yet to see a real Volkssturmer. Once the Americans have established themselves in a town the people start coming out of the cellars and before long the streets are flooded with them. They gaze at all the troops and peer in wonderment at our vehicles. More Polish, Russians and now even Chinese are encountered. Often half the town is made up of foreigners."* These men are most likely former prisoners recruited by force into the German Army, about to recover their freedom.

The next day, Archibald adds: *"Yesterday afternoon some of my fellow soldiers located a barber shop open for business. And before long I was getting my hair cut in a regular shop. The barber could speak fairly good English, having resided in England eight years or more. I asked him on a few points concerning Germany's future. Was surprised when he stated that Germany should not be governed by Germans but by an International Board or USA. As to Russia he is rather uneasy. I was always inclined to believe that the Germans are very nationalistic, but such doesn't seem to be the case. None of them care for the Prussians or Austrians. Having realized that we aren't out to do them harm (civilians), one would think that the people would have a little more loyalty toward the Army and State than what they do. They relish in telling you that 'Deutschland Kaputt' [Germany (is) broken] and that the Wehrmacht has taken off. One would imagine these people would have a little more pride."*

Once the cities are occupied, soldiers must manage civilians until the relevant authorities can deal with them. On April 10, Archibald describes the situation: *"The civilians have been running in and out all morning attempting to get passes for admittance into the residing towns. The Military Government has yet to take over and they are commencing to become quite a nuisance. Only persons working in the fields are eligible to leave town though. Went for a walk last evening just before dusk. The temperature was perfect and with the setting sun the swiftly blowing river with the village in the background made a picturesque scene. Hardly a building has been hit by the fortunes of war and the inhabitants are carrying on in a normal way. The people naturally put the blame of the war on someone else. In this sector it is the Prussians who provoked the war. Undoubtedly in East Prussia it would be someone else. Also, when one questions the people on the atrocities committed it is always the S.S. who are to blame. One would think that the S.S. consisted of some other race and were not Germans."* This remark is reminiscent of Montgomery's words, when he warned his troops about this kind of behavior in his letters on non-fraternization.

On April 18, the division continues its advance southward through Bavaria, in stifling heat after such a cold winter: *"Another extremely warm day. We have all the windows wide open and still it is rather uncomfortable. I took a nap this afternoon and feel much better for it. Traveling by vehicle is not as pleasant as before due to the clouds of dust that billow up. We seem to be traveling in a poorer section of Germany. The buildings are somewhat dilapidated, and farming is the main and only occupation. Terrain is quite level with few woods in its makeup. One can see village upon village off in the distance. The people seem somewhat religious. Although one still sees many religious ornaments hanging about, they are not as prevalent as before. Once in a while a radio can be found in working order, depending on whether the electricity is out. The radio is only powerful enough to get one or two stations. An efficient method to prevent the people from listening to foreign broadcasts. In many towns one finds more foreigners, mostly Russians, and Polish, than Germans. A rather queer set up but no friction seems to have developed."*

Four days after this letter, on April 22, Archibald is seriously wounded in action near Aalen. The 4th Division was moving southward, on the edge of Bavaria, halfway between its objective of Munich (cradle of the Nazi party), Stuttgart and Nuremberg.

Archibald would die of his wounds on May 4, 1945, the same day that German troops defending Bavaria, whom his unit was tasked to capture, lay down their arms. Only two days later, the entire German Army would surrender to the Allied forces.

Archibald was only 20 years old. His successful career in sports allowed him the opportunity to enter a prestigious university and, to prepare for his return from Europe, he carried a small dictionary in his combat helmet which he opened every day to learn a new word. Back at the beginning of October 1944, when his unit had just crossed the Siegfried Line and was making difficult progress in Germany, he wrote to his parents: *"Had forgotten all about my birthday until I received the card from Dad. It makes me shudder to think I'm about to enter my twentieth year and have accomplished so little. I seem to have been on the receiving end all my life and have yet to do the handing out. Well maybe I can fulfill a few of [my] ambitions someday."* Archibald Sayce now rests in his home town of Charlestown in New Hampshire.

Even as the weather warms up, this GI in Germany still wears a comfortable wool cap under his helmet. The latter is camouflaged with a net (found in Metz after the fighting), held here by a shoelace. The Americans aren't short of equipment or ammunition and in addition to his belt for Garand M1 ammo, this soldier wears a fabric bandoleer across his chest for additional clips. With a rifle slung over his shoulder, he reads a 'safe conduct' leaflet for Germans, who're surrendering by the thousands.

"The German soldier who carries this safe conduct is using it as a sign of his genuine wish to give himself up. He is to be disarmed, to be well looked after, to receive food and medical attention as required and to be removed from the danger zone as soon as possible." Dwight D. Eisenhower.

A MEANING TO WAR

The discouraged soldiers will accidentally discover the reason that led them to fight when the Nazis' crimes are exposed as the first Allies enter the camps. They'll liberate twenty-three 'labor' concentration camps, and six others intended for extermination...

The Red Army was the first to enter a concentration camp on July 24, 1944, in Lublin (Poland). The liberation of Majdanek camp, whose occupants had been sent on a death march by SS soldiers trying to erase the evidence of their crimes, preceded those of Belzec, Sobibor, Treblinka, Stutthof, Sachsenhausen and Ravensbrück, among the largest camps. The biggest of all, Auschwitz, where more than a million people died, is liberated by the Soviets in January 1945. Unlike the Anglo-Americans, who discover 'labor camps' in Germany (where prisoners work for German industry until dying of exhaustion), the Soviets in Poland encounter genuine extermination camps, where cruelty has no limits.

Six million Jews were killed in the Holocaust, half of them Polish. To this must be added the gypsy deportees, the disabled, prisoners of war, communists, homosexuals, Spanish republicans, alcoholics, trade union leaders, blacks, anti-socials and many more. A large proportion of them died in extermination camps (murdered from 1941 onwards in gas chambers with Zyklon B insecticide), while others died of hunger and disease, or were killed by mobile squadrons (1.4 million victims of the 'Shoah by bullets') or in Nazi ghettos.

Arriving in convoys, the men were executed first to avoid revolts, then the enterprise of death and its well-oiled machinery allowed a handful of SS to kill the equivalent of a large European city in one year. However, although rumors of the atrocity of the Nazi genocide have been circulating for some time (the Polish Home Army having passed on information to the Allies as early as 1942), Western Allied soldiers find them difficult to believe. In April 1945, they finally see the horror with their own eyes.

BERGEN-BELSEN

Hugh Stewart is a British film director who joined the Army Film and Photographic Unit in 1940. After covering the Allied landings in Tunisia and Normandy, as well as the fighting for Caen and the crossing of the Rhine, he witnesses near Celle (Germany) something more gruesome than anything he'd ever seen thus far: Bergen-Belsen concentration camp. Following its liberation by the 11th Armoured Division on April 15, 1945, Stewart insists on filming the 60,000 survivors, emaciated and sick, as they wander among more than 13,000 corpses abandoned in the camp's alleys. Stewart's images, capturing the empty eyes of prisoners behind the barbed wire, or the bodies pushed by bulldozers into mass graves, make the world aware of the scale of Nazi crimes. He describes it with terrible precision in a letter written four days later:

"Prisoners seem to be there for all sorts of reasons, a very large number for no other reason than that they were Jews or Poles. The Frenchman was in for espionage. One professor said something rude about Hitler. I know there were Germans, Poles, Russians, French, Italians, Hungarians, and other nationalities. The facts will be published elsewhere, but there were men, women and children of all nationalities, of all ages, of all stages of illness until death itself and corpses dead for weeks and possibly months. [...] The first thing I remember were groups of ragged dejected looking people behind barbed wire [...]. Suddenly I was conscious of the most appalling stench: the wind was blowing into my face. I could not see what caused the stench although I began to notice odd dead bodies lying around and nobody seemed to worry about it. As we went on further, I saw a group of about 20 bodies with their clothes off – men, women and children – just dumped in a pile.

VII - INTO THE REICH SPRING 1945

Live prisoners were squatting or walking near them quite unconcerned. Then I noticed something that was a further stage in degradation. Men and women performed their elementary needs of the body quite shamelessly out in the open and all muddled up. One of my officers told me he saw a woman use a corpse as something to sit on while she relieved her dysentery and I can well believe it. They got up without any attempt to wipe their posteriors. Everyone was pale and haggard beyond belief. Most of the corpses appeared to have died from hunger. Their limbs were like my wrist and their skin looked like rubber stretched over skeleton. They were discoloured in varying stages of decay and still the live ones carried on their existences as though they were not there at all.

After a short time, we came on a pile of dead female bodies, 80 yards by 30 yards, and about 3 feet high. There must have been at least 500 lying there thrown on top of one another so thin and so emaciated it was difficult to believe they had ever been people at all. Many of them were covered in horrible sores. The sight was something that I am quite unable to describe, and the smell was its equal. And yet even here there were people sitting down cooking a potato on a fire or lying in the sun. This spectacle was in full view of many children who were just as unreceptive as the adults. [...] As we were looking at this sight a crowd of internees gathered near us and I began to talk to them in my fragmentary German. I asked them what they wanted to do with the Nazis.

They all said, 'put them in a camp like this one'. One woman said, 'there is no good German but a dead one', but she was immediately contradicted by a man who said that their only friends were the 'Deutsche Banditten', who he explained to me were the communist partisans. What the fate of those people was when they were caught is impossible to conceive. As near as I could understand they helped internees to escape and tried to bring relief. [...] I went into one of the huts. Someone had attempted to clean them up but even so the smell was indescribable. Rags, dying men and ordure were on the floors and in the bunks. I was told by one man that several blocks of buildings were crammed full of dead and dying people. The dying were too weak to move and in many cases three bodies would be on one bunk, two of whom would be dead. Dying men motioned for food as we went by. Horrible sores covered their miserable bodies. We then went to the buildings where the SS guards (men and women) were locked up. Their job now consisted of collecting the dead bodies and a young officer with his men supervised the work. The British were full of a cold fury so intense that it was unbearable even to talk to them."

It was in Bergen-Belsen that the young German-born Jewish prisoner Anne Frank died of typhus, one month before its liberation. Her diary would later become one of the most widely read books in the world.

Dr. Fritz Klein, an SS camp 'doctor', standing in a mass grave after the liberation of Belsen. He will be executed for war crimes in December 1945.

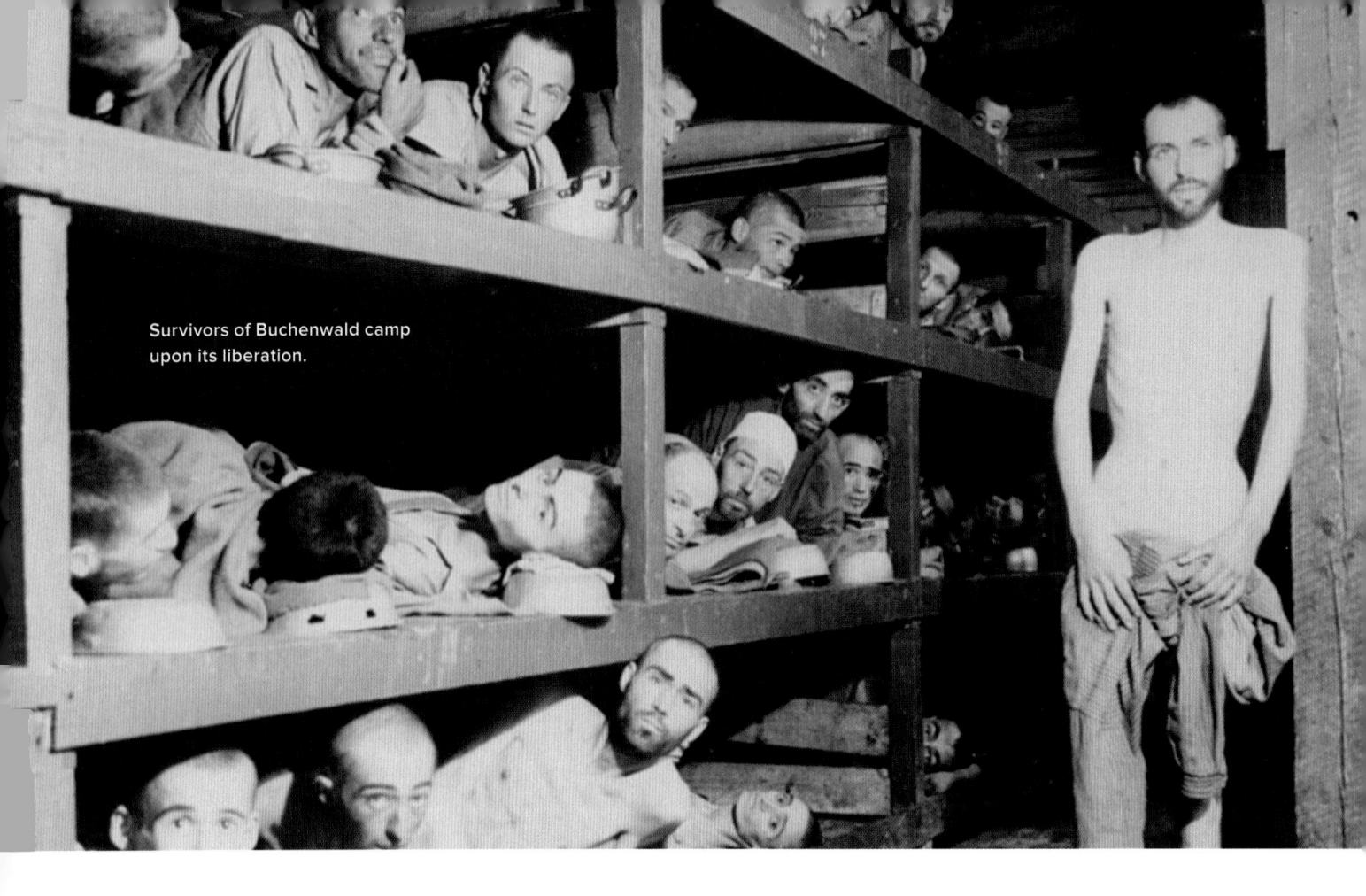

Survivors of Buchenwald camp upon its liberation.

BUCHENWALD

An American soldier stationed in Weimar shortly after the end of the war will decide to visit the nearby Buchenwald concentration camp, which had opened in July 1937, to discover what he had fought for. In a letter to his family, he writes: *"The first thing you see when approaching Buchenwald is a tall stone tower reminding one of a lighthouse. It is located about one hundred yards from the camp entrance. Only two months ago there was a small green lawn at the base of this monument. Today there rests before the tower those people who died after American troops entered the camp. People that were so poor that medical aid could no longer help them and perhaps some whom the Nazis had killed but had not the time to burn. Only a few of the graves were marked. One gave me a feeling of sadness for it was marked something like this: 1937-1945 Robert, Jehrmna. Whether he was French, Czech, Polish, Russian, I don't know, but these dates were significant. For eight long years he had waited for the great day when he would be free again. Eight long terrible years and then just before that day he passed away. Perhaps he was one of those beyond medical aid, or perhaps he had heard how close the Americans were and taunted his captors that at last his day was coming until they became so enraged they killed him. But the important thing to me was that he had managed to live in this hell-hole for eight years. He must have had something worth living for. Around the camp is a wire fence about ten feet high which is charged with electricity. [...] And to make doubly sure no one would escape there were watch towers every two hundred feet which were manned at all times by SS troopers. The camp has been cleaned up but just by looking at those who still remain and are waiting for transportation home one can get a good idea of how they suffered. Upon entering the camp I was seized upon by a Hungarian who had been a political prisoner. He was bald, looked twice his age, had only a few teeth and they were rotten. He offered to guide me around the camp. He first led me to a small cement building about 150 feet inside the gate. It looked like an ordinary building but it was much more for within its walls men were cremated. 150 of them every day. Human life is cheap here. At one side of the building is a hole. If any of the prisoners died of starvation or were killed by the Nazis they were thrown down this hole into the cellar of the building. There they were hung up on hooks just as you or I would hang up a half a beef. In the morning they were taken down from the hooks and placed in an elevator which carried them up to the ground floor where the furnaces were located. Then three at a time they were fed into those furnaces and when they opened the door again all that remained of what had once been a man was a handful of ashes. [...] As we walked along the Hungarian talked about the German civilians. 'They claim not to know what was going on here', he said, 'but they knew for many of us marched into Weimar every day to work in the factories and they knew in what condition we were'."*

VII - INTO THE REICH SPRING 1945

REVENGE

Guenther 'Gunner' Ahlf of the 95th US Division may have been born in Germany, but he's absolutely disgusted by these people he'd learned to respect: *"Have you been reading all these grim stories about the captured German concentration and prison camps? The Germans are stooping to bestiality and brutality. They know they're whipped but they'll be more fanatic than ever. If I were home I'd probably think it was a lot of propaganda, but it isn't. I've seen it with my own eyes and I've talked to too many who have seen it and even gone through it. I'm not ashamed of being German, but I have absolutely no feeling for any German in Germany. It doesn't bother me any more to throw people out of their homes – not even old people or women who weep and say they have no place to go. I'm not cruel or hard hearted, but these people allowed others to be beaten, starved, and tortured. No German over here is wholly innocent."*

Millions of forced laborers deported to Germany attempt to return home on their own while sowing revenge on their way. A soldier in Patton's Army in the Ruhr writes to his wife in April 1945: *"We have three large cans with boiling hot water to wash our mess kits in when we're done eating. In front of these there's another can we throw our garbage in. There's coffee, bones, garbage, cigarette butts, dirt, and everything imaginable in these cans. In the States they were picked up by negroes and the slop was given to the hogs. I saw something yesterday that damn near made me sick. These slave laborers (Russians, Poles, etc) that we freed and who now roam the streets ragged, undernourished and filthy went up to these garbage pails, dipped out a can full and proceeded to eat it. They ate all we had. Word must've got around because today there were more there. These people are a real problem now – there are 17 million in Germany. They go around in gangs and plunder and loot everything they can from the people. I don't feel sorry for the civilians because it was their boy Hitler who brought them here and they bled them long enough. A worker here got two slices of black bread and one watery bowl of potato soup per day. They were crowded in small filthy barracks and the only clothes they received was the rags the Germans people threw away. In one place there were 3,000 of them in a camp near a town that had 1,000 civilians. We came along and freed them and they went out in gangs, threw the civilians out of their homes, and broke and stole what they pleased. It seemed funny to have the Germans come to us in tears, pleading with us to help them and asking us to live in their homes. It serves them right. Naturally, we try to stop it as much as possible, but, primarily, we're still fighting the Germans."*

However, German civilians have much more to fear from the Red Army arriving from the East. For almost a year, the Soviets have been liberating a large number of camps in Poland and eastern Germany. Among the prisoners they found many compatriots and were hungry for revenge. An American soldier in the VIII Corps recounts at the end of the war: *"The Germans are trying hard to get through the American lines for protection from the Russians. I don't blame them. I too, would hate to face a man whose homeland I burned, whose children I had killed, whose wife I had raped. The ordeal would not be very pleasant. The roads are full of refugees fleeing into that part of Germany which the Americans are to occupy. They fear to stay in their homes for they know there will be reprisals for the things they have done. When I was near the Czech border, I heard them whisper the Russians are coming and then almost at once an exodus began to take place. West, west, west, always west. Old women pulling carts, men with packs on their backs, girls on bicycles, all heading west away from the Russians. I know what they would say at home but sometimes I think the Russians are right. You don't try to educate them to think your way. They either think your way or you kill them and just for good measure you kill a few of those who do decide to think your way."*

German civilians are regularly forced to help clean up the camps so they can realize the scale of the tragedy. This young woman, under the watchful eyes of the GIs, tries to contain her disgust at the bodies of 800 forced laborers who were murdered by their SS guards.

ALBERT VARDY

428 'Ghost' Squadron, Royal Canadian Air Force

Albert only got close to his dream of flying an aircraft by becoming a machine gunner in a bomber crew. Unfortunately, while participating in one of the last raids of the war in Europe, his aircraft is hit in northern Germany. Afraid of water, Albert will drown after his aircraft crash into the North Sea.

IN THE RCAF

Albert Edward Vardy was born in Bancroft, Ontario, on May 9, 1920. Like many young people at the time, he left school at the age of 12 to work on his father's farm, before joining a Canadian Artillery unit on January 7, 1943. After training, he was stationed in Halifax as a shooting instructor, but then chose to pursue his dream of becoming a pilot and exchanged his green uniform for the blue of the Air Force, obtaining a discharge to join the RCAF on November 11, 1943. Instead of a pilot, however, he became an air gunner and received his 'wings' on May 16, 1944 in Quebec.

Albert proposed to his girlfriend Thelma on July 3, five days before leaving Canada. He wrote to his parents from the ship that took him to Europe: *"I'll bet you can't guess where I am writing this letter from. Right out in the middle of the Atlantic Ocean. There is nothing to do only eat, sleep or wander around the deck so thought I might as well scratch a few lines. It will be mailed when I get across. [...] Believe me it's impossible to know until you have experienced it, what a feeling you have when you stand on the deck watching your beloved Canada disappearing in the distance and knowing that it may be a long time before you see either it or those you love again. I expected to feel a bit scared out here on the water but I've surprised myself. But if a man lets his imagination run wild, he could get in a bad state alright.* [...] *I'm already thinking about the return trip. What a joyful day that will be."* Albert will never return to Canada, disappearing at sea a few months later, in those depths he feared so much. As soon as he arrived in England on July 21, he had to take a swimming test. In order to force fate, one of his comrades pushed him into the pool, but Albert had to take additional swimming lessons to learn how to swim. Although he was making progress, his fear of water would never leave him.

Young pilot Donald Melvin 'Doc' Payne chose Albert and his best friend Earle 'Red' Casey (inseparable since their training) to complete his crew on August 13, 1944. Each man had to have detailed knowledge of the other crew members' work and Albert finally tried his hand at piloting. He wrote to his family: *"I have accomplished something that has always been my ambition. I can say now that I can really fly a plane myself. I have flown the bomber quite a bit now way up amongst the clouds. Of course, the 'skipper' is never far away."* However, Albert's real role would be as an air gunner in the Avro Lancaster X bomber number KB784. His training ended on February 6, 1945, when he joined one of the most famous squadrons of the Canadian Bomber Group: 428 'Ghost' Squadron, *"No more training. We are in the front line. No longer kids play."* He was promoted to flight sergeant on February 19. As the missions followed one after another, Albert already started to lose his first friends.

VII - INTO THE REICH SPRING 1945

Reading his letters, one might almost think he expects to experience a similar fate. In a letter his mother will receive after his death (the plane carrying his mail will also crash, with the letter itself being partly saved from the flames), he wrote: *"I happened to be looking through the casualty list today and saw where another one of the boys I signed up in the Army with had been killed in action. It was Bud Wright from Toronto. I was with him until I left the Army. He was transferred to the Infantry with 'Smitty'. It's been* [words lost in the fire] *how many of the old gang have been killed or wounded now. Guess it was a good thing I transferred. [...] It makes you think* [words missing] *find it best not to think too much about it. Just try and forget, but that is a hard thing to do especially when some of your* [words missing] *go out to their planes* [words missing] *with you is the same crew* [words missing]. *You say, 'Have a good trip boys', watch them take off and then the next day you see the one word 'Missing' after their names on the crew board. Believe me it will make anyone think."*

Albert in his flight suit.
In the turret of his un-pressurized bomber, temperatures at 19,000 feet can drop below -80°F (-62°C).

THE FIRST TEN MISSIONS

After participating in the bombing campaign to support *Operation Plunder*, the crew was at rest in Scotland. Albert took this opportunity to share his experiences with his father in a letter he wrote on March 17, less than a month before his death: *"I am still feeling fine and everything is going O.K. Of course, as you already know we are off Ops for the present. It's a rest alright but I would sooner keep going and get through a tour in a hurry, although, if we are off long enough the war will be over, we hope so anyway, unless they get the big idea of sending us to Burma. It's all supposed to be on a volunteer basis but if they don't get enough volunteers, well they have the power to do what they like about it. Germany is sure getting an awful hammering now. They talk about the heavy raids on London and other parts of England, but we can do more damage in one big raid than they do in weeks of their heaviest bombing. You no doubt hear plenty on the radio and see in the papers accounts of all the different raids but it really doesn't tell you much. It may say that 1,500 or maybe 2,500 bombers were over last night or did a lot of damage but unless you actually see the bombs go down and see the damage afterward, you could have no idea of what we are doing. It's simply beyond description. When you think of a thousand or so aircraft all carrying 5 to 11 tons of bombs plus a lot of incendiaries all dumping their load right fair on the heart of the city and all within 10 or 15 minutes, the destruction and devastation is terrible. The bomb load naturally varies with the different targets. If you have a long way to go naturally you have to take more fuel so that means a smaller bomb load; but it's still plenty at any time.*

When you think of it war is terrible, but then Jerry asked for it didn't he? And boy are we handing it out and not on a silver platter either. They may well squeal and complain, but they have forgotten the things they have done in the past six years. The millions of French, Greeks and Poles that have been brutally murdered. It practically makes me see red when I think of what they did in Poland in those torture camps. You have read it in the papers no doubt, where thousands a day were put in the crematoriums and their ashes sent to Germany as fertilizer. Could any man with a spark of self-respect and a sense of decency sit ideally by and watch that go on without raising a hand. I don't think so and all I can say is that the guys who failed to respond to the call of duty when the lives of millions of innocent people were at stake and the freedom of all the free nations of the world was hanging in the balance, aren't merely just Yellow, but in my opinion are branded for life as traitors to their own country and their fellow countrymen. I should hate very much to be among that number. I don't say this just because I am over here and think that everyone else should be. There are lots of guys who have every reason to stay at home providing they realize what we are going through, for their sake and appreciate it. But what gets me are the guys who have no particular reason for not giving a hand except they are cowards and even go out of their way to hinder the war effort. No doubt they will be better treated after the war than we will be."

A few days later, on March 31, Albert's bomber was on its way to Hamburg. As it was a daytime raid, it was particularly dangerous. Albert, in his turret with his double .50 caliber machine gun, and his friend Earle in the tail turret equipped with four .30 caliber guns, were watching for enemy fighters and on that day they faced major opponents: a group of Me262s suddenly attacked the fleet of bombers.

The German company Heinkel had developed the He112, a fighter superior to his rival, the Messerschmitt's Me109. Although both could reach about 300 mph, the He112 gained 19,000 feet in ten minutes and had a record range of 684 miles. However, Heinkel's links with Jews led the Reich's Ministry of Aviation to prefer the Messerschmitt model. Similarly, when Heinkel later developed the very first jet aircraft, the He280, the Ministry asked Heinkel to focus on its bombers, and Messerschmitt made history with the Me262 jet fighter (opposite). 1,100 units were made, but although it greatly surpassed the Allied aircraft in speed, it soon proved impractical. Nevertheless, it was to inspire the American and Russian post-war jet aircraft to a very large extent.

When a first Messerschmitt 262 shot down a Halifax bomber, which disappeared into the clouds below, Donald attempted a maneuver so that Albert could have a good angle of fire. The pilot remembered seeing Albert's bullets scattering the engine, fuselage and cockpit of the Me262. The speed of the latter couldn't save it, and the German aircraft thus began its fateful descent to the ground. This feat earned Albert the great admiration of his crew, who were already praising the calm and efficiency of the shooter.

But Albert's luck will change, and he's now living his last days. He writes a final letter to his mother on April 11, 1945: "Dear Mom, [...] We have a third of our tour in now, have ten done; and it's been anything but a boring tour. We have had plenty of excitement and have seen and done more things than I ever figured possible in such a short time. I got a great kick out of our last trip which wasn't long ago, a matter of hours. It was a daylight [raid] on a large city in the heart of Germany, there was no cloud and we could see the target perfectly and could see the big 'cookies' when they hit the ground. I think it was the best raid yet, it was handed over entirely to our Bomber Group because of our high record of bombing efficiency and I don't think one bomb missed the target. Most interesting to me was to see the Armies fighting as we passed over them and to see the towns, cities and country side all torn to pieces. It is also nice to fly over all those foreign countries in daylight and see what they actually look like. Especially the cities like Paris, Le Havre, Calais, Dunkirk, Brussels, Antwerp, Amsterdam, The Hague and of course lots of German cities which are just a mass of ruins.

I'll bet you were surprised to see the paper telling about us shooting down the Jerry [the Me262] – guess you hadn't got my letter by then did you? [...] I'm listening to the news right now and it sure sounds encouraging, cities that less than a week ago were the target for our bombs are now in our hands and the army has passed away beyond them. I see nothing to stop the boys from continuing their advance straight to Berlin and in a very short time.

What a day when they announce the complete occupation of Germany. You've sure got to hand it to the Jerries for backbone and determination: they are sure good fighters and no cowards and believe me I know from what I've seen. It takes nerve for a fighter pilot to fly straight into a stream of several hundred bombers in daylight knowing that everyone has six or eight guns turned on him plus all our fighter escort. It is simply a case of suicide, but he doesn't always go down alone I'm sorry to say. I think a lot of it may be the fanatical ideas taught to all Hitler Youth. But it is surely being stamped out and crushed now. [...] Well I guess this is about enough of this line of chatter, so will buzz for now and write a few lines to the One and Only, can't leave her out you know. So for now will say good night and God bless you, don't worry about me please. Lovingly, Bert."

VII - INTO THE REICH SPRING 1945

THE LAST RAID

On this fateful April 13, 1945, Albert embarks on what would be his final mission (it would also be one of the last raids of the Royal Air Force in Europe). His crew are ordered to participate in the bombing of the port of Kiel and in particular the submarines docked there. In total, 377 Lancaster and 105 Halifax bombers join the operation, which will nevertheless be considered ineffective: dropped from an altitude of 13,000 to 19,000 feet, the 871 tons of high-explosives will be dispersed around the objective. Two Lancasters, including Albert's, will also be lost for what would be a very limited result.

Albert's aircraft leaves Middleton Saint George base at 8:20 pm. During the bombardment, it's hit by anti-aircraft fire, injuring the pilot in the leg, left arm and hand. The plane is also in bad shape: its fuel tank has holes and two engines are damaged. The crew still manages to finish the mission, and begins to head back home. However, the situation becomes critical when the Lancaster is hit again south of Flensburg (Germany). The pilot, Don Payne, who can now see the ground under his feet through a gaping hole in the fuselage, decides to head for Sweden across the North Sea. As the Lancaster passes over the Danish coast at 12:10 am, the first engine shuts down. The others ignite and drop one by one, until the fourth and last engine is lost as well. The injured pilot has no choice but to try a landing on the water about 20 miles from Heligoland Island. However, the crew has never trained for such a maneuver and Don has no visual reference other than the whitecaps. The pilot's voice crackles in the loudspeakers: *"Dinghy, dinghy, prepare to ditch!"* Earle Casey, isolated in his turret in the back of the plane, only now learns that the plane has been hit. All the men abandon their posts with characteristic calm and join the most solid part of the bomber. Earle and his best friend Albert cling to each other as the procedure requires, and wait for the impact near the escape hatch.

The Lancaster hits the sea tail-first, but miraculously holds together. Unfortunately, the brutality of the impact throws the pilot out of the aircraft, still attached to his seat, through the window he'd opened for better visibility. When Don manages to reach the surface, the aircraft's nose is already sinking into the depths. After the men get out of the plane, despite their injuries they manage to join the inflatable boat that'd been ejected from the Lancaster's wing. Earle Casey, who has the same fear of water as his friend Albert, swims to the dinghy despite a broken shoulder, leg and tailbone. When the crew realizes that the inseparable duo isn't complete, it's already too late. The bomber has sunk into the icy waters of the North Sea, taking Albert Vardy with it.

The crew (left to right): Don 'Doc' Payne (pilot), F/S Albert Vardy (gunner), F/O George Riley (navigator), Sgt. Earle 'Red' Casey (tail gunner), Sgt. Eldon 'Baldy' Miller (wireless operator and gunner), and F/O Verne Banks (bomb aimer). Sergeant T. Sinclair (engineer), who was also with the crew at the time of the crash, is not in the photo.

Earle lost consciousness at the time of the crash and didn't see what had happened to his friend, but he's almost certain that he was killed on impact. The loss of their comrade is a terrible blow to the airmen's morale, who must now think of their survival, alone among the waves. They must deal with the wounded first by stopping the bleeding and tending to broken bones. They only have a small First Aid kit and no way to call for help. Unable to steer their circular dinghy, they've no choice but to wait for a miracle.

Soon, their meager rations are eaten and hunger and thirst hit back. Short of purification tablets for seawater, the survivors end up drinking their own urine. As the days go by, some of the men become delusional: one of them even passes an imaginary cup to his comrades. Only a copy of the New Testament that Earle Casey's mother had given him, and which had miraculously survived the crash, helps keep their hopes alive. They spend their days re-inflating the dinghy and bailing out water as rain and storms soon hit the crew, protecting themselves as best they can with a parachute. False hopes and mirages follow one another, undermining their morale even more. The group will see a submarine passing underneath them and continuing its course without noticing their presence, or mistakenly think they can spot the mainland, when in reality it's the foam of 7-foot-high waves that would soon almost destroy the dinghy. One of the men, discouraged and devastated by Albert's death, even tries to commit suicide by jumping into the water.

The survivors will spend twelve endless days drifting in these conditions, before reaching the mouth of the Elbe where a German Red Cross boat will finally come to their rescue on the afternoon of April 25. They'll then be immediately taken as prisoners of war and separated. Don Payne will march through Hamburg in a convoy of prisoners and have stones thrown at him by the inhabitants, despite his condition. He wouldn't blame them, however, as the city had been one of the main targets of his Lancaster. However, the Canadians would remain prisoners for only a few days and will be liberated on May 4 by the British, shortly before the end of the war. They'll be in a terrible physical condition, weighing only around 90 lbs [40 kg].

Albert died at the age of 24 on Friday 13: his sister's birthday. His parents are devastated. A few months earlier, their son had written to them: *"Please, for my sake, don't worry too much about me, as I feel sure that everything will come out alright, and should the worst come to the worst, I have the assurance that all is well and that I am ready to go."* On June 4, after his parents received the terrible news, pilot Don Payne will write to them: *"We fliers have a code, we assume the worst to happen, so we confide in one another... Bert made me promise to tell 'Mom and Dad not to take it too hard'. Our crew was the best in in Bomber Group Number 6, and Bert was a fighter... We are proud of your son Ma'am. The whole dog gone world is proud."* Don ends the letter with Bert's words: *"Please tell them not be make me unhappy by being unhappy themselves"*.

Badly shaken by his loss, Albert's father wouldn't leave his bed for several weeks.

Albert's body was never found, but his name is inscribed on a plaque at the Runnymede Memorial in Englefield Green, England. Next to it are the names of 20,450 missing airmen killed in air operations in Northwest Europe. In total, more than 116,000 men and women lost their lives fighting in the Commonwealth Air Forces (including 17,000 Canadians).

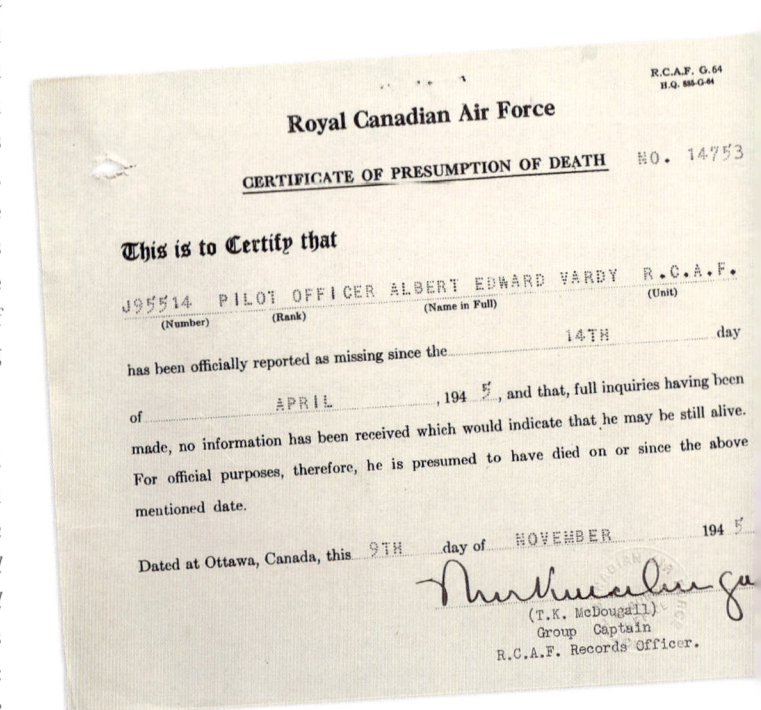

VIII

VICTORY
The Final Shots

On April 19, when the Ruhr Pocket had just been destroyed, the Soviets pushed the Germans back from the heights of Seelow, the last line of defense outside Berlin. The next day, on Hitler's birthday, the Red Army's artillery pounded the capital, which a week later was cut off from the rest of Germany. In his underground bunker near the Chancellery, Adolf Hitler, red with anger, accuses his officers of having made him lose the war. His anger is particularly aimed at Reichsführer-SS Heinrich Himmler, who'd tried to negotiate peace with the Western Allies in the hope of continuing the fight with them against the USSR. Himmler was eventually arrested by the Allies in May 1945, but committed suicide in prison. In the meantime, Hitler learned of the death of his Italian ally Benito Mussolini, who'd been shot by communist partisans on April 28, before he was hung upside down in a large square in Milan to be abused by the crowd.

On the afternoon of April 30, after marrying his mistress Eva Braun the day before, Hitler shoots himself in the head with a revolver, while his new wife bites into a cyanide capsule. While the Red Army (and its 2.5 million men) is only 300 yards from the bunker, Hitler's body is burned to avoid the same fate as Mussolini. It would still be found and identified by the Soviets, although Stalin will claim after the war that Hitler had fled to Latin America with the complicity of the Americans, in order to discredit his new enemies. Many loyal Nazis also commit suicide over the following days as resistance weakens in Berlin (the last volunteers to continue the fight are the Scandinavian 'Nordland' and the French 'Charlemagne' SS Divisions). The capture of Berlin on May 2, 1945, costs the Soviets 352,425 casualties, a quarter of which were killed.

A GI writes to his parents on May 2: *"Was just reading in the Army paper that Hitler is dead. That I do not believe. He is too danged rotten to just up and die. They say that Doenitz took his place as Führer. Well, all I can say is that I think Hitler has been running true to form and has taken it on the lamb and so this Doenitz is the scape goat. But if this paperhanger is alive and we find it out he will get it anyway. Let's hope he got the same medicine as Mussolini got. Mussolini was buried in the potter's field at Milan. He sure got a royal funeral, I don't think. Mother asked in one of her letters if I had heard the President's funeral service. No I missed it also. But we had memorial services here for him at the same time he was being buried at Hyde Park. Speaking about Hyde Park, I saw a place called that, but it was not at home it was at London. It was not a pretty place, they had a good many shelters dug throughout the place. It fairly bristled with Anti-Aircraft guns. One day that will be a pretty place again to walk through."*

A GI photographed this sign on the Reichsautobahn (Reich Motorway), indicating the direction of Berlin. All over Europe, the last German positions gave way one after the other, and the flags of the victors (such as these originals above, found in Lyon, France) flourished in the liberated villages.

ITALY FALLS FIRST

At the beginning of 1945, the Germans were still holding the Gothic Line. Their forces were by then made up of elderly or very young men (*"barely 13 or 14 years old"* according to a soldier in the 91st US Infantry Division), but their artillery was still causing bloodshed. An American sergeant in the 362nd Regiment wrote in a letter: *"Well, the Jerries are still throwing their old, worn out guns at us. Just a few minutes ago I saw an old battered bathtub sail through the air and land with a crash."* After a whole winter spent harassing the enemy in small-scale night attacks, the 5th Army resumed the offensive towards Bologna on February 18 and targeted German artillery positions in the Apennines (*Operation Encore*).

Supported on their flanks by American and British troops, the Poles liberated Bologna on April 21 after a violent bombardment. They were removed from the lines for good the next day, after sustaining 234 dead and 1,228 wounded in the battle.

It's still possible, over seventy years later, to observe traces of the fighting and shelling on the walls. Paintings indicating the nearest air raid shelters have also been preserved.

Operation Encore was only a preliminary step to the great spring offensive, *Operation Grapeshot*. The latter's success wasn't guaranteed, since the Allies only opposed twenty divisions to twenty-seven German divisions, who were eager for revenge following the recent bombings on Germany. Moreover, it's estimated that the ratio between attackers and defenders must be at least three to one for an attack to be successful. However, the Allies had a major asset since the arrival of the American 10th Mountain Division. Composed of top athletes and highly trained volunteers, this elite unit had no fear of the mountains and could even fight on skis. On April 9, the defenses at Bologna were violently bombarded when the 8th Army was back on the offensive. The 5th Army attacked five days later, with the 10th Mountain Division breaking through the defenses south of Bologna and opening the way to the city and the Po Valley.

The Poles had just learned that following the Yalta Conference on February 11, the British and Americans had offered part of Poland to Stalin (who'd installed a puppet communist government there) in the hope of obtaining Soviet help in the Pacific. One of the Polish units, the 5th Kresowa Division, was even named after the Kresy region, which was now given over entirely to the USSR. The Poles' morale was at its lowest and the commander of the II Polish Corps (General Wladyslaw Anders, a Russian prisoner in 1939 who was released after *Barbarossa* to reform a Polish army) even asked to have his troops withdrawn from the lines, with Churchill's agreement. But his men fought so well in Italy that they were irreplaceable as far as the Americans were concerned. Anders finally agreed to keep his troops on the front line for one last battle, taking Bologna on April 21. Nevertheless, the Polish government in London disappeared on July 5, 1945 in favor of the Warsaw government set up by Stalin, and Polish troops were excluded from the Victory parade.

Shoulder patch of the British 8th Army (1944 version), to which the Polish II Corps was attached.

While Bologna was falling, the Italian partisans fought in Milan and Turin. On April 22, the Po was reached in San Benedetto by the IV US Corps and Ficarolo by the XIII British Corps. The V Corps attacked the Venetian Line, but the German Army was already collapsing. The British rushed towards Venice, while the 10th Mountain Division took Verona on the 25th and the 'Buffalo Soldiers' of the 92nd Infantry Division liberated Genoa. Supported by Italian partisans, the Americans linked up with the French Resistance at the northwest border. In the east, the New Zealanders met Yugoslav partisans in their race to Trieste. Pursued into the Austrian mountains, German forces in Italy finally surrender on May 2, 1945. Captain Davis, who's been serving with the Royal Engineers since Sicily, writes to his wife: *"I have just heard that the war in Italy had ended and expect the war in the whole of Europe will end in a few days. It seems unbelievable that even part of the war is over, and I am rather proud that this theatre was the first to achieve victory because I feel that far too much publicity has been given to the Western Front."*

The front page of the *Oklahoma City Times* on May 2, 1945.

THE CANADIANS IN THE NETHERLANDS

In early 1945, *Operation Goldflake* redeployed all Canadian forces and certain British units to Western Europe from Italy. The move had to be made in the strictest secrecy, prohibiting all correspondence. Contact with civilians was also forbidden in order to protect the identity of the soldiers and their units. Al, an artilleryman from the 17th Field Regiment (Royal Canadian Artillery), 5th Armoured Division, thus landed in Marseille (France) in February 1945. While the British and Americans were crossing the Rhine and entering Germany, the Canadians took the road to the Netherlands. With the Dutch population suffering from a serious famine, liberating the country was now a serious concern. In parallel, operations *Chowhound* and *Manna* aimed to drop 11,000 tons of rations from bombers to keep the civilians from starving. Arnhem, still in enemy hands since *Market Garden* in September 1944, was the main objective of Harry Crerar's 1st Canadian Army.

This Canadian soldier in the Netherlands wears a Battledress dated 1945 with its original burgundy patch for the 5th Armoured Division (this rectangle was red for the 1st Infantry Division, blue for the 2nd, gray for the 3rd, and green for the 4th Armoured Division). Canadian uniforms are very similar to the British ones, but greener in color. This soldier carries a light pack on his back, a gas mask bag filled with various equipment, two ammunition pouches on his stomach and a British canteen, whose cover is already marked by three different men: a Seaforth Highlanders soldier, a Royal Engineer and a Royal Corps of Signals man (it was found in Brittany after the war). His helmet is the new MKIII model nicknamed 'Turtle', distributed from Normandy to Anglo-Canadians in replacement of the MKII (this original helmet, dated January 1944, was actually found in the Netherlands). It's covered with a two-tone net (green and brown) typical of Canadian troops, on which strips of burlap are attached for camouflage purposes, and an individual shell dressing, always within reach.

VIII - VICTORY SUMMER 1945

Al's regiment, unbeknownst to the Germans, was soon on 'The Island' between Nijmegen and Arnhem. It encountered little opposition and the excellent visibility offered the artillerymen prime targets. On April 2, *Operation Quick Anger* was a success and the capture of the area allowed the creation of a bridgehead on the Lower Rhine. Al then moved into position in Elst to cover the assault on Arnhem by the British 49th (West Riding) Division. On the 12th, the artillery carried out diversionary fire to the west of the city. Duped into thinking that this was the main attack, the Germans dropped a phenomenal amount of shells of all calibers there, depleting a large part of their ammunition stockpile. When the British launched their real assault to the southeast, the enemy had little left to defend itself. Two days later, the entire 5th Canadian Armoured Division stood in front of Arnhem and finally seized the city at first light.

With the silence surrounding *Operation Goldflake* finally lifted, Al could now write to his wife, which he did shortly before attacking Arnhem: *"Dearest Princess, [...] you say that that letter was the first in six weeks. I told you honey it would be that long. I thought you were going to be mad as hell at me. I am glad you understand. You know princess, as I have explained in my other letters, I really couldn't help it. You know that during that time I didn't write you wrote me about fifty-three pages all told. If I can get that many pages by not writing, I'd be better off not to write you darling (haha). Gosh honey, you don't know how much I look forward to your letters. They mean a lot to me. [...] Gosh I'm really sick of this being away from you. I think of you so darn much that I can hardly get anything done. I'm sure this war can't last much longer, I'll go nuts if it does. You ain't kidding. We have so much to say but I can't see nothing wrong saying it in letters. However if you think we should save it till we get together, we'll save it then. I have a lot to say but I don't know how to say it... Please don't get the impression that we are wasting our lives away. You might like me better when I come back because I have changed a bit in the ways of the world. And I'm sure darling that at our age we will be able to enjoy ourselves better than ever before. You wait and see darling, I'm sure we'll never regret it. Of course, I got to admit that I hate being away from you for so long. I swear I'll never do it again, princess."*

However, Al still has a long way to go. On April 17, nearly 200 Germans are reported north of Otterloo (there are actually between 600 and 900, fleeing to the west). The batteries are put on alert, but their positions are quickly overwhelmed as they fire at close range on the enemy attackers. With most of their guns destroyed, Al and his comrades are forced to use their rifles, sometimes resorting to hand-to-hand combat. They manage to hold their positions, surrounded for seven endless hours under a deluge of mortar shells. The Germans have infiltrated many positions, preventing the 4th Anti-Tank Regiment from helping the isolated artillerymen. The latter, who've not yet received their Sten machine guns after handing back their Thompsons in Italy, have no choice but to kill the enemy with their bare hands to recover weapons and grenades. A sergeant strangles a German while a comrade hits the enemy on the ground with the butt of his rifle.

The situation seems desperate and at sunrise, German fire only intensifies. But as the Canadians run out of their last ammunition, British Churchill tanks suddenly arrive from the east. The chaos is such that they mistakenly fire on what's left of some of the Canadian positions, before finally managing to coordinate their actions and clear the area with a flame thrower. When the tanks link up with the artillerymen, they expect to find only corpses. In reality, the Canadians suffered minimal losses, successfully defending their positions and inflicting 300 killed on their attackers. Instead, they're now quietly having breakfast in their foxholes.

Al and his regiment are back on the line a few days later, supporting the 5th Armoured Division in Leeuwarden and Delfzijl. The Westminster Regiment, in the pocket of Delfzijl where the Germans have withdrawn, is impressed by the responsiveness of the 17th RCA guns and the accuracy of their fire. With excellent visibility, the Canadians are able to score many direct hits, with one gunner even managing to sink a German ship with a single shell. The Germans at Delfzijl surrender on May 2. The ceasefire is ordered at 8 am on May 5, a few hours after the surrender of German forces in the Netherlands, Denmark and Northwest Germany.

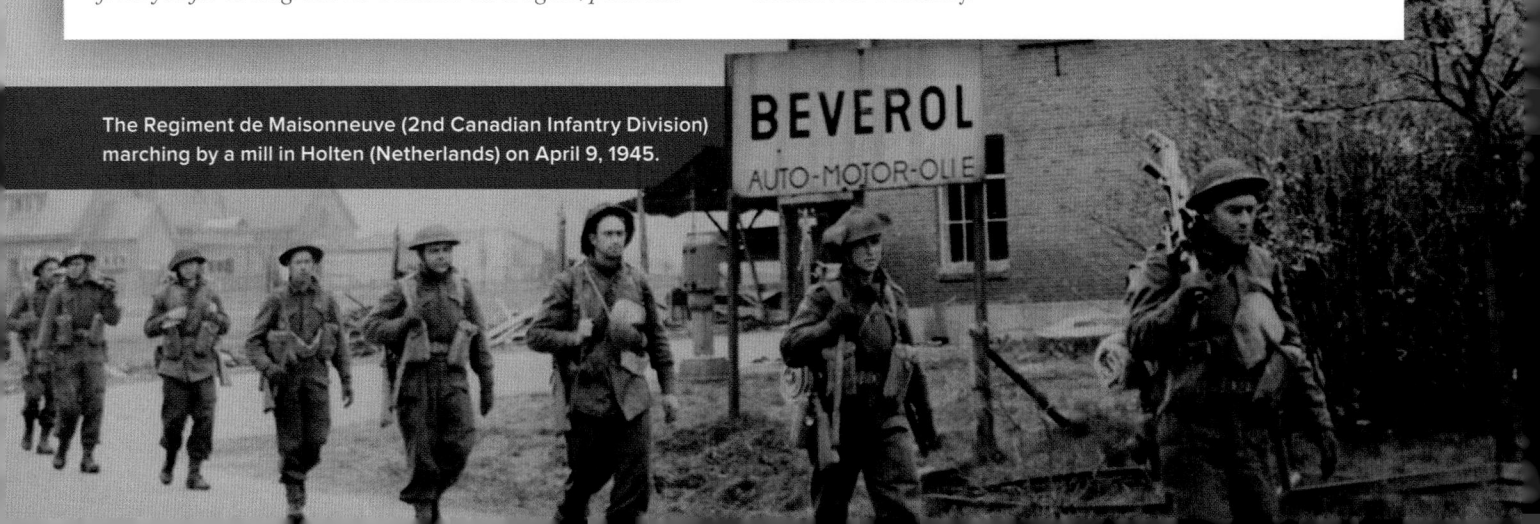

The Regiment de Maisonneuve (2nd Canadian Infantry Division) marching by a mill in Holten (Netherlands) on April 9, 1945.

IN THE CRADLE OF NAZISM

In late April, the Allies are driving across Germany in all directions. The American 20th Armored Division, which arrived on the front line at the beginning of the month, is rushing towards Munich, where the Nazi party was born. There, even in the last days of the war, resistance is still strong. Among the infantry soldiers mounting the tanks, Robert has just celebrated his twenty-fourth birthday. He writes in his diary on April 28, 1945: *"Were aroused the next morning at 0430, ate 10 in 1* [rations]*, and pulled out to cross the Danube for purposes of expanding the bridgehead. It was once again wet & cold (Hell! Doesn't the sun ever shine over here!). The Engineers had thrown up the pontoon bridge and we crossed the famous Danube. It's just like all the streams over here – narrow & very swift. We kept moving slowly and finally hit the German perimeter. We were all set for anything with guns full loaded and all tensed up! We ate C rations & headed into the Hagermann Forest. Our convoy stopped for about an hour and up ahead we heard the machine guns barking. Finally, we started to move again and passed through the town of* [Langenmosen]*. There were about a hundred prisoners and twenty dead Heinies lying along the road but no GI casualties. The next town was Schrobenhausen and much larger. We had to shell it for about 30 minutes before we moved in but after that it was a soft touch and we rolled right through, capturing about 300 prisoners and a German intact. Still no GI casualties. Outside of Schrobenhausen was another smaller town and the artillery shelled it for ten minutes before we moved in.*

Throughout Germany, the advance of the infantry was facilitated by heavy bombardments that destroyed every city, as seen here in Waldenburg on April 16, 1945 (63rd US Infantry Division).

Here were the first casualties. One of our M8 armored cars was hit by a Panzerfaust about three minutes before I got there. There were two dead GIs lying beside it and the other two were seriously wounded. From here on the story was all the same. We were a task force of tanks, infantry, artillery and weren't to be stopped by anything. We rolled through town after town on the way to Munchen [Munich]. *Our forward vehicles would shell and machine gun whatever opposition there was and after leaving behind a few men to herd together the prisoners, we'd keep rolling on – Weilenbach, Langenpettenbach, Munster, Pasenbach, Schrobenhausen. We killed approximately 30 Germans in each town and the remaining would give up."*

After advancing about 35 miles and taking dozens of towns in a very short space of time, the unit sets up defenses for the night. The next day, their experience of Germany would change completely. On April 29, Robert writes: *"We awakened the next morning feeling not bad having had only two casualties the day before. We cleaned our guns & moved out but slowly. We traveled about a mile and a half, then moved forward again into Dachau, and about this time all hell broke loose. Recon had reported the town clear the night before, but Jerry had slipped back in during the night. About half of each squad was riding the tanks & our 2nd platoon was well into the town before the fireworks started. They opened up on us with everything in the books and that was plenty. Our men were hit like flies on the tanks before they even knew what was happening. I crouched in our trench shaking in my shoes and watched the show. Over half the 2nd platoon was knocked off right in the main street and the wounded and dead were everywhere. We got our three machine guns into action against the building tops and darn near shot the town off the map. Our firepower was terrific, but Jerry had the advantage – he knew where we were & would see us. All we could do was blast where we thought he was. The 45th Infantry Division, a veteran outfit from away back, finally came in behind us and finished clearing the town of snipers. We licked our wounds and counted our casualties, about fifteen dead and thirty wounded from B Company."*

At the same time, the 45th Division, along with the 42nd Division and elements of the 20th Armored Division, is liberating the concentration camp northeast of Dachau. April 30, only one week before the end of the war, would be just as eventful: *"Awakened this morning early and moved out on our original mission, a larger airfield a half mile away. The artillery shelled it all night so there wasn't too much opposition. The Germans had removed all the planes and camouflaged them in the woods. We captured about 50 planes undamaged and the hangars weren't too bad. We moved another half mile against stiff opposition with the 45th – 10 of our tanks were knocked out and came upon a terrifically large military school for SS troops.*

VIII - VICTORY SUMMER 1945

The defenses were dug in for 500 yards in front of the building and were used for instructional purposes to the troops. They were used for more practical purposes now. A tough nut to crack for the 45th. We sat and watched them flush the bunkers & I can testify they had plenty of casualties. One of them was hit in the face about ten yards from our vehicle. His eye shot out and a bloody mess. He was writhing in agony, but the medics couldn't get to him. We were all under fire. About this time, I spied a Jerry coming up out of his foxhole for purposes which both he and I shall never know. He was about 300 yards away and as about three quarters of him came up to ground level I caught him in my sights and squeezed the trigger. I think I aged about ten years in that split second. That night we bivouacked in front of the school just outside of Munchen."

FINAL SHOTS OF THE WAR

When the Americans enter Austria and Czechoslovakia, the Soviets are in Vienna and Prague. Churchill, afraid that the Red Army would reach Denmark first, rushes his 2nd Army north to liberate the peninsula. German troops now hold only a few pockets in East Prussia, the Kurland Peninsula (Latvia), Czechoslovakia and Yugoslavia. On May 4, the Germans wish to negotiate their surrender with the Western Allies alone and buy time to move as many troops as possible to the West.

They eventually surrender unconditionally to SHAEF Headquarters in Reims on Monday, May 7, 1945 at 2:41 am. But to Stalin, Generaloberst Alfred Jodl's signature with high-ranking, mainly Western brass, isn't enough, especially at a time when Soviet troops are still fighting the Germans. The USSR demands a second signature in Berlin, which is completed by Generalfeldmarschall Wilhelm Keitel on May 9, at 00:01 am, while the ceasefire in the West comes into force. As a result of this, the Russians will celebrate the 1945 victory one day after the West.

An American lieutenant of the 119th Anti-Aircraft Artillery Battalion fires one of the last shots of the war in the West on May 7. He writes to his wife the next day: *"The surrender here was surprising, or rather the way it was taken by the men was surprising. It just didn't seem possible that we didn't have to fight any longer. We just accepted it for what it was, and tonight a few of the boys are knocking themselves out with a bottle they saved and everyone else is just going about his job as usual. The best thing about the whole day was the fact that we knocked down two Jerries on the last day. We're pretty happy about it too, for we've grown to hate these B------- and we'd just as soon kill'em as look at'em. [...] Anyway, from now on stop worrying, for I'm perfectly OK and 'cease fire' is to be at 0001 in the morning."*

Indeed, Churchill announces on the radio in the afternoon of May 8: *"Hostilities will end officially at one minute after midnight tonight, but in the interests of saving lives the 'Cease fire' began yesterday to be sounded all along the front"*. Officially, the very last shot is fired by another GI, Domenic Mozzetta of the 97th Infantry Division. His unit is now in Klenovice (Czechoslovakia), shortly after liberating the Flossenburg concentration camp just before the border. On patrol at 11:55 pm, Domenic hears a German sniper bullet whipping the air next to his ear. Firing four times towards the muzzle flash in front of him, he sees the sniper's body fall from the tree where he'd been hiding. Five minutes later, the ceasefire starts, and this fourth shot officially becomes the last of the European conflict. Today, a black granite memorial with a bas relief of an M-1 rifle marks the exact spot where it was fired. Of course, it should be noted that this was the last shot fired at the German enemy – Paul Pirat of the 3e division d'infanterie algérienne writes in his diary on May 8: *"Everyone shoots in the air. The Anti-Aircraft guns open fire to finish their ammo, these are the last shots fired. I empty my machine gun. At midnight and 1 second, the war is over."*

THE ATLANTIC POCKETS SURRENDER

Vincent is a sergeant in the American 366th Medical Battalion, 66th 'Black Panther' Division.

The black panther of the 66th Infantry Division. The animal represents the qualities of a good infantryman: boldness, agility and bravery. This patch belonged to Vincent.

The unit's journey had begun in a tragic way: at 5:30 pm on December 24, 1944, Christmas Eve, the Belgian ship *Leopoldville*, which carried a large number of the men to Cherbourg, was torpedoed by the German submarine *U-486* and hundreds of soldiers were killed 6 miles off the coast. While the 'Panthermen' were expected to help fend off the German attack in the Ardennes, they received new orders after being heavily weakened by the *Leopoldville* accident. Their new mission, as of January 1, was to relieve the 94th Division near the Lorient and Saint-Nazaire pockets: harbors in Brittany that were still in German hands. Vincent's unit was headed for Lorient.

The Keroman submarine base in Lorient still stands today!

The Keroman submarine base had been built in Lorient harbor in 1941, at the instigation of Admiral Dönitz. Three gigantic reinforced concrete structures were erected, capable of housing at least forty U-boats, which in turn were responsible for the loss of more than 500 Allied ships during the Battle of the Atlantic. For the Germans, the base was one of the most ambitious projects they'd set up during the war, and it was so well built that the Allies had to design a special bomb to try to destroy it. Even so, 'Tall Boy' only partially managed to damage the base and block its entrance for a few submarines, but at a terrible price: the city was completely blown off the map.

During the battle for France, around 95,000 German soldiers are cut off in the 'Festung' ports from the retreating Wehrmacht, and as the war draws to a close, they've been holding the pockets for nine months. There are 25,000 of them in Lorient. Allied patrols are organized, combat missions with infantry and armored vehicles conducted, but the many artillery batteries and the solid 15-mile-long German defensive belt compel French Forces of the Interior and GIs to dig in and try to contain the pocket indefinitely. On May 7, 1945, following the German surrender, the first contacts between the Allies and the defenders are made. The official ceremonies of surrender take place on May 10 for Lorient and on May 11 for Saint-Nazaire. In the meantime, the Germans have to clear access to the pockets, remove obstacles, fill anti-tank ditches, evacuate the area and park themselves in prison camps. French and American soldiers entering the Keroman base find a great deal of equipment in excellent condition (submarines, speed boats...) and share the loot according to established conventions. To Vincent, the end of the war is good news, of course, but he regrets the fact that work is finished for the infantryman, while for him and the other medics, it's only just begun!

On May 14, 1945, the 66th Division moves to Koblenz (Germany) to guard prison camps. It's here that Vincent writes the following letter to his wife two weeks later: *"Germany (I got this far – luckily!), Sunday May 27, 1945.*

My darling wife, [...] censorship has finally been lifted, but I guess my letter will be spot checked by the base censor – which is OK by me, as long as it's not our Company officer!! One thing I can say Marge, even though where we are now is like a prison – I'm darn glad to be out of the dirtiest part of France – Normandy and Brittany! I guess by now you know where we were – yep, fighting and DODGING the damned worst gun ever invented – the German '88' mil. There'll be plenty stories on this for years to come you can bet on that for there isn't one to equal the firepower of it! Our Division and the FFI's (worse than the Nazis!) were holding the pocket at Lorient and St Nazaire. Lorient was a complete wreck when we went in on May 7. This was a sub base and they really planned on staying for years. I never saw such cement and reinforced forts like they had in all my life! In some places even the new 11-ton bomb couldn't hurt it! Everywhere we went were tunnels with pictures and rooms like a house! I really think they could have held out forever if they had more food for we found loads and loads of ammunition but only enough food left for three days. They were kept supplied since last September, by subs & small ships. Our artillery took care of the ships recently!! [...]

A souvenir brought back by Vincent: "What WAS an airplane P-40 last week!"

VIII - VICTORY SUMMER 1945

The Germans in Lorient lived like kings. In one converted hospital summer resort on the Atlantic Ocean, my C.O., 15 men and myself had a sweet time 'capturing' 133 Nazi jerks who were glad to give up to our two armed guards we had with us. They had mines all over the place so at first souvenir hunting was risky after we did our job but finally we got stuff. I already sent the commander's swell portable phonograph and dagger etc., so let me know if and how you receive it. One Nazi even 'gave' (ha!) me his camera. These guys had their French girl collaborationists with them and some really beautiful German blond nurses.

I got some other stuff too that I can't mention now but all in all honey – everything seemed too quiet when we returned to Calan so in a few days we moved up here – where? Well here in Brodenbach, Germany. A picturesque place in the valleys of the famous 'wine' country, the Moselle river. [...] The only trouble is we're practically prisoners – we can't leave our area only on business – no fraternizing with Germans ($65 fine or 6 years) and what's worse they are nice to our face but hate our guts! Being here is worse than fighting the war for we have to treat them nice, which naturally takes us off our guard – and things can and have happened. We're not very far from Koblenz, which I'm happy to report is flat. These rats really got London's air blitz back double! The young kids here even look fanatic at us – good thing looks can't kill! By looking at the place we live tho' I can see why they liked Hitler for he gave them everything! The people here are all dressed well but I guess it's all French etc. stuff for they are dressed poorly except in Paris. One thing I can say dear the papers couldn't exaggerate anything in this war! Gosh I have so much to tell you Darling it gets me mad for I can't write fast enough, so I'll just ramble on OK?

If you're wondering how we happened to be put holding the 'French pockets or the forgotten war' (huh, guys died) well here it is. We were alerted in England on December 23 and told to be ready to pull out in 6 hours, and we were for if you remember this was when the Nazis were trying a break through or what was called the 'bulge' (they nearly made it). If they broke through the Ardennes the pockets of Lorient, Dunkirk, St Nazaire etc. were supposed to break out. Well on a rainy, snowy, foggy, damn cold Xmas Eve we started out on the Channel in an LST named the 'War Whoop' from Portsmouth, England. In front of us was a good-sized troop ship loaded with about 1,500 guys and equipment – well off we were to war and the Channel I say again is rougher than the Ocean! It was supposed to be an 8 hour-trip but between the weather and subs, well time went on and on. We couldn't see a thing on any side or hear for the wind howling but did detect subs around and when we landed at Cherbourg (also flat) we found out the troop ship went down on Xmas morning at 2:30 am [The *Leopoldville* he writes about here actually sank at 8:30 pm and carried 2,235 soldiers, 515 of whom went down with the ship and 248 others died from injuries or hypothermia. It's surprising that this part of the letter wasn't censored, since the men of the 66th Division were ordered never to speak about the incident. The file was only de-classified in 1996]. So I guess orders had to be changed fast for instead of heading for Belgium where our mail went we took over where the 94th Division was at Lorient. I won't say anymore dear for I've had worse Xmas's [sic] but can't remember when!! [...] I guess for some of us we were lucky for the 94th Division was sent up in the bulge and lost 3/4 of their personnel! But we had our share too.

We have a few Purple Hearts in the company. I damn near had one when an '88' hit across the street from me in a town called Locrest [probably Inzinzac-Lochrist, north of Lorient] and the street was only 25 or 30 feet wide, not much I wasn't scared – none of us were – baloney! Of course after about 10 or more rounds – you just don't give a damn! And never let anyone say they didn't hit the Red Cross and our ambulances or otherwise! We were perfect targets with all white helmets! I wish I had a gun here, more than ever! Well dear I guess I've told you 1/3 of the stuff I have done since that day I left you in the morning of September 11, 1944. [...] I'm ready to go to the CBI [China-Burma-India theater of war] rather than be a 'prisoner' in the Army of Occupation. [...] On April 26 when I last wrote the war was really blasting to a finish but we didn't know what we were doing! We had every big gun in the sector behind us and all day and night they didn't rest. Yeah I guess part of the 3rd Army will occupy too. [...] So Darling Wife – please, please wait a while longer for me."

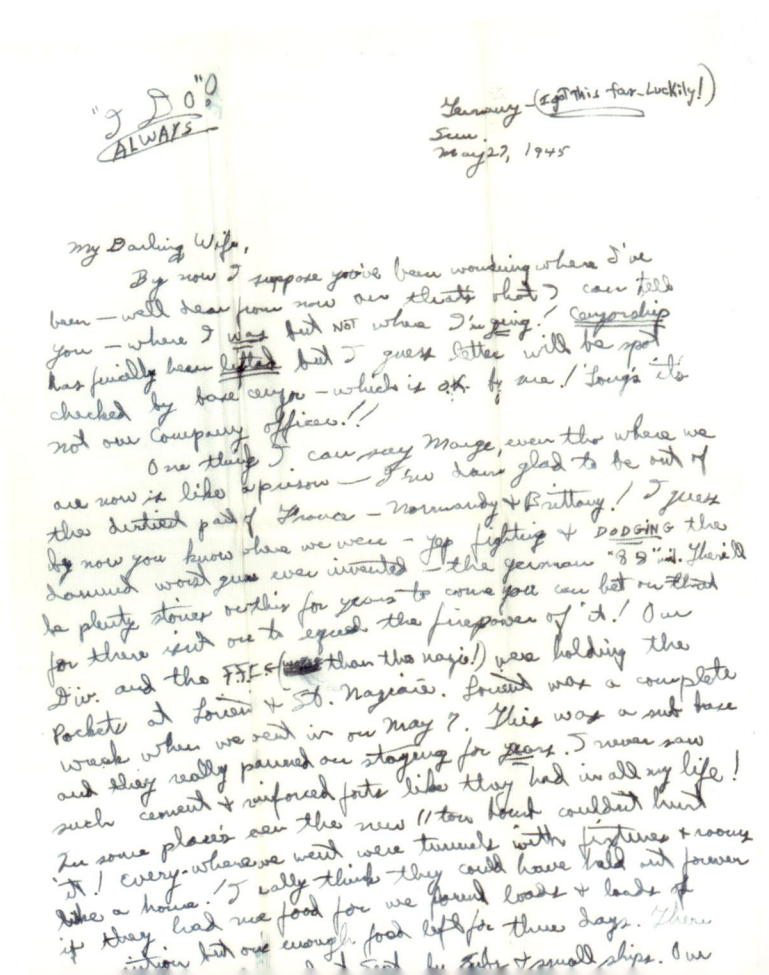

CELEBRATIONS

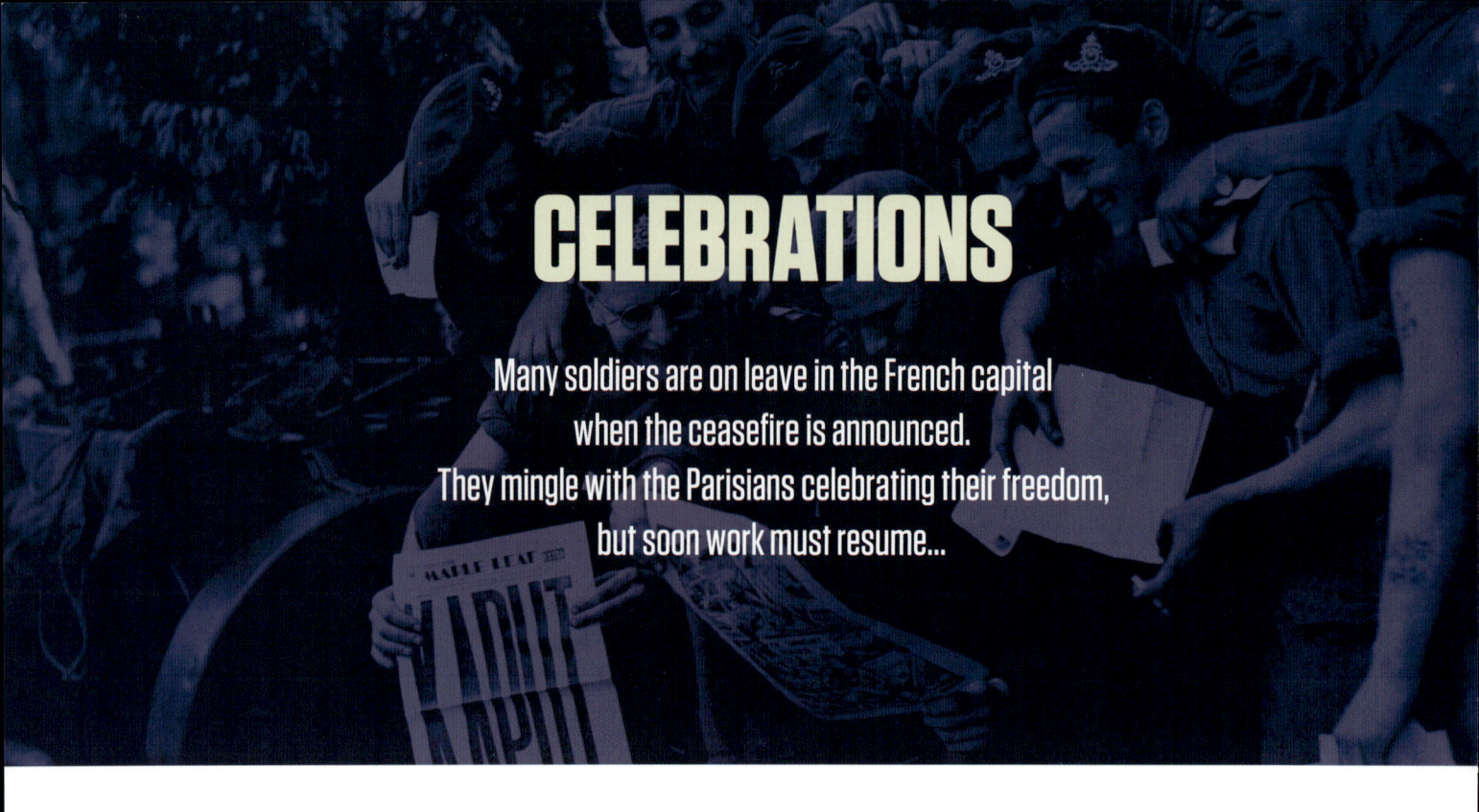

Many soldiers are on leave in the French capital when the ceasefire is announced. They mingle with the Parisians celebrating their freedom, but soon work must resume...

PARIS CELEBRATES VICTORY

Robert is assigned to SHAEF Communications Zone, Seine Section, which was established in Paris shortly after the liberation. The GI writes to his parents on May 8, 1945: "Well, this is really 'the' day here. At three o'clock this afternoon Churchill will announce the war officially over. It is about two o'clock now and there are formations of Boeing Flying Fortresses and different types of planes overhead. The streets are lined with flags and the people are in a real holiday mood. Last night I went to a show and when I walked up the Champs Elysees it was loaded with people. Planes were dropping colored flares and had their bright landing lights on. It was sure quite a sight. All of a sudden, a big cheer went up and the Arc de Triomphe blazed with light. What a night, but it promises to be more tonight, as today it will really be official. The street where I live is decorated from bottom to the top story. I sure wish you folks could see this place today! The people here are really happy it's over, and they sure deserve it. I'm wondering today how it looks at home. I sure wish I could see the celebrating around Seattle today. What makes it even better, it is a beautiful day, hardly a cloud and downright hot if you move very fast. There are parades scheduled too. Last night people walked arm in arm, singing and really having a time. I'll be drinking a toast to all of you today and am sure thinking of you. [...] Well folks, a better letter next time although I know you can't beat this news. What a day!"

Bernard is a captain in the 13th US Airborne Division, which has recently arrived in Europe. It's never seen combat, much to the frustration of its paratroopers, who were deployed to France to help finish the Battle of the Bulge, but the battle had ended before the unit was engaged. Similarly, even though it was to jump with the 17th US Airborne and the 6th British Airborne during *Operation Varsity*, it was dismissed at the last moment due to the lack of available aircraft. All subsequent operations in which the division was to participate in Germany were also canceled due to the rapid advance of Allied troops, meaning the war in Europe ended before it had even fired a shot. Bernard is nevertheless happy for the Parisians who are celebrating peace and he writes to his wife on May 9: "At last the war is over - over here! And what a celebration there was last night. It was really wonderful to see - millions of people on the street. The lights were almost all lit, the fountains going. Notre Dame illuminated. And from the Arc de Triomphe to the Place de la Concorde - just a seething mass of humanity. I was lucky enough to be able to stand on one pillar of the Arc and take a picture of the crowd - it was a tremendous sight!

VIII - VICTORY SUMMER 1945

Today is still a holiday – no classes either, so I am free to roam Paris and take more pictures which I shall do – walk down the Champs de Elysées [sic] and toward the Louvre, Luxembourg Palace – into the Park area – and I have 3 rolls of film to use. It's been quite an experience, and except for celebrating with you I think I'd rather be here at a time like this."

Frank belongs to the 28th US Infantry Division. He experienced the hedgerow fighting in Normandy, the horror of the Hürtgen Forest, the freezing winter in the Ardennes and the capture of the Colmar Pocket. On VE-Day (Victory in Europe), he's on leave in Paris and celebrates with the French. On May 11, he writes to his little sister: *"Well of course you know that a half of a war is over, boy am I glad – now all I have to do is sweat out the Pacific – I sure would like to get home though... When the war ended, I was in Paris. That's a nice place to be especially when they're all celebrating. Well I didn't know what was going on. Too much 'Cognac'. Boy was I loaded. Had a swell time anyway.*

The people there were all going crazy." Frank would finally leave the army in October 1945.

Once the celebrations are over, life resumes in Paris and the Americans discover another facet of the capital. A soldier in the 89th Infantry Division just returning from leave writes to his mother on 27 June: *"We arrived at about 11 am yesterday upon which I immediately searched out 'Rainbow Corner' and took a shower. Rainbow Corner is a cluster of buildings directed by the Red Cross, designed for the benefit of all personnel of the Allies. After the shower Ray (Fisher) and I ate at the Café de La Paix – something I've always wanted to do. We were very thirsty, and the beer was surprisingly good. And the world DOES pass by the doors of the Café de La Paix. And there is nothing half-way about the girls in Paris either. I mean, they are either very attractive or very repulsive. Nor do they seem very scrupulous. I did all I could do to defend my virtue from the advances of several charming young lovelies.*

A GI with a bookseller on the banks of the Seine, near Notre-Dame Cathedral. Below, a map of Paris for American troops on leave.

As I say, I had only sixteen hours. So any impressions I may have had are strictly fleeting. Parisians are quite like Americans. They love new things – and they love money. A bargain is a landmark in their lives. It's true, they try to 'do' the poor, defenseless, American GI. They wanted 98 francs for a haircut, shave, shampoo, and manicure, from me. That's the equivalent of two American dollars [about $28 nowadays]. I gave him 30 francs and he loved me for it. After lunch, I took a bus tour of the city. It was supposed to last two hours and stop at every place of interest. It did neither. It lasted an hour and a half, and they stopped only at the Eiffel Tower, Napoleon's Tomb, and the Arc de Triomphe. Oh, yes, we did get a fleeting glimpse of Notre Dame. I tried to take some pictures (35 mm film that I cut down to fit the camera – God knows how they'll turn out!), but I never had enough time. I was continually running for it. At Notre Dame, there were some mummers standing almost at the gate, selling things. First, some evil-looking wart would sidle up to you and ask without moving his lips if you'd care for some 'dirty pictures'. He'd flash you a glimpse of something pretty impossible. If you told him to beat it, some saintly looking babe would totter over to you, look at you with soulful eyes and try to sell you a picture of Mary Magdalene or a cross. They had you coming and going! I actually expected to find some of them inside the Cathedral. The war hasn't been kind to Notre Dame. Its exterior has the appearance of many moon's exposure to stone-termites. The interior is pretty bare. The Jerries took everything that could move. I took a shot which I hope turned out, no promises on any of those pictures. Napoleon's Tomb or Les Invalides was pretty impressive, flanked by stacks of steps, and topped by a gold (real they claim) dome. Inside is a huge, dimly lit alter, in front of which lies all that remains of the Emperor. He lies in a deep wide well, so that all who come to see him shall bow their heads in respect. After the tour, we went the rounds, looking for some good wine. That, apparently, is something you cannot get. It's pretty poor stuff – watery. Supper over, we danced with some WACs [Women's Army Corps] to a pretty good orchestra, at 'Rainbow Corner'. [...] We had arrived at the theater late, and the SRO sign was up. Stubbornly, we looked around, finding nothing in the orchestra or balcony. We decided to sit on the steps in the mezzanine, when we noticed that the middle front row of the latter was empty. So we packed there, wondering why no one was sitting in some of the best seats in the house. We were soon to learn. An usherette hustled up, screaming 'Pour les Généraux ! Pour les Généraux !'. 'What Generals?' I asked, looking around. There were no Generals. She persisted, saying that they were 'réservés' but fled when Ray and I tried to kiss her, albeit she was laughing. They were good seats. That's about all we had time for. Oh that ride back, Gosh! I slept all day today [...] The story here is about the same. I think we're going to move soon – where I don't know. We've turned in our rifles to be packed. We didn't turn them in when we took the boat ride here. So you see, I'm hesitant about ordering packages."

WELCOME FOR LEAVE TROOPS

To: Officers and Men Arriving in Paris on Leave.

You have been selected by your Commanding Officer as deserving of a pass to Paris.

As Commanding General of Seine Section, Communications Zone, ETOUSA, I welcome you to Paris. I want to assure you that I, as well as all the members of my command, desire greatly to do everything in our power to make your stay, however long it is, as enjoyable and worthwhile as possible.

Take advantage of the things that interest you among the great and varied number of activities Paris has to offer. We have endeavored to guide you and to aid you in doing this.

Call upon us, any of the personnel of Seine Section, for anything we can do to make your visit to Paris a truly pleasant and valuable experience.

PLEAS B. ROGERS
Brigadier General, USA
Commanding

THE UNITED STATES ARMY

PARIS

GUIDE FOR LEAVE TROOPS

A wooden cross for an iron cross? Prophetically, the reverse side of this Allied propaganda leaflet from 1942 shows the high price to pay for those seeking to earn the 'Eisernes Kreuz' medal – half a million German soldiers were killed on the Western European front until 1945. Dispersed by balloons, this original leaflet was collected by a civilian in Switzerland: *"About ten of those leaflets were falling on the south-eastern part of the old town of Neuchâtel. The soldiers of the territorial service searched for them frantically. At rue Saint-Honoré, I was able to collect just one copy without being seen."*

WHAT FUTURE FOR GERMANY?

An American combat engineer hears the news of the German surrender while on leave in Valkenburg, Netherlands. He writes to his brother a few days later, after returning to work in Germany: *"Still here along the Elbe river. Received Dad's May 8th V-mail yesterday. The end of this German war certainly was one of rumor and fake news, until one didn't even get enthused when the real word came. Besides, to us, everything continues as before. So it is difficult to get up steam about it. When I was in Valkenburg and saw the people parading, dancing in the streets, street lights shining, and windows in homes showing yellow light in friendly happy greeting – then I too felt that the war was over. Here the German people of course continued as before on VE-day and so did we. Things here seem to be safe – there are very few incidents happening in the area of German resistance or underground activity. We expected, at first, that the werewolves would prove to be vicious, but so far, they have kept holed up pretty well. All in all, I'd say your brother has survived and will survive this war OK."*

Occupation is not always easy, however, and men who've lost friends in battle have great difficulty accepting why the Germans aren't treated more harshly. Patton himself, according to one soldier, spends more time preparing for the future war against communism than acting for de-nazification (he'll consequently be relieved of command of his 3rd Army by Eisenhower and put in charge of the 15th Occupation Army). An infantryman writes in the summer of 1945: *"Don't talk to me about Patton – pardon me, General Patton. He's a disgusting old hypocrite! I'm disgusted with the way we are handling Germany. Instead of going in there, and showing them we mean business, we pamper and love them. A Heinie comes along and says 'There are no Germans prepared to run the government but Nazis. Nazis are the only governmental-experienced people we have!', so what do we do, we agree – and start co-operating with them. As long as we continue to do that – just that long will Nazism survive!"*

However, not everyone agrees with him. Kenneth, an American medic, writes from the French town of Nancy on May 27: *"They sure did fix Germany this time. I was reading just the other day that in Dresden alone they killed around 300,000 people by air raids alone* [in reality, this number had been multiplied ten times by Goebbels's German propaganda ministry. The raids on Dresden on February 13 and 14, 1945 and their hurricanes of fire caused the deaths of around 40,000 people. But Air Marshal Sir Arthur Harris's 'terror bombings' were already severely criticized after being more effective in creating refugee flows hindering the movement of the Wehrmacht than in undermining German industry.] *The way Germany is gutted she shall never I don't believe be any trouble. In Berlin if they ever decide to rebuild it will take 20 to 30 years to do the job. I don't think they will ever be able to count the German dead that lay buried in the ruins. It may sound hard, but we had to dump death on the German people to let them know just what war is because all her wars in the past were on other countries [sic] soil. This time the people have paid a price which they will never forget. They have not only sacrificed their sons but also their homes and a lot have lost their own lives. They (the people) are the ones responsible for this crime of the ages. Hitler was their instrument through which they hoped to gain world domination. Today they will be subjected to Military law.*

Already the schools in the first four grades have opened in Aachen under strict supervision of the Allies. The only hope for a peaceful Germany rests on the shoulders of these small children. You can't count on a thing from the adult. 'For a little child shall lead them', so says the Great Book. So the task of educating them is a hard one but by great pains it can be done. If the German Youth of the future puts as much zeal into peace as they have into waging war, Germany shall take her place as any other modern democratic nation in this world but if she fails then she is doomed to have armies of occupation in her country forever. We are determined this time that our blood shall not have been shed in vain and no more American homes robbed of their sons.

So you can see at a glance that Germany these few weeks since VE-day has been treated as a defeat[ed] foe and not as [a] bad little boy whose parents smile at his bad behavior. The German leaders of the Nazi party have been committing suicide. Well they can't face a trial for they know that they even digressed from the principals of modern warfare. It's nothing but plain murder that they sanctioned. So the criminal war board will extract the rightful penalty. Russia will see to that. She has no feeling of sympathy. She fights fire with fire. A great policy for dealing with barbaric hoodlums. When Germany is purged, and only then can you start the foundation of a new and decent Germany."

The new generation would indeed be the one to keep the peace for decades to come. In a park overlooking the Rhine in Germany, Henry Crookhorn enjoys a moment of serenity for the first time and writes to his wife: *"Looks more and more like the 15th Army will be the 'Army of Occupation' and that we'll be part of it although there's nothing official on it. The fellows would prefer it that way rather than go to the Pacific, as the better of two evils. At least we know what we got here and it's not bad at all, except they are getting pretty stingy with the food, as they have all these prisoners to feed now along with displaced refugees. [...] It was lonesome sitting there without you, but as I started to think about things in general, well I figured I was pretty lucky after all. Here I was relaxing on a park bench with peace and quiet around me, while on the other side of the world, guys were living and sleeping in mud holes getting shot at and suffering a million other tortures. Then I felt much better. Some little German kids came over to me and asked for chocolates and gum. They usually say, 'any gum, chum?'. Some GI taught them that phrase. Even tho' they are Germans, you can't resist. Kids are the same the world over, so cute and innocent. If only people would remain as kids, what a nice world this would be to live in. [...] I sure miss hearing from you. Well, one of these days, all this will be over with. It can't last forever, altho' at times it may seem that way. [...] I see by the papers that a lot of the guys are parading around New York with beaucoup battle stars and ribbons (fruit salad we call it). I'd like to be one of them. Well, when my turn comes, the novelty will be worn off and we'll be damn glad to get back to 'civils' again. Guess those suits of mine will be all out of style. What's the latest in Men's wear these days or are they still wearing zoot suits?"*

Twenty-four high-ranking Nazi officers were sentenced during the Nuremberg Trial from November 20, 1945 onwards. Accused of complicity, crimes against peace, war crimes or crimes against humanity, they pleaded "not guilty", putting all the blame on Hitler. Eleven of them were hanged.

BARBARA STUART

Camp Shows Unit 590, 6817th Special Service, USO

Millions of soldiers now want to go home, but in the meantime, they need to be entertained.
This is the role of the USO (United Service Organizations), which plays shows all around the world.
Barbara Stuart is a dancer and will travel through France to meet the troops.

Barbara Stuart was born on April 10, 1916 in New York. She started dancing very early and later worked with renowned ballet masters such as Pierre Vladimiroff, Anatole Vilzak and George Balanchine. She joined the American Ballet, which would later be called the New York City Ballet, and there met Lila Zali, a Russian immigrant ballerina, who soon became her closest friend.

As Barbara walked the streets of New York one day in December 1941, she was shocked to hear a loudspeaker broadcasting the latest news in the city: *"Pearl Harbor is under attack! War is declared!"* Barbara, Lila and another dancer immediately formed a small troupe, 'The Three Debs', to support the war effort in their own way: they would tour across the United States with the United Service Organizations and even accompany Jack Paar (USO Master of Ceremonies) to the South Pacific.

The United Service Organizations was created in 1941 by President Roosevelt to bring together various associations who wanted to support the morale of American troops. The purpose of the USO Camp Shows was to entertain Allied soldiers at home, abroad and in hospitals, with many celebrities of the time performing a variety of singing, dancing and theater shows, helping the men feel a little closer to home. The USO still performs the same function today!

The Three Debs

An American soldier wrote to his parents from the battlefields of France: *"Am a little tired and weary and won't be able to write a lot. [...] We are having a variety show at the Red Cross this evening and I think I will go. I need a change, have been putting* too many hours in and I need to get a change of mind. It's good these shows for the boys' morale and it sure needs boosting from time to time. Now morale is a funny thing it rises and falls just like an ocean swell, and precaution is taken by our commander to keep this thing called morale high, it's to the advantage to the whole outfit that it's kept that way. So hence these movies, dance bands, bingo parties, and variety shows."* Now that the fighting is over, it's still essential to occupy the bored, and sometimes traumatized, soldiers awaiting their return home, in order to avoid any bad behavior and accidents.

The 6817th Special Service Battalion is responsible for coordinating the various shows. Although not a combat unit, it's still militarily organized. Composed of 710 members (mostly former soldiers), the battalion is divided into three companies: the Soldier Show Company has the 'performers' (actors, singers, dancers, musicians, writers, directors, costume designers…), the USO Company has the drivers and technicians, and the HQ Company directs the whole battalion.

In 1944, Barbara and her troupe left for Europe, driving through bombed cities in convoys and performing the opera *Die Fledermaus* for the soldiers. They still live in much better conditions than the latter, as one of Barbara's fellow dancers would say: *"But I thought we were supposed to suffer!"*

Barbara writes to some friends in June 1945: *"This is the first real chance I have had to write as there has been no way of sending letters before and now we are being rushed through a preparation for going to the North of France. We leave here, Paris, which is headquarters and are on the road for about ten weeks. After that we return here for a week's rest. The voyage over was glorious and after some delay in England we came on and landed at Le Havre where the destruction is incredible. We are living in a beautiful house which has a charming garden. The only thing that mars its perfection is that ten of us sleep in army cots in the living room and there is a continuous line for the two available bathrooms. Some of the French people here have been through a lot, and they have been very helpful to us with laundry and such. I find myself doing most of the interpreting as not many of the girls speak French. Mine is very shaky but this practice is wonderful.* Up in Central Park [a Broadway musical] *arrived the day before us and have gone on the road."*

Back in the United States after the war, Barbara will meet a Russian immigrant, Max Rabinowitsh, through her friendship with Lila, and they will marry in 1947. A famous pianist in Hollywood, Max's playing will be heard in many films from the 1930s to the 1960s (including *Ben-Hur*). He'll go on tour with Barbara and the couple will settle in Laguna Beach, California, where Barbara and Lila will create the Pacific Ballet. Barbara would teach dance there and indulge her passion until her death on June 25, 1998.

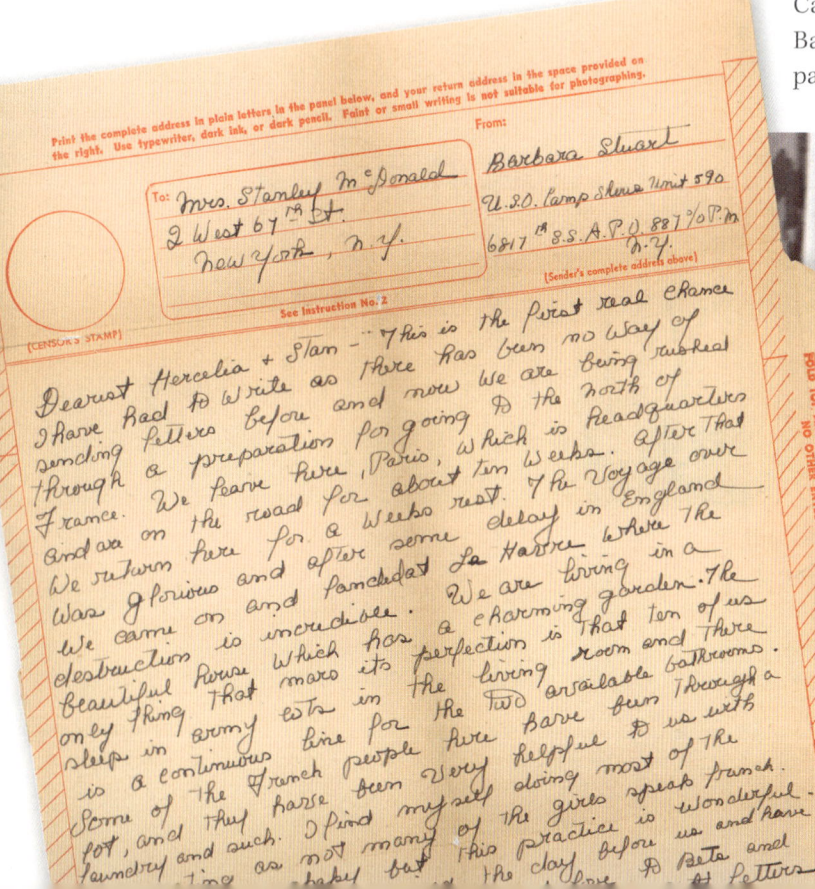

FLEMING McCONNELL

2nd / 7th Reconnaissance Regiment, 3rd Infantry Division, Canadian Army Occupation Force

Dreaming of adventure, Fleming is eager to do his duty in Europe.
Although disappointed to arrive after the German defeat, he'll travel through demolished European cities
and report on the occupation to his parents, illustrating his letters with many drawings.

Born in 1925 in the province of Manitoba, in the heart of Canada, Fleming studied in Calgary and Victoria, but chose to follow in the footsteps of his older brother, who served in Italy with the Canadian artillery (where he was wounded before leaving for Northern Europe). Fleming volunteered in 1944 and joined an armored unit at Camp Borden (Ontario). He initially wanted to become a mechanic or a truck driver, but as the weeks passed he became bored and envied the infantrymen, who were seeing some action. In February 1945, he finally left Canada.

Excited about the idea of liberating Europe, he found out he had to wait a little longer before setting foot on German soil, as a new training session awaited him in England. He was taught to shoot in a Sherman tank, but feared that he'd never have a chance to put that knowledge into practise, as he still had two months of training left and the news from the front suggested that the war would end soon. He regretted not having chosen the infantry, as infantrymen only stayed in England fewer than six weeks, and sometimes only one or two weeks depending on the needs for replacements. He met many Canadian veterans who shared their war stories, with everyone agreeing that the Germans were tough, especially young soldiers. Fleming wrote: *"One corporal told us about a Nazi they had finally captured after he had been conducting a one-man suicidal war in a house, against the Canadians.*

It turned out that his parents had been killed and his home devastated – and his city. 'What else is there for me to do but fight?' he asked." Fleming consequently spent time in pubs listening with admiration to the stories of wounded soldiers returning from the front.

He finally arrives on the continent in early June 1945 (*"too late for any fighting – but still, I am here"*) and joins his first regiment, the British Columbia Regiment (Duke of Connaught's Own) or 28th Armoured Regiment, attached to the 4th Canadian Armoured Division. It's been fighting ever since landing in France on July 28, 1944 and as Fleming says, *"The Regiment has been wiped out a couple of times (the tanks that is – not necessarily the crews) so it is supposed to be a good regiment."*

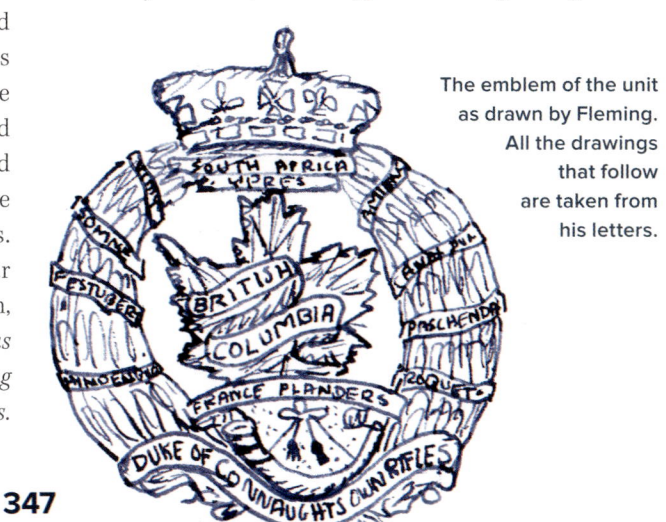

The emblem of the unit as drawn by Fleming. All the drawings that follow are taken from his letters.

His unit settles in Hengelo (misspelled by Fleming on his map), in the eastern Netherlands, very close to the German border. The welcome is warm, especially by the children who seem to adore the Canadians, but women and soldiers aren't allowed to fraternize.

There isn't much to do in this small town of 40,000 inhabitants, especially as movement is limited: many fighting units return to England and there are no means of transportation available. Fleming is bored... He writes to a friend: *"Amsterdam is out of bounds and also I hear the 1st* [Canadian] *Division is moving to England. Oh well – after I get home from my ten year occupational stint I may, just MAY get to see you. You'll be sorry when some sniper gets me or when an M.P. puts me in the glasshouse for 40 years for fraternizing! I have not been warned for occupation duties yet – and have my fingers crossed. As it is the 4th Division is the last to go home."*

His orders actually arrive shortly after this letter and Fleming is transferred to the 7th Armoured Reconnaissance Regiment of Montreal (17th Duke of York's Royal Canadian Hussars), 3rd Canadian Infantry Division. This prestigious regiment landed on Juno Beach on June 6, 1944, in one of the most fortified areas on the coast. It later won eleven 'Battle Honors' (acquired in each battle where it distinguished itself particularly well, earning the right to put the names of these battles on its flag) for its actions in Caen, Falaise, on the Scheldt or in the Rhine Valley. However, when the war ended, most of the original members returned to Montreal and were replaced by volunteers from other units. On June 1, 1945, the regiment is mobilized to participate in the occupation of Germany and renamed '2nd/7th Reconnaissance Regiment, Royal Canadian Armoured Corps, Canadian Army Occupation Force' on August 2, 1945. Fleming and his new unit are in charge of northwestern Germany and based in Bunde, close to the Dutch border, on the North Sea.

As many Allied soldiers have already returned home, the food situation improves in July 1945. The immediate release of many German prisoners of war also helps – those who'd been forcibly recruited with no connection to the Nazi party and were considered more useful for the reconstruction of the country. The Western Allies now only detain SS troops and those deemed to be a threat, all of whom will be released by 1948 (but the officers accused of war crimes would be tried accordingly). The ban on fraternization is also lifted, at last, and Fleming sets out to find a good German dictionary to talk with the locals.

He soon meets interesting people, as he writes on July 17: *"I went to one farmhouse near here for eggs and had a very pleasant chat. They had a brother living near Vancouver (working on this I got a promise for eggs – which is some feat here). The father had been through the first campaigns in Western Europe, and then he had fought on the Leningrad front for 3 years. He and his wife were honestly fed up and disgusted with the Nazis. They said that it was bad for Germany that she lost the war, but that it would have been a lot worse if she had won. That is the most truly repentant and encouraging remark I have heard from a German yet. The usual line is terrific complaints about the punishment which is being given Germany (hardly felt here at all) for the crimes of the Nazis 'and' (of course) 'WE aren't Nazis!' (as a matter of fact, this quarter is a former Nazi stronghold)."*

VIII – VICTORY SUMMER 1945

Relationships with civilians are more relaxed, and the Canadians are able do some sightseeing or engage in sports or artistic activities (Fleming hopes to join the regimental newspaper), but they must remain on their guard. Fleming always keeps his Sten machine gun at the ready, both to force respect and to protect himself from possible attacks: *"As to physical violence – there was a little in the next town a couple of weeks ago, but that was because the Germans expected the worst from the Canadians – now that they see that we are quite harmless they don't fear and hate us so much. Also, of course, we always carry weapons, and usually go in pairs. Still, when one sees the sneers, or the arrogance on the faces of the young fellows around here, one is not inclined to be too trusting."*

In late August, Fleming has the opportunity to go on leave to Brussels. He recounts his journey in this long and fascinating letter of August 25, 1945: *"Dear Ma' n' Pa' n' Grandmother, it was swell while it lasted, the only thing wrong being that it didn't last long enough. Yes, I may now say, with a worldly little cough that 'of course when I was in Brussels...' The capital of Belgium has been the object of my scrutiny for almost exactly 76 hours. It had a good going over believe me! A week ago Wednesday I was told to whip my stuff together to go on a weekend (72 hours). That Friday at 6 in the morning in a terrible rain we left Bunde in a truck (armoured car) and were taken to the river Ems, where the bridge was open to let barges through, we were transferred to a wee motor boat to cross. Then to truck and so on to Oldenburg where the Division assembled trucks at the large and most wonderful airfield for leave personnel. Into more trucks and off to Nijmegen – 185 more miles of very poor roads. Roads in Germany are generally bad – very much worse than Holland which has excellent concrete highways. At Zutphen we were crossing the famous 'Harry Crerar' bridge (longest Bailey bridge in the world, built by Canadians) when an M.P. stopped the truck at the end of the bridge. The roadway on the bridge is wood, and it was very wet – so Wham! Wham! Wham! Five big 'sixties' slid into each other as the drivers applied their brakes on the slippery road. We were in the middle one and were bounced around a bit but aside from smashed radiators there was no damage. It was quite something seeing the trucks behind us sliding along so smoothly and then whacking us!*

We went through Arnhem. Last time I was in Arnhem, in May, it was a picture of desolation. No one but the odd anti-looting patrol around at all, shops boarded up, broken glass everywhere, battle debris, smashed cars, broken weapons, clothes, petrol cans, barricades, overturned streetcars, everywhere desertion and desolation. Now, only three months later, the onetime corpse is alive and almost beautiful. Throngs of gaily dressed people, jams of traffic, flags, stores, everything as it should be – except of course the smashed houses, and the several acres that are just heaps of broken masonry. They also now have a real bridge across the Rhine at Arnhem to replace the one that was blown up after the paratroopers were pushed out. We were lucky enough to be held up 24 hours in Nijmegen and spent the period very pleasantly as the transit camp there is very pleasant indeed. Sunday morning, we boarded the leave train for Brussels and set off on our long slow trip. The coaches are all old LNER [London and North Eastern Railway] and not luxurious in the least. The engines are also all newly built English models, probably made expressly for this purpose. When one sees the sidings full of shot up, blown up, and blasted locomotives that were operating before the RAF pitched in one understands the locomotive shortage. And so on, through s'Hertogenbosch, Tilburg, Breda, and East Antwerp. One gets a wonderful view of Antwerp docks with miles of rows of cranes and beneath them many large ships. In Antwerp we buy vegetables from a hawker in the station, for cigarettes or Belgian francs. Guilders [Dutch currency]? *No chance!*

Then on to Brussels through some very lovely flat country. Belgium looks and smells warmer, more friendly than Holland. Rather ordinary entrance to Brussels (where we arrived about 4 pm), into the Gare du Nord and whisked off by an Army bus to the 'Beaver Apartments' - 'right in the heart of downtown Brussels!' Free accommodation and free meals.

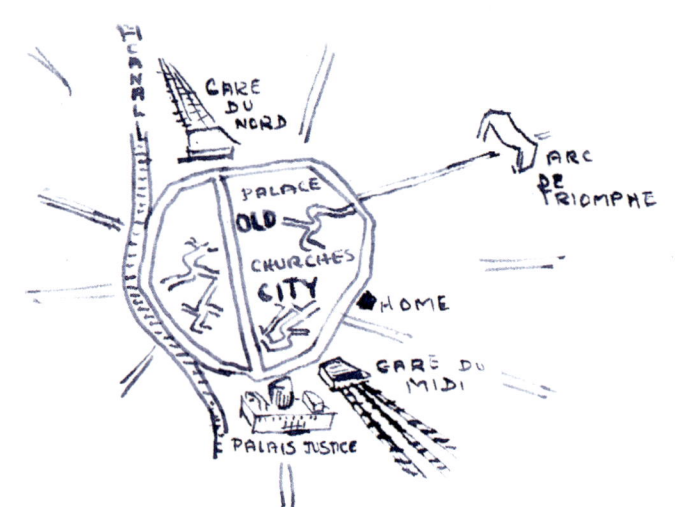

Just about everything was obtainable there, though at considerable prices. I could even have bought mom some real silk stockings (black market) but I lacked both the kazoom and the statistics. Incidentally if you want anything in lace please send me details. It is plentiful and not overwhelmingly expensive and apparently Brussels is the place to get it. But it seems to me we have all kinds of lace stuff at home. It was not per schedule, but I led a model misogynistic life when in Brussels, chiefly because it costs about 300 francs just to say hello to any passable babe (thanks to the Americans who swarm here). And are the women ever chic!

Facilities for Canadian servicemen are many and excellent and we also are allowed into all English and American canteens, theatres, etc. (all facilities are for all services which is excellent as all three – Canadian, US and English – have excellent facilities). At seven o'clock that night I was waiting for the guy I was traveling with in our room – sitting on my bed. I woke up at 11 pm and very disgusted went to bed properly. Bang went one night. Next day however I had a look see. Brussels is well laid out and as the street cars are free I soon got to know my way around. One cannot go by street names at all as the same street may have as many different names as there are blocks – or even turns – in it. I saw all the sights one should see from the staggeringly immense Palais de Justice (which the Germans damaged considerably when burning documents) to Mannekin Pis (which no German would dare to damage). I saw a lace maker at work, saw the King's Palace and his huge park with its Japanese pagoda and Chinese restaurant. The Churches are in some cases very beautiful from the outside but on the inside I did not like them at all – packed with statues, altars, hangings, paintings, prayer boxes, and so on. I quite fled in disappointment from the interior. We were also taken out to the national shooting gallery. It is here that the Jerries shot Edith Cavell in the last war [this British nurse saved the lives of many soldiers on both sides, but was sentenced to death by the Germans for helping 200 Allies flee occupied Belgium on October 12, 1915]. The four holes her stool had made where she sat when executed had been commemorated with the names of other patriots on a concrete slab, topped by a memorial statue. Jerry tore it all up and sent it away. We were also shown the shooting galleries used by the Jerries during this war for the execution of at the very least 350 people (graves of 250 can be seen).

I could go on for quite a while – the night I visited the red-light district and saw, among other things, three '17th Dukes' men trying to break up a tavern (the M.P.s finally took them away) to the hours or so I spent in Brussels's wonderful big store 'Bon Marché'.

And so on Wednesday at 4 pm we catch the train to Nijmegen and next morning take the truck again – arriving at Bunde at 11 pm Thursday night. Slightly disconcerted to find that (a) I was on guard (b) my troop had decamped along with my bedroll. Cold night, but now my bedroll and I are together again, separation only having cemented more firmly our deep affection. At the moment our troop (plus me) is looking after a camp of Yugoslav POWs, who are Royalists and hence find it unadvisable to go home. They are a very good bunch of chaps and they love us – saluting at all possible occasions. This camp, incidentally, used to be Stalag VI for Canadians and English. Not too bad a hole. Location is just over the border from Hengelo (remember). We are here 2 weeks – very good go."

Fleming's unit will serve as occupier until May 15, 1946, when the British 52nd (Lowland) Division takes over. The Regiment will be disbanded nine days later and Fleming would return to Canada. After the war, he'll study medicine and radiology, taking him from Toronto (Canada) to Massachusetts (USA), angiography in the United Kingdom, Norway and Sweden, and will have a distinguished career as a medical physicist. He passed away at Victoria Hospital on August 15, 2008.

VIII - **VICTORY** SUMMER 1945

"..*.#*..THIS B.... SO'N SO OF AN ARMY!
YOU'VE EVEN GOTTA GET UP FOR YOUR MEALS! *∂!"

With humor, Fleming sometimes sarcastically denounces certain realities, as on the back of the photo below, taken by a German photographer and sent to his mother. It could've been titled 'behind the scenes'.

351

POINTS

The Allies are looking forward to reuniting with their loved ones, but everything depends on the 'points' system set up by the army. For the lucky ones who've earned enough of them, it's a ticket to one of the many transit camps on the coast, and home. For the others, occupation awaits, or worse, the Pacific...

COUNTING THE POINTS

On May 11, 1945, Guenther 'Gunner' Ahlf of the 95th Infantry Division does the math: *"It doesn't look as though I'll be discharged for a while according to this points system which was finally released. The way I figure I have 24 points for the number of months in the service, 8 points for the number of months overseas, five points for a battle star, five points for a Purple Heart, and five points for a Bronze Star (when I get it). That's 49 points. You must have 85 to be considered for a discharge. Now if we had three children (12 points for each), I'd have 85 points. I'll have to spend 18 more months overseas in order to get the necessary 85 points, if I have to spend them over here it won't be so bad."* Gunner fears being sent to the Pacific to help defeat Japan's Imperial Army.

Marvin is in a Medical Collecting Company, whose role in combat was to recover the wounded on the battlefields and take them to the nearest aid station. He's served on several fronts since 1942, and even had a brush with death during a New Year's Eve bombing in the Ardennes. His company followed Allied troops across Germany and finished its race in Pilsen (Czechoslovakia) in mid-June 1945. On June 24, it returns to southeastern Germany, at Rankam, near the Czechoslovak border. The next day, Marvin writes to his girlfriend on correspondence paper recovered from a Nazi officer's desk (opposite): *"While in Pilsen, Ceskaslovensko (Czechoslovakia), I wrote you a V-mail. Stayed overnight with an ambulance company. I had a very enjoyable time. The most interesting to me were the people. They don't fall all over you with friendship. They seem more or less reserved which I think is very good. They are nice people and will be very friendly after they size you up. This city is the most active I've seen over here, it's clean and doesn't seem to have been badly hurt by the war. Another odd thing that struck me is so many male citizens well dressed, I believe there were more males than females about town. They have trolleys in operation so rode on two. I took a number of pictures. Was down to the train station. Many people going different places – reminded me of peace time in the States. We had a safe journey to Rankam last night. Received your June 12th letter Saturday just before going to Czechoslovakia so did not have time to answer it. [...] I believe the last letter I wrote you was while I was in charge of the German Military Hospital of Oberroning, Germany. We had German & white Russian POWs as patients. The Russians were in bad shape. Last full day I was there I helped dig a grave for a number of them. I have since come back to the company which is located in Rankam, a small village.*

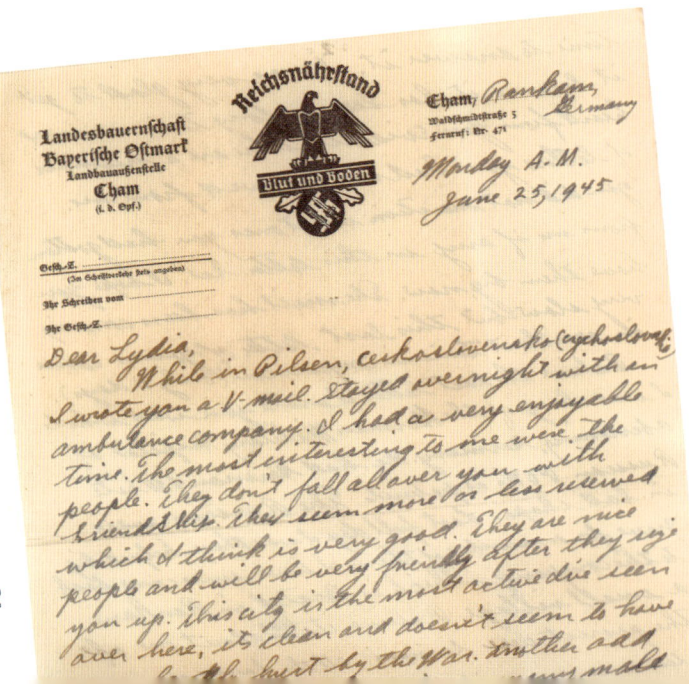

VIII - VICTORY SUMMER 1945

KILLING THE BOREDOM

One of the missions of the Army of Occupation is protecting German civilians and former prisoners of war, and it's not an easy task. The latter sometimes feel threatened by Allied soldiers traumatized by their experiences on the front, who now find themselves with too much time on their hands. Among the civilians' guardian angels is a corporal in a former Anti-Aircraft Artillery battalion who served in North Africa, Italy and Southern France: *"We are no longer AAA boys, we are SP. It stands for Security Police. We look after the people and prisoners etc. We are something like MPs, but we don't take care of traffic. But we keep an eye on the GIs so they don't harm the forced labor which were brought here by the Germans. This job is sure keeping us fellows very busy."* He writes again a month later: *"Darling, I'm having my hands full nowadays with these SS prisoners which we're now guarding. [...] I'm no longer with the 108th [Anti-Aircraft Artillery Gun Battalion]. I'm now with the 141st. As you know all of us fellows in the ETO were all put into different outfits according to the amount of points they have... So in that case we were put into an outfit which had men with the same number of points. [...] Boy, doesn't a thing like that make a fellow mad. For the simple reason it was us fellows which made the 108th make history in the army books. So now it is going home with other fellows just because they have a few more points than we have. There is [sic] only 27 men of the original gang going home with the 108th, because they have children so now they have over 85 points to go home. You know darling, the army always tries to do things to make the men disgusted."*

Lieutenant Richey (US Army Air Forces) writes to his wife at the desk of a German officer in April 1945.

Believe it has about one of the poorest-class Germans – all the houses are more or less run down and ill kept or very old. The house we live in is the opposite – naturally built by Hitler's click or authority. In fact this house is very nice having all the modern conveniences. It was a home for SS children – has miniature stools, low wash bowls, shallow swim place, sand box etc. Looks like a rustic hunting lodge from outside appearance. [...] Yes, I have more free time, now. Play ball once in a while, pull guard and dispensary duties, 24 hours each. We will be having a sightseeing trip now and then while we are not busy. May get more patients to handle and perhaps have to take over some more hospitals. Our company is in category 'T' which is the Army of Occupation which may be here from 6 months to 2 years. However, this does not mean I will remain here that long. If I am lucky, I may go home soon. I have enough points and 409s and 861s – Medical and Surgical technicians – are no longer considered essential. All I am sweating now is the transportation problem, so the paper says. I grow more anxious each day. I am sure I will make it before Christmas, tho'. It cannot be too soon till I am able to see you again. It is my desire to see and talk with Lydia who has been swell in writing me during the long and dangerous months over here. July 3 will make me 4 years in the Army and August will make me 3 years overseas. What a life. If it were not for God and happiness in my heart I do not know what would have become of me. I will be ever so happy when I return for good."

Marvin would soon set sail from Le Havre with his company and arrive in New York on November 13, 1945, along with 1,936 other soldiers returning from Europe.

Original shirt of an American corporal from SHAEF, bearing a late model of the shoulder patch designed by Eisenhower. Formerly black, symbolizing Nazi oppression, its background was changed to blue in July 1945 to represent peace. On top is the sword of liberation, "burning with the fire of justice", and a rainbow composed of the colors of the Allied flags. The American units in Berlin added a 'Berlin' label in 1951. Maintaining order in occupied Germany, this soldier wears the black armband of the Military Police.

While waiting for their return home, Allied soldiers go sightseeing and collect souvenirs. American Sergeant Theodore Beekman, who ended the war with the 100th Infantry Division, took the opportunity to visit Southern Italy and Southern Germany. In addition to local currency and stamps featuring Hitler's face, he brought back a camera and a German-made Walther pistol (as shown by this SHAEF authorization in the middle) to the United States.

VIII - VICTORY SUMMER 1945

Boredom and the temptation to celebrate victory with excess end up creating embarrassing situations for the officers, who're trying their best to handle their men. A lieutenant in an artillery unit attached to the American 83rd Infantry Division writes to his family just three days after VE-Day: *"Our battery played a game of baseball against the medics of a nearby field hospital. It was so very hot that the boys were weak from the heat. We lost after a very good showing. I have forgotten the score. I got to see some American nurses from a distance. If I had been alone I would have gotten more interested. [...] The rumors are all good and to listen to some there is a boat in Antwerp for us to catch as soon as we can get the orders. Some of the men have enough points to get out on and they are beginning to wonder how soon it takes effect. Now the officers are wondering how they can get out. If the same point system is used for us, I have sixty one and it takes eighty five to even be considered. [...] Remember the cook that we had trouble with back in Luxembourg? Well he has given us trouble again. I think I may have mentioned that he went on a tear and tried to shoot up a couple of the men. Well it seems that cooks go bad when they get drunk. One of the new men we got in back in Neuss on the Rhine has been giving us a little trouble and on VE-Day he got drunk and didn't show up for battery duty, so he was busted to a private. The next day Colonel Smith saw him out after curfew and tried to stop him and confined him to quarters without a guard. This morning he was not in them with the result that he really has gotten himself into a mess. He will have to put in at least a year and forfeit all pay and allowances and be dishonorably discharged. That is the price of some liquor. What a wonderful object lesson it will make for a temperance lesson."*

WAITING AT 'LUCKY STRIKE'

Richard belongs to the 89th Infantry Division. Having arrived in Le Havre on January 24, 1945, his regiment spent the month of February at Camp Lucky Strike, not far from the harbor. It then headed for Frankfurt and afterwards Koblenz, before crossing the Rhine on March 25. In April, Richard liberated a German factory in Seebach where 4,630 Russian and Ukrainian female prisoners were forced to manufacture bomb detonators. Meanwhile, the rest of the division discovered the horror of the Ohrdruf camp (part of Buchenwald) on April 4 – the very first concentration camp liberated by American troops. Richard and his comrades soon resumed their eastward progression towards the Mulde River and Czechoslovakia. When VE-Day finally came, he was sent back to France and the Lucky Strike transit camp, where he'd first entered Europe. Located near the sea between Fécamp and Dieppe, and only 20 miles from the port of Le Havre, Lucky Strike is the largest military base in Europe in 1945.

Built in September 1944 on a former German airfield, the camp covers more than 600 hectares and is part of the Normandy Assembly Area (NAA), along with various other camps named after popular cigarette brands. Although the men don't stay there for long, Lucky Strike is the main point of entry and exit for Allied soldiers in Europe and sometimes shelters up to 100,000 people. In addition to a hospital and an airfield, it's a real American city with shops, bars, a church, shows, and even its own ice cream factory!

The 89th Division is now in charge of welcoming the troops passing through the camp. Richard tells his mother: *"We left Elgersburg, Germany, May 27, arriving at Camp Lucky Strike June 2. It was quite a surprise. We expected to be stepping aboard 'the boat' at Le Havre. Our job since that time has been to process outfits that ARE going to step aboard the boat. The next thing we knew, we were being inactivated here. Inactivation consists of the transfer of most of the personnel in the outfit, and a subsequent replacement of this personnel. We were told that after the inactivated 89th reached the States, it would be deactivated – complete breaking up of the outfit. This would be done by the simple expedient of discharge. Meanwhile these men would carry on with the job of processing. Now, we don't know where we stand. Some General has thrown in a recommendation that the 89th remain intact. Out of 40 divisions committed at the same time the 89th stands head and shoulders above the rest on the record. I was talking with the Captain, the other night. He is all broken up over the breaking up of his company. I never saw a man change as he has done. He has a real affection for his men. He admitted last night that 'one' learned a great deal about men over here. He used to be the kind that said, 'a man who won't wear a tie will be careless in combat'. He has learned differently.*

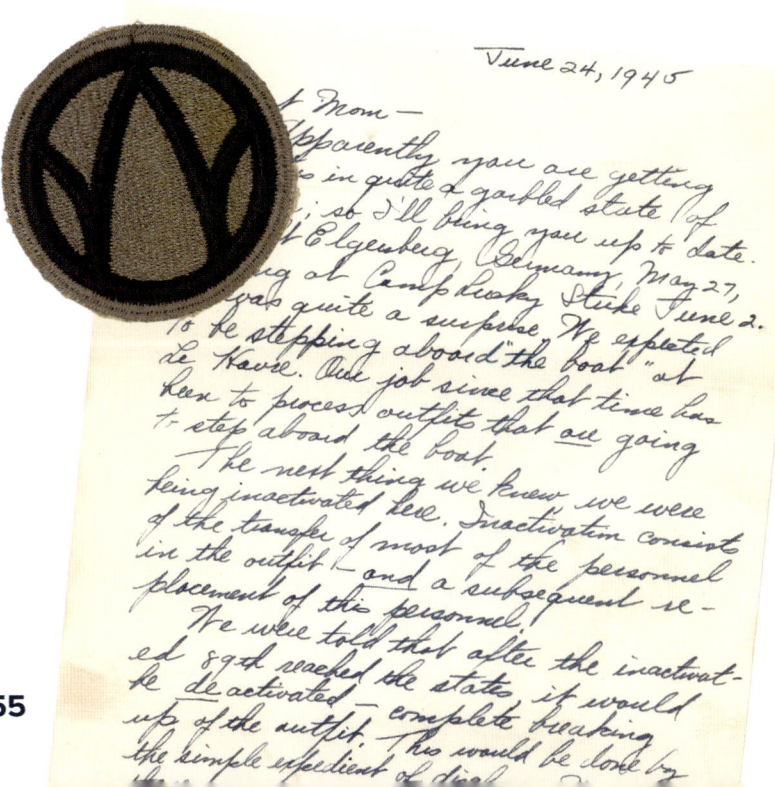

The day I first arrived at Camp Butner, I was a mess. I had ridden in a hot, dusty, sooty mail train that took from 8:00 am on day to 2:00 am the next day to get from Washington DC, to Durham, NC. All I had were the clothes I had arrived in. They were a part of me, and I was a part of them. The Captain had looked me up and down and had immediately formed an opinion of me – bad. He admitted last night that he had thought 'what kind of a joker is this?' Among other things, he asked me what kind of an outfit I'd like to go to – not that he could do anything about it (he's tried with a lot of fellows). I told him I'd like to go to school, he laughed. Anyhow, everything is now in a jumble. Men have been frozen in the outfit, but replacements come in anyway. Today the company strength soared from 187 to over 250! The general consensus of opinion is that we'll be back in the States before September."

Not having enough points to return home, Richard thinks about working as a journalist for the army. He learns French and questions the outfits leaving Europe about their journey through the war, in order to help write their stories for posterity. He soon finds a new position he loves: hosting a show on the camp radio. On June 18, after discussing current events and his division (whose emblem is a W in an O, as seen on the shoulder patch on the previous page), he closes his broadcast in the following manner: *"And so until tomorrow evening, this is Pfc. Dick H. asking if there is anyone who does not wonder if the inactivation of the 89th means not only the end of the Rolling W, but also the beginning of the Crawling Double-X".*

Robert Chenier, of the 8th Air Force, finally returned to Glens Falls, NY, after three years of service in Europe. With his field-made patch sewn with real silver thread, he kept his train ticket home, paid for by the army, as a souvenir.

THINKING ABOUT THE FUTURE

On August 18, 1945, a British civilian working for the Army writes to a friend and experienced surgeon in the 2nd New Zealand Division, who was still stationed in Italy: *"Dear Capt. H., [...] I have received a letter from the British Embassy in Prague this morning stating that the message was delivered and acknowledged by Miss H. You have certainly had a long separation and I hope things will go well for you both in the future. I wonder if you will be returning to this country. I had a letter from Major Caughley a few days ago and he had been on a wonderful 10 days tour of the Continent – the sort of thing that would have cost a fortune in peace time. Well, it is all over now, though the reconstruction is a terrific business and I only hope we are able to keep the spirit that has won the war going through this period. I personally can't get into a mood of rowdy rejoicing – have seen far too much of the tragedy of the last six years. I was lucky enough to have a ticket for the Thanksgiving Service in St. Paul's yesterday – it was a great occasion attended by the King and Queen, numerous Royalties and all the Diplomatic Corps. I am now anxiously waiting news of a young cousin who was caught with his Regiment in the fall of Hong Kong [1941] – we have only had one postcard since then so hope he is still alive – one wonders."*

Jack is a paratrooper in the Service Company of the 508th Parachute Infantry Regiment, 82nd Airborne Division. He joined the Army in February 1943 at the age of 19. He writes in August 1945 from Frankfurt – where the unit serves as Eisenhower's honor guard – to his parents in California: *"I'll give you a very brief summary of the things that have been happening since or rather during the past few weeks. The first, and the one of most importance, was when Sgt. Eyestone (Transport Sergeant) went home on points. This definitely left us shorthanded. According to the Army, no one man is indispensable, in the motor pool's estimation this is a gross understatement. [...] When one Corporal goes the duties seem to double up on us. You can guess by what I have already said that the peace-time army (that's a laugh) isn't exactly a picnic. But enough about this boring daily routine.*

Mom, I don't know where you got the idea that the points have been lowered to 50, because you were definitely misinformed. To date the points still stand at 85, however in the near future they will be lowered to 80, then to 75 and on down. Up to May 12 I have credit for 63 actual points, with my Purple Heart, I have 68, and judging from the latest reports I will lose my points for that, because I wasn't hospitalized. It seems as though being wounded isn't enough. They want you to be in the hospital for at least two months. I still haven't heard the last word on this so I can say I have 68 points with a question mark after it? However according to the Stars & Stripes, *'all men, who will not be in the Occupation forces will be home before Spring'. I will say that*

VIII - VICTORY SUMMER 1945

I won't be home by X-Mas, and I am quite sure of this. Nothing is definite so don't believe everything you hear or read. This place is full of rumors, so we disregard all rumors.

As for Ray [a woman he met in Europe, probably serving in a female branch of the army] and I, all I have along this line is bad news. We have had so much trouble getting together, that it is ceasing to be funny. In fact, in this regard, along with numerous others, we are definitely fed up with the British and American Armies. Ray was moved three weeks ago from Brussels to Oostend, Belgium. Then last week they moved her to Calais, France. I have been through all kinds of channels to get transportation to see her but all I received for my troubles was a very polite but a definite no. [...] As for my post war plans, I'm afraid that I will be quite a dependent. I have always had to depend upon my family, and it seems like being 21 and supposedly a man, I will have to continue in this status. I want to go on the farm, but if I do, I want at least one years college training. With no experience in farming, all I will be is a liability. The Army will finance my schooling, so nothing will be lost in this respect. I think this will be the best plan." The 508th PIR will go home on November 9, 1946. By this time, Jack would've been waiting for his departure at the Sissonne camp (France) since January 1 of the same year.

For his part, a Canadian artilleryman from the 1st Division already has a plan for the future. He writes to a friend: *"Only recently was I declared unfit for frontline duty anymore, so for the present I'm sitting away back here in Base, with lots of time to write those letters, neglected for so long. I'm in excellent health and spirits and I write with a very sincere wish that you are so, but with much finer circumstances to work under* [his friend is a school teacher in Canada]. *After two and a half years in Blighty, I came out here via Tunisia, with the first assault in July '43 and have, very fortunately, been with my original Battery continuously, until a rather rotten break occurred when we made the 'Push' from Cassino to Rome and the North. [...]*

We're all enjoying a hitherto forbidden fruit – thinking of our return home. I don't mind saying, Tom, it will look good to me, nearly 4 years absent. But, really, where my curiosity is bothering me, is in speculation about the future and the teaching profession in particular. As you may realize, many of us have already enlisted in the 'return-to-college' plan for rehabilitation and my service allows 4 years of such training. However, before planning along those lines, I would like some first-hand information, as to prospects and possibilities, from one who knows. I would deeply appreciate any help you could forward, because quite frankly, my whole life seems to be filled with such things as rations, ammunition, guns, barrages, targets and allied details and quite incapable of judging for myself on civilian matters."

For those who don't have the 'chance' of being declared unfit for duty, war must go on. The Anglo-Canadians expect to be shipped to Burma, and the Americans to the Pacific. James had landed in North Africa with the 2nd Armored Division in 1942, then served in Sicily, Normandy, Belgium and Germany. On April 29, 1945, seeing the war in Europe coming to an end, he wrote to his sweetheart: *"I hate to even think of going to the Pacific, it would just kill me. After being over here for over two long years, well I just couldn't take it. I find myself going nuts now, I get up in the morning to find myself pulling out my hair one at a time. The thought of being away from you for another two years, would be murder in itself. If I should go to the Pacific there is nothing I can do but go, but for God sake let me go home for a while anyway. Is that asking too much? If I should go there, there is but one thing left for us to do, and that is forget that we ever knew each other, and if something like this should happen it would be better for us both. I don't expect any girl to wait that long for anyone, yes even if their love is so strong that they are willing."*

Many units are preparing to leave again for the other side of the world, but fortunately, none of them will see combat there. Before their arrival or during the crossing, an unexpected event will mean the end of the Second World War for everyone.

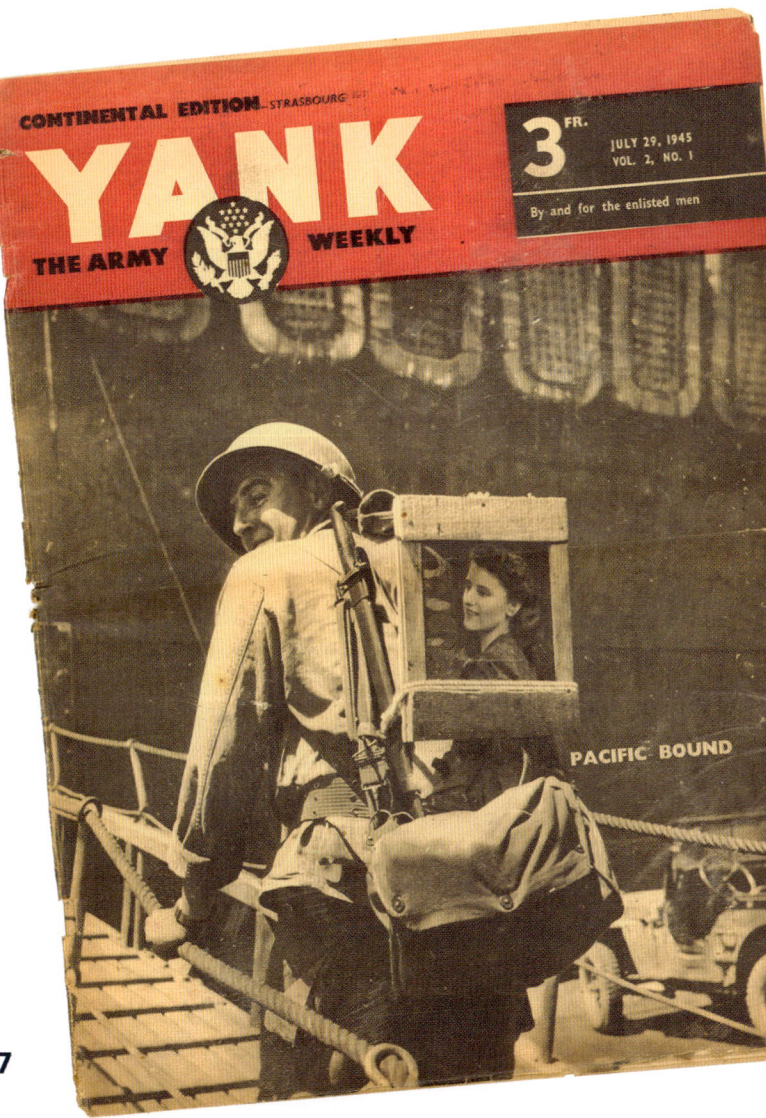

HARRISON FORRESTER

C Company, 48th Armored Infantry Battalion, 7th Armored Division

Having led an armored infantry company since landing in Normandy and being decorated multiple times for bravery in battle, Harrison isn't sure if or when he'll go home. As he watches his men leave for the United States, he expects to be shipped to the Pacific…

Harrison Smith 'Hassie' Forrester was born on February 16, 1918, in Georgia (United States). He earned a bachelor's degree in architectural science in South Carolina before enlisting in the Army as a 2nd lieutenant shortly after Pearl Harbor. In 1944, Harrison was a captain commanding C Company of the 48th Armored Infantry Battalion (7th Armored Division). He landed on Utah Beach on August 9 and traveled through Normandy to the Seine, leading the assault on its north bank on the 23rd. He experienced fierce fighting near Paris and then in Metz in September, which earned him not one but two prestigious Silver Star medals.

FROM HEROIC ACT TO HEROIC ACT

His first Silver Star citation (actions from August 14 to September 1) states: *"In the sweeping advance of the 7th Armored Division across France, Captain Forrester continuously led his Company in daring and successful forays against the enemy. On 15 August he personally led his unit in the capture of Tremblay without a single casualty to the company, although the town was strongly defended by machine guns and infantry troops. His superior leadership and sound tactics were also evident on 22 August, when he led his company in a frontal assault on Chevannes* [west of Melun]*, and captured two 88mm guns, one Mark IV tank, one 20mm gun and numerous automatic weapons and small arms. Again, on 29 August, he demonstrated his skillful employment of troops when he led two platoons into the town of Chaumuzy* [southwest of Reims]*, after driving out numerous Mark IV tanks and killing or capturing a large number of infantrymen. Captain Forrester's cool and courageous leadership inspired his men to successfully achieve difficult and dangerous objectives with a minimum loss of life."*

His second citation for a Silver Star wasn't long in coming and was for the capture of Marieulles (6 miles southwest of Metz) on September 18, 1944: *"The town was defended by approximately 500 infantry troops and numerous strategically emplaced anti-tank guns and automatic weapons. All approaches to the town were devoid of good cover and were accurately 'zeroed in' by heavy artillery to the north and east. Three times within 36 hours the battalion essayed an attack, but each time it was repulsed with heavy losses. With morale at its lowest point, Captain Forrester determinedly rallied his company and personally led his men in a fourth assault on the defenses of the town. By his courageous leadership and complete contempt for danger, he inspired his men to follow him through heavy artillery fire and take the town. Approximately 250 enemy troops were killed and a hundred captured in the course of the battle."*

Two days after this second feat of arms, Harrison received a German machine gun bullet in the thigh on September 20.

VIII - VICTORY SUMMER 1945

After his hospitalization, he returned to his company in Belgium on January 2, 1945, and led the recapture of Saint-Vith at the end of the month, where the fighting claimed many victims. In early March, when the battalion was supporting the 9th Infantry Division near Dottendorf (Germany), Harrison was wounded a second time, receiving a piece of shrapnel in the eye, but wasn't evacuated. Cities fell one after the other and prisoners multiplied.

Harrison (second from left) and his men.

Led by a brave officer, Harrison's company also included other outstanding heroes, one of whom, Corporal Thomas J. Kelly, was even awarded the Medal of Honor. Harrison testifies: *"My Company was attacking a small German village, and I had held back the first platoon before sending them up toward some woods to clear out some snipers who were holding up the other boys. Kelly was with the first platoon. Just before the men reached the woods two tanks spotted them and cut loose... while they were still in the open. Machine guns opened up on them, seventeen men were hit and went down, the rest of the group, Kelly among them, got back to the gully. But after a minute, Kelly said he was going back. I didn't know what he was up to, but I saw him go out. I watched him go along the wide-open field that had no more cover than a marble topped table. Little puffs of machine gun fire danced around his feet. After leading seven blinded men out of the line of fire Kelly returned ten times, each time bringing a wounded soldier down the hill, all the while under constant fire."* The town was secured the following day, at the cost of eight killed and thirty-two wounded (including fourteen seriously wounded) in Harrison's company.

NO REST FOR THE BRAVE

At the end of the war the battalion is in Badow (Germany), where it stays from May 5 to 20, 1945. During this period, it deals with 2,000 German prisoners, 5,000 civilian refugees and 100 Allied prisoners of war. The battalion then resumes its drive through Germany, gathering more and more prisoners along the way, before C Company finishes its race in Lobnitz in June. On the agenda: patrols, physical exercise and softball. Harrison writes to his wife on May 24: *"Well, yesterday Stars & Stripes came out with the news that really put a stop to any illusion I had of getting a furlough home – no more rotation to the States... Only those officers and men who are getting discharged or being redeployed via the States are getting home now under the present policy effective on 31 May... Hope to hell the policy changes, otherwise I'll be here indefinitely, or as long as my outfit remains... Even compassionate cases can't go home on rotation under the present policy... Lt. Good, one of my platoon leaders, has received confirmation through the Red Cross that his 7 months old daughter, which he has never seen, is suffering with a serious heart ailment and asthma; furthermore, the baby specialist says that death can be expected at any time... Even with this I doubt if there's even the faintest hope of him getting a furlough. I'm still working on it though.*

Harrison inspecting his troops in Germany, shortly after the end of the war. Only the helmet's liner is worn, the heavy steel shell being no longer necessary.

Incidentally, I hate to mention it, but should anything serious happen that would cause you to have to notify me immediately, be sure that you do so through your local Red Cross chapter instead of by telegram. They will of course notify me by telegraph after their investigation and verification – this will always save up to two weeks' time and often a month. [...] Sgt. Hobson has come back from furlough – he hasn't arrived yet, but is still at higher headquarters – I've sent for him, so he should arrive at any minute – I'm dying to see the old rascal... He had enough points to keep from him coming back but being an old army man, I guess he volunteered, the damn fool... At this particular time it's really 25th May and I was only able to complete two sentences yesterday having been stopped cold by an inventory of all organizational and personal equipment which was suddenly thrown in my lap simultaneously with an announcement that my supply sergeant was leaving immediately for the States to be discharged – so in addition to my numerous other duties I find that I'm also supply sergeant. [...]

Four hours later (after many interruptions): I am now playing bridge and writing at the same time – we just started, but from the looks of the first hand it doesn't look like I'm going to win. If this is a sample of what I'm going to be getting the rest of the night – one king and that's all. We were supposed to have a movie tonight but the damn projector broke before it even got started. Naturally everyone left the theater when it broke and now they just phoned that it's fixed again – it'll break again – it always does; so I won't go back again. The 'old man' and Bob Herntzman went to visit the Russians this afternoon. I was supposed to have gone but things didn't work out. They say that those Russians really throw quite a feast, not to mention beaucoup vodka... Oh well, I guess I saved myself a headache and indigestion. I'll just save my eating and drinking until I can have you along with it, OK?"

In July, C Company is relieved by the Red Army and moves to Eberstadt. The battalion conducts various 'raids' (*Operation Tallyho*) in search of SS soldiers hidden among civilians. On July 10 they arrest five SS troopers, several Nazi leaders and many former soldiers who haven't received a formal discharge. At the same time, the battalion is training for a possible deployment to the Pacific, with about 100 men being transferred to the 1st Armored Division to be sent to Japan.

On August 21, 1945, there are only 350 GIs left in the entire battalion, with many soldiers and officers being sent back to the United States. This is eventually the case for Captain Harrison Forrester, who now has 110 points thanks to his many medals. The division will eventually head for the United States in October and be deactivated there. Harrison will resume his work in architecture until his death on July 9, 2006.

BEFORE PEACE, THE PACIFIC

As they approach Japan, the Allies suffer terrifying losses in the Pacific islands and the soldiers in Europe are expected to land there to fill the ranks. The battles for Iwo Jima and Okinawa in particular are extremely bloody, and to avoid the scheduled invasion of Japan itself in November 1945, the new American President Harry S. Truman will make a decision that will change the world forever.

[It may seem irrelevant to talk about the Pacific War in this book, which primarily focuses on Western Europe, but the outcome of these seemingly distant battles will have a radical impact on the future of Europe, as will be seen later.]

CATASTROPHIC BEGINNINGS

Beaten by their non-commissioned officers to harden them up during training and indoctrinated from childhood to believe in their 'divine race' and in the fact that there's no greater honor than to die on the battlefield, Japanese soldiers are formidable fighters. Following the attack on Pearl Harbor, the Allies suffered a long series of defeats. In British Malaysia, Singapore fell on February 15, 1942, leading to the capture of 80,000 British, Indian and Australian prisoners of war and marking the greatest surrender in Commonwealth military history. The Japanese and their Thai allies also took control of the Dutch Indies and French Indochina. American forces resisted in the Philippines until May 8, 1942, when another 80,000 soldiers were captured. Around 12,300 Filipino and American prisoners died during the 'death march' of April 9, 1942, after three months of fighting for the province of Bataan on the island of Luzon. General Douglas MacArthur, Supreme Allied Commander in the Southwest Pacific, was forced to withdraw to Australia.

Like the Nazis, the Japanese would be responsible for the deaths of millions of non-combatant personnel and prisoners of war (more than 27% of the latter would die in captivity, a percentage seven times higher than the mortality rate in German and Italian camps). There were even reports of cannibalism committed by their Japanese jailers, and hundreds of thousands of Chinese civilians and Allied prisoners would be used as guinea pigs for various medical experiments and chemical or biological weapons testing (plague, typhoid, anthrax, cholera etc.).

THE TABLES TURN IN 1942

This long series of setbacks for the Allies, similar to the one they experienced at the same time in other parts of the world, ended in the summer of 1942. For the Americans, the Battle of Midway was the equivalent of El Alamein for the British or Stalingrad for the Soviets. Here, the US Navy inflicted heavy losses on the Japanese fleet between June 4 and 7, 1942. Convinced they were trapping the Americans, the Japanese fell into an ambush that cost them four aircraft carriers (which had taken part in the attack on Pearl Harbor six months earlier) and a heavy cruiser that would prove irreplaceable.

At the end of 1942, the Allies took the upper hand and began a long campaign to liberate the Pacific Islands one by one, as they moved towards Japan. While the Australians were fighting to fend off the Japanese advance in New Guinea, in August 1942 the Americans landed around 16,000 men from the US Marine Corps (US Navy infantrymen, whose presence in Europe was anecdotal) and US Army soldiers at Guadalcanal (Solomon Islands).

After six bloody months in the jungle at the mercy of booby-traps, snipers and 'Banzai' charges, the Americans finally took control of 'Henderson Field' airfield. In June 1943, *Operation Cartwheel* was launched to isolate the Japanese forward base at Rabaul and implement Admiral Chester Nimitz's 'Leapfrogging' idea, which involved bypassing the most defended islands and making small 'hops' towards Japan. A Marine in the 1st Division describes a typical island in a letter: *"It is mighty hot out here, then all of a sudden it will rain like hell. We have coconuts, rain, mud knee deep, and plenty of work."*

1st Marine Division service uniform.
The outfit's victory at Guadalcanal made it so popular that its shoulder patch bears the name of the island.

FROM ISLAND TO ISLAND

Arthur was among the men who dropped off soldiers and marines on the beaches. A former teacher, he became a US Navy lieutenant manning a landing craft attached to USS *Knox* (APA-46). Arthur had already participated in the following operations: the Mariana Islands (capture and occupation of Saipan, July 15-23, 1944), Tinian (July 24-28, 1944), Leyte (landings of October 20 and November 18, 1944) and Luzon (landings in the Lingayen Gulf, January 9, 1945). The US military had made significant progress since 1941 and as it approached Japan, fighting was becoming increasingly fierce. In a letter dated February 4, 1945, written on the atoll where he rested before participating in the Iwo Jima invasion, Arthur talked about his sadness at having spent Christmas and New Year's Day away from his family, although his brother, a Marine, was fighting nearby. So far, he'd been rather lucky, but this wasn't the case for several of Arthur's former students, who were killed in action. He wrote to a former colleague:

"What a heavenly day... and in what a helluva place. Thank the good lord for the mail or I know the devil would have had me by the coat tail. [...] The news concerning my own welfare is very brief due to the censors' efforts to make it such. However, I'm getting saltier everyday [...] This is a forsaken place... The worst yet. We are restricted to one atoll for recreation and the thing has already become a graveyard... of beer cans (the Americans will leave their mark... beer cans on every Pacific atoll). [...] Now we have lettuce, apples, oranges, celery, grapefruit etc. aboard. It's wonderful – but it wasn't so good for some 6 weeks that I can recall... We even had to extricate the weevils from the rice. This life is tough on the boys and do they long for the good old States. But I'm afraid it's going to be a while. We are optimistic though very much, and we think nothing of trespassing or humiliating one's dignity. It is not all without a hot foot or a nervous nature's reaction subjecting your safety, but we manage. They say all the world's a stage, and all its people merely actors. Yes and no... here the plays are all tragedies; they can be dramatic, but it isn't what the actor would want it to be. My mind goes berserk with the fanatical display of playing the hero role. You get over it... with sweat, blood and tears!"

American landing crafts carrying the first assault wave on Luzon, Lingayen Gulf, on January 9, 1945.

This Japanese flag was picked up as a souvenir from a corpse at a Japanese stronghold on Bougainville Island by American soldier Pat McDermott. According to him, *"the stains are blood and holes bullet holes"*.
'Buun Chokyu' at the top of the flag means *"May your military fortune be eternal!"* The name Fukuo Fujita (the big letters on the right) refers to the owner of the flag. Handwritten all around the red circle are the names of the soldier's family and friends. It was forbidden to mention your unit on this type of flag in order not to give intelligence to the enemy, but Fukuo Fujita was probably part of the 17th Japanese Army. The fighting for Bougainville lasted from November 1943 to the end of August 1945, when the last pocket of resistance finally fell. Above, Marine Raiders (US Marine Special Forces Unit) in the Bougainville jungle.

Typical uniform of a 4th Marine Division infantryman on Iwo Jima. This Marine uses the 'beach' side of his reversible helmet cover and wears the HBT P41 shirt and pants.

The shirt belonged to at least three different Marines (and was probably reused later in Korea): McNight, McElhenny and Wood.

On his back, the Marine carries a USMC field pack, also marked with the names of four Marines: Yeadon, Lombard, Doetsch and Tighe. On it are attached a camouflaged waterproof poncho and an old army shovel.

The USMC cross-flap canteen belonged to Marine Winfield R. Carlisle, 4th Engineer Battalion, 4th Marine Division, who fought in Kwajalein, Saipan and Tinian, where he was wounded on August 1, 1944. Nevertheless, he returned to his unit, and was on Iwo Jima in February 1945.

364

VIII - VICTORY SUMMER 1945

Operation Detachment started on February 19, 1945 on the volcanic island of Iwo Jima. Tasked with capturing three Japanese airfields (in order to use them to attack Japan), the Marines of the 3rd, 4th and 5th Divisions fought their way from the black sandy beaches to the Japanese galleries and pillboxes scattered over the 8-square-mile island. For the first time in the Pacific War, American casualties (killed and wounded) exceeded those of the Japanese. On Iwo Jima, the enemy fought with incredible fanaticism: of the 21,000 Japanese soldiers present at the beginning of the battle, only 216 were taken prisoner, often because they were too seriously wounded to resist capture. The others were all killed in action, committed suicide, or died of exhaustion in their bunkers. Some launched Banzai charges, faithful to the Gyokusai ideology (death rather than the dishonor of being taken prisoner), which along with the Bushido samurai code and propaganda equating the American soldier to a merciless animal, discouraged any attempt to surrender. On March 26, when the island was at last secured, 6,821 Marines had died in one month and 19,217 others were wounded.

In his letter of April 6, 1945, written shortly after the end of the battle of Iwo Jima, Arthur recounted the hell of the landings he was finally allowed to write about: *"You know, Hitler boasts that his troops in Italy are well seasoned fighters. They should be. Look at the peppering they are getting! For an old professor I guess I have come a long way too and am not entirely immune to peppering. I only hope that I continue to duck when I shouldn't be getting too darn curious. I guess I told you that my first real action was at Luzon... It was a thrilling orientation and I proved a good steady head under fire as I landed my wave... the 5th to hit the shores off Lingayen. It was a great day. Previous to that I had been at Pearl Harbor, the Marshall Islands (Majuro and Kwajalein), Los Negros and Manus Islands, New Britain, New Guinea, Leyte, Ulethia, Guam... then that rough party at Iwo Jima which you have undoubtedly read about. Iwo was really rough and for anyone to brag that he wasn't scared as hell would be a good liar. When you see those rockets and mortars take off in your direction you just wonder where to go. There is no answer but luck and fortune."*

The helmet cover of the US Marine Corps is reversible in order to adapt to different terrains (seen here on the 'jungle' side). This helmet's liner is stenciled with the name of its owner, Danley.

OKINAWA: THE LAST BATTLE

Jerry is in the 3008th Quartermaster Graves Registration Company, recovering the bodies of the combatants, often in the middle of the fighting, to identify and bury them in temporary cemeteries. He served in the Philippines before participating in the enormous landing on Okinawa, one of the last islands before Japan. It was the largest amphibious assault of the Pacific War and one of its deadliest battles. Attached to the 7th Infantry Division of the US Army, Jerry landed on Okinawa on April 1, 1945. The first few days were relatively easy and the northern part of the island was soon taken. He wrote to a friend on April 9, from *"Okinawa Shima, Japan"*:

"Sorry I haven't been able to answer your letter of March 4, any sooner as I have been doing a little traveling since I last wrote you. There I am now only about 325 miles from the southern tip of Japan. A little less than 2 hours from Tokyo by air. Getting pretty close to the Jap home land. I don't know just what the newspapers have reported about this operation, but I know very little about it even though I am here at the scene of action. One thing I know is that it isn't as tough as the invasion of the Philippines. We have had only one good air raid and several alerts when nothing came over. It looks to me as though the Japs have nothing left to throw at us of any importance. Their fleet is practically wiped out and they don't send any planes in great numbers over, so they can't have much left. I have been over a lot of this island and if they had put up a good fight here it would have been a lot tougher than it is. This island is strictly Japanese and has been always under Jap influence. The civilians are harmless and seem to want to be friends. Several Jap soldiers have been found to be dressed in women's clothing, but they are soon found out and captured. Some of them are pretty tough looking.

The essential jungle aid kit for the Marine or US soldier in the Pacific, from left to right: first aid bandage, powder for 'body-crawling insects', water purification tablets and insecticide bottle.

When we first arrived here the civilians that were found were put into enclosures but so many of them were coming out of the hills that they were all turned loose to return to what is left of their homes. It seems a shame that their homes have been destroyed but any building here is a potential stronghold for the enemy and has to be gotten rid of. I have seen a few civilians and they all bow from the waist in friendly recognition. That is Jap custom. They are very poor people and have such ancient methods of cultivation in their rice paddies. They live in wood houses of thatched or tile roofs, with either stone walls or a lot of trees around their houses because of being in a typhoon belt at certain times of the year. There are fairly decent roads which we are using, and the fleas are wicked. I think I have more of them on me than all the dogs at home. The mosquitoes are as bad, even though it is quite dry here at this time of year. The number of ships that was here on D-Day is unbelievable. Largest convoy yet in the history of the US. I never knew of so many in my life. The Navy deserves a lot of credit on this operation."

Only when they reached the limestone hills and caves in the heart of the island did the soldiers and marines encounter more sustained resistance. The Japanese launched their first counter-offensive on all fronts on the evening of April 12. The fighting was extremely violent, and the Battle of Okinawa lasted until the evening of June 21, totaling eighty-two days. At sea, kamikazes crashed their precious planes into the American fleet on purpose, killing 3,048 sailors and sinking 29 ships. The Americans suffered colossal losses and Jerry therefore had a lot of work: 12,281 Americans were killed on the island, plus more than 82,000 wounded, many of whom would inflate the number of deaths in the days and even months to come. As for the Japanese, they resisted with their usual determination and the Allies would thus count 110,071 enemies killed in action or by suicide.

In addition to this appalling number there were tens of thousands of civilians, men and women, who were forced by the Japanese to fend off the invader, or who volunteered to die for their Emperor Hiro Hito. Roger visited the island at the end of the battle and wrote on July 22: *"As we rode farther south, we began to see evidences of the battle. At one point about six medium tanks were strewn across a field also several smaller Jap tanks. The terrain was much too rough for tanks and they weren't used to much advantage. You could easily tell where the heavy fighting had started. Almost along an even line the trees became leafless and the ground pitted with shell craters. [...] I don't believe anything could be so leveled as Shuri [Castle]. The driver pointed out where the palace and castle had been – just a mass of rubble, there is not one structure standing or the shell of it..."*

DOWNFALL

August 1945. Now that the war in Europe is over, the Allies can commit all their forces for the final blow to Japan. The island of Okinawa would thus be used as the starting point for *Operation Downfall*, scheduled for November. The largest armada ever assembled is supposed to hit the shores in two separate invasions: *Operation Olympic* on November 1, 1945, on Kyushu (the South Island), then *Operation Coronet*, an even more colossal landing, scheduled for March 1946, near Tokyo. The latter would allow the capture of the main island of Honshu. Learning from what they'd witnessed on Iwo Jima and Okinawa, the Allies plan to engage nearly 1.5 million soldiers, hundreds of warships and thousands of bombers in response to the kamikaze behavior of the Japanese, who'd stop at nothing to defend their territory. The Japanese plan to oppose them with 2.3 million experienced soldiers supported by a militia of 28 million civilians: the *Ketsu-go* defense plan.

VIII - VICTORY SUMMER 1945

Both sides have already calculated an estimate of future losses. Allied casualties are estimated to reach hundreds of thousands of men during the campaign. As the Americans had seen with their own eyes during their recent battles, Japanese civilians would be called upon to defend their emperor and their families in 'Volunteer Fighting Corps', armed with bamboo spears and suicide bombs against well-equipped GIs. The Japanese themselves estimate that their deaths would reach 20 million men and women. They know that the war is lost. Nothing separates the Allies from Japan anymore and the massive bombing campaign in the summer of 1945 alone killed a quarter of a million Japanese. Tokyo and many other cities were blown off the map with napalm, so much so that by August, American airmen had virtually no targets left.

The Japanese therefore try to negotiate an armistice, which would preserve the borders of their Empire and protect the Emperor from a war crimes trial – a proposal the new American President Harry S. Truman firmly rejects. When his offer of unconditional surrender goes unanswered and wishing to avoid the imminent disaster of *Operation Downfall*, Truman decides to use nuclear weapons, which had been developed in the greatest secrecy and whose existence he's only just learned about. Eager to show the world a demonstration of US strength, and even without being sure of its success and the low availability of enriched uranium meaning there would be no second chance, he orders the bomb to be dropped on a firm target, without warning.

"JAPS QUIT"

In 1939 German physicist Albert Einstein, who'd emigrated to the United States in 1933, warned Roosevelt that the Germans were about to acquire a formidable weapon based on the fission of the atom (commando raids in Norway to destroy a heavy water plant had made it possible to slow down their plans). The *Manhattan Project* outpaced the Reich's own project in 1942, but would put an end to another war when the uranium bomb 'Little Boy' strikes the city of Hiroshima on the morning of August 6, 1945. The surprise is total, even for the crew of the Boeing B-29 *Enola Gay* who didn't expect such a high level of devastation. Around 80,000 civilians are killed in the explosion, along with 20,000 soldiers of the 2nd Japanese Army, while thousands more are poisoned by the radiation.

Three days later, on August 9 and still without news of the Emperor, the Americans drop the plutonium bomb 'Fat Man' on Nagasaki. Nearly 70,000 civilians are added to the list of the first victims of the nuclear era.

However, despite the violence of the explosions and strong criticism towards the Americans for deliberately targeting civilians, the casualty levels don't reach those of the Battle of Okinawa and are even farther from the *Downfall* predictions: paradoxically, Truman is convinced that he's just saved thousands of lives, and the 600,000 Japanese civilians killed, most of them in 1945, are considered to be small when compared to the 20 to 50 million Asian civilians (more than half of them Chinese, but also Indians, Javanese, Indochinese...) who were killed during the imperial invasions.

A 60,000-foot-high cloud of smoke rises from the industrial center of Nagasaki. 'Fat Man' has just exploded.

Allies around the world are very enthusiastic when they hear the news. A sergeant in a B-29 bomber squadron writes on August 8 from Guam Island: *"Gee, but the news sounds good, and those Japs are worried about the new bomb that is the talk of the day around here and all over the world. I do hope it will get this war over with but quick. I want to get back to my precious one."* On Okinawa, a GI assigned to the 10th Army Transportation Section writes: *"We got the report yesterday on the Air Forces new atomic bomb. They say one bomb has the potentiality of 2000 B-29s fully loaded. It is almost impossible to comprehend that. Think of the effect it will have. We ought to be able to bomb Japan out of the war now. It is too bad that all that power has to be used to destroy & not to create!"* He adds the next day: *"We have just received word that Russia has declared war on Japan. What a blow that must be to the Japs coming on the heels of the atomic bomb. It most certainly will shorten the war. One of the fellas said, 'I am going right down and pack my barracks bag!' I hope it won't be long till we can do that tho'..."*

The Soviet invasion of Manchuria (decided at the Yalta Conference and involving more than 15 million soldiers) is indeed triggered at the same time and the Red Army crushes the imperial troops. It's all too much for the Japanese Empire, whose surrender is announced on August 15 and signed on September 2, 1945, putting a definitive end to the Second World War. However, the last Japanese soldier, hidden in the jungle and still loyal to the Emperor, wouldn't surrender until December 1974!

At the 'Rainbow Corner' of the Red Cross in Paris, these GIs can finally take a breath: the war is over!

Jeffrey is a sailor on the USS *Piedmont*, a support destroyer that served in the battles of Iwo Jima and Okinawa, among others. On August 14, 1945, when Japan accepted the terms of the Allied Peace Treaty, the ship was about to leave Eniwetok to take over the Japanese fleet. On the 28th, it first drops anchor at Sagami Wan, on Honshu Island, then enters Tokyo Bay two days later to dock at the Yokosuka naval base.

On August 30, Jeffrey writes to an American combat engineer in Europe: *"Well, we're really here. I never thought two years ago in high school, I'd wind up in Tokyo. We sailed into the Bay yesterday, the day of the first initial entry. Enclosed is an envelope with a cancellation stamp for that date as a souvenir. The Postman stamped a few for us yesterday for that purpose. They might be worth quite a bit back in the States in a couple years. We've really taken over everything. What a job. I'm glad there wasn't any opposition. We can see a good part of Yokosuka Naval Base from here. Halsey and his staff moved in today.* [William 'Bull' Halsey Jr. is the commander of the US Navy Third Fleet. He announced to his ships in a communiqué: *"Cessation of hostilities. War is over. If any Japanese airplanes appear, shoot them down in a friendly way."* He is present on the deck of his flagship, the USS *Missouri*, when the Japanese sign their surrender there on September 2.]

It's a tremendous place. Yokohama is only a couple miles away too. We can see what's left of it pretty clearly with a glass. I guess it was one of the targets for the atomic bomb from the looks of it. A Japanese navigator came aboard yesterday to pilot us into the Bay. He came alongside on one of our destroyers while we were underway. They strung a line across, put him in a breeches buoy and pulled him over. It was all pretty dramatic. When they pulled him aboard he looked like a young kid; had coal-black hair, about 120 lbs., fair skin and looked quite intelligent. He must've known his stuff because we got here alright. The climate up here is swell; more like home, especially after 18 months of sweating it out. We are fairly close to the Missouri where the peace documents will be signed in a couple days. I wish I could get over and see the ceremony in person but there's not a chance. I doubt if I'll be able to get ashore while we're here but if I can I'll get you a few souvenirs."

From Yokosuka, USS *Piedmont* will provide the American troops occupying Japan with food and equipment, as well as hospital ships that will take care of the liberated Allied prisoners of war.

A NEW WORLD

Among these former prisoners is Anthony, a British soldier who had been held captive by the Japanese in a labor camp in Thailand after being captured in Singapore: *"At last my dream of dreams has come true. Once again a free man, and able to write to you. [...] Well dear, I hope you are very well. I am looking forward to seeing you, after 3 ½ years* [as a] *prisoner of war. It is like being born again, to eat good English food, as much as you want, to be able to wash with soap and wear clean white clothes. I could go on forever, tell you hardships we have been through, but don't worry, it is all over now. FREE AGAIN, and soon to be with you. Oh darling, it is you and I from now on. We are going to do great things, you and I."*

Operation Downfall will never be launched, much to the relief of the troops in the Pacific, but also in Europe and in the United States. This is true for Guenther Ahlf, whose 95th Division had returned home on June 29, 1945 and had started training immediately, ready to be shipped to the Pacific, without him having a chance to see his Betty again (the division was to be part of the invasion force of *Operation Coronet*). Still, *Downfall* would change the course of history. Its preparation was the main reason for the American refusal to participate in Churchill's post VE-Day plan, the aptly named *Operation Unthinkable*. Disgusted by reports of Soviet repression in countries liberated by the Red Army and eager to obtain a better agreement for Poland, the British Prime Minister planned to go to war against the USSR before the mass demobilization in the summer of 1945. Field Marshal Montgomery had even been ordered to collect captured German weapons for possible 'future use'. Indeed, in the final weeks of the war in Western Europe, many German soldiers surrendered on their own to the Americans in the hope of fighting alongside them against their future common enemy: the Soviet Union (a situation that will become real in 1955, when the Bundeswehr is established, to erase the memory of the Wehrmacht despite its 'experienced' officers). But as the United States wants to leave Europe as soon as possible, Churchill's plan is abandoned.

For his part, Stalin also considered invading France and Italy in 1944. However, even if the 400 Russian divisions ready to rush into a ruined Western Europe could probably not've been stopped (according to General Chtemenko, the invasion would have taken less than a month), Moscow was now within the reach of the American Air Force thanks to its new positions in Japan. In addition, the US nuclear demonstration had made quite an impact. This was actually the initial intention of the *Manhattan Project* (which led to the acquisition of the atomic weapon): intimidate today's ally, so that it doesn't become tomorrow's enemy. Yet the arms race has begun. The USSR will also acquire the nuclear bomb in 1949 and China, now a communist country, in 1964. The United Kingdom will be equipped in 1952 and France in 1960. Europe will thus be divided into two distinct blocs: NATO (1949) in the West, led by the United States, and the Warsaw Pact (1955) in the East, led by the USSR. They would fight indirectly in Korea (1950-1953), Vietnam (1964-1975), and will take sides in civil or decolonization wars throughout the world, without ever engaging in direct confrontation that could potentially end in nuclear disaster... This is the 'Cold War'.

From 1961 onwards, many German families will be separated by both physical and ideological borders. Until the fall of the Berlin Wall in 1989 (separating the two blocs), followed by the collapse of the USSR two years later, a two-speed Europe will develop in relative peace. Elfriede is a young German girl from Grosskayna, Merseburg Salle. On March 1, 1948, she writes in English to a former GI in the 1st Infantry Division, who'd passed through her home on his way to Czechoslovakia in the final days of the war: *"Dear Sir Knutson, nearly three years have passed, since we have heard nothing from each other. Still we hoped to receive a letter from you. You will be sure to remember us. We have spent five hours with you. Very often and gladly we think back on them. How are you? We suppose that you have arrived in your country safe and sound and attend to your professional duties. We are well in conformity to that time. How you will know, we belong to the Russian zone. There are no Russians in our town. The state according to the nourishment leaves much to be desired. There is a shortness of provisions and victuals and of the necessary clothing. We all hope that the future of Germany turns to its advantage. Certainly, you have read news on Germany and may imagine how the present situation is. We would be very glad to send us news. Hoping that you write us a letter. I greet you heartily, Yours, Elfriede and parents."*

Germany would recover in a few decades after the fall of the Berlin Wall and even become the main driving force of the European Union. Eisenhower had told his staff in June 1945: *"The success of this occupation can only be judged 50 years from now. If the Germans have at that time a stable prosperous democracy, then we shall have succeeded."*

Underneath this victory medal is a letter from the White House received by Private Herrold of the 76th Division and distributed to all members of the American forces: *"To you who answered the call of your country and served in its Armed Forces to bring about the total defeat of the enemy, I extend the heartfelt thanks of a grateful Nation. [...] We now look to you for leadership and example in further exalting our country in peace."*

GIs on their way back to the port of New York (1945).

Samuel is the older brother of Raymond Hurd, the GI in charge of collecting the bodies of his comrades from the 1st Infantry Division in the snow of the Ardennes (page 275). The latter is at last about to go home with the 99th Division, after having suffered many traumatic experiences in Sicily, Normandy, Belgium and Germany. Samuel has a lot of sympathy for his little brother, since he himself had gone through hell during the First World War (arriving in France on August 2, 1918, Samuel and the 52nd Pioneer Infantry Regiment participated in the terrible Meuse-Argonne offensive (26,000 Americans killed and nearly 96,000 wounded) in the final weeks of the conflict). On September 2, 1945, he writes to Raymond, not knowing that he's already on a boat bringing him home (explaining why the letter was returned to him):

"Dear Ray, Official – V-J-Day [Victory in Japan]! Hurrah! Now dag-nab-it. I hope the politicians will know enough to keep peace and not lose it for at least 1,000 years. Now if the peace lasts as long as Hitler's rule of Europe – which he said would last for Germany [for] 1,000 years – well! How come, here is another week gone and we did not hear from you. Could it mean that you are journeying around Sunny France again or are you sailing the briny deep? I got a very strong suspicion that you may be on the way home or even in the old US right now – and Boy! I sure hope you are here. How are your nerves holding out these days? Has the long rest after V-E Day given you any relief from war fatigue? Don't let things get you down. I know it's tough, but you will overcome all things and I am praying hard that God will heal the scars on your mind and soul. I know what he can do and in fact he is the only one who can do it. Just put your trust in him and let him take care of all the past as well as the future, and I know he will wipe the slate clean and make the future look rosy and happy. God only has the power to heal the mental scars that come from some of the awful things a fellow has to go through in war. I know from experience. I would not exchange the Peace he put in my heart for all the gold in the world, nor all the honor. [...] I just hope I live long enough to see you married to a fine lady and about a dozen little fellows climbing upon your knees. That will be the day!! I still have not found the lady I think is good enough for you so maybe you will have to look up one for yourself. My! My! Looks like I take a lot of interest in your private affairs. Well forgive me and hurry home."

EPILOGUE

THE PRICE OF PEACE

War changes people. On the battlefields young soldiers realized that their lives would never be the same again. An American officer attached newspaper clippings in a letter to his wife, in which he commented: *"They contain some interesting data, especially FDR's 'again and again and again' pledge in 1940 to keep every mother's son out of any foreign war, but here we are slapping around in the mud, minus 'galoshes' and a decent bit of grub, representing the richest country in the world, fighting supposedly to make the world safe for democracy; with the thousands of American homes broken up, fatherless children brought up in communities running rampant with greed, vice and prostitution. After the war when the 'boys' come home you'll see some changes. They are not taking all this misery over here for nothing. And they'll be an awful lot of bums too, floating around, because the Army sure can make one out of you. I see it every day, especially in these teenage boys with whom I first came in. A year and a half have made an awful lot of difference in them."*

Many also wondered if the sacrifice of their youth would really make a difference. Archibald Sayce, of the 4th Infantry Division, wrote in the Hürtgen Forest on the eve of his last birthday: *"The average soldier desires a hard peace for the Third Reich but believes wars will continue indefinitely. A rosy outlook, eh!! His sole aim is to get home as soon as possible and that is mostly what he speaks of. A majority of the fellows detest Europe, and never want to travel again."*

Once the censorship was lifted shortly after VE-Day, words became even harsher, as in this letter written by a GI in the 9th Infantry Division: *"Then came the invasion and darling I was so afraid that I was going to die and that I wouldn't see you anymore. [...] It's hell on a man's nerves honey when you see dead people all around you and you just know that you're next and you know you have so much to live for. [...] Months go by and all you hear is bullets and shells and bombs and all you see is guys like Vargo hitting the dirt for the last time. [...] You kill people without thinking of whether they have a wife and baby or if they have a mother. Honey, war is the most horrible thing that ever happened to any man. [...] I want to be home where I can be gentle to you and treat people like human beings instead of shoving a bayonet thru his guts."*

William White, in the 76th Division, wrote to his wife after his very first attack on the Siegfried Line, in February 1945: *"I thought of the Valentine [card] you sent me. I had to burn it before I went into the attack. I know what war is now. No one but God, the devil (the inventor) and the guys that have actually been up there know what it's like. It's a place where every one suddenly realizes no one can help them but God. And believe me, every one calls on him. It's a place where you walk, eat, and sleep with death always searching for you. It's a place where you learn fear and learn to conquer it. It's a place where you always have to be on the alert, where there is never any rest, and very little time to eat - if you have anything to eat. Some of the boys in my company were without food for as long as four days. I was lucky I was prepared for what happened. I had one K-ration per day. It's pretty hard to lay on the ground and hear men screaming for help, when you can't do anything for them, or to see men drowning and have to let them go. [...] Yes I had a lot of close calls, but I guess someone was praying so I'm still here. Twice, shells landed close enough to spit on them, but didn't go off. That's the time when you are very thankful to God."*

A HEAVY TOLL

American soldiers paid the highest price for the liberation of Western Europe. All fronts combined, they had more than 407,300 soldiers killed, two thirds of them on this continent. The British deplored almost as many deaths worldwide (383,700), but over a longer period of time and including those from their many colonies. Canada suffered 45,400, Australia 39,800, New Zealand and South Africa 11,900 military deaths each. As for France, it lost 92,000 soldiers killed in 1940, and more than 120,000 others in its battles for its liberation or in the POW camps (including colonial troops). Its Belgian and Dutch neighbors lost 12,100 and 17,000 soldiers respectively.

Over 200,000 Polish soldiers died in action, in the army in exile, in the Polish resistance (when the country was occupied by Germany and the USSR) or in captivity. With civilians deported and executed, Poland lost 5 million of its inhabitants, or 16% of its population, the highest ratio for all countries combined.

The Germans lost half a million men against the Western Allies and we can add a million deaths to this figure by counting its Hungarian, Romanian and Italian allies as well. However, it was on the Eastern Front that the Nazis suffered the most casualties. In the city of Stalingrad alone, where the failure of their invasion of the USSR materialized, they lost almost as many men as in all of Northwest Europe. A total of 2.3 million Germans died on the Eastern Front, but their Soviet enemies and former allies lost a staggering 8.7 million soldiers there! In addition to the military, 18 million Soviet civilians were killed in the German invasion and then the reconquest. The statistics are terrifying, but the main cause of such a high death toll might be Stalin himself. For example, he often prohibited the evacuation of civilians, as in Leningrad (today's St. Petersburg) in order to encourage his soldiers to fight harder to protect them. Caught in the crossfire and without any supplies during an 872-day siege, one and a half million civilians died, mainly from hunger (there were even many reports of cannibalism). One million opponents to the Stalinist regime also died in its labor camps: the 'Gulags'. As for the soldiers of the Red Army (especially in the disciplinary battalions), they were regularly executed by their own officers for 'treason' (Stalin's order No. 227: *"panic-mongers and cowards must be shot in place"* by 'blocking detachments'), or thrown into frontal assaults without adequate equipment.

In any case, civilians are the first victims of the war: they suffer deprivation, are condemned to exodus, sometimes deliberately exterminated or used as human shields by the occupier and bombarded by both enemy aircraft and the liberators. In the United Kingdom, 60,000 civilians died in Luftwaffe raids during the Blitz, but the Royal Air Force took revenge as early as 1942 by inflicting ten times more casualties on German civilians, without any real strategic value. Civilian deaths in Western Europe are estimated at 22 million people, more than the military losses. In addition to this enormous figure are the 6 to 11 million victims of the Holocaust. If we add the military deaths to the civilian deaths, we reach a total of more than 40 million deaths in Europe alone.

Worldwide, the Second World War killed more than 70 million people in just six years. No war in history has yet caused so many casualties and is almost five times that of the First World War, which took place only twenty-five years earlier. This toll is so heavy that our brains can't imagine the scale of the tragedy. It's therefore important to read the words of these men who'd gone through hell so that we can live in peace today. The letters of those who gave their lives, such as Desmond Finny, Jim and Vernon Miller, Ronald Whitehead, Leonard Wood, Cortland Kester, Melvyn Roat, Archibald Sayce, Albert Vardy and so many others are the only traces of their experience of the war, as they never came home to tell us themselves. Even those who were lucky enough to return have often kept silent about these dark years, hoping to forget their trauma and to try to rebuild their lives, but also because we, as civilians, can't understand what they experienced.

Through their words, we may have a vague idea of their pain, their fear and the horror of the conflict, but it helps us realize our own opportunities in life and that's the most important thing. As Winston Churchill so aptly put it: *"Those who fail to learn from history are condemned to repeat it"*. This time, humanity had gone so far in hatred and barbarism that the various belligerents havn't fought each other again for many decades... But for how long? As long as memory is preserved, hopefully

Remains of an American helmet found near Carentan, on the site of a former military hospital, 73 years later.

THANK YOU

ACKNOWLEDGMENTS

First of all, I would like to thank my wife Laëtitia, for reviewing the first draft and listening to me constantly talk about my project, and for accepting the personal sacrifices necessary to accomplish this extremely time-consuming undertaking; her parents, Nicole and Gérard and my own, Isabelle and Vincent for their corrections; Bertrand Froger for his advice and his keen eye; Matthieu Biberon and the team at Ouest-France Editions (the original French publisher) for their trust and of course Heather Williams for her help with the English manuscript and bringing the project overseas with Pen & Sword Books; Jim Howey for helping me acquire some of the most interesting letters in my collection, as well as his kindness and all the additional information he was able to provide; Louis Cabarat for accompanying me on several trips to Normandy; Federico Vitiello for his welcome in Italy and his precious help; James Lullo for guiding me through the next steps of this adventure; Melissa Masseron and Mathilde Mauris for their legal assistance; Andrew 'Andy' Newson for his work at the British archives at Kew; Matt Anderson of the 509th Parachute Infantry Association; Eric Belloc at the Airborne Museum in Sainte-Mère-Église; Lt-Col. Allix Lafille, Jean-Pierre Kuntzmann and Loïc Canevet of the 12th Cuirassiers; Jean-Marie Harmand and the Comité des défenseurs de l'ouvrage de La Ferté; Maryse Batillot from the town hall at Charmes; Marie Hoguet at the Utah Beach Landing Museum; Rachel Brett (British Library, London); Yuri Beckers (9thinfantrydivision.net); Corinne Denise and Sylvain Burgaud for the dagger and photos of Jean Denise; Lloyd Scott and Tom Sellen for their additional information on Leonard Wood; Jean-Charles Leroy; The members of the WW2 Talk forums and Passion Militaria in particular, for helping me when I started my collection, perfecting my knowledge and correcting my mistakes; and many others who supported me.

A big thank you to the friends who participated in my 'living mannequins' projects, accepting the odorous constraints of wearing wartime period uniforms (in order of appearance): Vincent Bonny; Cyril Masset; Thomas Chaignon; Jérémy Chanal; Pierre Simon; Pierre Tostain; Alexandre Gros; Federico Vitiello; Damien Buron; Clément Horvath (author); Laëtitia Beauvais and Thomas Font; Karl Stefic; Geoffroy Bouché; Charlemagne Boton; Alban Péan; Lucas Charvet; Victorien Draperon; Bertrand Froger; Clément Leconte; Pierre Seigne; Franck Grison; Jeffrey Lecomte; Pierre Durut; Guillaume De Sousa and Louis Cabarat. Thanks also to the actors of the films I produced to support the project.

It would obviously be impossible to know the identity of the men presented in this book without the trust placed in me by their relatives: Rick Alm (Rest in Peace) and Sarah Alm Weber; Laurie Siegel Columbia and Thomas Spier; Gloria Landon Bronson; Monique Pirat and Valérie Olampi; Martin Clavier; Cindy Louise Nemec and Federico Vitiello; Stuart Rabinowitsh; Steve and Jeremy Hayman and Marilynn Erickson; Serge Balloux; Vivien Roworth and Sharon Wakefield and Viv Wilson; Michael Crookhorn; Jim Friedrich; Katie Badura; Betty and Amber Ahlf; Tiphaine Francisco and Annette Pasquier; Maryse Vallières; Jeff and Jim Barrow; Nancy Robertson; Aileen McConnell; David Birnbaum; Desda J. Monaghan; Debi Collinsworth and Marilyn Mills; Robyn G. Pharr and Ellen Ferne Glemby and Peter Galbert; Randal and Leota Jentzen; Rob Alexander; Brad and Jenise Falk; Frances Stinnett; Tawna Whitford; Olwen Roden Kelly; Elizabeth Ada Harris Johnstone and Judith Jones and Ivan Naslovar; Mary Miller-Bishop and Vera Smith and Len Miller; Harrison Forrester Jr; Joanne K. Adlam and Lyn McOnie and Leonard John Old; Meagan Lace Follansbee; Cecil Newton (himself); John and Louise Finny; Samantha and Vera Galliers; Stephanie Tropp; Karin and Juliette Duhamel; Ashley Grimes; Barry and Laurie Keefe and the intermediaries too numerous to list.

Although searching for these descendants was a much longer and more expensive undertaking than I would've imagined, their contribution has contributed greatly to the stories you have discovered here. Of course, I can never thank all those men and women who fought for our freedom enough.

CREDITS

All photographs in this book were taken by the author Clément Horvath and are his exclusive property, with the exception of the following photographs: 'Fort de la Ferté' (Jean-Marie Harmand, comité des défenseurs de l'ouvrage de La Ferté), 'Jetée de Dunkerque' (Jérôme Morland), 'Port of Augusta, Sicily' and 'Reggio di Calabria' (Louis Cabarat), 'Monte Cassino' (Pino Valente), and 'Keroman Base' (André Fèvre, thanks to Yohann Bagot). These photographs have been retouched by the author.

The period photographs are primarily taken from the public domain collections of the American National Archives, the Imperial War Museum and the US Air Force. Photo p. 89: Bundesarchiv 1011-291-1230-13. Photo p. 208 (top): Public Archives of Canada. The unpublished and personal photographs of the soldiers presented in this book were published with the agreement of the families. All objects, letters, journals, uniforms, etc. presented in this book are or have been part of the author's personal collection, with the exception of the following pieces: Journal of the parachutist doctor Murray Goldman (p. 161, Airborne Museum in Sainte-Mère-Église), uniform of the 3rd Infantry Division in Anzio (p. 143, Federico Vitiello), uniform of the 101st Airborne in Bastogne (p. 272, Bertand Froger), and photographs of the liberation of Antwerp (p. 223, Ronald L T Jeltes). Thank you to the families who didn't hesitate to provide additional letters and documents to complete the portraits of their veterans.

British camera from the 1930s that belonged to the author's great-grandfather, Henri Cholet (5e Génie – a Combat Engineer regiment), evacuated from Dunkirk in the summer of 1940.

SOURCES

The main sources used in this book are original letters collected over the years. The comments reported therein have been verified to the closest extent possible. I also relied on documents and reports collected at the archives in Vincennes for French soldiers, Kew for British soldiers, numerous online sources for American soldiers (The National Archives, Fold3 etc.) and the Veterans Affairs of Canada website for Canadians. Various associations mentioned in the acknowledgments provided interesting documents and the expertise of enthusiasts from different internet forums helped perfect my knowledge (Passion Militaria, WW2 Talks, US Militaria Forum, World War Helmets among many others).

The journeys of the soldiers presented here were traced with the help of the following books (among others): *New Zealand Engineers, Middle East* (Joseph F. Cody); *Time Changes All Things* (Donald R. Amundson); *Rob Alexander's blog* (docalexander. wordpress.com); the 509th Parachute Infantry Association's website (Matt Anderson); *History of the Ontario Regiment, 1866-1951* (Alexander Andrew Schragg); *D-Day: The Files* (Richard Holmes); *Beyond Valor: World War II's Ranger and Airborne Veterans Reveal the Heart of Combat* (Patrick K O'Donnell); *We Were Young Once, and Brave* (Charles Leroux – *Chicago Tribune*, July 30, 1998); *Pray Hard* (Rick Alm & Sarah Alm Weber); *History of the Royal Warwickshire Regiment 1919-1955* (Marcus Cunliffe); *Journal de guerre 1939-1944* (Christian Girard); *Always a Brother* (Randal D. Jentzen); *A Trooper's Tale* (Cecil Newton); articles about Albert Vardy in *The Bancroft Times* (Luke Hendry); *Flyboy: Memoirs of a P-47 Pilot* (Kenneth Lane Glemby).

The general context has been built from many books, including this non-exhaustive list of those that have been most useful to me: *La Seconde Guerre mondiale* (Antony Beevor); *The Second World War: A Miscellany* (Norman Ferguson); *La Guerre perdue de 1940* (Pierre Stéphany); *Batailles sur les ponts de la Loire* (Guy Bonnet); *Dieppe 19 août 1942* (Olivier Richard); *Omaha Beach 6 juin 1944* (Joseph Balkoski); *The Battalion* (Robert W. Black); *Le Débarquement de Provence* (Raymond Muelle); *With the Jocks: A Soldier's Struggle for Europe* (Peter White); *The Words of War* (Marcus Cowper); *The War North of Rome* (Thomas R. Brooks); *The Victors* (Stephen E. Ambrose); *Les Poches de résistance allemandes* (Rémy Desquesnes); *Uniformes de la Seconde Guerre mondiale* (Peter Darman); *The British Soldier* (Jean Bouchery); *GI, guide du collectionneur* (Henri-Paul Enjames); *Histoire de la Première Armée Française Rhin et Danube* (Général de Lattre de Tassigny); *Arnhem: the Battle for the Bridges* (Antony Beevor); *La Seconde Guerre mondiale en 100 objets* (Maj. Gen. Julian Thompson & Dr. Allan R. Millett).

www.tillvictory.com

Originally published in France by Éditions Ouest-France
as *Till Victory : lettres de soldats alliés.*
First published in Great Britain in 2020 by Pen & Sword Military,
an imprint of Pen & Sword Books Ltd, Yorkshire - Philadelphia.

Copyright © Clément Horvath, 2020
ISBN 978 1 52678 273 1

The right of Clément Horvath to be identified as Author of this work
has been asserted by him in accordance with the Copyright, Designs and Patents Act 1988.
A CIP catalogue record for this book is available from the British Library.
All rights reserved. No part of this book may be reproduced or transmitted in any form or by any means,
electronic or mechanical including photocopying, recording or by any information storage and retrieval system,
without permission from the Publisher in writing.

Printed and bound in India by Replika Press Pvt. Ltd.

Pen & Sword Books Ltd incorporates the Imprints of Pen & Sword Books Archaeology, Atlas, Aviation, Battleground, Discovery, Family History, History, Maritime, Military, Naval, Politics, Railways, Select, Transport, True Crime, Fiction, Frontline Books, Leo Cooper, Praetorian Press, Seaforth Publishing, Wharncliffe and White Owl.
For a complete list of Pen & Sword titles please contact :

PEN & SWORD BOOKS LIMITED
47 Church Street, Barnsley, South Yorkshire, S70 2AS, England
E-mail: enquiries@pen-and-sword.co.uk
Website: www.pen-and-sword.co.uk

PEN AND SWORD BOOKS
1950 Lawrence Rd, Havertown, PA 19083, USA
E-mail: uspen-and-sword@casematepublishers.com
Website: www.penandswordbooks.com